# COMMERCIAL LAW
# IN SCOTLAND

AUSTRALIA
Law Book Co.
Sydney

CANADA and USA
Carswell
Toronto

HONG KONG
Sweet & Maxwell Asia

NEW ZEALAND
Brookers
Wellington

SINGAPORE and MALAYSIA
Sweet & Maxwell Asia
Singapore and Kuala Lumpur

# COMMERCIAL LAW IN SCOTLAND

By

### Professor Fraser Davidson, LL.B, Ph.D
*Alexander Stone Professor of Commercial Law*
*University of Glasgow*

### Laura J. Macgregor, LL.B, LL.M, Dip.LP
*Solicitor*
*Senior Lecturer in Commercial Law*
*University of Edinburgh*

THOMSON

™

W. GREEN

Published in 2003 by

W. Green & Son Ltd
21 Alva Street
Edinburgh EH2 4PS

www.wgreen.co.uk

*Typeset by J.P. Price, Chilcompton, Somerset*
*Printed and bound in Great Britain by*
*Bath Press Ltd, Lower Bristol Road, Bath*

No natural forests were destroyed to make this product;
only farmed timber was used and replanted.

A CIP catalogue record for this book is available from the British Library

ISBN 0 414 01385 9

© W. Green & Son Limited 2003

# DEDICATION

To Bill, Denis and Alexander.

# PREFACE

It is customary in works like these to ask, "what is commercial law"? This is of course a legitimate question, as it is not one of those subjects with clearly defined boundaries. No two works on the subject seem to cover exactly the same aspects, and among any group of students, academics or practitioners there would no doubt be widespread disagreement as to what falls within its scope. This is chiefly because commercial law is a portmanteau term for a series of quite distinct subjects, which impact in their various ways upon trade and commerce. This work is aimed mainly at students undertaking courses in commercial law or mercantile law at one of the Scottish law schools, and this largely determines its character, in that it follows (more or less) the Law Society prescription for the subject. This will no doubt mean that there will be practitioners who will feel that the book does not cover the whole range of commercial law, as they understand it. This is unavoidable. Even those authors who aim to be as comprehensive in their coverage as possible readily admit that there are areas, which some might regard as commercial law, which they have been forced to omit. To have expanded on our coverage, we would have had to include subjects which would have been of little interest to our main target audience, increasing the size of the work to unwieldy proportions, and also increasing its cost. That being said, there might seem to be one conspicuous omission, in that the work contains no treatment of company law. To that it might be rejoined that, while the relevance of company law to the commercial world cannot be doubted, even those works which aim to be comprehensive tend to exclude company law, which is regarded as very much a subject in its own right. To have given company law anything like an appropriate treatment would have come close to doubling the size of the work, thus upsetting its balance. It was thus thought preferable to omit it, especially given that there are several excellent company law texts on the market.

The other oft-asked question is whether there is such a thing as commercial law. In other words, does commercial law operate as a coherent system, or is it merely a label attached to a set of quite separate branches of the law, which are linked only by the fact that they impinge on commercial life? The latter position is closer to the truth. Each area of commercial law is quite distinctive. Many concern the way in which the law regulates specific contracts. Sometimes those contracts are regulated for the most part by the common law, in other cases, they are mainly regulated by statute. Areas like bankruptcy deal with a statutory process, while rights in security are partly created by contract, partly by statute, and partly arise at common law. Those areas based on the common law tend to form a coherent whole, upon the foundation of a limited number of general principles. Areas which are organised around a single, dominant statute also tend to feature a coherent code, whether that statute seeks to codify the common law, or imposes a specially designed conceptual framework on the law, or gives effect to an international convention. There are other areas, however, which are not quite so coherent. Increasingly, moreover, the demands of consumer protection and of membership of the European Union (the two often being linked) have seen accretions to the law which, whatever their social utility, do little for its conceptual integrity. To a lesser extent, the same might be said of the influence of English law. Furthermore, even those areas of law which remain internally consistent are not designed by reference to other areas of commercial law. This is not to say that the system as a whole is dysfunctional, rather that those who look for evidence of some overall design will be doomed to disappointment. Ours is not one of those systems which boasts an integrated commercial code. Nonetheless, although each area of law has developed along its own individual lines, there are numerous points at which two or more of the areas covered interact in practice. It is one of the aims of the book to detail those interactions, so that as well as gaining an understanding of the specific areas covered, the reader may gain an appreciation of how "commercial law" works.

Finally, we must record our appreciation for the assistance we have received in producing this book. Thus much thanks must go to our colleagues, Janeen Carruthers, Liz Crawford, Cowan Ervine, Jenny Hamilton, Parker Hood, Bill McBryde, Iain Macneil and Hector MacQueen and to Alexander Macgregor for his assistance with proofreading. Thanks also to all at Greens, especially the firm but fair Dr Valerie Malloch.

The law is stated as at May 1, 2003.

# CONTENTS

# Table of Cases

# TABLE OF STATUTES

# TABLE OF STATUTORY INSTRUMENTS

# Chapter 1

# SALE AND SUPPLY OF GOODS

## 1.1. INTRODUCTION:

Sources of legislation regulating the law of sale are both common law and statutory. The main statutory source is the Sale of Goods Act 1979, the complex historical development of which is examined below. This codifying statute has been much amended, most recently as a result of compliance with European directives. General common law principles are, however, also relevant. Sale is, of course, a contract, and therefore draws some of its rules from general contractual principles, for example, where one considers the issue of formation of contract. Other common law contractual principles appear, perhaps in amended form, within the 1979 Act. It can be seen, therefore, that the resultant scheme of regulation is a complex one. The analysis must also be drawn wider than merely sale, taking in hire, hire purchase and contracts for the supply of goods and services. If one issue were, amongst this mass of legal rules, to be highlighted as an important theme, it is the extent of consumer protection afforded by the legal principles. Important protections appear, for example, in the form of the statutory implied terms contained in ss.12 to 15 of the 1979 Act, and the controls on contracting-out of such protections applied by the Unfair Contract Terms Act 1977.

The first Act to codify the law on sale of goods was the Sale of Goods Act 1893. This statute was, however, a codifying statute only in so far as it applied in England. It was only once the Bill had been before Parliament for four years that provisions extending to Scotland were finally agreed. Prior to 1893 the law of sale in Scotland and England had contained important differences. The Scots law of sale, unlike English law, is based on Roman law.[1] Thus whereas one could say that the Act codified English law, it enacted important changes to Scots law. In 1979 a further consolidation Act was passed, and it is this Act which remains the point of reference for the law of sale in the UK.[2]

In view of the later addition of the Scottish provisions to the 1893 Act, it is perhaps not surprising that those provisions contained some defects which were later replicated in the 1979

---

[1] See W. Gordon, "Sale" in K. G. C. Reid and R. Zimmermann (eds), *A History of Scottish Private Law* (2000), Vol. II, Ch. 12.

[2] References to statutory provisions in this chapter are to the 1979 Act unless otherwise indicated. Prior to the 1979 Act the law had been amended in the Supply of Goods (Implied Terms) Act 1973.

Act. Important statutory reform has taken place in recent years which has resolved many, if not all, of the problems.

The most important statutory reform of the 1979 Act arose following joint consultation of the English and Scottish Law Commissions.[3] The joint report, published in 1987, resulted in the passing of the Sale and Supply of Goods Act 1994. This Act, more than any other, resolved the issues which had remained problematic for Scots law. In particular, it removed the English terms "condition" and "warranty" from the Scottish provisions, and it extended the protections for purchasers or consumers provided by the statutory implied terms to contracts other than sale.[4] A further joint report was published in 1993[5] which led to the Sale of Goods (Amendment) Act 1995 which strengthened the purchaser's rights where he or she buys part of a larger bulk of goods.

More recent amendments have been made by the Sale and Supply of Goods to Consumers Regulations 2002.[6] These regulations, which came into force on March 31, 2003, were passed in order to implement the European Directive on certain aspects of the sale of consumer goods and associated guarantees.[7] The Regulations introduce several important changes to the field of consumer protection, most notably by amending the implied term as to satisfactory quality; introducing the consumer's right to repair or replacement of goods; and regulating consumer guarantees.[8] Certain of the provisions of the Directive were mandatory and certain were optional. Thus, for example, Member States had the option of imposing a time limit of two months on consumers within which defects in goods would require to be notified to the seller.[9] Because this would have watered-down the protection currently available to consumers in the UK, this provision was not included in the 2002 Regulations. Similarly, other parts of the Directive were not included within the 2002 Regulations because UK law already provides a higher degree of consumer protection.[10] In this chapter, the 2002 Regulations are not commented on specifically. Rather, the changes which they effect are integrated into the general discussion.

## 1.2. DEFINITION OF A CONTRACT OF SALE OF GOODS

The definition of a contract of sale of goods is supplied in s.2(1) of the 1979 Act:

> "A contract of sale of goods is a contract by which the seller transfers or agrees to transfer the property in goods to the buyer for a money consideration, called the price."

The seller may transfer the property (*i.e.* the ownership) in the goods as part of the contract of sale.[11] However, the seller may agree to transfer property at some point in the future, or conclude a contract subject to a condition. In both of the latter cases the contract still falls within the definition given above and is described as an agreement to sell.[12] In a conditional

---

[3] See the eventual joint report: *Report on Sale and Supply of Goods* (Law Com. No. 160; Scot Law Com. No. 104, May 1987).

[4] See para. 1.2.

[5] *Sale of Goods Forming Part of a Bulk* (Law Com. No. 215; Scot. Law Com. No. 145, July 1993).

[6] SI 2002/3045, hereinafter "2002 Regulations".

[7] Directive 99/44 [1999] O.J. L171/12, See, in particular, the second DTI consultation paper on the implementation of the Directive, available from *www.dti.gov.uk/ccp/consultation.htm*.

[8] As is commented on below at para. 1.9., the changes protect consumers in sale, sale and supply of goods, hire and hire-purchase.

[9] Directive 99/44, Art. 5(2).

[10] Art. 8(2) of Directive 99/44 permits Member States to: ". . . adopt or maintain in force more stringent provisions . . . to ensure a higher degree of consumer protection."

[11] See also s.2(4).

[12] See also s.2(5).

contract, the condition may be either suspensive or resolutive. Where the condition is suspensive, performance of the obligation is delayed, or suspended, until the condition is purified. By contrast, where the condition is resolutive, the obligation is already in force, and purification of the condition brings the obligation to an end.[13]

Section 61(1) defines "goods" as: ". . . all corporeal moveables except money". So everything from a safety-pin to a supertanker falls within the definition, but incorporeal property such as copyright cannot be goods, nor can heritable property. That being said, the definition continues, "in particular 'goods' includes emblements, industrial growing crops, and things attached to or forming part of the land which are agreed to be severed before sale or under the contract or sale; and includes an undivided share in goods". Thus, where it was agreed that the buyer would enter the seller's land to fell and remove timber, the timber came within the latter part of the definition of goods.[14] Because ownership of land is usually from the heavens to the centre of the earth,[15] minerals usually form part of an ordinary title to land. They can, however, be transferred, as heritable property, under a separate title.[16] However, once minerals have been extracted, there is no reason why they cannot fall within the definition of "goods".[17]

The definition of goods has proved problematic in its application to computer software. Although a disk can clearly fall within the definition, this seems to ignore the real product, which is the software supplied on the disk. Such software may be downloaded over the internet, which places the contract outwith the Sale of Goods Act entirely, and, importantly, denies the buyer important protections under that Act.[18] Lord Penrose has defined a contract for the supply of computer software as: ". . . a contract *sui generis*, which may involve elements of nominate contracts such as sale, but which would be inadequately understood if expressed wholly in terms of any of the nominate contracts."[19] Sir Iain Glidewell in a leading English case, *St Albans DC v International Computers Ltd*,[20] indicated that while a disk fell within the definition of goods, the same could not be said of a computer program.[21] His comments were, however, *obiter*.

The term "goods" also includes an undivided share in the goods.[22] Section 5 further subdivides goods into "existing" and "future" goods. The former are goods owned or possessed by the seller at the time of sale, whereas the latter are goods to be manufactured or acquired by the seller after the making of the contract of sale. Clearly, the latter type of contract can only be an agreement to sell.[23] Goods may also be specific or unascertained, specific goods being goods identified and agreed upon at the time the contract is made,[24] and unascertained being neither so identified nor agreed upon. Subject to one exception (see para. 1.11.), it is only possible to have an agreement to sell unascertained goods. A sale transfers ownership of the property to the buyer, while an agreement to sell gives the buyer only a personal right against

---

[13] See H. MacQueen and J. Thomson, *Contract Law in Scotland* (2000), paras 3.59–3.62.

[14] *Munro v Liquidator of Balnagown Estates Co Ltd,* 1949 S.C. 49.

[15] *"a coelo usque ad centrum".*

[16] See explanation in R. Rennie, *Minerals and the Law in Scotland* (2001), Ch. 1.

[17] However, *cf. Morgan v Russell* [1909] 1 K.B. 357 at 365, *per* Alverstone C.J., although Walton L.J. at 366 reserved judgment on whether a contract for minerals which had not been worked at the date of the contract could be a contract for the sale of goods in terms of the 1893 Act.

[18] Specifically the implied terms relating to description, fitness for purpose and quality at ss.12, 13 and 14, commented on below.

[19] *Beta Computer Systems Europe Ltd v Adobe Computer Systems Europe Ltd,* 1996 S.L.T. 604 at 609.

[20] [1996] 4 All E.R. 481; [1997] F.S.R. 251, CA. See also the discussion in I. Lloyd, *Legal Aspects of the Information Society* (2000) paras 10–16 to 10–30.

[21] [1996] 4 All E.R. 481 at 492–494. Sir Iain Glidewell made an attempt to protect buyers of programs even though the contract for sale of a program fell outwith the Sale of Goods Act 1979. He indicated that the same implied terms which protect the buyer under a sale of goods contract (terms as to description, fitness for purpose and quality under ss.12, 13 and 14) could be implied into a contract for sale of a program as a matter of common law. Again, this was *obiter* and it will be interesting to see whether his view is taken up in a later case.

[22] Inserted by the Sale of Goods (Amendment) Act 1995, s.2.

[23] s.5(3).

[24] s.61(1).

the seller. The distinction between sale and agreement to sell is of vital importance in a variety of contexts, chiefly insolvency, where the buyer will lose out in a contest with the seller's liquidator or trustee in bankruptcy, should there be only an agreement to sell.

## 1.3. OTHER TRANSACTIONS

Many contracts do not fall within the Sale of Goods Act 1979. Where the contract involves exchanging goods for goods with no part of the consideration made up by money then the contract is treated as one of barter and not sale.[25] Where the contract is one of part exchange, such as the common example of sale of used cars, the consideration will usually be goods plus money. The legal analysis in such situations has tended to be that the contract is a contract of sale.[26] However, this may have been because, at that stage, only by defining the contract as one of sale would the purchaser receive the protection of the statutory implied terms. Similar protections are now provided to contracts of barter through the Sale and Supply of Goods Act 1994, and so there may no longer be any reason to class such contracts as contracts of sale.

Contracts for work and materials also previously presented a problem of definition given that they involve the provision of both goods and services. Again, the question has become less important because the 1994 Act extended to consumers under such contracts the same protections from the implied terms as were previously provided only to purchasers under sale contracts.

A number of other contracts pose difficulties of classification. Party A may agree to buy goods from party B on condition that B purchases goods from A. This contract, which may be described as "countertrade" could be classed as two contracts of sale, but given that both transactions occur in the same contract, it is probably better classified as a form of barter. Where goods are exchanged for previously purchased stamps, then the contract is regulated by the Trading Stamps Act 1964. The contract may also be any of the following types which are subject to separate regulation: credit sale, conditional sale, hire or hire purchase.[27] Whereas the first two types could be classed as types of sale, hire purchase cannot, given that there is no obligation on the hirer to buy the goods. A case which amply illustrates the difficulties inherent in classifying transactions is *Esso Petroleum Ltd v Customs and Excise Commissioners*[28] in which coins showing the images of members of the 1970 England World Cup Team were provided as free gifts to purchasers of Esso products. Two members of the House of Lords thought that there was no contract which related to the coins, the others thought that there was a contract, although one classed it as sale and two classed it, not very usefully, as a "collateral contract".

## 1.4. SALE OR SECURITY?

Section 62(4) provides that the Act does not apply to: "a transaction in the form of a contract of sale which is intended to operate by way of mortgage, pledge, charge, or other security." This section is aimed at so-called "sham sales". As is explored later in this book (see para. 6.3.), it is difficult, if not impossible, in Scots law to create a security over moveable property without taking possession of that property. Parties seek therefore, to enter into what may look like sale, but is, in truth, an attempt to take a security over moveables without taking possession of those

---

[25] *Widenmeyer v Burn, Stewart & Co Ltd,* 1967 S.C. 85; *Ballantyne v Durant,* 1983 S.L.T. (Sh. Ct.) 38.
[26] *Sneddon v Durant,* 1982 S.L.T. (Sh. Ct.) 39.
[27] See Consumer Credit Act 1974, Supply of Goods and Services Act 1982.
[28] [1976] 1 W.L.R. 1.

moveables. If A lends £2,000 to B, B can "sell" his car to A, but under an agreement that B will retain possession of the car. The idea is that A will sell the car back once repaid, there being no real intention to create a contract of sale, the car actually being used as security for the money lent by A to B. Thus if B became bankrupt, then A could argue that the car is in fact A's property. Because s.62(4) disapplies the Act to such sham sales, the property in the goods will not pass, and the security will be ineffectual.[29]

## 1.5. FORMATION OF THE CONTRACT

The normal rules of conclusion of contracts apply to contracts for the sale of goods. No particular formalities are required. The Consumer Protection (Cancellation of Contracts Concluded Away From Business Premises) Regulations 1987[30] regulate the formation of sale contracts in certain circumstances. When a business enters into a contract to supply a consumer with goods or services, and the contract is made away from the supplier's business premises, the supplier must give the consumer written notice of his or her right to cancel the contract within seven days.[31] The notice must be given at the time of entry into the contract, or if the consumer is at home when he or she offers to enter into the contract, at the time when that offer is made.[32] Failure to comply with these requirements renders the contract unenforceable.[33] Where the consumer exercises his or her right to cancel, any money paid must be refunded,[34] and the consumer has a lien (see para. 6.9.) over any goods supplied until repayment is made.[35] The latter protection does not apply where the consumer requests a visit,[36] nor in respect of goods intended for current consumption and supplied by regular roundsmen.[37] The issue of when a visit is unsolicited was considered in *Havair Ltd v Vile*.[38] The company had delivered leaflets to V's home inviting him to return a coupon requesting a visit from a salesperson. V argued that the delivery of the leaflet was itself a visit, but that argument was rejected and the Regulations were held not to apply.

A similar regime applies to contracts for the supply of goods or services to consumers made exclusively via distance communication[39] by virtue of the Consumer Protection (Distance Selling) Regulations 2000.[40] Most of the Regulations do not apply to contracts for the supply of goods intended for everyday consumption and supplied to the consumer's home or workplace by regular roundsmen.[41] Nor do they apply to contracts for the supply of accommodation, transport, catering or leisure services.[42] Generally, the Regulations require the supplier to provide the consumer with certain information, such as the main characteristics of the goods or services, the price and any delivery costs, and the right to cancel the contract, where appropriate.[43] Certain contracts cannot be cancelled by the consumer, *e.g.* where goods have been made to the consumer's specification, or are clearly personalised or perishable.[44] Certain

---

[29] See examples in *Robertson v Hall's Trustee* (1896) 24 R. 120; *Hepburn v Law,* 1914 S.C. 918; *Scottish Transit Trust Ltd v Scottish Land Cultivators Ltd,* 1955 S.C. 254.
[30] SI 1987/2117 (as amended).
[31] reg. 4(1).
[32] reg. 4(4).
[33] reg. 4(6).
[34] reg. 5(1).
[35] reg. 5(2).
[36] regs 3(1)(a) and (b).
[37] reg. 3(2)(b).
[38] [2000] C.L. 848.
[39] See the exclusions contained in reg. 5(1).
[40] SI 2000/2334 implementing Directive 97/7.
[41] reg. 6(2)(a).
[42] reg. 6(2)(b).
[43] reg. 7(1)(a).
[44] reg. 13(1)(c).

other types of contracts are excluded, *e.g.* contracts for the supply of newspapers,[45] for gaming services,[46] or for the supply of software or audio/video recordings which are unsealed by the consumer.[47]

Where the exceptions do not apply and, therefore, the consumer has the right to cancel, he or she must do so within a cooling-off period by giving to the supplier notice of cancellation.[48] Where the contract is cancelled, it is treated as if it had never been made.[49] The cooling-off period is seven working days beginning with the day after the day on which the consumer receives the goods.[50] Where the right to cancel has not been timeously intimated to the consumer, the cooling-off period is seven working days beginning with the day after the day on which the consumer is informed of this right.[51] If the supplier completely fails to intimate the right to cancel, the cooling-off period is three months and seven working days beginning with the day after the day on which the consumer receives the goods.[52]

Where the consumer cancels the contract, the price must be reimbursed within 30 days, and any related credit agreement is also cancelled.[53] The consumer is under a duty to restore the goods to the supplier and to take reasonable care of them until they are so restored.[54] He or she need not physically return the goods to the supplier. The consumer's only duty is to deliver the goods at his own premises.[55]

If the contract is not cancelled, the goods must be supplied within 30 days beginning with the day after the day on which the consumer sent his order to the supplier, although the parties may agree otherwise.[56] Finally, if the consumer's payment card (credit card, debit card, charge card or store card)[57] is used fraudulently in connection with a distance contract, then the consumer may cancel the payment or have any payment recredited by the card issuer.[58]

## 1.6. THE PRICE

The consideration for the goods is the price. Although the price will usually be fixed in the contract of sale, it may be determined in other ways. It may be left to be fixed in a manner agreed by the contract, or may be determined by a course of dealing between the parties.[59] If neither of these possibilities is open to the parties, the buyer is bound to pay a reasonable price for the goods.[60] The Act provides that what is a reasonable price is a question of fact which depends upon the circumstances of each case.[61] It was stated in one Scottish case[62] that a reasonable price need not be the market price[63] but must be fair and just to both parties,[64] and

---

[45] reg. 13(1)(e).
[46] reg. 13(1)(f).
[47] reg. 13(1)(d).
[48] reg. 10(1).
[49] reg. 10(2).
[50] reg. 11(2).
[51] reg. 11(3).
[52] reg. 11(4).
[53] reg. 15.
[54] reg. 17(3).
[55] reg. 17(4).
[56] reg. 19(1).
[57] reg. 21(6).
[58] reg. 21(1) and (2).
[59] s.8(1).
[60] s.8(2).
[61] s.8(3)—assuming of course that the absence of agreement on price does not indicate a fundamental lack of consensus, see *May and Butcher Ltd v R.* [1934] 2 K.B. 17, HL.
[62] *Glynwed Distribution Ltd v S Koronka & Co Ltd,* 1977 S.C. 1.
[63] 1977 S.C. 1 at 7–8, *per* Lord Kissen; at 11, *per* Lord Leechman.
[64] 1977 S.C. 1 at 8, *per* Lord Kissen; at 11, *per* Lord Leechman.

that circumstances might require a balancing of advantages and disadvantages to the seller and buyer.[65] The parties may agree that the price is to be fixed by the valuation of a third party, and where that third party fails to do so, the contract will be avoided.[66] If either of the contracting parties has been at fault in preventing the third party from carrying out the valuation, then the other contracting party has a right to sue him or her for damages.[67]

## 1.7. TIME

If a contract provides that time is of the essence in relation to a particular matter, then breach by one party of that stipulation will entitle the other party to rescind. In a contract of sale, unless the terms of the contract indicate that the parties intended otherwise, stipulations as to time of payment are not of the essence.[68] Whether any other stipulation as to time is or is not of the essence of the contract is a matter of interpretation of the terms of the contract.[69]

## 1.8. THE PASSING OF PROPERTY

The main purpose of the contract is to pass the property in goods (*i.e.* transfer ownership thereof) from seller to buyer. The regime which was imposed by the Sale of Goods Act 1893 in relation to passing of ownership of goods was very different from the pre-existing regime under Scots common law. At common law, the transfer of ownership required both the will or intention of the seller and delivery.[70] Under the 1979 Act the general rule is that property in goods (as ownership is described in the Act) passes when the parties intend it to pass.[71] In the case of unascertained goods, property cannot pass until the goods have been ascertained[72] although there is an exception to this rule in the case of unascertained goods which are part of an identified bulk.[73]

### (a) Rules for ascertaining intention

The parties may make their intentions in this regard perfectly clear, and usually do, while the Act specifically states that, in order to ascertain the intention of the parties, regard must be had to the terms of the contract, the conduct of the parties and the circumstances of the case.[74] However, after this process of interpretation has been completed, doubt may continue to exist as to the intentions of the parties. In such a case, use can be made of a number of rules contained in the Act which assist in ascertaining that intention. It should be noted, however, that such rules are only relevant where the intention of the parties is not clear. As Lord President Strathclyde explained:

---

[65] 1977 S.C. 1 at 8, *per* Lord Kissen.
[66] s.9(1).
[67] s.9(2). See also *Essoldo v Ladbroke Group* [1976] C.L.Y. 337, where the English courts granted an injunction preventing one of the parties from obstructing the determination of the price.
[68] s.10(1).
[69] s.10(2).
[70] Stair, *Institutions,* I,7,8 and III,2,5; Erskine, *Institute*, II,1,18; Bankton, *Institute* II,1,20; Bell, *Principles,* 1299, and *Commentaries,* I,177.
[71] s.17(1).
[72] s.16.
[73] See discussion at para. 1.8.(b) below.
[74] s.17(2).

"The rules in section 18 are merely intended to be a guide in ascertaining the intention of the parties. But, if the intention of the parties is quite plain . . . then the rules of section 18 do not come into play at all."[75]

*Rule 1* states:

"Where there is an unconditional contract for the sale of specific goods in a deliverable state the property in the goods passes to the buyer when the contract is made, and it is immaterial whether the time of payment or the time of delivery, or both, be postponed."

However, this is out of step with many modern transactions, especially sales to consumers. Thus Lord Diplock stated in *R. V. Ward Ltd v Bignall*[76]:

"In modern times very little is needed to give rise to the intention that the property in specific goods is to pass only on delivery or payment."[77]

The term "unconditional contract" probably refers to a contract with no conditions relating to the passing of property rather than a contract with no conditions whatsoever.[78] A "deliverable state" means that the goods are in such a state that the buyer would, under the contract, be bound to take delivery of them.[79] In *Gowans v Bowe & Sons*[80] in a contract for the sale of potatoes it was agreed that when the potatoes were mature the farmer would lift them and put them into pits on the farm. When the buyer wanted the potatoes, he was to send his workmen to lift the potatoes from the pits, clean and sort them, and put them into the buyer's bags. The farmer would then cart them to the railway station or harbour for the buyer. After the potatoes were put into pits, the seller went bankrupt. It was held that property in the potatoes had passed to the buyer. Lord Cullen explained:

". . . I am unable to regard such carting as something to be done to put the goods into a deliverable state. I think that, in the ordinary working out of such a contract, the potatoes would be delivered to the buyers when lifted by them from the pits and put into their own bags. According to the intention of the parties here, the carting was, I think, only a facility for removal after delivery."[81]

*Rule 2* states:

"where there is a contract for the sale of specific goods and the seller is bound to do something to the goods for the purpose of putting them into a deliverable state, the property does not pass until the thing is done and the buyer has notice that it has been done."

The *Gowans* case is an example of this rule. In that case the contract was for the sale of specific goods—the whole crop of potatoes. The seller was bound to put the potatoes into pits to put them into a deliverable state, and the buyer had been made aware that the seller had completed this task.

*Rule 3* states:

"where there is a contract for the sale of specific goods in a deliverable state but the seller is bound to weigh, measure, test, or do some other act or thing with reference to the goods for the purpose of ascertaining the price, the property does not pass until the act or thing is done and the buyer has notice that it has been done."

---

[75] *Woodburn v Andrew Motherwell Ltd,* 1917 S.C. 533 at 538.
[76] [1967] 1 Q.B. 534.
[77] [1967] 1 Q.B. 534 at 545, *per* Lord Diplock.
[78] But see *Varley v Whipp* [1900] 1 Q.B. 513 at 517, *per* Channell J.
[79] s.61(5).
[80] 1910 2 S.L.T. 17.
[81] 1910 2 S.L.T. 17 at 18, *per* Lord Cullen.

In *Nanka Bruce v Commonwealth Trust Ltd*[82] a sub-buyer was to weigh the goods, and the price paid by the buyer was calculated on the basis of this weight. It was held that the sale was not conditional on the weighing of the goods. The weighing was simply to check that the goods fitted the weight which has been represented. Property in the goods had passed prior to the weighing being carried out. Rule 3 would not have been appropriate, given that, in that case, the sub-buyer and not the seller was obliged to weigh the goods.

*Rule 4* states that:

> "when goods are delivered to the buyer on approval or on sale or return or other similar terms the property in the goods passes to the buyer—
> 
> (a) when he signifies his approval or acceptance to the seller or does any other act adopting the transaction;
> 
> (b) if he does not signify his approval or acceptance to the seller but retains the goods without giving notice of rejection, then, if a time has been fixed for the return of the goods, on the expiration of that time, and, if no time has been fixed, on the expiration of a reasonable time."

This rule, in common with the other rules, may be excluded by agreement between the parties.[83] In some cases it may be difficult to tell whether goods have, in fact, been provided by a seller to a buyer on a sale or return basis, or have been sent by a principal to an agent for the agent to sell on the principal's behalf.[84] If it is the former, the buyer is likely to be free to keep the whole proceeds of resale, whereas if at least a proportion of the resale price must be handed by the original buyer to the original seller, the buyer retaining a proportion of the price in payment of his fee it is likely to be regarded as the latter case. The importance of the distinction is seen where the contract stipulates that the property in the goods will not pass until the seller is paid in full. Were the contract to be regarded as a sale or return contract, then the second buyer might find that he or she is not the owner of the goods, where the first buyer fails to pay for them, whereas if the first buyer were reselling as the original seller's agent, the second buyer would receive good title to the goods.[85]

In one case, it appears that a retailer, on being sent goods by a wholesaler in order to effect sales to customers, became the purchaser himself on pledging the goods.[86] There are indications in the judgments that the Second Division was keen to ensure that the loss would not fall on the third party pawnbroker who had no knowledge of the relationship between the wholesaler and the retailer.[87] Property does not pass where the buyer fails to return the goods to the seller within the agreed period for reasons outwith his control, such as seizure by a creditor.[88]

*Rule 5* is divided into three parts.

*Part 1* provides that:

> "where there is a contract for the sale of unascertained or future goods by description, and goods of that description and in a deliverable state are unconditionally appropriated to the contract, either by the seller with the assent of the buyer or by the buyer with the assent of the seller, the property in the goods then passes to the buyer; and the assent may be express or implied, and may be given either before or after the appropriation is made."

---

[82] [1926] A.C. 77.

[83] *Weiner v Gill* [1906] 2 K.B. 574.

[84] *Weiner v Harris* [1910] 1 K.B. 285.

[85] *Weiner v Harris* [1910] 1 K.B. 285; and see para. 1.10. below, especially 1.10.(a).

[86] *Bryce v Ehrmann* (1904) 7 F. 5.

[87] *Bryce v Ehrmann* (1904) 7 F. 5 at 10, *per* the Lord Justice-Clerk Macdonald, and at 16, *per* Lord Moncreiff.

[88] *Re* Ferrier [1944] Ch. 295.

Because assent may be implied rather than express, it is sufficient if the buyer fails to respond to a notice from the seller that the goods are in a deliverable state and have been appropriated to the contract.[89] Express assent is not required. A useful analysis of the meaning of "unconditional appropriation" was made by Pearson J. in *Carlos Federspiel & Co SA v Charles Twigg & Co Ltd*.[90] He emphasised the consensual nature of appropriation:

> ". . . the element of common intention has always to be borne in mind. A mere setting apart or selection of the seller of the goods which he expects to use in performance of the contract is not enough. If that is all, he can change his mind and use those goods in performance of some other contract and use some other goods in performance of this contract."[91]

He continued:

> "To constitute an appropriation of the goods to the contract, the parties must have had, or be reasonably supposed to have had, an intention to attach the contract irrevocably to those goods, so that those goods and no others are the subject of the sale and become the property of the buyer . . .".[92]

He then suggested that the appropriating act was usually the last act to be carried out by the seller, although if the seller was due to carry out an "important and decisive" further act then property would not usually pass until that final act had been carried out.[93] So in *Hendy Lennox (Industrial Engines) Ltd v Grahame Puttick Ltd*[94] appropriation did not occur when generators were set aside and marked with the names of individual customers. Appropriation only occurred when the customers were sent invoices and delivery notes bearing the serial numbers of the generators to be delivered to them.

It should also be remembered that appropriation must be unconditional. So, if the contract stipulates, for example, that the property will only pass when the price is paid in full, that condition will prevail.

*Part 2* provides that:

> "where in pursuance of the contract, the seller delivers the goods to the buyer or to a carrier or other bailee or custodier (whether named by the buyer or not) for the purpose of transmission to the buyer, and does not reserve the right of disposal, he is to be taken to have unconditionally appropriated the goods to the contract."

This rule is, in effect, an example of appropriation. Giving of goods to a carrier may not mean that there has been appropriation, as in a case where a number of orders were despatched together to the same carrier with no indication of which goods are due to which customer.[95] The goods had not been ascertained so that property could not pass. Moreover, it must be appreciated that property will not pass if the seller reserves the right of disposal. So where goods are entrusted to a shipper under a bill of lading made out in the seller's favour, they remain at his disposal and no property passes.[96]

*Part 3* was added by the Sale of Goods (Amendment) Act 1995. It states:

> "where there is a contract for the sale of a specified quantity of unascertained goods in a deliverable state forming part of a bulk which is identified either in the contract or by

---

[89] *Pignataro v Gilroy* [1919] 1 K.B. 459.
[90] [1957] 1 Lloyd's Rep. 240.
[91] [1957] 1 Lloyd's Rep. 240 at 255, *per* Pearson J.
[92] [1957] 1 Lloyd's Rep. 240 at 255, *per* Pearson J.
[93] [1957] 1 Lloyd's Rep. 240 at 255–256, *per* Pearson J.
[94] [1984] 1 W.L.R. 485.
[95] *Healy v Howlett & Sons* [1917] 1 K.B. 337.
[96] See s.19(2) and para. 4.33.

subsequent agreement between the parties and the bulk is reduced to (or to less than) that quantity, then, if the buyer under that contract is the only buyer to whom goods are then due out of the bulk —

(a) the remaining goods are to be taken as appropriated to that contract at the time when the bulk is so reduced; and

(b) the property in those goods then passes to that buyer."

The effect of this part might be described as "appropriation by exhaustion."[97] Goods in a bulk are reduced to such an extent that the remaining amount is inevitably destined for one buyer alone. This is sufficient for appropriation and thus the passing of property.

## (b) Sales from an identified bulk

Sections 20A and 20B contain important provisions which must be read in conjunction with s.18 (r.5(3)). The law has always proceeded on the basis that it is a logical impossibility to sell unascertained goods.[98] Thus where, for example, there was an agreement to buy part of a bulk cargo,[99] no property could pass until that bulk had been divided into the appropriate fractions, because otherwise it was impossible to say exactly which goods the buyer owned. This could cause problems in insolvency situations, since if the seller went bankrupt (or into liquidation, if a company), the buyer would lose out in a contest for the goods with a liquidator or trustee in bankruptcy. This was the case even if the buyer had actually paid for the goods. In such a case, the liquidator or trustee would retain and resell the goods, leaving the buyer to pursue a claim as an ordinary creditor.[1] Pressure from certain commodity trade associations and concern that the parties to international sale contracts might select another legal system to govern their relations led to a report on the matter by the Law Commissions, and ultimately to an attempt to provide some protection for buyers in such situations by the addition of ss.20A and 20B by the Sale of Goods (Amendment) Act 1995.

Thus, where the buyer has paid in advance for a specified quantity of goods which are part of a bulk which has been identified by the parties,[2] he or she acquires an undivided share in the bulk, and becomes an owner in common with the other buyers and/or the seller.[3] So, if the owner of a cargo of 3,000 tonnes of coal sells 1,000 tonnes to each of three buyers, those buyers become owners in common of that cargo. Should the owner manage only to sell 1,000 tonnes to a single buyer before becoming insolvent, then he or she and the buyer become owners in common of the cargo.

It is important to bear in mind that these provisions only apply where the parties do not provide otherwise.[4] Also they apply only where the parties have agreed that the goods are to be supplied from an identified bulk, *i.e.* a mass or collection of goods of the same kind, which are contained in a defined space or area, and is such that any goods in the bulk are interchangeable with any other goods therein of the same number or quantity.[5] That identification may occur in the contract or by subsequent agreement,[6] such as where a buyer of grain is informed after the formation of the contract that the goods will be drawn from a particular cargo—as long as this

---

[97] Which was previously recognised by case law: see *The Elafi* [1982] 1 All E.R. 208; although the Act now makes it clear that property to what remains passes, even if it was less than the buyer contracted for.

[98] s.16.

[99] As is commonplace in the commodity trades: see Joint Report by the Law Commissions, *Sale of Goods Forming Part of a Bulk* (Law Com. No. 215; Scot. Law Com. No. 145, July 1993), para. 1.3.

[1] See *Re Wait* [1927] 1 Ch. 606; *Re London Wine Shippers* [1986] P.C.C. 121; but *cf. Re Stapylton Fletcher Ltd* [1994] 1 W.L.R. 1181.

[2] s.20A(1).

[3] s.20A(2).

[4] s.20A(2).

[5] s.61(1).

[6] s.20A(1)(a), see para. 4.3. of the Law Commissions' Joint Report for examples of situations which fall within the ambit of the provision (*op. cit.*, Law Com. No. 215; Scot. Law Com. No. 145, July 1993).

reflects the agreement of the parties. The provisions are not designed to apply where a seller receives an order to be filled from his general stock at his discretion, or even that both parties had a specific source in mind, if they did not actually agree that the goods would be drawn from that source. Moreover, they only apply when the buyer agrees to buy a specified quantity of goods from the bulk,[7] *i.e.* 1,000 tonnes from the bulk, but not one third or 20 per cent of the bulk. (A person purchasing a fraction or percentage of an identified bulk would acquire an undivided share of the goods, but would not be subject to the provisions of ss.20A and 20B.) Finally, they only apply when the buyer has paid for the goods or at least some of them.[8] Part payment of the price for any goods is treated as payment for a corresponding part of the goods.[9] So, if the buyer agrees to buy 1,000 tonnes of coal at £100 per tonne, and pays half the price in advance, *i.e.* £50,000, he is treated as having paid for 500 tonnes.

Section 20A(3) states that the size of share which the buyer has at any time is such share as the quantity he has paid for out of the bulk bears to the quantity of goods in the bulk at that time. So, if the buyer has paid for 1,000 tonnes out of a 3,000 tonne cargo, he is entitled to a one-third share of the cargo. Equally, if the liquidator of the seller company has sold and removed a further 1,000 tonnes from the cargo, leaving only 2,000 tonnes, then the buyer remains and, still entitled to 1,000 tonnes consequently, his share increases to one half.[10] More importantly, should in the above scenario 1,000 tonnes have instead been stolen or destroyed, the buyer is again entitled to the 1,000 tonnes he or she has paid for, and thus one half of the bulk. In other words s.20A(3) imposes the risk of any loss on the seller. On the other hand, s.20A(4) directs that if the aggregate of the shares of buyers exceeds the size of the bulk, the shares must be reduced proportionately.[11] So, if each of three buyers has bought and paid for 1,000 tonnes out of a 3,000 tonne cargo, and it transpires that there are only 2,700 tonnes in the cargo, the entitlement of each buyer, *inter se*, is reduced to 900 tonnes. This does not mean that any buyer is then contractually entitled to only 900 tonnes. Section 20B(3)(c) provides that nothing in either s.20A or s.20B affects the right of any buyer under his or her contract. Each of the buyers in the above scenario retains a claim against the seller for failing to deliver the appropriate amount of goods, which claim might of course be worth very little in an insolvency situation. Section 20A(4) simply attempts to achieve equity among buyers when it is practically impossible to deliver to each the amount he or she is due.

Ultimately, of course, a buyer will seek delivery of the goods due to him or her from the bulk. Where the buyer has paid for only some of the goods due to him or her, and some are delivered to him or her, it is assumed that the goods so delivered are goods for which he or she has paid.[12] In other words, where the buyer has ordered 2,000 tonnes of coal from the bulk, but paid only for 1,000, should 1,000 tonnes be delivered to him or her, it will be deemed to be the 1,000 tonnes he or she has paid for, and he or she will be precluded from arguing that he or she has received the other 1,000 tonnes and thus remains entitled to 1,000 tonnes from the bulk. At common law, the agreement of all common owners is required for any dealing with the property. This is clearly not practical in the current context, so any common owner is deemed to consent to:

(1) any delivery from the bulk to any other common owner of goods due to the latter under his contract,[13] and

---

[7] s.20A(1).

[8] s.20A(1)(b).

[9] s.20A(6).

[10] It would be possible for the amount of the bulk to increase, and for the share owned by the buyer thus to decrease, *e.g.* where a buyer has bought 500 gallons of oil held in a particular storage tank. At the time of entering into the contract, it contains 1,000 gallons, so his share is a half. Should another 1,000 gallons be deposited in the tank, his share would be a quarter.

[11] s.20A(4).

[12] s.20A(5).

[13] s.20B(1)(a).

(2) any removal or disposal by another common owner of goods which are part of the latter's share of the bulk.[14]

No cause of action accrues against anyone who acts in accordance with the above provisions, nor is there any obligation on any buyer to compensate another in respect of any shortfall in the goods received by that buyer.[15] These provisions, put crudely, operate on a "first come, first served basis". Take the scenario of three buyers who each buy and pay for 1,000 tonnes out of a 3,000 tonne cargo. One buyer takes delivery of his 1,000 tonnes, and it then transpires that there are only 2,700 tonnes in the cargo, so that the "entitlement" of each buyer was only 900 tonnes. The other buyers have no right against the first, as he was contractually entitled to the 1,000 tonnes of which he received delivery. An alternative scenario would be that one buyer buys and pays for 1,000 tonnes out of a 3,000 tonne cargo, while another agrees to buy the other 2,000 tonnes, but pays for only half. Although the latter's share in terms of s.20A is only 1,000 tonnes, he is contractually entitled to 2,000 tonnes, so that if he takes delivery of that amount, the other buyer may not complain, even if he faces a shortfall as a result.

## (c) Reservation of the right of disposal and retention of title

As has been illustrated above, the governing principle in the transfer of property in goods is the intention of the parties. Section 19 permits the seller to reserve the right of disposal in the goods until certain conditions are fulfilled. Even though goods have been delivered to the buyer, the seller retains the property in the goods until those conditions are fulfilled.

A practical example of the operation of this section is the use of retention of title clauses. Such clauses permit the parties to agree that the seller will retain the property in the goods notwithstanding delivery to the buyer, until the buyer has paid the price in full. Such clauses are relatively uncontroversial in Scots law, being, in effect, a contract of sale subject to a suspensive condition.[16] However, more complex clauses known as "all sums" clauses proved to be problematic for the courts. Such clauses provide that title to the goods is reserved until all sums due by the buyer to the seller in the context of all transactions between the two parties have been paid. Such clauses were initially considered to be an attempt to create a security over corporeal moveables without possession and therefore invalid.[17] Section 62(4) of the 1979 Act disapplies the Act in relation to such clauses. Eventually, the House of Lords held that such clauses were valid, considering them to be a simple application of the rules contained in s.17 and s.19(1) of the Act. The buyer was not attempting to create a security without possession because he or she had never had the property in the goods.[18]

However, even that decision created only a limited protection for a seller seeking payment. While such clauses allow a seller who is owed money by the buyer to assert ownership of the goods as against the buyer (or the buyer's liquidator or trustee in bankruptcy), no retention of title clause, whatever its form, allows a seller to assert ownership against a *bona fide* purchaser from the buyer. (See discussion of sales by buyers in possession in para 1.10.). Accordingly those drafting such clauses sought to confer a measure of protection by adding terms which provided that the proceeds of any sale of the goods by the buyer were to be held in trust for the original seller. Whilst such clauses may be effective in English law,[19] they are not effective in

---

[14] s.20B(1)(b).

[15] s.20B(2), (3)(a).

[16] *Archivent Sales & Development Ltd v Strathclyde RC,* 1985 S.L.T. 154, although in that case the retention of title clause was defeated by the operation of s.25 of the Sale of Goods Act 1979 which permits a buyer in possession to transfer the property in goods under certain conditions, see below. On sales subject to a suspensive condition, see Stair, *Institutions,* I,14,4.

[17] *Deutz Engines Ltd v Terex Ltd,* 1984 S.L.T. 273. For the rule against the creation of securities over corporeal moveables without possession, see Gloag & Irvine, *The Law of Rights in Security* (1897) pp.188–189 and see discussion at para. 6.3. below.

[18] *Armour v Thyssen Edelstahlwerke AG,* 1990 S.L.T. 891.

[19] *Aluminium Industrie Vaasen BV v Romalpa Aluminium Ltd* [1976] 1 W.L.R. 676.

Scots law, Lord President Emslie commented that ". . . the essential ingredients of a trust are entirely lacking . . .".[20] Another ingenious term sought to overcome the principles of accession and *specificatio* in the law of property by purporting to retain title to the goods, even where the original goods had been incorporated by the buyer into a new product or irreversibly changed in nature.[21] Since these goods would be regarded as new goods, such a term would be regarded, not as an attempt to retain ownership of goods, but as an assertion of some sort of right of ownership over goods which would not belong to the seller at common law. Given that such terms do not appear to receive effect even in England,[22] and in light of the hostility of the Scottish courts to certain forms of retention of title clauses, such a term is likely to be found invalid as an attempt to create a security without possession.[23]

## 1.9.   THE PASSING OF THE RISK

The passing of the property in goods is related to the passing of the risk, *i.e.* which party bears the risk if the goods are damaged or destroyed. Provisions on the passing of risk are contained in s.20 of the 1979 Act. However, the 2002 Regulations recently added an important amendment to this section, providing that s.20 is, effectively, ignored where certain criteria apply.[24] The contract must be a consumer contract, and the buyer must also be a "consumer". A "consumer contract" is a contract where one party deals in the course of a business and the other party does not so deal.[25] "Consumers" are natural persons acting for purposes outside their trade, business or profession.[26] Where the contract relates to the transfer of the ownership or possession of goods, the goods must also be of a type "ordinarily supplied for private use or consumption."[27] Following the amendments enacted by the 2002 Regulations, this latter limitation does not apply where the consumer is an individual,[28] the goods remain at the seller's risk until they are delivered to the consumer. There is therefore a blanket consumer protection rule on the passing of risk in what might be called "pure" consumer situations.[29]

Outside those "pure" consumer situations, unless the parties agree otherwise, the general rule is that the owner of the goods bears the risk of their damage or deterioration, in other words, the risk passes when the property passes. Thus s.20(1) stipulates:

> "Unless otherwise agreed, the goods remain at the seller's risk until the property in them is transferred to the buyer, but when the property in them is transferred to the buyer the goods are at the buyer's risk whether delivery has been made or not."

Importantly, therefore, risk does not depend upon actual possession of the goods.

The rule in s.20(1) is subject to two further exceptions. First, if delivery has been delayed through the fault of either party, the goods are at that party's risk as regards any loss which

---

[20] *Clark Taylor & Co Ltd v Quality Site Development (Edinburgh) Ltd,* 1981 S.C. 111 at 116, *per* Lord President Emslie.

[21] *Deutz Engines Ltd v Terex Ltd,* 1984 S.L.T. 273 at 274–275, *per* Lord Ross.

[22] See *Re Peachdart Ltd* [1984] 1 Ch. 131.

[23] See *Deutz Engines Ltd v Terex Ltd,* 1984 S.L.T.273 but *cf. Zahnrad Fabrik Passau GmbH v Terex Ltd,* 1986 S.L.T. 84.

[24] 2002 Regulations, reg. 4(2) adding new s.20(4) to the 1979 Act.

[25] Unfair Contract Terms Act 1977, s.25(1).

[26] 2002 Regulations, reg. 2.

[27] Unfair Contract Terms Act 1977, s.25(1).

[28] 2002 Regulations, reg. 14, inserting new s.25(1A) into the Unfair Contract Terms Act 1977, s.25(1).

[29] See also a similar amendment made to s.32, which deals with the effect of delivery to a carrier. S.32(1) provides that where the seller is authorised or required to send the goods to the buyer, delivery of goods to the carrier is deemed to be delivery of goods to the buyer. The 2002 Regulations, reg. 4(3), add a new s.32(4) to the 1979 Act. Its effect is that where the contract is a consumer contract and the buyer is a "pure" consumer, s.32 does not apply, and delivery of goods by the seller to the carrier is not deemed to be delivery to the buyer.

might not have occurred but for that fault.[30] An example of this rule in operation can be found in *Demby Hamilton & Co Ltd v Barden*[31] where the buyer delayed in providing instructions as to the delivery of apple juice in casks. When the apple juice went "off", the buyer was held to bear the risk of deterioration even though property in the goods remained with the seller. Secondly, nothing in s.20 affects the duties of either party as a custodier of the goods of the other party.[32] So the party in possession will remain liable for loss deriving from his or her negligence or that of his servants.

Certain of the provisions of the Act dealing with destruction of the goods follow the common law of contract. The Act provides that where there is a contract for the sale of specific goods and, without the seller's knowledge, they have perished at the time the contract is made, the contract is void.[33] A similar rule applies in a contract for the sale of specific goods where, without the fault of either party, the goods perish after the contract is entered into but before the risk passes to the buyer. The contract is again void.[34] It may not be easy to establish whether goods have perished. In *Asfar v Blundell*,[35] a vessel carrying dates was sunk during the course of a voyage. The defendant argued that there had been no change in nature of the dates, they "were still dates, composed of stone, skin, flesh . . ." even though they had been impregnated with sewage and had begun to ferment. Lord Esher M.R. stated that goods have perished if they are so changed in their nature "as to become an unmerchantable thing . . . which no buyer would buy and no honest seller would sell, . . .".[36] In this case the dates had undoubtedly changed in nature and become unmerchantable, and so it was held that no freight was payable. If the goods which are the subject of the contract have, in fact, never existed, neither s.6 nor s.7 will apply to make the contract void. The seller may be liable in damages for representing to the buyer that the goods exist.[37]

It was seen that s.20 is subject to the contrary agreement of the parties, and parties will commonly contract so as to ensure that the risk is borne by the party in possession, irrespective of ownership. So, for example, if a seller is successful in inserting a retention of title clause (see previous para) into the contract, he would almost invariably also include a term to the effect that the goods are at the buyer's risk, as soon as the latter acquires possession. By contrast ss.6 and 7 are not expressed to be subject to contrary agreement, so that it does not seem open to the parties to place the goods at either's risk, where s.6 or s.7 would render the contract void. It is implicit in all that has been said so far, that if the goods are at the buyer's risk when destroyed, then he or she remains liable for the price, while if they are destroyed while at the seller's risk, then (subject to s.7) he or she remains liable to fulfil the contract.

The interaction of the buyer's right to reject (see para. 1.12.) and the passing of risk is subject to doubt. It may be the case that the passing of risk is subject to the buyer's right to reject where the goods turn out to be defective or otherwise disconform to contract. It has been stated that even if the property has passed to the buyer, the risk always remains with the seller where the buyer has a right to reject, presumably subject to an obligation on the part of the buyer to take reasonable care of the goods while they are in his or her possession.[38]

---

[30] s.20(2).

[31] [1949] 1 All E.R. 435.

[32] s.20(3).

[33] s.6.

[34] s.7.

[35] [1896] 1 Q.B. 123.

[36] [1896] 1 Q.B. 123 at 128, *per* Lord Esher M.R.

[37] *McRae v Commonwealth Disposals Commission* (1951) 84 C.L.R. 377.

[38] See Atiyah, Adams, and MacQueen, *The Sale of Goods*, (10th ed., 2000), pp.352–353 citing *Head v Tatersall* (1870) L.R. 7 Ex. 7 as authority for this proposition. Some support for this view is perhaps to be found in a Scottish case decided after the passing of the Act: see *Kinnear v Brodie* (1901) 8 S.L.T. 475.

# 1.10.  SALES BY A NON-OWNER

Having discussed how the property in goods passes, it is appropriate to consider whether ownership of goods may be transferred if they are sold by someone who does not own them. Section 21(1) states:

> ". . . where goods are sold by a person who is not their owner, and who does not sell them under the authority or with the consent of the owner, the buyer acquires no better title to the goods than the seller had, unless the owner of the goods is by his conduct precluded from denying the seller's authority to sell."

This is an expression of the rule *nemo dat quod non habet*, or that no one can pass a better title than that which he had. The exception to this rule, *i.e.* the latter part which prevents the owner from denying the seller's authority to sell, is difficult to analyse. It resembles personal bar, or what is known as estoppel in English law. However, doubts have been expressed in English law as to whether it is based on estoppel, in particular because it is not limited to the usual type of estoppel which prevents the true owner from denying the seller's authority to sell, but, in addition, has the effect of permitting ownership of goods to pass. In particular, Lord Devlin commented:

> "We doubt whether this principle . . . ought really to be regarded as part of the law of estoppel. At any rate it differs from what is sometimes called "equitable estoppel" in this vital respect, that the effect of its application is to transfer a real title and not merely a metaphorical title by estoppel."[39]

It may be that the exception can be explained by reference to the apparent authority of an agent,[40] rather than personal bar.[41]

Further exceptions to the *nemo dat* rule exist, and, in common with the exception discussed above, they may rest upon the principle of apparent authority. The logic behind these exceptions was explained by Lord Denning as follows:

> "In the development of our law, two principles have striven for mastery. The first is for the protection of property: no one can give a better title than he himself possesses. The second is for the protection of commercial transactions: the person who takes in good faith and for value without notice should get a good title. The first principle has held sway for a long time, but it has been modified by the common law itself and by statute so as to meet the needs of our own times."[42]

These exceptions are considered below.

## (a) Sale by a mercantile agent

The Factors Act 1889 s.2(1) provides:

> "Where a mercantile agent is, with the consent of the owner, in possession of goods or of the documents of title to goods, any sale, pledge, or other disposition of the goods, made by him when acting in the ordinary course of business of a mercantile agent, shall . . . be as valid as if he were expressly authorised by the owner of the goods to make the same;

---

[39] *Eastern Distributors Ltd v Goldring* [1957] 2 Q.B. 600 at 611, *per* Lord Devlin.

[40] See para. 2.4.(b) below.

[41] *Eastern Distributors Ltd v Goldring* [1957] 2 Q.B. 600 at 611, *per* Lord Devlin, see *Corporeal Moveables—Protection of the onerous bona fide acquirer of another's property*, (SLC Memorandum No. 27, 1976), paras 27–28.

[42] *Bishopsgate Motor Finance Corporation Ltd v Transport Brakes Ltd* [1949] 1 K.B. 322 at 336–337, *per* Lord Denning.

provided that the person taking under the disposition acts in good faith, and has not at the time of the disposition notice that the person making the disposition has not authority to make the same."[43]

One may have assumed that if the mercantile agent had tricked the principal into leaving the goods with him, then that would prevent the operation of this section. However, the section simply requires the consent of the owner to the agent's possession. In *Pearson v Rose & Young*[44] the Court of Appeal held that the fact that the agent had obtained the registration book for the car subsequently sold by him by larceny by a trick was not important. The only question was whether the goods were in his possession with the consent of the owner. Lord Denning explained that consent may be provided for different purposes:

> "That means that the owner must consent to the agent having them for a purpose which is in some way or other connected with his business as a mercantile agent. It may not actually be for sale. It may be for display or to get offers, or merely to put in his showroom; but there must be a consent to something of that kind before the owner can be deprived of his goods."[45]

In other words, if an individual entrusts his car to a car dealer for the purpose of finding out what sort of offers might be made on it, any unsuspecting individual to whom the dealer sells the vehicle obtains a good title, even if the dealer tricked the owner into giving up possession. However, if the owner had given the dealer the car merely to be repaired, the dealer could not give a good title to a bona fide purchaser, as he does not have the goods in his capacity as a mercantile agent.

According to the Factors Act 1889, a mercantile agent is someone ". . . having in the customary course of his business as such agent authority either to sell goods or to consign goods for the purpose of sale, or to buy goods, or to raise money on the security of goods."[46] In other words, a mercantile agent is someone who customarily sells goods in the course of a business. So a car hire company was not a mercantile agent where it occasionally sold cars from its fleet.[47] It can be appreciated from this definition that a pawnbroker is a mercantile agent.

## (b) Sale by a seller in possession

Section 24 of the Act provides that:

> "Where a person having sold goods continues or is in possession of the goods, or of the documents of title to the goods, the delivery or transfer by that person, or by a mercantile agent acting for him, of the goods or documents of title under any sale, pledge, or other disposition there of, to any person receiving the same in good faith and without notice of the previous sale, has the same effect as if the person making the delivery or transfer were expressly authorised by the owner of the goods to make the same."[48]

The requirement for continuity of possession has been interpreted as continuity of physical possession only. It does not matter if the legal nature of the seller's possession has changed in nature, *i.e.* if the seller becomes an agent or custodier for the buyer.[49] The seller's continued possession of the goods may even be wrongful[50]—unlike s.2(1) of the Factors Act 1889 there is

---

[43] See para. 2.3.(b) below.
[44] [1951] 1 K.B. 275.
[45] *Pearson v Rose & Young* [1951] 1 K.B. 275 at 288, *per* Lord Denning.
[46] s.1(1), see also s.26 of the 1979 Act.
[47] *Belvoir Finance Ltd v Harold G. Cole Ltd* [1969] 1 W.L.R. 1877.
[48] See also s.8 of the Factors Act 1889.
[49] *Pacific Motor Auctions Proprietary Ltd v Motor Credits (Hire Finance) Ltd* [1965] A.C. 867; *Worcester Works Finance Ltd v Cooden Engineering Co Ltd* [1972] 1 Q.B. 182.
[50] *Worcester Works Finance Ltd v Cooden Engineering Co Ltd* [1972] 1 Q.B. 182.

no requirement in this section that the possession be with the consent of the owner. So someone who has sold goods, but who instead of delivering them to the buyer, purports to sell them again to a bona fide purchaser, gives a good title to the latter. But someone who sold goods, yielded possession to the buyer, and thereafter recovered possession, *e.g.* by hiring the goods from the buyer, would no longer be a seller in possession, and so would not be able to confer a good title if he or she purported to sell the goods.

The word "disposition" is interpreted widely. In *Worcester Works Finance Ltd v Cooden Engineering Co Ltd*[51] it was interpreted as including the repossession by the original owner from the seller in possession with that seller's consent. Seizure of the goods against the seller's will does not, however, amount to a disposition within the meaning of the section.[52] The recent case of *Michael Gerson (Leasing) Ltd v Wilkinson*[53] contains an unusual interpretation of the idea of the "delivery or transfer" which the seller in possession makes to the buyer in terms of s.24. A company, E, sold goods under a sale and leaseback arrangement to a finance company, MG, but without ever delivering them to MG. In other words E sold the goods to MG, which then leased them to E, E remaining in possession throughout. E then purported to enter a similar sale and leaseback arrangement in relation to some of the same goods (known as the sch. 3 goods) to another finance company, State. In neither case were the goods actually delivered to either of the finance companies. State then sold the Sch. 3 goods to another company, Sagebush. The Court of Appeal found that E amounted to a seller in possession in terms of s.24, and that there had been a constructive delivery of the Sch. 3 goods from E to State, followed by an immediate redelivery to E as a hirer. State therefore obtained good title to the Sch. 3 goods under s.24, and could resell them to Sagebush.

## (c) Sale by a buyer in possession

Section 25(1) provides that:

> "Where a person having bought or agreed to buy goods obtains, with the consent of the seller, possession of the goods or the documents of title to the goods, the delivery or transfer by that person, or by a mercantile agent acting for him, of the goods or documents of title, under any sale, pledge or other disposition thereof, to any person receiving the same in good faith and without notice of any lien or other right of the original seller in respect of the goods, has the same effect as if the person making the delivery or transfer were a mercantile agent in possession of the goods or documents of title with the consent of the owner."[54]

It can be appreciated that it is this provision which will often defeat retention of title clauses (discussed at para. 1.8.). Even though such a clause may ordinarily be effective to retain ownership of the goods in the seller, s.25(1) allows a buyer in possession to confer a good title on a bona fide purchaser. Section 25(2) specifically provides that a buyer under a conditional sale agreement (see para. 3.2.) is not a person who has bought or agreed to buy goods for the purposes of this section. A buyer under a sale or return contract is similarly not within the ambit of the section.[55] So if property in the goods has not already passed to a buyer under a sale or return contract, he or she cannot confer a good title on a bona fide purchaser, hence the discussion in para 1.8. of the importance of determining whether an individual has really taken goods on sale or return or is selling them as the seller's agent. Buyers from individuals who have taken goods on sale or return will often be protected by such individuals being regarded as mercantile agents.

---

[51] [1972] 1 Q.B. 210.
[52] See *The Saetta* [1994] 1 All E.R. 851.
[53] [2000] 3 W.L.R. 1645.
[54] See also s.9 of the Factors Act 1889.
[55] *Weiner v Harris* [1910] 1 K.B. 285.

Just as *Michael Gerson (Leasing) Ltd v Wilkinson*[56] is illustrative of the wide interpretation given by the courts to terms such as "possession" and "delivery" in the context of s.24, so *Four Point Garage Ltd v Carter*[57] is illustrative of the same approach to cases falling within s.25. The defendant agreed to buy a car from a dealer, F, and paid the full purchase price without taking possession of the car. F did not have the car, but intended to purchase it from the plaintiff, also a car dealer. F asked the plaintiff to deliver the car direct to the defendant, so that at no time did F take possession of the car. The plaintiff delivered the car to the defendant, but thought that he was leasing it to the defendant. The defendant thought that the car had been delivered to him by F. F then went into liquidation without paying the plaintiff. The plaintiff brought an action against the defendant claiming that the car had remained in his ownership. It was held that, through the operation of s.25, the defendant had obtained good title to the car. F had acted as a buyer in possession, even though he had at no time been in possession of the car. Simon Brown J. explained his reasoning on this point as follows:

> "There appears no possible good reason to differentiate under the statute between a case where, as here, the plaintiff sellers themselves deliver direct to the sub-purchaser and a case where . . . instead, the seller delivers to his buyer, who then forthwith delivers on to the sub-purchaser. Often no doubt the precise arrangement would depend on no more than the geographical interrelationship of the three parties."[58]

Clearly, the protection of the buyer acting in good faith, the defendant here, is a high priority. The result also ignores the requirement in s.25 that there be delivery or transfer of the goods by the buyer in possession. F, the buyer "in possession" did not actually deliver the goods to the defendant. As will be characteristic of the operation of s.25, F, the buyer in possession does not have good title to the goods, but is nevertheless able to pass good title to a buyer in good faith.

The buyer in possession must have the seller's consent to his possession, but it does not matter if the consent is subsequently withdrawn and the original contract is rescinded.[59] However, s.25 cannot operate to pass good title where the original seller had no title to the goods whatsoever. Thus where goods are stolen from A by B and B sells to C, who then sells to D, D does not obtain a good title, and D cannot claim that C is a buyer in possession with the consent of the seller.[60] In the opinion of Lord Goff, the original Factors Acts sought to give:

> ". . . protection to those who had dealt in good faith with factors or agents, to whom goods, or documents of title to goods, had been entrusted, to the extent that the rights of such persons should . . . .override those of the owner who had so entrusted the goods or documents to the factor or agent . . .".[61]

The Acts did not seek to "enable a factor or agent, entrusted with goods by a thief or a purchaser from a thief, to give a good title to a bona fide purchaser from him, overriding the title of the true owner."[62]

### (d) Sales of motor vehicles subject to hire purchase or conditional sale agreements

As stated above, s.25 is explicitly stated not to apply to conditional sale agreements.[63] Similarly, it cannot apply to sales by the hirer under a hire-purchase agreement (see para. 3.2.), given that

---

[56] [2000] 3 W.L.R. 1645.
[57] [1985] 3 All E.R. 12. This case also indicates that s.25 may defeat a retention of title clause, as also occurred in *Archivent Sales & Development Ltd v Strathclyde RC,* 1985 S.L.T. 154.
[58] [1985] 3 All E.R. 12 at 15, *per* Simon Brown J.
[59] *Newtons of Wembley v Williams* [1965] 1 Q.B. 560.
[60] *National Employers Mutual General Insurance Association Ltd v Jones* [1990] 1 A.C. 24.
[61] *National Employers Mutual General Insurance Association Ltd v Jones* [1990] 1 A.C. 24 at 58, *per* Lord Goff.
[62] *National Employers Mutual General Insurance Association Ltd v Jones* [1990] 1 A.C. 24 at 59, *per* Lord Goff.
[63] s.25(2).

he or she has not bought or agreed to buy the goods. However, such legal niceties tend not to be appreciated by most individuals who "buy" goods under conditional sale or hire-purchase agreements, who regard themselves as the owner of the goods. Normally, this has little practical consequence, as these goods are not often resold. The major exception to this practice is, of course, cars, which are routinely resold. Under the 1979 Act, an unsuspecting purchaser of a car which the seller held on H.P. found that he or she had no title. Because this was a distressingly frequent occurrence, the situation was addressed by ss.27 to 29 of the Hire-Purchase Act 1964. These sections apply to a party who has hired a motor vehicle under a hire-purchase agreement, or holds it under a conditional sale agreement and has not yet become the owner of the vehicle. Where that party makes a disposition[64] of the motor vehicle to a private purchaser acting in good faith and without notice of the relevant hire or conditional sale agreement, the disposition is valid.[65] It can be appreciated that the provisions aim to protect private but not trade purchasers. It makes no difference that the motor vehicle may have passed through the hands of several trade purchasers before reaching the private purchaser.[66] However, the first private purchaser to acquire the motor vehicle must do so in good faith. If he or she does not, then no subsequent purchaser can acquire good title to it.[67]

It might be added that someone who buys a vehicle from an individual who is hiring it under a contract of lease, rather than a contract of hire purchase, cannot be given a good title.[68]

### (e) Sale under a voidable title

Section 23 reflects the common law rule that where a seller has a voidable title to goods, but it has not been avoided at the time of sale, the buyer obtains a good title provided he or she acts in good faith and without notice of the defect in title.[69] It should be noted, however, that even after the buyer's title has been avoided, the buyer in possession may be able to pass good title under s.25.[70] It must be doubted whether this is the case if the contract is void *ab initio*.[71]

## 1.11. DUTIES OF THE SELLER

The seller is subject to a number of duties under the contract of sale.

### (a) Delivery

It is the duty of the seller to deliver the goods and of the buyer to accept and pay for them.[72] The word "delivery" is not used here in the sense of physical delivery, but rather "voluntary transfer of possession."[73] Thus, whether the buyer must collect the goods from the seller or the seller must send them to the buyer is a matter of interpretation of the terms of the contract.[74] In the absence of any provision to the contrary, the place of delivery is the seller's place of

---

[64] Disposition is defined in s.29(1) and includes ". . . any sale or contract of sale (including a conditional sale agreement), any . . . hiring under a hire-purchase agreement and any transfer of the property of goods in pursuance of a provision in that behalf contained in a hire-purchase agreement . . .".

[65] s.27(2).

[66] s.27(3).

[67] s.27(4).

[68] *Mitchell v Heys & Sons* (1894) 21 R. 600.

[69] See *MacLeod v Kerr,* 1965 S.L.T. 358.

[70] *Newtons of Wembley v Williams* [1965] 1 Q.B. 560.

[71] *Morrisson v Robertson* (1908) 15 S.L.T. 697.

[72] s.27.

[73] s.61(1).

[74] s.29(1).

business, or if he or she has none, his or her residence, but if the contract is for the sale of specific goods which the parties at the time the contract was made knew to be in some other place, that place is the place of delivery.[75] Where the seller is obliged to deliver the goods to the buyer in terms of the contract but there is no stipulation as to time, they must be sent within a reasonable time,[76] and delivery must be made at a reasonable hour.[77]

It has been stated that ". . . in ordinary commercial contracts for the sale of goods the rule clearly is that time is *prima facie* of the essence with respect to delivery."[78] Breach of the obligation of delivery on the part of the seller would therefore give the buyer the right to rescind. The buyer may, however, lose that right if, after the due date for delivery, the buyer continues to press for delivery.[79] The buyer in this position may stipulate a new time for delivery so that time can again be of the essence provided that the period stipulated is reasonable.[80]

## (b) Delivery of the wrong quantity

Where the seller delivers too few goods the buyer may reject them or keep them, paying at the contract rate.[81] Where he or she delivers too many goods the buyer may reject them all, or reject only the excess, or keep them all, paying at the contract rate.[82] In either case the buyer may not reject the whole of the goods delivered unless the shortfall or excess is material.[83] Each of the rules on delivery of the wrong quantity may be varied by the parties by agreement.

## (c) Duty to pass good title

Section 12(1) provides that it is an implied term of the contract of sale that the seller has a right to sell the goods, and, in the case of an agreement to sell, that he or she will have such a right at the time when the property is to pass. Lack of a right to sell does not necessarily mean that the seller does not own the goods. In *Niblett v Confectioners Materials Co Ltd*[84] the seller did not have a right to sell because the goods infringed a third party's trademark. This case must be contrasted with *Microbeads AC v Vinhurst Road Markings Ltd*[85] in which the goods which were the subject of the contract of sale again infringed a patent. However, that patent had been granted after the time of sale. Therefore, because at the time of sale there was no patent to infringe, there was no concomitant breach of the seller's duty under this section.

The buyer's remedy for breach of s.12(1) is rejection of the goods and return of the price. That this remedy can constitute significant protection for the buyer can be seen from cases such as *Warman v Southern Counties Car Finance Corporation Ltd*.[86] In this case the hirer exercised his remedy of rejection of a car. He was found entitled not only to the return of his instalment payments, but also the costs of insuring it, repairing it, and defending an action by the true owner. The party who had hired the car to him was held not entitled to claim anything for the hire of the car during the period in which the hirer had the use of it.

*Butterworth v Kingsway Motors Ltd*[87] is a further example of the buyer's right to rescind due to breach of the implied term contained in s.12(1), but is of greater interest for its analysis of

---

[75] s.29(2).
[76] s.29(3).
[77] s.29(5).
[78] *Hartley v Hyams* [1920] 3 K.B. 475 at 484, *per* McCardie J.
[79] *Hartley v Hyams* [1920] 3 K.B. 475; *Charles Rickards Ltd v Oppenheim* [1950] 1 K.B. 166.
[80] *Charles Rickards Ltd v Oppenheim* [1950] 1 K.B. 166.
[81] s.30(1).
[82] s.30(2)–(3).
[83] s.30(2D).
[84] [1921] 3 K.B. 387.
[85] [1975] 1 W.L.R. 218.
[86] [1949] 2 K.B. 576, note that this case was decided under the equivalent provisions of the hire-purchase legislation. See also *Rowland v Divall* [1923] 2 K.B. 500.
[87] [1954] 2 All E.R. 694.

the transfer of title to a car sold in breach of a hire-purchase contract. R sold the car while she held it on hire-purchase, mistakenly believing that she had the right to do so. Ownership of the car, however, remained with the hire company. However, she continued to make the hire payments when they became due. The car was then sold several times until R eventually discovered that she had had no right to sell it. The eventual buyer, B, rescinded the contract because of the breach by his immediate seller, K, of s.12(1) and obtained the return of the price. However, when R made the last payment due, title to the car vested in her, and, according to the court, perfected all of the other titles of parties who had bought and sold the car subsequent to the sale by her. The car eventually vested in K. The court left open the question whether B would have been entitled to rescind had K's title to the car been perfected prior to the raising of the action for reduction by B. The wider question is, given that the Act recognises a number of situations where someone who has no right to sell goods can nonetheless confer a good title on a bona fide purchaser (see para. 1.10.), whether the buyer may rescind the contract under s.12(1), even though the true owner of the goods cannot impugn his title. It is submitted that since there is still a clear breach of s.12(1) in such situations, rescission is open to the buyer.

In *McDonald v Provan (of Scotland Street)*[88] the seller unsuccessfully sought to use the doctrine of *specificatio* to avoid the duties imposed on him by s.12(1). F had welded together two halves of different cars, one half being part of a stolen car. He had then sold it to P who acted in good faith, and who then sold it to M, before it was removed by the police. P argued that, applying the doctrine of *specificatio,* the new car constituted an entirely new entity, and the right of property in it vested in the party who had constructed it, namely F. In rejecting this argument, Lord President Clyde commented:

> "The doctrine which the defenders seek to invoke is an equitable doctrine, not a strict rule of law, and the doctrine can only be invoked where there is complete *bona fides* on the part of the manufacturer . . . The result is that the defenders never did acquire an exclusive right of property in the composite vehicle and were thus not in the position of having an unqualified right to sell it to the pursuer. If so, they would be in breach of s.12(1)."

The companion of s.12(1) is s.12(2), under which the seller impliedly promises that the goods are free, and will remain free until the time when the property is to pass, from any charge or incumbrance not disclosed or known to the buyer before the contract is made, and also that the buyer will enjoy quiet possession of the goods.[89] The seller does not, under s.12(2), provide an absolute guarantee of the buyer's position against every disturbance which might occur, as there is no breach of the duty under this section where a third party wrongfully disturbs the buyer's possession.[90] The operation of s.12(2), is illustrated by the *Microbeads* case, considered above. It was noted that there was no breach of s.12(1) where the goods infringed a patent, because that patent had not been granted at the time of sale, so that at the time of sale the seller did have a right to sell the goods. Nonetheless, the fact that the buyer could not use the goods because of the patent meant that he could not enjoy quiet possession of the goods, so that there was a breach of s.12(2).[91]

---

[88] 1960 S.L.T. 231.

[89] The cases discussed in the context of s.12(1): *Niblett v Confectioners Materials Co Ltd* [1921] 3 K.B. 387; *Microbeads A.C. v. Vinhurst Road Markings Ltd* [1975] 1 W.L.R. 218; and *McDonald v Provan (of Scotland Street) Ltd,* 1960 S.L.T. 231, each contain discussions of potential breaches of s.12(2).

[90] *The Playa Larga* [1983] 2 Lloyd's Rep. 171.

[91] See also *Rubicon Computer Systems Ltd v United Paints Ltd* [2002] T.C.L.R. 453, CA, where it was held to be a breach of s.12(2) when the suppliers of a computer system installed a feature which allowed them to lock the buyers out of the system.

## (d) Duty to provide goods of correct description

Where goods are sold by description, there is an implied term under s.13 that the goods will correspond with their description. Obviously, all generic sales will be by sales by description, as where a buyer orders a ton of potatoes. Yet, according to Lord Wright, the class of goods sold by description is a wide one:

> "There is a sale by description even though the buyer is buying something displayed before him on the counter; a thing is sold by description, though it is specific, so long as it is sold not merely as the specific thing, but as a thing corresponding to a description, *e.g.* woollen undergarments, a hot water bottle, a second-hand reaping machine . . ."[92]

Section 13 specifically provides that the sale is not prevented from being a sale by description "by reason only that, being exposed for sale or hire, they are selected by the buyer." The description may not be in words but could be in images or numbers. In *Beale v Taylor*[93] a car was advertised for sale as "Herald convertible, white, 1961, twin carbs, £190". When he saw the car, the buyer checked the metallic disc on the back of the car which read "1200", reaffirming his view that the car was the first model of the "1200" to come out in 1961. The car was, in fact, made up of parts of two different models welded together. He successfully established that this was a sale by description.

Lord Diplock defined the characteristics which form part of the description in *Ashington Piggeries v Christopher Hill Ltd*:[94]

> ". . . description is confined to those words in the contract which were intended by the parties to identify the kind of goods to be supplied. It is open to the parties to use a description as broad or as narrow as they choose. But ultimately the test is whether the buyer could fairly and reasonably refuse to accept the physical goods proffered to him on the ground that their failure to correspond with that part of what was said about them in the contract makes them goods of a different kind from those he agreed to buy. The key to s.13 is identification."

The goods may be defective, and yet still conform to description. In the above case the plaintiffs sold feed-stuff to the defendants who were mink breeders. The foodstuff caused the death of thousands of mink because an ingredient, Norwegian herring meal, contained a toxic agent. The contract under which the herring meal was supplied provided that it was sold as "fair, average quality." It was held that this was not part of the description. The fact that it was contaminated was not a breach of s.13—herring meal was still herring meal, even if it was poisonous. Similarly in *Border Harvesters Ltd v Edwards Engineering (Perth) Ltd*[95] it was held that there was no breach of s.13 when a grain-dryer failed to achieve its stated capacity (*i.e.* did not achieve the desired quality), Lord Kincraig noting:

> "What was contracted for was described as a Kamas dryer; what was supplied was a Kamas dryer. What the dryer was capable of doing was . . . not part of the description."[96]

There is some confusion as to whether the buyer must prove that he or she actually relied on the description before a breach of s.13 can be established.[97] To require actual reliance is, perhaps, to state the position too forcefully. Weaker formulations of the test were offered in *Harlingdon & Leinster Enterprises Ltd v Hull Fine Art Ltd*.[98] A painting was advertised as being

---

[92] *Grant v Australian Knitting Mills Ltd* [1936] A.C. 85 at 100.
[93] [1967] 1 W.L.R. 1193, CA.
[94] [1972] A.C. 441 at 503–504.
[95] 1985 S.L.T. 128.
[96] 1985 S.L.T. 128 at 131. See also *Manchester Liners Ltd v Rea Ltd* [1922] 2 A.C. 74 at 80, *per* Lord Dunedin, relied on by Lord Kincraig in the *Border Harvesters* case.
[97] *Joseph Travers & Son v Longel Ltd* (1947) 64 T.L.R. 150 suggests that this is the case.
[98] [1991] 1 Q.B. 564.

by Gabriele Münter. An employee of the seller made it clear to a potential buyer that the seller knew nothing about the artist, whereas the buyers were dealers in German expressionist art and had examined the painting. After the purchase, when the painting turned out to be a forgery, the buyer tried, unsuccessfully, to establish a breach of s.13. Lord Justice Nourse explained:

> "It is suggested that the significance which some of these authorities attribute to the buyer's reliance on the description is misconceived. I think that that criticism is theoretically correct. In theory it is no doubt possible for a description of goods which is not relied on by the buyer to become an essential term of a contract for their sale. But in practice it is very difficult, and perhaps impossible, to think of facts where that would be so. The description must have a sufficient influence in the sale to become an essential term of the contract and the correlative of influence is reliance. Indeed, reliance by the buyer is the natural index of a sale by description."[99]

Alternatively, Lord Justice Slade indicated that it must be possible: ". . . to impute to the parties . . . a common intention that it shall be a term of the contract that the goods will correspond with the description."[1] Such tests will undoubtedly be difficult to apply. It is unfortunate that there is some ambiguity on this point. If actual reliance is a requirement then this might dilute the protection afforded to the buyer by this important section.

## (e) Duty to supply goods of the requisite quality and fitness

In terms of s.14, where the goods are sold in the course of a business, the goods supplied under the contract must be of satisfactory quality and fit for the buyer's purpose.[2] The expression "in the course of a business" has a wide meaning. The sale of the entire stock of a business was held to be a sale in the course of a business,[3] and the outcome of a recent case, *Stevenson v Rogers*,[4] suggests that it will only be purely private sales which fall outwith this definition. The Court of Appeal relied on the fact that this section had been amended,[5] explaining ". . . the requirement for regularity or dealing, or indeed any dealing, in the goods was removed."[6] Thus the sale of a fishing boat, the main asset of a fishing business, was held to be a sale in the course of a business.

The requirement that the goods must be sold in the course of a business means that the implied terms do not apply to purely private sales.[7] Yet the terms implied under s.14 also apply where the person selling in the course of a business is acting as an agent for a private individual, unless the buyer is aware that the principal is not acting in the course of a business or reasonable steps have been taken to bring this fact to the buyer's attention prior to the conclusion of the contract.[8] In *Boyter v Thomson*[9] it was held that this section applied whether the principal was disclosed or undisclosed.[10] In a situation where the principal is undisclosed

---

[99] *Harlingdon & Leinster Enterprises Ltd v Hull Fine Art Ltd* [1990] 3 W.L.R. 13; at 21 and 18, *per* Nourse L.J. The use of "essential term" is ambiguous: he may have been referring to a "condition" in English law, breach of which permits the buyer to rescind, as opposed to a warranty, breach of which only sound in damages, see ss.11(3) and 60. Following the amendments made by the 1994 Act, the terms "condition" and "warranty" are not relevant for Scots law. The text in Scotland is whether or not the breach is material, in which case the buyer can rescind, or non-material, in which case the buyer is limited to claiming damages only, see s.15B.

[1] *Harlingdon & Leinster Enterprises Ltd v Hull Fine Art Ltd* [1990] 3 W.L.R. 13 at 30, *per* Slade L.J.

[2] s.14(2)–(3).

[3] *Buchanan-Jardine v Hamilink*, 1983 S.L.T. 149.

[4] [1999] 1 All E.R. 613.

[5] See Sale of Goods Act (Implied Terms) Act 1973, s.3 which eventually became Sale of Goods Act 1979, s.14(2).

[6] *Stevenson v Rogers* [1999] 1 All E.R. 613, C.A. at 623, *per* Potter L.J.

[7] This is confirmed by s.14(1), which indicates that, except as provided for by the Act, there is no implied term about the quality or fitness of goods. There may, of course, be express terms.

[8] s.14(5).

[9] 1995 S.L.T. 875.

[10] See para. 2.7. below.

when the contract is concluded, once the buyer is aware of the principal's identity, the buyer must elect to sue either principal or agent.[11]

Goods supplied under the contract include packaging and instructions. In *Geddling v Marsh*[12] the plaintiff was injured when a bottle containing mineral water exploded. The seller was held to be in breach of s.14 even though the explosion was caused by a defect in the bottle, rather than the mineral water itself, and the bottle was returnable. In *Wormell v R H M Agricultural (East) Ltd*[13] the seller was found to be in breach of s.14 where defective instructions on tins of weedkiller rendered an otherwise effective product virtually useless.

According to the English courts, the terms implied under s.14 can extend to any foreign object supplied with the goods. In *Wilson v Rickett, Cockerell & Co*[14] the plaintiff had bought a consignment of coal from the defendant. Damage was caused to the plaintiff's house when a detonator which had been mistakenly included with the consignment exploded. The Court of Appeal rejected the argument that the goods supplied under the contract, coal, were of excellent quality and that the detonator was not supplied under the contract at all. Lord Denning stated: ". . . the section refers to the 'goods supplied under a contract of sale'. In my opinion that means the goods delivered in purported pursuance of the contract. The section applies to all goods so delivered, whether they conform to the contract or not . . ."[15] However, this decision is contrary to an earlier Scottish authority on almost exactly the same facts, *Duke v Jackson*.[16] Subsequent Scottish cases have sought to distinguish *Duke*,[17] and, in view of the convincing criticism which it received from the Court of Appeal in *Wilson v Rickett, Cockerell & Co*, *Duke* must surely be unlikely to be authoritative in the future.

Merely because goods meet the standard stipulated in the contract does not preclude them from failing to measure up to the implied terms.[18]

## (i) The meaning of "satisfactory quality"

Before examining in detail the implied term as to satisfactory quality, it should be noted that it has several limitations. It does not apply to any defect which is specifically drawn to the buyer's attention before the contract is made.[19] Nor does it apply where the buyer examines the goods before the contract is made, to any defect which that examination ought to reveal.[20] The 1973 amendments clarified one ambiguity relating to the buyer's examination of goods. Older authority suggested that the implied term might not apply where the buyer carried out a cursory examination, where the defect would have been revealed had the examination been carried out properly.[21] The wording of the above provision was amended from "such" examination to "that" examination. The implied term is therefore only excluded in respect of defects which would have been revealed by the type of examination that was *actually carried out*. This provides better protection for the buyer.

The 1893 Act referred to "merchantable" quality rather than "satisfactory quality", although that term was not defined in the Act. A large body of case law grew up around the term, and this undoubtedly helped frame the eventual statutory definition. The first attempt to define "merchantable quality" occurred in the Supply of Goods (Implied Terms) Act 1973 which

---

[11] See para. 2.7.(d) below.
[12] [1920] 1 K.B. 668.
[13] [1986] 1 All E.R. 769.
[14] [1954] 1 Q.B. 598.
[15] [1954] 1 Q.B. 598 at 607.
[16] 1921 S.C. 362.
[17] *Fitzpatrick v Barr*, 1948 S.L.T. (Sh. Ct.) 5.
[18] *Britvic Soft Drinks Ltd v Messer UK Ltd.* [2002] 3 All E.R. (Comm.) 321, CA: soft drinks met the appropriate British Safety Standard specified in the contract, but contained Benzene, and so could not be sold on to the public. Thus they were neither satisfactory in terms of s.14(2), nor fit for their purpose in terms of s.14(3).
[19] s.14(2C)(a).
[20] s.14(2C)(b).
[21] *Thornett & Fehr v Beers & Son* [1919] 1 K.B. 486.

provided that goods were of merchantable quality "if they are as fit for the purpose or purposes for which goods of that kind are commonly bought as is reasonable to expect having regard to any description applied to them, the price (if relevant) and all the other relevant circumstances".[22]

The Law Commissions in their joint report[23] made several criticisms of the term "merchantable." The term itself was thought to be out-of-date, and inappropriate in a consumer context. The focus on fitness for purpose did not take into account many aspects which were important to consumers such as appearance and finish and freedom from minor defects. Finally, the definition did not include durability or safety of the goods, characteristics which are obviously important.

Satisfactory quality is elaborated upon in s.14(2A). Goods are of satisfactory quality: ". . . if they meet the standard that a reasonable person would regard as satisfactory, taking account of the description of the goods, the price (if relevant) and all the other relevant circumstances." Quality is specifically stated to include the state and condition of goods, and the following (among others) are in appropriate cases aspects of the quality of goods: fitness for all the purposes for which goods of the kind in question are commonly supplied; appearance and finish; freedom from minor defects; safety and durability.[24] The 2002 Regulations recently added a new "relevant circumstance" to this list, namely, public statements on the specific characteristics of the goods made about them by the seller, the producer or his representative, particularly in advertising or on labelling where the contract is a consumer contract.[25] The "relevant circumstances" are commented on below, but, for the moment it should be noted that not all of these aspects will be relevant in every case—the section states that they are aspects of the quality of goods "in appropriate cases." Satisfactory quality is a relative concept, and goods of moderate or even poor quality will be satisfactory in certain circumstances.

Views are mixed on whether "satisfactory" quality is preferable to "merchantable" quality. The new concept clearly resolved certain ambiguities. However, the word "satisfactory" does not denote a very high standard in normal English usage, and may even be close to "mediocre." The Law Commissions' initial suggestion of "acceptable" quality was dropped. It may be that it is asking too much to frame a definition which will apply to all of the diverse consumer and commercial sales which fall within the ambit of the 1979 Act. That this difficulty is recognised by judges is clear from comments such as the following from Rougier J.:

> "Any attempt to forge some exhaustive, positive and specific definition of such a term, applicable in all cases, would soon be put to mockery by some new undreamt of set of circumstances."[26]

Case law interpreting the definition, rather than the actual definition itself, is of key importance. Although opinion on this point appears to be mixed, it is thought that the courts may consider older case law on "merchantable quality" as an aid to interpretation of "satisfactory quality."[27] Certain questions remain open. *Shine v General Guarantee Corporation,*[28] suggested that merchantable quality included not only the condition of the goods but also the reasonable expectations of the buyer. The buyer, a second-hand car enthusiast, succeeded in proving that the car he had bought was not merchantable because it had been immersed in water for over 24 hours and had been written off by its insurers. It is not clear whether satisfactory quality includes such reasonable expectations.

---

[22] reg. 7(2) inserted a new s.62(1A) into the 1893 Act.
[23] Joint Report No. 160/104.
[24] s.14(2B)(a) to (e).
[25] 2002 Regulations, reg. 3 inserting new s.14(2D)–14(2F) to the 1979 Act.
[26] *Bernstein v Pamson Motors (Golders Green) Ltd* [1987] 2 All E.R. 220 at 222, *per* Rougier J.
[27] See P. S. Atiyah, J. N. Adams and H. MacQueen, *The Sale of Goods*, (10th ed., 2000), at pp.158–159.
[28] [1988] 1 All E.R. 911.

## (ii) Aspects of the quality of goods

### Fitness for all common purposes

Older authority suggested that goods were of merchantable quality if they were fit for *any* of the common purposes of such goods.[29] The 1994 amendments refer to *all* common purposes, which is a much higher standard for the seller to attain. This is a significant improvement on the previous position. If brand new goods are not fit for one of the purposes for which they are usually supplied, then the seller must make this fact known to the buyer.[30]

Section 14(3) also concerns fitness for purpose, although it covers the situation where the goods are required for some particular purpose made known to the seller, whereas s.14(2) concerns fitness for ordinary purposes. If the buyer's purpose is an uncommon one, he or she should be able to fall back on the protection in s.14(3).

### Appearance and finish

This issue arose most frequently in relation to new cars. One can contrast Lord Justice Mustill in *Rogers v Parish (Scarborough) Ltd*[31] who considered that the quality of a new car includes "pride in the vehicle's outward and interior appearance" with Rougier J. in *Bernstein v Pamson Motors (Golders Green) Ltd*[32] who considered that whereas the buyer of a Rolls Royce would not: "tolerate the slightest blemish on its exterior paintwork; the purchaser of a motor car very much at the humbler end of the range might be less fastidious." Because appearance and finish are now specifically incorporated in the definition, this issue is no longer subject to doubt.

### Freedom from minor defects

The inclusion of this issue in the definition of satisfactory quality effectively reverses an infamous Scottish case, *Millars of Falkirk v Turpie*.[33] The sellers of a car had failed several times to rectify several minor defects. Mr Turpie sought to reject the goods because they were not of merchantable quality. The sellers refused to accept his rejection and brought an action for the price. It was held that because the fault was a comparatively minor one which could have been cured at the cost of £25, the new car *was* of merchantable quality. The Lord President (Emslie) indicated that such defects were to be expected in new cars. This was a common judicial view at that time. Similar sentiments were expressed by Rougier J. in *Bernstein v Pamson Motors (Golders Green) Ltd*[34] where he stated that the buyer of a new car "must put up with a certain amount of teething troubles and have them rectified" adding by way of explanation "no system of mass production can ever be perfect."[35] The specific reference to freedom from minor defects as one of the aspects of satisfactory quality should now ensure that there is no doubt as to what the buyer is entitled to expect.

### Safety

In contrast to the original wording of s.14, the amended wording now refers to safety. This issue should be relatively simple to assess. Goods safe in themselves may be rendered unsafe by inadequate or misleading instructions.[36]

---

[29] *M/S Aswan Engineering Establishment Co Ltd v Lupdine Ltd* [1987] 1 W.L.R. 1.
[30] Joint Report, Law Com. No. 160; Scot. Law Com. No. 104), para. 3.36.
[31] [1987] Q.B. 933 at 944, *per* Mustill L.J.
[32] [1987] 2 All E.R. 220 at 228, *per* Rougier J.
[33] 1976 S.L.T. (Notes) 66.
[34] [1987] 2 All E.R. 220.
[35] [1987] 2 All E.R. 220 at 228–229, *per* Rougier J.
[36] *Wormell v RHM Agricultural (East) Ltd* [1986] 1 All E.R. 769; reversed on another point on appeal [1987] 3 All E.R. 75.

## Durability

Certain dicta suggest that durability was an aspect of merchantability.[37] This issue is now put beyond doubt by the inclusion of this characteristic as part of satisfactory quality. The buyer must show that the goods were not durable at the time of supply by the seller, although it will usually not be possible to do so until some time after the initial supply. If goods break down soon after they have been purchased this will be a factor which the courts will take into account in assessing durability. However, they will also look at factors such as the frequency of use to which the goods were put, and any mistreatment of the goods. Price and description are also relevant to this assessment.

The most recent application of this part of the legislation provides some cause for concern for purchasers of second-hand vehicles. In *Thain v Anniesland Trade Centre*[38] the buyer purchased for £2,995 a five-year old Renault 19 which had done about 80,000 miles. The car developed a gearbox fault after two weeks of running which was so serious that the car had to be written-off. The court held that it was sufficient if the car was fit for its initial use, and that durability was not a quality reasonably to be expected of a second-hand car. The low price and high mileage were key issues in deciding what would be satisfactory to a buyer.

In most cases where the goods are found not to be of satisfactory quality because they are not durable, the buyer has the right to damages only given that the right to rescind will probably have been lost due to lapse of time.

## Public statements

The new relevant circumstance added by the 2002 Regulations is public statements on the specific characteristics of the goods made about them by the seller, the producer or his representative, particularly in advertising or on labelling. It applies only where the contract is a consumer contract.[39] "The producer" is given a wide definition, to catch "the manufacturer of goods, the importer of goods into the European Economic Area or any person purporting to be a producer by placing his name, trade mark or other distinctive sign on the goods."[40] The seller can escape this type of liability if he or she can show that, at the time the contract was made, he or she was unaware, and could not reasonably have been aware, of the statement; before the contract was made, the statement had been withdrawn in public; or the decision to buy the goods could not have been influenced by the statement.[41] The list of relevant circumstances is not, as has already been stated, an exclusive one, and public statements may still be relevant even though they do not fall within the terms of this new provision.[42]

## (iii) Implied term as to fitness for purpose

As explained above, fitness for all common purposes is one of the factors to be taken into account under s.14(2A) in assessing whether the goods are of satisfactory quality. However, a separate implied term as to fitness for purpose exists in s.14(3). Where the buyer, expressly or by implication, makes known to the seller any particular purpose for which the goods are being bought, the goods must be reasonably fit for that purpose whether or not that is a purpose for which such goods are commonly supplied, unless the circumstances show that the buyer does not rely, or that it is unreasonable for him or her to rely on the seller's skill or judgment.

---

[37] See Lord Diplock in *Lambert v Lewis* [1982] A.C. 225 at 276.

[38] 1997 S.L.T. (Sh. Ct) 102.

[39] 2002 Regulations, reg. 3, inserting new s.14(2D)–14(2F) to the 1979 Act.

[40] 2002 Regulations, reg. 6, inserting new definitions into 1979 Act, s.61(1). This definition contains similarities to the description of the party liable under the Consumer Protection Act 1987 in the context of defective products, see Consumer Protection Act 1987, s.2(2)(b).

[41] 2002 Regulations, reg. 3(2E)(a) to (c).

[42] 2002 Regulations, reg. 3(2F).

There is no duty on the buyer to make known an obvious purpose. Lord Wright explained in *Grant v Australian Knitting Mills Ltd*:

> "There is no need to specify the particular purpose for which the buyer requires the goods which is nonetheless the particular purpose, because it is the only purpose for which anyone would ordinarily want the goods."[43]

By contrast, if the goods have a number of purposes, in order to rely on s.14(3), the buyer will have to make known to the seller the particular purpose for which he or she, the buyer, will be using the goods.[44] The relationship with s.14(2) should be borne in mind: if the purpose for which the goods are used is a common purpose then the buyer will be able to argue that the goods are not of satisfactory quality in terms of s.14(2). However, where the buyer intends to use the goods for an unusual or extraordinary purpose and fails to make this known to the seller, he or she will probably fail under both s.14(2) and (3).[45] The goods may also appear to be unfit for their purpose, and yet it may be proved that this is due, not to a defect in the goods, but rather to some idiosyncrasy or abnormal feature of the buyer or the buyer's business. Should that be the case, there will be no breach of s.14(3). In order to rely on s.14(3) the buyer must make the seller aware of the idiosyncrasy. So, for example, a buyer was unsuccessful in proving that a Harris tweed coat was unmerchantable where she contracted dermatitis through wearing it, but it was proved that her skin was abnormally sensitive, and the coat would not have injured the skin of a normal person.[46]

Section 14(3) is subject to the proviso that the implied term will not apply where the seller can show that the buyer has not relied, or it would not be reasonable for him or her to rely, on the seller's skill and judgment. The onus lies on the seller, and, generally, reliance will be presumed. As Lord Wright commented in *Grant v Australian Knitting Mills*:

> "The reliance will seldom be express: it will usually arise by implication from the circumstances: thus to take a case like that in question, of a purchase from a retailer, the reliance will be in general inferred from the fact that a buyer goes to the shop in the confidence that the tradesman has selected his stock with skill and judgement: . . ."[47]

If the buyer knows that the seller has no choice as to the goods sold, there may be no reliance, for example, where the seller is only permitted to sell one type of beer from a pub and the buyer is aware of this fact.[48] The buyer may similarly fail to prove reliance where the buyer has greater expertise in the market in question than the seller. Nevertheless, even where the seller is manufacturing goods to the buyer's directions, the buyer may still be relying on the seller to carry out the process competently.[49] A defect may be discovered by the buyer through an examination prior to the contract being concluded. In such a case, a claim under s.14(2) is ruled out due to the buyer's awareness of the defect. However, a claim under s.14(3) might be possible. Although one might have thought that, in such a case, the buyer is not relying on the seller's skill and judgment, he may be relying on the seller to rectify the defect.[50] Otherwise, pre-contractual knowledge of a defect will mean that the buyer does not rely on the seller's skill and judgment, unless perhaps the seller advises the buyer that the goods will still be fit for their purpose despite the defect.

## (f) Implied terms in sales by sample

Under s.15 there is an implied term that:

---

[43] [1936] A.C. 85 at 99, *per* Lord Wright.

[44] *Flynn v Scott,* 1949 S.C. 442.

[45] *B. S. Brown & Son Ltd v Craiks Ltd,* 1970 S.C. (H.L.) 51.

[46] *Griffiths v Peter Conway Ltd* [1939] 1 All E.R. 685. See also *Slater v Finning Ltd,* 1996 S.L.T. (H.L.) 916.

[47] [1936] A.C. 85 at 99.

[48] *Wren v Holt* [1903] 1 K.B. 610.

[49] *Ashington Piggeries v Christopher Hill Ltd* [1972] A.C. 441.

[50] *R & B Customs Brokers v UDT Ltd* [1988] 1 W.L.R. 321.

(1) the bulk will correspond with the sample in quality[51];
(2) the buyer will have a reasonable opportunity of comparing the bulk with the sample[52]; and
(3) the bulk will be free of any defect making the goods unsatisfactory which would not be apparent on a reasonable examination of the sample.[53]

A sale is by sample where there is an express or implied term in the contract to that effect.[54]

## (g) Attempts to exclude liability for the implied terms

Generally, it is not open to the seller to argue that he could not have discovered the defect. Liability for breach of the implied terms is absolute in this respect.[55] The Unfair Contract Terms Act 1977 prevents the seller from excluding the duties imposed on him to pass good title under s.12.[56] This obligation applies regardless of the type of contract at issue, *i.e.* whether or not it is a consumer contract.

Turning to the other implied terms, *i.e.* those in s.13 (conformity with description), s.14 (quality or fitness) and s.15 (sale by sample), the ability to exclude such terms depends upon whether the contract is a consumer contract or not, using the definition of consumer contract contained in s.25(1) of the Unfair Contract Terms Act 1977 as amended by the 2002 Regulations.[57] If the contract is a consumer contract, the attempt to exclude the duties of the seller is void.[58] In all other cases, the attempt to exclude will be subject to a fair and reasonableness test.[59] The onus of proving that the contract is not a consumer contract rests on the party who claims that it is not *i.e.* the party trying to exclude liability. The changes which the 2002 Regulations made to the definition of a consumer must be borne in mind here.[60] Previously, where the contract related to the transfer of ownership or possession of goods, a contract would only be a consumer contract where the goods were of a type ordinarily supplied for private use or consumption. As a result, attempts to exclude the implied terms in sale of goods cases in relation to a consumer would only be automatically void where the goods were of this nature. Where goods were supplied to a consumer but were of a type normally supplied for use in a business, the lesser test of whether it was fair and reasonable to incorporate the exclusion clause applied. Following the 2002 amendments, this limitation is disapplied where the consumer is an individual. Individuals are now protected, and attempts to exclude the implied terms are automatically void, regardless of the individual's intended purpose for the goods purchased. Where the consumer is *not* an individual, the position remains unchanged. For attempts to exclude the implied terms to be void, where the contract is for the transfer of ownership or possession of goods, the goods must still be of a type ordinarily supplied for private use and consumption. If the goods are not of this nature, the attempt to exclude the implied term is subject to the lower test of whether it was fair and reasonable to incorporate the exclusionary term. It should be recalled, however, that this relates only to attempts to exclude the implied terms in ss.to 13, 15. Attempts to exclude the implied term relating to the passing of good title in s.12 are always void, regardless of the characteristics of the buyer.

The 2002 Regulations also made relevant amendments where goods are purchased at auctions. The more stringent test for exclusion clauses, *i.e.* the one which imposes the sanction of voidness, does not apply where the consumer buys second hand goods sold by public auction

---

[51] s.15(2)(a).
[52] ss.14(2C)(c) and 15.
[53] s.15(2)(c).
[54] s.15(1).
[55] *Frost v Aylesbury Dairy Co Ltd* [1905] 1 K.B. 608.
[56] UCTA, s.20(1)(a) .
[57] See the discussion of this definition at para. 1.9. above.
[58] UCTA, s.20(2)(i).
[59] UCTA, s.20(2)(ii) and see *Britvic Soft Drinks Ltd v Messer UK Ltd* [2002] 3 All E.R. (Comm.) 321, CA.
[60] See the discussion of this definition at para. 1.9. above

at which individuals have the opportunity of attending in person or where the buyer is not an individual and the goods are sold by auction or competitive tender.[61] The lesser test of whether it was fair and reasonable to incorporate the exclusion clause is applicable in such situations.

Where the "fair and reasonableness" test applies, the onus of proving that the exclusion was fair and reasonable lies on the party who so contends.[62] Guidelines for the court to use in applying the fair and reasonable test are contained in Sch. 2 to the Act. The guidelines are specifically stated to apply to contracts of sale and supply of goods. Relevant factors include the relative bargaining strengths of the parties, whether the term was customary in the trade and whether there were alternative means of meeting the buyer's requirements.

### (h) Implied terms in other contracts—the Sale and Supply of Goods Act 1982

#### (i) Types of contracts within the ambit of the Act

Thus far, the discussion in this chapter has been limited to sale contracts only. There are, however, many other types of contracts in which consumers are involved in which they require a similar degree of protection. Important protections are found in the Sale and Supply of Goods Act 1982. The protections fall into two parts. The first part includes contracts for the transfer of property in goods other than sale, hire-purchase and donation. Effectively this class would contain contracts of barter and contracts for the supply of work and materials. The definition of a contract for the "transfer of goods" is "a contract under which one person transfers or agrees to transfer to another the property in goods, other than an excepted contract."[63] Excepted contracts, to which the provisions do not apply, are sale and hire-purchase. Such contracts are already protected by other statutes.[64] The fact that services are provided in addition to goods and the nature of the consideration are both irrelevant—the contract remains a contract for the transfer of goods.[65] The protections contained in the second part of the Act relate to contracts of hire.[66] A contract of hire is: "a contract under which one person ("the supplier") hires or agrees to hire goods to another, other than an excepted contract." Hire purchase is an excepted contract. For both parts the actual protections are very similar to those which apply under the Sale of Goods Act 1979.[67]

#### (ii) The consumer's remedies

It would be unsatisfactory if consumers did not benefit from the protection provided from the implied terms in other contracts as they do in the context of sale. Similar protections in relation to hire-purchase had been available since the Supply of Goods (Implied Terms) Act 1973. However, in Scotland, the same protections were not available in other consumer contracts. This contrasted with the position under English law where similar protections were available by virtue of the Supply of Goods and Services Act 1982, an Act which did not apply to Scotland. This anomaly was resolved in 1994.[68] Where the contract is a consumer contract,[69] the same statutory implied terms apply in contracts of barter, contracts for the provision of work and materials, and contracts of hire as they do in the context of sale.[70]

---

[61] 2002 Regulations, reg. 14, inserting new s.25(1B) into the Unfair Contract Terms Act 1977, s.25(1).

[62] UCTA, ss.20(2), 24 and 25 as amended by the Act 1979, s.63(1) and Sch. 2, paras 21 and 22.

[63] s.11A(1).

[64] In sale the buyer is already protected by the implied terms in the 1979 Act, and in hire purchase the hirer is protected by the Supply of Goods (Implied Terms) Act 1973.

[65] s.11A(3).

[66] s.11G.

[67] See ss.11B–11F for contracts for the transfer of goods and ss.11H–11K for hire.

[68] The Sale and Supply of Goods Act 1994 inserted a new Part 1A (ss.11B–11K) into the Supply of Goods and Services Act 1982.

[69] "Consumer contract" is defined by reference to s.25(1) of the Unfair Contract Terms Act 1977 commented on below. .

[70] "Satisfactory quality" is confusingly defined for both contracts for the transfer of goods and contracts of hire, necessitating reading s.11J(3), the interpretation section, and Sch. 2, para. 6(10) together.

The amendments recently enacted by the 2002 Regulations to the implied terms in the context of sale have similarly been applied to other consumer contracts. Thus, provisions similar to those governing the seller's liability for public statements have been applied to contracts for the transfer of goods,[71] contracts of hire[72] and contracts of hire-purchase,[73] in all cases only where the contract is a consumer contract.[74]

The general scheme of remedies visible in the context of contracts of sale, namely the ability to rescind for a material breach, and the ability to claim damages for a non-material breach[75] was also applied to contracts for the transfer of goods by the 1994 Act.[76] It is not surprising, therefore, to see that the new hierarchy of remedies contained in the 2002 Regulations including repair and replacement has been applied to contracts for the transfer of goods[77] in the same way as it has to contracts of sale. The same pattern of remedies depending upon whether or not the breach was material was not extended to contracts of hire by the 1994 Act. The Law Commissions considered that the protections offered by Scots common law were sufficient. As a result, the amendments contained in the 2002 Regulations providing the consumer with a right to repair or replacement do not apply in cases of hire or hire-purchase.

As is the case in contracts of sale, the implied terms in the context of contracts other than sale rely on the definition of "consumer contract" found in the Unfair Contract Terms Act 1977 as amended by the 2002 Regulations commented on above.[78]

### (iii) Attempts to exclude the statutory implied terms

The discussion in this part assumes that the exclusionary term in question has been incorporated into the contract, a factor which is governed by common law principles.

As stated above, the Unfair Contract Terms Act 1977 controls attempts to exclude the implied terms. As expected above (see para. 1.11.(g)); it is impossible to exclude the duties imposed on the seller to pass good title under s.12.[79] This is regardless of the type of contract at issue, *i.e.* whether or not it is a consumer contract.

In relation to the other implied terms, *i.e.* those in s.13 (conformity with description), s.14 (quality or fitness) and s.15 (sale by sample), the ability to exclude such terms depends upon whether the contract is a consumer contract or not. The definition of "consumer contract" is that contained in the Unfair Contract Terms Act 1977 as amended by the 2002 Regulations.[80] If the contract is a consumer contract, the attempt to exclude the duties of the seller is void.[81] In all other cases, the attempt to exclude will be subject to a fair and reasonableness test.[82]

The same regime applies to attempts to exclude the implied terms in contracts for the transfer of goods and contracts of hire,[83] and hire-purchase.[84] Section 21 of the Unfair Contract Terms Act 1977 provides that in all cases the implied term relating to title cannot be excluded, and the other implied terms cannot be excluded in consumer contracts,[85] although in other contracts they can be excluded subject to the reasonableness test.

---

[71] 2002 Regulations, reg. 8, inserting new s.11D(3A)–(3C), and (10) into the Sale and Supply of Goods Act 1982.

[72] 2002 Regulations, reg. 11, inserting new s.11J(3A)–(3C) and (10) into the Sale and Supply of Goods Act 1982.

[73] 2002 Regulations, reg. 13, inserting new s.10(2D)–(2F) and (8) into the Supply of Goods (Implied Terms) Act 1973.

[74] "Consumer contract" is defined by reference to s.25(1) of the Unfair Contract Terms Act 1977: see new s.11M(5) and s.11J(10) referring to s.11F(3) of the 1982 Act, and s.12A(3) of the Supply of Goods (Implied Terms) Act 1973.

[75] 1979 Act, s.15B.

[76] Sale and Supply of Goods Act 1982, s.11F .

[77] 2002 Regulations, reg. 9, inserting new Pt 1B, ss.11M–11S into the Sale and Supply of Goods Act 1982.

[78] See the discussion of this definition at para. 1.9. above.

[79] UCTA, s.20(1)(a).

[80] See the discussion of this definition at para. 1.9. above.

[81] UCTA, s.20(2)(i).

[82] UCTA, s.20(2)(ii).

[83] Supply of Goods and Services Act 1982, ss.11B–K.

[84] Supply of Goods (Implied Terms) Act 1973, ss.8–11, although a right to reduction of the price was already provided in Scots law in terms of the Contract (Scotland) Act 1997, s.3.

[85] See the discussion of this definition at para. 1.9. above.

# 1.12. THE BUYER'S REMEDIES

What are the buyer's remedies when the seller is in breach of the duties outlined in the previous paragraph? The scheme of remedies available to the buyer has been amended in important respects by the 2002 Regulations. Previously, where the goods did not conform to the contract, the buyer's only remedies were a right to damages in the case of a breach by the seller of any term of the contract, and the right to rescind and reject the goods if the breach was material.[86] Additional protection was provided where the contract was a consumer contract, in that any breach by the seller of any of the implied terms under ss.13–15 was deemed to be a material breach.[87] New remedies have been added where the buyer is a consumer, namely the right to have the goods repaired, replaced, the price reduced[88] and a further right to rescind.[89] Despite limited authority to the contrary, Scots law did not previously contain a right of repair or replacement.[90] The new remedies take the form of a new Pt 5A of the Act, headed "Additional Rights of Buyers in Consumer Cases." This serves to stress that consumers are given these remedies alongside the pre-existing remedies of rejection and damages afforded to all buyers under s.15B(1).

## (a) The new remedies in general

In common with certain other amendments made by the 2002 Regulations, the new rights apply only where the contract is a consumer contract, and the consumer is a "pure" consumer, in the sense that he or she is a natural person acting for purposes which are outside his trade, business or profession.[91] They arise where the goods do not conform to the contract at the time of delivery,[92] and the lack of conformity is defined as where there is either a breach of an express term of the contract or one of the implied terms in ss.13, 14 or 15.[93]

Although, in principle, the relevant time for assessing conformity is the time of delivery, the Regulations contain an extended meaning for the word "delivery." The protections extend to any goods which do not conform within the period of six months after delivery.[94] This provision is known as a "reversed burden of proof."[95] Any lack of conformity which becomes apparent within six months of delivery is deemed to have existed at the date of delivery. The seller requires to prove otherwise by establishing either that the goods did conform at the date of delivery or that the extension is incompatible with the nature of the goods or the nature of the lack of conformity.[96] So, for example, the provision will not apply in the case of goods which are not in their nature durable. The reversed burden of proof does not apply to the buyer's existing right to damages or rescission under s.15B(1) of the 1979 Act.

---

[86] s.15B(1).

[87] s.15B(2).

[88] A right to reduction of the price was already provided in Scots law in terms of the Contract (Scotland) Act 1997, s.3.

[89] 2002 Regulations, reg. 5, which inserts a new Pt 5A to the 1979 Act.

[90] *Lindley Catering Investments v Hibernian FC Ltd*, 1975 S.L.T. (Notes) 56; *Strathclyde Regional Council v Border Engineering Contractors Ltd*, 1998 S.L.T. 175. The Scottish Law Commission indicated relatively recently that they favoured the existing pattern of remedies and would not favour the introduction of a right to cure as the primary remedy: see *Remedies for Breach of Contract* (Scot. Law Com. No. 174, December 1999), para. 7.21. The right to rescind is, of course, already available under s.15B(1)(b) of the 1979 Act.

[91] 2002 Regulations, reg. 5, inserting new s.48A into the 1979 Act, and reg. 2. The definition is slightly wider than that which appears in Directive 99/44 (". . . purposes which are outside his trade, business or profession"). The UK Government chose the wider definition for the sake of conformity with Directive 93/13 on unfair terms in consumer contracts, see second DTI consultation paper (above n.7), p.7.

[92] 1979 Act, s.48A(1)(b).

[93] 1979 Act, s.48F.

[94] 1979 Act, s.48A(3).

[95] Second DTI Consultation paper.

[96] 1979 Act, s.48A(4).

## (i) The right of repair or replacement in detail

The buyer has the right to have the goods repaired or replaced by the sellers,[97] and the seller must repair or replace within a reasonable time but without causing significant inconvenience to the buyer.[98] A new definition of "repair" is inserted into the 1979 Act, namely to bring the goods into conformity with the contract.[99] Necessary costs must be borne by the seller, including labour, materials and postage.[1] The seller can, however, escape these remedies in certain situations: first, where the remedy is impossible; secondly, where the grant of one remedy (*e.g.* repair) would be disproportionate in comparison to the other (*e.g.* replacement); and, thirdly, where either remedy would be disproportionate to the other remedies introduced into the Act by the 2002 Regulations, namely reduction in price, or rescission.[2] The issue of whether the remedy is "disproportionate" depends on whether the costs are unreasonable, taking into account the value which the goods would have had if they had conformed to the contract, the significance of the lack of conformity and whether the other remedy could be effected without significant inconvenience to the buyer.[3] The Act now indicates that the nature and purpose for which the goods were acquired are both relevant to the assessment of what amounts to a reasonable time or significant inconvenience.[4] It can be appreciated from this that it is for the buyer to indicate in the first instance the remedy he or she would prefer, but that protections are provided to the seller when that remedy is inappropriate. So in relation to many if not most low-cost goods, it would not be open to the buyer to insist on repair, because its cost may well be significantly greater than that of replacement.

It is open to the buyer to apply to the court for an order of specific implement requiring the seller to repair or replace.[5] The court also has a wide power to order payment of damages or repayment of the price.[6]

## (ii) The right of reduction of the purchase price and rescission in detail

The rights of reduction of the purchase price or rescission are subsidiary rights. They are only available[7] if the buyer is unable to require the seller to repair or replace on grounds of impossibility, disproportion of the remedy sought,[8] or failure by the seller to repair or replace within a reasonable time and without significant inconvenience to the buyer as detailed above.[9]

Where the buyer is seeking to rescind the contract, the court may order that any reimbursement that the buyer obtains be reduced to take account of the use that he or she has had of the goods since they were delivered.[10] This may be contrasted with the right to rescind the contract under s.15B(1), where the buyer is entitled to recover the price without any reduction to reflect the use of the goods which he or she has had. On the other hand, the right of rescission and rejection under s.15B(1) may not be exercised once the buyer has accepted the goods, a restriction which does not apply to the additional rights under Pt 5A. As is the case with repair or replacement, the court has a wide power to order payment of damages or repayment of the price.[11]

---

[97] 1979 Act, s.48B(1)(a) and (b).
[98] 1979 Act, s.48B(2)(a).
[99] 1979 Act, s.61(1).
[1] 1979 Act, s.48B(2)(b).
[2] 1979 Act, s.48B(3).
[3] 1979 Act, s.48B(4).
[4] 1979 Act, s.48B(5).
[5] 1979 Act, s.48E(2).
[6] 1979 Act, s.48E(6).
[7] 1979 Act, s.48C(2).
[8] 1979 Act, s.48B(3).
[9] 1979 Act s.48B(2).
[10] 1979 Act, s.48E(5).
[11] 1979 Act, s.48E(6).

### (iii) Assessment of the new remedies

The 2002 Regulations have made an important change to the nature of the buyer's remedies. Ultimately, the consumer wants the goods which he or she paid for, and the right to repair or replacement ensures that he or she achieves this goal. The new rights to reduction of the price or rescission are "subsidiary" in nature, as explained above. Thus, they provide the buyer with a remedy where the seller ultimately fails to repair or replace. However, the buyer's primary right should be recovery of the purchase price. The buyer may prefer to rescind in order to avoid the delay and administrative problems inherent in achieving repair or replacement, especially if the relationship between the seller and the buyer has irretrievably broken down. The primary right to rescind is retained given that the buyer's rights under s.15B(1) are unchanged by the 2002 Regulations. Nonetheless, if the buyer does require the seller to repair or replace the goods, he or she may not rescind the contract and reject the goods under s.15B(1) until he has given the seller a reasonable time to effect that replacement or repair.[12]

### (b) Right of partial rejection

Under s.35A, unless, as a matter of interpretation of the contract, the parties have a contrary intention, the buyer has four options where some or all of the goods do not conform to the contract. The buyer may:

(1) accept all the goods;
(2) reject all the goods;
(3) reject only the disconforming goods;
(4) reject some of the disconforming goods.

Where the contract is a contract by instalments, the same right of partial rejection is conferred in respect of each instalment.[13] The buyer's rights in this respect are subject to an important qualification: acceptance of any of the goods in a commercial unit is deemed to be acceptance of all the goods in that unit.[14] A commercial unit is a unit the division of which would seriously impair the value of the goods or the character of the unit, *e.g.* a pair of shoes or a set of encyclopaedias.

### (c) Loss of the right to reject

It has been noted that the buyer has the right to rescind the contract and reject the goods in response to a material breach of contract. However, by virtue of s.35(1), the buyer may lose the right to reject goods conferred by s.15B(1) where he or she has "accepted" the goods. He or she may be deemed to have accepted them where he or she expressly intimates acceptance; or does an act inconsistent with the seller's ownership; or retains the goods for a reasonable period of time without intimating rejection. This section is however subject to the buyer's right to examine the goods under s.35(2). A buyer who has not previously examined the goods is not deemed to have accepted them until he or she has had a reasonable opportunity of examining them to ascertain that they are in conformity with the contract (or in the case of a sale by sample, of comparing the bulk with the sample.)

Where the buyer neglects to examine the goods at the proper time and only examines them much later, he or she will be deemed to have accepted them.[15] However, a recent case suggests that the courts may treat the buyer leniently when it comes to assessing what is a reasonable period within which to reject. In *Truk (UK) Ltd v Tokakidis GmbH*[16] goods were delivered to

---

[12] 1979 Act, s.48D.
[13] s.35A(2).
[14] s.35(7).
[15] *Pini & Co v Smith & Co* (1895) 22 R. 699.
[16] [2000] 1 Lloyd's Rep. 543.

the buyers in June, and it was only when a further prospective buyer became interested in the goods that the unsatisfactory nature of the goods came to light. Further discussions took place between the original seller and buyer, and it was only in March of the next year that the goods were rejected. In holding that rejection had taken place within a reasonable time, Judge Raymond Jack commented:

> ". . . where goods are sold for resale, a reasonable time in which to intimate rejection should usually be the time actually taken to resell the goods together with an additional period in which they can be inspected and tried out by the sub-purchaser."[17]

Judge Jack also emphasised that what is a reasonable period is a matter which depends on the circumstances of the case and may involve a balancing of the opposing interests of the buyer and seller.[18]

Special protection is provided to consumers by s.35(3) which states that the buyer cannot lose the right of examination of the goods under s.35(2) by agreement, waiver or otherwise. Thus, the common practice of forcing the buyer to sign an "acceptance note" (which indicates that the goods have been accepted in good condition) once goods have been delivered but before the buyer has had an opportunity to examine the goods does not exclude the buyer's right of examination where the buyer is a consumer.[19] The corollary of this is that a buyer who is not a consumer can exclude his rights in this way. However, the seller would have to show that it is fair and reasonable to exclude the buyer's rights in this way in terms of UCTA 1977.

Section 35(4) provides that the buyer is deemed to have accepted the goods when, after the lapse of a reasonable time, he or she retains the goods without intimating to the seller that he or she has rejected them. Section 35(5) specifically states that, in assessing this issue, the question of whether the buyer has had a reasonable opportunity of examining the goods to ascertain whether they are in conformity with the contract is material. It is difficult to give guidance on what will constitute acceptance through lapse of reasonable time. It is essentially a question of fact, and conflicting case law exists,[20] particularly in relation to the rejection of defective cars.[21] Much depends on the complexity of function. What is a reasonable time in relation to a toothbrush, will not be reasonable in relation to a nuclear submarine. It will also be appreciated from *Truk* that the idea of a reasonable time may be significantly extended if it is reasonable for the buyer to delay testing the functioning of goods.

Any attempt within a consumer contract to stipulate a period within which the buyer must reject goods would be regarded as an attempt to restrict the buyer's rights and would be void in terms of the Unfair Contract Terms Act 1977.[22] In a non-consumer contract case, such a clause would be subject to the reasonableness test.[23]

---

[17] [2000] 1 Lloyd's Rep. 543 at 551, *per* Raymond Jack J.

[18] [2000] 1 Lloyd's Rep. 543 at 550, *per* Raymond Jack J.

[19] For an example of a non-consumer contract where an acceptance note had the effect of barring the buyer from subsequently rejecting the goods, see *Mechans Ltd v Highland Marine Charters*, 1964 S.L.T. 27.

[20] See *Burrell v Harding's Exx.*, 1931 S.L.T. 76 where a buyer purchased a reredos which he understood, because of an innocent misrepresentation by the seller, dated from the 15th Century. More than two years later the buyer was held entitled to reject when he discovered that part of it was a modern copy. Compare *Leaf v International Galleries* [1950] 2 K.B. 86 where the buyer had bought a painting which he understood, due to a misrepresentation by the seller, was a Constable. The buyer was found not entitled to rescind five years later. These cases may be complicated by the fact that the relationship between rescission for breach under the 1979 Act and rescission for innocent misrepresentation has not been fully analysed by the Scots courts: see Atiyah, Adams, and MacQueen, *The Sale of Goods*, (10th ed., 2000), at pp.529–532.

[21] See *Bernstein v Pamson Motors (Golders Green) Ltd* [1987] 2 All E.R. 220, where the buyer retained the car for three weeks and covered 140 miles. This was thought by Rougier J. to be too long a period to allow the buyer to reject. Compare *Rogers v Parish (Scarborough) Ltd* [1987] Q.B. 33, where the buyer was found entitled to reject even though he had retained the car for six months and covered 5,500 miles.

[22] s.20(2)(a)(i).

[23] s.20(2)(a)(ii). For an example of a clause in a non-consumer which failed the reasonableness test see *R W Green Ltd v Cade Bros Farms* [1978] 1 Lloyd's Rep. 602.

The buyer is not deemed to have accepted the goods merely because he or she asks for, or agrees to, their repair by the seller nor where the goods are delivered to another purchaser under a sub-sale or other disposition.[24] The "reasonable time" after which the buyer is deemed to have accepted the goods is suspended while the goods are being repaired. However, if the buyer attempts to repair them himself or herself, or to have them repaired without reference to the seller, then this would probably be regarded as an act inconsistent with the seller's ownership, excluding the right of rejection.

It might be added that there is no necessary connection between the passing of the property (see para. 1.8.) and the question of whether the goods have been accepted. Property in goods may pass to the buyer long before he or she actually sees them. Obviously, if they turn out to be defective, he or she may reject them. Equally, where there is a retention of title clause in the contract, the buyer may have been using the goods for a significant period of time without being their owner. In such circumstances, he or she would be deemed to have accepted them.

## (d) The buyer's personal remedies

A buyer may have a right to claim damages from the seller. Sometimes he or she will be able to exercise this alongside the remedy of rejection. Sometimes it will be his or her only remedy, because the breach is not of an order that would give him or her the right to reject, or where he or she has lost that right through accepting the goods, or where rejection is not practically possible because no goods were delivered in the first place.

### (i) Damages for non-delivery

Where the seller wrongfully neglects or refuses to deliver the goods to the buyer, the buyer may maintain an action against the seller for damages for non-delivery.[25] Their measure is the estimated loss directly and naturally arising, in the ordinary course of events, from the seller's breach,[26] and where there is an available market for the goods, *prima facie*, the measure is the difference between the contract and market prices at the time when they ought to have been delivered, or if no time was fixed, at the time of refusal to deliver.[27] The operation of this formula is seen in *Williams Bros Ltd v Agius*[28] where the buyer of coal was awarded damages reflecting the difference between the contract price of 16s 3d per ton and the market price of 23s 6d per ton, even though the buyer had contracted to resell the coal at 19s per ton, the House of Lords reasoning that he would have to buy at the market price in order to fulfil his own contract. A buyer will, of course, be subject to the normal contractual duty to mitigate his loss, which in the case of an anticipatory breach may oblige him to acquire replacement goods without delay.[29] However, he is not bound, in mitigation, to accept the seller's offer of goods of an alternative make.[30]

### (ii) Damages for defective goods

Once again, the measure of damages is the estimated loss directly and naturally arising, in the ordinary course of events, from the seller's breach.[31] Where defective goods are rejected, the

---

[24] s.35(6).

[25] s.51(1).

[26] ss.51(2) and 53A(1).

[27] s.51(3).

[28] [1914] A.C. 510.

[29] See *e.g. Kaines (UK) Ltd v Osterreichische Warrenhandelgesellschaft* [1993] 2 Lloyd's Rep. 1, CA, where in a highly volatile market damages were calculated on the basis that the buyer should have bought alternative goods as soon as the seller indicated that he would not perform, rather than reflecting the difference between the contract price and the (much higher) market price at the scheduled date of delivery.

[30] See *Allen v W. Burns Tractors Ltd,* 1985 S.L.T. 252, buyer's damages reflected the higher cost of obtaining from a different source the goods he had ordered.

[31] s.53A(1).

buyer will, *prima facie*, be entitled to damages calculated on the basis that the goods have not been delivered. Where the buyer elects to retain defective goods the measure of damages will, *prima facie*, be the difference between the value of the goods at the time of delivery and their value had the contract been fulfilled.[32] If defective goods cause the buyer physical injury[33] or damage to his property,[34] damages should reflect this fact, while in certain cases consumers have even been successful in recovering damages for inconvenience or distress.[35] Claims for loss of profit may be allowable, if these should have been within the contemplation of the parties.[36] It has also been held that where the goods were acquired for resale to the public, damages could include the cost of recalling defective goods[37]

### (e) The buyer's right to specific implement

Where there is a contract to deliver specific or ascertained goods, and these have not been delivered, s.52 allows the buyer to ask the court to order that the contract be performed specifically. This provision is stated to be supplementary to the right of specific implement in Scotland.[38] Theoretically, therefore, as the remedy of specific implement is a general right in respect of breach of contract,[39] that remedy should be available on a wider basis than conceded by s.52, *i.e.* in respect of unascertained goods. Nonetheless, since the courts have traditionally asserted a discretion to withhold the remedy in appropriate circumstances,[40] this remains a purely theoretical possibility, because even where the goods are ascertained the courts will decline to award implement where the buyer can obtain replacement goods on the open market.[41]

## 1.13. THE BUYER'S DUTIES

Needless to say, the buyer has duties in addition to rights under the contract.

### (a) To pay for the goods

The buyer must accept and pay for the goods in accordance with the contract of sale.[42] Although the parties may vary this rule by agreement, delivery of the goods and payment of the price are stated to be concurrent conditions: "the seller must be ready and willing to give possession of the goods to the buyer in exchange for the price and the buyer must be ready and willing to pay the price in exchange for possession of the goods."[43] As noted above,[44] time is not usually of the essence in contracts of sale, and so the seller will not have the right to rescind if payment is not made timeously. However, the contract of sale may expressly confer on the seller the right of resale where the buyer has failed to pay timeously (or otherwise defaults).[45] If

---

[32] s.53A(2).
[33] *Godley v Perry* [1960] 1 W.L.R. 9.
[34] *Wilson v Rickett Cockerell & Co Ltd* [1954] 1 Q.B. 598.
[35] *Bernstein v Pamson Motors (Golders Green) Ltd* [1978] 2 All E.R. 220.
[36] See *e.g. George Mitchell (Chesterhall) Ltd v Finney Lock Seeds Ltd* [1983] 2 A.C. 803.
[37] *Britvic Soft Drinks Ltd v Messer UK Ltd.* [2002] 3 All E.R. (Comm.) 321, CA.
[38] s.52(4).
[39] *Stewart v Kennedy* (1890) 17 R. (H.L.) 1.
[40] *Moore v Paterson* (1881) 9 R. 337 at 351, *per* Lord Shand.
[41] *Union Electric Co v Holman & Co,* 1913 S.C. 954 at 958, *per* Lord President Dunedin.
[42] s.27.
[43] s.28.
[44] See para. 1.7.
[45] s.48(4).

the seller, having reserved this right, actually sells the goods, the original contract of sale is rescinded, although this is subject to the seller's right to claim damages against the original buyer.[46] In two other situations the unpaid seller has a right of resale: first, where the goods are perishable; and, secondly, where the seller has given notice to the buyer of his intention to resell.[47] Although the Act does not specifically address the effect of resale in the latter two situations, it has been held that resale has the effect of rescinding the original contract of sale, and the seller is entitled to any profit on resale.[48]

### (b) To take delivery

The buyer is obliged to take delivery of the goods within a reasonable time,[49] although failure to do so will not usually justify rescission unless the failure or refusal amounts to a repudiation of the contract.[50] Where the goods are perishable, it is assumed that time is of the essence, and a failure to take delivery will justify the seller's rescission and resale.[51] If the buyer has been requested to take delivery but fails to do so within a reasonable time of the request, he or she is liable for any loss caused by such failure and also for a reasonable charge for the care and custody of the goods.[52]

### (c) To accept the goods

The buyer has a duty to accept the goods.[53] Wrongful rejection entitles the seller to rescind.

## 1.14. THE REMEDIES OF THE SELLER

The seller, of course, has certain personal remedies where the buyer defaults—the right to sue for the price of the goods and/or damages. But where a seller has not been paid, he or she may be able to exercise certain remedies based on his or her possession of the goods.

### (a) The possessory remedies of the unpaid seller

For the purposes of the protections contained under s.39, the seller is "unpaid" where the whole of the price has not been paid or tendered,[54] (so that a seller is unpaid if any of the price is outstanding), or when a bill of exchange or other negotiable instrument has been received as conditional payment and it has been dishonoured.[55] An unpaid seller has three rights which are exerciseable even though property in the goods has passed to the buyer:

(1) a lien on the goods or right to retain them while he or she is in possession of the goods;
(2) where the buyer is insolvent, a right to stop the goods in transit after he or she has given up possession of them;
(3) a right of resale.[56]

---

[46] s.48(4).
[47] s.48(3).
[48] *R. V. Ward Ltd v Bignall* [1967] 1 Q.B. 534.
[49] s.37(1).
[50] s.37(2). For an example of a case where time of delivery was held to be of the essence of the contract, see *Shaw, MacFarlane & Co v Waddell & Son* (1900) 2 F. 1070.
[51] *Sharp v Christmas* (1892) 8 T.L.R. 687.
[52] s.37(1).
[53] s.27.
[54] s.38(1)(a).
[55] s.38(1)(b).
[56] s.39(1)(a), (b) and (c).

## (i) Lien

Section 41(1) sets out three situations in which the unpaid seller is able to exercise his or her right of lien, *i.e.* his or her right to retain possession until paid:

(1) where the goods have been sold without any stipulation as to credit; in other words, where it has not been agreed that the buyer should be permitted a certain period within which to make payment;

(2) where the goods have been sold on credit but the term of credit has expired; *e.g.* where the buyer has been given two months to pay, but has not done so at the end of this period;

(3) where the buyer becomes insolvent,[57] *i.e.* where he or she has ceased to pay his or her debts in the ordinary course of business, or cannot pay his or her debts as they become due.[58] In this case the right can be exercised even where the contract allows the buyer a period of credit. The Act takes the view that the seller should not be obliged to yield the goods to a buyer who is unable to pay.

The Act lays stress on continuity of possession rather than the character of possession, because even if the seller is in possession of the goods as the buyer's custodier or agent, the right remains exerciseable.[59] Where part delivery has been made, the right may be exercised over the remainder, unless the circumstances indicate an agreement to waive the right over the remainder.[60]

The seller's lien may be lost in the following circumstances:

(a) when the seller delivers the goods to a carrier or custodier for the purpose of transmission to the buyer without reserving the right of disposal of the goods; thus if the seller gives the goods to a haulier to be sent to the buyer or to a warehouseman to be held for the buyer, the right is lost. The same is true if he or she ships them to the buyer under a bill of lading (see para. 4.33.) made out in the buyer's favour. Yet if that bill of lading is made out in his or her own favour, he or she is regarded as having retained a right of disposal, and so may still exercise the right of lien.

(b) when the buyer or his or her agent lawfully obtains possession of the goods;

(c) by waiver.[61]

If the seller relinquishes possession, then the right of lien is lost for good. It cannot be resurrected by the seller regaining possession.[62] A buyer who has rejected the goods cannot claim to be an unpaid seller for the purpose of exercising a right to retain the goods until the price is returned.[63]

## (ii) Stoppage in transit

Where the buyer is insolvent, an unpaid seller who has relinquished possession can stop the goods in transit, resuming possession until the buyer pays the price.[64] This right can only be exercised as long as the goods are in transit, so it is important to be able to determine how long

---

[57] s.41(1)(a), (b) and (c).

[58] s.61(4).

[59] s.41(2).

[60] s.42.

[61] s.43.

[62] *London Scottish Transport Ltd v Tyres (Scotland) Ltd,* 1957 S.L.T. (Sh. Ct.) 48; *Hostess Mobile Catering v Archibald Scott Ltd,* 1981 S.L.T. (Notes) 125.

[63] *J. L. Lyons & Co Ltd v May and Baker Ltd* [1923] 1 K.B. 685.

[64] s.44.

the transit lasts. The Act states that goods are in transit from the time they are delivered to a carrier or custodier for transmission to the buyer, until the buyer or his or her agent takes delivery of them.[65] Obviously, if a carrier is the buyer's agent, then the goods are effectively in the hands of the buyer and there is no transit.[66] If the buyer (or agent) obtains delivery before the goods arrive at their appointed destination, the transit is at an end.[67] If, after the goods have arrived at their appointed destination, the carrier or custodier acknowledges to the buyer (or agent) that he or she holds the goods on his or her behalf, the transit is at an end, and it does not matter that a further destination has been indicated by the buyer.[68] However, if the buyer rejects the goods and the carrier or custodier continues in possession, the transit continues, even though the seller has refused to have the goods back.[69] Where the carrier or custodier wrongfully refuses to deliver the goods to the buyer or the buyer's agent, the transit is at an end.[70] Finally, where part delivery has been made, the remainder of the goods may be stopped in transit, unless the circumstances indicate an agreement to give up possession of all the goods.[71]

Stoppage in transit may be effected either by the seller retaking actual possession of the goods or by the giving of appropriate instructions to the carrier or custodier.[72] If the goods are in the physical possession of the employee of the carrier or custodier, and the instructions are given to the carrier, they must be given in sufficient time to allow the carrier to communicate them to the employee to prevent delivery to the buyer.[73] When the goods have been stopped in transit, they must be redelivered to, or according to the directions of, the seller, who bears the expenses of redelivery.[74] If proper instructions are not given, the carrier will not be responsible for the consequences. Indeed, if the unpaid seller refuses to take delivery of the goods or to give directions for their delivery, and refuses to pay freight due to the carrier, he or she will be liable to the carrier in damages equivalent to the amount of freight.[75] On the other hand, if the carrier ignores timeous instructions to halt delivery, and delivers the goods to the buyer, he or she will be liable in damages to the seller.[76]

### (iii) Effect of resale by the buyer

What if the buyer, against whom either of the possessory remedies is sought to be exercised, turns out to have resold the goods? The answer is that the rights of lien and stoppage are effectual against a sub-buyer unless the seller assented to the resale.[77]

In the context of his discussion of s.47(1) in *Mordaunt Bros v British Oil & Cake Mills Ltd*,[78] Pickford J. observed:

> ". . . the assent which affects the unpaid seller's right of lien must be such an assent as in the circumstances shews that the seller intends to renounce his rights against the goods. It is not enough to shew that the fact of a sub-contract has been brought to his notice and

---

[65] s.45(1).
[66] See s.45(5) which indicates that when the goods are delivered to a ship chartered by the buyer, it is a question of fact whether they are in the master's possession as a carrier, or as the buyer's agent.
[67] s.45(2).
[68] s.45(3).
[69] s.45(4): it is submitted that this provision prevails over s.45(3).
[70] s.45(6).
[71] s.45(7) For an example of an unsuccessful attempt to argue that the sellers had agreed to give up possession of all the goods, see *Mechan & Sons Ltd v North Eastern Railway Co*, 1911 S.C. 1348.
[72] s.46(1).
[73] s.46(3).
[74] s.46(4).
[75] *Booth Steamship Co Ltd v Cargo Fleet Iron Co Ltd* [1916] 2 K.B. 570.
[76] *Mechan & Sons Ltd v North Eastern Railway Co*, 1911 S.C. 1348.
[77] s.47(1).
[78] [1910] 2 K.B. 502.

that he has assented to it merely in the sense of acknowledging the receipt of the information . . . The assent . . . means an assent given in such circumstances as shew that the unpaid seller intends that the sub-contract shall be carried out irrespective of the terms of the original contract."[79]

It was also stated that the assent might be more easily inferred where the transaction entered into with the sub-buyer is for specific as opposed to unascertained goods.[80] The seller has been held to have assented to a sub-sale where he or she was aware that the price was to be paid by the buyer to him or her from the proceeds of the sub-sale.[81]

The principle in s.47(1) is subject to the specific exception that where a document of title has been transferred to a buyer, and the buyer transfers the document to a person who takes it in good faith and for value, then if a sale has been entered into between buyer and sub-buyer, the seller's right of lien or stoppage in transit is defeated,[82] and if a pledge or disposition other than a sale is entered into, the seller's right of lien or stoppage in transit can only be exercised subject to the rights of the pledgee (*e.g.* pawnbroker) or transferee.[83] So if goods are shipped, and a copy of the bill of lading (see para. 4.33.) is sent to the buyer, the transference of this bill of lading to the sub-buyer will allow him or her to demand possession of the goods from the original seller.[84]

## (iv) Seller's right of resale

Although the exercise of the seller's rights of lien or stoppage in transit does not automatically rescind the contract,[85] resale by a seller who has exercised these rights will confer a good title on the buyer.[86] Additionally, the seller is given an express power of resale where the goods are perishable or where he or she gives notice of his or her intention to resell, and the price is not paid or tendered within a reasonable time.[87] The seller may also recover damages from the buyer for any loss occasioned by the breach of contract.[88] Where the seller has expressly reserved the right of resale in case of the buyer's default, and the buyer does, in fact, default, the resale is treated as an implied rescission of the contract and the seller may have a claim for damages.[89] This means that the seller is selling his or her own goods in the resale and is therefore entitled to retain any profit on the resale.[90]

## (b) The seller's personal remedies

Apart from remedies based on possession of the goods, a seller confronted with a breach of contract by the buyer has certain personal remedies against the buyer, namely, to sue for the price and to sue for damages. The advantage of being entitled to sue for the price is that the seller is under no obligation to mitigate his or her loss by looking for a new buyer.

---

[79] [1910] 2 K.B. 502 at 507, *per* Pickford L.J.
[80] [1910] 2 K.B. 502 at 507, *per* Pickford L.J. See also *D. F. Mount Ltd v Jay & Jay (Provisions) Co Ltd* [1960] 1 Q.B. 159 at 168, *per* Salmon J.
[81] *D. F. Mount Ltd v Jay & Jay (Provisions) Co Ltd* [1960] 1 Q.B. 159.
[82] s.47(2)(a).
[83] s.47(2)(b).
[84] See *Cahn v Pockett's Bristol Channel Steam Packet Co Ltd* [1899] 1 Q.B. 643.
[85] s.48(1).
[86] s.48(2).
[87] s.48(3).
[88] s.48(3).
[89] s.48(4).
[90] *R. V. Ward Ltd v Bignall* [1967] 1 Q.B. 534.

## (i) Action for the price

The seller may sue for the price:

- where the property has passed and the buyer wrongfully neglects or refuses to pay.[91] However, the seller cannot claim where the property in the goods has not passed due to the wrongful act of the buyer;[92]
- where the price is payable on a day certain irrespective of delivery, and the buyer wrongfully neglects or refuses to pay, whether or not the property has passed or goods have been appropriated to the contract.[93]

The day certain rule is something of an anomaly, in that it allows the seller to claim the price, even when no property has passed. The meaning of a "day certain" is ambiguous. Obviously it can be a specific date, but the authorities indicate that a date fixed by reference to some future or contingent event is not a day certain. So in one case where payment was to be made on submission of an invoice, this was not payment on a day certain,[94] whereas in another a contract which provided for payment of specific instalments on completion of stages of the work was stated to be payment on a day certain.[95] It would seem inequitable that a seller who rescinds the contract in response to failure to pay on a day certain should be able to claim the price without delivering the goods, yet such is the logic of an English decision of the House of Lords,[96] although it appears that Scots law might prevent such a result.[97]

## (ii) Damages for non-acceptance

Where the buyer wrongfully neglects or refuses to accept and pay for the goods, the seller can sue for damages for non-acceptance.[98] This may be the seller's only remedy, but where the property in the goods has passed, the seller may choose to sue for damages, rather than exercising his or her option of suing for the price. The measure of damages is the estimated loss directly and naturally resulting in the ordinary course of events from the buyer's breach of contract.[99] Where there is an available market for the goods, the measure will be the difference between the market price and the current price when the goods ought to have been accepted, or if no time was fixed for acceptance, at the time of refusal to accept.[1]

The seller may recover damages even if it seems that, looking at the transaction as a whole, the seller has not made a loss. In one case, following breach by the buyer, the seller had been able to sell the goods for more than the contract price.[2] Nevertheless, the seller was awarded the difference between the contract and the market price at the date of breach. The following statement was approved in the case:

"... the seller cannot recover from the buyer the loss below the market price at the date of the breach if the market falls, nor is he liable to the purchaser for the profit if the market rises."[3]

---

[91] s.49(1).
[92] *Colley v Overseas Exporters* [1921] 3 K.B. 302.
[93] s.49(2).
[94] *Henderson & Keay Ltd v A. M. Carmichael Ltd*, 1956 S.L.T. (Notes) 58.
[95] *Workman Clark & Co v Lloyd Brazileno* [1908] 1 K.B. 968, although the case contains very little discussion of s.49(2) of the Act.
[96] *Hyundai Heavy Industries Co Ltd v Papadopoulos* [1980] 1 W.L.R. 1129.
[97] See *Lloyds Bank plc v Bamberger*, 1993 S.C. 570 at 573F–G, *per* Lord Justice-Clerk Ross.
[98] s.50(1).
[99] s.50(2).
[1] s.50(3).
[2] *Campbell Mostyn (Provisions) Ltd v Barnett Trading Co* [1954] 1 Lloyd's Rep. 65.
[3] *A. K. A. S. Jamal v Moolla Dawood, Sons & Co* [1916] 1 A.C. 175 at 179, approved by Somervell L.J. in *Campbell Mostyn (Provisions) Ltd v Barnett Trading Co* [1954] 1 Lloyd's Rep. 65 at 68.

On the other hand, if the contract price and the market price at the time of breach are identical, and the goods can be readily resold at that price, then the seller may only receive nominal damages.[4] Where supply exceeds demand the seller will usually be entitled to the profit lost on the sale.[5] Jenkins L.J. explains matters in *Charter v Sullivan*[6] as follows:

> "The number of sales he can effect, and consequently the amount of profit he makes, will be governed . . . either by the number of cars he is able to obtain from the manufacturers, or by the number of purchasers he is able to find. In the former case demand exceeds supply, so that the default of one purchaser involves him in no loss, for he sells the same number of cars as he would have sold if that purchaser had not defaulted. In the latter case supply exceeds demand, so that the default of one purchaser may be said to have lost him one sale."[7]

## 1.15. CONSUMER GUARANTEES

Although this is not strictly speaking related to the contract of sale of goods, it would be remiss not to point out that the 2002 Regulations contain new protections for consumers in relation to guarantees.[8] The consumer guarantee is defined as:

> "any undertaking to a consumer by a person acting in the course of his business, given without extra charge, to reimburse the price paid or to replace, repair or handle consumer goods in any way if they do not meet the specifications set out in the guarantee statement or in the relevant advertising."[9]

"Consumer" is given the normal definition supplied by the 2002 Regulation, a natural person contracting for purposes which are outside his trade, business or profession.[10] A guarantee is further defined in s.15(1) as a contractual obligation owed by the guarantor under the conditions which are set out in the guarantee itself and also in any associated advertising. This contrasts with the position under Scots law where guarantees could be classed as promises or unilateral obligations.[11] Where goods are supplied with a guarantee, the guarantee takes effect when the goods are delivered.[12] Certain minimum standards are set, including the fact that the guarantee must be in plain intelligible language[13] and must be in English where the goods are offered within the UK.[14] It must include essential particulars such as the duration and territorial scope together with the name and address of the guarantor.[15] Where the consumer requests a copy of the guarantee it must be provided to him or her within a reasonable time,[16] and this particular provision binds not only the guarantor but any person who offers the goods which are the subject of the guarantee for sale or supply.[17] The consumer also has the right to

---

[4] *Charter v Sullivan* [1957] 2 Q.B. 117.
[5] *W. L. Thompson Ltd v Robinson (Gunmakers) Ltd* [1955] Ch. 177.
[6] [1957] 2 Q.B. 117.
[7] [1957] 2 Q.B. 117 at 124–125, *per* Jenkins L.J.
[8] 2002 Regulations, reg. 15.
[9] 2002 Regulations, reg. 2. See also reg. 15(1) which provides that the guarantee is a contractual obligation owed by the guarantor under the conditions which are set out in the guarantee itself and also in any associated advertising.
[10] 2002 Regulations, reg. 2.
[11] See M. Hogg, "Scottish Law and the European Consumer Sales Directive", 2001 E.R.P.L., 337 at 349.
[12] 2002 Regulations, reg. 15(1).
[13] 2002 Regulations, reg. 15(2).
[14] 2002 Regulations, reg. 15(5).
[15] 2002 Regulations, reg. 15(2).
[16] 2002 Regulations, reg. 15(3).
[17] 2002 Regulations, reg. 15(4).

apply for an order of specific implement in relation to certain of his or her rights under this section.[18]

It is common for consumers in the UK to be offered an extended warranty relating to consumer goods. Such extended warranties, purchased by the consumer, apply for perhaps two to five years, and are generally expensive. Retailers encourage consumers to buy them by indicating that they provide the consumer with the comfort of knowing that their goods will be automatically replaced should they break down within the warranty period. Such extended warranties have always been controversial given that, in buying such a warranty, in effect, the consumer is paying for protections which he or she probably already possesses under the implied terms of the 1979 Act. In conformity with the terms of the original Directive, such warranties are not covered by the 2002 Regulations because guarantees are defined as being "given without extra charge".[19] It is unfortunate that the opportunity to protect consumers against such warranties was not taken in the Directive.

---

[18] In relation to rights under 2002 Regulations reg. 15(2), (4) or (5).
[19] 2002 Regulations, reg. 2.

# Chapter 2

# AGENCY

## 2.1. INTRODUCTORY ISSUES

### (a) General

An agent has been described as "a person who has authority to act for and on behalf of another (called the principal) in contracting legal relations with third parties; and the agent representing the principal creates, alters, or discharges legal obligations of a contractual nature between the latter and third parties."[1] Not all of the aspects of agency can be included in a short definition, but this definition encapsulates the essence of agency which is the ability to create and discharge legal relations for another party. In exchange for payment of a fee, the principal is able to benefit from the agent's expertise in negotiating contracts. The principal may appoint an agent who is based in a foreign country, allowing the principal to make use of the specialised knowledge of local market conditions which the agent possesses. The international aspect of agency is of key importance, particularly since the enactment of the 1986 Commercial Agents Directive[2] which was implemented in Great Britain by the Commercial Agents (Council Directive) Regulations 1993.[3] The Directive aims to protect commercial agents, and its impact on the Scots law of agency has been extensive.

The extent of the agent's authority is an important issue. If the agent exceeds his or her authority then this may jeopardise the validity of the contract which the agent has entered into on the principal's behalf. In certain circumstances, the contract may be valid, for example, where the agent can rely on his or her apparent authority, or where the principal may ratify the agent's actions, as is explored below. Nevertheless, it is often difficult to ascertain whether the principal or, in fact, the agent is bound in the contract which the agent has attempted to conclude with a third party on the principal's behalf.

The manner in which the agent acts is also important. The form of the contract entered into will often depend upon the amount of information which was imparted to the third party by the

---

[1] T. B. Smith, *A Short Commentary on the Law of Scotland* (1962), p.774.

[2] EC Council Directive 86/653 ([1986] O.J. L132/17) on the co-ordination of the laws of Member States relating to self-employed commercial agents.

[3] SI 1993/3053 (amended by SI 1993/3173 and SI 1998/2868).

agent. Issues such as whether the agent made it clear to the third party that he or she was acting for a principal, and whether that principal was named by the agent, can be determinative of the contractual relationships formed.

## (b) Agency and mandate

Mandate differs from agency in that mandate is a gratuitous contract. In mandate, the mandant is the equivalent of the principal and the mandatary the equivalent of the agent. Many of the mandatary's rights and duties are similar to those of the agent in agency. The advocate's contract is a contract of mandate, even though the advocate does not, of course, act gratuitously.[4]

## (c) Capacity

The extent to which an agent and a principal must have capacity to contract is an area which is subject to a surprising amount of doubt. Given that the agent is acting as the extended arm of the principal, the principal should not be able to enlarge his or her contractual capacity by employing an agent. A principal who has no contractual capacity will lack the ability to appoint an agent, and will not be personally bound by contracts which the agent purports to enter into on his or her behalf. A good illustration of the consequences of lack of capacity on the principal's part is that of promoters of limited companies. The aim of a promoter is to set up a limited company, and he or she may purport to act as an "agent" for the company (the principal) at a time when the company has not yet been formed. In such a situation the promoter does not bind the company, even if the company has benefited from the supply of goods and services under the contracts entered into by the promoter.[5] The promoter is personally bound under any such contracts.

The contractual capacity of the agent is a more difficult issue. In the context of the agent's ability to enter contracts on the principal's behalf, the agent's capacity is not particularly important. The aim of the agent/principal relationship is to bind the principal in a contract with a third party. The agent's lack of capacity should not prejudice the formation of such a contract. The same considerations clearly do not apply where the agent is suing or being sued by a principal or a third party. In such a situation, the agent's lack of capacity may mean that an action for enforcement of the particular contract, whether concluded between agent and principal or agent and third party, cannot be raised.

## (d) Constitution

The principal and agent may have entered into an actual written contract, and indeed, where the Commercial Agents (Council Directive) Regulations 1993 apply, either party has the right to receive from the other, on request, a signed written document setting out the terms of the agency contract including any terms subsequently agreed.[6] In cases not governed by the Regulations, a written agreement is not required, an oral agency agreement being possible. If the agency agreement is a written agreement, it may be described as a factory and commission or a power of attorney.[7]

It is usually assumed that the agent and principal have entered a contract, whether that be written or oral. However, an agency relationship may arise where the agent begins to act on the

---

[4] A more detailed discussion of mandate can be found in *Stair Memorial Encyclopedia* (2002 Reissue) (*"SME Reissue"*) "Agency and Mandate", paras 18–28.

[5] Companies Act 1985, s.36C(1) (added by the Companies Act 1989, s.130(4)). See also *Tinnevelly Sugar Refining Co. Ltd v Mirrlees, Watson & Yaryan* (1894) 21 R. 1009.

[6] Commercial Agents (Council Directive) Regulations 1993, SI 1993/3053, reg. 13.

[7] A power of attorney authorises the agent to administer the affairs of a principal who is unable to do so himself or herself, whether that be through absence abroad or illness.

principal's behalf with the principal's consent.[8] In such a situation it is less clear that an actual contract actually exists. It is also more common to refer to an agency "relationship" rather than an agency "contract." It may be that the agency relationship arises simply through implication from the facts.

## 2.2. THE COMMERCIAL AGENTS (COUNCIL DIRECTIVE) REGULATIONS 1993

The Commercial Agents Directive 1986[9] was implemented in Great Britain[10] by the Commercial Agents (Council Directive) Regulations 1993.[11] The regulations took effect from January 1, 1993 and apply to all agency agreements in force as at that date. They apply to the activities of commercial agents in Great Britain, regardless of the nationality of that commercial agent.[12] In order to understand the provisions of the Regulations, it is important to consider the aim of the Directive. This aim is visible in the Treaty of Amsterdam, Art. 136, which refers to the "need to promote improved working conditions and an improved standard of living for workers:" The preamble to the Directive itself also refers to the harmonisation of conditions for commercial agents to ensure their uniform protection throughout the European Union.[13]

Bearing these aims in mind, it is not surprising that the effect of the individual regulations is intensely protective of the commercial agent. Scots and English agency law has traditionally assumed an equality of bargaining power between principal and agent, and has even been even more protective of the principal in view of the agent's ability to enter into contracts beyond the confines of his or her authority. Because of this difference of approach, integrating the Regulations into the common law has proved problematic.[14] The Regulations are, in general, a very complex piece of legislation. For example, certain of the individual regulations can be excluded by the contracting parties, whereas others are mandatory. Each individual regulation must be checked to ascertain whether it may be excluded or not.

### (a) Definition of a commercial agent

A commercial agent is defined in the Regulations as follows:

> "A self-employed intermediary who has continuing authority to negotiate the sale or purchase of goods on behalf of another person (the 'principal'), or to negotiate and conclude the sale or purchase of goods on behalf of and in the name of that principal."[15]

In certain respects this definition requires further comment. A commercial agent may be an individual, a company or a partnership.[16] The definition refers to the sale or purchase of goods, ruling out agents who provide services. The commercial agent must have a "continuing

---

[8] *Barnetson v Petersen Bros* (1902) 5 F. 86; *Morrison v Statter* (1885) 12 R. 1152.

[9] EC Council Directive 86/653 ([1986] O.J. L382/17) on the co-ordination of the laws of the Member States relating to self-employed commercial agents.

[10] Great Britain includes England, Wales and Scotland. For Northern Ireland, see the Commercial Agents (Council Directive) Regulations (Northern Ireland) 1993, SR 1993/483, effective from January 13, 1994.

[11] SI 1993/3053 (amended by SI 1993/3173 and SI 1998/2868).

[12] reg.1(2). For an analysis of the international application of the regulations see *Stair Memorial Encyclopedia* (2002 Reissue) (*"SME Reissue"*) "Agency and Mandate", paras 37–41.

[13] EC Council Directive 86/653 ([1986] O.J. L382/17), preamble.

[14] See the discussion of the agent's rights under the Regulations to either indemnity or compensation on termination commented on at para. 2.9. below.

[15] reg.2(1) ("commercial agent").

[16] See *AMB Imballaggi Platici Srl Pacflex Ltd* [1999] 2 All E.R. (Comm.) 249.

authority" thus ruling out one-off transactions—the commercial agent must have a continuing relationship with the principal.[17] Given that the commercial agent must act in the name of the principal, where the agent acts on behalf of an undisclosed principal, a situation which is possible only in the UK and not in the rest of the European Union, the Regulations will not apply.[18]

## (b) "Negotiate"

The word "negotiate" has been interpreted in English cases on the Regulations. In *Parkes v Esso Petroleum Company Ltd*[19] Lord Justice Morritt relied on the ordinary English meaning of "negotiate", adding:

> "This definition does not require a process of bargaining in the sense of invitation to treat, offer, counter-offer and finally acceptance, more colloquially known as haggle. But equally it does require more than the self-service by the customer followed by payment in the shop of the price showed on the pump."[20]

Clearly the commercial agent must have some sort of active role in selling to or buying from customers. There will, no doubt, be other types of business where the customer selects the goods for himself, and the agent's role is so inactive that he or she falls outwith the definition of a commercial agent.

## (c) Exclusions

Certain types of business are expressly excluded from the definition of a commercial agent, namely:

(1) an officer of a company or association who is empowered to enter into commitments binding on that company or association[21];
(2) a partner acting on behalf of his firm[22];
(3) a person acting as an insolvency practitioner[23];
(4) a commercial agent whose activities are unpaid (a mandatary in Scots law)[24];
(5) a commercial agent acting on commodity exchanges or in the commodity market;[25] and
(6) the Crown Agents for Overseas Governments and Administrations, as set up under the Crown Agents Act 1979, or its subsidiaries.[26]

The Regulations do not apply where the agent's activities are "secondary."[27] The definition of secondary was a matter which was left to the discretion of the individual Member States. The definition in the British regulations is extremely complicated, and involves reading certain specific regulations in conjunction with the Schedule. Paragraph 2 of the Schedule defines the normal activities of a commercial agent, indicating by implication what is secondary. The

---

[17] The issue of whether the Regulations apply to an agent who does not have a direct contractual relationship with the principal *i.e.* a sub-agent is a controversial one. An English decision which had indicated that such a contractual link was not required in order for the Regulations to apply (*Light v Ty Europe Ltd* [2003] E.W.H.C. 174 (Q.B.)) was recently overturned (*Light v Tye Europe Ltd*, C.A., July 25, 2003).

[18] See the discussion of undisclosed principal in para. 2.7 below.

[19] [1999] 1 C.M.L.R. 455, Ch. D.

[20] (1999) 18 Tr.L.R. 232 at 238, CA.

[21] reg. 2(1)(i).

[22] reg. 2(1)(ii).

[23] reg. 2(1)(iii).

[24] reg. 2(2)(a).

[25] reg. 2(2)(b).

[26] reg. 2(2)(c).

[27] reg. 2(3), (4).

activities of a commercial agent are described as the sale and purchase of goods,[28] where transactions are normally individually negotiated and concluded on a commercial basis,[29] and procuring a transaction on one occasion is likely to lead to further transactions in those goods with that customer, or to transactions with customers in the same geographical area.[30] This picture of what constitutes acting as a commercial agent is further expanded in para. 3, which details factors suggesting that the situations fall within para. 2, *i.e.* what is part of the commercial agent's normal activities:

(a) the principal is the manufacturer, importer or distributor of the goods;
(b) the goods are specifically identified with the principal in the market in question rather than, or to a greater extent than, with another person;
(c) the agent devotes substantially the whole of his time to representative activities (whether for one principal or for a number of principals whose interests are not conflicting);
(d) the goods are not normally available in the market in question other than by means of the agent;
(e) the arrangement is described as commercial agency.[31]

Paragraph 4 lists factors which suggest that the agent does not fall within para. 2, *i.e.* the agent's activities *are* secondary, namely where:

(i) promotional material is supplied direct to potential customers;
(ii) persons are granted agencies without reference to existing agents in a particular area or in relation to a particular group;
(iii) customers normally select goods for themselves and merely place their order through the agent.[32]

The Regulations also contain a presumption that the activities of mail order catalogue agents for consumer goods and consumer credit agents do not fall within para. 2 and are therefore secondary.[33]

Deciding whether or not an agent's activities are secondary, and therefore that he or she is not covered by the Regulations, is a complicated exercise. A great deal of information on the agent's working practices may be required, which can then be analysed in the light of the complex provisions in the Schedule to the Regulations.

## 2.3.   The Agent's Authority

As stated above, the extent of the agent's authority has an important impact on the success of the aim of agency: the constitution of a contractual relationship between principal and third party. Ideally, the extent of the agent's authority will be spelled out in the contract between principal and agent. The agent's authority may, however, be implied. Thus, an agent may have specific powers which are available to him or her because he or she is a member of a particular profession, or because of surrounding circumstances. A solicitor has implied powers which allow him or her to carry out certain actions without the express consent of his or her client. Established case law may assist in the determination of whether any particular action is or is

---

[28] Sch., para. 2(a).
[29] Sch., para. 2(b)(i).
[30] Sch., para. 2(b)(ii).
[31] Sch., para. 3(a)–(e).
[32] Sch., para. 4(a)–(c).
[33] Sch., para. 5.

not within an agent's implied authority.[34] For example a solicitor has implied authority to order a search for incumbrances in conveyancing transactions,[35] but not to enter a contract on behalf of a client[36] nor to obtain an overdraft facility for that client.[37] It should be noted that, although the advocate's contract is a contract of mandate, the solicitor's contract is an agency contract.

## (a) General and special agents

A general agent is an agent who is employed to carry out all of the business of a particular principal, or at least, all of the business of the principal of a particular kind, whereas a special agent is employed to carry out one particular transaction. Although this issue is not entirely free from doubt, a solicitor appears to be a general agent.[38] The distinction between general and special agents is an important one given that it shapes the type of implied authority which that agent has.[39] If the agent is a general agent, the third party may assume that that agent has all the powers which an agent of that type would usually possess. If the agent is a special agent, his or her implied powers will only be such as are necessary to carry out the single transaction which he or she has been appointed to carry out.

## (b) Mercantile agents

Care must be taken in the use of agency terminology. The term "commercial agent" is likely to denote an agent falling within the ambit of the Commercial Agents (Council Directive) Regulations 1993.[40] Although the scope of the Regulations is wide, many agents are not governed by the Regulations (for example, those dealing in services, not goods) and so the use of the term "commercial agent" as a general term is not appropriate.

Historically, agents were sometimes described as either "factors" or "brokers." The distinction between factors and brokers was important: a factor was usually entrusted with possession of goods, and sold the goods in his or her own name.[41] By contrast, a broker did not usually take possession of goods, nor sell goods in his or her own name, and acted more as an intermediary.[42] This distinction is less important in a modern context, although it continues to be visible in some areas: auctioneers are classed as factors, whereas stockbrokers and insurance brokers are, not surprisingly, brokers. The word "factor" is now used in a more specialised sense.[43]

The term "mercantile agent" acquired a specific meaning through the operation of the Factors Acts.[44] A mercantile agent is defined as an agent who "in the customary course of business" has "authority either to sell goods, or to consign goods for the purpose of sale, or to buy goods, or to raise money on the security of goods."[45] Such an agent, through the operation of the Act, has the ability to pass title to the principal's goods, where the principal has not consented and would not have consented to the agent's particular transaction. The relevant section stipulates that where the mercantile agent is in possession of goods or documents of

---

[34] For a full discussion of this issue, see *Stair Memorial Encyclopedia* (2002 Reissue) (*"SME Reissue"*) "Agency and Mandate", paras 51–54.

[35] *Fearn v Gordon and Craig* (1893) 20 R. 352.

[36] *Danish Dairy Co v Gillespie*, 1922 S.C. 656 at 665, *per* Lord President Clyde, at 667, *per* Lord Skerrington, and at 671, *per* Lord Cullen.

[37] *Commercial Bank of Scotland v Biggar*, 1958 S.L.T. (Notes) 46.

[38] See, however, Bell, *Principles*, s.219(7) who classes a solicitor as a special agent.

[39] See the explanation given by Lord Young in *Morrison v Statter* (1885) 12 R. 1152 at 1154.

[40] SI 1993/3053 (amended by SI 1993/3173 and SI 1998/2868).

[41] *Cunningham v Lee* (1874) 2 R. 83 at 87, *per* Lord President Inglis.

[42] *Cunningham v Lee* (1874) 2 R. 83 at 87, *per* Lord President Inglis.

[43] It is more common to use the word "factor" to describe someone who manages property or flats or other heritable property on another's behalf. It may also refer to the practice of debt-factoring.

[44] See s.2(1) Factors Act 1889, applied to Scotland by the Factors Act 1890. See also the discussion at 1.10.(a) above.

[45] Factors Act 1889, s.1(1).

title with the consent of the owner, any sale, pledge or other disposition of the goods made by him when acting in the ordinary course of business, is as valid as if he were expressly authorised by the owner of the goods to make the same.[46] As a result, the third party transacting with the mercantile agent need have few concerns over the agent's lack of authority. There are certain qualifications, however. The third party must act in good faith, and must not have notice of the agent's lack of authority to make the disposition.[47]

### (c) *Del credere* agency

When an agent contracts on behalf of a principal, he or she does not normally provide the principal with a guarantee of the solvency of the third party with whom, as a result of the agent's efforts, the principal has concluded a contract. If such a guarantee is, in fact, given, the agency is known as *del credere* agency.[48] The agent will, of course, charge a fee for the provision of this extra service. As with other types of agency, the agency relationship may be created expressly or by implication.[49] Aside from the provision of the guarantee, in other respects *del credere* agency operates in the same way as any normal agency relationship.

## 2.4. AGENT ACTING OUTSIDE HIS AUTHORITY

The operation of the Factors Acts explained above, is one example of an agent who, despite his or her lack of authority, has the ability to enter into valid contracts on the principal's behalf. Other concepts of the law of agency may be used to validate that agent's actings notwithstanding a lack of authority. The two most important principles which have this effect are ratification and ostensible or apparent authority.

### (a) Ratification

Even if the agent entered into a contract on the principal's behalf without having first obtained the requisite authority, the principal may be able to ratify the agent's actings. Valid ratification creates privity of contract between the principal and the third party. It can be either express or implied from the principal's conduct,[50] and it may operate in different ways: it may validate a particular transaction where the agent had failed to obtain the requisite authority to carry out that transaction, or it may operate where the "agent" was not, in fact, an agent at all. The agent may simply have purported to act for a specific principal.[51] In the latter case, ratification effectively creates the agency relationship.

Ratification is retrospective in effect: privity of contract between principal and third party is deemed to exist from the moment the agent entered into the contract on the principal's behalf, as though the agent had been validly authorised at that time. The retrospective nature of ratification can lead to some curious results where the third party attempts to withdraw from the contract after it has been concluded by the agent but before ratification. The retrospective effect renders the third party's attempt to withdraw ineffective.[52] This runs counter to the requirement of *consensus in idem* in contractual relations.

---

[46] Factors Act 1889, s.2(1).

[47] Factors Act 1889, s.2(1).

[48] *Lloyd's Exrs v Wright* (1870) 7 S.L.R. 216.

[49] *Lloyd's Exrs v Wright* (1870) 7 S.L.R. 216; *Stein's Assignees v Brown* (1828) 7 S. 47.

[50] *Ballantine v Stevenson* (1881) 8 R. 959; *Barnetson v Petersen* (1902) 5 F. 86.

[51] See J. J. Gow, *Mercantile and Industrial Law of Scotland* (1964) pp.517 and 520; Laura Dunlop *et al* (eds), Gloag and Henderson, *The Law of Scotland* (11th ed., 2001) para. 21.04; *Alexander Ward & Co Ltd v Samyang Navigation Co Ltd*, 1975 S.C. (H.L.) 26, 1975 S.L.T. 126.

[52] *Bolton Partners v Lambert* (1889) 41 Ch. D. 295; *Bedford Insurance Co v Instituto de Resseguros do Brasil* [1985] Q.B. 966 at 981, *per* Parker L.J.; *Presentaciones Musicales v Secunda* [1994] Ch. 271. Although the authorities on this point are English, there is no reason to suspect that a different result would be reached in Scots law.

Ratification is subject to stringent requirements, all of which must be fulfilled before it can be effective. The requirements are considered below.

### (i) Principal in existence

The principal must be in existence at the time the agent entered into the contract with the third party on the principal's behalf. The example given above of a promoter entering into a pre-incorporation contract falls foul of this rule. The company is unable to ratify because it was not in existence at the time the promoter/agent entered into the contract.[53]

### (ii) Principal must have legal capacity

The principal must have had legal capacity both at the time the agent entered into the contract, and at the time of ratification.[54] The principal must have legal capacity at the time the agent purports to enter into the contract as a result of the retrospective nature of ratification. If, following ratification, the principal is treated as having reached *consensus in idem* with the third party at the time the agent entered into the contract, then the principal must have the capacity to reach *consensus in idem* at that time. Although there is no specific Scottish authority on this point, it is suggested that the principal must also have legal capacity when he or she ratifies. This is because ratification is a legal act which must therefore be carried out by a party with legal capacity.

Previously, it was impossible for the shareholders to ratify the actings of a director or agent of the company, where the agent had entered into a contract which was outside the objects of the company as contained in the objects clause.[55] Under the Companies Act 1985, the shareholders may ratify the actings of the director or agent by special resolution, and can also relieve the directors of liability, again, by special resolution.[56]

A puzzling case on the issue of capacity and ratification is *Alexander Ward & Co Ltd v Samyang Navigation Co Ltd*.[57] Solicitors raised an action for debt at a time when no directors were in office. The question before the court was whether the company acting through liquidators could ratify the raising of the action. It was held that the company was a competent principal at the time of raising of the action, and ratification was possible. Lord Hailsham explained that because the company was competent either to appoint directors or authorise proceedings in general meeting at the time at which the solicitors raised the action, then it followed that it was a competent principal, even if it had not carried out either of these steps at the relevant time.[58]

### (iii) Agent must enter transaction as an agent

Where the agency relationship has not been constituted, and the principal, through ratification, effectively seeks to "create" the agency relationship, the agent must have entered into the contract with the third party as an agent and not on his or her own account.[59] Whether the "agent" has named the principal in this situation is not important—it is sufficient simply for the "agent" to make it clear that he or she acts for an unidentified principal.[60]

---

[53] Companies Act 1985, s.36C(1) (added by the Companies Act 1989, s.130(4)). The Companies Act provisions effectively gave statutory form to the pre-existing common law: see *Tinnevelly Sugar Refining Co Ltd v Mirrlees, Watson & Yaryan* (1894) 21 R. 1009; *Kelner v Baxter* (1866) L.R. 2 C.P. 174; *Cumming v Quartzag Ltd*, 1980 S.C. 276.

[54] *Boston Deep Sea Fishing and Ice Co Ltd v Farnham* [1957] W.L.R. 1051.

[55] *Ashbury Railway Carriage and Iron Co Ltd v Riche* (1875) LR 7 H.L. 653. This issue is unlikely to arise in a modern context due to the width of the objects clause and the operation of ss.35A and 35B of the Companies Act 1985.

[56] Companies Act 1985, s.35(3) (substituted by the Companies Act 1989, s.108).

[57] 1975 S.C. (H.L.) 26.

[58] 1975 S.C. (H.L.) 26 at 47.

[59] *Weir v Dunlop & Co* (1861) 23 D. 1293; *Reid's Trustees v Watson's Trustees* (1896) 23 R. 636.

[60] The implications of acting for a disclosed and named principal, a disclosed and unnamed principal, and an undisclosed principal are considered at para. 2.7. below.

This rule can be illustrated by a famous English case, *Keighley, Maxsted & Co v Durant.*[61] The agent had received authority from the principal to buy corn subject to a maximum price. The agent was unable to buy at that price, and bought at a higher price, intending the transaction to be a joint speculation by the principal and him. After the transaction, the agent duly informed the principal, and the principal, happy with the agent's actings, purported to ratify the contract. When the agent failed to take delivery of the goods, the principal was sued by the seller. The principal was found not liable for failing to take delivery of the goods because he was not a party to the contract. Because the agent had not intended to enter into the contract purely in a representative capacity, the contract had been formed between seller and agent.

Unfortunately, a Scottish case, *Lockhart v Moodie & Co,*[62] appears to reach a conflicting result. A and B had entered into a joint venture agreement for the purchase of yarn. A authorised B to buy yarn at a maximum price of 1s 11d per spindle. B purchased yarn at a greater price, 1s. 11¼d., buying in his own name and not disclosing to the seller any involvement on the part of A. B became bankrupt and the seller sued A for the sums due. The First Division found A liable, but only to the extent of the approved price. This result may be explained on the basis that the principal is the joint venture[63] and that ratification is carried out by that joint venture, a view which is consistent with the opinion of Lord President Inglis in the case.[64] This explanation goes some way towards avoiding the problematic issue that, for ratification to operate successfully, the agent must not be entering into the transaction on his own account. However, it is difficult to avoid the conclusion that the agent did enter into the contract at least partly on his own account. The case therefore remains something of an anomaly. It was not discussed in *Keighley Maxsted*, and it seems not to have been subsequently referred to in any Scottish case. Gloag also identified *Keighley Maxsted* as the authoritative case.[65]

### (iv) Time limits

If the act which is being ratified is subject to a timescale, then the principal must ratify within that timescale. The most famous example of this principle is the case of *Goodall v Bilsland*[66] in which the agent, a solicitor, was authorised to object to the renewal of a licence at the licensing court. Because he was unsuccessful with his objection, he appealed to the Licensing Appeal Court, but without first obtaining the principal's authority for the raising of the appeal. The appeal had to be raised within a specific timescale and the principal's subsequent ratification came outwith that timescale and was therefore ineffective. This result is difficult to reconcile with the retrospective effect of agency. As stated above, once ratification has taken place, the act of the agent is deemed to be the act of the principal. The raising of the action by the agent should therefore have been deemed to be the act of the principal and thus should have been timeously effected. Judgments in the cases which consider the retrospective nature of ratification, which are mostly English, have not fully explored the implications of the rule providing for retrospective effect.

### (v) Contract must not be void or illegal

If the contract which was entered into by the agent is affected by illegality, or is void, then ratification will have no effect.[67] The contract remains invalid.

---

[61] [1901] A.C. 240.

[62] (1877) 4 R. 859.

[63] A joint venture is a type of partnership which is formed for one specific purpose, see para. 9.2.

[64] (1877) 4 R. 859 at 866.

[65] Gloag, *op. cit.,* p.143.

[66] 1909 S.C. 1152. See also the English cases of *Bird v Brown* (1850) 19 L.J. Ex. 154 and *Dibbins v Dibbins* [1896] 2 Ch. 348.

[67] *Bedford Insurance Co Ltd v Instituto de Resseguros do Brasil* [1985] Q.B. 966 at 986, *per* Parker L.J.

## (vi) Principal must make an informed choice

As already noted, the principal can be deemed to have ratified through his or her conduct. However, before such an inference may be made from the principal's conduct, he or she must be aware of all the relevant facts. In *Forman v The Liddesdale*[68] an agent was authorised to instruct repairs to a ship which had been damaged when it was stranded. The agent instructed repairs which went beyond mere "stranding damage" and amounted to refurbishment of the ship. After the repairs had been carried out, the principal used the ship. It was held that simple acceptance and use of the repaired ship did not amount to ratification of the agent's actions.

## (b) Ostensible/apparent authority

Where the agent does not possess the requisite authority to carry out a specific transaction, that transaction may still be valid through the operation of ostensible authority. Ostensible authority operates to prevent the principal from acting in such a way as to give to the third party the impression that the agent is properly authorised, and then subsequently seeking to deny that the agent was authorised. Ostensible authority can therefore be seen as a device which protects the third party, and acts as a type of personal bar in relation to the principal.[69] In English law, it has been described as follows:

> " . . . a legal relationship between the principal and the contractor created by a representation, made by the principal to the contractor intended to be and in fact acted on by the contractor, that the agent has authority to enter on behalf of the principal into a contract of a kind within the scope of the 'apparent authority' so as to render the principal liable to perform any obligations imposed on him by such a contract."[70]

If the third party is successful in his or her attempt to prove the existence of ostensible authority, then the agent's lack of authority is not cured. The agent remains unauthorised. The principal is merely prevented from relying on the agent's lack of authority and the third party is protected.

Other requirements must be fulfilled to establish ostensible authority successfully. The principal must create the impression of authority through a direct representation or through his or her own conduct. There must also be a causal link between that representation or conduct and the third party's belief, in other words the third party must believe that the agent is authorised as a direct result of the principal's representation. It follows, therefore, that if the third party actually knows that the agent is not authorised, even in the face of conduct of the principal suggesting otherwise, then ostensible authority cannot arise.[71] Finally, the third party must have relied on that representation and have suffered loss through that reliance.

One of the leading Scottish cases on ostensible authority, *International Sponge Importers Ltd v Watt*,[72] does not, unfortunately, provide a clear exposition of the principle. Cohen, a commercial traveller, was authorised to sell sponges on behalf of International Sponge Importers Ltd. Cohen often called upon a firm of saddlers, Watt & Co, to sell sponges. The usual method of payment for the sponges was for Watt to make out a cheque in the name of the company and send it direct to the company. On certain occasions in the past, Cohen had collected cheques from Watt made out to the company. On four previous occasions, Cohen had also induced Watt to pay by providing cheques made out in Cohen's name and handed directly to him, or in cash. Cohen absconded owing sums to the company. Both the Court of Session

---

[68] [1900] A.C. 190.

[69] For recent confirmation that ostensible authority is a form of personal bar, see *Bank of Scotland v Brunswick Developments (1987) Ltd (No. 2)*, 1997 S.C. 226 at 243, *per* Lord President Rodger.

[70] *Freeman & Lockyer v Buckhurst Park Properties (Mangal) Ltd* [1964] Q.B. 480 at 503, *per* Diplock L.J. whose speech was approved by Lord Hope in the Scottish case of *Dornier GmbH v Cannon*, 1991 S.C. 310 at 314.

[71] *Colvin v Dixon* (1867) 5 M. 603.

[72] 1911 S.C. (H.L.) 57.

and the House of Lords decided that the principal could not recover the sums due from the customers. Certain of their Lordships reached this decision on the basis that the principal had tacitly consented to this method of dealing by the agent because he had failed, through his inaction, to prevent it.[73] This argument appears to have its basis in ostensible authority. However, there are difficulties inherent in analysing this situation as one involving ostensible authority. As stated above, the principal must create the impression of the requisite authority through a representation or his or her conduct. In this case, it is the principal's inaction which creates the impression of authority. At least one other judge appeared to decide the case on the basis of implied authority.[74] Such an argument relies on the fact that it is part and parcel of the normal powers of a commercial traveller to accept cheques made out in his or her principal's name, cheques made out in his or her own name, or cash. These opinions illustrate how difficult ostensible authority is to differentiate from implied authority, and how the same set of facts may often be explained using either concept.

If the requirement of a representation or conduct on the part of the principal can be fulfilled by simple inaction by the principal, as was the case in *International Sponge Importers*, then it is only a small step from there to establish ostensible authority where the representation is made entirely by the agent. Such a situation has been advocated in English academic writings,[75] and at least one Scottish case could provide the necessary authority for this approach.[76] In an important English case, *First Energy (UK) Ltd v Hungarian International Bank Ltd*[77] the requirement of a representation or conduct on the part of the principal was applied in such a weak manner, that the case could arguably be authority for the proposition that a representation from the agent alone is sufficient in English law. The agent, Jamison, was a senior manager in charge of the Manchester office of HIB. Jamison had been negotiating with First Energy, and sought to arrange finance for them. First Energy were aware that Jamison was not authorised to grant the finance arrangement on his own. Jamison nevertheless took it upon himself to confirm the finance facility in a letter signed by him alone. The bank later sought to repudiate the transaction on the basis of Jamison's lack of authority. The Court of Appeal held that although Jamison did not have the authority to grant the loan facility, he did have apparent authority to communicate to First Energy that head office approval of the loan had been obtained. The court held that the principal was bound by the agent's actings.

The judges in the Court of Appeal approached the problem in different ways. Steyn L.J. and Nourse L.J. took a practical approach, indicating that it would be unreasonable for a third party such as First Energy to bear the burden of establishing the extent of the agent's authority.[78] Lord Steyn identified two types of apparent authority. The first is the apparent authority to enter into the loan facility. This Jamison did not have. It would have required a representation on the part of the principal which was lacking, and would also have been impossible as a result of First Energy's actual knowledge of Jamison's lack of authority. The second is the apparent authority to make representations to clients on behalf of the principal. Such representations could encompass communicating head office approval. Lord Steyn indicated that this apparent authority to make representations arose from the position in which Jamison had been placed: he had been "clothed with ostensible authority to communicate that head office approval had been given . . ."[79]

Steyn L.J. also classified ostensible authority as a type of implied or usual authority, which is unfortunate given what has been stated above on the risk of confusing these issues. In his view, there are two meanings of "usual authority":

---

[73] See *International Sponge Importers Ltd v Andrew Watt & Sons*, 1911 S.C. (H.L.) 57 at 65, *per* Lord Low (Second Division) and at 67, *per* Lord Chancellor, Lord Loreburn (H.L.).

[74] Lord Ardwall: see 1911 S.C. (H.L.) 57 at 67.

[75] I. Brown, "The agent's apparent authority: paradigm or paradox?" [1995] J.B.L. 360.

[76] *Smith v Scott & Best* (1881) 18 S.L.R. 355, although the case may be explained using implied authority.

[77] [1993] 2 Lloyd's Rep. 194.

[78] [1993] 2 Lloyd's Rep. 194 at 200 and 203, *per* Steyn L.J. and at 208, *per* Nourse L.J.

[79] [1993] 2 Lloyd's Rep. 194 at 204. A similar phrase: ". . . clothed with the trappings of authority" appears in the commentary to the Restatement Third, *Agency*, Tentative Draft No. 2, para. 2.03, Comment c.

"First, it sometimes means that the agent had implied actual authority to perform acts necessarily incidental to the performance of the agency. Secondly, it sometimes means that the principal's conduct in clothing the agent with the trappings of authority was such as to induce a third party to rely on the existence of the agency . . .".[80]

Thus, on the facts before him, Jamison had possessed the second type of usual authority.

Lord Steyn's approach is likely to lead to even greater confusion in what is, already, a very confused area. His two classes seem to be nothing other than, respectively, implied authority and ostensible authority, the latter involving minimal action on the part of the principal. The case has taken ostensible authority a long way from its acknowledged logical underpinnings of personal bar in Scots law or estoppel in English law.[81] One might have hoped that the case would not prove to be influential, especially given that it is contrary to earlier English House of Lords authority.[82] However, the amount of coverage which it is given in English agency textbooks suggests otherwise. Judicial reconsideration of the whole concept of ostensible authority is required.

In *International Sponge Importers* the third party's impression of the extent of the agent's authority was based on the method by which contracts had been concluded in the past. A recent English case suggests that the fact that contracts were concluded in a specific manner in the past cannot amount to a representation by the principal that contracts will *only* be concluded in the same manner in the future.[83] Ostensible authority is likely to arise in certain factual situations. It may arise where the agent was previously authorised, but the agent's authority has ceased. If that agent continues to act as though he or she was authorised, then ostensible authority may arise. In view of this fact, it is particularly important for a principal to inform existing customers that the agent's authority or employment has ceased. If he or she succeeds in properly informing all customers, then ostensible authority cannot arise. This requirement is given statutory form for partnerships in the Partnership Act 1890.[84] As has already been stated, for ostensible authority to be established, there must be a causal connection between the principal's representation and the third party's reliance. If the third party is aware of the cessation of the agent's authority, then the principal's failure to inform him or her is irrelevant—ostensible authority will not arise.[85] The principal may inform clients by using a circular or advertisement.

Another area where ostensible authority may arise is where a general agent has exceeded his authority. Because the agent is a general agent, third parties may reasonably assume that the agent has the wide powers which are usual for that type of agent to possess. This will clearly not be the case with special agents. However, it is difficult to analyse general agency as a species of ostensible authority. It is the agent's job-title, not any specific representation or conduct on the party of the principal, which creates the impression of authority. As such, the powers which a general agent holds are better explained as examples of implied authority, rather than ostensible authority.

## 2.5.  THE AGENT'S DUTIES/PRINCIPAL'S RIGHTS

### (a) Duty to follow instructions

The agent is under a duty to perform the contract of agency according to its terms at common law. The principal's instructions must be clear, and the agent will not be liable for any losses

---

[80] [1993] 2 Lloyd's Rep. 194 at 201, *per* Steyn L.J.
[81] *Rama Corporation v Proved Tin and General Investments Ltd* [1952] 2 Q.B. 147 at 149–150, *per* Slade J.
[82] *Armagas v Mundogas SA* [1986] A.C. 717.
[83] *Pharmed Medicare Private Ltd v Univar Ltd* [2003] 1 All E.R. 321.
[84] Partnership Act 1890, s.36.
[85] *North of Scotland Banking Corp v Behn Müller & Co* (1881) 8 R. 423 at 429.

caused as a result of the ambiguity of the instructions.[86] Under the Commercial Agents (Council Directive) Regulations 1993, the commercial agent is under a similar duty to "comply with reasonable instructions given by [the] principal."[87] If the agent acts in such a way as to breach his or her express instructions then he or she will be liable to the principal for any loss caused.[88]

If the principal does not provide express instructions, the agent may still be bound to comply with duties which are usual in the particular trade in which the agent is working.[89]

## (b) Duty of skill and care

The agent has a duty to perform the agency contract with skill and care, although the extent of this duty may vary. The institutional writers Erskine and Bell equated the agent's duty with that of ". . . a prudent man in managing his own affairs."[90] Where the agent is a professional person his or her duty is that of a reasonably competent and careful member of that profession.[91] The agent's duty may vary depending upon a variety of other factors such as the custom in the particular trade, any course of prior dealings between the parties, and the particular circumstances of the case.[92]

If the agent breaches his or her duty of skill and care, the principal may claim damages for breach of contract,[93] although in the context of such an action the court may take into account any relevant conduct of the principal such as the giving of defective instructions.[94] A recent Scottish case suggests that if the agent's duty is framed in an extremely broad manner such as to amount to an absolute discretion, the agent will not be liable in damages to the principal for defective performance except perhaps where he or she has completely failed to exercise the discretion or acted in a wholly unreasonable manner.[95]

## (c) Duty to keep accounts

Although the agent is under a duty to keep accounts, such accounts need not be written ones. The course of the relationship between the agent and the principal may indicate that a verbal accounting only is required.[96]

## (d) Agent's fiduciary duty/requirements of good faith

### (i) Duty of good faith

The agent is often stated to be under a fiduciary duty. An alternative explanation is that the agent is under specific duties which arise as a result of the requirements of good faith. Bell's explanation of the duty sets a high standard: "An agent is bound to maintain the most entire good faith, and make the fullest disclosure of all facts and circumstances concerning the principal's business."[97] The Commercial Agents (Council Directive) Regulations 1993 impose

---

[86] *Ireland v Livingston* (1872) L.R. 5 H.L. 395.

[87] Commercial Agents (Council Directive) Regulations 1993, SI 1993/3053, reg. 3(2)(c).

[88] *Gilmour v Clark* (1853) 15 D. 478; *Wright v Baird* (1868) 6 S.L.R. 95; *Bank of Scotland v Dominion Bank (Toronto)* (1891) 18 R. (H.L.) 21.

[89] Bell, *Commentaries*, I, 517.

[90] Bell, *Commentaries*, I, 516; Bell, *Principles*, s.221; Erskine, *Institutes*, III, 3, 37.

[91] *Cooke v Falconer's Representatives* (1850) 13 D. 157 at 172, *per* Lord Fullerton; *Beattie v Furness-Houlder Insurance (Northern) Ltd*, 1976 S.L.T. (Notes) 60. In the case of solicitors, see the analysis by R. Rennie, *Solicitors' Negligence*, (1997), paras 3.02 *et seq*.

[92] *Hastie v Campbell* (1857) 19 D. 557 at 561, *per* Lord President McNeill, at 564, 565, *per* Lord Curriehill; *Alexander Turnbull & Co Ltd v Cruikshank and Fairweather* (1905) 7 F. 791.

[93] *Salvesen & Co v Rederi Aktiebolaget Nordstjernan* (1905) 7 F. (H.L.) 101.

[94] *Mackenzie v Blakeney* (1879) 6 R. 1329.

[95] *Glasgow West Housing Association v Siddique*, 1998 S.L.T. 1081.

[96] *Russell v Cleland* (1885) 23 S.L.R. 211.

[97] Bell, *Principles*, s.222.

on commercial agents a duty to look after the interests of the principal and act dutifully and in good faith.[95] That duty to act in good faith is expanded upon in the Regulations where three particular aspects of the duty are detailed. Those aspects do not, however, form an exhaustive list of what constitutes acting in good faith. The commercial agent must:

(1) make proper efforts to negotiate and, where appropriate, conclude the transactions he is instructed to take care of;[96]

(2) communicate to his principal all the necessary information available to him;[97] and

(3) comply with all reasonable instructions given by his principal.[98]

## (ii) Duty to account

One of the most important aspects of the agent's fiduciary duty is the duty to account to the principal for all benefits received by the agent in the course of performance of the principal's business contract.[99] For this duty to arise, the sums received must have been received in the course of the agency business and not as a result of any other business carried out by the agent.[1] The duty extends to benefits other than money, including anything over and above the agent's agreed remuneration.[2] The duty is not sufficiently wide to prevent the agent from working for another principal in addition to the original principal, even if this means competing with the original principal.[3] Such a "non-competition" clause cannot be implied into the agency contract and would require to be inserted as an express term.[4]

A breach of this duty by the agent results not in an action of damages on the part of the principal, but rather in an action of accounting.[5] If the principal is successful in such an action, the agent must pay over the gain which he or she has made in breach of the duty. This differs from an action of damages where the principal's damages would be measured by reference to his or her loss. Given that the character of the action is disgorgement of gains, the agent must actually have made a gain or profit from breach.[6] In addition to raising an action of accounting against the agent, the principal may have the right to rescind the contract with the third party if the agent and the third party colluded to defraud him or her.[7]

## (iii) Duty not to disclose confidential information

The agent is under a duty not to disclose or make use of any confidential information concerning the principal's business which has come into the agent's knowledge through performance of the agency contract. This duty may not necessarily end with termination of the agency relationship.[8]

---

[95] Commercial Agents (Council Directive) Regulations 1993, reg. 3(1).

[96] SI 1993/3053, reg. 3(2)(a).

[97] SI 1993/3053, reg. 3(2)(b).

[98] SI 1993/3053, reg. 3(2)(c).

[99] Neilson v Skinner & Co (1890) 17 R. 1243, at 1251, per Lord Young; Trans Barvil Agencies (UK) Ltd v John S Baird & Co Ltd, 1988 S.C. 222, at 227, per Lord McCluskey.

[1] Manners v Raeburn and Verel (1884) 11 R. 899; Lothian v Jenolite Ltd, 1969 S.C. 111 at 125, per Lord Walker.

[2] Trans Barvil Agencies (UK) Ltd v John S. Baird & Co Ltd, 1988 S.C. 222 at 231, per Lord McCluskey.

[3] Lothian v Jenolite Ltd, 1969 S.C. 111.

[4] Lothian v Jenolite Ltd, 1969 S.C. 111 at 123, per Lord Wheatley. An express term had been inserted into the agency contract in Alexander Graham & Co v United Turkey Red Co Ltd, 1922 S.C. 533.

[5] Sao Paolo Alpargatas SA v Standard Chartered Bank Ltd, 1985 S.L.T. 433; Trans Barvil Agencies (UK) Ltd v John S Baird & Co Ltd, 1988 S.C. 222 at 231, per Lord McCluskey.

[6] Sao Paolo Alpargatas SA v Standard Chartered Bank Ltd, 1985 S.L.T. 433. See also, at 438, Lord Grieve's approval of a dictum from Lord Upjohn in Boardman v Phipps [1966] 3 W.L.R. 1009 at 1070 where he sets out a four-stage test to be used in analysing whether the agent has a duty to account.

[7] Huntingdon Copper and Sulphur Co Ltd v Henderson (1877) 4 R. 294 at 302, per the Lord Ordinary (Lord Young).

[8] Liverpool Victoria Legal Friendly Society v Houston (1900) 3 F. 42. See the conflicting case of Earl of Crawford v Paton, 1911 S.C. 1017, although in this case the information may not have been confidential, see Lord Dundas at 1026 and Lord Salvesen at 1028.

### (iv) Transactions between principal and agent

The agent is under a duty not to enter into any transactions with the principal which would allow the agent to make a profit at the principal's expense.[9] This duty may be part of a wider duty on the agent not to enter into situations in which the agent's interests conflict with the principal's.[10] There are several cases which illustrate this rule in the context of solicitor/client relationships. If a solicitor arranged a sale of property for the client without disclosing that the solicitor himself or herself was the buyer, then this would constitute a clear breach of the duty.[11] An example of such a breach occurred in *McPherson's Trustees v Watt*[12] in which a solicitor acted for his client, trustees, in the sale of four houses. Unknown to the trustees, the solicitor proposed to buy two of the houses himself, and arranged for the remaining two to be sold to his brother. Lord Blackburn explained the conflict of interest present in such cases as follows:

> "The mere fact that the agent was in circumstances which made it his duty to give his client advice puts him in such a position that, being the purchaser himself, he cannot give disinterested advice—his own interests coming in contact with his client's, that mere fact authorises the client to set aside the contract if he chooses so to do."[13]

Even if the solicitor discloses, and obtains the client's agreement to his or her role as a buyer, this may still constitute a breach of the duty.[14] In such a situation, the solicitor may also be in breach of his or her duty to provide the client with independent advice.

If the agent was instructed to buy goods from a third party on the principal's behalf but, instead of doing so, buys goods from himself or herself on the principal's behalf, the principal may choose to rescind the contract and claim from the agent any profit which the agent made through the transaction.[15]

### (v) Duty not to delegate

It is perhaps misleading to state that the agent is under a duty not to delegate any work which he or she is required to carry out in the performance of the agency contract. The duty is subject to numerous exceptions and it is probably more accurate to state the reverse: that the agent has the right to delegate except in particular circumstances. The duty not to delegate was originally an application of the general rule of contract law which provides that where *delectus personae* is present, *i.e.* where the agent has been chosen to carry out work because of special skill which he or she possesses, then the choice of that agent excludes performance by another.[16] The institutional writers Stair and Erskine indicated that the agent could delegate where the agent's task was one which did not involve any particular skill.[17] It is always open to the parties to stipulate expressly in the agency contract that certain tasks may or may not be delegated.

As in many parts of the law of agency, the custom of a particular trade has an impact on whether the agent has the ability to delegate. The agent may be required to carry out a task which is clearly outside his or her expertise. In such a situation the agent has the implied power to delegate such a task in order to perform the agency contract properly.[18] An example of the

---

[9] *Cunningham v Lee* (1874) 2 R. 83 at 89, *per* Lord Ardmillan.

[10] *Huntingdon Copper and Sulphur Co Ltd v Henderson* (1877) 4 R. 294 at 307, *per* Lord Mure, and at 299, *per* Lord Young.

[11] *Cleland v Morrison* (1878) 6 R. 156; *Rigg's Executrix v Urquhart* (1902) 10 S.L.T. 503.

[12] (1877) 5 R. (H.L.) 9.

[13] *McPherson's Trustees v Watt* (1877) 5 R. (H.L.) 9 at 21.

[14] *Cleland v Morrison* (1878) 6 R. 156 at 172, *per* Lord Young.

[15] Bell, *Principles*, s.222.

[16] McBryde, *op.cit.*, paras 12–42—12–43.

[17] Stair, *Institutions*, I, 12, 7; Erskine, *Institute*, III, 3, 34.

[18] Erskine, *Institute*, III, 3, 34; Bell, *Commentaries*, I, 517.

operation of this rule is the solicitor's ability to instruct local agents where the original solicitor's case is being heard in a different part of Scotland.[19] The original solicitor has the implied power to delegate.

The contractual structure which is created following delegation is an issue which is subject to some confusion in Scots law. Delegation may have one of two effects: the new agent may completely replace the original agent and enter into a direct contractual relationship with the principal; or the new agent may enter into a contract with the original agent, creating a chain of contracts joining principal, original agent and new agent. The former situation is more correctly described as novation[20] and the latter as sub-contracting. Whether novation or sub-contracting has occurred will depend upon the interpretation of both the original agency contract and the agreement between the original agent and new agent, and also the particular facts and circumstances. For example, if the principal has consented to the arrangement then it is more likely that novation rather than sub-contracting has occurred.[21] This follows because novation leads to more serious consequences for the principal and therefore requires the principal's consent. The original agent is removed from the contractual structure entirely, leaving the principal more financially exposed.

### (vi) Relief

The agent has a duty to relieve the principal of the principal's liability where the agent has entered into a contract in excess of his or her authority. An example of this can be found in *Milne v Ritchie*[22] where the agent had instructed builders to build a house for the principal but had agreed a price which was in excess of that authorised by the principal. Although the principal was bound to pay to the builders the agreed price, the principal had a right to an action against the agent for recovery of the excess which the principal was bound to pay.[23]

## 2.6.   AGENT'S RIGHTS/PRINCIPAL'S DUTIES

### (a) Principal's duties

### (i) Commercial Agents (Council Directive) Regulations 1993

As has been noted above, the commercial agent is under a general duty of good faith towards the principal in terms of the Commercial Agents (Council Directive) Regulations 1993.[24] The principal similarly owes a general duty of good faith towards the commercial agent under the same Regulations. The principal's duty is drafted in much the same way as the agent's duty, namely non-exclusive specific examples of the operation of that duty are included in the Regulations. The examples are considered in the paragraphs which follow.

The principal must provide the commercial agent with the necessary documentation relating to the goods concerned[25] and obtain for the commercial agent the information necessary for the agent's performance of the agency contract.[26] The principal must also: "notify his

---

[19] *Robertson v Foulds* (1860) 22 D. 714.

[20] McBryde, *op.cit.* paras 12–14—12–16 and 25–18—25–22.

[21] For a more detailed discussion of this problem, see *Stair Memorial Encyclopedia* (2002 Reissue) (*"SME Reissue"*) "Agency and Mandate", para. 100.

[22] (1882) 10 R. 365.

[23] *Milne v Ritchie* (1882) 10 R. 365 at 366, *per* Lord Young.

[24] Commercial Agents (Council Directive) Regulations 1993, SI 1993/3053 (amended by SI 1993/3137 and SI 1998/2868).

[25] Commercial Agents (Council Directive) Regulations 1993, SI 1993/3053, reg. 4(2).

[26] SI 1993/3053, reg. 4(2)(b).

commercial agent within a reasonable time once he anticipates that the volume of commercial transactions will be significantly lower than that which the commercial agent could normally have expected."[27] The latter duty, which is an onerous one, deserves specific comment. It forces the principal to monitor the relevant market closely and thus may run counter to the commercial realities of the situation. Local agents are often employed in a particular country where the principal has no commercial presence. In such a case the agent is more likely to have greater knowledge of local market conditions than the principal, and thus is better placed to predict a reduction in the volume of transactions. The duty also runs counter to the principal's usual practice of keeping such business information confidential.

The principal must advise the commercial agent within a reasonable time whether he accepts or refuses a transaction which the commercial agent has procured for the principal, and of any non-execution by the principal of a transaction arranged by the commercial agent.[28] This duty is a difficult one for UK agency lawyers to understand and may perhaps indicate the divergence of business practices in agency relationships throughout the European Union. In Scots law, the agent, when he or she concludes a contract on the principal's behalf, immediately creates privity of contract between the principal and the third party. There is no period of time during which the principal has the opportunity to decide whether to accept or reject the contract.

## (b) Agent's rights

### (i) Remuneration and commission at common law

The agency will usually contain an express right to remuneration. His or her remuneration may be calculated on the basis of commission on sales concluded by him or her in favour of the agent. The agency contract may, however, be silent on the issue, in which case there is a rebuttable presumption in favour of remuneration exists where the work carried out forms the agent's livelihood.[29] The courts will consider evidence from the particular trade in order to establish the rate of remuneration, although such evidence may equally indicate that no remuneration is payable. Where the agent is not a professional person, that agent's remuneration may be due on a *quantum meruit* basis.[30]

The agent's right to commission will usually be expressly stipulated in the agency contract. Even if it is so stipulated, it may be no easy matter to apply the contractual provisions to the situation at hand. Where the agent's role is to find a contracting party for the principal, the problematic issue is usually whether the eventual contract between principal and third party has been entered into as a direct result of the agent's efforts or whether the principal and third party would have entered into a contract in any event, without the agent's intervention. As a general rule, the agent's entitlement to commission arises where the transaction was "brought about, or materially contributed to" by the actings of the agent.[31] The principal may also be under a duty not to act to "frustrate" payment of the agent's commission, for example, by entering into a contract with another party expressly to avoid making payment of commission to the agent.[32]

---

[27] SI 1993/3053, reg. 4(2)(b).

[28] SI 1993/3053, reg. 4(3).

[29] *Mackersy's Executors v St Giles Cathedral Managing Board* (1904) 12 S.L.T. 391, *Campbell v Campbell's Executors* (1910) 47 S.L.R. 837.

[30] *Robb v Kinnear's Trustees* (1825) 4 S. 108; *Kennedy v Glass* (1890) 17 R. 1085.

[31] *Walker, Fraser & Steele v Fraser's Trustees*, 1910 S.C. 222 at 229, *per* Lord Dundas. See also *A R Bennet & Co Ltd v Bow's Emporium Ltd*, 1928 S.C. (H.L.) 19 at 20, *per* Lord Shaw; *Robertson v Burrell* (1899) 6 S.L.T. 368; *Douglas Goodfellow and Partners v Gordon*, 1987 S.C.L.R. 684.

[32] *Dudley Bros & Co v Barnett*, 1937 S.C. 632. English law may differ on this point: see the analysis in *Stair Memorial Encyclopedia* (2002 Reissue) (*"SME Reissue"*) "Agency and Mandate", para. 111, n.1.

## (ii) Remuneration and commission under the Commercial Agents (Council Directive) Regulations 1993

The Regulations provide the commercial agent with a right to remuneration where the agency contract is silent. The commercial agent is entitled to:

"the remuneration that commercial agents appointed for the goods forming the subject of his agency contract are customarily allowed in the place where he carries on his activities and, if there is no such customary practice, a commercial agent shall be entitled to reasonable remuneration taking into account all aspects of the transaction."[33]

The Commercial Agents Regulations also contain detailed provisions which protect the commercial agent's right to commission. He or she is entitled to commission on transactions concluded during the period covered by the agency contract:

(1) where the transaction has been concluded as a result of his action;[34] or
(2) where the transaction is concluded with a third party whom he has previously acquired as a customer for transactions of the same kind.[35]

Commission may also be payable where the commercial agent "has an exclusive right to a specific geographical area or to a specific group of customers and where the transaction has been entered into with a customer belonging to that area or group."[36] Even after termination of the commercial agency contract the agent may have the right to commission where a transaction is "mainly attributable to his efforts"[37] during the agency contract and the transaction is entered into within a reasonable time after termination or if the order of the third party reached the principal or the commercial agent before the agency contract terminated.[38] The commercial agent's right to commission is not, however, unqualified. It is not due where the transaction will not be executed for a reason for which the "principal is not to blame."[39] The concept of "blame" is not present in UK contract law, but presumably the effect is that commission will not be due where the principal is not in breach. It does not, however, cover situations of frustration, which are dealt with in another part of the Regulations.[40]

## (iii) Continuation of the principal's business

Where the agent is remunerated by commission only, his or her continued remuneration depends upon the continuation of the principal's business. Although there is little case law on this issue in Scotland, the English courts have considered whether it is possible to imply a term into the agency contract binding the principal to continue with his or her business so as to secure the agent's right to commission. It has been found that, as a general rule, no such term is to be implied into the agency contract.[41] Despite the force of this general rule, the agency contract may be framed in such a way that the natural interpretation is that the principal has undertaken a binding obligation to continue his or her business.[42]

---

[33] Commercial Agents (Council Directive) Regulations 1993, SI 193/3053 (amended by SI 1993/3173 and SI 1998/2868), reg. 6(1).
[34] SI 1993/3053, reg. 7(1)(a).
[35] SI 1993/3053, reg. 7(1)(b).
[36] SI 1993/3053, reg. 7(2).
[37] SI 1993/3053, reg. 8(a).
[38] SI 1993/3053, reg. 9.
[39] SI 1993/3053, reg. 11(1)(b).
[40] SI 1993/3053, reg. 16.
[41] *Patmore v Cannon* (1892) 19 R. 1004; *State of California (SS) Co Ltd v Moore* (1895) 22 R. 562; *Rhodes v Forwood* (1876) 1 App Cas 256; *Gardner v Findlay* (1892) 30 S.L.R. 248 at 250, *per* Lord Low; *L French & Co v Leeston Shipping Co Ltd* [1922] 1 A.C. 451.
[42] *Turner v Goldsmith* [1891] 1 Q.B. 544, CA; *Reigate v Union Manufacturing Co (Ramsbottom) Ltd* [1918] 1 K.B. 592.

## (iv) Reimbursement, relief and lien

The agent has a right to be reimbursed by the principal for all expenses which he or she has incurred in the proper performance of the agency contract.[43] If the sums were expended by the agent in a course of action which constituted improper rather than proper performance of the agency contract, then the sums will not be recoverable. An example of improper performance can be seen in *Tomlinson v Scottish Amalgamated Silks Liquidator.*[44] The agent, a company director, was unsuccessful in his attempt to recover his expenses for defending an action for fraud. Such expenses were not part of the proper performance of the agency contract. Indeed, had the charge been found relevant, the director would have been acting wholly contrary to his duties under the agency contract.

The agent is entitled to relief from any liabilities which have accrued as part of the proper performance by him or her of the agency contract.[45] As with reimbursement, the right to relief can be lost if the agent has acted contrary to the agency contract, for example by seeking to defraud or conceal material facts from the principal.[46] The right to relief has also been qualified by the custom of a particular trade.[47]

The agent has a lien, or right to retain the principal's goods in his possession, as security against payment of his or her commission or remuneration. The lien may be general or special: a general lien allows the agent to retain goods in security of any transaction carried out by the agent on the principal's behalf, not necessarily a transaction involving the goods retained, whereas a special lien allows the agent only to retain goods which are the subject of the transaction out of which the debt concerned has arisen. Commercial or mercantile agents,[48] solicitors[49] and stockbrokers[50] are able to exercise general liens, which enable them to retain the principal's goods against payment of the general balance due by the principal. Accountants possess only the more limited special lien.[51]

# 2.7. CONTRACTS WITH THIRD PARTIES

The aim of an agency transaction is to create privity of contract between the principal and the third party. However, such privity may not be attained, and, instead, a contract may be concluded between the agent and the third party. In identifying the contracting parties, in agency as in any other type of contract, the courts must look to the intentions of the parties. It has often been stated that, in order to decide this issue, one must ascertain whether the third party intended to give credit to the principal or to the agent.[52] In other words, was the third party relying on the financial standing of the principal or the agent when entering into the contract? If the third party contracted on the credit of the principal, then he or she has formed a contract with the principal, or the agent *mutatis mutandis.* However, this particular approach is not obvious from an analysis of the cases. Instead, the courts consider the manner in which the agent has acted and the amount of information he or she has disclosed to the third party. Three particular situations have been identified:

---

[43] *Drummond v Cairns* (1852) 14 D. 611; *Marshall Wilson Dean and Turnbull v Feymac Properties Ltd,* 1996 G.W.D. 22–1247.

[44] 1935 S.C. (H.L.) 1.

[45] *Stevenson v Duncan* (1842) 5 D. 167 .

[46] *Robinson v Middleton* (1859) 21 D. 1089.

[47] *Dinesman & Co v Mair & Co,* 1912 1 S.L.T. 217.

[48] *Sibbald v Gibson and Clark* (1852) 15 D. 217 at 221, *per* Lord Justice-Clerk Hope.

[49] *Drummond v Muirhead and Guthrie Smith* (1900) 2 F. 585.

[50] *Glendinning v John D Hope & Co,* 1911 S.C. (H.L.) 73.

[51] *Findlay (Liquidator of Scottish Workmen's Assurance Co Ltd) v Waddell,* 1910 S.C. 670.

[52] Bell, *Principles,* s.224A; Bell, *Commentaries,* I, 541, Lord McLaren's note; *Carsewell v Scott & Stephenson* (1839) 1 D. 1215; *Miller v Mitchell* (1860) 22 D. 833 at 846, *per* Lord Neaves, and at 849, 850 *per* Lord Ivory.

(1) where the agent acts for a disclosed and named principal;
(2) where the agent acts for a disclosed but unnamed principal;
(3) where the agent acts for an undisclosed principal.

Each situation is considered below.

## (a) Agent acts for a disclosed and named principal

Where the agent discloses to the third party both the fact of the agency and the identity of the principal, the general rule is that the contract will be formed between the third party and the principal, and the agent will not incur personal liability in any contract with the third party.[53] Even where the principal is not expressly named, but the third party could, with relative ease, identify the principal, the contract is still formed between the principal and the third party.[54] However, this general rule of non-liability for the agent can be rebutted by evidence to the contrary. Such evidence may exist as a matter of custom, *i.e.* the custom of the particular trade may dictate that the contract is concluded between agent and principal and the agent accepts personal liability.[55]

## (b) Written contracts

If a written contract has been entered into, this question may be solved by the operation of the general presumption that the party executing a written document intends to accept personal liability under it. This presumption is difficult to rebut and the onus lies on the agent to prove that he or she did not intend to accept personal liability.[56] The strength of this presumption is illustrated by cases in which attempts to overturn it failed even though the third party was aware that the agent was acting in a representative capacity[57] or where the terms of the contract were consistent with the agent acting in a representative capacity, but he signed it without qualifying his signature.[58]

It is not only the agent's method of signature which is relevant, however. The court must interpret the contract as a whole.[59] In one of the leading Scottish cases, the agent, a sales manager for two companies, sought to employ a sub-agent.[60] He sent a letter on the headed notepaper of one of the companies confirming the arrangements, which he signed using his personal signature. The court held that the agent had failed to discharge the onus that he, having personally signed the contract, and not the company, was bound by it.

Even if the agent adds after his or her signature a description of the capacity in which he or she is signing the contract, this may not be sufficient to rebut the presumption of personal liability. It has been held that where a director and secretary signed a contract adding the designations "director" and "secretary" and the name of the company after their signatures, this was not sufficient to rebut the presumption.[61] The designations were merely descriptive of the agents' roles. Instead, the agent must make his or her representative capacity clear, for

---

[53] *Miller v Mitchell* (1860) 22 D. 833; *Fenwick v Macdonald, Fraser & Co Ltd* (1904) 6 F. 850; *Stone and Rolfe Ltd v Kimber Coal Co Ltd,* 1926 S.C. (H.L.) 45.

[54] *Armour v T. L. Duff & Co,* 1912 S.C. 120 at 124, *per* Lord Guthrie.

[55] For example, solicitors grant letters of obligation in conveyancing transactions where it is customary for certain of the obligations to be personal obligations binding the solicitor rather than the client: *Johnstone v Little,* 1960 S.L.T. 129, OH, *cf. Digby Brown & Co v Lyall,* 1995 S.L.T. 932; or stockbrokers who deal with one another as principals even though they are clearly acting in a representative capacity, *Maffett v Stewart* (1887) 14 R. 506.

[56] *Stewart v Shannessy* (1900) 2 F. 1288.

[57] *Lindsay v Craig,* 1919 S.C. 139; *Gibb v Cunningham and Robertson,* 1925 S.L.T. 608; *Muirhead v Gribben,* 1983 S.L.T. (Sh. Ct.) 102.

[58] *Brown v Sutherland* (1875) 2 R. 615.

[59] *Brebner v Henderson,* 1925 S.C. 643 at 645, 647, *per* Lord President Clyde; *Stone and Rolfe v Kimber Coal Co Ltd* 1926 S.C. (H.L.) 45.

[60] *Stewart v Shannessy* (1900) 2 F. 1288.

[61] *Brebner v Henderson,* 1925 S.C. 643; although *cf. McLean v Stuart,* 1970 S.L.T. (Notes) 77.

example by adding "as agent for and on behalf of" or *"per procuration"*. The operation of this rule in statutory form can be found in the Bills of Exchange Act 1882 in so far as it applies to the drawer, indorser or acceptor of a bill[62] (see para. 5.3.).

Where the agent is acting on behalf of an unincorporated association which has no legal capacity, even words clearly indicating that he or she does not intend to undertake personal liability will be insufficient to avoid liability on his or her part.[63] This is an example of the rule discussed above that the principal must have legal capacity for agency to operate successfully.[64]

## (c) Agent acts for a disclosed but unnamed principal

In this type of situation the agent makes the fact that he or she is acting in a representative capacity clear, but fails to name his or her principal. There is, unfortunately, very little authority on this issue in Scots law and, consequently, much confusion.[65] The identity of the contracting parties may be established by applying the rule outlined above, namely, ascertaining whose credit the third party was relying on when he or she entered into the contract.[66] Alternatively, the cases may be resolved using the doctrine of election. The third party may have alternative actions against principal and agent, and must elect which of the two to hold liable.[67] The cases discussed below are perhaps the only clear examples of these two solutions.

In *Lamont Nisbet & Co v Hamilton*[68] the agents were managing owners of a ship who instructed insurance brokers to insure the ship. When the agents went into liquidation, the insurance brokers brought an action against the owners of the ship for payment of insurance premiums. The insurance brokers were unsuccessful. The court held that they had, all along, taken the agents as their contracting parties. Lord President Dunedin reached this result by asking who the third party, the pursuers, gave credit to, and concluding that it was to the agents.[69] The insurance brokers were aware that the agents were acting in a representative capacity. The name of the principal, the owner of the ship could easily have been ascertained from the Register of Owners.[70]

In *Ferrier v Dods* an auctioneer had been instructed to sell a horse. The auctioneer was, obviously, acting in a representative capacity, but the name of the principal was not disclosed. The buyer was unhappy with the quality of the horse, and considered that there had been a breach of the warranty given that the horse was sound. After the auction, once he had found out the identity of the seller, the buyer had returned the horse to the seller. It was held that the buyer would have been entitled to sue either the principal or the agent, but that, having returned the horse to the principal, he had elected to hold the principal liable as his debtor. The opinions in the case focus mainly on the issue of election, and not whose credit the purchaser looked to when he made the purchase.

The position is clearer where the agent refuses to identify his unnamed principal. The agent will be personally liable. *Gibb v Cunningham and Robertson* provides an example of the operation of this rule. A solicitor refused to name his clients, and was therefore found liable to implement a contract which he had concluded on their behalf.[71]

---

[62] Bills of Exchange Act 1882, s.26(1).

[63] For example a church congregation in *McMeekin v Easton* (1889) 16 R. 363; and unincorporated clubs in *Thomson v Victoria Eighty Club* (1905) 43 S.L.R. 628 and *Cromarty Leasing Ltd v Turnbull*, 1988 S.L.T. (Sh. Ct.) 62.

[64] See para. 2.1.(c) above.

[65] See the comments of Lord Prosser in *P & M Sinclair v Bamber Gray Partnership*, 1987 S.L.T. 674 at 676.

[66] *Lamont Nisbet & Co v Hamilton*, 1907 S.C. 628.

[67] *Ferrier v Dods* (1865) 3 M. 561.

[68] 1907 S.C. 628.

[69] *Lamont Nisbet & Co v Hamilton*, 1907 S.C. 628 at 635, 636, *per* Lord President Dunedin.

[70] See *Armour v T. L. Duff & Co*, 1912 S.C. 20.

[71] 1925 S.L.T. 608. This may, however, be the simple application of the presumption that the signatory of a written contract is personally bound by it.

## (d) Agent acts for undisclosed principal

In this situation the agent is acting in a representative capacity, but this fact is entirely concealed from the third party. That third party, unaware of the existence of a principal, will consider that he or she has concluded a contract with the "agent". After the third party has concluded a contract, the principal may disclose his or her existence and, provided that the agent has acted within his or her authority,[72] may sue the third party direct. The third party may also choose to sue the principal rather than the agent once the principal is disclosed. Liability is, however, alternative and not joint and several. Lord Young explained alternative liability as follows:

> ". . . if a person really acting for another goes into the market and buys as if for himself, he binds himself, but if the party from whom he buys finds out his true position then he can treat him as an agent only. He cannot have two principals to deal with, and no double remedy is allowed."[73]

It is contrary to the normal rules of formation of contract to permit the principal to intervene in a contract in this way. It results in the third party being treated as having reached *consensus in idem* with a party of whom he or she was previously unaware. Various attempts have been made to identify the legal basis of the concept of the undisclosed principal, but there is no generally accepted explanation.[74] The concept is usually justified simply by its commercial utility.[75]

Once the principal has disclosed himsel for herself, the third party must elect to sue either the agent or the principal.[76] Election can be express, or can be inferred from conduct.[77] Once the third party has elected, his or her election is final.[78] Although this point is not entirely free of doubt, where the pursuer institutes proceedings against the relevant party but matters do not proceed to decree, then an election has not taken place.[79] Only if decree has been obtained can it be stated that election has occurred. However, receiving a dividend on bankruptcy has been held to be the equivalent of pursuing a party to judgment and therefore the equivalent of decree.[80]

In certain situations the principal is barred from acting in this way. This may occur as a matter of interpretation of the contract concluded between the agent and the third party. Such an interpretation may arise in a number of ways: the contract may contain a clause indicating that the named contracting party is the sole contracting party[81]; the definition of the contracting party may exclude an undisclosed principal by implication; or the existence of an undisclosed principal may be excluded as a matter of interpretation of the contract as a whole.[82] The undisclosed principal is also barred from acting in this way where his or her concealment is

---

[72] *Hutton v Bulloch* (1874) L.R. 9 Q.B. 572.

[73] *Meier & Co v Kuchenmeister* (1881) 8 R. 642 at 646, *per* Lord Young.

[74] See, *e.g.* N. Seavey, *The Rationale of Agency* (1920) Yale Law Journal 859; W. Müller-Freienfels, "The Undisclosed Principal" (1953) 16 Modern Law Review 299; R. Barnett, *Squaring Undisclosed Agency with Contract Theory* (1987) 75 California Law Review 1969.

[75] G. H. L. Fridman, *The Law of Agency*, (7th ed., 1996) 254; F. M. B. Reynolds (ed.), *Bowstead and Reynolds on Agency* (17th ed., 2001), para. 8–071.

[76] *Bennett v Inveresk Paper Co* (1891) 18 R. 975 at 983, *per* Lord McLaren; *Laidlaw v Griffin*, 1968 S.L.T. 278.

[77] *Ferrier v Dods* (1865) 3 M. 561, the facts of which are discussed above. Election was inferred from the buyer's conduct of returning the horse to the seller.

[78] *David Logan & Son Ltd v Schuldt* (1903) 10 S.L.T. 598; *British Bata Shoe Co v Double M Shah Ltd*, 1980 S.C. 311.

[79] *Meier & Co v Kuchenmeister* (1881) 8 R. 642; *Black v Girdwood* (1885) 13 R. 243, although this case concerned a partnership and liability was thus joint and several and not alternative; *Craig & Co v Blackater*, 1923 S.C. 472. This may not be the position under English law, see the discussion in *Stair Memorial Encyclopedia* (2002 Reissue) ("*SME Reissue*") "Agency and Mandate", para. 156.

[80] *David Logan & Son Ltd v Schuldt* (1903) 10 S.L.T. 598.

[81] *United Kingdom Mutual Steamship Assurance Association v Nevill* (1887) 19 QBD 110; *J. A. Rayner (Mincing Lane) Ltd v Department of Trade and Industry* [1990] 2 A.C. 418 at 516, *per* Lord Oliver.

[82] *Humble v Hunter* (1842) 12 Q.B. 310; *J. A. Salton & Co v Clydesdale Bank Ltd* (1889) 1 F. 110.

carried out with the purpose of deceiving the third party. The leading case is *Said v Butt*,[83] where the undisclosed principal used an agent to buy a ticket for the first night of a theatre performance. He used an agent because he knew that the managing director of the theatre would not sell a ticket to him personally, because of allegations which he had previously made against the managing director. When he arrived at the theatre on the night of the performance, he was refused admission. It was held that he could not intervene on this contract. The reasoning used by the judges in this case is far from clear. It may be a case which rests on mistake rather than on an abuse of the ability to act as an undisclosed principal. It seems that this case is not authority for the proposition that an undisclosed principal is barred from intervening where the third party would not have contracted with him.[84]

## 2.8. WHERE THE AGENT EXCEEDS HIS AUTHORITY

### (a) Liability of the agent

If the agent has exceeded his or her authority, and the principal can neither ratify the agent's actions nor rely on the doctrine of ostensible authority, then no contract is formed between the principal and the third party. The agent may, however, be personally bound in the contract, for example, where he or she had acted for a non-existent principal, or where the principal had no capacity to contract. Indeed, where the agent purports to enter into a contract with a third party where the principal is in existence but the agent lacks the authority to do so, the agent will not be personally bound.[85] However, outside these particular examples there is no general rule that the agent who exceeds his or her authority is always bound in a contract with the third party.

The third party has other remedies which may be used against the agent to recoup his or her losses. If the agent has fraudulently or negligently misrepresented his or her authority, then the third party may have an action against the agent for damages in delict and the delictual measure of damages will apply.[86] Where the agent has been neither fraudulent nor negligent, the third party may yet have a contractual action for breach of warranty of authority.[87] The measure of damages in the latter action is the loss which the third party has suffered as a result of not having the principal as a contracting party.[88] It follows, therefore, that if the contract which the third party intended to enter into with the principal would have been a losing bargain, the third party has suffered no loss as a result of the agent's misrepresentation and can recover no damages.[89] As is the case in other examples of misrepresentation, the agent's misrepresentation must have actually caused the loss. The third party will not, therefore, be able to recover damages where he or she already knew that the agent was not authorised and did not rely on the agent's misrepresentation.

In one case it was argued that the principal had a similar action for breach of warranty of authority against the agent.[90] Although the principal was successful in his action, this type of action has a different basis than those discussed above. It arises from the agency contract between the principal and agent, and is, in effect, an action for breach of the agent's duties under the agency contract.

---

[83] [1920] 3 K.B. 497.
[84] *Bowstead and Reynolds on Agency,* para. 8–081.
[85] Bell, *Commentaries*, I, 543.
[86] See Gloag, *op. cit.,* p.154. There is very little authority on this issue in Scots law.
[87] *Anderson v Croall & Sons* (1903) 6 F. 153.
[88] *Anderson v Croall & Sons* (1903) 6 F. 153.
[89] *Irving v Burns,* 1915 S.C. 260.
[90] *Salvesen & Co v Rederi Aktiebolaget Nordstjernan* (1905) 7 F. (H.L.) 101.

## 2.9.　TERMINATION OF THE AGENCY CONTRACT

### (a) Termination under the Commercial Agents (Council Directive) Regulations 1993

Minimum periods of notice of termination are imposed by the Commercial Agents (Council Directive) Regulations 1993. These requirements apply to both parties. Either agent or principal must provide one month's notice in the first year of the agency contract; two months in the second year; and three months thereafter.[91]

The Regulations contain rights on the part of the agent to receive either a "compensation" or "indemnity"[92] payment on termination of the agency contract.[93] This part of the Regulations has proved by far the most controversial part, and has given rise to some difficult and conflicting case law in Scotland and England.

### (b) Indemnity and compensation—general provisions

The contracting parties cannot, by agreement, avoid payment of either compensation or indemnity, although the indemnity provisions must be expressly opted into.[94] Thus, if the contract is silent on the issue then compensation and not indemnity is payable. The commercial agent's rights can be time-barred. He or she must notify the principal within a year of termination of the agency contract if he or she wishes to pursue the entitlement.[95]

The commercial agent's rights to either indemnity or compensation may be excluded in certain situations. It is excluded where the principal has terminated as a result of the commercial agent's breach or default caused by frustration of contract.[96] It is also excluded where the commercial agent himself or herself has terminated the agency contract although termination may be justified in two separate situations: first where the principal is in breach of the agency contract[97]; and secondly where termination occurs due to the "age,[98] infirmity or illness of the agent in consequence of which he cannot reasonably be required to continue his activities."[99] Finally, it is excluded where the commercial agent has assigned his or her rights and duties under the agency contract to another person, with the consent of the principal.[1]

### (c) The indemnity provisions

The commercial agent's right to indemnity seeks to secure for him or her the benefit of the work which he or she has carried out prior to termination which would otherwise accrue to the principal.[2] His or her entitlement arises if and to the extent that:

> (1) he or she has brought the principal new customers or has significantly increased the volume of business with existing customers and the principal continues to derive benefits from the business with such customers; and

---

[91] SI 1993/3053, reg. 15(2)(a)–(c).

[92] The words "indemnity" and "compensation" should be used with care. They have a particular meaning under the Regulations which is entirely different from their usual meaning in the Scots law of contract.

[93] SI 1993/3053, regs 17 and 18.

[94] SI 1993/3053, reg. 17(2).

[95] SI 1993/3053, reg. 17(9).

[96] SI 1993/3053, reg. 18(a), read in conjunction with reg. 16.

[97] SI 1993/3053, reg. 18(b)(i).

[98] Although see *Frape v Emerco International Ltd*, 2002 S.L.T. 371 in which compensation was held to be payable where the contract "terminated" on the agent's 65th birthday, as agreed in the contract.

[99] SI 1993/3053, reg. 18(b)(ii).

[1] SI 1993/3053, reg. 18(c).

[2] *Moore v Piretta PTA Ltd* [1999] 1 All E.R. 174.

(2) the payment of this indemnity is equitable having regard to all the circumstances and, in particular, the commission lost by the commercial agent on the business transacted with such customers.[3]

Payment of the indemnity is subject to a maximum, namely one year's commission based on the average of either the last five years of the agency, or, if the agency has lasted less than five years, the annual average over the period of the agency.[4]

## (d) The compensation provisions

The compensation provisions seek to compensate the commercial agent for the damage he or she suffers as a result of termination of his or her relationship with the principal. Such damage is deemed to occur particularly when the termination takes place in either or both of the following circumstances, namely circumstances which:

(1) deprive the commercial agent of the commission which proper performance of the agency contract would have procured for him whilst providing his principal with substantial benefits linked to the activities of the commercial agent; or

(2) have not enabled the commercial agent to amortize the costs and expenses that he has incurred in the performance of the agency contract on the advice of his principal.[5]

These circumstances are, however, merely two examples, and do not form an exhaustive list of the situations in which the agent will be entitled to claim compensation.[6] Following a number of recent cases, it seems clear that "termination" is interpreted widely to include situations where the contract comes to an end on its natural expiry.[7] Compensation may therefore be payable in such situations, for example, where it was agreed in the agency contract that the contract would terminate on the agent's 65th birthday.[8]

The method of calculation of compensation has proved highly controversial. The leading case in Scotland is *King v T. Tunnock Ltd.*[9] Mr King had been employed by Tunnocks as an agent selling Tunnock's products since 1962. His family had had a long connection with the company, his father having worked for them before him. In 1994, Tunnocks closed their bakery section, and terminated the agency relationship with Mr King. There was no written agency agreement and Mr King was given no payment in lieu of notice, nor any indemnity nor compensation. An Extra Division of the Inner House found that Mr King was entitled to compensation. The controversial part of the judgment lies in the use by the Inner House of principles of French law as a guide to calculation of the amount of compensation. The source of the compensation provisions is, of course, the original Directive which the UK Regulations implemented. It is acknowledged, however, that the Directive "borrowed" the concept of compensation from French law.[10] The Inner House was referred to the established practice in France of awarding the pursuer two years' loss of average gross commission.[11] Their Lordships then used this French judicial custom to assist in their assessment of Mr King's compensation, although they noted that "even in France the two year rule is only a benchmark and can be varied at the discretion of the judge".[12] Several factors in Mr King's case supported his claim for a relatively high amount of commission, for example, the long duration of the agency

---

[3] SI 1993/3053, reg. 17(3).
[4] SI 1993/3053, reg. 17(4).
[5] SI 1993/3053, reg. 17(7)(a) and (b).
[6] See *King v Tunnock Ltd,* 1996 S.C.L.R. 742, later overturned: see *King v Tunnock,* 2000 S.C. 424.
[7] *Whitehead v Jenks & Cattell Engineering Ltd,* February 2, 2001, unreported; *Frape v Emerco International Ltd,* 2002 S.L.T. 371; *Light v Ty Europe Ltd* [2003] 1 All E.R. (Comm.) 568.
[8] *Frape v Emerco International Ltd,* 2002 S.L.T. 371.
[9] 1996 S.C.L.R. 742, reversed in *King v Tunnock,* 2000 S.C. 424.
[10] See *Bowstead and Reynolds on Agency,* para. 11–046.
[11] *King v T. Tunnock Ltd* 2000 S.C. 424 at 430.
[12] *King v T. Tunnock Ltd* 2000 S.C. 424 at 439.

relationship and the high level of commission which had been generated by it. Their Lordships awarded him the relatively high amount of compensation of £27,144, which represented two year's gross commission.

The approach taken by the Inner House was severely criticised in a later English case, *Barrett McKenzie v Escada (UK) Ltd.*[13] The judge clearly found problematic the suggestion that he should apply a French judicial custom which does not appear in the UK Regulations. However, a later English case has confirmed that the approach of the Inner House is the correct one, although the court exercised their discretion to award the plaintiff less than two year's gross commission.[14]

In two further English cases, *Ingmar GB Ltd v Eaton Leonard Inc*[15] and *Tigana Ltd v Decoro Ltd*,[16] the approach of the Inner House has been confirmed as the correct one. It is interesting to note, however, that in both cases the English Court of Appeal exercised its discretion in order to award that agent less than two year's gross commission. In *Tigana Ltd v Decoro Ltd*,[17] Mr Justice Davis listed several factors which he suggested ought to be taken into account in the calculation of compensation. These include the length of the agency relationship, whether the principal appointed the agent as an exclusive or a non-exclusive agent; and the extent to which the agent is free, following termination, to deal with customers with whom he or she dealt during the agency relationship.

### (e) Termination at common law

The agency relationship may terminate by agreement or simply on the expiry of the period of time stipulated for performance.[18] The contract may also terminate because the purpose for which it was entered into comes to an end.[19] If the parties have not expressly agreed a date of termination or formula for calculating the same, then the courts will ascertain the date of termination as a matter of interpretation of the agency contract as a whole.[20]

The principal may decide to revoke the agency contract,[21] although the right to revoke may be excluded as a matter of interpretation of the contract.[22] Where the principal does revoke, he or she must relieve the agent of any losses suffered by him or her where revocation occurs before the agent has completed ongoing transactions.[23] An attempt by the principal to revoke where that is not within his or her power may lead to liability to the agent in damages, again as a matter of interpretation of the agency contract.[24] The agent may have the right to payment of commission on termination.

The agent may also have the ability unilaterally to revoke the agency contract. He or she may be liable to the principal in damages where, for example, he or she delays in informing the principal of his or her revocation[25] or renounces at a critical time.[26]

### (f) Frustration of the agency contract

The agency contract, like any other contract, may be frustrated by the occurrence of unexpected events. Following frustration, both parties will be released from performance of

---

[13] [2001] All E.R. (D) 78, February 1, 2001.

[14] *Ingmar GB Ltd v Eaton Leonard Inc* [2001] All E.R. (D) 448, Q.B. See also *Parry v Dionex (UK) Ltd* (Sh. Ct) 2002 G.W.D. 22–721.

[15] [2001] All E.R. (D.) 448.

[16] [2003] E.W.H.C. 23 (Q.B.).

[17] [2003] E.W.H.C. 23 (Q.B.).

[18] *Brenan v Campbell's Trustees* (1898) 25 R. 423; *Ferguson and Lillie v Stephen* (1864) 2 M. 804.

[19] *Price & Co v Tennent* (1844) 6 D. 659; *Black v Cullen* (1853) 15 D. 646.

[20] *Stevenson v North British Rly Co* (1905) 7 F. 1106.

[21] *Walker v Somerville* (1837) 16 S. 217; *Douglas Goodfellow and Partners v Gordon,* 1987 S.C.L.R. 684.

[22] *Galbraith and Moorhead v Arethusa Ship Co Ltd* (1896) 23 R. 1011.

[23] Erskine, *Institute,* III, 3, 40.

[24] *Galbraith and Moorhead v Arethusa Ship Co Ltd* (1896) 23 R. 1011.

[25] Erskine, *Institute,* III, 3, 40.

[26] Erskine, *Institute,* III, 3, 40.

their future obligations under the contract, although rights which have accrued prior to frustration are enforceable by the parties. The cessation of the principal's business will frustrate the agency contract given that the very purpose for which the agency relationship was created has ceased. The courts are very reluctant to imply a term into the agency contract binding the principal to continue with his particular business.[27] Although the principal may, following such termination, be liable to the agent in damages for losses suffered in the context of ongoing transactions,[28] no damages will be payable for the agent's expenditure made in anticipation of the continuation of the contract.[29]

Frustration of the agency contract can also be caused by impossibility of performance[30] or supervening illegality.[31] The sequestration or liquidation of the principal or agent will have a similar effect.[32] The death of either the principal[33] or the agent[34] also terminates the agency relationship, but this is subject to several exceptions. Older case law indicates that an agent is entitled to continue to manage the affairs of a principal even after that principal's death but only in order to finalise the principal's financial affairs.[35] The personal representatives of a deceased principal may also ratify the agent's actings.[36] Whilst the insanity of the principal does not necessarily terminate the agency contract,[37] the agent's insanity will terminate the contract. Where the agency is a factory and commission or power of attorney the factory and commission may continue notwithstanding the mental incapacity of the granter, subject to certain conditions.[38]

---

[27] *SS State of California Co Ltd v Moore* (1895) 22 R. 562 at 567, *per* Lord Adam, and at 567, *per* Lord McLaren.

[28] Erskine, *Institute,* III, 3, 40.

[29] *London, Leith, Edinburgh and Glasgow Shipping Co v Ferguson* (1850) 13 D. 51; *Patmore & Co v B Cannon & Co Ltd* (1892) 19 R. 1004.

[30] *Rhodes v Forwood* (1876) 1 App. Cas. 256.

[31] *Hugh Stevenson & Sons Ltd v AG für Cartonnagen-Industrie* [1918] A.C. 239.

[32] For the principal's liquidation, see *SS State of California Co Ltd v Moore* (1895) 22 R. 562.

[33] *Pollok v Paterson* 10 Dec 1811 F.C. 369 at 376, *per* Lord Meadowbank; *Kennedy v Kennedy* (1843) 6 D. 40; *Lord Advocate v Chung,* 1995 S.C. 32.

[34] Erskine, *Institute,* III, 3, 40.

[35] See *Campbell v Anderson* (1829) 3 W. & S. 384; *Pollok v Paterson* Dec. 10, 1811 F.C. 369 at 376, *per* Lord Meadowbank; although *cf. Kennedy v Kennedy* (1843) 6 D. 40.

[36] Stair, *Institutions,* I,12,6; Erskine, *Institute,* III,3,41.

[37] *Pollok v Paterson* Dec. 10, 1811 F.C., at 375, *per* Lord Meadowbank and 377.

[38] Law Reform (Miscellaneous Provisions)(Scotland) Act 1990, s.71(1). This will only apply where the factory and commission or power of attorney was entered into after the date of the section coming into force, namely January 1, 1991: see s.75(3)(b). "Mental incapacity" means that a person is incapable of managing his property or affairs by reason of mental disorder (including personality disorder) within the meaning of the Mental Health (Scotland) Act 1984, s.1(2): LR(MP)(S) Act 1990, s.71(2). The definition of "mental disorder" in MH(S)A 1984, s.1(2) was amended by the Mental Health (Public Safety and Appeals) (Scotland) Act 1999 (asp 1), s.3(1).

# Chapter 3

# CONSUMER CREDIT

This chapter will mainly concern itself with an examination of the Consumer Credit Act 1974. However, it may be useful to begin with an examination of how credit may be provided and the legal nature of those arrangements.

## (1) TYPES OF CREDIT

The idea of credit may seem superficially simple, but there is a variety of types of credit and a variety of ways to classify the giving of credit. However, a relatively simple classification is the distinction between lender credit and vendor credit.

## 3.1. LENDER CREDIT

Is quite straightforward. Essentially it involves one party lending another money. This can take the form of a loan from a financial institution, typically a bank or building society. Loans may be at fixed rates with standard monthly repayments, but can easily feature variable rates and repayments. Bank overdrafts are also a form of loan, the amount and the rate of interest typically fluctuating, and the borrower not generally being committed to make fixed repayments. Some arrangements can have features of both devices, such as where a debtor makes regular repayments on an amount owed, but is then permitted to extend his borrowing up to an agreed (often the original) figure—revolving credit. Prior to the passing of the Consumer Credit Act 1974, the making of loans was governed by the Moneylenders Acts, but as banks and building societies were exempted from that legislation, many loans were governed purely by the common law. As will be seen, assuming that they meet the prerequisites for the application of the Act, all such forms of credit now fall within the scope of the Consumer Credit Act 1974.

Sometimes the loan is secured. This might be through a simple guarantee. Alternatively, the borrower might assign his right to a payment from a third party, *e.g.* under a life assurance policy. Or he might pledge an item of moveable property, as where goods are pawned.[1] Or he might grant a standard security over heritable property, what might be called a mortgage by the layperson (see para. 6.8.). While certain types of security were governed by detailed legislation, such as the Pawnbrokers Acts, others again were governed, more or less exclusively, by the common law. As will be seen, generally if the basic transaction is governed by the Consumer Credit Act 1974 so too is any associated security transaction.

## 3.2. VENDOR CREDIT

While a loan may obviously be used to purchase goods, and indeed the borrower may be formally restricted by the terms of the agreement to use it for that purpose, vendor credit is credit actually supplied by the seller (or owner) of goods to the buyer (or hirer) to finance the transaction between them. It takes various forms.

### (a) Hire-purchase

The reason why reference had to be made in the previous paragraph to hirers and owners is because of the contract of hire-purchase, which is probably the most common form of vendor credit. Essentially, such an agreement sees the debtor making payments for the "hire" of the goods, with an option but not an obligation to purchase the goods either on paying the final instalment, or on paying a further sum. That sum can be purely nominal and usually is. In *Close Asset Finance v Care Graphics Machinery Ltd*[2] a "hirer" was bound to make payments in respect of goods, amounting to several million pounds over a number of years. Thereafter, it had an option to purchase the goods for £50. It was argued that this was a sale agreement, since no reasonable person would fail to exercise the option clause. It was held that as the hirer was not legally obliged to buy the goods, the contract could not be one of sale and must be a contract of hire-purchase. It might be added that the most common form of hire-purchase transaction involves a trader selling goods to a finance company, which then "sells" them to the debtor on hire purchase. The debtor then has no direct contractual relationship with the trader,

---

[1] There is a detailed and complex regime dealing with pawn under ss.114–122 of the Consumer Credit Act 1974. It will not be addressed in this chapter, but rather in the Chapter on Rights in Security: see para. 6.4.

[2] [2000] C.C.L.R. 43.

although it is possible that the trader might be bound by any promises made to the debtor, or be delictually liable to him, whether for misrepresentations or otherwise.[3] The distinction between hire-purchase and simple hire is, of course, that under the latter contract there is no intention to sell the goods and the hirer has no option to purchase. It is however, not uncommon for certain hire contracts to extend over the economic life of the goods and to involve hire charges which are the equivalent of the sale price of the goods and the charge which might be levied for credit. Even before the passing of the Consumer Credit Act 1974, hire-purchase was the subject of detailed legislative control, while hire was essentially governed by the common law. Now, both are addressed by the Act.

### (b) Credit sale and conditional sale agreements

A conditional sale agreement is simply a contract of sale where the passing of the property is subject to a suspensive condition, typically the payment of the final instalment of the price. A credit sale agreement may often appear identical in that both types of transaction see the price paid in instalments, but the critical difference is that in a credit sale, although the goods are sold on credit, property in them usually passes immediately the contract is made. The crucial difference between credit or conditional sale and hire purchase, is that in the former the buyer is bound to purchase the goods. So in *John G. Murdoch & Co Ltd v Greig*[4] where the contract referred to hire payments, the fact that the "hirer" was bound to purchase the goods meant that the contract was one of sale. Similarly, in *Forthright Finance v Carlyle*[5] a "hire-purchase" agreement bound the "hirer" to make a number of payments. After he had made the final payment he would become the owner of the goods, unless he exercised an option not to receive title to the goods. Phillips L.J. opined[6]:

> "This contract has all the ingredients of a conditional sale agreement. The option not to take title, which one would only expect to be exercised in the most unusual of circumstances does not affect the true nature of the agreement."

Although both credit and conditional sale agreements are contracts for the sale of goods, they are dealt with differently by the Consumer Credit Act 1974. Despite being conceptually quite distinct, conditional sale is mainly regulated alongside hire-purchase, as was the case under the more recent hire-purchase statutes. While credit sale did receive some limited acknowledgement under that legislation, it is not specifically recognised by the Consumer Credit Act 1974, although it would normally be regarded as a debtor-creditor-supplier agreement under that Act (see para. 3.15.).

## 3.3. OTHER FORMS OF CREDIT

### (a) Check trading

This involves a voucher purchased by a customer from a check trader, which allows the former to purchase goods to that value from any shop prepared to accept the check. The most well known form of check trading in Scotland involves checks issued by the Provident Clothing and Supply Company. When the customer uses the check to buy goods, he is charged the cash price, and the amount is marked on the back of the check, allowing him to spend the rest of the

---

[3] *Andrews v Hopkinson* [1957] 1 Q.B. 229.
[4] (1889) 16 R. 396.
[5] [1994] 4 All E.R. 91.
[6] at 97b.

check elsewhere. The check trader then reimburses the retailer, typically subject to a discount. The customer pays off the amount of the check in instalments (usually weekly), the total of these instalments amounting to rather more than the amount of the check, the difference thus representing interest paid on the amount borrowed. While, the exact legal nature of check trading has never been determined by the higher courts, it resembles a form of money lending (and thus now potentially subject to the Consumer Credit Act 1974), and this is the view taken of it by an English county court.[7] The transaction between customer and retailer is certainly nothing more than a simple contract of sale.[8]

## (b) Credit cards

Credit cards are, of course, extremely widely used. They have certain affinities with check trading in that the card issued by the credit card company to a customer may then be used to purchase goods or services from any business prepared to accept the card. When a card is used to acquire goods or services, the customer signs a voucher permitting the business to claim payment from the credit card company. On presentation of the voucher, the credit card company then pays the business for the goods or services—usually subject to a discount—and recovers the full amount from the customer. Some credit cards require the customer to repay the whole amount incurred on a card during a particular period at the end of that period, *e.g.* American Express cards. Most cards, however, while permitting such repayment, allow customers to use the card up to a pre-arranged limit, and to repay as much or as little as the customer wishes (subject to a specified minimum payment) during each period. Interest is, of course, charged on the outstanding balance. The network of relationships described above is often slightly more complex in that businesses are often recruited for credit card companies by third parties known as merchant acquirers. Merchant acquirers may then make payments on behalf of the company, and levy a charge thereon.

The legal nature of credit card transactions was considered in *Re Charge Card Services.*[9] The Court of Appeal held that there were three essential contracts involved in the use of a credit card. These were:

(1) the contract between credit card company and the retailer by virtue of which the retailer agrees to accept payment via the card and the credit card company agrees to pay the retailer for the goods or services purchased (usually subject to a discount);

(2) the contract between credit card company and the cardholder whereby the latter is issued with the card which enables him to purchase goods, and agrees to pay the company the price he was charged for those goods (plus interest if necessary);

(3) the contract between the retailer and the cardholder whereby the former sells goods and services to the latter on the basis that payment via the card was accepted in substitution for payment by cash.

This means that the retailer[10]: "must . . . be taken to have accepted the company's obligation to pay in place of liability on the customer to pay [the retailer] direct."

Thus the cardholder's obligation to the retailer is entirely discharged by tendering the card in payment, and does not revive if the credit card company fails to pay the retailer. Equally, the cardholder is liable to pay the credit card company, whether or not the company pays the retailer. It seems to follow from the above analysis that, if the card is used in circumstances where the company is under no obligation to pay, *e.g.* where a credit limit has been exceeded, the use of the card does not discharge the customer's obligation to pay the retailer. It is then an

---

[7] *Premier Clothing Co Ltd v Hillcoat,* reported in Report of the Committee on Consumer Credit (1971) Cmnd. 4596, para. 4.1.64.

[8] *Davies v Commissioners of Customs and Excise* [1975] 1 W.L.R. 204.

[9] [1989] Ch. 497.

[10] *per* Sir Nicholas Browne-Wilkinson V.C. at 513H–514A.

interesting question whether he would be liable to pay the full amount for the goods or services, or the discounted amount the retailer expected to receive from the credit card company. The status of credit card transactions under the Consumer Credit Act 1974 is considered in detail below (see para. 3.41.)

It might be added that payment for goods and services via a debit card involves immediate payment from the customer's bank account through an electronic transfer of funds. There is no substitution of a right of payment by the customer by a right of payment by the bank. Depending on the state of the customer's bank account, such transactions may or may not involve the granting of credit by the bank to the customer. In the *Charge Card* case it was unsuccessfully argued that payment by credit card was analogous to payment by cheque, as it was common ground that payment by cheque or any other bill of exchange was conditional, the buyer's liability remaining if the cheque were not honoured.[11] Where payment by cheque is accompanied by the use of a cheque guarantee card, then the holder of that card has authority from the bank to make an offer to the retailer, which if acted upon, creates contractual relations between the bank and the retailer.[12] If the conditions relating to the use of the card are observed, the bank undertakes to meet the sum for which the cheque is drawn, whether or not its customer has sufficient funds in his account. This is not however a contract of guarantee (cautionary obligation), but rather an independent contract between bank and customer.[13] Nonetheless, even where a guarantee card is used, it is probable that payment by cheque remains conditional, and does not discharge the buyer's liability if, despite the use of the card, the cheque is dishonoured.[14] In other words, use of a cheque guarantee card does not substitute a right of payment by the bank for a right of payment by the customer. Instead it adds a parallel right of payment by the bank.

### (c) Retailer's revolving credit

Some retailers operate a system whereby the customer makes regular fixed payments (usually monthly) allowing him to obtain goods or services from the retailer on credit up to a specified multiple of his payments. For example, a customer who is bound to pay £30 per month might be allowed 10 times that amount, *i.e.* £300, in credit at any one time. As each payment is made, the customer is permitted to obtain goods or services provided the credit limit is not exceeded. Interest would usually be charged on the amount of credit outstanding at the end of each month. The legal nature of such arrangements is undecided. They are not direct cash loans, as the amount of credit is dependent upon the value of the goods or services obtained. They are certainly not hire-purchase transactions. There is however, some support that they amount to a series of credit sales,[15] and thus potentially subject to the Act.

## 3.4. Introduction to the Act—The Crowther Report

The law of consumer credit is largely comprehended in the Consumer Credit Act 1974. But the genesis of that Act lies in the 1971 Report of the Committee on Consumer Credit[16]—the Crowther Report. The Report found that the then existing law relating to credit transactions was seriously defective, *inter alia* because:

---

[11] *ibid.*, at 511D–E and see *McLarens's Trs v Argylls Ltd*, 1915 2 S.L.T. 241.

[12] *First Sport Ltd v Barclays Bank plc* [1993] 3 All E.R. 789 at 794e–g, *per* Evans L.J. Scots law might regard the bank as making a promise.

[13] *ibid.*, at 795d.

[14] *Re Charge Card Services* [1987] Ch. 150 at 166C, *per* Millett J.

[15] See *N.G. Napier Ltd v Patterson,* 1959 J.C. 48; and authorities cited in Report of the Committee on Consumer Credit (1971) Cmnd. 4596, para. 4.1.64.

[16] Cmnd. 4596.

- transactions were regulated according to historical legal form rather than their substance and function,
- the law was excessively technical,
- the law failed to distinguish between consumer and commercial transactions, and conferred inadequate protection upon consumers.

The Committee felt that piecemeal reform of the law would not be adequate. Instead it recommended repeal of the great mass of existing legislation and its replacement by two Acts. One would be designed to harmonise the treatment of all forms of consumer credit, strengthening the position of the consumer, and creating effective enforcement mechanisms. The other would restructure the general law of credit and security. The government however was not convinced of the necessity of the latter measure,[17] and pressed ahead only with the former recommendation. The result was the Consumer Credit Act 1974, a discussion of which follows.

# (2) THE LICENSING SYSTEM

## 3.5.   INTRODUCTION

The impact of legislation designed to protect consumers is considerably enhanced by the creation of effective enforcement machinery. Large parts of the pre-Act regime depended entirely upon individual consumers for enforcement. Money-lending and pawnbroking featured licensing systems, but these were largely ineffective because of the decentralised nature of these systems and the lack of a single authority responsible for enforcement. Thus responsibility for the overall administration and enforcement of the 1974 Act and associated Regulations is that of the Office of Fair Trading (OFT), with enforcement at local level being the responsibility of weights and measures authorities. One of the main controls created by the Act is a comprehensive licensing system operated by the OFT. Thus under s.21(1) a licence is required to carry on a consumer credit or consumer hire business, or indeed[18] an ancillary credit business. An ancillary credit business is any business which involves any of the following activities[19]:

- credit brokerage (introducing credit seekers to credit providers);
- debt-adjusting (helping to renegotiate credit based debts);
- debt-counselling (giving advice about credit based debts);
  debt-collecting;
- operating a credit reference agency (a business which supplies information about the financial standing of individuals).

It should be noted that consumer credit, consumer hire or ancillary credit need not be the main business carried on. If any of these is a regular activity carried on in the course of one's main business, then a licence is required. The requirement of regularity would mean that a business which, for example, only occasionally lent money would not require a licence,[20] while under the moneylenders legislation the Court of Appeal has held that the circumstances under which a person lends out his capital may qualify him to be regarded as an investor rather than carrying on a business.[21] The only types of body exempt from the licensing requirements are local

---

[17] See Reform of the Law of Consumer Credit (Cmnd. 5427), para. 14.
[18] Under s.147.
[19] See s.145.
[20] *R v Marshall* (1990) 90 Cr. App. Rep. 93; *Hare v Schurek* [1993] C.C.L.R. 47.
[21] *Wills v Wood* [1984] C.C.L.R. 7.

authorities,[22] and any body corporate empowered by statute to carry on a business, *e.g.* the Post Office.[23]

## 3.6.   TYPES OF LICENCE

There are two types of licence—a standard licence and a group licence. The most usual type of licence will be a standard licence. It is issued to a named person, whether an individual, a firm, an unincorporated body or company,[24] and authorises him to carry on business under the name(s) specified in the licence, but no other.[25] The membership of a firm or unincorporated body may fluctuate without entailing any consequences for the holding of the licence, but if the business ceases to be carried on under the firm name the licence ceases to have effect.[26] The OFT may issue a group licence where examination of individual applications is not thought to be required in the public interest,[27] although it can exclude named persons from the scope of a group licence.[28] Solicitors holding practising certificates are currently covered by a group licence issued to the Law Society of Scotland.

### (a) Categories of standard licence

There are six categories of standard licence, reflecting the various types of licensable activity. These are:

A—Consumer Credit Business.   This is defined as "any business so far as it comprises or relates to the provision of credit under regulated consumer credit agreements".[29] Thus if a business provides credit, but not under such agreements, as where it lends only to companies or lends only sums in excess of £25,000 (see next paragraph), then it need not obtain a licence. However, if it ever provides credit under regulated consumer credit agreements, a licence will be required, even if this represents only a very minor part of its business.

B—Consumer Hire Business.   This is defined as "any business so far as it comprises or relates to the hiring of goods under regulated consumer hire agreements".[30]

C—Credit Brokerage.   This is the effecting of introductions of individuals who desire to hire goods or obtain credit to businesses which offer these facilities or to other credit brokers.[31] The definition is not restricted, however, to the introduction of individuals seeking to enter into regulated agreements (see para. 3.12.). So, a person such as an estate agent or solicitor who introduces persons seeking mortgages (which are not generally governed by the Act) to lenders is a credit broker.[32] Also a credit broker would be someone who introduces those seeking credit to a business which makes agreements which are "exempt" under the Act (see para. 3.17.), unless they are exempt because the number of payments is so small.[33] In other words, it is still credit-brokerage to introduce individuals to a business which lends money at a rate which is so low that the agreements are exempt, but it is not credit-brokerage for a business which sells goods to introduce individuals to a another business which will lend them money to buy those

---

[22] s.21(2).
[23] s.21(3).
[24] s.22(1)(a).
[25] s.24.
[26] s.36(5).
[27] s.22(1)(b).
[28] s.22(6).
[29] s.189(1).
[30] s.189(1).
[31] s.145(2).
[32] s.145(2)(a)(ii).
[33] s.145(3)(b).

goods, as long as the money is to be repaid within 12 months and in no more than four instalments. The category of credit-broker embraces not only credit and mortgage brokers, but also businesses which introduce their customers to finance companies. However, a business which displays application forms for a particular company's credit card is not a credit broker, as it does not effect an introduction.[34]

D—Debt-Adjusting and Debt-Counselling.    Debt-adjusting is defined[35] as, in relation to debts due under consumer credit or consumer hire agreements, negotiating with the creditor or owner on behalf or the debtor or hirer, terms for discharging a debt, or taking over in return for payments by the debtor or hirer, his obligation to discharge a debt. Also covered would be "any similar activity concerned with the liquidation of a debt".[36] This might cover the situation where a car dealer, in taking in part-exchange a car held on hire-purchase, obtains a settlement figure from the finance company, and discharges this as part of the deal for purchasing a new car.[37] Certainly falling within the main definition would be situations where a credit card company allow customers to switch amounts owing to other companies to its card. Any business which only took over responsibility for debts over £25,000 would not require to be licensed, as such debts would not be "due under consumer credit agreements".

Debt-counselling is the giving of advice to debtors or hirers about the liquidation of debts due under consumer credit or consumer hire agreements.[38] It would not cover the giving of advice to those about to enter such agreements. Although certain voluntary organisations which commonly provide advice of this kind may not be thought of as businesses, it must be remembered that "business" under the Act includes "profession",[39] so that such organisations would require to be licensed.

E—Debt Collecting.    Debt collecting is the taking of steps to procure payment of debts due under consumer credit or consumer hire agreements.[40] This would cover not merely those who collect debts on behalf or creditors, but also those who are assigned those debts (generally for a consideration) and then collect the debts on their own behalf.

F—Credit Reference Agency.    This is a business which furnishes persons "with information relevant to the financial standing of individuals, being information collected for the agency for that purpose". The requirement that the information be collected for the purpose of furnishing to others serves to exclude a whole host of organisations which routinely collect such information for their own purposes, and may sometimes furnish it to others.

If a business carries on more than one of these activities, it will require the appropriate licence for each activity. In practice, if more than one category is required, a single licence will be issued which covers the appropriate categories.


## 3.7.    SPECIFIC EXCLUSIONS

Certain individuals are specifically excluded from the need to obtain certain categories of licence. Thus solicitors engaged in contentious business and advocates acting as advocates are not to be treated as doing so in the course of any ancillary credit business.[41] This means that any need for licence category C, D, E or F which might otherwise arise will be prevented from doing so. Solicitors not engaged in contentious business are not subject to the exclusion, but

[34] *Brookes v Retail Credit Cards Ltd* [1986] C.C.L.R. 5.
[35] s.145(5)(a)–(b).
[36] s.145(5)(c).
[37] But see but see R. Goode, *The Consumer Credit Act* (Butterworths, 1979), para. 1002.
[38] s.145(6).
[39] s.189(1).
[40] s.145(7).
[41] s.146(1), (3).

will be covered in respect of things done in the course of their practice by the group licence obtained by the Law Society of Scotland, except in so far as anything they do would fall within categories B or F. A creditor, owner or supplier may often collect payments or discuss the debt will the debtor or hirer. Nonetheless, he is not to be treated as being involved in debt-adjusting, debt-counselling or debt-collecting, and nor is anyone who acquires those debts through acquiring the business.[42] Finally, anyone who is not acting as an employee, and who asks someone to enter either a regulated consumer hire agreement, or a debtor-creditor-supplier agreement where the creditor is to be the supplier, and effects the introduction by canvassing off trade premises, is not to be treated as a credit broker.[43] The typical situation which this provision is designed to address is that of the individual who acts as an agent for a mail order company, and who canvasses applications from friends and acquaintances to acquire goods on credit from the company's catalogue. The policy of the Act is that such individuals need not be licensed. Yet canvassing is defined as making oral representations to the consumer during a visit to any place where the consumer may be.[44] While the exclusion therefore plainly applies to the situation where the agent visits the consumer's home, it does not appear to apply to the situation where canvassing occurs in the agent's home, as the agent could hardly be described as visiting her or his own home. The upshot is therefore that individuals who conduct such activities from home should technically be licensed[45]

## 3.8. OBTAINING A LICENCE

A standard licence is obtained by applying to the OFT, and under s.25(1) a licence must be granted if the OFT is satisfied that the applicant is a fit and proper person to engage in the activities covered thereby, and that the name(s) under which he applies to be licensed is not misleading or otherwise undesirable.[46] In relation to the former criterion, the OFT in terms of s.25(2) must take into account any circumstances appearing to be relevant, but in particular any evidence that the applicant (or any employee, agent or associate[47]—past or present[48]) has committed any offence involving fraud, dishonesty or violence, or contravened any statutory provision regulating the provision of credit to individuals or other transactions with individuals, or committed acts of unlawful discrimination in connection with the business, or engaged in deceitful or oppressive or unfair or improper business practices. Thus the OFT may decide to refuse a licence where the applicant has not actually broken the law, but has, for example, pursued a policy of providing credit to those who cannot afford it, or employed high pressure sales methods. Equally, an applicant need not be guilty of fraud, etc. in relation to a consumer in order to be deemed an unfit person. Thus it was decided in *North Wales Motor Auctions Ltd v Secretary of State for Trade*[49] that the OFT (in fact the Director-General of Fair Trading, as the legislation then stood) was entitled to refuse a license on the basis that the controller of the applicant company had been convicted of defrauding the Inland Revenue, the judge indicating that as the granting of a licence was a privilege, the refusal of a licence could not be a punishment. If the OFT is minded to refuse an application, or to grant it on terms different

---

[42] s.146(6).

[43] *ibid*.

[44] s.48(1).

[45] See further Goode, *op. cit.,* para 1002; P. Dobson, *Sale of Goods and Consumer Credit Act* (6th ed., Sweet & Maxwell, 2000), para. 22.16.

[46] See further Goode, *op. cit.* pp.363–365.

[47] Defined in s.184.

[48] Or where the applicant is a body corporate any person appearing to be the controller thereof or an associate of such a person.

[49] [1981] C.C.L.R. 1.

from those applied for, then it must give the applicant its reasons and invite the applicant to submit representations in support of his application.[50] Thereafter, the OFT may grant or refuse the licence, or grant it in different terms. An appeal against the determination of the OFT lies to the Secretary of State, and thence on a point of law to the Inner House.[51]

## 3.9. RENEWAL, REVOCATION, ETC OF LICENCE

A licence will operate for five years.[52] Thereafter the holder must apply for its renewal. If during the currency of a licence the OFT is of the opinion that if the licence expired it would be minded to renew it on different terms, then it may look to vary it. If it is of the opinion that it would be minded to refuse to renew it, then it may look to suspend (for a fixed or indefinite period) or revoke it. Before it takes any such action, it must inform the licensee of the action it is minded to take and invite representations from the licensee.[53] An appeal again lies to the Secretary of State and the Inner House as described above. Where a licence is revoked or suspended the OFT may authorise a licensee to carry into effect agreements made before the revocation or suspension.[54] A licensee may apply to the OFT to end the suspension of a licence.[55] A licence will automatically terminate upon the occurrence of certain events such as where the licensee dies, has his estate sequestrated, or becomes incapable of managing his own affairs,[56] but termination will be deferred for 12 months within which time the licensee's business may be carried on by an authorised person.[57] The holder of a licence must give notice to the OFT within 21 working days of any change in,[58]

(1) the officers of a body corporate licencee; or in the officers of a body corporate which is the controller of a licensee; or
(2) the officers of a licensee which is an unincorporated body; or
(3) the members of a licensee which is a partnership.

Moreover, a body corporate licencee must notify the OFT that a person has become or ceased to be its controller within 21 working days of becoming aware of it.[59] Where a change in a partnership has the result that the business ceases to be carried on under the licence, the licence ceases to have effect.[60]

## 3.10. EFFECT OF OPERATING WITHOUT A LICENCE

A licence covers all lawful activities done in the course of the licensed business whether by the licensee or any agent or employee.[61] It is however an offence to engage in any of the activities

---

[50] s.27.
[51] ss.41–42.
[52] Consumer Credit (Period of Standard Licence) (Amendment) Regulations 1991, SI 1991/1817.
[53] ss.31–33.
[54] s.32(5).
[55] s.33.
[56] ss.37(1), 38(1).
[57] See s.37(3) and SI 1976/1002.
[58] s.36(2).
[59] s.36(2)(b).
[60] s.36(5).
[61] s.23(1).

described by the Act without a licence.[62] More importantly, a regulated agreement made while unlicensed cannot be enforced against a debtor or hirer without an order from the OFT, unless it is a non-commercial agreement.[63] It may be noted that a creditor or owner is unlicensed in regard to a particular agreement if it is beyond the scope of his licence, while a non-commercial agreement is defined as an agreement which is not made in the course of the licensee's business.[64] Rather surprisingly in *Hare v Schurek*[65] the Court of Appeal held that the word "business" should be interpreted as referring to a consumer credit or consumer hire business. Accordingly, when a car dealer entered into an isolated hire-purchase agreement, this agreement was treated as not being made in the course of a business, and was thus a non-commercial agreement. A creditor or owner who falls foul of these provisions might seek a validating order, which will treat all agreements made during the period in which he was unlicensed as if he had been licensed.[66] Application for a validating order must be made by the unlicensed person to the OFT, who unless it decides to make the order requested, must:

(1) inform the applicant, giving its reasons, that it is minded to refuse the application or grant it on different terms to those applied for; and
(2) invite representations in support of the application.[67]

In deciding whether or not to grant such an order, the OFT must consider, in addition, other relevant factors[68]:

- how far debtors or hirers under regulated agreements made during the period were prejudiced by the trader's conduct;
- whether it would have been likely to grant a licence had it received an application;
- the degree of culpability in failing to obtain a licence.

The OFT may, if it thinks fit, limit any order to specified agreements or those of a specified description or made at a specified time, or make the order conditional on the doing of specified acts by the applicant.[69] In much the same way, a person who carries on an ancillary credit business without the requisite licence cannot enforce any agreement for his services against the other party unless he obtains a validating order from the OFT.[70] So, for example, an unlicensed credit broker who agrees (with either the credit seeker or credit granter) to introduce a credit seeker to a credit granter in return for a commission, is unable to sue for that commission without an order. Finally, a regulated agreement made by a debtor or hirer introduced to the creditor or owner by a credit broker who was unlicensed at the time of the introduction is unenforceable against the debtor or hirer without a validating order from the OFT.[71] The aim of this provision is to persuade businesses who use credit brokers to ensure that those credit brokers are properly licensed. In *Citibank Trust v Gregory*[72] a debtor introduced by an unlicensed credit broker entered into a non regulated agreement. It was held that the validity of this agreement was unaffected. However, as the credit broker was carrying on an ancillary credit business without a licence, he could not sue the debtor for his commission.

---

[62] s.39(1).
[63] s.40(1).
[64] s.189(1).
[65] [1993] C.C.L.R. 47.
[66] s.40(2).
[67] s.40(3).
[68] s.40(4).
[69] s.40(5).
[70] s.148.
[71] s.149.
[72] 1992, unreported.

## 3.11. REFORM OF THE LICENSING SYSTEM

At the time of writing the DTI is engaged in a consultation process regarding possible reform of the licensing regime.[73] This has to be set in the context of a Consumer Credit Directive currently being drafted by the EU, which is likely to propose a system of registration for all lenders and credit intermediaries in the EU. The sorts of reforms being considered include:

- the replacement of the existing six categories of licence by a single category, subject to OFT power to restrict the scope of individual licenses;
- longer duration periods for licenses, perhaps indefinite, but subject to enhanced monitoring of licence holders;
- application fees to vary according to the size or turnover of the applicant, or determined by the amount of enforcement activity generated by particular sectors of the industry;
- application fees to be significantly higher than renewal fees;
- empowering the OFT and local authority trading standard departments to make compliance visits to licence holders and to enter premises and inspect books and other records;
- empowering the OFT to lay down rules of conduct for licence holders, breach of which would invite enforcement action;
- conferring upon the OFT a new range of intermediary enforcement powers short of licence revocation, including administrative fines, the power to order practices to cease and to demand undertakings as to future conduct, the power to attach conditions to the licence, and the power to issue an immediate suspension of a licence;
- removing the Secretary of State from the process of appeals against licensing decisions;
- automatically revoking licenses where custodial sentences are imposed under the Act.

It is also suggested that the current fitness test compares unfavourably with that which operates under the Financial Services and Markets Act 2000, in that the former is based on very limited information and focuses on past behaviour. Thus it is proposed that the amount of information required be extended and subject to basic checking. The OFT may be enabled or even required to lay down statutory rules of conduct, breach of which will led to sanctions. It may be subject to a formal duty to issue detailed guidance on the nature of the test and how it will be applied in different sectors.

# (3) THE CONCEPTUAL STRUCTURE OF CONSUMER CREDIT—REGULATED AGREEMENTS

## 3.12. INTRODUCTION

As well as providing for the overall control of the credit industry through the licensing system, the Act looks to regulate individual credit transactions. It was anticipated that the Act would regulate all forms of consumer credit, but as will be seen, there are certain forms which fall outwith the scope of the Act, while the Act comprehends certain agreements although no consumer is involved. In essence, however, the Act applies to all regulated agreements. These are consumer credit agreements, consumer hire agreements and exempt agreements.

---

[73] *Consultation Document on the Licensing Regime under the Consumer Credit Act 1974*, December 2002.

## 3.13. CONSUMER CREDIT AGREEMENT

A consumer credit agreement is a personal credit agreement by which the creditor provides the debtor with credit not exceeding £25,000.[74] (This figure is currently under review.) In *National Westminster Bank plc v Story*[75] it was surprisingly held that where the bank agreed to supply S with £35,000 of credit via an overdraft facility of £15,000, a loan of £15,000, and a loan of £5,000, that should be treated as a single agreement to lend £35,000, which was not regulated by the Act. A debtor for this purpose can include a business as long as it is not a corporate body.[76] Credit is defined by s.9(1) as including "a cash loan or any other form of financial accommodation". This means that not only loans but hire purchase, credit sale and conditional agreements fall within the definition. Hire purchase agreements indeed are specifically included.[77] However, in *Joyce v Barlow*[78] it was said that a deferment of payment in the absence of a contractual right to defer was a mere indulgence and not a financial accommodation amounting to credit.

In calculating the amount of credit supplied, the total charge for credit is not taken into account.[79] The meaning of the total charge for credit is prescribed by Regulations of immense complexity.[80] As might be expected, interest charges are part of the total charge for credit. Thus in a situation where an individual borrows £24,000 and is required to repay sums amounting to £30,000, the total charge for credit is obviously £6,000, the amount of credit is £24,000, so that the transaction falls within the £25,000 limit and is thus a regulated agreement. Similarly, if under a hire-purchase agreement the hirer is bound to make 30 monthly payments of £1,000, but the cash price of the goods is £24,000, the total charge for credit is again £6,000, the amount of credit £24,000, and the transaction is a regulated agreement. More generally, the Regulations seek to ensure that any payment which requires to be made in order to obtain the credit is regarded as part of the total charge for credit, even if the payment requires to be made by a relative of the debtor rather than the debtor himself. Among the types of charges included are those payable under:

(1) transactions entered into as a condition of making or in compliance with the credit agreement;
(2) security transactions;
(3) any credit brokerage contract related to the credit agreement.

At the same time, certain charges are excluded from the total charge for credit. These are:

(a) default charges;
(b) charges which would also be payable by a cash customer. It has been held that if cash customers receive a discount which is not extended to credit customers, then the sum represented by the discount should be regarded as part of the total charge for credit[81];
(c) charges for the care, maintenance or protection of goods or land. It is, for example, not uncommon in hire-purchase contracts that the hirer will be obliged to enter a contract ensuring the maintenance of the goods;
(d) variable bank charges on current accounts. This deals with the situation where a loan is granted on condition that the borrower maintains a current account with the bank.

---

[74] s.8(1).
[75] *The Times,* May 14, 1999, CA.
[76] s.189.
[77] s.9(3).
[78] 1999 C.L. February 262.
[79] s.9(4). An item which is part of the total charge for credit does not cease to be so, merely because time is allowed for its payment: *Humberclyde Finance Ltd v Thompson* [1997] C.C.L.R. 23.
[80] See ss.20(1), 189(1). Consumer Credit (Total Charge for Credit) Regulations 1980, SI 1990/51.
[81] *R. v Baldwin's Garage* [1988] Crim L.R. 438.

Charges on the current account which vary according to the use made of it are not part of the total charge for credit;

(e) charges relating to membership of certain organisations. It is quite common for members of particular clubs, associations, trade unions and the like to be able to obtain credit on favourable terms from certain lenders. Even if it is a condition of the credit agreement that the borrower remains a member of that organisation, the membership subscription will not be part of the total charge for credit, provided it entitles him to other benefits besides the receipt of credit, and provided he was a member before applying for the credit;

(f) insurance premiums under certain types of policy, *i.e.*

    (i) a policy where the debtor, although obliged to insure, has a free choice of insurer;

   (ii) a policy in respect of risks relating to land where the acquisition of the land is financed by the credit agreement, and the particular insurer is dictated by someone else who has an interest in the land;

  (iii) a policy taken out before the debtor applies to enter the credit agreement, *e.g.* where money lent on the security of a house obliges the debtor to maintain his existing house insurance policy;

  (iv) a policy which is not mandatory under the regulated agreement;

   (v) a life insurance policy the proceeds of which are to be used to repay the debt, *e.g.* a mortgage endowment policy;

  (vi) a motor vehicle insurance policy.

## 3.14. Types of Credit Agreement:

The Act sub-divides credit agreement into a variety of types.

### (a) Fixed sum and running account credit

Fixed sum credit means precisely that—the amount of credit is established and does not vary.[82] A loan would be one example—so would an H.P. agreement. Running account credit allows the debtor to obtain from time to time, cash, goods or services from the creditor or a third party.[83] Examples would be an overdraft, a store card or a credit card. A running account credit agreement is a regulated agreement if the credit limit does not exceed £25,000. The credit limit is the maximum permitted debit balance, ignoring permissible temporary advances.[84] This might mean that it would be easy to evade the application of the Act simply by applying no credit limit or an unrealistically high credit limit, knowing that the amount of credit supplied at any one time will not actually exceed four or perhaps even three figures. Accordingly, s.10(3)(b) provides that the agreement will still be regarded as a regulated agreement if:

(1) the debtor cannot draw more than £25,000 at any one time; or

(2) the rate of the total charge for credit rises, or some other condition favouring the creditor comes into operation, if the debit balance rises above a given amount (of £25,000) or less); or

(3) when the agreement is made it is probable, having regard to its terms and all other relevant circumstances, that the debit balance will never rise above £25,000.

---

[82] s.10(1)(b).
[83] s.10(1)(a).
[84] s.10(3)(a).

There are various reasons why a distinction is drawn between fixed sum and running account credit. First, as noted above, running account credit is subject to special rules as to how it is decided whether the arrangement is within the £25,000 limit. Secondly, the criteria as to whether an agreement is exempt vary according to which category it occupies. Thirdly, in a running account credit agreement, the debtor automatically gets periodic statements of account. Fourthly, the information to be supplied in adverts and quotations will differ as will the prescribed form of the agreements.

## (b) Restricted and unrestricted use credit

This distinction is made in line with the recommendation of the Crowther Committee that credit should be dealt with according to the purpose it serves, rather than its legal form. It is particularly helpful in distinguishing between debtor-creditor and debtor-creditor-supplier agreements, and in working out whether an ancillary agreement qualifies as a linked transaction under the Act. A restricted use credit agreement under s.11(1) involves the credit being used to finance a specific transaction between the debtor and either the creditor or another person (the supplier). A typical example of this would be an H.P. agreement. An unrestricted use credit agreement under s.11(2) sees the debtor free to use the credit as he wishes. A good example of this would be an overdraft. In terms of s.11(3), an agreement which provides that credit must be used for a specific purpose will still count as an unrestricted use credit agreement, if the credit is provided in such a way as to leave the debtor free to use it as he chooses (albeit in breach of contract). Essentially then, when the credit is intended to finance a transaction with a supplier, the funds must be transferred directly to the supplier if the agreement is to be seen as a restricted use credit agreement.

## (c) Debtor-creditor agreements and debtor-creditor-supplier agreements

Every credit agreement must be either a debtor-creditor agreement or a debtor-creditor-supplier agreement. The Act is interested in agreements where there is a business connection between the creditor and the supplier, taking the view (see para. 3.41.) that the fate of the credit and supply contracts should be to some degree intertwined. These are debtor-creditor-supplier agreements. Debtor-creditor-supplier agreements may involve only two parties, such as where the supplier of goods and services also makes available the credit.[85] One example would be a store card. Another would be an H.P. agreement where the trader sells the goods to the finance company, which then supplies both the goods and credit to the debtor. Alternatively, three parties may be involved, as where a restricted use credit agreement is used to finance a transaction between the debtor and supplier under existing arrangements or in contemplation of future arrangements between the creditor and the supplier.[86] Check trading (see para. 3.3.) provides an example of this. Another example would be the use of a credit card, whereby the card-issuer has arranged with the supplier that it will furnish the credit to finance the purchaser of goods and services. Use of a debit card such as SWITCH ordinarily creates neither a debtor-creditor agreement nor a debtor-creditor-supplier agreement, as no credit is normally granted. If a customer is permitted to draw on an overdraft via a debit card, the purchase of goods or services with this facility on the face of it would create a debtor-creditor-supplier agreement. However, the Act specifically prevents this outcome,[87] and the use of the card as described creates a simple debtor-creditor agreement. Use of a credit card simply to obtain money also creates a debtor-creditor agreement. The same is true when a debit card is used to obtain money by drawing on an overdraft facility. If the money is obtained from a retailer through a "cash-back" facility, that retailer is simply to be regarded as the lender's agent, and not a party to the transaction.

---

[85] s.12(a).
[86] s.12(b).
[87] s.187(3A).

An unrestricted use credit agreement made by the creditor under pre-existing arrangements with the supplier, in the knowledge that the credit is to be used to finance a transaction between the debtor and the supplier, also falls to be regarded as a debtor-creditor-supplier agreement. So if, for example, you need a loan to buy a car and the dealer sends you round to a finance company with which he has an understanding, the loan being made in the knowledge that it will be used to purchase the car sets up a debtor-creditor-supplier agreement, even though there is no formal restriction on the use of the money. The crucial element is the connection between the creditor and supplier. If a creditor lends a debtor money to acquire a car, then it does not matter that the creditor is aware of the purpose of the loan or even of the identity of the supplier, if there is no arrangement between the creditor and supplier. This is a debtor-creditor agreement, not a debtor-creditor-supplier agreement.[88]

## 3.15. CONSUMER HIRE AGREEMENTS

Under s.15 this is an agreement whereby an individual hires goods, and

(1) is not an H.P. agreement;
(2) is capable of subsisting more than three months;
(3) the hirer is not required to make payments exceeding £25,000;
(4) the hirer is not a body corporate.

The first condition is designed to draw a distinction between hire proper and hire purchase, which is in essence a form of credit and is regulated in a different way under the Act. The second condition is designed to exclude short-term hire, such as daily or weekly vehicle rental. It may be noted that an agreement for an indefinite period or for a definite period of, say, a year does not cease to fall within the condition merely because either party is entitled to terminate at any time. Equally, an agreement which stipulates a hire period of three months, but which allows for the option of renewal, also falls within the condition. In both cases the agreement is *capable* of subsisting more than three months.[89] In relation to the third condition, in deciding whether the £25,000 figure is exceeded VAT is taken into account.[90] But if an item is hired for a year at a rental of £1,000 per week, the hirer having the option of terminating at any time upon giving a weeks notice, the agreement still falls within the condition. Although if the agreement runs its anticipated course the hirer will certainly make payments exceeding £25,000, but the way the agreement is constituted he is not actually *required* to do so. The key to determining whether the condition is met is to ascertain the hirer's minimum possible liability under the agreement.

## 3.16. CREDIT-HIRE AGREEMENTS

This is not a category of agreement recognised by the Act, but a strange hybrid emerging from commercial practice. Typically, such agreements arise where a motorist whose car has been disabled in an accident is permitted to hire a replacement for the period during which his own car is out of commission. The hire charges do not have to be paid until the conclusion of an action for damages against the other motorist, which the lessor is given the right to pursue in

---

[88] s.13.
[89] But see *Burdis v Livsey* [2002] 3 W.L.R. 762, CA.
[90] *Apollo Leasing Ltd v Scott,* 1984 S.L.T. (Sh. Ct.) 90.

the motorist's name. The lessor then looks to deduct the cost of its services from damages recovered on behalf of the motorist. In *Dimond v Lovell*[91] it was contended that such arrangements did not involve the provision of credit. According to Lord Hoffmann,[92] the argument of the company was that the:

> "services provided to D were not only the use of the car but also the pursuit of her claim. If one treats these obligations as forming part of an entire contract, [the company] could not recover any part of the consideration unless it had not only allowed D the use of the car, but also brought the claim for damages to a conclusion. Only at this point would [the company] become entitled to payment and therefore the provision for 'credit' was not really credit at all. Payment was not postponed beyond the date at which it would in any event have first become payable."

Yet this argument foundered on the fact that the company had a right but not a duty to pursue the claim. Accordingly, in allowing D to defer payment until damages had been obtained from L, the company was indeed providing her with credit. Thus such an agreement may amount to a consumer credit agreement, and possibly also a consumer hire agreement under the Act.

## 3.17.  EXEMPT AGREEMENTS

Under s.16 and associated orders certain types of agreement which would otherwise be regulated agreements are excluded from the scope of the Act. The categories include:

- certain types of consumer hire agreement where the consumer leases metering equipment from a public telecommunications operator or gas, electricity or water authorities;
- certain types of consumer credit agreement where the creditor is either a local authority or a specified organisation or an organisation of a specified description (*e.g.* certain specified building societies, friendly societies, insurance companies, charities, trade unions, land improvement companies), and the agreement is secured by a heritable security. This exemption would tend to exclude most mortgages and other loans secured on land;
- fixed sum debtor-creditor-supplier agreements (other than H.P. or credit sale agreements or those secured by pledge, *i.e.* pawn) where the number of payments to be made by the debtor is four or less and those payments are made within a period of 12 months beginning with the date of agreement. It has been held that the period of 12 months must include the date of the agreement, so that where the final payment in respect of an agreement entered into on March 3, 1997 fell to be made on March 3, 1998, the period allowed for payment was one day longer than that prescribed by the Act, with the result that the agreement was not exempt[93];
- debtor-creditor-supplier agreements financing the purchase of land where the number of payments to be made by the debtor is four or less;

---

[91] [2000] 2 All E.R. 897, HL.

[92] At 903g–h; He also points out the advantages of this sort of arrangement from a consumer's point of view at 910b–c, "By virtue of her contract, she obtained not only the use of the car but additional benefits as well. She was relieved of the necessity of laying out the money to pay for the car. She was relieved of the trouble and anxiety of pursuing a claim . . . She was relieved of the risk of having to bear the irrecoverable costs of successful litigation and the risk . . . of having to bear the expense of unsuccessful litigation." However, companies do not render those extra services free. A charge for them is typically built into the cost of hire. It was the view of their Lordships that the cost of those extra services were not recoverable from the other party. Damages under this head would be limited to an amount equivalent to the bare cost of hiring a replacement car.

[93] *Zoan v Rouamba* [2000] 2 All E.R. 620, CA. See also *Murphy v Madden* 2000 G.W.D. 13–460; *Ketley v Gilbert* [2001] 1 W.L.R. 986, CA. But *cf. Burdis v Livsey* [2002] 3 W.L.R. 762, CA.

- debtor-creditor-supplier agreements for running account credit where all indebtedness is extinguished at the end of a specific accounting period (*e.g.* certain types of American Express account where the debtor is required to repay the amount of credit in full at the end of each month);
- debtor-creditor agreements where the cost of credit is low, *i.e.* where the rate of interest does not exceed the higher of 13 per cent or 1 per cent above the base rate of the major banks in operation 28 days before the date on which the agreement was made. It would be extremely rare for a commercial lender to make such a low cost loan, but this exception would embrace the practice of certain businesses of making loans to employees on very favourable terms;
- consumer credit agreements connected with foreign trade.

## 3.18. SMALL AGREEMENTS

The Act continues to apply to regulated agreements no matter how small the sum involved. However it is recognised that it would be unduly burdensome to require creditors to comply with all the provisions of the Act where small sums are involved. Accordingly, the provisions of the Act relating to formalities and cancellation rights (see paras 3.32., 3.35.) do not apply to small agreements. These are regulated consumer credit or consumer hire agreements where the credit given or hire payments do not exceed £50.[94] But a conditional sale or hire-purchase agreement can never be a small agreement.[95] Nor can any agreement which is secured otherwise than by a guarantee or indemnity.[96] Again, if a transaction which involves credit in excess of £50, is split into two or more agreements, these cannot be small agreements.[97]

## 3.19. NON-COMMERCIAL AGREEMENTS

The provisions of the Act relating to formalities and cancellation rights (see paras 3.32., 3.35.) similarly do not apply to non-commercial agreements. These are regulated consumer credit or consumer hire agreements not made by the creditor owner in the course of a business carried on by him.[98] This provision is directed towards the situation where a private individual provides credit, such as loans between friends or family. Yet the word "business" was interpreted in *Hare v Schurek*[99] as referring to a consumer credit or consumer hire business, despite the plain words of the Act suggesting no such restriction. Thus a hire-purchase agreement entered into the course of a car-dealing business was treated as a non-commercial agreement.

## 3.20. MULTIPLE AGREEMENTS

These are either agreements which are divided into different parts falling under different categories under the Act, or an agreement which is indivisible but the terms of which place it in

---

[94] s.17(1).
[95] *ibid*.
[96] *ibid*.
[97] s.17(3).
[98] s.189(1).
[99] [1993] C.C.L.R. 47.

more than one category.[1] As regards the former type the principle to be followed is that each part is to be treated as a separate agreement and dealt with accordingly, while an agreement of the latter type must be treated as falling into each category. An example of the former type is a contract between bank and customer which operates under significantly different provisions depending on whether or not the customer is overdrawn. Where the customer is not overdrawn, no credit is being given and thus the agreement is not regulated by the Act at all. Where he is, it is clearly a regulated debtor creditor agreement. Another example is that of credit-hire agreements (see para. 3.16.), which can be both consumer hire and consumer credit agreements. An example of the latter type is the issue of a credit card which also allows cash to be drawn. If used in this way, it clearly creates a debtor-creditor relationship, while if used as a credit card it creates a debtor-creditor-supplier relationship. The agreement falls into both categories and is regulated accordingly.

## 3.21. LINKED TRANSACTIONS

The Act acknowledges that when a regulated agreement is entered into, it may be accompanied by certain ancillary agreements, *e.g.* when a television is hired or bought on credit, the consumer may be persuaded to enter into a maintenance contract or a contract insuring the set against damage. The view the Act takes is that where such agreements are clearly linked to the main contract then any rights enjoyed under the main agreement in relation to withdrawal, cancellation or early settlement equally apply to the main agreement. A linked transaction is entered into by the debtor or hirer (or a relative) and any other party. To qualify as a linked transaction in terms of s.19 it must:

(1) be a transaction entered into in compliance with the main agreement, *e.g.* if it is a condition of obtaining a loan that the customer takes out ill health or unemployment insurance; or

(2) be financed by a debtor-creditor-supplier agreement involving three parties, *e.g.* if a car dealer sends the consumer along to a finance company to obtain a loan to purchase a car, the contract for the sale of the car is a linked transaction. (Similarly if a credit card is used to buy goods, the sale contract is a linked transaction.), or

(3) be a transaction initiated by,

    (a) the creditor or owner or his associate;

    (b) a person who in the negotiation of the transaction is represented by a credit broker who is also a negotiator in antecedent negotiations for the principal agreement;

    (c) a person who, at the time the transaction is initiated knows that the principal agreement has been made or contemplates that it might be made,

and that person initiated it by suggesting it to the debtor or hirer (or his relative), who enters into it:

    (i) to induce the creditor or owner to enter into the principal agreement, or

    (ii) for another purpose related to the principal agreement, or

    (iii) where the principal agreement is a restricted use credit agreement for a purpose related to a transaction financed or to be financed by the principal agreement,

The types of situation which fall within category (3) include the situation where the creditor or dealer simply persuades the debtor to enter into a maintenance contract, or where the creditor

---

[1] s.18.

simply refuses to enter into the main agreement unless the debtor enters into a maintenance contract (without making it a formal condition of the former contract that the debtor enters the latter).

It may be noted that any agreement for the provision of a security (*e.g.* a guarantee) cannot be a linked transaction.[2]

# (4) SEEKING BUSINESS/SEEKING CREDIT

Having introduced the conceptual framework employed by the Act, before proceeding to examine how the Act controls the operation of regulated agreements, it is useful to consider how the Act safeguards the consumer at the pre-contractual stage, through controls on advertising, quotations and canvassing. Some attention will also be paid to safeguards for individuals seeking credit.

## 3.22. RECOVERING FEES FROM CREDIT BROKERS

Consumers may approach credit-brokers seeking an introduction to a source of credit. The Act aims to offer some protection against the possibility of a credit-broker charging a substantial fee for seeking to obtain credit, while aware that the consumer is unlikely to receive credit. So where the consumer wants to make a consumer credit or consumer hire agreement, or a credit agreement to finance the purchase of a house, or a credit agreement secured on land, if the credit-broker's introduction does not lead to a relevant agreement within six months thereof, the consumer cannot be liable to pay the broker a fee or commission in excess of £5. If he has already paid, he is entitled to recover any sum in excess of £5.[3]

## 3.23. CREDIT REFERENCE AGENCIES

It is very important for those involved in the business of giving credit to know whether a potential customer is a good risk. Thus organisations have emerged specialising in collecting information regarding the credit histories of individuals, which information they will sell to credit-givers. These are credit reference agencies. The difficulty for the consumer is that he can be refused credit essentially because of the information supplied by one of these agencies, without ever discovering that this is the case. Thus under s.157 a creditor owner or negotiator must, within seven working days of receiving a written request from the consumer, supply the name and address of any credit reference agency from which information had been sought about his financial standing.[4] Naturally, a creditor or owner in this context would include prospective creditors or owners. This obligation does not apply to any request made more than 28 days after the termination of negotiations.[5] It is an offence to fail to comply with such a request.[6]

---

[2] s.19(1).
[3] s.155.
[4] s.157(1); Consumer Credit (Credit Reference Agency) Regulations 2000, SI 2000/290.
[5] s.157(2).
[6] s.157(3).

A consumer which is a firm or unincorporated body can under s.158 then make a written request to a credit reference agency to provide a copy of any file it hold on the firm or body, at the same time tendering a fee of £2. Assuming the agency has been provided with such particulars as it may reasonably require in order to identify the file, it must respond within seven working days, even if it is only to indicate that it does not hold a file on the consumer.[7] A "file" means any information kept about the consumer by the agency, however stored, and reduced to a transcript in plain English if not stored in plain English.[8] Along with the file the credit reference agency must provide a statement indicating the consumer's right under s.159 to have wrong and prejudicial information corrected or removed from the file.[9] Failure to comply with any provision of s.158 is an offence.[10] A consumer who is an individual has similar rights under the more general terms of s.7 of the Data Protection Act 1998.

An alternative procedure to s.158 exists under s.160 in the case of requests from business consumers. The s.160 procedure is designed to recognise the fact that provision of the file would be very likely to reveal the agency's sources, and that these sources would be unlikely to continue to furnish information if they were aware that confidentiality could not be guaranteed. Accordingly, if the agency wishes to escape the application of s.158, it must apply to the OFT. The OFT may direct that the s.160 procedure shall apply instead if satisfied that:

(1) compliance with s.158 would adversely affect the service provided by the agency to its customers; and

(2) it is probable that business consumers would not be prejudiced by the direction.

If the direction is made, the agency, when it receives a request from a business consumer, then has the option of proceeding under s.158 or, within the prescribed period, of giving the consumer such information included in or based on entries in the file as the OFT may direct, together with a statement of the consumer's right under s.159 and his right under s.160(4). The latter is a right, within 28 days of receiving the above information or such longer period as the OFT will allow, to give notice that he is dissatisfied with the information. If he pays the required fee, and satisfies the OFT that he has taken such steps as are reasonable with a view to removing the cause of his dissatisfaction, the OFT may direct the agency to give the consumer a copy of the file, and the OFT may then disclose to him such information thereon as it thinks fit. As ever, failure to comply with s.160 is an offence.

When the right[11] to have wrong and prejudicial information corrected or removed from the file is exercised, the credit reference agency must, within 28 days of receiving the relevant notice from the consumer, inform him that it either has made the appropriate corrections or deletions or has taken no action, and give him a copy of any amended entry.[12] Within 28 days of being so notified (or if not notified, within 28 days of the expiry of the period during which he should have been notified), a consumer, unless he has been informed that the incorrect entry has been deleted, may serve a further notice requiring it to add to the file an accompanying notice of correction (not exceeding 200 words).[13] This means that the consumer can suggest his own correction if the agency declines to amend, or makes an amendment with which he disagrees. The idea is that the agency would then have to include a copy of the consumer's amendment when supplying information including or based on the challenged entry.

The agency then has a further 28 days to indicate that it intends to comply.[14] However, if it appears to the agency that it would be improper to publish such amendment because it is

---

[7] s.158(1); Consumer Credit (Credit Reference Agency) Regulations 2000, SI 2000/290.
[8] s.158(5).
[9] s.158(2).
[10] s.158(4).
[11] Under s.159(1).
[12] s.159(2).
[13] s.159(3).
[14] s.159(4).

incorrect, defamatory, frivolous, scandalous, or otherwise unsuitable, then it may refer the matter to the relevant authority, who may make such an order as it thinks fit.[15] The consumer may also make such a reference should the agency fail to respond within the 28 day period.[16] The relevant authority will be the OFT where the consumer is a firm or unincorporated body, but otherwise will be the Information Commissioner.[17] It is an offence to fail to comply with such an order.[18]

## 3.24.  ADVERTISING

The controls imposed by s.43 of the Act apply to any advertisement in any medium which indicates that the advertiser is willing to provide credit or hire facilities. It has been held that a car advertisement which bore also the name and logo of a finance company is not such an advertisement as it did not actually state that the advertiser was willing to provide credit.[19] Also comprehended are adverts advertising credit brokerage services or the services of the credit or hire business to which the credit broker introduces customers, and adverts issued by a debt adjusting or debt counselling business indicating that it is willing to advise on debts or engage in transactions concerned with the liquidation of debts.[20] The Act also creates exceptions to its regime. Thus advertisements do not fall under its control if the advertiser does not carry on a consumer credit or consumer hire business, or a business in the course of which he provides credit to individuals secured on land. Nor is an advertisement within the Act if it indicates that:

- credit is available only to a body corporate; or
- the credit must exceed £25,000 and that no security is required or any security is to consist of property other than land; or
- (where goods are to be hired) the advertiser is not willing to enter a consumer hire agreement.

Exceptions created by statutory instrument[21] include:

- advertisements relating to certain consumer credit agreements where the number of payments does not exceed a certain number or the total charge for credit does not exceed a certain rate—This means that AMEX adverts are not within the controls;
- advertisements relating to certain consumer credit agreements connected with trade with a country outside the UK;
- advertisements relating to certain consumer hire agreements for the hire of metering equipment used in connection with the supply of electricity, gas or water.

Controls upon the form and content of advertisements are prescribed by Regulations made under s.44 of the Act.[22] These Regulations are immensely detailed, but in effect they demand that information should be presented clearly, legibly and "together as a whole". They also stipulate that advertisements must provide information about any personal factors which will be taken into account in considering whether to offer credit. Mortgage advertisements must make it clear that the borrower's home is at risk if payments are not kept up. The charge for credit must be expressed as an annual percentage rate "APR", so that the relative cost of credit has

---

[15] s.159(5)(b).
[16] s.159(5)(a).
[17] s.159(8).
[18] s.159(6).
[19] *Jenkins v Lombard North Central* [1984] 1 W.L.R. 307.
[20] s.151(1).
[21] See Consumer Credit (Exempt Advertisements) Order 1985, SI 1985/621.
[22] Consumer Credit (Advertisements) Regulations 1989, SI 1989/1125.

to be immediately ascertainable, and the APR must be prominently displayed. Advertisements are divided into three broad types—simple, intermediate and full—and the Regulations indicate what sort of information must, must not and may be included in each type. Simple advertisements are limited in the information which *may* be displayed—only the advertiser's name, address, telephone number, logo and occupation or general nature—although if they do not also indicate that he is willing to hire goods or provide credit then they are not subject to the controls of the Act at all.[23] The regime applicable to simple advertisements is designed to allow advertising of the name of a business through devices such as calendars. Intermediate advertisements *must* specify name, address or telephone number, and an indication that terms can be obtained by application to that address or number. Full advertisements will include considerably more information such as details of the cost of credit including the APR and the frequency and amount of payments. Certain expressions cannot be used, while prescribed warnings must accompany advertisements of certain transactions. The Regulations do not apply to advertisements aimed solely at business customers.

It is an offence to contravene the above Regulations. It is also an offence under s.46 if an advertisement contains information which is false or misleading in a material respect. Successful prosecutions have been brought where expressions such as "nought per cent APR and 0 per cent finance" have disguised the fact that cash customers can obtain a better deal.[24] It is now indeed the case that advertisements are specifically prohibited from using such expressions as "interest free" unless the total amount paid by the debtor would not exceed the cash price of goods.[25] A more specialised type of offence is created by s.45 where an advertisement states a willingness to provide restricted use credit for the supply of goods and services and these goods or services are not provided for cash. This is designed to deal with the situation where, for example, a mail order firm offers seemingly favourable credit terms, disguising the fact that the lack of a cash price prevents the consumer making a sensible comparison. Where an offence is committed, it is also committed by anyone who devised or published the advertisement, although the latter has a defence if he can prove that he had no reason to suspect that publication would be an offence.[26]

## 3.25. QUOTATIONS

Section 52 authorises the making of Regulations regarding the form and content of any document by which a person who carries on a consumer credit or consumer hire business, gives prospective customers information about the terms on which he is prepared to do business, and requiring such persons to provide quotations to individuals who seek them. Detailed Regulations were made indicating how credit or hire trader or credit-broker should respond to a request for a quotation, and prescribing the form and content of any such quotation.[27] The content was very similar to the information supplied in a full advertisement. However, a review conducted in 1994 found that few consumers ever requested a quotation, and recommended the repeal of the Regulations.[28] They were duly revoked[29] and the replacement Regulations[30]

---

[23] *Jenkins v Lombard North Central* [1984] 1 W.L.R. 307.
[24] *Metsoja v H. Norman Pitt & Co Ltd* [1990] C.C.L.R. 12.
[25] Consumer Credit (Advertisements) Regulations 1989, reg. 7(c); and see *Ford Credit plc v Normand,* 1994 S.L.T. 318.
[26] s.47(1)–(2).
[27] Consumer Credit (Quotations) Regulations 1989, SI 1989/1126.
[28] OFT, *Consumer Credit Deregulation.*
[29] Consumer Credit (Quotations) (Revocation) Regulations 1997, SI 1997/211.
[30] Consumer Credit (Content of Quotations) and Consumer Credit (Advertisements) (Amendment) Regulations 1999, SI 1997/2725.

no longer demand that the trader respond to a request for a quotation. Rather they insist that specific "health warnings" should accompany quotations made in relation to certain transactions. So where, for example, a loan is to be secured on the customer's home, the quotation should say "Your home is at risk if you do not keep up repayments on a mortgage or other loan secured on it".

## 3.26.  CANVASSING

The Act seeks to prohibit the doorstep peddling of loans. Thus canvassing debtor-creditor agreements off trade premises is a criminal offence.[31] Canvassing signifies soliciting a consumer to enter a regulated agreement by making oral representations during a visit which was not previously arranged.[32] Indeed even if the visit was arranged an offence is still committed if the request was not in writing and signed by (or on behalf of) the person making it.[33] Trade premises mean the business premises, not only those of the creditor, but also a supplier, the canvasser or even the debtor.[34] So no offence is committed if the representative of a finance company visits the debtor's shop to persuade him to borrow money. Nor is an offence committed if a debtor is persuaded to enter into an agreement off trade premises, where the canvasser had not visited for that purpose, e.g. where a loan is agreed as the result of a chance encounter at a social event.[35] As a result of a determination by the Director General of Fair Trading it is not an offence for a representative of a bank to canvass off trade premises in order to persuade a customer to accept an overdraft on his current account. Obviously, it is not a criminal offence to canvass debtor-creditor-supplier agreements such as H.P. agreements. Finally, it is a criminal offence to canvass off trade premises the services of a credit broker, debt adjuster or debt counsellor.[36]

## 3.27.  CIRCULARS TO MINORS

By virtue of s.50, it is an offence, with a view to financial gain to send to a person under 18 a document inviting him to borrow money, obtain goods or services on credit, hire goods or even apply for information about any of these things. However, if a circular which happens to be sent to a minor indicates that the particular facility is not open to anyone below 18, then it does not invite that minor to obtain the facility.[37] It has also been held that if a sender can show that applications from minors were refused as a matter of policy, any such communication would not be sent to a minor "with a view to financial gain", and thus no offence is committed where the minor receives such a document.[38]

## 3.28.  UNSOLICITED CREDIT TOKENS

It is an offence under s.51 to supply a credit token unless in response to a written and signed request. A credit token is something supplied by someone carrying on a consumer credit

---

[31] s.49(1).
[32] s.48(1).
[33] s.49(2).
[34] s.48(2).
[35] s.48(1)(a).
[36] s.154.
[37] *Alliance & Leicester Building Society v Babbs* [1993] C.C.L.R. 77.
[38] *ibid.*

business who undertakes that cash, goods or services will be supplied by him on its production, or that where on its production a third party supplies cash, etc. he will pay for them in return for payment to him by the recipient of the token. This covers store cards and credit cards. An offence is committed under this provision even if the token does not amount to an actual offer to give credit, such as where further formalities are necessary before credit may be obtained.[39] It might be argued that debit cards such as Switch, bank cash cards and guarantee cards are not covered, as they do not involve the grant of credit. It is not an offence to renew an existing token. Nor is it an offence to respond to an oral request for a token in respect of a small debtor-creditor-supplier agreement.

# (5) ENTERING INTO AGREEMENTS

## 3.29. INTRODUCTION

Part V of the Act sets up a number of protections for individuals who might enter into consumer credit agreements. However, there are certain types of agreement which are excluded from all the provisions of Pt V except those provisions relating to antecedent negotiations (see below). These are[40]:

(1) non-commercial agreements (see para. 3.19.); and
(2) agreements which meet *all* of the following criteria, being:

- a small agreement (see para. 3.18.);
- for restricted use credit; and
- a debtor-creditor-supplier agreement.

An example would be a credit sale agreement where the amount of credit does not exceed £50. In addition, there are a couple of exclusions which only apply where the OFT thinks fit, and where it considers the exclusion to be in the interests of debtors.[41] These are[42]:

- a debtor-creditor agreement to finance the making of such payments arising on, or connected with the death of a person as may be prescribed, and
- a debtor-creditor agreement enabling the debtor to overdraw on current account. Indeed in this instance if the creditor is a bank, the OFT must allow the exclusion unless it considers it would be against the public interest to do so. The aim is to allow bank overdrafts with minimum formality.

The provisions of Pt V are examined in the succeeding paragraphs.

## 3.30. PRE-CONTRACTUAL INFORMATION

Regulations may be made under s.55 requiring specified information to be disclosed to a prospective debtor or hirer. As yet, none have been made.

## 3.31. ANTECEDENT NEGOTIATIONS

The Act impinges on pre-contractual negotiations through the concept of antecedent negotiations. These are[43] any negotiations with the debtor or hirer conducted by:

---

[39] *Elliott v Director General of Fair Trading* [1980] 1 W.L.R. 977.
[40] s.74(1)(a), (2).
[41] s.74(3).
[42] s.74(1)(b)–(c).
[43] s.56(1).

(1)  the creditor or owner; or

(2)  a credit-broker who supplies the creditor with goods to be supplied to the debtor under a debtor-creditor-supplier agreement involving two parties (*e.g.* when an individual looks to buy furniture from a shop on H.P., and the shop sells the furniture to the finance company which then enters into an H.P. agreement with the individual); or

(c)  the supplier in a debtor-creditor-supplier agreement involving three parties (*e.g.* the store from which goods are bought using a credit card).

Negotiations begin when the negotiator and the debtor first enter into communication, including communication by advertisement, and include all representations made by the negotiator to the debtor and any other dealings between them.[44] The point of all of this is that in categories (2) or (3) above the negotiator is treated as acting both for himself and as the creditor's agent (*i.e.* the creditor is liable for the negotiator's misrepresentations, etc). The Act seeks to preclude any attempt to avoid this, in that an agreement is void to the extent that it purports to make the negotiator the debtor's agent, or to relieve the creditor of liability for the negotiator's acts or omissions.[45] As regards (2) the agency only extends to representations "in relation to the goods sold or proposed to be sold" by the dealer to the creditor. This is an important qualification. In *U.D.T. v Whitfield*[46] W was interested in acquiring a new car on H.P., although he already had a car on H.P. The car dealer offered him a trade-in allowance which would be more than sufficient to pay the outstanding balance in relation to the existing H.P. agreement, and undertook to clear off that balance. The remaining amount owed on the new car was to be financed by H.P. agreement with U.D.T. In the event, the dealer failed to clear off the balance under the first agreement. W argued that U.D.T. was liable for the dealer's failure to fulfil this obligation. The county court agreed, taking the view that as far as W was concerned, the purchase of the new car, the trade-in agreement and the undertaking to pay off the outstanding sum on the old car were a single transaction. Thus the promise to pay off the outstanding sum could be regarded as a representation "in relation to the goods sold?" Yet in *Powell v Lloyds Bowmaker Ltd*,[47] which featured very similar facts, that reasoning was explicitly rejected. The sheriff insisted that "the goods sold" meant only the new car, so that the finance company could not be liable for any representation made by the dealer as regards paying the sum outstanding on the car being traded in. The Court of Appeal has since ruled that *Whitfield* is correct and *Powell* is wrong.[48]

## 3.32.  FORM AND CONTENT OF AGREEMENTS

Regulations made under s.60 prescribe the form and content of any agreement.[49] In terms of form, requisite information must be given prominence and be easily legible and distinguishable. Financial information must be presented as a whole. Prescribed content includes:

- a prominent heading on the first page stating the legal nature of the agreement (*e.g.* Hire-Purchase Agreement regulated by the Consumer Credit Act 1974);
- the names and addresses of the parties;
- the cash price (where appropriate);
- the amount of any required deposit or advance payment;

---

[44] s.56(4).
[45] s.56(3).
[46] [1987] C.C.L.R. 60.
[47] 1996 S.L.T. (Sh. Ct.) 117.
[48] *Forthright Finance Ltd v Ingate* [1997] 4 All E.R. 99.
[49] Consumer Credit (Agreement) Regulations 1983, SI 1983/1553 as amended.

- the amount or limit of credit;
- the APR;
- the total amount payable;
- details of the timing and amount of payments;
- details of default charges;
- details of any security provided by the debtor or hirer;
- details of rights, obligations and remedies under the Act.

There must also be a signature box for the debtor or hirer. Finally, the agreement must contain all express terms.[50] The agreement must be signed by the debtor or hirer (in the signature box) and by or on behalf of the creditor or owner.[51] The agreement must be in proper form and contain all the prescribed information when signed. Signature of a document which is lacking any of these details is inept. If any term is not legibly presented, then not only is there a breach of the Act,[52] but the term might not be enforceable under the Unfair Terms in Consumer Contracts Regulations 1999. Indeed even if all the requirements of the Act are complied with, a term might not be enforceable under the Regulations merely because it is expressed in language which, though perfectly clear to a lawyer, is not plain and intelligible to a layperson.[53]

## 3.33. COPIES OF THE AGREEMENT

If the creditor or owner has already signed the agreement when the debtor or hirer signs, the latter must receive a copy of the agreement there and then.[54] If the creditor or owner has not signed, then as well as the debtor or hirer receiving a copy on signing the agreement, he is entitled to receive a second copy within seven days of the creditor or owner signing.[55] Copies of credit-token agreements need not be sent within seven days, as long as they as supplied before or at the same time as the credit token.[56] In addition the debtor or hirer can always demand a further copy of the agreement at any time during its currency on payment of a fee of £2.[57] Special rules apply where a prospective regulated agreement is to be secured on land. These rules do not apply to bridging loan agreements or restricted use credit agreements to finance the purchase of the land, *i.e.* ordinary mortgages.[58] The rules therefore are directed towards second mortgages, and seek to ensure that the debtor is not pressurised into entering them without a chance to reflect on the transaction. In such cases, the prospective debtor must receive a copy of the unexecuted agreement, containing a notice indicating his right to withdraw and how it may be exercised.[59] This copy is for him to consider rather than sign, and at least seven days must elapse before he is sent a copy to sign.[60] During the intervening period the creditor must not approach him in any way, unless the debtor specifically so requests.[61] The creditor must continue to refrain from contact for a further seven days after this copy is sent for signature, or until the debtor has signed and returned it if this is earlier.[62] The right to receive this copy to consider is in addition to the normal rights to receive copies under ss.62-63 (see above).

---

[50] s.61(1)(b).
[51] s.61(1)(a).
[52] s.61(1)(c).
[53] See SI 1999/2083, reg. 7.
[54] s.63(1).
[55] ss.62(1), 63(2).
[56] s.63(4).
[57] ss.77–79.
[58] s.58(2).
[59] s.58(1).
[60] s.61(2)(b).
[61] s.61(2)(c).
[62] s.61(3).

## 3.34.   WITHDRAWAL

Where the creditor or owner has not signed when the debtor or hirer signs, the latter is entitled to withdraw at any time before the former signs. This may be done by notice to any of the following[63]:

- the creditor or owner;
  any credit-broker or supplier who was the negotiator in antecedent negotiations;
- anyone who in the course of a business negotiated on behalf of the *debtor or hirer*.

Notice may be given orally or in writing and no particular form is required as long as the intention to withdraw is communicated. Withdrawal has the same effect as cancellation (see next para).

## 3.35.   CANCELLATION

Under s.67 a regulated agreement may be cancelled if two conditions are met:

- Oral representations by the negotiator (or his representative) must have been made in the presence of the debtor in the course of antecedent negotiations. A representation will be any statement which might be capable of inducing the debtor to enter into the agreement, although it is not necessary that these representations should actually have induced the agreement or have been intended to do so.[64] Essentially what is involved is some degree of pre-contractual interaction. The question of who counts as a negotiator is discussed under the heading of antecedent negotiations earlier in this paragraph. If goods are purchased from a finance company on hire purchase, then the dealer would be a negotiator. However, a company which hires goods cannot be a negotiator.[65]
- The agreement must have been signed by the debtor or hirer other than on the trade premises of the creditor or owner, or the negotiator, or any party to a linked transaction (other than the debtor or hirer or any relative). This condition tends to restrict the category of agreements which are cancellable. Basically, it is aimed at giving an individual a period of reflection when they are persuaded to enter into an agreement during a visit to their home. However, it must be remembered that the emphasis of the provision is on where the agreement is signed. If after considerable pressure during a home visit, an individual agrees to enter into an agreement, but the agreement is actually signed on trade premises, the agreement is not cancellable. Yet, if an individual goes to the creditor's premises in search of credit, but for whatever reason the agreement is signed in that individual's home, it is cancellable.

There are cases which are excepted from the cancellation provisions. These are agreements exempted from the provisions of Pt V by s.74 (see para. 3.17.) plus agreements secured on land, agreements where credit is restricted to the purchase of land, and bridging loans in connection with the purchase of land.[66] These latter cases are exempt because the policy of the Act is not to allow agreements related to land to be cancellable, because of the legal complications which

---

[63] s.57.
[64] *Moorgate Services v Kabir* [1995] C.C.L.R. 74, CA.
[65] *Lloyd's Bowmaker Leasing Ltd v McDonald* [1993] C.C.L.R. 65.
[66] s.67.

cancellation might create in such circumstances. However, it might be remembered that in certain such cases the prospective debtor is permitted a period of uninfluenced reflection before entering into the agreement (see para. 3.33.).

Where an agreement is cancellable, s.64 demands that every copy of the agreement must contain a notice in the prescribed form, indicating the right to cancel, how and when it may be exercised, and the name and address of a person to whom notice of cancellation may be sent. If a second copy of the agreement is not required (see para. 3.37.), a separate notice detailing the cancellation information must be posted within seven days of the agreement being made.

## Mechanics and effect of cancellation

The receipt of the above notice or the second copy is important for the exercise of the right to cancel under s.69. Cancellation may be effected at any time within the cooling off period, which runs from the point at which the debtor or hirer signs the agreement, until five days after the receipt of the second copy or notice. Notice of cancellation, which must be in writing, but need not be in any particular form as long as it effectively communicates its intention, may be sent to anyone to whom a notice of withdrawal might have been sent, or to anyone specified in the agreement. If notice is posted, then it is deemed to be served at the date of posting, even if it never arrives.[67]

Subject to certain exceptions, a notice of cancellation will cancel the agreement and any linked transaction, and will withdraw any offer to enter into a linked transaction.[68] Any sum paid under the agreement or a linked transaction will be repaid, and any sum payable ceases to be so.[69] A debtor or hirer has under s.70(2) a lien for any sums to be repaid on any goods in his possession under the cancelled agreement. Otherwise, s.72 dictates that any goods held must be returned, although the debtor or hirer need not take the initiative in doing so. Rather, he can hand them over at his own premises, having received a written request to do so, although he is bound to take care of them in the meantime.[70] Moreover, the debtor or hirer need not return perishable goods, goods supplied in an emergency, or goods which are consumed or incorporated in something else prior to cancellation at all.[71] Obviously, he will be unable to return services supplied prior to cancellation. Clearly, in certain cases the effect of cancellation is that the trader will lose out financially. This is mitigated to some degree by the Act providing that where goods have been supplied in an emergency, or are incorporated in something else prior to cancellation, the debtor must still pay the cash price for them despite cancellation.[72] Within 10 days of cancellation the creditor or owner must return to the debtor or hirer any goods given in part exchange or pay a sum equivalent to the part-exchange allowance.[73] The Act also guards against the possibility that a debtor might be able to keep the amount of a loan simply by cancelling the loan agreement. So if the agreement is not a debtor-creditor-supplier agreement for restricted use credit (*e.g.* a hire-purchase agreement), then if the credit has already been supplied when it is cancelled, the agreement continues in force so far as it relates to the repayment of credit and the payment of interest.[74] Nonetheless, no interest is payable on any sum repaid within a month of service of the notice of cancellation, or (if repayment was to be in instalments) before the date when the first instalment was due.[75] Moreover, where

---

[67] s.69(7).
[68] s.69(1)(c).
[69] s.70(1).
[70] s.72(3)–(5).
[71] s.72(9).
[72] s.69(2).
[73] s.73.
[74] s.71(1).
[75] s.71(2).

repayment is to be in instalments, the debtor is not liable to make any repayment unless he receives a written request from the creditor in a form prescribed by regulations, stating the amounts of the remaining instalments.[76]

## 3.36. ON-LINE AGREEMENTS

It is worth noting that in December 2002 the DTI issued a Consultation Document on Facilitating the Conclusion of Credit and Hire Agreements Electronically under the CCA. Depending on the outcome of the consultation exercise, the provisions relating to the form and content of agreements and to related issues such as copies of the agreement and cancellation may have to undergo radical amendment.

## 3.37. PROPER EXECUTION OF THE AGREEMENT

Under s.65 a regulated agreement which is not properly executed cannot be enforced against the debtor or hirer without the permission of the court (see para. 3.50.). Retaking possession of goods or land to which the agreement relates is specifically stated to amount to enforcement.[77] Thus a creditor or owner who might otherwise be entitled to recover goods or land, requires the assistance of the court to do so where the agreement is not properly executed. No restriction is placed on the right of the debtor or hirer to enforce an agreement which is not properly executed. To be properly executed the document embodying the agreement:

(1) must be in prescribed form and contain all prescribed terms;
(2) must be signed as prescribed by the parties;
(3) must be legible;
(4) must contain all the terms of the agreement, apart from implied terms;
(5) if the agreement is cancellable, must contain the prescribed information regarding cancellation rights and their exercise.

Moreover all copies of the agreement must have been supplied as required.[78]

## 3.38. SECURITY

Often a creditor or owner will be reluctant to enter a credit or hire transaction without the benefit of some kind of security. Where security is provided by or at the request of a debtor or hirer, it is governed by the Act.[79] Otherwise, where the security is provided without reference to the debtor or hirer, *e.g.* where a finance company insists that a dealer agrees to indemnify it against loss before it is prepared to buy goods from the dealer to sell to a debtor on hire purchase, the security does not fall within the scope of the Act. Where a security is governed by the Act, then if the regulated agreement is not enforceable, neither is the security,[80] although of

---

[76] s.71(3); Consumer Credit (Repayment of Credit on Cancellation) Regulations 1983 (SI 1983/1559).
[77] s.65(2).
[78] See ss.61–64.
[79] s.189(1).
[80] s.113.

course the fact that a security is not enforceable would not of itself affect the enforceability of the regulated agreement. Moreover, the security agreement must be in writing and signed by or on behalf of the surety[81] (the provider of the security). It must comply in form and content with the Consumer Credit (Guarantees and Indemnities) Regulations 1983,[82] and in particular must contain all express terms in legible form.[83] A copy of the security agreement and the regulated agreement and any other document referred to in the latter must be given to the surety at the time the security is provided, although if the security is provided before the regulated agreement is entered into, a copy of the latter (and any other document referred to therein) must be provided within seven days of it being made.[84] Failure to comply with any of these formalities means that the security is improperly executed and thus may only be enforced by court order.

# (6) MATTERS ARISING DURING THE COURSE OF THE AGREEMENT

## 3.39. RIGHT TO INFORMATION

At any time during the currency of a regulated agreement, a debtor or hirer has the right to request from the creditor or owner a copy of the agreement and a statement of the account between them. This statement will include, in the case of a fixed-sum credit agreement, information as to the amount already paid, the amount which has become payable but is as yet unpaid (including the various amounts comprised in that total sum, and the date each fell due), and the total sum which will become payable (again detailing the various amounts comprised in that total sum and the date each will fall due).[85] In the case of a running-account credit agreement, this statement will include information as to the state of the account, any amount currently payable, and the amounts (assuming the debtor does not draw further on the account) which will later become payable (including the dates these fall due).[86] In the case of a consumer hire agreement, this statement will include information as to the amount which has become payable but is as yet unpaid (again including the various amounts comprised in that total sum and the date each fell due).[87] Parallel provisions exist to confer on a person providing a security under a regulated agreement a copy of the agreement, a copy of the security agreement and a statement of the account.[88] In all the above cases the request must be in writing and a fee of £1 must be paid, but none of the above provisions apply to a non-commercial agreement. In addition, the debtor under a regulated consumer credit agreement (whether non-commercial or not) may make a written request (in this case without having to pay a fee) for a statement of the amount required to pay off the entire debt, which statement should show how that amount is arrived at.[89] In this case a rebate will be due for early settlement (see para. 3.44.).

If the creditor or owner does not respond accurately to any such request as is mentioned in the previous paragraph within 12 days of receiving it, then he is not entitled to enforce the agreement (or the security agreement where the request comes from a person providing security) while he remains in default.[90] An offence is committed if he continues in default for a

---

[81] s.105(1), (4)(a).
[82] SI 1983/1556, and see s.105(2)–(3).
[83] s.105(4)(b)–(c).
[84] s.105(4)(d), (5)(a), (b).
[85] s.77.
[86] s.78.
[87] s.79.
[88] See ss.107–109.
[89] s.97 and Consumer Credit (Settlement Information) Regulations 1983 (SI 1983/1564.
[90] ss.77(4)(a), 78(6)(a), 97(3)(a), 107–109.

month.[91] He is, however, bound by any statement supplied, so that if the figure quoted is too low, *e.g.* where the creditor tells the debtor that £1,000 is required to settle the debt when the figure should really be £10,000, then the debtor may rely upon that information.[92] This is subject to the power of the court to offer such relief from the operation of the rule as may be just.[93] It may also be noted that the English courts have held creditors to be bound by statements provided to debtors other than under these statutory provisions, as a result of the doctrine of estoppel.[94] It may be that a debtor may be able similarly to rely on personal bar.

## 3.40.  IMPLIED TERMS

A regulated agreement may also be a contract of sale of goods and thus subject to the implied terms as to title and quality. Almost identical terms to those implied under ss.12 to 15 of the Sale of Goods Act 1979 are implied in contracts of hire-purchase under ss. 8 to 11 of the Supply of Goods (Implied Terms) Act 1973 and in contracts of hire under ss.7 to 10 of the Supply of Goods and Services Act 1982. It should be noted, however, that remedies under contracts of hire continue to be governed by the common law.

## 3.41.  CONNECTED LENDER LIABILITY

Often traders and finance houses are very closely connected. Thus, although the common law would see supply contracts and credit contracts as entirely independent, the Act takes the view that in certain circumstances breach of the former should have consequences for the creditor.[95] Accordingly, s.75 provides that if a debtor under a debtor-creditor-supplier agreement involving three parties, which is made under or in contemplation of arrangements between the supplier and creditor, has in relation to a transaction financed by the agreement a claim against the supplier in respect of a misrepresentation or breach of contract, he shall have a like claim against the creditor. In other words, in a three party debtor-creditor-supplier transaction the creditor is jointly and severally liable with the supplier for the latter's misrepresentation and breach of contract.

There are certain exceptions to this provision. It does not apply to a non-commercial agreement, nor to a claim which relates to any single item to which the supplier has attached a cash price not exceeding £100 or more than £30,000.[96] So if a connected lender provides a loan to allow an individual to purchase a number of items of electrical equipment, while the creditor will be jointly and severally liable with the supplier should a cooker malfunction, if a kettle priced at £70 malfunctions, then a claim cannot be brought against the creditor. This is so even if the claim against the supplier greatly exceeds £100, as where the kettle explodes causing the buyer severe injury.

Given that the creditor shares liability for breach of the supply contract, the question whether the cost of credit can be recovered is a difficult one. It would not seem to be a head of damages for breach of the supply contract, unless it could be argued that the loss flowed directly from the supplier's breach of contract. It might be easier to recover such damages if the

---

[91] ss.77(4)(b), 78(6)(b), 97(3)(b), 107–109.
[92] s.172(1)–(2).
[93] s.172(3).
[94] See *e.g. Lombard North Central v Stobart* [1990] C.C.L.R. 53.
[95] For the rationale, see the Crowther Report, para. 6.6.22. *et seq.*
[96] s.75(3)(a)–(b).

claim was for misrepresentation. One hesitates, however, to be overly dogmatic regarding the operation of this section, in light of *U.D.T. v Taylor*.[97] There the sheriff principal accepted that where a purchaser of a car had a right to rescind the contract of sale (the supply contract), s.75 conferred a similar right to rescind the accompanying loan contract (the credit contract). This seems dubious, but was followed in another sheriff court case.[98] On the other hand, in *Jarrett v Barclays Bank plc*[99] the Court of Appeal has suggested that "like claim" means "like cause of action", albeit that the remedies available against the creditor will differ from those against the supplier. In *Renton v Henderson's Garage (Nairn) and U.D.T.*[1] s.75 was wrongly applied to a two party debtor-creditor-supplier transaction, where the finance company purchased a vehicle from the supplier and itself sold it on a conditional sale basis to the debtor. Yet the practical outcome was identical, given that the debtor was in a direct contractual relationship with the finance company regarding the sale of the car.

## Credit cards and connected lender liability

It has been argued by the credit card industry that credit card transactions would not fall within s.75 as, *inter alia*, a fourth party is involved—a "merchant acquirer" who recruits retailers willing to accept the card, and may well also pay their accounts, obtaining payment in return from the card issuer. Yet it is likely that the courts would still regard this situation as involving an "arrangement" between the supplier and creditor, and indeed the sheriff court has accepted that s.75 applies to credit card transactions.[2] The Act specifically prevents payments by debit card being subject to s.75.[3] The Act only applies to regulated agreements made on or after July 1, 1977. Thus it is argued that if the credit card agreement was entered into before that date, s.75 will not apply, and it does not matter how often a "new" card has been issued. At the same time, if that agreement has been varied by agreement of the parties after July 1, 1977, then it is treated as having been terminated and a new agreement made.[4] Accordingly, s.75 should then apply. An alternative argument is that a debtor-creditor-supplier agreement is created not when the credit card agreement is entered into, but each time the card is actually used, so that all credit card transactions are subject to s.75, no matter when the credit card agreement was entered into. Those companies which entered into agreements before the key date have indicated that they will voluntarily accept s.75 liability, but only to the extent of the credit used on that particular purchase. There is also an argument that s.75 may not apply in relation to credit card purchases made abroad. Again, this issue turns on when the debtor-creditor-supplier agreement is created. If it is created when the credit card agreement is entered into, then the argument cannot stand, as Scots/English law would govern the relationship between debtor and creditor, so that s.75 would apply. If however, it is created when the card is actually used, then the law of the foreign jurisdiction would apply, so that s.75 could not be relied upon. In *Jarrett v Barclays Bank plc*[5] the Court of Appeal entertained a claim against the bank in terms of the misrepresentation and breach of contract by the vendors under a time-share agreement (partly financed by the use of a credit card), despite the fact that the Portugese courts were acknowledged as having exclusive jurisdiction to hear the claim against the vendors. A final question attending the use of credit cards is what is the position under s.75 in respect of a transaction entered into by an authorised user of the card, *e.g.* the spouse or child of the card-holder. The simple answer would appear to be that as the card-holder bears liability in such transactions, the user would be regarded as their agent, so that s.75 would apply straightforwardly.

---

[97] 1980 S.L.T (Sh. Ct.) 28.
[98] *Forward Trust Ltd v Hornby* [1995] C.C.L.R. 574.
[99] [1999] Q.B. 1 at 15G, *per* Morritt L.J.
[1] [1994] C.C.L.R.29. See also *Porter v General Guarantee Corporation* [1982] C.C.L.R. 1.
[2] *Dalglish v National Westminster Bank plc*, 2001 S.L.T. (Sh. Ct) 124.
[3] s.187(3A).
[4] s.82(2).
[5] [1999] Q.B. 1.

## 3.42.  MISUSE OF CREDIT CARDS

On the subject of credit cards, the Act seeks to offer some protection for consumers against the misuse of credit tokens. Thus under s.66 the debtor cannot be liable for any unauthorised use of a credit token unless he has either signed it (or a receipt for it), or used it. Once it has been thus accepted, if it is misused by a person in possession with the debtor's consent, the latter is liable for all loss.[6] If it is accidentally lost or stolen, s.84(1) restricts the debtor's liability to £50. The debtor is not in any case liable for any loss arising after the creditor has been given notice that it is lost stolen or otherwise liable to misuse.[7] A credit token agreement must therefore contain the name, address and telephone number of a person to whom notice of loss must be given, and if it fails to do so the debtor will not be liable for the creditor's loss.[8] Again, no liability can arise where a credit card is used fraudulently in connection with a contract to which the Consumer Protection (Distance Selling) Regulations 2000 apply.[9]

## 3.43.  APPROPRIATION OF PAYMENTS

A debtor or hirer may have more than one regulated agreement with the same creditor or owner. Rather than make a number of separate payments every week, month, etc, he may obviously make a single undifferentiated payment. When that payment would not be sufficient to meet the total sums then due, s.81(1) provides that he has the right (which he would in any case have at common law) to appropriate the sum to any one or more of the debts, and in such proportions as he thinks fit. Should he fail to make an appropriation, then if any of the agreements is an H.P., conditional sale or consumer hire agreement, or an agreement in relation to which a security is provided, then the payment is appropriated to sums due under the various agreements "in the proportions which those sums bears to one another".[10] Thus if the debtor has three agreements under which he respectively pays £600, £300 and £100 per month, and instead of tendering a cheque for £1,000 in a particular month, he submits a cheque for £300, he is regarding as paying respectively £180, £90 and £30 in respect of those three agreements. Of course, where none of the agreements falls into one of the above categories, the creditor, in the absence of an appropriation by the debtor, may appropriate the amount as he thinks fit. In the English case of *Julian Hodge Bank Ltd v Hall*[11] H had only one agreement, a regulated H.P. agreement. He owed both arrears and interest thereon. He made a payment in respect thereof which was less than the total amount of the arrears and interest. As H had failed to appropriate, the creditor was held entitled to do so. The Court of Appeal held that the creditor's appropriation was not effective until communicated to the debtor, but was then irrevocable.

# (7) TERMINATION AND DEFAULT

## 3.44.  EARLY DISCHARGE BY THE DEBTOR

A regulated agreement may be terminated early by the debtor serving notice on the creditor and making full payment of the amount due.[12] The debtor will be entitled to a rebate on the

---

[6] s.84(2).
[7] s.84(3).
[8] See Consumer Credit (Credit Token Agreements) Regulations 1983 (SI 1983/1555).
[9] SI 2000/2334, reg. 21.
[10] s.81(2).
[11] [1998] C.C.L.R. 14.
[12] s.94.

charge for credit, calculated according to a complex formula.[13] The debtor would be entitled to demand a statement of the amount required to pay off the entire debt (see para. 3.39.). If an agreement is thus terminated it will also terminate the liability of the debtor (or his relative) under a linked transaction other than a contract of insurance or guarantee.[14]

## 3.45. TERMINATION OF CONSUMER HIRE AGREEMENT BY HIRER

While it may commonly be assumed that a hirer will hire goods for as long as he requires them, the agreement may bind him to a certain minimum period of hire. It is possible for this period to be extremely lengthy, and there had been signs over the years that certain businesses were committing hirers to arrangements which would see the latter pay at least as much as they might expect to pay if they were acquiring the goods on hire purchase. In such cases, hirers would obviously never become the owners of these goods, nor enjoy any of the protections of the hire-purchase legislation.[15] Accordingly, by virtue of s.101, however long the contractual period of hire may be, a hirer under a regulated consumer hire agreement may terminate the agreement if it has been running for at least 18 months. The hirer must give notice equivalent to the shorter of three months and the period between hire payments. The right does not apply to agreements:

(1) which require the hirer to pay more than £1,500 p.a.;
(2) where the hirer hires the goods for business purposes, and he selects goods which the owner then acquires from another at his request;
(3) where the hirer requires the goods to hire to another in the course of business.

These exceptions reflect the fact that the right is designed to protect consumer rather than business hirers and are designed to meet the concerns of commercial equipment leasing companies.

## 3.46. TERMINATION OF H.P. AND CONDITIONAL SALE AGREEMENTS

A debtor under such an agreement may terminate it and return the goods at any time before the final payment falls due by giving notice to the person authorised to receive payments under the agreement.[16] The debtor remains liable for all payments due prior to termination. He must also bring his payments up to half the total price, assuming that he has not already crossed this threshold. The agreement may stipulate a lesser but not a greater sum, while the court can itself order payment of a lesser sum, if it considers that sufficient to compensate the creditor, although it cannot relieve the debtor of existing liability.[17] The amount payable may be increased if the debtor has failed to take reasonable care of the goods. This right may assist a

---

[13] s.95. That formula is prescribed by the Consumer Credit (Rebate on Early Settlement) Regulations 1983 (SI 1983/1562). The DTI consulted in August 2002 about making the formula fairer to borrowers and ensuring that they are better informed about how it operates.
[14] s.96.
[15] *Galbraith v Mitchenall Estates Ltd* [1965] 2 Q.B. 473.
[16] s.99.
[17] s.100(3).

debtor who faces the prospect of default due to financial difficulties. Yet often such debtors cannot take advantage of it, as agreements commonly contain accelerated payments clauses. These indicate that if the debtor defaults on any payment, *all* payments to be made under the agreement (including of course the final payment) immediately become due. Such clauses would be penal in nature unless they offer the debtor some rebate for early settlement, but as they invariably do, thus far they have been held to be effective.[18] Even so, such a clause must now surely be challengeable, where the debtor is a consumer, under the Unfair Terms in Consumer Contracts Regulations 1999.[19] It may be pointed out that, despite its terms, such a clause cannot have immediate effect, as the creditor will require to serve a default notice (see para. 3.48.) before becoming entitled to an accelerated payment. Indeed, even on the expiry of the period allowed to remedy the default, the debtor may escape the effect of the clause by seeking a time order (see para. 3.51.). If, however, the clause does operate, the debtor will be entitled to claim either the rebate for early settlement allowed by the Act (see above) or the rebate allowed by the clause, whichever is more advantageous.

It may further be observed that where H.P. and conditional sale agreements fall outwith the scope of the Act, it is not uncommon to find minimum payments clauses, which commit debtors to paying very substantial sums where they elect to terminate the agreement. Because such sums, which very often are far in excess of any loss the creditor can suffer as a result of the termination, are payable upon the occurrence of a specified event, rather than upon a breach of contract, they cannot be considered to be penalties.[20] This has led Lord Denning to remark[21]:

> "Let no one mistake the injustice of this. It means that equity commits itself to this absurd paradox: it will grant relief to a man who breaks his contract, but will penalise the man who keeps it."

This has led to the courts at times treating what appears to be a straightforward notice of termination as an indication of a debtor's intention to default, thus allowing them to consider whether such payments were indeed penalties.[22] It must also now be questioned whether such clauses would be valid in terms of the Unfair Terms in Consumer Contracts Regulations 1999.

## 3.47. REPOSSESSION OF GOODS UNDER H.P. AND CONDITIONAL SALE AGREEMENTS

Of course a debtor may simply default without seeking to terminate, and ultimately the creditor may look to repossess the goods. The Act provides a limited degree of protection for a debtor who has paid a reasonable number of instalments by prescribing in s.90 that the creditor must obtain a court order to repossess the goods when the debtor is in default but has paid one third of the total price. If the creditor seeks to repossess in breach of the Act, s.91 provides that the agreement terminates, the debtor is entirely released from liability and can indeed recover all sums already paid. In *Kassam v Chartered Trust PLC*[23] K, having paid 40 per cent of the price of a car he had taken on H.P., decided he wanted to sell the car and handed it over to a car dealer. The Chartered Trust repossessed the car from the dealer without a court order. The Court of Appeal held that the provisions of ss.90 to 91 applied if the dealer held the car on behalf of K, but not if he held it as a party who had agreed to buy the car. Even apart from

---

[18] *Wadham Stringer Finance Ltd v Meaney* [1981] 1 W.L.R. 39.
[19] SI 1999/2083, Sch. 2, para. 1(e); and see Office of Fair Trading, *Unfair Contract Terms Bulletin,* No. 3, p.12.
[20] *EFT Commercial Ltd v Security Change Ltd (No. 1),* 1993 S.L.T. 128.
[21] In *Bridge v Campbell Discount Co* [1962] A.C. 600 at 626.
[22] *ibid.*
[23] [1998] R.T.R. 220.

these provisions, a court order is required by s.92 if the creditor wishes to enter upon any premises to take possession of goods (this provision also applies to goods hired by a consumer). Failure to observe the provisions of s.92 allows the debtor to recover damages for a breach of statutory duty.[24] None of these provisions applies if the debtor voluntarily consents to repossession.[25] Nor does s.90 apply where the creditor simply recovers goods abandoned by the debtor,[26] nor where the debtor voluntarily terminates the agreement. Yet the courts are slow to find that voluntarily termination has occurred. In *U.D.T. (Commercial) Ltd v Ennis*[27] the Court of Appeal held that a letter which stated "I am writing to inform you that I wish to terminate my agreement with you as I find I cannot fulfill the terms stated.", did not amount to a voluntary termination, as the debtor did not understand the consequences.

## 3.48. SERVICE OF DEFAULT NOTICE

The Act does not permit the creditor immediately to enforce his rights where the debtor is in breach. Thus under s.87 where the debtor is in breach the creditor must serve a default notice in prescribed form[28] before he can:

- terminate the agreement,
- demand earlier payment of any sum (as under an accelerated payment clause—see above),
- recover possession of any goods or land,
- treat any of the debtor's rights as terminated, restricted or deferred,
- enforce any security.

By contrast, a notice need not be served before the creditor may treat the debtor's right to draw on credit (*e.g.* under an overdraft or credit card) as restricted. Nor need a notice be served if the creditor merely wishes to sue for sums already due. When a notice requires to be served, it must indicate:

- the nature of the breach,
- what must be done to remedy it, if it is remediable, or the sum (if any) to be paid as compensation if it is not (the Act recognises the possibility of a breach being neither remediable nor compensatable),
- the consequences of failure to remedy the defect or pay the sum.

If the notice misstates any material particular, *e.g.* the amount the debtor requires to pay, it is invalid.[29] Otherwise the debtor must be given at least seven days to take the appropriate action, and if he does so, the breach is treated as never having occurred.[30] If the debtor fails to take the appropriate action within the relevant period, then obviously the creditor can proceed to exercise the available remedies. It should be noted that s.87 does not confer any remedies on the creditor. He is simply temporarily prevented from exercising certain of those he would have under the agreement.

### Non-default notice

The creditor must similarly give the debtor at least seven days notice before exercising a right to do any of the things mentioned in the above paragraph, which right is conferred by the

---

[24] s.92(3); and see *Ahmed v Toyota Finance,* 1996 G.W.D. 27–1566. If the goods are on hire, the hirer might also seek financial relief under s.132.
[25] s.173(3).
[26] *Bentinck v Cromwell Engineering Co* [1971] 1 Q.B. 324.
[27] [1968] 1 Q.B. 54.
[28] Enforcement, Default and Termination Notices Regulations 1983 (SI 1983/1561) as amended.
[29] *Woodchester Lease Management Services Ltd v Swain* [1999] C.C.L.R. 8, CA.
[30] s.89.

agreement although the debtor is not in breach.[31] This would cover the type of situation where, for example, the creditor is entitled to terminate the agreement at will, or upon the happening of a certain event. These provisions only apply to agreements which have a specified period of duration.

# (8) JUDICIAL CONTROL

## 3.49. GENERAL POWERS

The Act gives the sheriff considerable and flexible powers in relation to the agreement, which are generally exercised through the making of one or more of the orders created by the Act. In making these orders, the court has, under s.135, a general power to make the order conditional on a party doing specified acts, or to suspend the operation of the order for a particular period or until something is done. The court has power under s.136 to amend an agreement so as to give proper effect to any order. However, the court cannot extend the period for which a hirer is entitled to goods.[32] It has been held that s.136 does not give a court a wide power to adjust an agreement so as to amount to rewriting it, but merely power to make orders ancillary to the making of other orders.[33] Nor does the court have any power to make a "just" order, where any of the specific orders considered below cannot be made.[34]

## 3.50. ENFORCEMENT ORDERS

As has been seen (in para. 3.37.), when an agreement has been improperly executed, s.127 dictates that the creditor must obtain an enforcement order before he may enforce the agreement. Indeed where the agreement is cancellable, the agreement cannot be enforced even with such an order if there has been[35]:

- any failure to supply the requisite copies and the creditor has not supplied the debtor with a copy of the executed agreement prior to the commencement of court proceedings, or
- a breach of the provisions as to providing notification of the right to cancel.

Nor can the court make an order where the agreement fails to set out certain basic terms,[36] or is not signed by the debtor.[37] These basic terms are:

- a term stating how the debtor or hirer is to discharge his obligation to make payments under the agreement,
- a term stating any power of the creditor or owner to vary the amount payable,
- a term stating (in the case of a credit agreement) the amount of credit (or the credit limit) and the rate of interest on credit,

although in *Hatfield v Hiscox*[38] the judge held that the failure to state of the relevant documents "Credit Agreement regulated by the Consumer Credit Act 1974" and to state the relevant

---

[31] ss.76, 98.
[32] s.135(3).
[33] *J & J Securities v Lee,* 1994 C.C.L.R. 44.
[34] *Murie McDougall Ltd v Sinclair,* 1994 S.L.T. (Sh. Ct) 74.
[35] s.127(4).
[36] As prescribed by the Consumer Credit (Agreements) Regulations 1983 (SI 1983/1553), Sch. 6.
[37] s.127(3).
[38] 1998 C.C.L.R. 68; compare *Kemp v Ling,* 1998 C.L.Y. 2502; *Bhoyrub v Cazdow,* 1999 S.C.L.R 539.

protection and remedies available to the customer, all as required by the Consumer Credit (Agreements) Regulations 1983, did not amount to a failure to set out the the the prescribed terms. Rather, it was an "omission of information", so that the court was not precluded from enforcing the agreement. In *Dimond v Lovell*[39] (more fully discussed in para. 3.16.) the car-hire agreement was regarded as wholly unenforceable because the agreement failed to state the amount of credit. This was, of course, because the car-hire company was entirely unaware that it was granting credit. As the consumer had, in effect, used the car for free, the car-hire company could not recover the cost of hiring the car from the person responsible for damaging the consumer's own car. In *Wilson v First County Trust (No. 1)*[40] a document fee was wrongly added to the amount of a loan, rather than being described as part of the charge for credit. The Court of Appeal opined that if it was obliged to hold the agreement unenforceable in those circumstances, then s.127(3) was incompatible with the provisions of the European Convention on Human Rights protecting the right to property and guaranteeing a fair trial.

In those cases where the court has a discretion to make an order, in deciding whether it should do so, the court must have regard to the prejudice caused by the contravention, and the degree of culpability involved.[41] If it grants the order the court may also reduce[42] or extinguish any sum payable by the debtor or hirer or any surety.

## 3.51. TIME ORDERS

Under s.129, time orders may be sought by the debtor in two contexts: (1) where court action has been taken against him to enforce a regulated agreement, and (2) where he has been served with a default or non default notice. Such an order may be used for two broad purposes, first, to give the debtor a specified period of time to remedy any breach other than non-payment, and secondly, to reschedule the time and amounts of payments, having regard to the debtor's means. There seems to be some conflict in the authorities as to whether only sums due at the date of the order can be thus rescheduled, or all sums due under the agreement may be rescheduled.[43] In *Southern District Finance v Barnes*[44] it was suggested that if the creditor is seeking repossession of the land held in security for a loan, he is effectively demanding payment of all sums payable under the agreement, so the whole amount may be rescheduled. Of course, where an accelerated payments clause (see para. 3.45.) has operated, all sums under the agreement have inevitably become due.

Although in terms of factors to be taken into account, specific reference is only made to the debtor's means, the court refused to make an order in *First National Bank plc v Syed*[45] when there were considerable arrears, a very poor default record, and the payments which the debtor could afford would not even meet interest accrued. Similarly, in *Murie McDougall Ltd v Sinclair*[46] an order was refused when, under the proposed instalments, a loan intended to be paid off in a period of four years would have taken over 40 years to pay. It was further held that the powers of the court do not extend to varying the contractual rate of interest.

Section 130 deals with the situation where a debtor has made an offer to pay by instalments which the creditor has accepted. There a time order may be made without regard to the

---

[39] [2000] 2 All E.R. 897, HL.

[40] [2002] Q.B. 74. See also *McGinn v Grangewood Securities Ltd, The Times,* May 30, 2002, CA.

[41] s.127(1).

[42] As in *Rank Xerox v Hepple* [1994] C.C.L.R. 1.

[43] Cases like *J & J Securities v Lee* [1994] C.C.L.R. 44, assert the former, while cases like *Cedar Holdings v Thompson* [1993] C.C.L.R. 31, assert the latter.

[44] [1995] C.C.L.R. 52, CA.

[45] [1991] 2 All E.R. 250.

[46] 1994 S.L.T. (Sh. Ct) 74.

debtor's means, and in the case of H.P. or conditional sale agreements may deal with sums not yet due.

It is not clear whether the power to make time orders is intended to afford the debtor only temporary relief, or to allow the court very significantly to extend the term of the agreement.[47]

The DTI Consultation Document of March 2003, *Tackling Loan Sharks—and More!*, proposes to amend the legislation to make it clear that the latter is permissible, insisting that the court when using a time order considers the relief available under s.136 as regards amending the terms of the agreement, *e.g.* by adjusting the rate of interest. It also proposes to allow a borrower to apply for such an order to apply for a time order at any time during the agreement, rather than only when in default. It is further proposed that default notices be required to provide better information about the use of time orders. Finally, at the moment lay representatives cannot represent debtors who are seeking time orders before Scottish courts. It is proposed that lay representation be permitted.

## 3.52.   H.P. AND CONDITIONAL SALE—RETURN AND TRANSFER ORDERS

Under s.133 these can be made where, in relation to an H.P. or conditional sale agreement, an application for an enforcement or time order has been made, or the creditor has brought an action to recover possession of the goods. A return order is simply an order for the return of goods to the creditor. A transfer order is only feasible where the goods under the agreement are divisible. It transfers the title to part of the goods to the debtor, returning the remainder to the creditor. It is subject to the limitation that the amount already paid exceeds the part of the total price referable to the transferred goods by at least one-third of the unpaid balance of the total price. This can be represented algebraically by the formula $V = P - \frac{1}{3}U$, V standing for the maximum value of goods which may be transferred, P standing for the amount already paid, and U standing for the amount remaining unpaid. Notwithstanding a return or transfer order, a debtor may, at any time before the goods enter the possession of the creditor, pay the unpaid balance, fulfil any other conditions (if any), and claim the goods.[48] If the debtor fails to comply with a return or transfer order, the creditor may ask the court to revoke the order and instead order the debtor to pay for the goods retained.[49]

This section is designed to give the court the option, at least in those few cases where the goods under the agreement are divisible, to ensure that the debtor who has paid significant sums under the agreement, but cannot continue with it, is not left with nothing to show for his payments. The $V = P - \frac{1}{3}U$ formula, ensures that the court cannot intervene unless at least one-quarter of the price has been paid, and ensures that the creditor receives some degree of compensation for disappointed expectations and the fact that he will receive back second hand goods. So, in a case where the total price of the goods[50] is £6,000, and £1,500 has been paid, the operation of the formula will prevent any transfer order being made. (the amount paid—P—is £1,500, while the amount unpaid—U—is £4,500, so one-third of that figure is also £1,500.) The formula also sees the amount permitted to be transferred to rise sharply, the more of the price that has been paid. So, if in the above scenario £3,000 has been paid, the maximum value of goods which might be transferred is £2,000. But if £4,500 has been repaid, the maximum value of goods which might be transferred is £4,000. In other words a 50 per cent increase in the

[47] *Southern District Finance v Barnes* [1995] C.C.L.R. 52, CA, and see views of Lord Bingham in *Director General of Fair Trading v First National Bank* [2002] 1 All E.R 97 at 109–110.

[48] s.133(4).

[49] s.133(6).

[50] Including the deposit: s.133(2); and any sum payable on the exercise of an option to purchase: s.189(1).

amount paid, leads to a 100 per cent increase in the amount which might be retained. It must be emphasised that the formula is a restriction on judicial generosity. The court may not return goods to a higher value, but it may return goods to a lower value than allowed by the formula. Indeed it may be practically forced to do so, as where for example V = £4,000, and the goods held under the agreement are two items worth £5,000 and £1,000 respectively. It is also within the discretion of the court to decide not to make a transfer order at all. As to the question as to how value is ascribed to the goods held under the agreement, that will be done by the agreement itself, or failing that by the court.[51]

## 3.53. PROTECTION ORDERS

In terms of s.131, on the application of a creditor or owner, the court may make such order as it thinks just for the protection from damage or depreciation of his property or any property subject to a security, pending the outcome of proceedings under the Act. Such an order might restrict or prohibit the use of the property, or give directions as to its custody.

## 3.54. EXTORTIONATE CREDIT BARGAINS

Under s.137 the court is given extremely wide powers to reopen a credit bargain so as to do justice between the parties where it finds that bargain to be extortionate. It should be noted that a credit bargain is defined as any agreement where credit of any amount is provided to an individual. Thus, unlike the various orders under the Act, the power to reopen an extortionate credit bargain is not confined to regulated agreements. So a remedy may be sought under these provisions even where the credit exceeds £25,000. It may also be observed that the power does not apply to hire agreements. Hirers should instead seek financial relief under s.132 (see para. 3.56.). A credit bargain need not be a single agreement. It covers any transaction (*e.g.* arrangement fees) taken into account in calculating the total charge for credit.[52]

Under s.139(1) the debtor or any surety may take proceedings to have the bargain reopened, or may bring up the issue in any proceedings to which they are parties, or any proceedings to enforce the agreement or any security or linked transaction, or in any proceedings where the amount paid or payable under the credit agreement is relevant. The English courts have suggested that it may be possible for the court to raise the issue on its own initiative,[53] but it has been held in the sheriff court that this is incompetent.[54] The latter seems to be the correct view, as a DTI Consultation Document has suggested conferring precisely this power on the courts—although the DTI does not intend to pursue this suggestion.[55]

Where it is alleged that a credit bargain is extortionate, it is for the creditor to prove the contrary.[56] A credit bargain is extortionate if it requires the debtor (or a relative) to make payments which are grossly exorbitant, or otherwise grossly contravenes the principles of fair dealing[57]. In deciding whether a bargain is extortionate the court must have regard to any evidence relating to:

---

[51] s.133(7).
[52] s.137(2)(b)(ii).
[53] *First National Bank plc v Syed* [1991] 2 All E.R. 250 at 252, *per* Dillon L.J.
[54] *U.D.T. v McDowell,* 1984 S.L.T. (Sh. Ct) 10.
[55] See two documents entitled *Tackling Loan Sharks—and More: A Consultation Document on Modernising the Consumer Credit Act 1974,* August 2001, and March 2003.
[56] s.171(7).
[57] s.138(1).

- prevailing interest rates when the agreement was made;
- the debtor's age, experience, business capacity and state of health;
- the degree to which the debtor was under pressure at the time of the bargain and the nature of that pressure;
- the degree of risk undertaken by the creditor, taking into account the value of any security;
- the creditor's relationship with the debtor;
- whether or not a colourable cash price was quoted for any goods or services included in the bargain (this contemplates the situation where an apparently reasonable charge for credit conceals the fact that the cash price being employed is considerably higher than someone actually paying cash would pay);
- as regards a linked transaction, the extent to which it was reasonably required for the debtor's protection or was in the creditor's interests;
- any other relevant consideration.

It can be appreciated that several of the above factors may cut both ways. It may also be added that only those factors prevailing at the time of entry into the contract may be taken into account, so that it cannot be considered whether a credit bargain has become extortionate in light of the failure of the lender to lower interest rates in line with the market.[58]

When a bargain is reopened, the court may in terms of s.139(2) "for the purpose of relieving the debtor or a surety from payment of any sum in excess of that fairly due and reasonable", in effect rewrite the agreement—altering its terms, setting aside any obligation in whole or in part, ordering the repayment or part repayment of any sum, directing the return of property held as security, etc. There have been a number of cases where the provisions have been invoked, but these largely turn on the particular concatenation of facts. So while an APR of 39 per cent has been reduced to 30 per cent,[59] and APR of 42 per cent reduced to 21 per cent,[60] as in both cases the fact that security was provided for the loan was thought to render a higher than usual interest rate unnecessary, an APR of 48 per cent has been regarded as acceptable where there was a genuine risk being taken by the lender, and the borrower (unlike the other two cases) had business experience.[61] Thus it would be dangerous to seek to draw any principles of general application therefrom. It may be noted, nonetheless, that the Master of the Rolls in *Wills v Wood*[62] has emphasised that a bargain must be "extortionate" not merely "unwise", while in *Coldunell Ltd v Gallon*[63] the Court of Appeal was impressed by the fact that the creditor had "acted in the way that an ordinary commercial lender would be expected to act".[64] Likewise, Dyson L.J. in *Broadwick Financial Services Ltd v Spenceri*[65] noted that the test of extortionate was "very high", and not met simply because a lender does not inform borrowers that its mortgage rate does not reflect general variations in interest rates.

It may be added that certain terms which might be thought to be extortionate may also be challenged under the Unfair Terms in Consumer Contracts Regulations 1999.[66] The result of a successful challenge would render the term unenforceable.[67]

---

[58] *Paragon Finance plc v Nash*, [2002,] 2 All E.R. 248, CA. Although the court was prepared to imply a term into the contract that a lender would not operate a variable interest rate clause unreasonably, in the sense of dishonestly, for an improper purpose, capriciously or arbitrarily: see Dyson L.J. at 263g–h.

[59] *Devogate v Jarvis* (1987) unreported.

[60] *Prestonwell Ltd v Capon* (1987) unreported.

[61] *Ketley v Scott* [1981] I.C.R. 283.

[62] (1984) 128 S.J. 222.

[63] [1986] 1 All E.R. 429.

[64] But *cf. Devogate v Jarvis, Prestonwell Ltd v Capon (supra)*.

[65] [2002] 1 All E.R. (Comm.) 446.

[66] SI 1999/2083.

[67] *Falco Finance Ltd v Gough* [1999] C.C.L.R. 16.

## 3.55. REFORM OF THE EXTORTIONATE CREDIT PROVISIONS

It can be appreciated that the tests set by the above provisions are very demanding for a consumer to meet, and indeed few consumers have met them over the years. It is thought that fewer than 30 cases have been decided over the years, none in Scotland, and not that many in favour of consumers.[68] It was acknowledged over 10 years ago that the protections created by the Act were insufficient.[69] Subsequent research has revealed the widespread use of contracts which could be considered as wholly or partly extortionate, but a general unwillingness on the part of consumers to initiate proceedings, because of lack of resources or a fear of going to court—many of these consumers were among the most vulnerable people in society.[70] Accordingly, at the time of writing, the DTI is consulting on radical reform of the law in this area. Among the proposals put forward by the DTI Consultation Document of March 2003, *Tackling Loan Sharks—and More!*, are that:

(1) the "extortionate" test be replaced by a simple fairness test;
(2) the range of factors relevant to the question of fairness be expanded to include:

- whether the interest rate charged at the date of the bargain (and subsequently) is excessive in light of general interest rates, rates charged in that sector of the market, and rates charged by that provider;
- whether costs and charges are reasonable, having regard to the interest rate charged, whether they represent the creditor's actual loss from the debtor's default and the extent to which the debtor was made aware of them;
- whether the lender (or broker) engaged in any business behaviour or activity which was deceitful, oppressive, or otherwise unfair or improper;
- the lender's care and responsibility in making the loan, including the inquiries made to ensure that the debtor could afford the repayments,

(3) lenders be prohibited from charging interest on arrears at above the contractual rate;
(4) lenders be prohibited from charging interest on charges and fees under the agreement unless the fee/charge remains unpaid after a specified time period, *e.g.* allowing the debtor 28 days to pay any fee or charge before interest can be levied thereon;
(5) lenders be prohibited from charging compound interest, *i.e.* interest on unpaid interest;
(6) bodies such as the OFT to be entitled to seek a declaration that a particular practice was unfair;
(7) the creation of an accessible dispute resolution system, possibly (from the consumer's standpoint) low cost or no-cost, which might be an adjunct to or a replacement for the court process.

The document also asks whether there may be a need to set interest rate ceilings, or to set presumptive rates, which could only be exceeded with the prior approval of the OFT. (Although the DTI is not convinced that there is a need for such provisions.) Also being considered is whether there is a need to expand on the information required to be supplied to debtors, so that they are made aware, in particular, of any charges which may be levied on them, and the circumstances under which this may happen. Another possibility is to empower the OFT to issue restitution orders as a means of compensating consumers, who have not sought redress, in respect of particularly unfair practices.

---

[68] See *Tackling Loan Sharks—and More!* DTI Consultation Document, March 2003.
[69] OFT, *Unjust Credit Transactions*, 1991.
[70] Kempson and Whiley, *Extortionate Credit in the UK*, DTI 1999, and see also National Association of Citizens Advice Bureaux, *Daylight Robbery*, 2000.

## 3.56.  FINANCIAL RELIEF FOR HIRERS

Under s.132, where the owner of goods recovers them through or without taking court action, the hirer may request the court to order repayment of part or all of the sums repaid, and that the obligation to pay any sums owed shall cease. If it appears to the court just to do so, having regard to the extent of the enjoyment of the goods by the hirer, it may grant such an application in whole or in part. The provision is clearly designed to allow courts to afford a hirer, who has lost the goods, some degree of relief in situations where he might have to pay practically the full cost of hire without getting the corresponding benefit. Yet the courts thus far have shown little interest in exercising this discretion In *Automotive Financial Services Ltd v Henderson*[71] H, having agreed to lease a car for three years, returned it after six months, and ceased the monthly payments. A Ltd, as it was entitled to do under the agreement, rescinded and claimed the total of the sums due on termination of agreement. He requested relief under s.132, but relief was denied by the sheriff. The case for the defenders was that the pursuers having received six months hire payments and having resold the car, had already recouped more than the original value of the car. Therefore it was unjust that they should be able to recover the whole amount of the sums due on termination of agreement. It was suggested that it would be just to order payment of a lesser sum. This argument did not impress the sheriff, who observed,[72]:

> "The pursuers carry out a financing operation and clearly make their money by charging sums for the hire of a vehicle which, if totalled up add up to a figure some way over the price of the vehicle if that were simply bought by the customer. To suggest that the payments made should somehow entitle the customer to relief seems to me to be an unlikely proposition unless the defenders can set out a good reason why the pursuers should be satisfied in the commercial sense with what they have received. The defenders have not attempted to do so. Looking at the matter in another way, they have not even started to suggest that the payment sought is by way of a penalty."

The sheriff was held by the Sheriff Principal on appeal to have properly exercised his discretion.

---

[71] 1992 S.L.T. (Sh. Ct) 63.
[72] *ibid.*, at 64I–J.

# Chapter 4

# CARRIAGE OF GOODS

## 4.1. INTRODUCTION

Goods often have to be transported considerable distances, whether at the instance of a seller or buyer or otherwise, and a carrier is often employed to effect that transport. A contract of carriage is a contract for the hire of work and services, its essence being that the carrier is hired to carry goods safely from A to B in his own vehicle. If a seller agrees to transport goods to the buyer using his own vehicle, that is not a contract of carriage. Nor is it a contract of carriage if an individual merely hires a vehicle in order that he or his employees might collect goods he has ordered. There are three main forms of carriage—by land, sea and air and we shall outline the main features of the legal regimes relating to each, touching also on the issues raised by multimodal transport, *i.e.* where two or more of the above modes have to be combined.

# (1) CARRIAGE BY LAND

## 4.2. COMMON CARRIER

A carrier will either be a private carrier or a common carrier. A common carrier is someone who holds himself out as prepared to convey goods for anyone who chooses to contract with him.[1] He does not cease to be a common carrier just because in so holding out he places limitations on the places to which he will go,[2] or the type of goods he will carry,[3] or indicates that he will carry only under particular conditions.[4] Although whether a carrier falls to be regarded as a common carrier is essentially a question of fact,[5] it has been held that removal firms are not common carriers.[6] Moreover, by virtue of statute neither railway companies,[7] nor anyone providing a "universal postal service",[8] may be regarded as common carriers. It is also the case that standard form contracts in those industries which appear to involve common carriers tend to make it clear that they contract only on the basis that the carrier is not a common carrier.

Certain results flow from being a common carrier. First, he is taken to be making a continuing offer to carry (subject to any limitations as described above), which is open to be accepted by anyone.[9] If he refuses to carry goods when asked, he will be liable in damages,[10] unless the refusal is justified. Such refusal may be justified if:

- there is no capacity in his vehicle(s)—he is not bound to find extra capacity just because he is approached by a customer[11];
- the goods are not tendered at an appropriate time for loading[12];
- the consignor refuses to pay the freight in advance when asked to do so[13]—if the carrier carries the goods without requesting advance payment, he may not then demand payment until the carriage is complete, and is thus liable if he refuses to continue unless paid[14];
- carriage of the goods would be dangerous for himself, his employees, his vehicle, or other goods[15]—the consignor is liable to anyone who suffers loss or injury as a result of him entrusting dangerous goods to any carrier, common or otherwise, without advising the carrier of this.[16] It is not sufficient to label packaging as dangerous without properly advising the carrier of the nature of the danger[17];
- the goods are not adequately packed[18];
- the goods are of a nature that it is unreasonable to expect the carrier to carry, *e.g.* where they are of immense size[19];

---

[1] *Barr & Sons v Caledonian Railway Co* (1890) 18 R. 139.
[2] *Johnson v Midland Railway Co* (1849) 4 Exch. 367.
[3] *Dickson v Great Northern Railway Co* (1886) 18 Q.B.D. 176.
[4] *Great Northern Railway Co v L.E.P.* [1922] 2 K.B. 742.
[5] *Pearcey v Player* (1883) 10 R. 564.
[6] *ibid.*
[7] Transport Act 1962, s.43(6).
[8] Postal Services Act 2000, s.99.
[9] *Nugent v Smith* (1875) 1 C.P.D. 19 at 27.
[10] Bell, *Principles* s.159.
[11] *Spillers & Bakers v Great Western Railway Co* [1911] 1 K.B. 386 at 392.
[12] *Garton v Bristol & Exeter Railway Co* (1861) 30 L.J.Q.B. 273 at 293.
[13] *Wyld v Pickford* (1841) 8 M. & W. 443.
[14] *Barnes v Marshall* (1852) 18 Q.B. 785.
[15] *Barnfield v Goole & Sheffield Transport Co* [1910] 2 K.B. 94.
[16] *Cramb v Caledonian Railway Co* (1892) 19 R. 954.
[17] *ibid.*
[18] *Sutcliffe v Great Western Railway Co* [1910] 1 K.B. 478 at 503.
[19] *Date v Sheldon* (1921) 7 Ll.L. Rep. 53 at 54.

- the goods are of a value out of all proportion to the security measures he would have to take.[20]

A common carrier is bound by any rates advertised,[21] but in any case may not charge more than reasonable freight.[22] If he does charge more than is reasonable, then an action lies for the excess,[23] although as long as he does not exceed what is reasonable he is not bound to charge everyone the same rate.[24]

   The reason why a common carrier may refuse to carry goods of a value out of all proportion to the security measures he would have to take, is that he is strictly liable for the loss of or damage to the goods, even though there is no negligence on his part.[25] This is obviously a principle of central importance. There are a number of exceptions to this rule of strict liability. Thus the rule does not apply when the damage results from:

- an act of God, in the sense of a natural event which the carrier could not have predicted or guarded against, *e.g.* a sudden flood.[26] While an accidental fire would fall into this category, statute makes not only common carriers, but also private carriers liable for such damage.[27];
- an act of the Queen's enemies, in the sense of armed forces of a foreign power, rather than mere rebels or rioters[28];
- the inherent vice of the goods—this means a natural characteristic of the goods which lead to their damage, as where a horse became restless and injured itself trying to escape,[29] or where wine fermented and exploded during transit.[30] Naturally, a carrier cannot escape liability if an animal suffers injury because it is imperfectly secured[31];
- the fault of the consignor, as where the goods are inadequately addressed[32] or packaged,[33] or where the consignor insists on stowing the goods himself and does so ineffectively.[34]

It should also be noted that even where an exception applies, a common carrier will still be liable, if he or his employees by their negligence contributed to the loss,[35] or aggravated it once it had arisen.[36] Again these defences are not available if the carrier has deviated from the agreed route, unless the loss would have resulted even without the deviation.[37] While a common carrier will be liable for damage caused by unjustifiable delay in carriage,[38] if the delay was unavoidable, as where it was occasioned by an accident for which the carrier was not responsible, then no liability arises.[39] Of course, if delay is foreseeable, then the carrier will still be liable, unless he has warned the consignor of the possibility of delay.[40] This might arise, for example, where the carrier is aware that probable delays on a particular route might damage

---

[20] *McManus v Lancashire & Yorkshire Railway Co* (1859) 28 L.J. Ex. 353.
[21] *Campbell v Ker*, February 24, 1810, F.C.
[22] *Pickford v Grand Junction Railway Co* (1841) 8 M. & W. 372.
[23] *Baxendale v London and South West Railway Co* (1866) L.R.1 Ex. 137.
[24] *Great Western Railway Co v Sutton* (1866) L.R. 4 H.L. 226 at 237.
[25] Bell, *Principles*, s.235.
[26] *Makins v London & North Eastern Railway Co* [1943] K.B. 467.
[27] Mercantile Law Amendment (Scotland) Act 1856, s.17.
[28] *Curtis v Matthews* [1919] 1 K.B. 425.
[29] *Ralston v Caledonian Railway Co* (1878) 5 R. 671.
[30] *Farrar v Adams* (1711) Buller N.P. 69.
[31] *Paxton v North British Railway Co* (1870) 9 M. 50.
[32] *Hunter v Caledonian Railway Co* (1858) 20 D. 1097.
[33] *Gould v South Eastern Railway Co* [1920] 2 K.B. 186.
[34] *Rain v Glasgow & South-Western Railway Co* (1869) 7 M. 439.
[35] *Burns v Royal Hotel (St Andrews)*, 1958 S.C. 354.
[36] *Notara v Henderson* (1872) L.R. 7 Q.B. 225.
[37] *James Morrison & Co Ltd v Shaw, Savill and Albion Co Ltd* [1916] 2 K.B. 783.
[38] *Crawford v London, Midland & Scottish Railway Co*, 1929 S.N. 66.
[39] *Anderson v North British Railway Co* (1875) 2 R. 443.
[40] *McConnachie v Great North of Scotland Railway Co* (1875) 3 R. 79.

perishable goods. It might be added that where a delay does threaten perishable goods, a carrier who is unable to obtain the instructions of the consignor as to their disposal, is constituted as an agent of necessity to sell them.[41]

## 4.3. STATUTORY LIMITATION ON LIABILITY OF COMMON CARRIER

The strict liability of a common carrier at common law could clearly operate very onerously, particularly where the contents of very small packages turned out to be of immense value. Thus the Carriers Act 1830, s.1 provides that no common carrier shall be liable for loss or injury to a parcel or package containing certain types of article, the total value of which exceeds £10, unless the nature and value of such articles is declared to the carrier on delivery and any increased charge is paid. The types of article covered by the Act are generally things which tend to be valuable and/or fragile, *e.g.* gold, silver, precious stones, timepieces, paintings.[42] To entitle the carrier to levy the increased charge, he must affix in a conspicuous part of his premises a legible notice stating the increased charge.[43] If he fails in this, he may not levy the increased charge, and is liable to refund the excess,[44] but does not forfeit the protection of the Act.[45] Where the consignor has made the requisite declaration and paid any increased charge, he is entitled to recover the value of any goods lost, plus the amount of any increased charge,[46] although the carrier may attempt to prove that the actual value of the goods is less than their declared value.[47] If the consignor has either not made the requisite declaration, or not paid any properly levied increased charge, then he may not recover the value of the items lost or damaged, although if the items consigned were a mixture of articles covered by the Act and articles outwith its scope, the carrier remains strictly liable for the loss of the latter category of goods.[48] It might be added that the carrier cannot claim the protection of the Act where the loss or damage results from the dishonesty of his employee.[49] Nor does the Act absolve an employee from any personal liability, *e.g.* as might arise as a result of his dishonest or negligent behaviour.[50] It is always open to a carrier to make a special contract with a consignor, excluding the effect of the Act, and perhaps either excluding or limiting any liability to that consignor.[51]

## 4.4. PRIVATE CARRIER

If a carrier is not a common carrier, then he must be a private carrier. By definition, none of the consequences of being a common carrier apply to a private carrier. Thus he does not make a standing offer to carry, and thus can decide with whom he will contract. Moreover, he is not restricted as to the terms on which he will contract, in particular as to the amount of freight he

---

[41] *Forth Tugs Ltd v Wilmington Trust Co,* 1985 S.C. 317.
[42] See s.1.
[43] s.2.
[44] s.3.
[45] *Rusk v North British Railway Co,* 1920 2 S.L.T. 139.
[46] s.7.
[47] s.9.
[48] *Treadwin v Great Eastern Railway Co* (1868) L.R. 3 C.P. 308.
[49] s.7.
[50] s.8.
[51] s.6.

charges. Nor is he subject to the strict liability of the common carrier. However, he does undertake to exercise reasonable care in the exercise of the contract.[52] And while it is for the consignor to prove negligence or breach of duty,[53] the fact that goods delivered to him in good condition are then delivered by him in a damaged state is *prima facie* evidence of fault.[54]

## 4.5. EXCLUSION OF LIABILITY

The Unfair Contract Terms Act 1977 applies to all contracts of carriage.[55] Thus any contractual term or notice which purports to exclude or restrict liability for breach of any duty to take reasonable care or exercise reasonable skill, which duty arises in the course of a business out of a term of a contract or at common law, shall only have effect if it was fair and reasonable to incorporate it into the contract.[56] Equally, a term in a consumer or standard form contract, which purports to exclude or restrict liability for breach of contract only receives effect if it was fair and reasonable to incorporate it into the contract.[57] Thus any exclusion or limitation clause in a contract with a private carrier or a special contract with a common carrier is potentially liable to being struck down by the 1977 Act. It is also the case that an exclusion clause in a standard form contract of carriage with a consumer may be struck down as unfair under the Unfair Terms in Consumer Contracts Regulations 1999.[58] Yet nothing in that Act prevents a common carrier entering into a special contract with a consignor, which excludes his strict liability at common law. It should be pointed out, however, that a common carrier may not exclude liability by notice, only by agreement.[59] Without going into the law as to formation of contracts, it may also be observed that an issue may sometimes arise as to whether an exclusion or limitation clause is properly incorporated into the contract.[60] Moreover, exclusion or limitation clauses are construed *contra proferentem*. Thus in a contract with a common carrier such a clause would have to make it clear whether it intended to exclude strict common law liability, liability for negligence, liability for breach of contract, or all of these things. In *Graham v Shore Porters Society*[61] when the clause simply baldly excluded liability, it was construed as excluding only strict common law liability, leaving liability for negligence or breach of contract unaffected. Again, liability for negligence will usually only be held to be excluded if the clause explicitly says so, or this is the only meaning it can reasonably bear.[62] It has been held that unjustified deviation from the agreed route prevents a carrier relying on exclusion or limitation clauses.[63] There would appear to be no logical reason why this should be so, provided the exclusion clause were sufficiently widely drawn to accommodate such a breach of contract. Yet to the argument that the question whether a party can rely on an exclusion clause to justify his own serious breach has long been acknowledged to be a matter of construction rather than principle, it might be responded that Lord Wilberforce in Photo Productions Ltd v Securicor Transport Ltd[64] suggested that the deviation cases were sui generis and subject to special rules.[65]

---

[52] *Boomsma v Clark & Rose*, 1983 S.L.T. (Sh. Ct) 67.
[53] *Copland v Brogan*, 1916 S.C. 277.
[54] *Sutton & Co v Ciceri & Co* (1890) 17 R. (H.L.) 40.
[55] s.15(2)(c).
[56] ss.16(1)(b), 25(1).
[57] s.17(1).
[58] 1999 (SI 1999/2083).
[59] Carriers Act 1830 s.4.
[60] *McCutcheon v MacBrayne (David) Ltd*, 1964 S.L.T. 66.
[61] 1979 S.L.T. 119.
[62] *Page v London, Midland & Scottish Railway Co Ltd* [1943] 1 All E.R. 455.
[63] *Lord Polwarth v North British Railway Co*, 1908 S.C. 1275.
[64] [1980] A.C. 827 at 845F.
[65] But see Lloyd L.J. in *The Antares* (No. 1 and 2) [1987] 1 Lloyd's Rep. 424 at 430.

## 4.6.   DURATION OF LIABILITY

A carrier's duties operate from the point at which the goods are delivered to him[66] (or his agent or employee), until he delivers the goods to the consignee or to another carrier to continue their journey.[67] That being said, it is possible for the parties to settle the duration of carriage by agreement, *e.g.* by stipulating that it (and thus any duty attached thereto) terminates when the goods are delivered to the consignee's address, whether or not he is there to receive them. Where the goods are not to be delivered to the consignee's premises, as where the consignee is supposed to collect them from the carrier's local office, the consignee must be informed of their arrival and allowed a reasonable time to collect them, the carriage being deemed to continue during that period.[68] Moreover, if the consignee refuses or delays to receive the goods, or turns out not to exist, then the character of the carrier's stewardship of the goods alters to that of a mere depositary or warehouseman, thus liable only to take reasonable care of them until the consignor receives them back.[69] It does not amount to delivery simply to leave the goods at the carrier's premises,[70] nor to hand them over to his employees en route,[71] unless they have been instructed to collect them.[72] Obviously, if the carrier misdelivers the goods, he will be liable for any loss. Yet in turn he may recover the value of the goods from the person to whom they were wrongly delivered, unless he is personally barred from doing so.[73] If, on the other hand, the carrier delivers to the correct address and to an apparently authorised person, he is not liable if that person misappropriates the goods.[74]

## 4.7.   THE CARRIER'S LIEN

Once the contract has been carried out, a carrier has a special lien over the goods for the freight charges under the contract,[75] but has no general lien in respect of outstanding charges under other contracts of carriage involving that consignor.[76] Yet such a general lien can be created by contract,[77] and most standard form contracts will do so. It was seen in the context of sale of goods how an unpaid seller of goods who exercises the right to stop goods in transit may instruct the carrier to redeliver the goods.[78] This right yields to a carrier's special lien, so that a carrier may refuse to redeliver the goods unless the freight charges are paid. However, the right will prevail over a general lien, unless the seller was a party to the agreement creating that lien.[79]

---

[66] *Bain v Brown* (1824) 3 S. 256.
[67] *Gilmour v Clark* (1853) 15 D. 478.
[68] *Chapman v Great Western Railway Co* (1880) 5 Q.B.D. 278 at 281, *per* Cockburn C.J.
[69] Bell, *Principles*, s.235; *Metzenburg v Highland Railway Co* (1869) 7 M. 919.
[70] Bell, *Principles*, s.162.
[71] *ibid.*
[72] *ibid.*
[73] *Caledonian Railway Co v Harrison & Co* (1879) 7 R. 151.
[74] *British Traders Ltd v Unique Transport Ltd* [1952] 2 Lloyd's Rep. 236.
[75] *Scottish Central Railway Co v Ferguson, Rennie & Co* (1864) 2 M. 781.
[76] *Peebles & Son v Caledonian Railway Co* (1875) 2 R. 346.
[77] *Great Eastern Railway Co v Lord's Tr.* [1909] A.C. 109.
[78] Sale of Goods Act 1979, s.46(4).
[79] *United States Steel Products Co v Great Western Railway Co* [1916] 1 A.C. 189.

# (2) INTERNATIONAL CARRIAGE

The above account, like the rest of the book, states the law as it applies to Scotland. However, without going into the intricacies of private international law, if a transaction has an international dimension, it is by no means certain that it would be governed by Scots law. We are obviously not going to consider how various foreign systems might treat carriage of goods by land, but the UK is a party to certain international conventions which govern international carriage of goods by land, so that the principles governing most contracts of that nature are clear.

# (3) INTERNATIONAL CARRIAGE OF GOODS BY ROAD

## 4.8.   THE GENEVA CONVENTION

The UK is a party to the Geneva Convention on Contracts for the International Carriage of Goods by Road, which receives effect through the Carriage of Goods by Road Act 1965. The Convention applies to contracts of carriage of goods by road for reward where the places of uplifting and delivery are in two different countries, at least one of which is a party to the Convention.[80] Obviously, the Convention does not apply where carriage occurs wholly within the UK, and nor does it apply to carriage between the UK and the Channel Islands[81] or the Republic of Ireland.[82] There are also specific exclusions in respect of furniture removal and the carriage of mail or funeral consignments.[83] The Convention does not generally apply to multimodal transport, *e.g.* carriage partly by road and partly by sea.[84] Yet it does apply if goods are carried for part of the journey by some other means, as long as they never leave the vehicle, *e.g.* where a lorry carrying goods spends part of the journey aboard a ferry.[85] That being said, for the Convention to apply there must be an international element to the carriage of goods. The Convention would not apply, for example, if a lorry carried goods from Glasgow to Dover, was then placed on a ferry, and immediately unloaded on reaching France.[86] Where the Convention does apply, and loss, damage or delay occurs during carriage by the other mode of transport, then the carrier's liability will usually be determined according to the law applicable to the other mode of transport.[87] Finally, it may be observed, that although parties may not contract out of the Convention,[88] they may contract into it, by invoking its terms when it would not otherwise apply.[89]

---

[80] Art. 1(1).
[81] *Chloride Industrial Batteries Ltd v F & W Freight Ltd* [1989] 1 W.L.R. 823.
[82] Art. 1(5).
[83] Art. 1(4).
[84] But see *Quantum Corp Ltd v Plane Trucking Ltd* [2002] 2 Lloyd's Rep. 25, CA.
[85] Art. 2(1).
[86] *Princes Buitoni v Hapag-Lloyd Aktiengesellschaft* [1991] 2 Lloyd's Rep. 383.
[87] Art. 2(1).
[88] Art. 41(1).
[89] *Princes Buitoni v Hapag-Lloyd Aktiengesellschaft* [1991] 2 Lloyd's Rep. 383.

## 4.9.   CONSIGNMENT NOTE

While the Convention says nothing about the contract's constitution, each contract must be confirmed by a consignment note, signed by both parties[90]—one for each party and one to accompany the goods.[91] The note must contain key particulars and statements,[92] and should contain a description of the goods if they are dangerous.[93] The carrier will not be liable for any loss which derives from inadequacy of particulars in the note.[94] On receiving the note, the carrier must check whether statements in the note as to such things as the condition of the goods are accurate, and if he cannot check, he must enter his reservations on the note.[95] The note is *prima facie* evidence of the receipt of the goods, the making of the contract and any conditions mentioned therein.[96] Failure to issue the note has no effect on the validity of the underlying contract, which continues to be subject to the Convention.[97] However, if it is not issued, or even if it fails to indicate that the carriage is subject to the provisions of the Convention, the carrier cannot rely on the limitations on his liability described below.[98]

## 4.10.   DISPOSAL AND DELIVERY

The consignment note must indicate the destination of the goods and the consignee's name and address.[99] The consignor has control over the goods and may alter the place of delivery or indicate a new consignee or stop the goods in transit.[1] The only limitations on this right is that any instructions given must not divide the consignment,[2] or interfere with the carrier's undertaking or prejudice the consignors or consignees of other consignments he is carrying.[3] Otherwise, the carrier must obey any instructions given,[4] and is liable for any loss or damage resulting from his failure to do so.[5] The consignor loses control over the goods when:

- the consignee receives his copy of the consignment note,[6]; or
- when the goods arrive at the designated delivery place, and the consignee produces a receipt and requires their delivery and the delivery of his copy of the consignment note,[7]; or
- when the goods fail to arrive at their contractual destination, and the consignee seeks to enforce his contractual rights.[8]

If carriage or delivery is rendered impossible, the carrier must seek instructions from the party entitled to dispose of the goods.[9] If they are still in transit, he may take the steps he considers

---

[90] Art. 4.
[91] Art. 5(1).
[92] See Art. 6.
[93] Art. 22(1).
[94] Art. 7.
[95] Art. 8.
[96] Art 9; but *prima facie* evidence can of course be rebutted: see *Ulster-Swift Ltd v Taunton Meat Haulage Ltd* [1975] 2 Lloyd's Rep. 502.
[97] Art. 4.
[98] Art. 7(3).
[99] Art. 6(1)(d) and (e).
[1] Art. 12(1).
[2] Art. 12(5)(c).
[3] Art. 12(5)(b).
[4] Art. 12(2).
[5] Art. 12(7).
[6] Art. 12(2).
[7] Art. 13(1).
[8] Arts 12(2) and 13(1).
[9] Art. 14(1).

to be in that party's best interests.[10] That may mean their unloading, storage or sale. Sale is possible without instructions if[11];

- the goods are perishable or their condition warrants sale; or
- the storage expenses would be disproportionate the value of the goods; or
- if after a reasonable time he has not received reasonable instructions to the contrary from the party entitled to dispose of the goods.

It is that party who is entitled to the proceeds of sale.[12]

## 4.11. LOSS, DAMAGE OR DELAY

The carrier is *prima facie* liable for any loss, damage or delay occurring during carriage.[13] Delay occurs when the goods have not been delivered within the agreed time limit, or if there is none, within a reasonable time.[14] If the goods have not been delivered within 30 days of the agreed time limit, or if there is none, within 60 days of the carrier receiving the goods, they are treated as lost.[15] However, the carrier is not liable if the loss, damage or delay is caused by[16]:

- the wrongful act or neglect of the claimant;
- the claimant's instructions (if not attributable to the wrongful act or neglect of the carrier);
- the inherent vice of the goods—the frozen food being carried on a refrigerated vehicle has no inherent vice[17];
- circumstances which he was unable to avoid and the consequences of which he was unable to prevent, *e.g.* when goods are violently hijacked.[18] In deciding whether the carrier could have avoided the peril, it must be shown that he did his utmost, short of carrying precautions to unreasonable extremes. Acting as a normal prudent carrier would act is not enough.[19]

The burden of proof in relation to these exceptions lies on the carrier.[20] He is further exempted from the special risks inherent in[21]:

- carriage in open, unsheeted vehicles, when this has been expressly agreed and specified in the consignment note,[22];
- absent or inadequate packing of goods liable to wastage or damage if not properly packed[23];
- the handling, loading, stowage or unloading of goods by the sender or consignee or persons acting for them[24];
- the nature of goods which particularly exposes them to loss or damage, especially through breakage, rust, decay, desiccation, leakage, wastage, or the action of moth or

---

[10] Art. 14(2).
[11] Art. 16(3).
[12] Art. 16(4).
[13] Art. 17(1).
[14] Art. 19.
[15] Art. 20(1).
[16] Art. 17(2).
[17] *Ulster-Swift Ltd v Taunton Meat Haulage Ltd* [1975] 2 Lloyd's Rep. 502.
[18] *G. L. Cicatiello SRL v Anglo-European Shipping Services Ltd* [1994] 1 Lloyd's Rep. 678.
[19] *J. J. Silber Ltd v Islander Trucking Ltd* [1985] 2 Lloyd's Rep. 243.
[20] Art. 18.
[21] Art. 17(4).
[22] Art. 17(4)(a).
[23] Art. 17(4)(b).
[24] Art. 17(4)(c).

vermin[25]—although this exemption does not apply where the carriage is performed in a specially equipped vehicle, unless the carrier can show that it was properly chosen, maintained and employed.[26] It may be added that the fact that goods are susceptible to damage through over-freezing does not make them liable to "decay"[27];

- insufficient or inadequate marking or numbering of packages[28];
- the carriage of livestock[29]—as long as he can show he took all proper steps for their care.[30].

Where he can show that the loss or damage could be attributed to any such risk, this will be presumed to be the case,[31] and it falls to the claimant to prove otherwise.[32]

## 4.12.  THE LIABILITY OF THE SENDER

The sender of goods may also be liable to the carrier under the Convention. So he is liable for any loss, damage or expense attributable to:

- inaccuracy or inadequacy of the consignment note[33];
- defective packaging, unless apparent or known to the carrier on receipt of the goods[34];
- the absence, irregularity or inadequacy of documents or other information required to be given to the carrier for the purpose of completing customs or other formalities[35];
- the dangerous nature of the goods, unless the carrier is made aware of such danger.[36]

## 4.13.  COMPENSATION AND LIMITS THEREON

If a carrier is held liable for loss of or damage to the goods, compensation is assessed by reference to their value at the place and time at which they were accepted for carriage.[37] Value is determined according to the commodity exchange price, failing which the current market price, or failing both the normal price for goods of that kind and quality.[38] Liability for loss is moreover limited to 8.33 units of account per kilo of gross weight short.[39] However, if the sender, on payment of an agreed surcharge, declares in the consignment note a specific value, it is the declared value which sets the limit of the carrier's liability.[40] The carrier must also refund the carriage charges, customs duties, and other charges in respect of carriage.[41] In the case of

---

[25] Art. 17(4)(d).
[26] Art. 18(4).
[27] *W Donald & Son (Wholesale Meat Contractors) Ltd v Continental Freeze Ltd*, 1984 S.L.T. 182.
[28] Art. 17(4)(e).
[29] Art. 17(4)(f).
[30] Art. 18(5).
[31] Art. 18(2).
[32] Art. 18(3).
[33] Art. 7(1).
[34] Art. 10.
[35] Art. 11(2).
[36] Art. 22(2).
[37] Art. 23(1).
[38] Art. 23(2).
[39] Art. 23(3).
[40] Art. 24.
[41] Art. 23(4) and see *Sandeman Comprimas SA v Transitor y Transporter Integrales SL* [2003] 3 All E.R. 108, C.A.

damage amounting to less than total destruction, compensation reflects the amount by which the goods have diminished in value, and a proportionate amount of the charges, etc. must be refunded.[42] Yet compensation for damage cannot exceed the amount payable for total loss.[43] Liability for delay is limited to the amount of the carriage charges.[44] Yet if the sender has fixed the amount of a special interest in delivery by stipulating it in the consignment note, the carrier may be liable up to that amount in the case of delay, damage or non-delivery, in addition to his normal liability.[45] The carrier may not avail himself of any provision excluding or limiting his liability, or shifting the burden of proof, if the loss, delay or damage was caused by his wilful misconduct, or by any default regarded as such by the law of the country in which the proceedings are held.[46] The limitation provisions apply to delictual and restitutionary as well as contractual claims,[47] and embrace all individuals for whom the carrier is responsible.[48] In terms of establishing liability, taking delivery without checking the condition of the goods, or without giving a general indication of loss or damage to the carrier, is *prima facie* evidence of receipt in good condition.[49] Reservations must be intimated at the time of delivery if the loss or damage is apparent, and within seven days of delivery if it is not.[50] Where the goods are delayed, written reservation must be sent to the carrier within 21 days of delivery if compensation is to be payable.[51]

## 4.14. MULTIPLE CARRIERS

It may be that the sender enters into separate contracts with a number of different carriers in respect of the same consignment. Yet if the main carrier himself employs one or more carriers for different stages of the journey, each becomes a party to the main contract by his acceptance of the goods and the consignment note,[52] thus each becoming responsible for the entire carriage. Where this happens, proceedings may be brought against the first and last carriers as well as the carrier responsible for the portion of the carriage wherein the loss, damage or delay occurred, or against any combination of the three.[53] In *Parr v Clark & Rose Ltd*[54] it was held that while, in terms of Art. 4, failure to issue a consignment note has no effect on the validity of the underlying contract, which continues to be subject to the Convention, failure to provide a succeeding carrier with the consignment note is fatal to the potential liability of that carrier under Art. 34.

An action can only be raised[55]:

- in the court of a contracting state agreed between the parties; or
- in the court of the country where the defender is ordinarily resident, or has his principal place of business, or where is situated the branch or agency through which the contract was made; or
- in the court of the country where the carrier received the goods;

---

[42] *William Tatton & Co Ltd v Ferrymasters Ltd* [1974] 1 Lloyd's Rep. 203.
[43] Art. 25.
[44] Art. 23(5).
[45] Art. 26.
[46] Art. 29(1).
[47] Art. 28(1).
[48] Art. 28(2).
[49] Art. 30(1).
[50] Art. 30(2).
[51] Art. 30(3).
[52] Art. 34.
[53] Art. 36.
[54] 2002 S.C.L.R. 222.
[55] Art. 31(1).

- in the court of the country where the goods are supposed to be delivered.

No action may be raised if an action on the same grounds between the same parties is pending in a court of one of the states described above.[56]

As between the carriers themselves, the assumption is that the carrier responsible for the loss or damage should bear the ultimate liability for compensation, and that any other carrier who has had to meet a claim may therefore seek an indemnity or contribution.[57] Where more than one carrier is responsible, they bear a proportionate share of the loss,[58] and if it is not possible to determine who is responsible, then each carrier bears a share of the loss which reflects his share of the payment for carriage.[59] A similar apportionment occurs if a carrier who was partially or wholly liable to meet a claim becomes insolvent.[60] Although the question of contribution can be dealt with as ancillary to the main action,[61] separate contribution proceedings can only be brought before court of the country where the carrier from whom contribution is sought is ordinarily resident, or has his principal place of business, or where is situated the branch or agency through which the contract was made.[62] It should be noted that all provisions relating to indemnity or contribution are subject to contrary agreement between the carriers.[63] If the carrier from whom indemnity or contribution is claimed has had notice of the main proceedings, and has had an opportunity of entering an appearance therein, he may not dispute the validity of any payment made by the carrier seeking indemnity or contribution, if the amount of that payment was determined by the court.[64] The right to recover against another carrier may not be enforced, however, until the carrier seeking indemnity or contribution has actually made the payment.[65]

## 4.15.  LIMITATION OF ACTIONS

Any action arising from the contract of carriage is time-barred after a year, or after three years if wilful misconduct is involved. The limitation period runs[66]:

- in the case of delay, damage or partial loss, from the date of delivery;
- in the case of total loss, from the 30th day after the expiry of the agreed time limit for delivery, or if there is no time limit, from the 60th day from the date when the carrier received the goods;
- in all other cases on the expiry of three months from the making of the contract.

The making of a written claim suspends the running of the period, until the carrier rejects the claim in writing.[67] The limitation period also applies to claims for indemnity or contribution as between carriers, running from the date of the final judicial decision fixing compensation, or in the absence of a judicial decision, from the actual date of payment.[68]

---

[56] *ibid.*, and see *Andrea Merzario Ltd v Internationale Spedition Leitner Gesellschaft* [2001] 1 Lloyd's Rep. 490.

[57] Art. 37(a).

[58] Art. 37(b).

[59] Art. 37(c).

[60] Art. 38.

[61] *Cummins Engine Co Ltd v Davis Freight Forwarding (Hull) Ltd* [1981] 1 W.L.R. 1363.

[62] Art. 39(2).

[63] Art. 40.

[64] Art. 39(1).

[65] *ITT Schaub-Lorenz Vertriebgesellschaft GmbH v Birkart Johann Internationale Spedition GmbH* [1988] 1 Lloyd's Rep. 487.

[66] Art. 32(1).

[67] Art. 32(2).

[68] Art. 39(4).

# (4) INTERNATIONAL CARRIAGE OF GOODS BY RAIL

## 4.16. INTRODUCTION TO INTERNATIONAL CARRIAGE OF GOODS BY RAIL

The UK is a party to the 1980 Berne Convention concerning International Carriage by Rail, which receives effect through the International Transport Conventions Act 1983. That Convention in Appendix B contains the Uniform Rules concerning Contracts for the International Carriage of Goods by Rail. They apply to contracts of carriage of goods under a through consignment note made out for carriage over the territories of at least two contracting states, and exclusively over listed railway lines,[69] including for this purpose certain road, canal and shipping services which are complementary to rail services.[70] The carrier must carry the goods in complete wagon loads, provided he has the facilities to do so,[71] and the carriage can be undertaken without delay.[72] Certain articles are unacceptable,[73] *e.g.* goods which are too heavy to be carried by rail, while others, such as livestock, may be carried under conditions.[74]

## 4.17. CONSIGNMENT NOTE

The Rules only apply if a consignment note is made out,[75] and the consignor must present a separate note for each consignment of not more than a single wagon load.[76] The note provides evidence of the making of the contract and its contents,[77] and must be produced in the event of a claim.[78] There are two standard forms of consignment note.[79] That which demands *grand vitesse* requires the goods to be dispatched within 12 hours of receipt and for them to travel at least 300 kilometres every 24 hours. That which demands *petite vitesse* requires the goods to be dispatched within 24 hours of receipt and for them to travel at least 200 kilometres every 24 hours. The contract is made as soon as the carrier has accepted the goods and consignment note,[80] the consignor being responsible for all inaccuracies and irregularities in the note,[81] and for attaching any documents required for customs.[82] The consignor will also be responsible for the packing and marking of the goods if that is necessary,[83] while responsibility for loading goods depends entirely on the provisions which apply at the relevant station.[84] The carrier is entitled to ascertain the numbers of packages and weight of the goods and verify that they are as described in the note.[85]

---

[69] Art. 1(1).
[70] Art. 2(2).
[71] Art. 3(2).
[72] Art. 3(3).
[73] Art. 4.
[74] Art. 5.
[75] Art. 1(1).
[76] Art. 12.
[77] Art. 11.
[78] Art. 28.
[79] Art. 27.
[80] Art. 11(1).
[81] Art. 18(1).
[82] Art. 25.
[83] Art. 19.
[84] Art. 20(2).
[85] Arts 21–22.

## 4.18.  CARRIAGE

The consignor may stipulate the route,[86] and during the carriage may modify the instructions given in the note, by indicating a new consignee or destination, or stopping the goods in transit, or ordering their return.[87] Carriage ends, however, when the consignment note is handed to the consignee, or he accepts the goods, or where they reach their destination and the consignee demands their delivery and that of the note, or where they reach the territory of the country of destination and the consignor has not undertaken to pay the carriage charges in that country.[88] If carriage has been prevented, the carrier must decide whether to alter the route or to ask the person entitled to dispose of the goods for instructions.[89] Instructions must always be sought if it is impossible to continue the carriage.[90] Those instructions may be sent to the station from which the goods were sent or the station at which they are held. If the instructions are sent to the latter station, or involve the changing of the consignee or destination, the consignor must enter them on his copy of the consignment note given to the carrier.[91] If instructions are not given within a reasonable time, the carrier may act in accordance with the provisions in force at the station at which the goods are held or at the place of delivery.[92] Should such action involve the sale of the goods, the proceeds are held at the consignor's disposal, subject to deduction of the carriage charges.[93] Should carriage or delivery become possible, then carriage should resume or the goods should be delivered without seeking instructions.[94]

## 4.19.  LIABILITY OF CARRIER

The carrier is liable for delay, damage or loss during carriage.[95] Broadly the same exemptions from liability that apply in the case of carriage by road (see para. 4.11.) apply also in this case. Where the goods have to be carried by sea as well as rail, then (assuming the Convention applies) the carrier may also exempt himself from liability in respect of negligent handling of the ship, its unseaworthiness (if he can show he is not at fault), and other perils of the sea.[96] If goods have to be carried by road as well as rail, the Geneva Convention applies, unless it can be shown that the loss or damage could only have occurred while the goods were on the railway. Provisions relating to limitation of liability in respect of loss are similar to those under the Geneva Convention (see para. 4.13.), save that liability for loss is limited to 17 (as opposed to 8.33) units of account per kilo of gross mass short.[97] As regards liability for delay, if that delay caused actual loss or damage, compensation may not exceed three times the amount of the carriage charges, and may not in any case exceed the amount payable for a total loss.[98] Liability for damage should reflect the amount by which the goods have diminished in value.[99] The maximum compensation limits are doubled where loss, damage or delay is attributable to

---

[86] Art. 15.
[87] Art. 30.
[88] Art. 30(4).
[89] Art. 33(1).
[90] Arts 33(2) and 34(1).
[91] Art. 33(4).
[92] Arts 33(6) and 34(6).
[93] *ibid*.
[94] Arts 33(7) and 34(2);).
[95] Art. 36.
[96] Art. 48(1).
[97] Art. 40(1).
[98] Art. 43(5).
[99] Art. 42.

the carrier's gross negligence, and entirely removed if attributable to his wilful misconduct.[1] The carrier which accepted the goods will always be liable, as will the carrier of destination, but any intermediate carrier is only liable if the delay, damage or loss occurred on its system.[2] A carrier can only be sued in the courts of his own state.[3] Acceptance of the goods extinguishes all rights of action, subject to the following exceptions,[4]:

- where wilful misconduct or gross negligence is proved;
- claims for delay in delivery can be made within 60 days of acceptance;
- claims for partial loss or damage remain open if the loss or damage was pointed out before acceptance;
- claims for loss or damage which is not apparent are open if the carrier is asked to account for it within seven days of acceptance.

Provisions regarding limitation of actions once again resemble those under the Geneva Convention.[5]

## 4.20. CARRIAGE CHARGES

The carrier is entitled to payment of charges calculated in accordance with legal tariffs, which may also have to be published if the particular state so requires.[6] He may also levy special surcharges[7] and claim for disbursements.[8] Such tariffs must be applied to all users.[9]

# (5) CARRIAGE BY AIR

## 4.21. INTRODUCTION TO CARRIAGE BY AIR

At the time of writing carriage of goods by air is mainly governed by the Warsaw Convention for the Unification of Certain Rules Relating to International Carriage by Air as amended by the Hague Protocol, the Guadalajara Convention and the Montreal Protocols.[10] Domestic carriage is essentially regulated by a version of that regime.[11] However, as the Warsaw Convention regime is intended to be supplanted by the Montreal Convention of 1999,[12] which substantially updates it, we shall concentrate on the provisions of that Convention, although it is not yet in force. Given the similarity of its provisions, much of the case law under the Warsaw Convention will remain relevant.

---

[1] Art. 44.
[2] Art. 55(3).
[3] Art. 56.
[4] Art. 57.
[5] Art. 58; and see para. 4.15.
[6] Art. 6.
[7] Art. 24.
[8] Art. 6(9).
[9] Art. 6(3).
[10] See Carriage by Air Act 1961 (as amended); Carriage by Air (Supplementary Provisions) Act 1962.
[11] Carriage by Air (Application of Provisions) Order 1967 (SI 1967/480) (as amended).
[12] Carriage by Air (Implementation of the Montreal Convention 1999) Order 2002 (SI 2002/263).

## 4.22.   SCOPE OF CONVENTION

Carriage is international if, under the agreement of the parties, the place of departure and the destination are situated within different Convention states, whether or not there is a break in the carriage, or even if they are situated within the same Convention state as long as there is an agreed stopping place in another state, whether or not that other state is a Convention state.[13] So a flight from Glasgow to London is not international, but a contract to fly goods from Glasgow to Paris via London is international, even the Glasgow to London leg. Similarly, a contract which contemplates goods being flown from London to Belfast does not involve international carriage, whereas a contract which contemplates goods being flown from London to Belfast via Dublin does. Any provision which seeks to apply a different law, or which seek to alter the rules as to jurisdiction is null and void.[14] As far as jurisdiction is concerned, a pursuer may choose to raise an action against a carrier in a Convention state[15]:

- which is the domicile of the carrier; or
- which is the domicile of its principal place of business;, or
- where it has a place of business through which the contract was made; or
- which is the place of destination.

No court in any other state has jurisdiction and under the Warsaw Convention English courts have been prepared to grant injunctions to prevent actions being raised in such states,[16] while if an action is raised in one of the states described above, a plea of *forum non conveniens* cannot succeed.[17] Nonetheless, despite the above rules, disputes may still be settled by arbitration, as long as the forum (as selected by the claimant) is in one of the states mentioned above.[18] The arbitrator is bound to apply the provisions of the Convention.[19]

A carriage which is to be performed by successive carriers is deemed to be a single undivided carriage, if the parties regard it as a single operation.[20] It does not matter if there is more than one contract, and if the carriage as a whole is international, it does not matter if any contract(s) is performed entirely within the territory of a single state.[21] Each carrier is deemed to be a contracting party in so far as the contract relates to that part of the carriage under his supervision.[22] The consignor of goods has an action against the first carrier, the person entitled to the goods has an action against the last carrier, and both have an action against the carrier who performed the leg where the destruction, loss, damage or delay occurred, the carriers being jointly and severally liable.[23]

## 4.23.   AIR WAYBILL

The Convention contemplates that the consignor deliver a document known as an air waybill, although any other means which provides a record of the carriage may be substituted, in which case the consignor may request a cargo receipt .[24] Where there is more than one package being

---

[13] Art. 1(2).
[14] Art. 49.
[15] Art. 33.
[16] *Deauville v Aeroflot Russian International Airlines*[1997] 2 Lloyd's Rep. 67.
[17] *Milor S.R.L. v British Airways plc* [1996] Q.B. 702.
[18] Art. 34.
[19] *ibid*.
[20] Art. 1(3).
[21] *ibid*.
[22] Art. 36(1).
[23] Art. 36(3).
[24] Art. 4.

sent, the carrier may demand a separate waybill for each package, or if waybills are not being employed, the consignor may demand separate cargo receipts.[25] Each waybill must have three copies, all of which must be handed over with the goods.[26] The first copy should be marked "for the carrier", and signed by the consignor.[27] The carrier holds on to this copy. The second should be marked "for the consignee", and signed by both the consignor and the carrier.[28] This copy travels with the goods. The third should be signed by the carrier, and is given to the consignor once the goods have been accepted.[29] The waybill or cargo receipt is *prima facie* evidence of the conclusion of the contract, the acceptance of the goods, and the conditions of carriage,[30] but failure to comply with the provisions as to such documentation, does not undermine the contract, which continues to be subject to the provisions of the Convention including the provisions as to limitation of liability.[31]

The waybill or cargo receipt must contain[32]:

- an indication of the places of departure and destination;
- if these places are within the territory of a single state, an indication of an agreed stopping place in another state;
- an indication of the weight of the consignment.

It is the consignor's duty to ensure that the contents of the waybill, or the details he supplies for insertion in the cargo receipt are accurate, and he must indemnify the carrier against all loss arising from their incorrectness or inadequacy.[33] A similar duty is owed by the carrier to the consignor in respect of statements the carrier inserts in the cargo receipt on its own behalf.[34] The statements in the waybill relating to the number of packages and the weight, dimensions and packing of the goods are *prima facie* evidence of the facts stated, but those relating to the volume and condition of the goods do not, unless either these facts have been checked by the carrier in the consignor's presence, and this is stated in the waybill or cargo receipt, or the statements relate to the apparent condition of the goods.[35]

Under Art. 9 of the Warsaw Convention, if the carrier allowed goods to be loaded without a waybill in proper form having been completed, he was disabled from relying on the limitation of liability provisions described in the next paragraph. There is no equivalent provision in the Montreal Convention.

As well as the waybill, the consignor must furnish such information and attach to the waybill such documents as are required to meet customs and other formalities required before the goods may be delivered.[36] Again, he will be liable to the carrier in respect of any loss caused by the absence, insufficiency or irregularity of any such information or documents, unless the loss is attributable to the fault of the carrier or his servants or agents.[37]

---

[25] Art. 8.
[26] Art. 7(1).
[27] Art. 7(2).
[28] *ibid.*
[29] *ibid.*
[30] Art. 11(1).
[31] Art. 9.
[32] Art. 5.
[33] Art. 10(1)–(2).
[34] Art. 10(3).
[35] Art. 11(2).
[36] Art. 16(1).
[37] *ibid.*

## 4.24.  CARRIER'S LIABILITY

The carrier is strictly liable for loss of or damage to the goods during carriage by air, *i.e.* during the period in which the goods are in his charge, whether or not they are actually airborne.[38] He is strictly liable for damage caused by delay, unless he shows that all reasonable measures were taken to avoid the damage, or that it was impossible to take such measures.[39] Moreover, he is not liable for loss of or damage to the goods resulting from one or more of the following[40]:

- the inherent defects, quality or vice of the goods[41];
- their defective packaging unless performed by him or his servants or agents;
- an act of war or armed conflict;
- an act of a public authority in connection with the entry, exit or transit of the cargo (*e.g.* goods destroyed or impounded by customs officials).

The carrier may also raise the defence of contributory negligence.[42]

Although, subject to the points made above, the carrier is strictly liable, that liability is subject to a limit based on the weight of the goods, unless at the time the goods were handed over the consignor made a special declaration of interest in delivery at the destination, and if so required, paid an extra sum.[43] In that latter case the carrier would be liable to pay up to the amount declared by the consignor, unless he were able to prove that the amount declared was actually greater than the consignor's interest in delivery at the destination.[44] If only part of the goods are lost or damaged, only the weight of the goods concerned can be taken into account in assessing compensation, unless the value of the other goods is also affected.[45] So where a machine was sent in separate packages, one of which was badly damaged, it was the weight of the machine as a whole which formed the basis for assessing compensation, as the other packages were practically worthless without the damaged section.[46] It should be added that the carrier's liability is entirely unlimited in respect of his own acts or omissions or those of his employees or agents acting in the scope of their employment, if done with intent to cause damage or done recklessly and with knowledge that damage would probably result.[47] Knowledge here means actual knowledge, rather than knowledge an individual might reasonably be expected to have.[48] If goods are stolen by the carrier's cargo loaders, then he is liable, but if a member of his flight crew perpetrates the theft, the carrier will not be liable, as dealing with cargo is not in the course of such an individual's employment.[49] It is possible for a carrier to stipulate higher limits on his liability than laid down by the Convention, or agree to unlimited liability, but any provision of the contract relieving him of liability, or attempting to impose lower limits on his liability than laid down by the Convention, will be null and void.[50] He may also waive his defences under the Convention.[51]

---

[38] Art. 18.
[39] Art. 19.
[40] Art. 18(2).
[41] See *Winchester Fruit Ltd v American Airlines Inc.* [2002] 2 Lloyd's Rep. 265.
[42] Art. 20.
[43] Art. 22(3).
[44] *ibid.*
[45] Art. 22(3).
[46] *Applied Implants Technology Ltd v Lufthansa Cargo AG* [2000] 2 Lloyd's Rep. 46.
[47] Art. 25(5).
[48] *Nugent v Michael Goss Aviation Ltd* [2000] 2 Lloyd's Rep. 222.
[49] *Rusterberg Platinum Mines Ltd v South African Airways* [1977] 1 Lloyd's Rep. 564.
[50] Art. 26.
[51] Art. 27.

## 4.25. DISPOSITION AND DELIVERY

Under Art. 12(1) the consignor may at any time withdraw the goods, or insist they be held at any place where the plane stops, or demand their return to the place of departure, or direct that they be delivered to someone other than the consignee named in the waybill, as long as he meets the expense of any such step, and does not exercise the right in a way which prejudices the carrier or other consignors. The carrier may ignore the consignor's instructions only if what is asked is impossible, and the consignor must be informed of this forthwith.[52] If the carrier carries out the consignor's instructions, without requiring the production of the copy of the air waybill or cargo receipt delivered to the latter, he will be liable for any damage thereby caused to any person lawfully in possession of that document.[53] Once the goods have reached their destination, they are then at the disposal of the consignee rather than the consignor,[54] and the carrier must notify the former of their arrival, unless the contract directs otherwise.[55] The consignee is then entitled to demand delivery of the goods on the payment of any outstanding charges and the fulfilment of any conditions in the contract.[56] Should the consignee decline to accept the goods or proves impossible to communicate with, the goods remain at the disposal of the consignor.[57]

## 4.26. MAKING CLAIMS

Where the goods are damaged, the person entitled to delivery must complain in writing to the carrier as soon as the damage is discovered, and certainly within 14 days of the date of their receipt[58]. A carrier cannot be a "person entitled to delivery". Thus where the carrier with whom the consignor contracted subcontracted the actual carriage, and sent a complaint regarding damage to the goods to the actual carrier, it was held that proper notice had not been given.[59] Receipt of the goods without complaint by the person entitled to delivery is *prima facie* evidence that they have been delivered in good condition and in accordance with the carriage documents.[60] Damage here includes partial loss.[61] Where the goods are delayed, the complaint must be made within 21 days of them being placed at the disposal of the person entitled to delivery.[62] If these time limits are not adhered to, no claim may be made against the carrier for anything short of fraud.[63] Where the carrier admits the loss of the goods, or they have not arrived within seven days of the date when they should have arrived, the consignee is entitled to sue under the contract.[64] Loss presumably includes destruction in this context. Although no mention is made of the consignor making a claim where the goods are lost, it must be assumed that the consignor is the appropriate claimant where the goods remain in his ownership.[65] If the carriage is performed by successive carriers under one undivided carriage,

---

[52] Art. 12(2).
[53] Art. 12(3).
[54] Arts 12(4), 13(1).
[55] Art. 13(2).
[56] Art. 13(1).
[57] Art. 12(4).
[58] Art. 31(2).
[59] *Compaq Computer Manufacturing Ltd v Circle International Ltd,* 2001 S.L.T. 368.
[60] Art. 31(1).
[61] Carriage by Air Act 1961, s.4A.
[62] Art. 31(2).
[63] Art. 31(4).
[64] Art. 13(3).
[65] Compare *Thomas Cook Group Ltd v Air Malta Co Ltd* [1997] 2 Lloyd's Rep. 399, with *Ahmet v British Airways plc* [1997] A.C. 430.

the consignor may sue the first carrier in respect of loss, damage or delay, the consignee may sue the last carrier, and each may sue the carrier who was performing when the loss, damage or delay occurred, the carriers being liable jointly and severally.[66] Any right to damages under the Convention is extinguished if an action is not brought within two years of the date when the goods arrived at their destination, or ought to have arrived, or that date when the carriage actually stopped.[67]

# (6) CARRIAGE OF GOODS BY SEA

## 4.27. INTRODUCTION TO CARRIAGE OF GOODS BY SEA

If the carrier of goods by sea is a common carrier, then he is subject to the usual strict liability at common law in largely the same way as a common carrier by road.[68] Yet it would be very rare for a shipping company to be treated as a common carrier,[69] as almost none hold themselves out as willing to carry the goods of anyone who approaches them, and indeed almost all will explicitly contract on the basis that common law liability is limited or excluded altogether. The contract of carriage will usually take the form of either a charterparty or a bill of lading.

## 4.28. CHARTERPARTIES

This is a contract for the hire of the carrying capacity of a ship or some defined portion thereof, and is usually resorted to when a party wishes to ship a large quantity of goods. Theoretically, the contract may be entered into orally,[70] although invariably such contracts in modern times would be in writing, and would almost certainly adopt a standard form. Charterparties tend to take the form of either voyage charterparties, where the charterer gains the use of the vessel for a single voyage, or time charterparties, where he has the use of the vessel for a particular period of time. There is also an arrangement known as a demise charterparty. Under a demise charterparty the charterer leases an entire ship for a given period of time, gaining full possession of and control over it during that period, and so may determine such matters as its route.[71] A demise charterparty is therefore not a contract of carriage at all. The charterer does not ask the shipowner to carry goods for him. Instead, by leasing the ship, he is entitled to use it for whichever purpose he chooses, including carrying cargo. Usually, though not invariably, he gains the ship unmanned and so may appoint his own crew. Yet whether he appoints his own crew or simply uses the crew provided by the shipowner, they are regarded as working for him. Thus if the ship collides with another through the negligence of the crew, he rather than the shipowner is liable,[72] while if the master signs a bill of lading (see para. 4.32), he does so on behalf of the charterer rather than the shipowner, so that the charterer rather than the shipowner is liable to the holder of the bill for loss or damage to the cargo.[73] All this is very different to the position under true charterparties, which we shall now consider in detail.

---

[66] Art. 36(3).
[67] Art. 35(1).
[68] *Woods v Burns* (1893) 20 R. 602.
[69] Rare, but not unheard of: *A Siohn & Co Ltd v R H Hagland & Son (Transport) Ltd* [1976] 2 Lloyd's Rep. 428.
[70] *Nordstjernan SB v Salvesen* (1903) 6 F. 75.
[71] *Whistler International Ltd v Kawasaki Kisen Kaisha Ltd* [2001] 1 A.C. 638.
[72] *Clarke v Scott* (1896) 23 R. 442.
[73] *Baumwoll Manfactur v Furness* [1893] A.C. 8.

# 4.29. IMPLIED TERMS IN CHARTERPARTIES

## (a) Seaworthiness

It is an implied term in every charterparty that the vessel is seaworthy, either at the time of loading,[74] or in a time charterparty from the commencement of the contract.[75] If that duty is fulfilled, the owner will not be liable for loss due to the vessel becoming unseaworthy during the voyage.[76] Seaworthiness is not an absolute concept, but depends on the circumstances of the case, including the sort of voyage which is being attempted, and the type of cargo which is being carried. Thus the standard demanded of a ship carrying goods from Scotland to Australia, would not usually be the standard demanded of a ship carrying goods from Oban to Mull. Equally, while the question of whether a ship's refrigeration units are operating effectively would not bear on its seaworthiness if it were carrying iron ore, the matter would be different if it were carrying meat.[77] Seaworthiness does not mean unsinkability. If the ship is as fit as an ordinarily prudent owner would demand in light of the voyage to be undertaken, it meets the requirement, even if it proves unable to deal with freak conditions.[78] Essentially, the ship must be able to withstand the voyage,[79] cope with its cargo,[80] be adequately equipped,[81] have a crew which is adequate in terms of size and competence,[82] and have sufficient fuel.[83] It has also been said that the test of seaworthiness is whether an ordinarily prudent owner would have remedied the defect had known of it.[84] This serves to stress that a latent defect, which an owner neither knew or could have known about, can make a ship unseaworthy,[85] and it will not avail an owner to argue that he believed the vessel to be seaworthy on entirely reasonable grounds, nor even that he did all he could to make it seaworthy.[86] The onus of proving a ship is unseaworthy rests on the charterers, but will be relatively easy to discharge if the circumstances are suggestive of unseaworthiness, as where a ship breaks down very shortly after setting sail.[87] The implied term as to seaworthiness may be excluded, but only the clearest and most unambiguous of language will suffice to do so.[88]

## (b) Reasonable dispatch

It is an implied term in every charterparty that the vessel is able to embark on the voyage with reasonable dispatch.[89] Again, this term may be excluded.[90]

## (c) Deviation

It is an implied term in every charterparty that the vessel shall not unjustifiably deviate from its route. That route may be prescribed in the contract, otherwise it will be by the most direct

---

[74] *Cunningham v Colvills, Lowden & Co* (1888) 16 R. 295.
[75] *Giertsen v Turnbull & Co*, 1908 S.C. 1101.
[76] *ibid.*
[77] *Maori King (Cargo Owners) v Hughes* [1895] 2 Q.B. 550.
[78] *McFadden v Blue Star Line* [1905] 1 K.B. 697.
[79] *Steel & Craig v State Line Steamship Co* (1877) 4 R. (H.L.) 103.
[80] *Kopitoff v Wilson* (1876) 1 Q.B.D. 377.
[81] *Adam v J & D Morris* (1890) 18 R. 153.
[82] *The Jute Express* [1991] 2 Lloyd's Rep.55; *The Eurasian Dream* [2002] 1 Lloyd's Rep. 719.
[83] *Park v Duncan & Son* (1898) 5 S.L.T. 280.
[84] *Gilroy, Sons & Co v Price & Co* (1892) 20 R. (H.L.) 1.
[85] *The Glenfruin* (1885) 10 PD 103.
[86] *Steel & Craig v State Line Steamship Co* (1877) 4 R. (H.L.) 103.
[87] *Klein v Lindsay*, 1911 S.C. (H.L.) 9.
[88] *Nelson Line Liverpool Ltd v James Nelson & Son Ltd* [1908] A.C.16.
[89] *Suzuki v Benyon* (1926) 42 T.L.R. 269.
[90] *The Takafa* [1990] 1 Lloyd's Rep. 536.

geographical route, unless some other route is more usual.[91] It may be that there are several usual routes, in which case it would be permissible to follow any of these.[92] The term is only breached by voluntary deviation, not where deviation occurs by error.[93] The term deals with unjustifiable deviation. Deviation is justifiable in order to attempt to save life, but not in order to save property. So in *Scaramanga v Stamp*[94] it was permissible to deviate to help the crew of a ship in distress, but the owner was liable to the charterer for the loss of the cargo when the ship was itself lost in seeking to salvage the ship in distress. Deviation is also justifiable in order to protect the ship or cargo from imminent danger such a storm,[95] or to effect necessary repairs.[96]

The contract can, of course, specifically authorise deviation, but any such term, however widely expressed, will not be construed so as to ensure the main object of the contract is defeated, so that while the calling into ports which are broadly on the route of the voyage is permissible, deviation entirely away from the route of the voyage cannot be justified.[97] It might be added that exclusion and limitation clauses do not operate in relation to losses sustained during unjustifiable deviation, unless they explicitly cover this situation.[98] Unjustifiable deviation prevents the owner claiming demurrage[99] (see para. 4.31.), and permits the charterer to rescind.[1]

### (d) Dangerous goods

It is an implied term in every charterparty that the charterer will not ship dangerous goods,[2] although of course there is no breach where the parties are aware that a potentially dangerous cargo is to be carried. Goods may be dangerous because of the threat they impose to the ship or the remainder of the cargo,[3] or simply because their presence might cause the ship to be detained by the authorities.[4]

## 4.30. LOADING

If the ship is not already at the loading port, the charterparty may indicate a date by which it must arrive there, and failure to adhere to this will constitute a material breach.[5] Even if no such date is stipulated, the implied term that the vessel embarks on the voyage with reasonable dispatch will place the shipowner in breach if he does not proceed to the loading port within a reasonable period of time.[6] By the same token, if no port is nominated as the loading port in the charterparty, then if the charterer does not nominate a port either within the period specified in the charterparty or within a reasonable time, he will himself commit a material breach.[7] It is suggested that the charterer is under a duty to nominate only safe ports for both

---

[91] *The India City* [1939] A.C. 562.
[92] *ibid.*
[93] *Rio Tinto Co Ltd v Seed Shipping Co* (1926) 42 T.L.R. 381.
[94] (1880) 5 C.P.D. 295.
[95] *Donaldson Bros v Little & Co* (1882) 10 R. 413; but see *Whistler International Ltd v Kawasaki Kisen Kaisha Ltd* [2001] 1 A.C. 638.
[96] *Karlshamns Oljefabriker v Monarch Steamship Co,* 1949 S.L.T. 51.
[97] *Glynn v Margetson & Co.* [1893] A.C. 351.
[98] *Cunard Steamship Co v Buerger* [1927] A.C.1.
[99] *United States Shipping Board v Bunge y Born Ltde Sociedad* [1925] All E.R. 173.
[1] *Hain SS Co Ltd v Tate & Lyle Ltd* [1936] 2 All E.R. 597.
[2] *Chandris v Isbrandtsen-Moller Co Inc* [1951] 1 K.B. 240.
[3] *Ministry of Food v Lamport and Holt Line Ltd* [1952] 2 Lloyd's Rep. 371.
[4] *Mitchell, Cotts & Co v Steel Bros & Co Ltd* [1916] 2 K.B. 610.
[5] *Allison & Co v Jacobsen & Co* (1904) 11 S.L.T. 573.
[6] See *McAndrew v Adams* (1834) 1 Bing NC 29—failure to proceed to that port without deviation amounts to breach.
[7] *The Timna* [1971] 2 Lloyd's Rep. 91.

loading or unloading, although this matter will usually be regulated by an express term of the contract. A safe port is one which the ship can in the normal course of events safely enter, use and depart.[8] If a ship is damaged by an abnormal event in an otherwise safe port, the charterer will not be liable.[9] A port which is physically safe may be unsafe if, for example, the ship is liable to detention by the authorities.[10] The shipowner may refuse to enter an unsafe port,[11] but he may waive the right to refuse by knowingly accepting the nomination of an unsafe port.[12] He may always claim damages if he suffers loss by entering an unsafe port,[13] unless the particular type of loss could not be foreseen.[14] Unless the contract provides otherwise, the charterer is responsible for bringing the goods to the ship,[15] and the shipowner is then responsible for its loading,[16] proper stowage[17] and unloading.[18]

## 4.31. LAYTIME AND DEMURRAGE

A ship is an enormously costly capital asset, and over a period of time the return on this asset will depend on how many voyages can be attempted. In large measure this lies in the hands of the shipowner, but the speed at which the ship can be loaded and unloaded often depends on the charterer. Thus the contract will usually specify periods within which the cargo must be loaded and unloaded/uplifted. Such periods are known as laytime or lay-days. The contract will usually specify sums the charterer must pay if these periods are exceeded. These sums are known as demurrage, which is essentially a form of liquidated damages.[19] If the contract contains no provision for laytime, then loading and unloading must be completed within a reasonable time having regard to the circumstances.[20] So factors such as adverse weather conditions, the adequacy of cargo handling facilities, and labour shortages may bear on what is regarded as a reasonable time.[21] Where the contract does provide for laytime, then it does not matter why the laytime has been exceeded, and the charterer will be liable for demurrage however blameless he may be for the delay, unless of course the contract exempts him in certain situations, or unless the delay is actually attributable to the shipowner or persons for whose actions the shipowner is responsible.[22] If the contract does not provide for demurrage, then actual damages will be payable if the laytime is exceeded, or in the absence of laytime, if the loading and unloading is not completed within a reasonable time.[23] The same is true if demurrage is payable for a fixed period, and this period is exceeded. If the provisions as to demurrage do not specify a fixed period, then the shipowner may only claim demurrage, rather than actual damages, no matter how long the period during which the ship is detained, although if the ship is detained for an unreasonably long period, the period of demurrage may be terminated by the owner rescinding the contract and claiming damages.[24]

---

[8] *The Evia* [1983] 1 A.C. 786.
[9] *ibid.*
[10] *ibid.*
[11] *The Kanchenjunga* [1990] 1 Lloyd's Rep. 391, HL.
[12] *ibid.*
[13] *ibid.*
[14] *The Lucille* [1984] 1 Lloyd's Rep. 244, CA.
[15] *Glengarnock Iron & Steel Co Ltd v Cooper & Co* (1895) 3 S.L.T. 36.
[16] *ibid.*
[17] *Canadian Transport Co Ltd v Court Line Ltd* [1940] A.C. 394.
[18] *Ballantyne & Co v Paton & Hendry,* 1911 2 S.L.T. 510.
[19] *Moor Line Ltd v Distillers Co Ltd,* 1912 1 S.L.T. 147.
[20] *Ardan Steamship Co Ltd v Weir & Co* (1905) 13 S.L.T. 373.
[21] See variously *Carlton Steamship Co v Castle Mail Packets Co* [1898] A.C. 486; *J & A Wyllie v Harrison & Co* (1885) 13 R. 92; *Rickinson, Sons & Co v Scottish Co-operative Wholesale Society,* 1918 1 S.L.T. 329.
[22] *Aktieselkabet Dampskibet Hansa v Alexander & Sons,* 1919 2 S.L.T. 166; *The Mass Glory* [2002] 2 Lloyd's Rep. 244.
[23] *Moor Line Ltd v Distillers Co Ltd,* 1912 1 S.L.T. 147.
[24] *Lilly & Co v Stevenson & Co* (1895) 2 S.L.T. 434.

Depending on the terms of the contract, laytime commences when the ship has arrived and is ready to load or unload, as the case may be.[25] If the charterparty indicates that the ship must dock in a particular berth in a given port, then the ship cannot be treated as having arrived until it reaches that berth, although the charterer will still be liable in damages if the ship is delayed in reaching that berth through his fault.[26] However, if the charterparty simply indicates that the ship must dock in a given port, then the ship can be treated as having arrived as soon as it reaches the port and is at the effective disposal of the charterer—as was the case in *The Johanna Oldendorff*[27] where the ship was held to have arrived notwithstanding that she was 17 miles from her usual discharging berth. Laytime will not commence where a ship is physically ready to load or unload, but loading or unloading is not practically possible, as where the ship is affected by quarantine restrictions[28] Still, laytime will commence if lack of readiness is attributable to the charterer's fault.[29]

# (7) BILLS OF LADING

## 4.32.  INTRODUCTION TO BILLS OF LADING

While charterparties are employed if a shipper requires the capacity of an entire vessel, if a smaller consignment of goods is to be sent, a device known as a bill of lading will be usually be resorted to instead. Commonly, a shipper will ascertain when a ship is sailing to the port for which the goods are destined, book space on that ship, and at the appropriate time will send them to the port of departure along with a shipping note which contains details of the goods. That note will be signed by the carrier and acts as a receipt for the shipper. The goods will then be loaded. Thereafter, the shipper will prepare a bill of lading containing details of the goods shipped, which is presented to the carrier. The carrier, checks it, amends it if necessary, and issues the bill of lading. (Alternatively, the carrier may himself prepare and issue the bill of lading from information supplied by the shipper.) The bill then serves three separate functions. First, it is a document of title to the goods. Thus very often it will be forwarded by air to the port of destination. If the shipper is the buyer, he will forward it to himself or his agent, so that he may claim the goods on their arrival. If he is the seller, he will forward it to the buyer, or perhaps to a bank to be given to the buyer in return for payment. Secondly, it is a receipt for the goods. Thirdly it embodies the terms of the contract of carriage.

## 4.33.  THE BILL AS A DOCUMENT OF TITLE

A bill may be made out in favour of the bearer, but almost invariably in modern times it will be made out in favour of a named person (usually the shipper) or to his order. Until the goods have been delivered to the person entitled to them,[30] constructive possession of and property in the goods may be transferred by transferring the bill.—Whoever has the bill may claim the goods. However, if a bill made out in favour of a named person does not contains words such as "or order", or if it contains words such as "not transferable" or "not negotiable", then it may

[25] *Micosta S.A. v Shetland Islands Council*, 1986 S.L.T. 193.
[26] *Wake v Stevenson & Co* (1894) 2 S.L.T. 87.
[27] [1974] A.C. 479.
[28] *John and James White v The Steamship Winchester Co* (1886) 13 R. 524.
[29] *Vergottis v Wm Cory & Son.* [1926] 2 K.B. 344; and see *The Happy Day, The Times*, July 26, 2002.
[30] *Hayman & Son v McLintock* (1907) 15 S.L.T. 63.

not be transferred, and delivery may be made only to that named person.[31] A bearer bill may be transferred by simple delivery. A bill made out in favour of a named person may be transferred by indorsement. If indorsement takes the form of a simple signature, then the bill becomes a bearer bill, while if the name of the person to whom possession and/or ownership is to be transferred is added (indorsement in full), the bill is then treated as made out in his favour. That person in turn can indorse the bill, although if words such as "or order" were not added to his name, further transfer by him is prevented. As described above, a bill of lading must appear very like a negotiable instrument such as a bill of exchange, and in this context it is often useful to think of it in this way (see para. 5.2.). However, there is one major difference. As Lord Devlin puts it in Kum v Wah Tat Bank Ltd[32]

> "It is well settled that 'negotiable' when used in relation to a bill of lading means simply transferable. A negotiable bill of lading is not negotiable in the strict sense; it cannot, as can be done by the negotiation of a negotiable instrument, give the transferee a better title than the transferor . . ."

Thus in Lloyd's Bank v Bank of America[33] the buyer of goods, having pledged them to the bank, was given a bill of lading covering them by the bank, with a view to reselling them in order to be able to repay the bank. In fact, he instead pledged them again to a second bank, handing over the bill of lading, and absconded with the proceeds. It was held that, as the buyer's title was defective, the second bank did not obtain a good title merely by transfer of the bill of lading.

In England, it has been held that the transfer of a bill of lading does not transfer ownership of the goods, if the parties intend otherwise, so that the transfer may simply create a pledge if that is the parties' intention.[34] In Scotland the authorities are divided between those which seem to concede this possibility, and those which insist that there can be no security without actual possession, so that transfer of the bill must transfer the property in the goods, irrespective of the parties' intention.[35]

Although the above discussion has proceeded on the basis that a single bill of lading will be employed, it is not uncommon for a set of three bills to be issued, one being retained by the shipper, one being carried by the master along with the goods, and one being sent to the person to whom they are being delivered. It is important to understand that each bill is signed, and each has the status of an original bill, rather than a copy of the original. There are advantages in this practice, *e.g.* if the bill is sent to the consignee by air mail, he may use the bill to pledge or resell the goods long before the goods actually arrive. However, the existence of three bills relating to the same consignment clearly carries with it the potential to cause problems. Invariably each bill contains a clause indicating that once delivery is made under one bill, the others are rendered void. Nonetheless, it is quite possible for someone who holds more than one copy of the bill to indorse different copies to different individuals. It has been held that the master of a ship has no further duty than to deliver the goods to the first person to present a bill, and that he is not obliged to insist on the presentation of all three.[36]

## 4.34. THE BILL AS A RECEIPT

A bill of lading is a receipt acknowledging the quantity and condition of the goods shipped.

---

[31] *Henderson & Co v Comptoir D'Escompte de Paris* (1873) L.R. 5 P.C. 253.
[32] [1973] 1 Lloyd's Rep. 439 at 446.
[33] [1938] 2 K.B. 147.
[34] *The Kronprinsessan Margareta* [1921] 1 A.C. 486; and see the views of Mustill L.J. in *The Delfini* [1990] 1 Lloyd's Rep. 252 at 268.
[35] Compare *North Western Bank Ltd v Poynter, Son and Macdonalds* (1894) 2 S.L.T. 311, with *Hamilton v Western Bank of Scotland* (1856) 19 D. 152.
[36] *Glyn Mills, Curie & Co v East and West India Dock Co* (1882) 7 App. Cas. 591.

## (a) The mate's receipt

As a bill may take some time to complete, it is not unknown for the master of the ship or the firm in charge of loading operations to issue a document known as a mate's receipt, to cover the period between receipt of the goods and the issue of the bill of lading. In *Nippon Yusen Kaisha v Ramjihan Serogwee*[37] Lord Wright notes:

"A mate's receipt is not a document of title to the goods shipped. Its transfer does not pass property in the goods, nor is its possession equivalent to possession of the goods. It is not conclusive, and its statements do not bind the shipowner, as do the statements in a bill of lading signed with the master's authority. It is however, *prima facie* evidence of the quantity and condition of the goods received, and *prima facie* it is the recipient or possessor thereof who is entitled to have the bill of lading issued to him."

In *Kum v Wah Tat Bank Ltd*[38] the Privy Council acknowledged a peculiar custom of trade whereby mate's receipts were used as documents of title in the same way as bills of lading, but held that the particular mate's receipt could not be so regarded, as it bore the words "not negotiable". However the main purpose of the document is simply to acknowledge that the goods are now held by the carrier. It will be given up when the bill of lading is produced and thereafter ceases to have any function.

## (b) Clean bills of lading

Bills of lading are either clean or claused. A bill is claused when some reservation is expressed thereon by the carrier as to the quantity or condition of the goods. Otherwise the bill will be clean. It can be important for the bill to be clean, if the shipper wishes to sell the goods or raise credit upon them, and indeed many contracts make payment conditional on the delivery of a clean bill of lading. A bill is still regarded as clean even though it simply notes that the goods are in "apparent" good order or condition, or even if it states "weight, measure, quantity, conditions, contents and value unknown", the important point being that no specific reservation is stated.[39] Moreover, the bill refers to the condition of the goods at the time of loading, so that if it is subsequently amended to note damage or destruction during the voyage, it does not cease to be clean.[40]

## (c) Receipt as to quantity

At common law the rule was that the bill of lading was *prima facie* evidence of the quantity of goods shipped.[41] This was only a *prima facie* rule, so that it could be displaced by clear evidence that the quantity stated in the bill was erroneous,[42] but such evidence did have to be very clear.[43] However, s.4 of the Carriage of Goods by Sea Act 1992 now indicates that a bill of lading which represents goods which have been shipped on board a vessel, or have been received for shipment on board a vessel, and which has been signed by the master or any other person authorised by the carrier to sign bills, is conclusive evidence of shipment or receipt. That being said, where the bill states that weight or quantity is unknown, the bill is not even *prima facie* evidence of the quantity of goods shipped,[44] and it may be submitted that such words would exclude the effect of s.4, as the bill does not *represent* the goods shipped.

---

[37] [1938] A.C. 429 at 445.
[38] [1973] 1 Lloyd's Rep. 439.
[39] *The Galatia* [1980] 1 W.L.R. 495.
[40] *ibid.*
[41] *Smith & Co v Bedouin Steam Navigation Co Ltd.* (1895) 23 R. (H.L.) 1.
[42] *Craig Line Steamship Co v North British Storage and Transit Co* (1920) 2 S.L.T. 418,.
[43] *Dampskibsselkabet Svenborg v Love and Stewart Ltd,* 1916 S.C. (H.L.) 187.
[44] *Craig Line Steamship Co Ltd v North British Storage and Transit Co* (1920) 2 S.L.T. 418.

Moreover, and more importantly, s.4 does not apply at all where the Hague-Visby Rules apply in terms of the Carriage of Goods by Sea Act 1971 (see para. 4.37.). Where the Hague-Visby Rules do apply, the shipper may demand the issue of a bill showing either the number of packages or pieces, or the quantity or weight, as the case may be, as he has furnished in writing.[45] This is then *prima facie* evidence of the receipt of the goods described therein.[46] This of course means that the carrier may seek to prove that the details contained in the bill are erroneous, but he may not do so when the bill has been transferred to a third party acting in good faith.[47] The effect of the rules is to prevent reliance on a "weight or quantity unknown" clause. In *The River Gurara*[48] the Court of Appeal held that where goods were containerised, the rule related to the number of packages said to be within the containers, rather than the number of containers, even though the carrier had no way of checking what was in the containers, although he could seek to show that there was not in fact the stated number of packages in the containers.

## (d) Receipt as to condition

Almost invariably, a bill will state that the goods have been shipped "in good order and condition". This can obviously only relate to external condition, as is well illustrated by an Australian case where the goods being shipped in a container, the statement was taken to mean that the container appeared to be in good order and condition.[49] Unless the master qualifies the bill in some way, the use of these words will then afford *prima facie* evidence, as between the shipper and shipowner, that the goods were in good condition when shipped.[50] Of course, as only *prima facie* evidence is afforded, the shipowner is entitled to seek to prove that they were not in fact in good condition.[51] However, English authority suggests that in a contest with an indorsee of a bill acting in good faith, the shipowner will be barred from arguing that the goods were not in fact in good condition.[52] Scottish authority is to the contrary,[53] but it may be that the English position would now be preferred. Of course, if the bill is qualified, as where the master marks the bill "many bags, stained, torn and resewn", then the shipowner will be not be barred from arguing with an indorsee about the condition of the goods.[54] However, qualifications would have to be specific. Marking the bill "condition unknown" has not been treated as qualifying the statement as to good condition.[55] Where the Hague-Visby Rules apply, the shipper may demand the issue of a bill showing the apparent order and condition of the goods,[56] and such a bill is *prima facie* evidence of the receipt of the goods in that condition.[57] Again the carrier may not seek to prove the contrary when the bill has been transferred to a third party acting in good faith.[58]

---

[45] Art. 3, r.3.
[46] Art. 3, r.4.
[47] *ibid.*
[48] [1998] Q.B. 610.
[49] *The TNT Express* [1992] 2 Lloyd's Rep. 656.
[50] *Craig and Rose v Delargy* (1879) 6 R. 1269.
[51] *Crawford and Law v Allan Line Steamship Co,* 1912 S.C. (H.L.) 56.
[52] *Compania Naviera Vasconzada v Churchill and Sim* [1906] 1 K.B. 237.
[53] *Craig and Rose v Delargy* (1879) 6 R. 1269.
[54] *Canadian and Dominion Sugar Co Ltd v Canadian National (West Indies) Steamships Ltd* [1947] A.C. 46.
[55] *The Skarp* [1935] P. 134.
[56] Art. 3, r.3.
[57] Art. 3, r.4; and see *The David Agmashenebeli* [2002] 2 All E.R. (Comm.) 806.
[58] *ibid.*

## 4.35.   THE BILL AS AN EMBODIMENT OF THE TERMS OF THE CONTRACT OF CARRIAGE

As the contract of carriage is normally entered into prior to the issue of a bill of lading, the bill does not constitute the contract, but it does provide evidence of the fact of the contract and of its terms.[59] However, anything expressed in the bill cannot contradict the terms of the contract already agreed between the parties.[60]

## 4.36.   TRANSMISSION OF CONTRACTUAL RIGHTS UNDER BILLS OF LADING

Although a bill has for a long time been regarded as a document of title, so that ownership of the goods can be transferred by transferring the bill, the contract of carriage strictly remains between the original parties. So as a result of privity of contract, the purchaser of goods would not be able to sue if the goods were damaged or destroyed during the voyage, as the contract lay between the shipper and the carrier. This was remedied by the Bills of Lading Act 1855 which transferred the shipper's rights against the carrier to any individual who acquired property in the goods as a result of consignment or indorsement of the bill. However, this Act did not protect an indorsee who did not acquire property in the goods, or who acquired property other than through indorsement. Consequently, s.2(1) of the Carriage of Goods by Sea Act 1992 now confers the right to sue the carrier upon a lawful holder of a bill, as if he were a party to the original contract. Similar rights are conferred upon those entitled to the goods under sea waybills and ship's delivery orders (see para. 4.39.), and the Secretary of State has power to extend the Act to electronic bills of lading.[61] A holder of a bill is the named consignee in possession of the bill, or a person in possession of the bill as the result of indorsement or of simple delivery in the case of a bearer bill, and he is to be treated as the lawful holder where he takes the bill in good faith.[62] In this context, an individual is in good faith where he acts honestly.[63] When the holder of the bill acquires the rights of the shipper, the shipper loses those rights,[64] but the former may exercise his rights for the latter's benefit should the latter suffer loss.[65] Just as the holder may enforce the contract as if he were an original party, he will become liable under the contract, but only if he demands or takes delivery of the goods, or makes a claim under the contract.[66] This qualification is inserted to prevent commercial lenders who become holders of bills being made liable on the contract. Only the current holder can be made liable. If an indorsee of a bill indorses the bill onwards he ceases to be liable.[67]

---

[59] *Harland and Wolff Ltd v Burns and Laird Lines,* 1931 S.L.T. 572.
[60] *The Ardennes* [1951] 1 K.B. 55.
[61] s.1(5).
[62] s.5(2).
[63] *The Aegean Sea* [1998] 2 Lloyd's Rep. 39.
[64] s.2(5).
[65] s.2(4). There may remain an independent right to sue in delict where loss is sustained through the goods being negligently given up: see *East West Corp v Dampskibsselskabet af 1912 A/S* [2002] 1 All E.R. (Comm.) 676; upheld at [2003] EWCA Civ. 83; .
[66] s.3.
[67] *The Berge Sisar* [2002] 2 A.C. 205, HL.

## 4.37. BILLS OF LADING—REGULATION OF THE TERMS OF THE CONTRACT BY THE HAGUE-VISBY RULES

It has long been recognised that some statutory regulation of the terms of the contract of carriage by sea under a bill of lading was necessary, to prevent shipping companies imposing draconian terms on their customers. There has been some effort to co-ordinate such efforts on an international basis to ensure uniformity of treatment. These efforts have not been wholly successful, and at the time of writing there are three major international conventions bearing on the subject—the Hague Rules, the Hague-Visby Rules and the Hamburg Rules. Maritime nations around the world will have enacted legislation based on one of these Conventions. Currently the UK operates on the basis of the Hague-Visby Rules as incorporated into our law by the Carriage of Goods by Sea Act 1971.

### (a) The application of the rules

The rules apply to contracts for carriage of goods by sea,[68] during the period between loading and discharge,[69] and have been held to apply while goods were briefly stored on shore during the course of a voyage.[70] The contract of carriage must be covered by a bill of lading (or similar document of title).[71] Thus the Rules do not apply to charterparties, but do apply to bills of lading issued in relation to a ship under charterparty.[72] They will have effect with regard to the carriage of goods between ports in two different states, if either the bill of lading is issued in a contracting state, or the carriage is from a port in a contracting state.[73] Indeed they even apply where the carriage is between ports within the UK.[74] Additionally, they can be invoked by the parties in that they have effect if the contract provides that they, or the legislation of any state giving effect to them, are to govern the contract.[75] The Rules impose obligations and confer rights on the parties, as briefly described below.

### (b) Provision of seaworthy vessel by carrier

At common law, the term implied in charterparties that a seaworthy vessel must be provided is also implied in bills of lading. However, s.3 of the Carriage of Goods by Sea Act 1971 states that there is no absolute undertaking to supply a seaworthy ship. Instead the carrier before and at the beginning of the voyage is obliged to exercise due diligence[76]:

- to make the ship seaworthy;
- to properly man, equip and supply it;
- to make the holds, refrigerating and cool chambers, and all other parts of the ship in which goods are carried fit and safe for their reception, carriage and preservation.

The carrier will not be liable for any damage due to unseaworthiness, if he has complied with the above duties,[77] but if he is in breach of any of those duties, he may not rely on any defences or limitations on liability provided by the Rules.[78] If damage has been caused by unseaworthiness, the carrier has the burden of proving that he exercised due diligence to make the ship seaworthy.[79]

---

[68] Art. I(b).
[69] Art. I(e).
[70] *Mayhew Foods Ltd v Overseas Containers Ltd* [1984] 1 Lloyd's Rep. 317.
[71] Art. I(b); and see *The Happy Ranger* [2002] 2 All E.R. (Comm.) 24, CA.
[72] Art. V.
[73] Art. X.
[74] s.1(3).
[75] Art. X.
[76] Hague-Visby Rules, Art. III, r.1.
[77] Art. IV, r.1.
[78] *Maxime Footwear Ltd v Canadian Government Merchant Marine Ltd* [1959] A.C. 589.
[79] Art. IV, r.1.

## (c) Care of cargo by carrier

While common law liability for loss of or damage to cargo is strict, the Hague-Visby Rules provide substantial protection for the carrier. In the first place however, they dictate that he must "properly and carefully load, handle, stow, carry, keep, care for and discharge the cargo."[80] "Properly" means in accordance with a system which is sound, in light of the knowledge the carrier has about the goods.[81] However, the rules then provide a lengthy list of circumstances where the carrier is not liable. He may voluntarily accept liability in relation to all or any of these exceptions,[82] but may not add to the list.[83] The list is far too lengthy to set out here,[84] but it may be noted that it includes perils of the sea, and any neglect or default in the navigation and management of the ship, as well as any cause not arising from his fault or the fault of those for whom he is liable. The Rules also limit the carrier's liability for loss of or damage to the goods, according to a formula laid down therein.[85] The carrier will be discharged from any liability unless suit is brought within one year of the delivery of the goods, or of the date when they should be delivered.[86] Under Scots law, suit is synonomous with action, which is required to be commenced by summons.[87]

Arresting a vessel on the dependence of an action is not the same as raising an action, and is not enough to prevent a claim being time barred.[88]

## (d) Deviation by carrier

Any deviation in attempting to save life or property, or which is otherwise reasonable is not a breach of the Rules or of the underlying contract, and the carrier is not liable for loss or damage resulting therefrom.[89] In *Stag Line Ltd v Foscolo, Mango & Co*[90] in considering what amounted to a reasonable deviation Lord Atkin opined:

> "The true test seems to be what departure from the contract voyage might a prudent person controlling the voyage at the time make and maintain, having in mind all the relevant circumstances existing at the time, including the terms of the contract and the interests of all parties concerned, but without obligation to consider the interests of any one as conclusive."

In that case it was held not to be reasonable to deviate in order to land engineers who had been carrying out tests on the ship, whereas in *The Daffodil B*[91] it was reasonable to deviate to have a generator repaired. An unreasonable deviation disables the carrier from relying on the defences and limitations under the Rules.[92]

## (e) Carrier's rights in relation to dangerous goods

If the carrier discovers that goods of an inflammable, explosive or dangerous nature have been shipped without his consent, he may land or destroy them or render them harmless, without

---

[80] Art. III, r.2; but only where he has consented to carry out those tasks: see *Jindal Iron & Steel Co Ltd v Islamic Solidarity Shipping Co Jordan Inc.* [2002] 2 All E.R. (Comm.) 364.

[81] *Albacora SRL v Westcott and Laurance Line Ltd,* 1966 S.C. (H.L.) 19.

[82] Art. V.

[83] Art. III, r.8; and see *The Starsin* [2003] 2 W.L.R. 711, HL.

[84] See Art. IV, r.2.

[85] Art. IV, r.5.

[86] Art. III, r.6; and see *The Sonia* [2002] 2 All E.R. (Comm.) 984.

[87] *R M Supplies (Inverkeithing) Ltd v EMS Trans Schiffahrisges mbH & Co* 2003 S.L.T. 133.

[88] *ibid.*

[89] Art. IV, r.4.

[90] [1932] A.C. 328 at 343.

[91] [1983] 1 Lloyd's Rep. 498.

[92] *Stag Line Ltd v Foscolo, Mango & Co* [1932] A.C. 328.

being liable to compensation, the shipper indeed being liable for any expenses resulting from such shipment.[93]

## 4.38. CHARTERPARTIES AND BILLS OF LADING

So far the discussion has proceeded on the basis that a shipper of goods will either charter a ship to carry the goods, or send them as consignment in a general ship, employing a bill of lading. Yet it is not uncommon for the master of a ship to issue a bill of lading to the charterer. In this case, while the bill may serve as a receipt and document of title, the contract between the parties is governed by the charterparty and not the bill.[94] However, if the bill is indorsed to a third party, then it will govern the contract with the indorsee.[95] Even though a ship is under charter, some part of the cargo may yet be carried under a bill of lading. In this context, if, when the bill of lading is made out, the holder is aware of the charterparty, his contract may be with the charterer, otherwise it must be with the shipowner.[96] Nonetheless, under a demise charterparty (see para. 4.32.), the holder of a bill always contracts with the charterer.[97] Bills may often specify a few conditions, and then indicate "all other terms as per charterparty". That does not mean that every term in the charterparty will be incorporated into the bill. Certain clauses are obviously only intended to govern the relationship between shipowner and charterer, and so will not be incorporated.[98] Otherwise, it is really a matter of construction, as to whether a particular term is intended to be incorporated.[99] Obviously, a term which is inconsistent with an actual term of the bill cannot be incorporated.[1]

## 4.39. ALTERNATIVES TO BILLS OF LADING

It should not be assumed that a bill of lading will invariably be employed in those situations where it might be thought appropriate. Other documents are increasingly supplanting them. Although the status of a bill of lading as a document of title presents obvious advantages, it can carry disadvantages as well. The carrier must give possession of the goods to whoever produces the bill. Given that three copies of the bill are often made, the possibility for fraud exists. The other side of the coin is that if the carrier delivers the bill to someone who does not produce a bill of lading, he will be liable if that person turns out not to be entitled to the goods, and it will not avail him to show that he reasonably believed that person to have a right to the goods.[2] Thus carriers are understandably reluctant to relinquish possession except on production of the bill—an attitude which may lead to frustration for the owner if the arrival of the bill is delayed. Consequently, many cargoes are carried under sea waybills, documents which may set out the terms of the contract, but which are primarily receipts. They are not documents of title, and are not negotiable, so that ownership of the goods cannot be transferred by transferring the waybill.

---

[93] Art. IV, r.6.
[94] *Hill Steam Shipping Co Ltd v Hugo Stinnes Ltd,* 1941 S.L.T. 303.
[95] *Karlshamns Oljefbriker A/B v Monarch Steamship Co,* 1949 S.C. (H.L.) 1.
[96] *The Rewia* [1991] 2 Lloyd's Rep. 325.
[97] *Baumwoll Manafactur von Carl Scheiber v Furness* [1893] A.C. 8.
[98] *The Miramar* [1984] A.C. 676.
[99] Compare *The Phonizien* [1966] 1 Lloyd's Rep. 150; with *The Annefield* [1971] P. 168: incorporation of arbitration clauses. Private international law issues may also arise in this context, see *The Epsilon Rosa (No. 2)* [2002] 2 Lloyd's Rep. 701.
[1] *Hill Steam Shipping Co Ltd v Hugo Stinnes Ltd,* 1941 S.L.T. 303.
[2] *Mortis Exports Ltd v Dampskibsselskabet AF 1912 A/S* [2000] 1 All E.R. (Comm.) 91.

Essentially, possession of the goods should only be relinquished to the person specified in the waybill, and this should be done on proof of identity, without any need to produce the waybill. Although the terms of the Carriage of Goods by Sea Act 1992 apply to waybills the Hague-Visby Rules do not, although they may presumably be applied by agreement. It may be however, that the holder of a bill of lading sells parts of the cargo to different individuals. To enable them to obtain possession of the goods, he would issue a number of ship's delivery orders to the carrier. Again, a ship's delivery order is not a document of title, but simply an order to the carrier to deliver particular goods to a named person. It is possible for such "documents" to take electronic form.

## 4.40. FREIGHT

Freight is the sum payable for carriage of goods by sea. Where goods are carried under a charterparty, or a bill of lading or otherwise, it is either calculated according to the quantity of goods carried, or a fixed sum is agreed upon, which is payable regardless of the quantity carried—so-called lump sum freight. Unless the contract stipulates to the contrary, it is only payable on delivery of the goods.[3] So failure to deliver, even if caused by events outside the carrier's control disentitles him to freight, unless it is actually the fault of the owner of the goods that they have not been delivered.[4] If the goods are damaged, or there is short delivery, then the owner of the goods is entitled to deduct an appropriate amount from the freight, unless the carrier is not liable for the loss.[5]

### (a) Liability for freight

In *The Success*,[6] Hobhouse L.J. opines:

> "[C]arriage is for reward and the personal liability to pay the reward is a contractual liability . . . The personal liability is that of the person with whom the performing carrier has contracted to carry the goods. This person is normally the shipper. But the shipper may be shipping as the agent of the connsignee, in which case the contract will be with the consignee . . . [T]he inclusion of the words 'freight prepaid' in a bill of lading does not of itself show that the shipper is not to be under any liability for the freight if it has not in fact been paid . . . Indeed, a request to the carrier that he issue a freight prepaid bill of lading before the freight has in fact been paid would normally imply a personal undertaking by the person making the request that it would be paid"

By virtue of s.3 of the Carriage of Goods by Sea Act 1992, liability extends to any holder of a bill of lading who demands or takes delivery from the carrier, or who makes a claim against the carrier. It has been held that taking delivery means the voluntary transfer of possession, and simply co-operating in the unloading of the cargo does not amount to taking delivery.[7]

### (b) Pro rata freight

Obviously, if the goods are not delivered to the agreed destination, freight will not normally be payable. However, if the parties agree that delivery should be made at a place short of the

---

[3] *The Karin Vatis* [1988] 2 Lloyd's Rep. 330, CA.
[4] *Gaudet v Brown* (1873) L.R. 5 P.C. 134.
[5] *Gehrckens v Love and Stewart* (1905) 12 S.L.T. 720; contrast the position in England: *Thomas v Harrowing SS Co* [1915] A.C. 58.
[6] [1997] 2 Lloyd's Rep. 641 at 643.
[7] *The Berge Sisar* [2001] 1 Lloyd's Rep. 663, HL.

contractual destination, or such agreement can be inferred, then freight *pro rata itineris* is payable, *i.e.* a proportionate amount depending on how much of the journey has actually been completed.[8] No such agreement will be inferred unless the shipowner was ready and able to complete the voyage.[9] It is not enough that the goods are accepted at the intermediate port simply because the master of the ship insisted on leaving them there.[10] It must be possible to infer that the owner of the goods has voluntarily accepted delivery at that port and relinquished his right to have the goods delivered to their original destination.[11]

## (c) Advance freight

The contract may sometimes stipulate that freight or some part thereof is payable "in advance", or at a certain point in time, or on the happening of a certain event. In England, the rule appears to be that in such cases the freight is payable even though the goods are never delivered[12] (and of course the contract may be explicit on this point).[13] There would also appear to be Scottish authority to this effect.[14] Yet It has been argued[15] that the case of *Watson & Co v Shankland*[16] is authority for the view that in Scotland the rule is that freight must be repaid where the goods are not delivered, unless the contract clearly stipulates otherwise. However that was certainly not the basis on which the case was ultimately decided by the House of Lords,[17] and it has since been treated as not dealing with advance freight at all, and thus as not laying down any general rule.[18]

## (d) Back freight

If the delivery of the goods at the port of unloading is prevented by something outside the shipowner's control, *e.g.* the goods not being picked up, he may decide to transport them elsewhere, *e.g.* back to the port of unloading. All the expenses of doing so are recoverable from the shipper as "back freight".[19]

## (e) Dead freight

If under a charterparty the shipper is bound to supply a full and complete cargo, any failure to do so will render him liable for "dead freight".[20] This is essentially a claim for damages, calculated by reference to the difference between what he has earned by carrying the cargo, and what he would have earned had the obligation been fulfilled.[21] Obviously then, no question of dead freight can arise when the contract provides for lump sum freight. The principle applies not merely where a deficient cargo is supplied, but whenever the shipper fails to supply the cargo contracted for. So where the charterparty was for the shipping of a number of tugs, but these could not be loaded because their dimensions had been misdescribed, the shipowner was held to be entitled to sail without them, and to claim dead freight in respect of them.[22]

---

[8] *Christy v Row* (1808) 1 Taunt 300; *Hill v Wilson* (1879) 4 C.P.D. 329.
[9] *St Enoch Shipping Co Ltd v Phosphate Mining Co* [1916] 2 K.B. 624.
[10] *Metcalfe v Britannia Ironworks Co* (1877) 2 Q.B.D. 423.
[11] *Vlierboom v Chapman* (1844) 13 L.J. Ex 384.
[12] *Civil Service Co-operative Society v General Steam Navigation Co* [1903] 2 K.B. 756.
[13] *Great Indian Peninsular Railway Co v Turnbull* (1885) 53 L.T. 325.
[14] *Leitch v Wilson* (1868) 7 M. 150.
[15] See *Stair Memorial Encyclopaedia of the Laws of Scotland*, Vol. 21, para. 659.
[16] (1871) 10 M. 142.
[17] See (1873) 11 M. (H.L.) 51.
[18] *Peacock (Iberia) Coal Co Ltd. v Olsen, Johnston & Co Ltd* (1943) 60 Sh. Ct Rep 173.
[19] *Mossgiel Steamship Co v Stewart* (1900) 16 Sh. Ct Rep 289.
[20] *McLean and Hope v Fleming* (1871) 9 M. (H.L.) 38.
[21] *ibid*.
[22] *Raeburn and Verel v Tonnelier* (1894) 11 Sh. Ct Rep 336.

## 4.41.  GENERAL AVERAGE

This is an ancient principle, which entered the *Digest* of Justinian from the law of Rhodes, and which has become part of the law of practically every maritime nation. It is premised on the view that there are three interests involved in any voyage, the ship, the cargo and the freight (or shipowner, cargo owner and person entitled to claim the freight—the same individual may occupy more than one of these roles). In ordinary circumstances, if for example, the ship was damaged by bad weather, then the loss would be borne by the shipowner alone. However, if any interest suffers a sacrifice in order to save the venture as a whole, then the principle of general average dictates that the three interests together bear the cost of the sacrifice. So, where part of a ship's equipment was cut up for fuel in order to keep a pump going so that the ship and its cargo would not be lost, it was held that the principle applied.[23] There are various elements involved in the application of the principle:

- There must be a danger to the whole adventure. If only the ship or only the cargo is threatened, then the principle cannot apply. So where local inhabitants forced the captain of a beached ship to sell its cargo at much less than its value, the principle did not apply, as there was no danger to the ship.[24]
- That danger must be real, not merely apprehended, however reasonable that apprehension might be.[25]
- The sacrifice must be real and intended to save the adventure. So while the principle would apply if the master of a ship cut away a mast to save the ship and the cargo, there is no real sacrifice in cutting away a mast which has already been damaged beyond repair.[26] Equally, where a sacrifice is made as a result of an order given by the authorities, it cannot be claimed that the master intended it to save the adventure.[27]
- The danger must not be attributable to the fault of the party who is claiming contribution. So a shipowner cannot claim in respect of a sacrifice occasioned by the ship being unseaworthy.[28] That being said, if the party would not have been liable for his fault, as where such liability is contractually excluded, then a contribution can be claimed.[29]

Although it is easiest to conceive of general average it terms of the sacrifice of some part of the ship or its equipment, or the jettisoning of some part of the cargo, a claim might also be incurred in respect of vital expenditure, *e.g.* the cost of refloating a ship which has been driven aground.[30] The determination of general average contribution takes place at the conclusion of the voyage and under the law of the place of delivery of the cargo.[31] However, this rule, like any other relating to general average, is subject to contractual modification or exclusion, and it is commonplace to incorporate into the contract a set of rules known as the York-Antwerp Rules, which modify the above principles in certain respects.

---

[23] *Harrison v Bank of Australia* (1872) L.R. 7 Exch. 39.
[24] *Nesbitt v Lushington* (1792) 4 Term Rep. 783.
[25] *Watson & Son Ltd v Fireman's Fund Insurance Co* [1922] 2 K.B. 355.
[26] *Shepherd v Kottgen* (1877) 2 CPD 585.
[27] *Athel Line Ltd v Liverpool and London War Risks Association Ltd* [1944] K.B. 87.
[28] *The Evje (No. 2)* [1978] 1 Lloyd's Rep. 351, CA.
[29] *The Carron Park* (1890) 15 P.D. 203.
[30] *Kemp v Halliday* (1865) 34 L.J.Q.B. 233.
[31] *Simonds v White* (1824) 2 B. & C. 805.

## 4.42. MULTI-MODAL TRANSPORT

There has been a tendency to discuss carriage of goods by road, rail, air and sea, as if they were mutually exclusive, and it may indeed be that goods are covered by different contracts during the various stages of their journey. Yet, especially with the rise of containerisation, it is not uncommon for a contract with a single carrier to be entered into covering all stages of a journey. The carrier may then issue a "through" bill of lading under which he undertakes to carry goods to their destination.[32] Alternatively, he could issue a combined transport document to cover the entire journey. The legal status of such documents is unclear. It is unlikely that they are documents of title, and they may not attract the operation of the Hague-Visby Rules. Even though they may cover the whole journey, different legal regimes will apply to road, rail, sea and air elements of the carriage.[33] This means that the documents have to be very carefully designed, to deal with each aspect of the carriage, for example, invoking the Hague-Visby Rules in case they are held not to apply as a matter of course. Fortunately, sets of rules to govern multi-modal transport contracts have been designed by bodies such as the International Chamber of Commerce, which can be invoked by agreement, and which will provide a clear answer to the various questions which might arise.

---

[32] See *e.g. Coli Shipping (UK) Ltd v Andrea Merzario Ltd* [2002] 1 Lloyd's Rep. 608.
[33] *Mayhew Foods Ltd v Overseas Containers Ltd* [1984] 1 Lloyd's Rep. 317; *Quantum Corpn Inc. v Plane Trucking Ltd* [2002] 1 W.L.R. 2678, CA.

# Chapter 5

# NEGOTIABLE INSTRUMENTS

## 5.1. INTRODUCTION

Negotiable instruments are essentially documents, ownership of which entitles the owner to the payment of a sum of money, the amount of which is apparent on the face of the document. Ownership is generally easily transferred, sometimes by indorsement (see para. 5.6) by the current owner, followed by delivery to the new owner, sometimes by mere delivery. Yet, more importantly, unlike many other rights to payment, the transferee is generally not affected by flaws in the title of the transferor—hence the idea of negotiability. As Willes J. puts it in *Whistler v Forster:*[1]

> "The general rule of law is undoubted, that no-one can acquire a better title than he himself possesses. *Nemo dat quem non habet.* To this there are some exceptions, one of which arises out of the rule of the law merchant as to negotiable instruments. These being part of the currency, are subject to the same rule as money and if such an instrument be transferred in good faith, for value, before it is overdue, it becomes available in the hands of the holder, notwithstanding fraud which would have rendered it unavailable in the hands of a previous holder."

To put things another way, if, for example, a seller in a sale of goods contract assigns his right to be paid, the assignee is subject to any defence the buyer could have pleaded against the assignor. But if payment has been made using a negotiable instrument, such as a bill of exchange (see para. 5.2), then should that instrument be negotiated, the new owner is not subject to any contractual or other defences that the buyer may plead against the seller. Indeed, so much are negotiable instruments treated as equivalent to cash, that any contractual or other defences that the buyer may normally plead against the seller will not be available should the seller himself seek to enforce the bill against the buyer.[2]

---

[1] (1863) 14 C.B. (N.S.) 248 at 257.
[2] *Nova (Jersey) Knit Ltd v Kammgarn Spinnerei GmbH* [1977] 2 All E.R. 463, HL.

By the same token, the absence of negotiability can help distinguish documents which on the face of it appear to be negotiable instruments. Thus a bill of lading (see para. 4.32.) is a document of title which is transferred by indorsement and delivery, just like a negotiable instrument. However, as a bill of lading does not confer on the transferee a better title than the transferor, it is not negotiable, and so cannot be a negotiable instrument.[3] Negotiable instruments, as is elaborated below, are not a creation of law, but of commercial practice which the law has recognised—the so called law merchant. For that reason there is not a fixed and unchanging list of negotiable instruments recognised by the law. As Bigham J. noted in Edelstein v Schuler[4] in deciding that all bearer bonds were negotiable instruments:

> "The law merchant is not fixed and stereotyped; it has not yet been arrested in its growth by being moulded into a code; it is . . . capable of being expanded or enlarged to meet the wants and requirements of trade . . . the effect of which is that it approves and adopts from time to time the usages of merchants which are found necessary for the convenience of trade."

Documents which at the moment are recognised as negotiable instrument include share warrants issued to the bearer, whereby a company states that the bearer is entitled to specified shares,[5] scrip certificates issued to the bearer, whereby the government or a company certifies that the bearer is entitled to be issued with certain bonds or shares,[6] and treasury bills, which are essentially promissory notes (see para. 5.15.) issued by the government. A bankers draft is also a negotiable instrument, being an order to pay a certain sum of money issued by a bank to itself (e.g. by one branch to another). It would tend to take the form of a bill of exchange (see para. 5.2), but as the drawer and the drawee are the same person—the bank—s.5(2) of the Bills of Exchange Act 1882 entitles the holder to treat it as either a bill of exchange or a promissory note.[7] Travellers' cheques take various forms, and depending on which form they take, they may resemble bankers drafts, bills of exchange or promissory notes. However, whatever their precise form, an invariable aspect of travellers' cheques is that the customer signs them on purchase and again when they are cashed or negotiated, and they will not be honoured unless the two signatures match. Some commentators argue that this makes the order/promise to pay conditional, which means that they do not meet the definition of either a bill of exchange or a promissory note.[8] Others see the second signature as simply a formality establishing the holder's right to be paid, and not affecting the unconditional nature of the instrument.[9] However, even if the former view is correct, and travellers' cheques are not bills of exchange or promissory notes, there is an argument that they are a type of negotiable instrument in their own right, given that they are treated as such by the business community.[10]

An IOU simply evidences indebtedness and so is not a negotiable instrument,[11] although if it also contains a promise to pay, it may be treated as a promissory note.[12] The Inner House has held that a building society withdrawal form is not a bill of exchange,[13] and it could be said with certainty that any such form is not a negotiable instrument in its own right.

Bills of exchange, cheques and promissory notes are the most common forms of negotiable instrument. We shall look at the essential characteristics of each.

---

[3] See Lord Devlin in *Kum v Wah Tat Bank* [1971] 1 Lloyd's Rep. 439 at 446, PC.
[4] [1902] 2 K.B. 144 at 154.
[5] *Webb, Hale & Co v Alexandria Water Co Ltd* (1905) 93 L.T. 339.
[6] *Goodwin v Robarts* (1875) L.R. 10 Exch. 337; *Rumball v Metropolitan Bank* (1877) 2 Q.B.D. 194.
[7] See *Universal Import Export GmbH v Bank of Scotland*, 1995 S.L.T. 1318.
[8] *Chitty on Contracts* (28th ed., 1999) para. 34–174.
[9] R. Goode, *Commercial Law* (2nd ed., 1995), p.685.
[10] *Ashford v Thos Cook & Son (Bankers) Ltd* (1970) 471 P. 2d 531.
[11] *Thiem's Tr v Collie* (1899) 1 F. 764.
[12] *Muir v Muir*, 1912 1 S.L.T. 304.
[13] *Weir v National Westminster Bank*, 1994 S.L.T. 1251.

## 5.2. BILLS OF EXCHANGE

The concept of a bill of exchange was first developed more than 700 years ago by the Lombard Merchants. The basic idea is simple. Tam, a Scottish merchant, having sold his goods in Milan, would really like to convert his money into pounds Scots. The easiest way of so doing is to seek out a money changer, who will be able to effect the conversion. But then Tam will have to travel back to Scotland with a great deal of money—a fairly risky practice in medieval Europe. Thus instead the Milanese money changer—we shall call him Adolphus—gives Tam a document which instructs Jim, a money changer in Glasgow, to pay Tam a given sum. This is a bill of exchange. Adolphus is the drawer, Jim the drawee, and Tam the payee. In most cases Tam would present the bill to Jim and obtain payment. Jim would signify acceptance of liability by signing the front of the bill, becoming the acceptor. However, Tam may wish to raise funds on his journey home. Accordingly, he might sell the bill to Clement, a money changer in Paris, signing the back so that Clement becomes the payee.

The front of the bill looks like this

---

To Jim

Pay Tam One Thousand Pounds Scots on sight

*Adolphus*

Accepted

*Jim*

---

The back of the bill looks like this

---

*Tam*

---

As Tam has not signed the bill over to a named individual, the above bill has become payable to the bearer—whoever has the bill in their possession from now on. That means that henceforward the right to be paid under this bill can be transferred simply by transferring possession. In order to enhance the negotiability of bills of exchange, the practice soon emerged of drawing up some bills so that they were expressed to be payable to the bearer to begin with. The law in most European countries including England and Scotland quickly recognised the validity of the sorts of transactions described above, and the *lex mercatoria* or law merchant became common throughout Europe. The common law of both Scotland and England was then codified in the Bills of Exchange Act 1882.[14] This measure will henceforward be referred to as "the 1882 Act".

---

[14] See *McLean v Clydesdale Bank* (1883) 11 R. (H.L.) 1 at 3, *per* Lord Blackburn.

The Review Committee on Banking Services in their 1989 Report on Law and Practice defined the modern functions of bills of exchange as follows[15]:

(1) a means of settling a debt;
(2) a form of currency;
(3) a method of providing short term finance;
(4) a means of guaranteeing another's obligations.

The first two functions are straightforward. As regards the first, we are all familiar with the process of paying a bill by a cheque (a particular type of bill of exchange—see para. 5.12.). In relation to the second, a bill might be circulated almost exactly as if it were a type of money, and indeed bank notes have evolved from a particular type of negotiable instrument known as a promissory note. As far as the third is concerned, a party to a transaction such as a sale may lack ready access to funds, or else may simply wish a period of credit. Paying for goods via a bill which is payable at some point, say three months, in the future would permit this. If the seller in such a transaction wished more immediate access to money, he might choose to sell the bill to another person or institution, *e.g.* a bank, typically at a discount in light of the fact that it is not immediately payable. One would, of course, expect such a seller to charge rather more for the goods in the first place, to reflect the fact that he must either wait for payment, or sell the bill for less than its value. An alternative arrangement would be for the seller to draw a bearer bill payable three months in the future directly on the buyer. The buyer will then accept liability under the bill, and the seller may then either wait for payment in due course, or immediately sell the bill to a third party. The fourth function might arise where, for example, A is reluctant to sell B goods on credit or lend money to him. In order to provide A with some security for payment, C might draw up a bill in favour of A, payable at a future date. If B fulfils his obligation, then the bill can be destroyed or returned to C, but if B reneges, A would look to obtain payment under the bill. A variant on this situation would be for B himself to draw up a bill or bills in favour of A, payable at a future date, as a form of security for performance of his obligations.

## 5.3. THE ESSENTIALS OF A BILL OF EXCHANGE

### (a) Definition

Turning now to the current law relating to bills, s.3(1) of the 1882 Act defines a bill of exchange as "an unconditional order in writing addressed by one person to another, signed by the person giving it, requiring the person to whom it is addressed to pay on demand or at a fixed or determinable future time a sum certain in money to or to the order of a specified person or to bearer"

If a document does not comply with the above definition in every respect, it cannot be a bill of exchange.

### (b) Unconditional order

Although a bill may be courteously phrased, it must be imperative. So "please pay" is an order. "We hereby authorise you to pay" is not.[16] An order to pay the bill out of a specified fund is conditional, but a mere indication that payment may be drawn from a particular fund or a

---

[15] Cmnd 622, para. 8.04.
[16] *Hamilton v Spottiswoode* (1849) 154 E.R. 1182.

particular account may be debited is not.[17] An indication that the bill should only be paid if a receipt form is signed by the payee makes the instrument conditional, but an instruction to the payee to sign such a form does not.[18] Similarly, an indication why the bill has been drawn up does not make it conditional.[19] Section 3(2) of the Act further provides that an instrument which orders any act other than the payment of money cannot be a bill. So, for example, an instrument which ordered both the payment of money and the employment of staff could not be a bill.[20]

## (c) In writing

Although originally bills were manuscript in form, s.2 of the 1882 Act specifically directs that a bill may be printed. There would appear to be no reason why a bill should not be in any form which allows reproduction of the written words, *e.g.* photocopying. Matters of practicality will dictate that bills should be written in as permanent a medium as possible, but this is not a legal requirement, and there is authority to suggest that a bill may validly be drawn up in pencil.[21] From time to time stories arise, real or apochryphal, wherein bills are written on eggs, or shirts or cows, and indeed bills can be written on any medium which will bear writing, save metal.[22] Needless to say, however, bills are very rarely written other than on paper. Again, it is unusual but possible for a bill to take up more than one page, as long as it is a single instrument.[23] A bill need not be written in English.[24]

## (d) Addressed by one person to another

That is by the drawer to the drawee. A bill can be addressed to two or more drawees, but not in the alternative nor in succession.[25] If a person draws a bill on himself, as in the case of a bank draft, then the holder has the option of treating the instrument as either a bill of exchange or a promissory note.[26] The same option is afforded where the drawee is fictitious, or lacks contractual capacity. If no drawer's name appears on the bill, anyone accepting liability thereunder is treated as having issued a promissory note.[27]

## (e) Signed by the person giving it

Although s.18(1) indicates that the drawee can accept liability before it is signed by the drawer, the latter's signature is vital to create a valid bill. The bill does not become valid merely because the drawer subsequently signs the bill as an indorser.[28] Thus if the drawer never signs *qua* drawer, the acceptor cannot be made liable on that bill.[29] Suggestions that an acceptor in such circumstances may become liable as the maker of a promissory note are surely misguided, as the drawee only undertook to pay the holder because directed to do so by the drawer.[30] Although it is almost invariable for the drawer to sign in the bottom right hand corner of the

---

[17] s.3(3).

[18] See respectively, *Bavins Jnr & Sims v London & South Western Bank Ltd* [1901] 1 Q.B. 270; *Nathan v Ogdens Ltd* (1903) 93 L.T. 553.

[19] s.3(3)(b).

[20] *Dickie v Singh,* 1974 S.L.T. (Notes) 3.

[21] *Geary v Physic* (1826) 5 B & C 234.

[22] Coinage Act 1870, s.5.

[23] *K.H.R. Financings Ltd v Jackson,* 1977 S.L.T. (Sh.Ct.) 6.

[24] *Arab Bank Ltd v Ross* [1952] 2 Q.B. 216.

[25] s.6(2).

[26] s.5(2) and see *Universal Import Export GmbH v Bank of Scotland,* 1995 S.L.T. 1318.

[27] *Mason v Lack* (1929) 45 T.L.R. 363.

[28] *South Wales & Cannock Chase Coal Co v Underwood* (1899) 15 T.L.R. 157.

[29] *McCall v Taylor* (1865) 19 C.B., N.S. 301; although the document may be valid as an acknowledgment of debt, see *Lawsons Exrs. v Watson* (1907) 15 S.L.T. 245.

[30] Compare *Stoessiger v S.E. Ry Co* (1854) 3 E & B 549; with *Mason v Lack* (1929) 140 L.T. 696.

bill, this is a matter of practice rather than principle, and a bill will be valid no matter where he signs. Thus a promissory note was held to be valid where the maker wrote "I, John Stiles, promise to pay", without further signature.[31] Signature may include the application of a facsimile signature by means of a rubber stamp), and signature by initials or mark will suffice if it can be shown that this was the drawer's usual method of signature.[32]

Section 23 of the 1882 Act states that nobody can be liable on a bill, whether as drawer, indorser or acceptor, who has not signed it as such. This of course means, first, that a drawer cannot be liable if his signature is forged (but see para. 5.9.), and secondly that he cannot be liable if he appended his signature to a document without the intention of drawing up a bill of exchange (although if he has been negligent, he may be barred from denying the validity of his signature[33]). However, if someone signs a bill, whether as drawer, indorser or acceptor, in a trade or assumed name, he will be liable as if he had signed his own name.[34] Moreover, if a partner signs in the name of a firm, this is equivalent to the signature of all persons liable as partners in that firm.[35]

The phrase "liable as partners" indicates that seeming partners are bound in the same way as actual partners. By the same token, a firm will not be liable when a partner signs his own name on a bill, even if he is acting on behalf of the firm, although when chequebooks were issued to members of a firm which bore the name of that firm, all members were bound when one partner signed his own name under the printed name of the firm.[36] In the not infrequent situation where a partner shares the name of the firm, he is presumed to sign in its name.[37] However, if this presumption is rebutted, then the bill does not bind the other members of the firm, and it is immaterial that the holder believed the bill to be that of the firm rather than the individual concerned.[38] Despite all of the foregoing, it must not be assumed that the members of a firm will invariably bind the firm simply by signing the firm name. Such an outcome must depend on whether a partner in that firm would be regarded as having authority to sign a bill. If the firm has actually authorised him to do exactly that, then the matter is straightforward. But if it has not, then the firm is only bound if the partner has ostensible authority to sign. It is generally accepted that in firms involved in trade, *i.e.* the buying and selling of goods, partners have such authority, whereas in other firms they do not.[39] Therefore with non-trading firms, anyone who takes a bill signed by a partner must rely on him having actual authority. But if one takes a bill from a trading firm, any partner's signature binds the firm. It does not matter that within that firm he lacks authority to sign bills, unless of course the person taking the bill is aware of that lack of authority. But even in that case, the firm would be liable to a subsequent holder of the bill who had given value for it and had no notice of the limitation.[40] It may be added that even in a non trading firm a partner has ostensible authority to draw a cheque.[41]

Section 91(1) of the Act, moreover, lays down the general rule that wherever a signature is required, it is sufficient that it should be provided by a duly authorised representative. Authority may be actual or ostensible, and although the Act *prima facie* regards an unauthorised signature as a nullity, s.24(1) indicates that the drawer may ratify the signing of the bill. Should an agent sign a bill in the name of the principal, and it transpires that he lacks authority, he cannot be liable on the bill, as his own signature does not appear on it. But he may be liable in damages to the holder on the basis that he has warranted his authority.[42] On

[31] *Taylor v Dobbins* (1720) 1 Stra. 399.
[32] See respectively, *Goodman v J Eban Ltd* [1954] 1 Q.B. 550; Bell, *Principles*, s.323.
[33] *Foster v McKinnon* (1869) L.R. 4 C.P. 704.
[34] s.23(1), and see *Wilde v Keep* (1834) 6 C. & P. 235.
[35] s.23(1).
[36] *Ringham v Hackett, The Times,* February 8, 1980 CA.
[37] *Yorkshire Banking Co v Beatson* (1880) 5 C.P.D. 109.
[38] *ibid.*
[39] *Wheatley v Smithers* [1906] 2 K.B. 321; and see *Paterson Brothers v Gladstone* (1891) 18 R. 403.
[40] *Lewis v Reilly* (1841) 1 Q.B. 349.
[41] *Backhouse v Charlton* (1878) 8 Ch. D. 444.
[42] *Anderson v Croall* (1903) 6 F. 153; *West London Commercial Bank v Kitson* (1883) 12 Q.B.D. 157.

the other hand, if an agent draws up a bill and signs his own name, then only he is liable, even if the holder knew that he was signing as an agent.[43] Section 26(1) of the 1882 Act states that anyone who signs a bill, but adds words to his signature to indicate that he signs as an agent or in a representative capacity, will not be liable. But it continues that the mere addition of words describing him as an agent or representative will not exempt him from liability. So if someone signs a bill, and adds words such as "Agent", "Manager", "Secretary" or "Director", those words will generally be taken to be merely descriptive and the signatory will be personally liable on the bill.[44] However in *Bondina Ltd v Rollaway Shower Blinds Ltd*,[45] when the latter company's name was preprinted on a cheque as drawer, the fact that its directors simply added their personal signatures did not make them liable, the Court of Appeal taking the view that it was strikingly obvious that the cheque was drawn up on behalf of the company alone. In deciding whether a signature is that of principal or agent s.26(2) provides that the interpretation most favourable to the validity of the bill is adopted. Thus in *Rolfe Lubell & Co v Keith*[46] goods were to be paid for by a bill of exchange drawn on the buying company, the seller further demanding that the directors of the company indorse the bill in their personal capacity. K indorsed the bill, but added the words "director" and "for and on behalf of the company" to his signature. It was held that these words should be discounted and K be regarded as signing as an individual. As the company was already liable on the bill, its validity would not be reinforced by an indorsement on its behalf.[47] Again, where an individual makes it clear that he signs as a representative, but the body on behalf of which he signs lacks capacity, he will be personally liable.[48]

Section 25 of the 1882 Act states that a signature by procuration operates as notice that the agent has a limited authority to sign, and that the principal is only bound if the agent was acting within the actual limits of his authority. It is generally assumed that this provision only applies where a signature is explicitly by procuration, *i.e.* where the signature is accompanied by the expression "per pro" [the principal], rather than extending to all forms of representative signature.[49] There appears to be some doubt as to whether the principal is only bound if the agent was acting within his actual authority, or whether the agent need only be acting within his ostensible authority.[50]

Although bills are usually signed on behalf of companies by an authorised officer, it is possible for such a person merely to sign the name of the company.[51] It is a requirement of s.349(1) of the Companies Act 1985 that any bill, cheque or promissory note purporting to be signed on behalf of the company must bear its name in legible characters. Anyone who signs an instrument which does not meet this requirement will be personally liable thereon, unless it is duly paid by the company.[52] Persons have been held liable under this provision where there has been the most trivial misdescription or omission, and even where the misdescription is the fault of the person seeking to enforce liability.[53]

## (f) Payable on demand or at a fixed or determinable future time

Section 10(1) indicates that a bill is payable on demand if those words are used, or if it is expressed to be payable on sight or on presentation, or if no time is mentioned. A fixed time is

---

[43] *Leadbitter v Farrow* (1816) 5 M. & S. 345.
[44] *Brebner v Henderson,* 1925 S.C. 643.
[45] [1986] 1 W.L.R. 517.
[46] [1979] 1 All E.R. 860.
[47] See also *Scottish & Newcastle Breweries v Blair,* 1967 S.L.T. 72.
[48] *McMeekin v Easton* (1889) 16 R. 363.
[49] *Alexander Stewart of Dundee Ltd v Westminster Bank Ltd* [1926] W.N. 271.
[50] Compare *Bryant Powis and Bryant Ltd v Quebec Bank* [1893] A.C. 170; with *Midland Bank Ltd v Reckitt* [1933] A.C. 1; and see *Union Bank v Makin* (1873) 11 M. 499.
[51] Companies Act 1985, ss.36A, 37.
[52] s.349(4).
[53] See *Scottish & Newcastle Breweries v Blair,* 1967 S.L.T. 72; *British Airways Board v Parish* [1979] 2 Lloyd's Rep. 361; contrast *Durham Fancy Goods Ltd v Michael Jackson (Fancy Goods) Ltd* [1968] 2 Q.B. 839.

a specified future date. A determinable future time may be a specified time after the date of the bill or after "sight" (when the drawee sees the bill). Most bills will be dated, but a bill is not invalid just because it is not dated,[54] (although banks are not bound to honour undated cheques[55]), nor because it is ante-dated or post-dated.[56] If the bill is undated, s.20 permits any holder to insert the date. Section 12 further provides that where a bill is expressed to be payable at a fixed period after date, but is left undated, any holder may insert the true date. If the holder mistakenly but in good faith inserts the wrong date, s.12 renders the bill enforceable by a holder in due course as if the true date was entered. Section 12 deals in similar fashion with the situation where the acceptance is left undated on a bill payable at a fixed period after sight.

Alternatively, a determinable future time may be a specified time after the happening of an uncertain event which is nonetheless bound to occur, *e.g.* the death of the drawer.[57] A document which fixes the time of payment by reference to a contingent event, *e.g.* the marriage of the drawer, is not a valid bill, even if the event does occur.[58] Nor is a document a bill if payable "on or before" or "by" a particular date,[59] or "after" a particular date. Equally a document payable so many days after acceptance is not a bill, as the drawee may not accept.[60] In *Hong Kong & Shanghai Banking Corporation Ltd v GD Trade Co Ltd*[61] a bill was drawn up using a printed form which indicated that it was payable "at . . . sight", the idea being that the drawer would insert a particular period in the gap. In this case the drawer inserted the words "90 days after acceptance", and because the gap was too narrow, typed over the word "sight". The Court of Appeal held that while a bill expressed to be payable "90 days after acceptance" could not be valid, it was clear that there was no intention to delete the word "sight". That meant that the bill was payable 90 days after acceptance or sight and thus valid. This case illustrates how the courts tend to favour a construction in favour of validity where this is possible. That tendency perhaps went too far in *Novaknit Hellas SA v Kumar Bros International Ltd*[62] where a bill under a contract of sale was expressed to be payable either "60 days from shipment", or "60 days from presentation of documents", the underlying contract having stipulated that the bill was to be presented for acceptance with shipping documents relating to the goods. The Court of Appeal found itself able to hold that this meant that the bills were effectively payable 60 days from sight, since the bills would be presented at the same time as the documents, ignoring the fact that this relied on a contingency. It might be added that in both these cases the Court of Appeal expressed the *obiter* opinion that even if a bill were intially invalid as faling to meet this part of the definition, it could be rendered valid if the acceptor indicated a definite date for payment.

### (g) A sum certain in money

Section 9(1) states that a bill may provide for payment in instalments, with interest at a stated rate, or in a foreign currency, with or without an indicated or ascertainable rate of exchange. A direction to pay in gold dust or iron would not be valid,[63] and the validity of a bill drawn in Euros is doubtful. Section 9(2) provides that if the sum is expressed in both words and figures, but the two do not coincide, the former prevails. There is English authority to suggest that if a bill directs payment of £X "with interest", without specifying the rate of interest, then it is still

---

[54] s.3(4)(a).
[55] *Griffiths v Dalton* [1940] 2 K.B. 264.
[56] s.13(2).
[57] *Roffey v Green* (1839) 10 A & E 222.
[58] s.11.
[59] *Williamson v Rider* [1963] 1 Q.B. 89; *Claydon v Bradley* [1987] 1 W.L.R. 521.
[60] *Korea Exchange Bank v Debenhams (Central Buying) Ltd* [1979] 1 Lloyd's Rep. 548.
[61] [1998] C.L.C. 238.
[62] [1998] C.L.C. 971.
[63] *McDonald v Belcher* [1904] A.C. 429; *Dixon v Bovill* (1856) 3 Macq (H.L.) 1.

valid, as 5 per cent is the understood rate.[64] However, the Scottish courts would not regard that as a valid bill.[65] It is submitted that a bill which indicates a variable interest rate would similarly not be valid.[66] Section 9(2) dictates that interest runs from the date of the bill unless the contrary is stated, and if the bill is not dated, it runs from the date of issue.

### (h) To the order of a specified person or to bearer

If a bill is not payable to the bearer, the payee must be named or otherwise indicated with reasonable certainty.[67] Section 7(2) indicates that there can be several payees, either as joint or alternative payees, and that a bill may be made payable to the holder of an office. It is arguable that a bill which indicates no payee should be treated as payable to the bearer.[68] A bill payable to a fictitious or non-existent person is certainly payable to the bearer,[69] as was the case in *Clutton & Co v Attenborough & Son*[70] where a clerk induced his employer to sign cheques made payable to "George Brett", although neither of them knew anyone of that name. The clerk then indorsed the cheques as "George Brett" and sold them to the defendants for value. They cashed the cheques and the employer was held not to be entitled to recover the money from them, as although they held under a forged indorsement, the bill being legally a bearer bill, the indorsement was unnecessary and so could be disregarded.

Even if the bill is made payable to an existing person, it will be treated as payable to a fictitious person if the drawer never intended that the payee should be paid. That was the result of *Bank of England v Vagliano Bros*[71] where a merchant's clerk drew up a number of bills using the names of existing customers of the merchant as drawer and payee. The merchant duly accepted these bills. The clerk forged indorsements on the bills and obtained payment from the bank. The question then arose whether the bank could debit the merchant's account. He argued that it could not, having paid out under a forged indorsement. The House of Lords, however held that as the clerk had never intended the named payee to receive payment, the latter should be regarded as fictitious, and the bill thus payable to the bearer. As the bank had paid the bill to the bearer, it could debit the acceptor's account. However, matters are quite different if the drawer genuinely intends that the payee should be paid, albeit that intention is induced by another's fraud. So in *Vinden v Hughes*[72] a clerk made out a number of cheques in favour of his employer's existing customers, and obtained his employer's signature to each. He then forged the indorsements of the customers and sold the cheques to H. It was held that H was not entitled to the amount of these cheques, as he held them on forged indorsements. On the question whether the payees should be treated as fictitious (thus rendering indorsement unnecessary) Warrington J. observed[73]:

> "It was not a fiction to the employer then. It was intended to be, and was to him at that moment, a perfectly real transaction. He believed that he owed the sum of money represented by the cheque to the person whose name appeared upon it, and he signed the cheque in that belief."

"Cash" is not a specified person, so that a bill expressed to be payable "to cash" is not a valid bill under the Act, although it may be treated as a form of negotiable instrument payable to the bearer.[74]

---

[64] *Re Tillman* (1918) 34 T.L.R. 322.
[65] *Lamberton v Aiken* (1899) 1 F. 189.
[66] *Bank of Montreal v A & M Investments Ltd* (1982) 136 D.L.R. (3d) 181.
[67] s.7(1), and see *Adam Associates (Strathclyde) Ltd v CGU Insurance plc,* 2001 S.L.T (Sh. Ct) 18.
[68] *Daun & Vallentin v Sherwood* (1895) 11 T.L.R. 211.
[69] s.7(3).
[70] [1897] A.C. 90.
[71] [1891] A.C. 107.
[72] [1905] 1 K.B. 795.
[73] At 806.
[74] *Orbit Mining and Trading Co Ltd v Westminster Bank Ltd* [1963] 1 Q.B. 794, see especially Sellers L.J. at 811.

## 5.4. Negotiable Instruments and the Consumer Credit Act 1974

If a slight digression may be essayed, should a bill be expressed to be payable, say, "90 days after sight", then if it is given as payment for goods or services, a form of credit is effectively being extended. It might therefore be possible to obtain payment in a credit transaction through a negotiable instrument, rather than using the normal forms of contract. The attraction for a creditor is that negotiable instruments are not usually rendered unenforceable because of problems regarding the transaction to which they relate. In any case, it would always be open to the creditor to sell the instrument. The problem for the debtor is that many of the rights conferred by the 1974 Act could easily be circumvented by the use of negotiable instruments described above. Accordingly, except in the case of non-commercial agreements[75] (see para. 3.4.), payment under a regulated consumer credit or consumer hire agreement may not be made by any form of negotiable instrument other than a cheque,[76] while no negotiable instrument including a cheque can be used as security for any sum due under such an agreement,[77] *i.e.* retained as an effective guarantee of payment. Even if payment has been made by cheque, the creditor can only negotiate the cheque to a bank.[78] Any contravention of these provisions means that the regulated agreement is enforceable against the debtor or hirer only by order of the court.[79] Where a person knowingly takes a negotiable instrument in breach of these provisions, he is not entitled to enforce it, and is not a holder in due course[80] (see para. 5.7.). That being said, the bill may yet be enforced by a holder in due course, although the creditor must then indemnify the debtor or hirer.[81]

## 5.5. Incomplete Bills

Under s.20(1), where someone signs a blank sheet of paper and delivers it for conversion into a negotiable instrument, the act of delivery confers *prima facie* authority to complete the bill for any amount, using the signature as that of a drawer, acceptor or indorser. That authority is not confined to the person to whom the paper is delivered, but extends to any subsequent holder.[82] However, delivery and the intention to create a bill are both imperative. A person who has not lawfully obtained such a paper cannot rely on s.20, while someone who merely appends their signature to a piece of paper with no intention of creating a bill cannot be liable.[83] Section 20(1) also states that anyone in possession of a bill which is deficient in a material particular has *prima facie* authority to complete it . An example of this and of a signature being used as that of an indorser can be seen in *McDonald (Gerald) & Co v Nash & Co.*[84] McDonald was willing to sell goods to a third party, only if payment was guaranteed by Nash. Thus M drew a bill on the third party in his own favour. N then indorsed it. As things then stood, despite his indorsement, N was not liable on the bill, as it had not been indorsed to him. The House of Lords held that under s.20(1) M was entitled to place his signature, *qua* payee, above that of N's, so that the bill was properly indorsed to N and he became liable thereon.

---

[75] Consumer Credit Act 1974, s.123(5).
[76] *ibid.*, s.123(1).
[77] *ibid.*, s.123(3).
[78] *ibid.*, s.123(2).
[79] *ibid.*, s.124(1).
[80] *ibid.*, s.125(1).
[81] *ibid.*, s.125(3)–(4).
[82] *McLean v McEwan* (1899) 1 F. 381.
[83] see respectively *Russell v Banknock Coal Co* (1897) 24 R. 1009 at 1018; *Smith v Prosser* [1907] 2 K.B. 735 at 753.
[84] [1924] A.C. 625.

In terms of s.20(2), to make such a bill enforceable against a person who became a party prior to its completion, it must be filled in within a reasonable time and strictly in accordance with the authority given. It has been held that 18 months is not a reasonable time within which to complete a cheque.[85] As far as acting in accordance with the authority given is concerned, this means that, for example, if authority is given to A to complete a bill for a sum of £1,000, and he completes it in respect of £100,000, he cannot enforce it. However, given that a person who is given an incomplete bill is generally assumed to have authority to complete it as he wishes, the burden of proof of his lack of authority rests on the party disputing that authority.[86] Yet, if a bill is after its completion negotiated to a holder in due course, then s.20(2) assumes that it was completed timeously and with authority.[87] In other words, in the last example, a holder in due course would be entitled to enforce the bill for £100,000. In order to be a holder in due course, the bill must have been negotiated to the holder after completion. So an individual cannot be a holder in due course, despite having bought it in good faith, if he is the designated payee of the bill, nor where he himself completed it.[88] Yet even if an individual is not a holder in due course, the person who signed an incomplete instrument may be personally barred from denying its validity, if that individual has relied on it to his detriment.[89] Obviously, a bill can be enforced according to its apparent tenor against an individual who became a party to it after its completion.

## 5.6. NEGOTIATING A BILL

A negotiable bill is payable either to order or to the bearer, and an order bill is one which is either payable to order, or is payable to a particular person and does not contain words prohibiting transfer or indicating an intention that it should not be transferable.[90] So a bill which states "Pay Smith or order" is an order bill and thus negotiable, but the same could be said of a bill which simply states "Pay Smith". If a bill does contain words prohibiting transfer or indicating an intention that it should not be transferable, then it is valid as between the original parties, but is not negotiable.[91] Such an intention can obviously be deduced from the appearance of words such as "not negotiable" on the bill, or the fact that it states "Pay Smith only".[92] It was at one time thought that a bill expressly payable "to order" could not be made non-transferable.[93] However in *Hibernian Bank v Gysin*[94] the bill was payable to " the order of the Irish Casing Co Ltd only" and also bore the words "not negotiable". The Court of Appeal held that it was clearly intended not to be negotiable. It may be suggested that a bill which states "Pay to the order of Smith only" might still be treated as negotiable.

A bearer bill is negotiated simply by delivery.[95] A bill payable to a named payee is transferred by indorsement[96] and delivery. Nothing further is required to transfer the right to a bill. Lord Neaves says in *Connal & Co v Loder*[97]:

> "The privilege of a negotiable document is that it passes in its own corpus the thing it represents without intimation."

[85] *Griffiths v Dalton* [1940] 2 K.B. 264.
[86] *Anderson v Somerville, Murray & Co* (1898) 1 F. 90.
[87] See *McMeekin v Russell* (1881) 8 R. 587.
[88] See respectively, *Herdman v Wheeler* [1902] 1 K.B. 361; *France v Clark* (1884) 26 Ch. D. 257.
[89] *Lloyds Bank Ltd v Cooke* [1907] 1 K.B. 794.
[90] s.8(2), (4).
[91] s.8(1).
[92] *Hibernian Bank v Gysin* [1939] 1 K.B. 483.
[93] *National Bank v Silke* [1891] 1 Q.B. 435.
[94] [1939] 1 K.B. 483.
[95] s.31(2).
[96] s.31(3).
[97] (1868) 6 M. 1095 at 1102.

A bill payable to the order of two or more payees (or indorsees) must be indorsed by all of them, unles the one indorsing has authority to indorse for the others.[98] In practice indorsement means the payee signing the back of the bill,[99] or perhaps an attached slip of paper—an allonge—used when there is no room for further signatures on the back of the bill. Apart from this an indorsement must be written on the bill itself.[1]

In *K.H.R Financings Ltd v Jackson*[2] the Sheriff Principal observed:

> "the purpose of the provision is to enable a bill to operate as a negotiable instrument by ensuring that one piece of paper contains all the writing constituting the obligations of the bill and the names of the parties to it."

A simple signature is a general indorsement. This converts the bill into a bearer bill and subsequent negotiation may occur through mere delivery.[3] A special indorsement occurs where the indorser adds the name of the transferee to his signature, so that the bill is only payable to the designated individual.[4] Any holder may transfer the bill specially or generally. So the fact that a bill may have been specially indorsed on five occasions does not prevent the next holder indorsing it generally and transferring it as a bearer bill. Equally, the holder of a bill which has become a bearer bill may negotiate it to a named indorsee by writing above the general indorsement a direction to pay the bill to a specific person.[5] Whether a bill which was drawn up as a bearer bill can be specially indorsed is uncertain. Australian authority says that it cannot.[6] A bill may be restrictively indorsed by adding the word "only" to the transferee's name.[7] This prevents further negotiation of the bill, although the bill may expressly authorise the indorsee to transfer his rights.[8] In that case, all subsequent indorsees take the bill with the same rights and subject to the same liabilities as that indorsee.[9] Indorsement must be of the entire bill.[10] An indorsement which purports to transfer only part of the amount payable, or which purports to transfer the bill to two or more persons severally does not negotiate the bill,[11] *e.g.* where in a bill for £200 the indorser writes "pay only £50", or "pay Smith £150 and Jones £50". Such "indorsements" may, however, act as valid payment instructions.[12] Where a bill purports to be indorsed conditionally, the condition may be disregarded by the payer.[13]

If one indorses a bill, one becomes potentially liable to any subsequent party, should the bill be dishonoured.[14] Yet this can be prevented by adding the words "without recourse" to one's signature. If a bill payable to a named payee is transferred without indorsement, s.31(4) indicates that the transferee gets a title as complete as that of the transferor. In *Hood v Stewart*[15] Lord Justice Clerk Macdonald observed of this provision:

> "The title obtained by transference is not necessarily the same as the title obtained by indorsement. It is well known that an indorser may confer on an indorsee a better title than he himself possessed. This cannot happen in the case of mere transference. The transferee

[98] s.32(3).
[99] Although indorsement on the front of the bill is theoretically possible: *Young v Glover* (1857) 3 Jur. (N.S.) Q.B. 637.
[1] s.32(1).
[2] 1977 S.L.T. (Sh. Ct) 6.
[3] s.34(1).
[4] s.34(2).
[5] s.34(4).
[6] *Miller Associates (Australia) Pty Ltd v Bennington Pty Ltd* [1975] 2 N.S.W.L.R. 506.
[7] s.35(1).
[8] s.35(2).
[9] s.35(3).
[10] s.32(2).
[11] *ibid.*
[12] *Heilbut v Nevill* (1869) L.R. 4 C.P. 354.
[13] s.33.
[14] s.55(2).
[15] (1890) 17 R. 749 at 753.

acquires the title of the transferor, and nothing more. Hence such exceptions may be stated to the pursuer's title as might have been stated to the title of the transferor. As in an assignation, *utitur iure auctoris* and if the title of his author is bad, his own is no better."

## 5.7. HOLDERS

### (a) Holder of a bill

A bill can only be negotiated by a holder.[16] A holder is, by virtue of s.2 the bearer of a bearer bill, or the payee or indorsee in possession of a non-bearer bill. So anyone in possession of a bearer bill is inevitably a holder, however he obtained the bill. However, if a bill is expressed to be payable to "Alan Brown", then only Alan Brown can be the holder. Again, if Alan Brown indorses the bill specially to "Charlotte Dick" then only Charlotte Dick can be the holder. The Act speaks of holders, holders for value and holders in due course. Different rights attach to each category of holder, although it must be remembered that a holder for value will, by definition, be a holder, and a holder in due course will, by definition, be both a holder and a holder for value. As noted above, only a holder may negotiate a bill. Equally only a holder (or someone acting on his behalf) may present the bill for acceptance[17] or for payment.[18] Only a holder can sue on the bill,[19] or insert the date of issue or acceptance where this is omitted.[20] Only a holder can convert a bearer bill into an order bill,[21] and a bill can only be discharged by payment in due course, if that payment is made to a holder.[22]

### (b) Holder for value

Under s.27(2), where value has at any time been given for a bill, the holder is deemed to be a holder for value as regards the acceptor and all persons who became parties to the bill prior to value being given. This means that a holder for value may enforce the bill against such persons. The provision is designed to circumvent the rule of English law that a party may not enforce an obligation for which he has not provided consideration, and is arguably otiose in Scotland.[23] Section 27(3) further provides that where a person has a lien on a bill he is a holder for value to the extent of the lien.

### (c) Holder in due course

To have a complete array of rights under a bill a holder must be a holder in due course. A holder in due course is defined as by s.29(1) as someone who has taken a bill complete and regular on the face of it under the following conditions:

- that he became holder of it before it became overdue, and without notice that it had been previously dishonoured (if that were the case);
- that he took it in good faith and for value, and when the bill was negotiated to him he had no notice of any defect in the title of the person who negotiated it.

---

[16] s.31.
[17] s.41(1)(a).
[18] s.45(3).
[19] s.38(1).
[20] s.12.
[21] s.34(4).
[22] s.59(1).
[23] *Law v Humphrey* (1876) 3 R. 1192.

Every holder is *prima facie* deemed by s.30(2) to be a holder in due course.

## (d) Who is a holder?

Although the payee is within the definition of a holder, it has been held that a holder in due course must be someone to whom a bill has been negotiated.[24] However if the original payee negotiates the bill and subsequently becomes an indorsee, he can qualify as a holder in due course.[25]

## (e) Complete and regular on the face of it

This means that although one can have authority to complete an incomplete bill in terms of s.20, anyone who does so can never be a holder in due course (although an indorsee from such an individual could). The face of the bill includes the rear, so that any irregularity relating to indorsements would mean the bill was not regular on its face,[26] although it is not irregular for indorsements to appear out of sequence.[27] A bill is complete even though not yet accepted by the drawee,[28] although the same would not be true if any other key signature were missing. It is not irregular for a bill to be postdated,[29] but any material alteration would be irregular. It is irregular for there to be any discrepancy between the words and figures used on a cheque.[30]

## (f) Not overdue when transferred

This will be obvious when a bill is payable on a certain date. When a bill is payable on demand, it is overdue when it appears to have been in circulation for an unreasonable length of time.[31] A person who takes an overdue bill gets no better title than that which the person who negotiated it to him had.[32]

## (g) Without notice of dishonour

By virtue of s.36(5), a person who takes a bill knowing it to have been dishonoured gets no better title than that which the person who negotiated it to him had.

## (h) Good faith

A holder in due course must take a bill in good faith. By virtue of s.90 a person who acts negligently but honestly is acting in good faith. However, Lord Blackburn in *Jones v Gordon*[33] opines that if the facts show that a person:

> "must have had a suspicion that there was something wrong, and that he refrained from asking questions not because he was an honest blunderer or a stupid man, but because he thought—I suspect there is something wrong, and if I make further enquiry, it will no longer be my suspecting it but my knowing it, and then I shall not be able to recover—I think that is dishonesty"

So in that case a man was not acting in good faith where he paid £200 for bills worth over £1,700 on their face.

---

[24] *R. E. Jones Ltd v Waring & Gillow* [1926] A.C. 670; *Williams v Williams*, 1980 S.L.T. (Sh.Ct.) 25.
[25] *Jade International Steel v Robert Nicholas Steels Ltd* [1978] Q.B. 917.
[26] *Arab Bank v Ross* [1952] 2 Q.B. 216.
[27] *Lombard Banking Ltd v Central Garage & Engineering Ltd* [1963] 1 Q.B. 220.
[28] *National Park Bank of New York v Berggren & Co* (1914) 30 T.L.R. 387.
[29] *Hitchcock v Edwards* (1889) 60 L.T. 636.
[30] *Banco di Roma S.p.A. v Orru* [1973] 2 Lloyd's Rep. 505.
[31] s.36(3).
[32] s.36(2).
[33] (1877) 2 App.Cas. 616 at 629.

## (i) Value

By virtue of s.2, value means valuable consideration. In terms of s.27(1), this might include a debt owed by the person who is liable on the bill. Similarly, someone who has a lien over the bill sufficient to make him a holder for value under s.27(3) has been held to have given sufficient consideration to make him a holder in due course.[34] The Court of Appeal in *Clifford Chance v Silver*[35] has suggested that it is enough if one qualifies as a holder for value, so that it might be enough if a previous holder had given value for the bill, even if the current holder had not. This seems dubious.

## (j) Without notice of defect in title

A holder in due course must have no notice of any defect in the title of the person who negotiated the bill to him. Section 29(2) states that a person's title is defective, in particular, where he obtained the bill (or its acceptance) by fraud, duress, force and fear, or other unlawful means, or for an illegal consideration, or where he negotiates it in breach of faith, or fraudulently. So if A draws up a bill in favour of B, and fraudulently persuades C to accept it, B's title is not defective because he has not obtained the bill by fraud.[36] (If he had been aware of the fraud then his title might be defective.) Notice can of course be express notice of a defect of title, but would include being told that there is something wrong with the bill, without knowing precisely what that was.[37] Indeed, in this context although, once again, a person will not be held to have notice where he foolishly ignores facts that would prompt a sensible person to make inquiries, if the circumstances suggest that he suspected that there might be something wrong with the bill, but deliberately avoided making inquiries, notice will be imputed to him. To return to the views of Lord Blackburn in *Jones v Gordon*:[38]

> "A wilful or fraudulent absence of inquiry into the circumstances, when they are known to be such as to invite inquiry, will, if . . . abstinence from inquiry arose from a suspicion or belief that inquiry would disclose a vice in the bills, amount to general or implied notice."

It should also be remembered that the 1882 Act only requires a holder in due course to have no notice of any defect in the title of the person who negotiated the bill to him, when it was negotiated to him. So subsequent knowledge of any such defect should not affect his status as a holder in due course.

## (k) Status of a holder in due course

By virtue of s.38(2), a holder in due course holds the bill free from any defect in the title of prior parties, and is immune from any personal defences which could have been pleaded against prior parties. He can enforce the bill against any party who is liable on it. Thus a holder can enforce a bill even if it has been stolen or is affected by fraud. As Willes J. put it in *Whistler v Forster*:[39]

> "The general rule is undoubted that no one can acquire a better title than he himself possesses: *nemo dat quem non habet*. To this rule there are some exceptions, one of which arises out of the rule of the law merchant as to negotiable instruments. These being part of the currency, are subject to the same rule as money: and if such an instrument be transferred in good faith, for value, before it is overdue, it becomes available in the hands

---

[34] *Barclay's Bank Ltd v Astley Trust Ltd* [1970] Q.B. 527.
[35] [1992] 2 B.L.R. 11.
[36] *R.E. Jones Ltd v Waring & Gillow* [1926] A.C. 670.
[37] *Raphael v Bank of England* (1855) 17 C.B. 161.
[38] (1877) 2 App.Cas. 616 at 625.
[39] (1863) 14 C.B. 196.

of the holder, notwithstanding fraud which would have rendered it unavailable in the hands of a previous holder."

The above represents the main advantage of being a holder in due course. But there are various other rights and protections accorded only to a holder in due course.

- Thus where a bill payable at a fixed period after date is issued undated, s.12 indicates that should the holder in good faith and by mistake insert a wrong date, the bill shall operate and be payable as if the date inserted were the true date. However, if the bill finds its way into the hands of a holder in due course, then the above result follows even if the wrong date were not inserted by mistake nor in good faith. So, for example, if a bill expressed to be payable 30 days after acceptance is accepted on July 1, but that date is omitted, should the holder deliberately insert August 1 as the date of acceptance, an unsuspecting subsequent holder seeking to present the bill for payment on August 31could be told that it is overdue. But if that subsequent holder is a holder in due course, then the bill is treated as if payable on August 31.
- It was noted above (para 5.5.) that under s.20(1), where someone signs a blank sheet of paper and delivers it for conversion into a negotiable instrument the act of delivery confers *prima facie* authority to complete the bill for any amount, using the signature as that of a drawer, acceptor or indorser, but that under s.20(2) to make such a bill enforceable against a person who became a party prior to its completion, it must be filled in within a reasonable time and strictly in accordance with the authority given. However, if a bill is after its completion negotiated to a holder in due course, then s.20(2) assumes that it was completed timeously and with authority.
- It is noted in the next paragraph that while, by virtue of s.21(1), no party can be liable on a bill whether as drawer, acceptor or indorser, until it has been delivered, where a bill is in the hands of a holder in due course s.21(2) *conclusively* presumes it has been validly and unconditionally delivered by all prior parties.
- It is noted in the next paragraph that s.48 provides that if a bill is dishonoured by non-acceptance or non-payment, then the holder loses his right of recourse against the parties to the bill where he fails to give notice of dishonour to the drawer and each indorser. Any party to whom notice is not given is discharged from liability. However, if a bill is dishonoured by non-acceptance, and subsequently negotiated to a holder in due course, then by virtue of s.48(1), while the previous holder could not enforce the bill against prior parties, the holder in due course can.
- It is noted below (para 5.9.) that, by virtue of s.54(2), an acceptor cannot argue against a holder in due course that the drawer or payee does not exist, or that the drawer's signature is a forgery, or that the drawer lacked capacity or authority to draw up the bill, or that the drawer or any payee lacked capacity to indorse the bill. Similarly, by virtue of s.55(1)(b), the drawer cannot argue against a holder in due course that the payee does not exist, or lacked capacity to indorse the bill, while s.55(2)(b) precludes an indorser from disputing with a holder in due course the genuineness of the drawer's signature and all indorsements prior to his own.
- Section 62(2) provides that while the holder of a bill can renounce the liability of any party to the bill, such renunciation will not affect the rights of a holder in due course, who lacks notice of the renunciation.
- It is noted below (para 5.11.) that, under s.64(1), material alteration avoids the bill in relation to everyone who became a party prior to the alteration, except where such a party consents to the alteration. However, a bill may still be enforced, according to its original tenor, by a holder in due course, if the alteration is not apparent.

Section 29(3) states that a holder who derives title through a holder in due course has the rights of that holder, even though he is himself not a holder in due course, *e.g.* where a holder in due course has negotiated the bill to him as a gift, as long as he is himself not a party to any fraud or illegality affecting the bill.

## 5.8. CONDITIONS FOR LIABILITY

Having considered how the right to be paid under a bill may be transferred, it is time to look at who may be liable on a bill of exchange. There are various conditions which have to be met before an individual can become so liable.

### (a) Capacity

Section 22(1) directs that one can only become liable on a bill if one has contractual capacity. However, although a party who lacks capacity cannot be liable, s.22(2) provides that if a bill is drawn or indorsed by such a person, it remains enforceable against other parties.

### (b) Delivery

Every contract on a bill is incomplete and revocable until delivery of the instrument in order to give effect to that contract. Section 21(1) provides that no party can be liable on a bill, whether as drawer or indorser, until it has been delivered. So although A may draw up a bill in favour of B, he is not liable on it until it is delivered to B. Similarly, if B indorses the bill to C, he will not liable to C until it is delivered to C. Delivery is also generally necessary to make an acceptor liable. So, if in the above example the bill is drawn on D, should B present it to D for acceptance, D will not be liable until he has accepted the bill, *and* returned it to B. Nevertheless, an acceptor can also become liable by merely signing the bill, and giving notice that he has done so to the person entitled to payment.[40] Delivery may be an actual physical transfer of possession, or it may be constructive, as where an agent holding the bill for the drawer (or indorser) comes to hold it for the payee (or indorsee). By virtue of s.21(2), delivery may be conditional, in which case delivery will only be regarded as having occurred where that condition has been met. Thus in *Martini & Co v Steel and Craig*[41] when custody of the bill was given to the payee on the understanding that actual delivery would not occur until certain conditions were fulfilled, the bill was held not to have been delivered. Where the bill is no longer in the possession of a party who signed it, s.21(3) presumes that he has delivered it. Where a bill is in the hands of a holder in due course, s.21(2) *conclusively* presumes it to have been validly and unconditionally delivered by all prior parties. So if in the example at the beginning of this paragraph B indorses the bill gratuitously to C, and D refuses to accept liability, A might seek to repudiate liability by suggesting that B stole the bill from him after he signed it, so that it was never delivered. Because the bill is no longer in A's hands, delivery is presumed. However, if he can prove that B did indeed steal the bill, then it is treated as not having been delivered, and he is not liable to either B or C. Yet had B indorsed the bill to C for value, C would be a holder in due course, and it could not be argued against him that the bill had not been delivered. Equally, in the Martini case the question whether the condition had been fulfilled would have been irrelevant, if a holder in due course was seeking to enforce the bill.

### (c) Signature

It would not be entirely true to say that one cannot be liable on a bill if one does not sign it, but in most cases that will be so. Accordingly, one cannot be liable if one's signature is forged upon a bill, as s.24 deems that signature to be "wholly inoperative". If the forged signature is that of the drawer, then as the bill has not been "signed by the person giving it" in terms of s.3(1), it might be argued that the bill is entirely invalid. Yet this is not strictly the case, as an indorser is precluded by s.55(2)(b) from disputing with a holder in due course the genuineness of the drawer's signature, while s.54(2) precludes an acceptor from arguing against a holder in due

---

[40] s.21(1).
[41] (1878) 6 R. 342; *cf. Dextra Bank & Trust Co Ltd v Bank of Jamaica* [2002] 1 All E.R. (Comm.) 193, PC.

course that the drawer's signature is a forgery. Forgery of the drawee's signature as acceptor certainly does not invalidate the bill, and the drawer and any indorser will remain liable on it, although of course the drawee will not be. Forgery of an indorsement breaks the chain of liability. Consider the following example.

Adams draws a bill on Baker in favour of Cole. Baker accepts liability. Cole indorses the bill to Davis. As things stand, Adams Baker and Cole are all potentially liable to Davis. Evans then steals the bill and transfers it to Fox, forging Davis's signature. Fox then indorses it to Gill. When Gill comes to enforce the bill, then not only is it not enforceable against Davis. Under s.24, Davis's signature is treated as wholly inoperative. Thus it as if it were missing.

The front of the bill looks like this

| |
|---|
| To Baker<br><br>Pay Cole One Thousand Pounds on 1st June 2004<br><br> *Alan Adams* <br><br>Accepted<br><br>*Brian Baker* |

The back of the bill looks like this

| |
|---|
| Pay Davis<br><br>    *Chris Cole*<br><br>Pay Fox<br><br>    *David Davis*<br><br>Pay Gill<br><br>    *Fred Fox* |

But in law the back of the bill looks like this

| |
|---|
| Pay Davis<br><br>    *Chris Cole*<br><br>Pay Gill<br><br>    *Fred Fox* |

The signatures on the bill, as the law sees them, may be represented as follows:

| Adams | Baker | Cole | Blank | Fox |
|---|---|---|---|---|
| | (Acceptor) | (Indorser to | | (Indorser to Gill) |
| (Drawer) | | Davis) | | |

As far as Gill and Fox are concerned, the bill lacks an essential indorsement (Davis's) if they are to enforce it. So even if either qualifies to be regarded as a holder in due course, he could not enforce the bill against Adams, Baker or Cole. However, under s.55(2)(a) anyone who indorses a bill promises to subsequent holders that it will be paid. Thus Gill can enforce the bill against Fox. Evans is not liable on the bill, as his signature does not appear on it. He does not become an indorser merely by forging Davis's indorsement. He is nonetheless delictually liable to Fox for fraud. Meanwhile, the forgery does not affect the bill's essential validity, and if recovered by its true owner—Davis—it can be enforced in the normal way. It may be added that in determining who is a subsequent party, where there are two or more indorsements on a bill, s.32(5) deems each indorsement to have been made in the order in which it appears on the bill, unless the contrary is proved.

Discussion of s.24 has so far proceeded on the basis that a signature is inoperative because it is forged, but it may be inoperative because it is unauthorised. The question of authority is considered at para. 5.3. and it is not proposed to repeat that discussion here. Section 24, however, contemplates that an unauthorised signature, unlike a forged signature, may be ratified. There is nonetheless English authority that, despite the terms of s.24, a forged signature may be adopted.[42] Section 24 also contemplates that an individual may be seen as precluded from saying that his purported signature is forged or that a signature is unauthorised—the principle of personal bar. This may arise where the individual has already claimed that the signature is genuine, as in *Leach v Buchanan*,[43] or where he discovers the forgery but fails to reveal it, as in *Greenwood v Martins Bank*.[44] The latter case featured a husband who had discovered that his wife had been forging his signature on cheques, but did not inform the bank. The House of Lords held that he was under a duty to inform the bank of these forgeries, and his failure to do so amounted to a representation that his signature was genuine. Lord Tomlin commented[45]:

"Mere silence cannot amount to a representation, but when there is a duty to disclose, deliberate silence may become significant and amount to a representation."

It is suggested that personal bar would not operate, if disclosure could not have been made in time to prevent the detriment which was suffered by the person who relied on the signature.[46]

## 5.9. WHO IS LIABLE ON A BILL?

Having considered the prerequisites of liability, it is time to ask which parties may be liable on a bill.

### (a) The drawee

It is obviously assumed that the person on whom a bill is drawn will pay the bill. However, until a drawee accepts liability he is not a party to a bill, and thus not liable thereon, although failure

---

[42] *Greenwood v Martins Bank* [1932] 2 K.B. 371 at 379, *per* Scrutton L.J.
[43] (1802) 4 Esp. 226.
[44] [1933] A.C. 53.
[45] at 57.
[46] *McKenzie v British Linen Co* (1881) 6 App. Cas. 82.

to accept liability may place him in breach of an obligation to the drawer.[47] Nonetheless, if a drawee has funds available for the payment of the bill, s.53(2) directs that the bill operates as an assignment of the sum of the bill in favour of the holder[48] from the time the bill is presented to the drawee—the "funds attached" rule. In other words, when the bill is presented, the holder gains a right to any of the drawer's funds held by the drawee up to the amount of the bill.[49] So in *British Linen Bank v Carruthers*[50] a cheque for £161 was presented to the bank. The bank refused payment as the customer had only £136 in his account. When the customer went bankrupt the trustee in bankruptcy claimed all of the funds of the bankrupt held by the bank. However, the payee of the cheque argued that its presentation gave him a right to the £136. The court agreed, Lord Shand observing,[51]:

> "The result of the presentation of the cheque was to give a right to the funds of the drawer which the banker had in his hands at the time."

In order to determine whether there are "funds available" under s.53(2), a bank is entitled to combine all its customer's accounts. So a cheque would not amount to an assignation of funds in an account where, taking a customer's accounts as a whole, he is overdrawn.[52] Nor can it be argued that an overdraft facility creates "funds available".[53]

## (b) The acceptor

Usually, the bill will be paid by the acceptor. Where a drawee accepts, s.54(1) provides that he is undertaking to pay the bill according to the tenor of his acceptance (see next paragraph). Section 54(2) states that an acceptor cannot refuse payment to a holder in due course on the basis that the drawer does not exist, or that the drawer's signature is a forgery, or that the drawer lacked capacity or authority to draw up the bill, or that the payee does not exist or lacked capacity to indorse. Yet the same provision allows an acceptor to refuse payment, on the basis that an essential indorsement has been forged. It should be remembered that where the payee is a fictitious person, s.7(3) treats the bill as payable to the bearer, and hence negotiable by delivery. Therefore, in such a case, the acceptor cannot refuse to pay on the basis that the payee's indorsement has been forged, as such indorsement is not essential.

It is possible under s.65, although almost unheard of in practice nowadays, for a stranger to the bill to accept the bill to save the honour of any party who might be liable on it, should the drawee refuse to accept or the acceptor fail to pay. For this to happen, first, the bill must have been protested for dishonour by non-acceptance (see next paragraph), or protested for better security. (Section 51(5) provides that where the acceptor becomes bankrupt or insolvent or suspends payment before the bill matures, the holder may cause the bill to be protested for better security against the drawer and indorsers.) Secondly, the bill must not be overdue. Thirdly, the acceptor for honour must not be a party already liable on the bill. (Bizarrely, this might mean that a drawee who has refused to accept, might nonetheless accept for the honour of the drawer.) Fourthly, the holder must consent to this acceptance. By virtue of s.66(1), the acceptor for honour by accepting the bill engages that, if the bill has been duly presented to him, he will pay it according to the tenor of his acceptance, if the following conditions are met. First, the bill must have been duly presented for payment by the drawee, and not been paid by the drawee. Secondly, it must have been protested for non-payment. Thirdly, he (the acceptor

---

[47] *Hopkinson v Forster* (1874) L.R. 19 Eq. 74.

[48] So if anyone other than the holder seeks to present the bill, there will be no assignation: see *Dickson v Clydesdale Bank Ltd,* 1937 S.L.T. 585.

[49] That right may be invoked not only against the drawee, but against parties with competing assignations: *Watt's Trs v Pinkney* (1853) 16 D. 279.

[50] (1883) 10 R. 923.

[51] at 928.

[52] *Kirkwood & Sons v Clydesdale Bank Ltd,* 1908 S.C. 20.

[53] *Sutherland v Royal Bank of Scotland,* 1997 S.L.T. 329 at 340G-H.

for honour) must receive notice of these facts. Section 66(2) then makes him liable to the holder and to all parties to the bill subsequent to the party for whose honour he accepted.

## (c) The drawer

Section 55(1)(a) stipulates that the drawer of a bill, by drawing it, engages that it will be accepted and paid according to its tenor, and that if the bill is dishonoured he will compensate the holder and any indorser who is compelled to pay it (see below), provided that the requisite proceedings on dishonour are taken. If the bill is not accepted, then the drawer will have primary liability. If it is accepted but not paid, his liability is secondary to that of the acceptor. If called on to pay by a holder in due course, s.55(1)(b) provides that he cannot escape liability just because the payee does not exist or had no capacity to indorse. In terms of s.16(1), a drawer can always avoid liability by drawing up a bill "without recourse", although a payee might well be reluctant to take a bill in that form.

## (d) An indorser

Section 55(2)(a) stipulates that an indorser, by signing the bill, engages that it will be accepted and paid according to its tenor, and that if the bill is dishonoured he will compensate the holder and any subsequent indorser who is compelled to pay it, provided that the requisite proceedings on dishonour are taken. Under s.55(2)(b), he also guarantees to a holder in due course that the drawer's signature and all indorsements prior to his own are genuine. Accordingly, if a bill is stolen, and an indorsement forged, the original parties to the bill will not be liable to the holder, but the indorser will be. Once more, s.16(1) permits an indorser to exclude liability by indorsing "without recourse".

An illustration may help us understand the relationships involved. Let us take the example of Dodd, who draws a bill on Abel, in favour of a named payee Pratt, who then indorses it to Ion, who indorses it to Jones, who in turn indorses it to the current holder Hart.

The front of the bill looks like this

---

To Abel


Pay Pratt One Thousand Pounds on 1st June 2001


*Dylan Dodd*

---

The back of the bill looks like this

---

Pay Ion

    *Paul Pratt*

Pay Jones

    *Ian Ion*

Pay Hart

    *John Jones*

---

Suppose Abel, the drawee, refuses to accept liability. The chain of liability is thus:

Dodd      —      Pratt      —      Ion      —      Jones      —      Hart

The drawer would be ultimately liable, but Hart could equally seek to make all or any one of Pratt, Ion or Jones liable, the drawer and all indorsers being jointly and severally liable to the holder if a bill is dishonoured.[54] If Jones was made liable, he could proceed against all or any of Ion, Pratt and Dodd, while if Ion was made liable, he could proceed against either or both of Pratt or Dodd.

If Abel accepts liability, the chain looks like this:

Abel      —      Dodd      —      Pratt      —      Ion      —      Jones      —      Hart

The only real difference is that Abel becomes primarily liable, but if Abel should fail to pay, the chain of potential liability is as before. English authority suggests that if an acceptor fails to pay, any indorser who has been obliged to pay may also seek an indemnity from him.[55]

Suppose instead that Ion stole the bill from Pratt, forging the latter's indorsement. The situation might be represented thus:

Abel   —   Dodd   —   Pratt                          Jones   —   Hart

As Jones and Hart both take on a forged indorsement, they have no rights against the prior parties to the bill—Abel, Dodd and Pratt. Yet Jones would be liable to Hart. The chain of liability, as between the original parties remains in effect, and a new chain has been created. I is not liable *on the bill* to either Jones or Hart, as he has not indorsed it, but would be personally liable to Jones for fraud.

## (e) The quasi-indorser

Section 56 stipulates that where a person signs a bill otherwise than as a drawer or acceptor, he incurs the liabilities of an indorser to a holder in due course. The sort of situation contemplated is where someone who is not a holder of a bill nonetheless adds his signature to it to guarantee it will be paid. Consider the example just given. Suppose Jones had been reluctant to take the bill from Ion, but is persuaded to do so, because Brown, a person he knows to be of sound financial standing, agrees to add his signature under the indorsement of Ion. Jones then indorses it to Hart, and it is dishonoured while in his hands. When he looks to enforce it, along with the other signatures on the bill, he will find that of Brown. Brown cannot be an indorser, as he never owned the bill, so the Act treats him *as if* he were an indorser. Thus Hart can make Brown liable on the bill along with the others. Had Ion indorsed the bill to Hart gratuitously, Hart would not have given value for it, and thus would not be a holder in due course. Could he enforce the bill against Brown? This depends on how s.56 is interpreted. It may mean that Brown is only liable to a holder in due course, but the preferable interpretation is that anyone who signs the bill as Brown did incurs to subsequent parties the type of liabilities an indorser would incur to a holder in due course. A quasi-indorser is probably entitled to the rights of a true indorser, such as having to receive notice of dishonour in order to be made liable.[56] A quasi-indorser will not be liable to prior parties.[57]

---

[54] *Rouquette v Overmann* (1875) L.R. 10 Q.B. 525 at 537, *per* Brett L.J.
[55] *Duncan Fox & Co v North and South Wales Bank* (1880) 6 App. Cas. 754.
[56] *Lombard Banking Ltd v Central Garage and Engineering Co Ltd* [1963] 1 Q.B. 220.
[57] *Walker's Trs v McKinlay* (1880) 7 R. (H.L.) 85; but see *McDonald (Gerald) & Co v Nash & Co* [1924] A.C. 625.

## (f) Accommodation parties

An accommodation party is a person who has gratuitously signed a bill as drawer, acceptor or indorser in order to accommodate another party. A typical example would be where an individual who is short of money—A—draws up a bill which is payable to the bearer at a certain point in the future and persuades someone of impeccable financial standing—B—gratuitously to accept the bill. Given that the bill is accepted by a person of substance, A should be able to sell it in order to raise the money he needs. The hope is that when the bill becomes payable, A's financial situation will have improved sufficiently for him to be able to provide B with funds to meet the bill. Alternatives to the above scenario would be for A to draw a bill payable to B, which B indorses gratuitously, again allowing A to sell it, or where B simply gratuitously draws a bill in favour of A. But what happens if A cannot provide B with funds? Section 28(2) says that an accommodation party is nonetheless liable on the bill to a holder for value, even though that holder knew him to be an accommodation party, although he is not liable to the party accommodated. So if B has gratuitously drawn or indorsed a bill in favour of A, the bill cannot be enforced against him by A. Section 28 also speaks of an accommodation bill. Although the term is not defined, it can only be a bill where an individual has been accepted gratuitously, to "accommodate" the drawer.

In this context, the concept of a referee in case of need may be mentioned. Although this is now practically unheard of in practice, s.15 leaves it open to the drawer or any indorser to insert in the bill the name of a person to whom the holder may resort in case of dishonour. This referee in case of need is not, properly speaking, liable on the bill, and it is in the option of the holder to resort to him or not.

## (g) Negotiator of a bearer bill

A bearer bill is transferred by delivery, so anyone who negotiates it will not sign it and thus s.58(2) confirms that he will not be liable on the bill. This applies not only to bills drawn up as bearer bills, but also to bills which have become bearer bills through indorsement. Nonetheless, under s.58(3), anyone who thus negotiates a bearer bill warrants to his *immediate* transferee, that the bill is what it purports to be (*i.e.* is not affected by forgery),

- that he has the right to transfer the bill;
- that he is not aware of any fact which would render the bill valueless.

If any of these warranties is breached, he will be liable in damages. If the holder of a bearer bill should actually indorse it, then s.56 makes him liable on the bill as if he were an indorser.

## 5.10. How is a Bill Enforced?

Having considered who might be liable on a bill, the next question which arises is how the holder actually obtains payment.

## (a) Presentment for acceptance

If a bill is payable on demand or on sight or on presentation, or at any time after a certain date, then there is no need to present it for acceptance. Yet it may often be thus presented, as the fact that the drawee has accepted liability will obviously aid its ultimate enforceability, as well as enhancing its negotiability. Section 39 insists that a bill *must* be presented for acceptance in the following instances:

- where it expressly stipulates that it shall be presented for acceptance—even bills payable on demand must be presented for acceptance in such a case;

- where it is drawn payable elsewhere than the residence or place of business of the drawee. Section 45(4) assumes that these will be the places where the bill will be paid, so it is important to know whether the drawee will accept it if payable elsewhere. If the holder of such a bill does not have time to present it for acceptance before presenting it for payment on the day that it falls due, s.39(4) excuses the delay, and does not discharge the drawer or any indorser;
- where it is drawn payable at a certain period after sight. Here acceptance is obviously necessary to determine the date when the bill matures (becomes payable). Unless a holder of such a bill presents it or negotiates it within a reasonable time, he will lose his right of recourse against the drawer and prior indorsers.[58] In determining what is a reasonable time, regard must be had to the nature of the bill, trade usage and the facts of the case.[59]

There are rules as to how the bill must be presented. Thus s.41(1)(a) directs that presentment must be made by or on behalf of the holder to the drawee, or to some person authorised to accept or refuse acceptance on his behalf, at a reasonable hour on a business day and before the bill is overdue. Section 92 defines a business day as any day from Monday to Friday, apart from bank holidays, Good Friday and Christmas Day. (Section 18(2) allows a bill to be accepted though overdue, and s.10(2) then treats it as a bill payable on demand.) Secondly, where a bill is addressed to two or more drawees, who are not partners, s.41(1)(b) demands that presentment must be made to them all, unless one has authority to accept for all. Thirdly, where the drawee is dead, s.41(1)(c) states that presentment *may* be made to his personal representative. Fourthly, where the drawee is bankrupt, s.41(1)(d) states presentment *may* be made to him or his trustee. (Presentment is optional in these instance, see below). Finally, where authorised by agreement or usage, s.41(1)(e) renders presentment by post sufficient.

Under s.41(2), presentment (in those cases where otherwise necessary) is excused, and the bill may be treated as dishonoured by non-acceptance, where it cannot be effected by reasonable diligence, or where the drawee is dead, bankrupt, fictitious or lacks capacity. The same applies if the bill is not properly presented, but the drawee refuses to accept on some other ground. However, s.41(3) states that presentment is not excused, just because the holder has reason to believe that the bill will be dishonoured.

Under s.43(1), a bill is dishonoured by non acceptance:

(1) where it is duly presented for acceptance in accordance with the above rules, and acceptance is either refused or cannot be obtained within 24 hours,[60] or

(2) where presentment for acceptance is excused, and the bill is not accepted.

When a bill is dishonoured by non-acceptance, s.43(2) gives the holder an immediate right of recourse against the drawer and any indorser, and renders presentment for payment unnecessary. But if the bill is presented for acceptance, and is not accepted within 24 hours, then s.42 insists that the presenter must treat it as having been dishonoured, otherwise the holder will lose the aforesaid right of recourse.

## (b) Qualified acceptance

Under s.19(1), an acceptance may either be general or qualified. It has been said[61]:

> "the words of qualification must be incorporated into the acceptance, or at least so connected with the acceptance as obviously to form part of it; and must be also be such as to indicate clearly and unequivocally the nature of the restriction they are meant to introduce."

---

[58] s.40(1)–(2).
[59] s.40(3).
[60] See *Bank of Van Diemen's Land v Bank of Victoria* (1871) L.R. 3 P.C. 526.
[61] *per* Lord Watson in *H Meyer & Co Ltd v Jules, Decroix, Verley et Cie* [1890] A.C. 520 at 525.

So if there is any doubt whether apparent words of qualification written by the acceptor are truly intended to qualify the acceptance, they may be ignored and the acceptance treated as general. The Act identifies five ways in which an acceptance may be qualified, but these examples should not be regarded as exhaustive.[62] According to s.19(2) then, a qualified acceptance may be:

- conditional (*i.e.* where payment is dependent on the fulfilment of a stated condition[63];)
- partial (*i.e.* for part of the amount only);
- local (*i.e.* to pay only at a particular place. An indication that the bill will be paid at a specified place is not qualified, unless it is clear that the bill will only be paid there and not elsewhere. So in *Bank Polski v Mulder*[64] the fact that a bill was accepted payable at Amsterdam did not mean that the acceptance was qualified, as words such as "only" or "and not elsewhere" had not been added. Sometimes an acceptance will indicate that it is payable at a particular bank. This is again a general acceptance[65]);
- qualified as to time (*e.g.* where the acceptor indicates that he will not pay a bill drawn payable one month after sight until three months after sight);
- accepted by some of the drawees but not all. (section 6 allows a bill to have joint, but not alternative, drawees.)

Under s.44(1), a holder faced with a qualified acceptance may either take it or treat the bill as dishonoured by non acceptance. If he takes it, he should obtain the consent of the drawer and all prior indorsers, as by virtue of s.44(2), their lack of consent will discharge them from liability. Yet, if a drawer or indorser receives notice of a qualified acceptance, and does not dissent within a reasonable time, consent will be implied by s.44(3). Under s.44(2), consent is not required for the taking of a partial acceptance, as long as all parties are notified. The bill is then treated as dishonoured for the balance.

## (c) Presentment for payment

Unless presentment for payment is excused (see below), a bill must be duly presented for payment, failing which the drawer and any indorser will be released from liability by s.45. Nevertheless, due presentment is not necessary to make an acceptor liable where the bill has been generally accepted.[66] Indeed, even if the terms of an acceptance require presentment for payment, in terms of s.52(2) the acceptor will not be discharged by failure to present on the day the bill matures (see below), unless this is expressly stipulated.

## (d) How is a bill duly presented?

It must be presented at the right time, and at the right place. If a bill is not payable on demand, s.45(1) demands that presentment be made on the day it falls due, not the day before, or the day after.[67] In terms of s.14(1), a bill is due on the last day of the time of payment fixed by the bill, or if that is not a business day, on the next succeeding business day (s.14(1)). So if a bill dated November 25 is payable one month after that date, it will be due on December 27 (or on

---

[62] *Decroix, Verley et Cie v H. Meyer & Co Ltd* [1890] 25 Q.B.D. 343.

[63] See, *e.g. Craig v Howie* (1817) 6 Pat 261.

[64] [1948] 1 K.B. 497.

[65] *Ex p. Hayward* (1887) 3 T.L.R. 687.

[66] s.52(1), and see *McNeill v Innes, Chambers & Co,* 1917 2 S.L.T. 5.

[67] See respectively *Hamilton Finance Co Ltd v Coverley Westray Walbaum & Tosetti Ltd* [1969] 1 Lloyd's Rep. 53; and *Yeoman Credit Ltd v Gregory* [1963] 1 W.L.R. 343; *Neill v Dobson, Molle & Co Ltd* (1902) 6 F. 625.

December 29, if December 27 is a Saturday). Section 14(3) directs that where a bill is payable at a fixed period after sight, the time begins to run from the date of acceptance, or from the date of noting or protest (see below) if the bill is noted or protested for non-acceptance or non-delivery. If a bill is payable on demand, then s.45(2) provides that it must be presented within a reasonable time after its issue to make the drawer liable, and within a reasonable time after its indorsement to make an indorser liable. In determining what is a reasonable time, s.45(2) states that regard must be had to the nature of the bill, trade usage and the facts of the case. All that being said, very different rules apply if one is seeking to enforce the bill through summary diligence (see below).

Section 45(3) demands that presentment be made by the holder or his authorised agent to the drawee or his authorised agent at the proper place at a reasonable hour on a business day. A reasonable hour would tend to mean business hours. The proper place is any place specified in the bill, whether specified by the drawer or acceptor.[68] If no such place is specified in the bill, then, under s.45(4)(b), the proper place is the acceptor's address if given in the bill. So if a bill is drawn on (and accepted by) "Messrs Law & Co, Solicitors, 800 Buchanan Street, Glasgow," 800 Buchanan Street is the proper place. Moreover, in *Neill v Dobson, Molle & Co Ltd*[69] the bill being addressed to the acceptor at his home address, presentment at his business address was held improper. If no address is given, then under s.45(4)(b), the proper place is the acceptor's place of business if known, failing which his ordinary residence if known. If all else fails, s.45(4)(d) directs that the proper place is anywhere the drawee or acceptor can be found, or his last known place of business or residence. If the bill is presented at the proper place, but no person authorised to pay or refuse payment can be found, s.45(5) does not require further presentment. If a bill is drawn on or accepted by two or more persons who are not partners, and no place of payment is specified, then s.45(6) insists that presentment must be made to them all. Where the drawee or acceptor is dead, and no place of payment is specified, s.45(7) directs that presentment must be made to a personal representative, assuming that one exists and he can be found.

Section 46(1) excuses delay in presentment when caused by circumstances beyond the control of the holder, and not imputable to his default, misconduct or negligence. Such circumstances may even embrace postal delay.[70] Where the cause of delay ceases to operate, that provision insists that presentment must be made with reasonable diligence. Presentment may be dispensed with altogether in certain circumstances. These are rather narrower than the circumstances in which presentment for acceptance is excused. Thus presentment for payment is *not* dispensed with where the acceptor is dead, bankrupt or lacks capacity. It is of course the case that presentment for payment is not necessary where it has already been dishonoured by non-acceptance.[71] Presentment for payment is also dispensed with where:

- it cannot be effected with reasonable diligence.[72] So in *Cornelius v Banque Franco-Serbe*[73] a cheque was drawn on a bank in Amsterdam. Shortly thereafter, the German army occupied Amsterdam, rendering presentment practically impossible, and indeed illegal. In those circumstances, failure to present did not relieve the drawer of liability. However, s.46(2)(a), states that the fact that the holder has reason to believe that the bill will be dishonoured does not dispense with the necessity of presentment. In *Hamilton Finance Co Ltd v Coverley Westray Walbaum & Tosetti Ltd*[74] a bill was presented on the day before the due date and returned dishonoured. It was

---

[68] s.45(4)(a), and see *Barclays Bank plc v Bank of England* [1985] 1 All E.R. 385.

[69] (1902) 6 F. 625.

[70] *Hamilton Finance Co Ltd v Coverley Westray Walbaum & Tosetti Ltd* [1969] 1 Lloyd's Rep. 53. Presentment may be made by post where authorised by agreement or usage: s.45(8).

[71] s.43(2).

[72] s.46(2)(a).

[73] [1942] 1 K.B. 29.

[74] [1969] 1 Lloyd's Rep. 53.

held that even this fact did not dispense with the necessity of presentment on the due date, and failure to do so released the drawer and indorsers from liability;

● the drawee is a fictitious person[75];

● presentment is waived.[76] By virtue of s.16(2), it is always possible for a drawer or any indorser to expressly waive any of the holder's duties as far as he is concerned, by so writing on the bill. But waiver may be implied, *e.g.* by a party promising to pay the bill, despite being aware that due presentment has not occurred, and that this has discharged him from liability[77];

● as regards the drawer, where the drawee or acceptor is not bound, as between himself and the drawer, to accept the bill, and the drawer has no reason to believe that the bill would be paid if presented.[78] This would obviously embrace the situation where the drawer draws a bill on someone with whom he has no relationship, but the most common example of the situation contemplated by this provision would be where someone draws a cheque on a bank account which he knows lacks sufficient funds to cover the cheque, assuming of course he has no overdraft facility or has exceeded it. Where the provision applies, failure to present would not release the drawer from liability, but any indorser would still be released;

● as regards any indorser, where the bill was made or accepted for his accommodation, and he has no reason to believe that the bill would be paid if presented.[79]

By virtue of s.67(1), where a dishonoured bill has been accepted for honour, or contains the name of a referee in case of need (see previous paragraph), it must be protested for non-payment (see below), before it is presented for payment to the acceptor for honour or referee in case of need.

Where the address of the acceptor for honour is in the same place that the bill is protested, s.67(2) states that it must be presented to him not later than the day following its maturity. Otherwise, it must be forwarded for presentment to him not later than the day following its maturity. By virtue of s.67(3), delay in presentment or non-presentment are excused in the same circumstances as discussed above.

A bill is dishonoured by non payment when it is duly presented for payment and payment is refused or cannot be obtained, or where presentment is excused and the bill is overdue and unpaid.[80]

## (e) Notice of dishonour

If a bill is dishonoured by non acceptance or non payment then the holder has an immediate right of recourse against the parties to the bill.[81] However, an immediate right of recourse is not the same thing as an immediate right of action, and the latter can only arise where notice of dishonour is received.[82] Section 48(1) indeed states that where a bill is dishonoured by non acceptance or non payment, notice of dishonour must be given to the drawer and each indorser, and any such party to whom notice is not given is discharged from liability. That being said, if a bill is dishonoured by non-acceptance, and subsequently negotiated to a holder in due course, then while the previous holder could not enforce the bill against prior parties, s.48(1) allows the holder in due course to do just that. Again, where a bill is dishonoured by non-acceptance and notice of dishonour is given, s.48(1) states that notice of dishonour by non

---

[75] s.46(2)(b).

[76] s.46(2)(e).

[77] *Singer v Elliott* (1887) 4 T.L.R. 34; and see *McTavish's J.F. v Michael's Trs.,* 1912 1 S.L.T. 425, part payment would have amounted to implied waiver had it not been made in error.

[78] s.46(2)(c); and see *Bank of Scotland v Lamont* (1889) 16 R. 769.

[79] s.46(2)(d).

[80] s.47(1).

[81] ss.43(2), 47(2).

[82] *Kennedy v Thomas* [1894] 2 Q.B. 759 at 765, *per* Davey L.J.

payment need not then be given, unless the bill has been accepted in the meantime. (It is entirely competent for a bill previously dishonoured by non-acceptance to be accepted[83].) Section 52(3) makes it clear that there is no need to give notice of dishonour to an acceptor.

By virtue of s.49(1), notice must be given by (or on behalf of) the holder, or by (or on behalf of) an indorser who, at the time of giving it, is himself liable on the bill. This means not only that an indorser must have himself received timeous (see below) notice in order to give valid notice, but also that someone who has indorsed "without recourse" cannot give valid notice. If notice is given by the holder, then as a result of s.49(3), it operates for the benefit of all subsequent holders, and for the benefit of all prior indorsers who have a right of recourse against the party to whom notice is given. So, if the holder, having given notice of dishonour, then negotiates the bill, the new holder is entitled to enforce the bill against the party receiving notice.

As regards how notice given by the holder might operate for the benefit of an indorser, an example might help. Brown draws a bill on Andrews in favour of Curry, who indorses specially to Don, who indorses specially to Evans, who indorses specially to Fox. Fox presents the bill for acceptance to Andrews, who refuses to accept. If Fox duly sends notice of dishonour to Brown, then the rights of Curry, Don and Evans against Brown are also preserved. If Fox were to send notice of dishonour to all prior parties, then everyone's rights in the chain of liability are preserved, i.e. Evans against Brown, Curry and Don, Don against Brown and Curry, Curry against Brown.

If, on the other hand Fox were to send notice of dishonour only to Evans, then no other party's right of recourse is preserved, as only Fox has a right of recourse against Evans. In this last scenario, Fox's own rights against the other parties depend on notice of dishonour being duly sent by the appropriate indorser. Section 49(4) states that notice given by an indorser entitled to give notice operates for the benefit of the holder and all indorsers subsequent to the party to whom notice is given. So, assuming that Fox were to send notice of dishonour only to Evans, if Evans then duly sends notice of dishonour only to Don, then he preserves both his and Fox's right against Don (but against no other party). Again, if Evans duly sends notice of dishonour only to Brown, then he preserves everyone's right against Brown (but against no other party). And if he were to send notice of dishonour to all prior parties, then everyone's rights in the chain of liability would be preserved.

Often what will happen in the type of scenario above will be that each party will in turn send notice of dishonour to the person who indorsed the bill to him, with the payee (Curry) ultimately giving notice to the drawer (Brown). If that happens, then the rights of the holder against all the other parties will be preserved, as will the rights of each indorser against all parties prior to him. However, there may be problems if any indorser fails to give notice, or, as is more likely given that he would have to give notice to preserve his own rights, fails to give notice as prescribed by the Act. So if Fox were to send notice of dishonour only to Evans, and Evans failed to send due notice to Don, Fox loses any right of recourse against anyone but Evans. Thus, unless the holder is entirely confident that the person who indorsed the bill to him has funds to meet the bill, the safest course of action is to send notice of dishonour to all prior parties.

The fact that a party may be aware of the dishonour does not remove the need to give him notice).[84] However, in *Hamilton Finance Co Ltd v Coverley Westray Walbaum & Tosetti Ltd*[85] the holder was a subsidiary company of the indorser, their businesses being carried on from the same office largely by the same person. In those circumstances, it was held that it would have been absurd to require him to have given himself notice of dishonour. Notice need be in no particular form. So it might be given in writing or orally, the crucial thing being whether the bill is properly identified, and the fact of dishonour properly communicated.[86] It may be added

---

[83] s.18(2).
[84] *Re Fenwick, Stobart & Co* [1902] 1 Ch. 507.
[85] [1969] 1 Lloyd's Rep. 53.
[86] s.49(5).

that, by virtue of s.49(7), a written notice need not be signed, and an insufficient written notice may be supplemented and validated orally. Indeed that provision also indicates that a misdescription of the bill, will not vitiate the notice, unless the recipient is actually misled. He would have the burden of proving he was misled.[87] Under s.49(6), it is sufficient notice to return the dishonoured bill to the party in question, and s.49(15) provides that if a notice is properly addressed and posted, it is regarded as validly given to the addressee, even if it never arrives.

Section 49(12) directs that notice may be given as soon as the bill is dishonoured, and must be given within a reasonable time thereafter. Notice is not "given" until it is actually received. Thus, while notice would be bad if it was received before dishonour, if dishonour is anticipated, it is perfectly valid for notice to be sent before a bill is dishonoured, as long as it arrives after dishonour has occurred.[88] Section 49(12) states that in the absence of special circumstances notice is not deemed to have been given within a reasonable time unless:

(1) where the person giving and receiving notice reside in the same place, it is given or sent off in time to reach the latter on the day after dishonour; or

(2) where those persons reside in different places, it is sent off on the day after dishonour, if there is a post at a convenient hour on that day, and if there is not, by the next available post.

The same place probably means the same city.[89] An example of "special circumstances" justifying some delay in the giving of notice is to be found in The Elmville[90] where the drawer was the master of a ship, and some inquiries had to be made in order to determine his exact whereabouts.

Where a party to a bill receives due notice of dishonour, s.49(15) subjects him to the same time constraints in giving notice to antecedent parties. Suppose the drawer, payee/indorser and current holder of a bill all live in Glasgow. Should the bill be dishonoured, the holder must send notice of dishonour to the payee/indorser in time for it to arrive the next day. Similarly in order to preserve his remedy against the drawer, the payee/indorser must then send notice to the drawer in time for it to arrive on the day after he received his own notice. If the drawer lived in Edinburgh, the payee/indorser would have to send him notice on the day after the payee/indorser received his own notice. Had the payee/indorser received his own notice two days after dishonour, i.e. outwith the time contemplated, then unless there are special circumstances, he will be released from liability. That means that any notice given by the payee/indorser to the drawer will be ineffective, even if given timeously, as in order for it to be valid under s.49(1), notice must be given by the holder or by an indorser who, *at the time of giving it,* is himself liable on the bill. In other words, by releasing the payee/indorser from liability in this way, the holder will also release the drawer, unless of course the holder has himself given timeous notice to the drawer.

Section 49(13) further states that where a bill is dishonoured in the hands of an agent, he may either himself give notice to the parties liable on the bill, or give notice to his principal. In the latter case, he must do so within the same time as if he were the holder, and the principal on receipt of this notice has the same time for giving notice as if the agent had been an independent holder. This provision has particular significance when bills are presented on a customer's behalf by his bank. Assuming the parties are in different places, if the bank chooses to give notice to its principal (the customer), it would not have to send him notice until the day after dishonour, and the customer would not have to send notice to any party liable on the bill until the day after he received notice from the bank.

---

[87] *Eaglehill Ltd v Needham (J) Builders Ltd* [1973] A.C. 992.

[88] *ibid*.

[89] See *Hamilton Finance Co Ltd v Coverley Westray Walbaum & Tosetti Ltd* [1969] 1 Lloyd's Rep. 53 at 73, *per* Mocatta J.

[90] [1904] P. 319.

Where the drawer or indorser is bankrupt, s.49(10) allows notice to be given either to him or the trustee. Where the party giving notice knows that the drawer or indorser is dead, s.49(9) demands that notice be given to a personal representative, if there is one and he can be found with the exercise of reasonable diligence. It seems to follow that notice to a deceased party will be valid, if the party giving notice was unaware of the former's demise. Equally, if there is no personal representative, or he cannot be found, it would appear that notice is excused. Where drawers or indorsers are jointly liable on a bill, otherwise than as partners, s.49(11) demands that notice be given to each, unless one has authority to receive notice for the others. Presumably, if notice is only given to one such party, then he will be relieved of liability, along with the party or parties with whom he was jointly liable.

Delay in giving notice of dishonour is excused by s.50(1) where it is caused by circumstances beyond the control of the party giving notice, and not imputable to his default, misconduct or negligence. When the cause of delay ceases to operate, notice must be given with reasonable diligence. In *Studdy v Beesty*[91] notice of dishonour could not be given timeously because the indorser was no longer living at the address he had given. However, before he raised an action against the indorser, the holder learned of the latter's new address. As he clearly could have given notice before raising the action, failure to do so was held not to be excusable.

Section 50(2) allows notice of dishonour to dispensed with altogether:

- where after the exercise of reasonable diligence, notice cannot be given or does not reach the party sought to be charged;
- by waiver, express or implied. Notice may be waived before the time for giving due notice has arrived,or after the omission to give due notice. So where the drawer told the holder, before the bill was due, that he would to call to see whether it had been paid, this was held to amount to a waiver.[92] And a promise to pay, whether made before or after time for giving due notice has arrived, is generally treated as a waiver.[93] In *Lombard Banking Ltd v Central Garage and Engineering Co Ltd*[94] Scarman J. observed that the courts had been ready to imply waiver from very slight evidence. Thus he was willing to imply waiver from the fact that, despite the indorser being a director of the plaintiff company, and aware of the dishonour and the reasons for it before the plaintiffs themselves knew of it, he did not raise the issue of lack of notice until an action had been brought, and then only in an application to amend his defence,

as regards the drawer,

- where he and the drawee are the same person. There is no point in giving notice to the person who has himself dishonoured the bill;
- where he is the person to whom the bill is presented for payment. The same point could be made here. What might distinguish this case from that immediately above is that the drawer might receive the bill in a representative capacity;
- where the drawee is a fictitious person or lacks capacity. Here the drawer would be well aware that the bill had no chance of being honoured;
- where the drawee or acceptor, is as between himself and the drawer under no obligation to accept or pay the bill, *e.g.* where a cheque is drawn on an overdrawn account;
- where he has countermanded payment (and thus himself ensured dishonour—an example would be a stopped cheque),

as regards an indorser,

---

[91] (1889) 60 L.T. 647.
[92] *Phipson v Kneller* (1815) 4 Camp. 285.
[93] See respectively *Coulcher v Toppin* (1886) 2 T.L.R. 657; *Cordery v Colville* (1863) 32 L.J.C.P. 210.
[94] [1963] 1 Q.B. 220 at 233.

- where the drawee is a fictitious person or lacks capacity, and the indorser was aware of that fact at the time of indorsement. The qualification reflects the fact that while the drawer must know that the bill had no chance of being honoured, an indorser might be entirely innocent of that fact;
- where he is the person to whom the bill is presented for payment;
- where the bill was accepted or made for his accommodation (see para. 5.7.).

## (f) Noting and protest

Noting occurs where, at the behest of the holder, a solicitor who is a notary public presents the bill to the drawee for acceptance or payment. When this is refused, the notary will mark on the face of the bill the date, the fact that it protested for non-acceptance (p.n.acc.) or non-payment (p.n.p.), and his name or initials together with the abbreviation N.P. Noting may occur irrespective of whether a bill is protested, such as where the holder employs the services of a notary public in order to establish conclusively the dishonour of a bill. However, usually noting will occur as a precursor to formal protest of the bill. A protest is a certificate containing a formal declaration of protest. Section 51(7) states that it must contain a copy of the bill, be signed by the notary, and must specify:

(1) the person at whose request the bill is protested; and,
(2) the place and date of protest, the cause or reason for protest, the demand made, and the answer given, if any, or the fact that the drawee or acceptor cannot be found.

In *Bartsch v Poole & Co*[95] a bill was to be paid at the office of the drawer. It was dishonoured when presented, and the protest recited that it had been presented to a clerk, who had indicated that no funds had been provided to meet the payment. It was held that the clerk, being the employee of the drawer, could hardly be regarded as authorised to refuse payment on behalf of the acceptor. So the true reason for dishonour was that the acceptor could not be found. As the protest failed to recite this, it was invalid. As far as the date of protest is concerned, s.51(4) provides that a bill may be noted on the day of dishonour and must be noted no later than the next business day. A protest may then be drawn up later, and ante-dated at the date of noting.[96] The protest takes effect from the date of noting.[97] If the date of protest differs at all from the date of noting as marked on the bill, then once again the protest is invalid.[98] Section 51(9) excuses delay in noting or protesting where it is caused by circumstances beyond the control of the holder, and not imputable to his default, misconduct or negligence, but continues that when the cause of delay ceases to operate, the bill must be noted or protested with reasonable diligence.

Section 51 insists that a bill be protested at the place where it is dishonoured, and protest will not be valid if effected elsewhere.[99] However, if it is presented by post and returned dishonoured, it may be protested at the place to which it is returned—on the day of return if received during business hours, otherwise not later than the next business day.[1] Where it is drawn payable at the place of business or residence of someone other than the drawee, and dishonoured by *non-acceptance,* it *must* be protested *for non-payment* at the place where it is payable, and no further presentment to the drawee is necessary.[2] Where the services of a notary cannot be obtained at the place where the bill is dishonoured, any householder or substantial resident can protest the bill.[3] Indeed, in at least one case the holder has been prevented from

---

[95] (1895) 23 R. 328.
[96] s.93.
[97] s.51(4).
[98] *Macpherson v Wright* (1885) 12 R. 942.
[99] *Sommerville v Aaronson* (1898) 25 R. 524.
[1] s.51(6)(a).
[2] s.51(6)(b).
[3] s.94 and Sch. 1; *Sommerville v Aaronson* (1898) 25 R. 524.

recovering the expenses of sending a notary from some distance away to the place where the bill was dishonoured, the sheriff taking the view that householder protest should have been resorted to.[4]

Section 51(2) indicates that where the bill is a foreign bill, it must be protested or the drawer and indorsers will be discharged. (Under s.4 an inland bill is a bill appearing to be drawn and payable within the British Islands, or drawn within the British Islands upon some person resident therein. Any other bill is a foreign bill). Moreover, s.44(2) states that where a foreign bill has been part accepted, it must be protested as to the balance. Again, s.67(1) insists that where any dishonoured bill has been accepted for honour, or contains a reference in case of need (see para. 5.8.), it must be protested for non-payment, before being presented for payment to the acceptor for honour or referee. Moreover, s.67(4) says that where a bill is dishonoured by the acceptor for honour, it must be protested for non-payment by him. Apart from the above special cases, the protest of an inland bill is optional. Yet, s.98 deems it necessary if one wishes to do summary diligence on an inland bill (see below). Section 51(9) indicates that the need for protest is dispensed with by any circumstance which would dispense with notice of dishonour. But the fact that the bill is lost, destroyed or wrongly detained will not excuse lack of protest, as in such circumstances protest may be made on a copy or written particulars of the bill.[5]

Section 51(3) provides that a bill which has been protested for non-acceptance may subsequently be protested for non-payment. And where the acceptor becomes bankrupt or insolvent before a bill matures, s.51(5) entitles the holder to protest it, so that he can have better security against the drawer and any indorsers when the bill does mature.

## (g) Measure of damages on dishonour

Assuming that notice of dishonour has been duly given, and (where appropriate) the bill has been duly noted and protested, the holder may proceed to enforce his rights. Thus s.57(1) allows him to recover (as liquidated damages) from any party who is liable on the bill:

- the amount of the bill;
- interest from the time of presentment for payment, if the bill is payable on demand, otherwise from the time of maturity;
- the expenses of noting and (where necessary) protesting the bill.

If the bill on its face provided for the payment of interest, s.9(1)(a) would regard such interest as part of the amount of the bill. Unless the bill provided otherwise, such interest would run from the date of the bill, or if undated, from the date of issue.[6] As far as interest on the amount of the bill is concerned, the rule laid down by the Act that interest runs from the time of maturity where a bill is not payable on demand, applies even if payment is not sought until some time after maturity.[7] However, the court may, if justice so requires, withhold (in whole or in part) any interest recoverable as damages.[8] Equally, if the bill on its face provides for the payment of interest at a given rate, the court has a discretion to award interest recoverable as damages at the same or a different rate.[9] Because the expenses of protesting the bill may only be recovered where protest is necessary, they cannot be recovered where, e.g. the bill is protested for better security.[10] Any party who is liable on the bill, means the drawer and any indorser, assuming that the bill has not been drawn or indorsed without recourse. Similarly, any party who is thus made liable on the bill can recover what he has paid in damages from any

---

[4] *McRobert v Lindsay* (1898) 5 S.L.T. 317.

[5] s.51(8).

[6] s.9(3).

[7] *Bank Polski v Mulder (K.J.) & Co* [1942] 1 K.B. 497.

[8] s.57(3); and see *Ledeboter (N.V.) & Vander Held's Textiehandel v Hibbert* [1947] K.B. 964.

[9] *ibid.*

[10] *Re English Bank of the River Plate* [1893] 2 Ch. 438.

prior party, *i.e.* the drawer and prior indorsers, and the drawer himself can recover from the acceptor—but not from a drawee who refuses to accept.[11]

### (h) Enforcement by summary diligence

In Scotland it is possible to enforce the bill without resort to court action, as s.98 specifically provides for the continuation of the Scottish procedure of enforcement by summary diligence. For summary diligence to be competent, the bill must be duly presented, noted and protested.[12] Although due presentment is required, the holder will not lose his right to enforcement by summary diligence merely because he has not presented the bill at the time dictated by s.45 of the Act (see above). In *McNeill & Son v Innes, Chambers & Co*[13] it was pointed out that under the pre-existing law of Scotland, summary diligence was competent as long as a protest for non-acceptance was registered within six months of the date of the bill, or a protest for non-payment was registered within six months of the date on which payment became due. Thus since s.98 specifically stated that the Act does not in any way alter or affect the law as to summary diligence in Scotland, these rules must still apply, despite the terms of s.45. Registration must be in the Books of Council and Session, or the books of the sheriff court enjoying jurisdiction over the person against whom diligence is to be done. A warrant can then be obtained to charge the party liable to pay the amount due, failing which the holder can do diligence on his estate (*e.g.* arrest funds).

Summary diligence is only competent where the bill is entirely complete and regular on its face. Thus it is not competent against someone who has signed the bill only by initials, nor where the bill has evidently been torn up and pasted together again, nor where it appears to have been cancelled, albeit mistakenly, nor where liability is accepted subject to conditions.[14] Nor is it competent against someone who is not subject to the jurisdiction of the Scottish courts.[15] It has been held not to be competent on a cheque.[16]

## 5.11. DISCHARGE OF A BILL

Although the previous section considered the dishonour of a bill, most bills will not be dishonoured but discharged. Once a bill has been discharged, s.36(1)(b) states that it ceases to be negotiable. There are various ways in which a bill may be discharged.

### (a) Payment in due course

The most obvious way in which a bill may be discharged is by payment in due course.[17] Under s.59(1), this is payment on or after maturity by or on behalf of the drawee or acceptor to the holder, in good faith and without notice of any defect in the holder's title. Section 59(2) insists that payment in due course by a drawer or indorser, does not discharge the bill, as of course the bill will remain in force to allow them to enforce the liability of prior parties. Indeed, by virtue

---

[11] s.57(1).

[12] *Neill v Dobson, Molle & Co Ltd* (1902) 6 F. 625.

[13] 1907 S.C. 540.

[14] See respectively *Munro v Munro* (1820) Hume 81; *Thomson v Bell* (1850) 12 D. 1184; *Dominion Bank v Bank of Scotland* (1889) 16 R. 1081; *Summers v Marianski* (1843) 6 D. 286.

[15] *Charteris v Clydesdale Banking Co* (1882) 19 S.L.R. 602.

[16] *Glickman v Linda,* 1950 S.L.T. 19.

[17] So in *Coats v Union Bank of Scotland,* 1930 S.L.T. 292, HL, it was held that while three parties were jointly and severally liable on a cheque which they had drawn up, once it had been paid, it was discharged, leaving them only jointly liable for the underling debt which it had secured. Thus no single party could be sued for more than a third of the debt.

of s.59(2)(b), if an indorser pays the bill, he can recover it—s.52(4) insists that a holder must hand over the bill to a party who pays it—strike out his and subsequent indorsements, and negotiate it again. The same would be true of a drawer who pays a bill payable to his own order. Under s.37, an acceptor who paid a bill before maturity would be entitled either to cancel it (see below), or to put it back in circulation, having sold it to some third party. But if a drawer pays a bill payable to a third party, while he may enforce payment against the acceptor, s.59(2)(a) prohibits him from reissuing it. If the drawer or an indorser makes only part payment, the holder may seek to recover the full amount from the acceptor,[18] unless the holder renounces his rights (see below) on receiving part payment.

It will be seen that payment must be made to the holder. This means that since a "holder" is defined in s.2 as the bearer or the payee or indorsee in possession, payment to a bearer who has stolen the bill nonetheless discharges the bill. The same result follows if the holder has a defective title. However, it will be remembered that s.24 indicates that a forged signature is wholly inoperative, so anyone who holds upon a forged indorsement cannot be regarded as a holder. Consequently, payment to such a person will not discharge the bill.

Finally, s.59(3) directs that an accommodation bill is discharged when paid in due course by the party accommodated. In other words, if A accepts liability on a bill in order to accommodate his friend B, the bill will only properly be discharged when paid by B.

## (b) Acceptor becoming holder

Section 61 provides that the bill is discharged when the acceptor becomes the holder on or after maturity, i.e. when the person liable to pay is also the person entitled to be paid. This result does not follow should the acceptor become the holder before maturity, as it would always be open to him to negotiate the bill.

## (c) Express waiver

Section 62(1) provides that the bill is discharged when the holder, at or after maturity, absolutely and unconditionally renounces his rights against the acceptor. That renunciation must be in writing, unless the bill is delivered up to the acceptor. Clearly, renunciation before maturity does not discharge the bill. Renunciation in writing need not be signed by the holder, but must be[19]:

> "an absolute and unconditional renunciation of rights. It is not necessary to put these words in, but that must be the effect of the document. Then the document is not to be a note or memorandum of the renunciation or of an intention to do it, but it must be itself the record of the renunciation."

In *Edwards v Walters,*[20] E, the holder of a promissory note handed it over to the daughter of the maker, W (equivalent to both a drawer and acceptor) on the maker's death, orally stating it to be a gift. When E died, his representative successfully sued W's executors on the note. It was held there was no renunciation in writing, neither had the note been delivered to W.

Section 62(2) further provides that the liabilities of any party may "in like manner" be renounced by the holder before, at or after maturity. However, the provision continues that this cannot affect the rights of a holder in due course who has no notice of the renunciation. Certain aspects of the meaning of this provision are not clear. Thus can a holder renounce the liabilities of the drawer merely by returning the bill to him? Moreover, will that in turn renounce the liabilities of any indorsers, given that otherwise they would have a right of recourse against the drawer?

---

[18] *Barclays Bank Ltd v Aschaffenburger Zellstoffwerke A.G.* [1967] 1 Lloyd's Rep. 387.
[19] *Re George* (1890) 44 Ch. D. 627 at 632.
[20] [1896] 2 Ch. 157.

## (d) Cancellation

Section 63(1) provides that the bill is discharged by cancellation, apparent on its face, by the holder or his agent. Cancellation might be effected by striking out key words or signatures, or writing "cancelled" across the face of the bill, or tearing up the bill.[21] Unintentional or mistaken or unauthorised cancellation does not discharge the bill, but the holder has the burden of proof here.[22] The holder can cancel the liability of any party by cancelling that party's signature. In this case s.63(2) directs that any indorser who would have a right of recourse against such party is also discharged.

## (e) Alteration

Although, strictly speaking, a bill cannot be discharged by alteration, s.64(1) states that material alteration avoids the bill in relation to everyone who became a party prior to the alteration, except where such a party consents to the alteration. However a bill may still be enforced *according to its original tenor* by a holder in due course if the alteration is not apparent. An alteration is apparent if the potential holder looking at the bill with reasonable care would see that it had been altered.[23] In any case an altered bill remains enforceable against the party making the alteration and subsequent parties. Presume, for example, that Abel draws a bill on Bone for £100 in favour of Cole, who indorses it specially to Dean. Bone accepts liability. The bill is then altered by Dean, so that it is for £100,000, although the fact of the alteration is not apparent to anyone who might see the bill. Dean then indorses it specially to Earl, who gives £99,000 for it in good faith. Earl in turn indorses it specially to Fox, who gives £98,000 for it in good faith. Although the bill is *prima facie* avoided in relation to Abel, Bone and Cole (who became parties prior to the alteration), Fox, as a holder in due course, may enforce it against them according to its original tenor, *i.e.* for £100. In addition, he can enforce it for £100,000 against the party making the alteration (Dean) and any subsequent party (Earl). It may be noted that accidental alteration does not avoid a bill.[24]

The alteration must be material. The following are material in terms of s.64(2):

- the date,
- the sum payable (as where a condition as to the payment of interest is added[25]),
- the time of payment,
- the place of payment.

It has also been held that alteration of the name of the payee is material,[26] as is the alteration of the place where the bill is drawn so that an inland bill becomes a foreign bill (even though this was to the disadvantage of the party making the alteration).[27] More generally, Brett L.J. opined in *Suffell v Bank of England*[28]:

> "Any alteration seems to me to be material if it would alter the business effect of the bill."

Obviously, if a gap in a bill is filled in as authorised by the Act, this does not amount to an alteration.[29]

The drawer or acceptor of a bill is under no duty to subsequent holders to take precautions against material alterations being made.[30] So, in the above example, the fact that Abel draws a

---

[21] *Smith v Prosser* [1907] 2 K.B. 735.
[22] s.63(3); and see *Bank of Scotland v Dominion Bank* (1891) 18 R. (H.L.) 21.
[23] *Woollatt v Stanley* (1928) 138 L.T. 620.
[24] *Hong Kong and Shanghai Banking Corporation v Lo Lee Shi* [1928] A.C. 181.
[25] *Payana Reena Saminathan v Pana Lana Palaniappa* [1914] A.C. 618.
[26] *Slingsby v District Bank* [1932] 1 K.B. 544.
[27] *Koch v Dicks* [1933] 1 K.B. 307.
[28] (1882) 9 Q.B.D. 555 at 568.
[29] *Foster v Driscoll* [1929] 1 K.B. 470.
[30] *Schofield v Earl of Londesborough* [1896] A.C. 514.

bill so that it is easy to alter from £100 to £100,000 will not allow even a holder in due course to sue him for the larger sum.

## (f) Prescription

Although again, a bill cannot be discharged by prescription, any obligation under a bill (or a promissory note) may be extinguished by prescription. If five years elapses from the appropriate date without any relevant claim being made in relation to the obligation, then the obligation will prescribe.[31] The "appropriate date" is the date when the bill is payable.[32] A relevant claim is a claim made for implement of the obligation either in appropriate proceedings or through lodging a claim for sequestration or liquidation.[33] Alternatively, the execution of any diligence to enforce the obligation can be a relevant claim.[34] Appropriate proceedings means court or arbitration proceedings.[35]

## 5.12. CHEQUES

Nowadays the most commonly used form of bill of exchange is a cheque. A cheque is defined by s.73 as a bill of exchange drawn on a banker and payable on demand. The provisions of the 1882 Act apply equally to cheques except where otherwise provided. Thus, starting from the premise that a cheque is just an ordinary bill of exchange, in this section we are going to look at how the Act treats cheques differently. Indeed it should be noted that there are situations where cheques are treated differently due to banking practice. Thus, although s.3(4)(a) states that bills need not be dated, no bank will pay a cheque which is undated, and their right to refuse to do so has been upheld by the courts.[36]

### (a) Presentment of cheques

As a cheque is payable on demand, it will never be presented for acceptance—only for payment. While, under s.45, failure to present a bill for payment within a reasonable time discharges the drawer and indorsers, s.74 states that failure to present a cheque within a reasonable time only discharges the drawer to the extent that he is actually damaged by the delay. As this will only arise if the bank is unable to pay, it rarely arises in practice.

### (b) Crossings on cheques

One way in which cheques differ from ordinary bills of exchange is that cheques may be crossed, and of course banks now supply pre-printed cheque forms which are already crossed. A crossing is simply two parallel transverse lines on the face of a cheque. The words "and company" or any abbreviation thereof may be added, as might the words "not negotiable". Under s.76(1), this is a general crossing. A crossing becomes a special crossing when the cheque bears across its face the name of a bank. Section 76(2) then regards the cheque as specially crossed to that bank. With a special crossing, the two parallel transverse lines are not necessary, but usually appear. A crossing is a material part of the cheque, and so any obliteration, alteration or addition (except as mentioned above) to a crossing will amount to a

---

[31] Prescription and Limitation (Scotland) Act 1973, s.6, Sch. 1, para. 1(e).
[32] *ibid.*, s.6(3).
[33] *ibid.*, s.9(1).
[34] *ibid.*
[35] *ibid.*, s.4.
[36] *Griffiths v Dalton* [1940] 2 K.B. 264.

material alteration under s.64 (see previous paragraph). That being said, a cheque, like any other bill, has no status as an instrument until delivered to the payee. Accordingly, any obliteration or alteration of the "crossing" before that point does not amount to a material alteration, as the cheque does not exist as a cheque before delivery. So, for example, a drawer might seek to "open" the crossing on a pre-printed, pre-crossed cheque form of the type issued by most banks to their customers by writing "pay cash" on the face of the cheque and initialling those words.[37]

## (c) Who may cross a cheque

A drawer may cross a cheque generally or specially, while any holder may cross an uncrossed cheque generally or specially, or turn a cheque crossed generally into a special crossing.[38] Moreover, s.77(4) allows any holder to add the words "not negotiable" to a crossed cheque. A collecting banker (*i.e.* the bank which receives payment of a cheque on behalf of its customer) may cross a cheque specially to himself, while the banker to whom the cheque is specially crossed may specially cross it to another banker for collection.[39] It is difficult to see the purpose of the former provision, but the latter allows a bank, which is not a member of the clearing system, to cross it to a bank which is, so that payment can be received (see below).

## (d) Effect of crossing

A cheque which is crossed generally must be presented for payment through a bank account. In other words, if you hold a cheque in your favour, you must pay it into your bank account. It cannot simply be cashed. A specially crossed cheque may only be presented for payment through the named bank. The main purpose of crossings on cheques therefore is to safeguard against fraud. Section 79(1) states that a cheque which is specially crossed to more than one bank should not be paid, except where it is specially crossed by one bank to another for collection. This would arise where a cheque is specially crossed to a bank which is not a member of the clearing system, and thus that bank has to specially cross it to a bank which is a member of the system in order that payment can be received. (The clearing system operates on the basis that it is not practical for banks to present each cheque individually to each paying bank. So as between themselves the clearing banks send cheques in batches to a clearing house, with a view to establishing on a day-to-day basis whether a given bank is overall in debit or credit to any other. That indebtedness is then settled between the banks in a single transaction. Each individual cheque will nonetheless still ultimately make its way to the branch where the drawer holds his account. If honoured, then it has "cleared". If dishonoured, then that fact will have to be fed back into the clearing system.)

The words "and company" historically came to be added to crossings when the drawer did not know the name of the payee's bank, so employed the words to indicate the intention that the cheque be paid through a designated bank, leaving the payee to insert the name of the appropriate bank. Thus those words by themselves have no particular legal significance. Cheques marked not negotiable can still be transferred but not "negotiated", *i.e.* the holder can assign the right to receive payment, but the transferee obtains no better title than the transferor.[40] As Vaughan Williams L.J. puts it in *Great Western Railway Co v London and County Banking Co*[41]:

> "The section does not say that the person to whom the payee of the cheque gives a crossed cheque marked "not negotiable" shall not become the transferee of the cheque,

---

[37] *Smith v Union Bank of London* (1875) 1 Q.B.D. 31.
[38] s.77(1)–(3).
[39] s.77(6), s.77(5).
[40] s.81.
[41] [1900] 2 Q.B. 464 at 474–475.

but merely that he shall not take a better title than that which the person from whom he took it had. The transferability of the cheque is not affected by the words not negotiable but only its negotiability."

Thus a bank which had negotiated a cheque marked not negotiable was held liable to the drawer, as the person who had negotiated it to the bank (the original payee) had induced the drawer to draw up the cheque by fraud. When the case reached the House of Lords, Lord Lindley observed that[42]: "everyone who takes a cheque which is marked 'not negotiable' takes it at his own risk, and his title to the money is as defective as his title to the cheque itself."

The use of the words "a/c payee" were intended to indicated that a cheque should only be paid into the account of the named payee, thus offering greater protection against fraud. However, the practice of using these words was not contemplated by the 1882 Act, so that the pre-1992 cases indicate that while the use of the words did not render the cheque invalid, nor did they affect its negotiability.[43] They were not to be treated as a direction to the paying bank,[44] but as a warning to the collecting bank that it might be liable for the tort of conversion (a wrong unknown in Scotland) if it received payment on behalf of anyone other than the named payee, and that person turned out not to have a good title to the cheque.[45] In 1992 however, the Cheques Act of that year added a new s.81A to the Act. If the cheque bears the words "account payee" or "a/c payee", with or without the word "only", it is not transferable. The original payee remains the owner, and it cannot be enforced by any transferee. There is no reason why the drawer of a cheque should not strike out the words "a/c payee" which appear on the pre-printed cheque forms issued by most banks to their customers, and if he appends his signature to this alteration, it should theoretically be effective. It is, however, doubtful whether in practice banks would take this view.

### (e) Payment of crossed cheque

Section 80 states that if the bank on which the cheque is drawn, in good faith and without negligence, pays a crossed cheque in accordance with the crossing, both it and the drawer will be in the same position as if payment had been made to the true owner of the cheque. Suppose Abel owes Carr £1,000. He draws a cheque for that amount on the Bishop Bank in favour of Carr. Dodd steals the cheque from Carr, forges Carr's indorsement, and pays it into his own account with the Ecclesiastical Bank. Should the Bishop Bank pay on the cheque, it will be treated as if it had paid Carr, and may debit Abel's account. Meanwhile, Abel is treated as if he had paid his debt to Carr. (For the position of banks who pay on forged indorsements see the next paragraph.)

Moreover, s.81A(2) states that a bank,

> "is not to be treated for the purposes of s.80 as having been negligent by reason only of its failure to concern itself with any purported indorsement of a cheque which . . . is not transferable."

The exact meaning of the above provision is unclear. It certainly permits a bank to ignore an indorsement of a cheque crossed a/c payee. However, it may absolve a bank from liability where it pays a cheque marked a/c payee to an indorsee who is not the named payee, as long as it is not otherwise negligent.

Subject to this, s.79(2) indicates that if a bank pays a crossed cheque other than in accordance with the crossing—*i.e.* if it pays a cheque crossed generally other than to a bank or a cheque crossed specially other than to the named bank—it will be liable to the true owner for

---

[42] [1901] A.C. 414 at 424.

[43] *Akrokerri (Atlantic) Mines Ltd v Economic Bank* [1904] 2 K.B. 465; *A L Underwood Ltd v Bank of Liverpool* [1924] 1 K.B. 775.

[44] *Importers Ltd v Westminster Bank Ltd* [1927] 2 K.B. 297.

[45] *Universal Guarantee Property Ltd v National Bank of Australia* [1965] 2 All E.R. 98.

any loss sustained. So in *Phillips v The Italian Bank*[46] the bank paid over the proceeds of two crossed cheques in favour of P to one of his employees. It was held liable to P for the amount of these cheques. The only exception under s.79(2) is where the cheque does not appear to have been crossed, or to have had a crossing which has been obliterated or improperly altered. In such a situation a bank paying is protected as long as it acts in good faith and without negligence. A cheque which has had a crossing altered otherwise than authorised by the Act is usually treated as void, as having been subject to a material alteration.[47]

## 5.13.   OTHER PROTECTION OF BANKS

Banks are in a difficult position regarding cheques. The consequences of wrongful dishonour can be serious, while if a cheque is wrongly paid, the bank usually cannot debit the customer's account. At the same time, a bank which collects payment on a cheque for someone other than the true owner may, at least in England, be liable to the latter. Thus certain protections are accorded to banks. We have already seen that the common law affords some protection where customers have facilitated alteration or are otherwise barred from relying on forgeries, and we have just noted the protections afforded by ss.80 and 81A. These are not the only statutory protections.

### (a) The paying bank

Where the signature of the drawer is forged, the bank which pays has no protection, and cannot debit the drawer's account. However if a bank pays a cheque (or any bill) upon a forged or unauthorised indorsement, then s.60 will treat it as having paid the cheque in due course, as long as it pays in good faith and in the ordinary course of business. This means that the bank can debit the drawer's account, and that the payee has no claim on the drawer. A bank may obviously be acting in good faith, even though negligent. It is also possible for a bank to be acting in the ordinary course of business, though negligent. In *Carpenters' Co v British Mutual Banking Co Ltd*[48] this was the view taken by the majority of the Court of Appeal of a situation where a bank, over a period of time, allowed an employee of the plaintiff, who banked at the same branch as his employer, to pay into his account a large number of cheques made out in favour of his employer's various suppliers, having forged the indorsements on those cheques. It has, however, been suggested that to pay an uncrossed cheque for a large sum over the counter, on the basis that it had been indorsed, would not be in the ordinary course of business, where the person looking to receive payment is not the sort of person whom one would expect to be receiving a large sum of money.[49]

Allied to this, the Cheques Act 1957, s.1, states that where a bank pays a cheque drawn on it, which is not indorsed or is irregularly indorsed, in good faith and in the ordinary course of business, it incurs no liability by this fact alone. (An irregular indorsement is one where there is some doubt as to whether it is the indorsement of the payee—as where a cheque made out to John Smith is indorsed "J. Smith".[50] It is not necessarily invalid.). This provision, like s.60, is designed to remove the need for banks to concern themselves with indorsements. In particular, it was designed to remove the need for paying banks to insist on indorsement to the bank by the payee before making payment. Indorsement was thought to be necessary, as it gave the

---

[46] 1934 S.L.T. 78.
[47] See ss.64, 78.
[48] [1938] 1 K.B. 511.
[49] See *Bank of England v Vagliano Brothers* [1891] A.C. 107 at 117–118; *Auchteroni & Co v Midland Bank* [1928] 2 K.B. 294 at 304.
[50] See Lord Denning in *Arab Bank v Ross* [1952] 2 Q.B. 216 at 227.

bank the protection of s.60. In other words, if a cheque was payable to Adam Abel, and the bank was unable to tell whether the person seeking payment was Adam Abel (as would be most likely), then indorsement would protect it. If the person seeking payment was Adam Abel, then indorsement would be ordinarily effective. If he were not, and was obliged to forge the signature of Adam Abel, then s.60 will treat it as having paid the cheque in due course, despite the forged indorsement. The Cheques Act 1957 was intended to allow banks protection if they simply paid the payee, without bothering about indorsement. However, a circular of London Clearing Bankers of September 23, 1957 suggested that banks should still require indorsement in certain circumstances, including where cheques are paid over the counter. Arguably then, a bank which pays a cheque over the counter is not acting in the ordinary course of business, and thus does not have the protection of s.1. The provision therefore has not quite had the liberating effect intended. It should also be noted that s.1 is quite narrow in scope. It does not deal with the case where a cheque lacks a necessary indorsement—*i.e.* it does not help a bank which allows Bertha Black to pay a cheque made payable to Adam Abel into her own account, in the absence of Adam Abel's indorsement.

## (b) The collecting bank

Under s.4 of the Cheques Act 1957, if a banker in good faith and without negligence receives payment of a cheque either for a customer or for itself (crediting the customer's account), and the customer has no title or a defective title, the bank does not incur any liability to the true owner simply by receiving payment. What is negligence in this context? In *Marfani v Midland Bank Ltd*[51] Diplock L.J. observes:

> "What facts ought to be known to the bank, and what facts are sufficient to cause it to suspect that the customer is not the true owner must depend on current banking practice, and change as that practice changes. Cases decided thirty years ago, when the use by the general public of banking facilities was much less widespread, may not be a reliable guide to what the duty of a careful bank is today.
>
> Where the customer is in possession of the cheque and appears to be the holder, the bank is entitled to assume that the customer is the owner of the cheque unless there are facts which are known or ought to be known to the bank which would cause a reasonable bank to suspect that the customer is not the true owner"

A possible example of negligence might be a bank which allows an employee to pay into his account a cheque drawn on his employer.[52] Negligence might also arise where payment of a cheque crossed a/c payee is received on behalf of anyone other than the named payee.[53]

It is, however, perhaps worth remarking that s.4 protects the collecting bank against liability for the tort of conversion, a wrong which has no counterpart in Scotland. There is clear authority that under Scots law a collecting bank cannot be liable to the true owner where it receives payment merely as an agent for its customer.[54] Where it receives payment on its own behalf, such as where it gives cash for a cheque over the counter, and then obtains payment from the bank on which the cheque is drawn, then it should qualify to be regarded as a holder in due course. By virtue of s.2 of the Cheques Act 1957 this would even be so if the cheque were payable to a named payee, and there had been no indorsement. That means therefore that in those cases where a holder in due course would be unable to enforce the cheque, *e.g.* where the signature of the drawer or any indorser is forged, the bank will be liable to make repayment.

[51] [1968] 1 W.L.R. 956 at 972.
[52] *Lloyd's Bank Ltd v E.B. Savory & Co* [1933] A.C. 201.
[53] *Honourable Society of the Middle Temple v Lloyd's Bank plc* (1999) C.L. March 38.
[54] *Clydesdale Bank v Royal Bank of Scotland* (1876) 3 R. 586; and see *McLaughlin v Allied Irish Bank plc* 2001 S.L.T. 403.

## (c) Bank's duty of care

The law of negligence may also affect the way a bank may handle a cheque. Often a customer will not or cannot (as in the case of a company) draw cheques itself. Sometimes a bank may have to dishonour cheques drawn by agents where the circumstances should give rise to suspicions. It has been said that a bank should "make such enquiries as would be appropriate and practical if the bank in question has or a reasonable bank would have, grounds for believing that the authorised signatories are misusing their authority for the purpose of defrauding the principal".[55] On the other hand a bank was held not to have been in breach of duty when it continued to allow a solicitor to draw large cheques on his firm, even though it was aware he had a gambling problem.[56] The Court of Appeal said that what was required was that no reasonable cashier would pay without consulting a superior, and no superior would authorise payment without inquiring further. May L.J. noted[57]:

> "The principal obligation is upon the bank to honour its customer's cheques. There is nothing in the contract which would require a bank to consider the commercial wisdom or otherwise of the particular transaction. To a large extent the bank's obligation is automatic or mechanical. Presented with a cheque the bank must honour it save in exceptional circumstances".

Moreover, a bank was not in breach of its duty of care when it paid out on a cheque for £20,000 on an account with a nil balance, after its customer had presented a signed blank cheque to a business associate[58].

## (d) The bank as a constructive trustee

English cases suggest that a bank may be liable as a constructive trustee where it knowingly credits money to its customer's account which the customer has received in trust for another.[59] Knowledge would also appear to be crucial in Scotland. In *Style Financial Services v Bank of Scotland*[60] Lord Ross delivering the opinion of the Inner House commented:

> "There is no fiduciary relationship between a bank and customer in respect of money paid into a bank. The relationship between the bank and customer is one of debtor and creditor . . . When money is paid into an overdrawn account, the bank is not bound to enquire how the payer came by the money . . ., but is entitled to set it off against the debt on the overdrawn account."

It was further held that where sums are paid into an overdrawn account they cannot be pursued, Lord Ross continuing[61]:

> "Once the sums have been paid into the account and have served to reduce the debit balance, they have ceased to exist, and accordingly cannot be traced."

Thus the bank was entitled to use cheques which an agent had received on behalf of his principal to reduce the former's overdraft. On the other hand, it could be argued that the bank has in such circumstances received money to which it was not properly entitled, and the question of whether there might thus be a restitutionary claim was left open in *Mercedes Benz Finance Ltd v Clydesdale Bank plc.*[62] Of course it is quite common for customers to receive

---

[55] *per* Brightman J. in *Karak Rubber Co Ltd v Burden (No. 2)* [1972] 1 All E.R. 1210 at 1231.
[56] *Lipkin Gorman v Karpnale* [1992] 4 All E.R. 409.
[57] At 421.
[58] *Verjee v CBC Bank Trust Co (Channel Islands) Ltd* [2001] 1 Lloyd's Rep. Bank 279.
[59] See *e.g. Polly Peck International plc v Nadir (No 2)* [1992] 4 All E.R. 769.
[60] 1996 S.L.T. 421 at 424H.
[61] At 425C.
[62] 1996 S.C.L.R. 1005.

money on behalf of third parties, paying the funds into a designated account. If the bank is or should be aware of this relationship, it may be liable to the third party if it allowed the customer to pay such funds into his own account, as in *Style Financial Services v Bank of Scotland (No. 2)*[63] where the bank was not liable for paying cheques payable to S into the (overdrawn) account of S's parent company, as S had clearly authorised the bank to do so.

## 5.14. The Banker-Customer Relationship

Although it is not necessary to understand the nature of the banker-customer relationship in order to understand the nature of a cheque, an understanding of certain aspects of that relationship casts light on whether cheques need be honoured.

### (a) Bank's duty of repayment

The customer is the creditor of the bank. As Lord Mackay puts it in *Royal Bank of Scotland v Skinner*[64]:

> "After some fluctuation of opinion, it is now well settled that the relationship between customer and banker is neither a relation of principal and agent nor a relation of a fiduciary nature, trust or the like, but a simple relation of debtor and creditor. The bank is not in the general case the custodier of money. When money is paid in, despite the popular belief, it is simply consumed by the bank, which gives an obligation of equivalent amount."

Consequently, the bank is under a duty to repay money to the customer according to the terms of their agreement, whether by paying the money directly to the customer or by honouring a cheque. Of course, if there is no money in the account, or *a fortiori* if the account is overdrawn, this duty no longer applies, unless the bank has undertaken to provide overdraft facilities.[65] Where a customer in writing a cheque is drawing on an overdraft facility, the bank is his creditor. A bank is under no duty to provide such a facility, even if it has done so in the past.[66]

In this context, it is important to be aware that a bank is generally entitled without prior notice to mass all a customer's accounts together in order to decide whether he is in credit, unless of course it has been agreed that the accounts should be kept separate.[67] On the other hand a bank cannot mass accounts of different types together without giving notice to the customer.[68] If a customer deposits money with the bank without indicating the account to which it is to be ascribed, the bank may appropriate the payment as it thinks fit, and thus may choose to pay the money into an overdrawn account.[69]

Also important in this context is how long a period must elapse before a customer is permitted to draw on cheques paid into the account. This really depends upon the contract between the bank and the customer, but it is usual to insist that a customer may not draw on a cheque before it has cleared.[70] A bank which wrongfully dishonours a cheque will be liable in damages. It is assumed that a business customer's reputation will be damaged, so that he will be entitled to substantial damages without proof of loss,[71] as well as damages for any actual loss

---

[63] 1997 S.C.L.R. 633.
[64] 1931 S.L.T. 382 at 384.
[65] *Fleming v Bank of New Zealand* [1900] A.C. 577.
[66] *Ritchie v Clydesdale Bank* (1886) 13 R. 866.
[67] *National Westminster Bank Ltd v Halesowen Pressworks and Assemblies Ltd* [1972] A.C. 785.
[68] *Kirkwood & Sons v Clydesdale Bank Ltd,* 1908 S.C. 20.
[69] *Jackson v Nicoll* (1870) 8 M. 408.
[70] *Westminster Bank Ltd v Zang* [1966] A.C. 182.
[71] *King v British Linen Co* (1899) 1 F. 928.

of business he can prove. A private customer, on the other hand, has traditionally been assumed to be entitled to purely nominal damages unless he can prove actual loss, but the Court of Appeal has recently suggested that a presumption of damage should now be made as regards personal transactions, given the modern importance of an individual's credit rating.[72] English cases also tend to suggest that wrongful dishonour is defamatory.[73]

A bank is under no duty to advise customers of the most advantageous type of account.[74]

## (b) Revocation of authority to pay

A bank's authority to pay may be revoked in a number of situations.

### (i) Death of customer

Section 75(2) states that a bank's authority to pay its customer's cheques is terminated by notice of his death. So a bank may continue to honour its customer's cheques until it receives notice of his death. However, if the bank has funds to cover the cheque, s.53(2) provides that presentation of the cheque after the bank has received notice of his death will operate as an assignation of those funds. In deciding whether funds are available for payment, all the customer's accounts of whatever kind may be massed together.[75] A bank which pays a cheque after having received notice of its customer's death can neither debit the account or pursue the payee.[76]

### (ii) Countermand of payment

Where a cheque is "stopped" by a customer requesting that it not be paid prior to it actually being paid, s.75(1) directs that the bank must not pay the cheque. Obviously, if the bank does not receive notice of countermand before it pays the cheque, then the notice is of no effect. This view was taken to its logical extreme in *Curtice v London City & Midland Bank*,[77] where payment was held not to have been effectively countermanded when notice having reached the bank after it was closed, it was placed in the letter box, but due to an oversight not actually picked up until two days later, by which time the cheque had been paid. It was, however, suggested in that case that if the bank's failure to receive timeous notice was due to its negligence, then it might be liable to the customer in damages. If the bank receives timeous notice, but nonetheless pays the cheque, it may not debit the customer.[78]

Varying the normal rule in Scotland (see para. 5.9.), a cheque presented in those circumstances does not operate as an assignation in favour of the payee. Instead, s.75A deems the bank to have no funds to pay the cheque. Although the bank is not liable on a stopped cheque, the drawer of the cheque will still be liable thereon.[79]

The question arises as to the effect upon the above principles of the use of a cheque guarantee card. The commercial utility of cheques might be compromised by the rule that they need only be honoured if the customer has funds to meet them. Traders might be reluctant to accept cheques if they are uncertain of whether they will be honoured. Thus the banking industry has developed the guarantee card. In essence, the guarantee card amounts to a promise or contractual undertaking on the part of the relevant bank that if the conditions

---

[72] Compare *Gibbons v Westminster Bank* [1939] 2 K.B. 882; with *Kpohraror v Woolwich Building Society* [1996] 4 All E.R. 119.

[73] *Davidson v Barclay's Bank Ltd* [1940] 1 All E.R. 316.

[74] *Suriya v Midland Bank plc, The Times*, March 29, 1999 CA.

[75] *Kirkwood v Clydesdale Bank*, 1908 S.C. 20.

[76] *Credit Lyonnais v George Stevenson & Co Ltd* (1901) 9 S.L.T. 93; but see *Barclays Bank Ltd v W J Simms Son & Cooke (Southern) Ltd* [1980] Q.B. 677.

[77] [1908] 1 K.B. 293.

[78] *Burnett v Westminster Bank* [1966] 1 Q.B. 742.

[79] *McLean v Clydesdale Bank* (1883) 11 R (H.L.) 1.

attached to the card are met, the bank will pay the cheque, even if the customer has insufficient funds to meet it. The conditions attached to such typically include that the cheque is signed in the payee's presence by the person whose signature appears on the card; that the payee writes the card number on the reverse of the cheque; that the amount of the cheque does not exceed a certain sum (usually £100); that therefore no more than one cheque can be used in respect of a single transaction; that the cheque is signed before the expiry of the card. *First Sport Ltd v Barclay's Bank plc*[80] concerned the requirement that the signature on the cheque should correspond to the signature on the card. The signature on the stolen card had been altered to resemble the signature on the stolen cheque. The Court of Appeal controversially held that the bank is required to honour the cheque in those circumstances. The bank, of course, was unable to debit its customer, as the cheque had not been signed by him. If clearly enough drawn, the conditions attaching to the use of the card could, of course, allow the bank to refuse payment in the above circumstances, or else to debit the customer's account. If the latter course were adopted, however, the relevant term might be challengeable under the Unfair Terms in Consumer Contracts Regulations 1999,[81] in those cases where the customer is a consumer.

It is generally assumed that by using the card, the customer precludes himself from "stopping" the cheque. This could be analysed in terms of the customer giving up the right of countermand. However, assuming that the parties cannot agree to override s.75(1), an alternative analysis would see any countermand as a breach of the customer's contract with the bank, entitling the bank to damages to the extent of the value of the cheque. The former view is the more practical, if not the most theoretically satisfying. If a bank wrongfully refused to honour a cheque backed by the use of a guarantee card, then the payee would clearly have a right of action against it. Moreover, given that the rule that a cheque acts only as conditional payment is arguably not displaced by the use of the card, the payee would also have a right of action against the drawer.[82]

## (iii) Sequestration and winding up

When an individual is sequestrated, his entire estate (including any bank account) vests in the permanent trustee as at the date of sequestration.[83] The sequestrated individual may not deal with the estate.[84] This means that a sequestrated customer may no longer write cheques, and the bank's authority to honour them is withdrawn. However, if a cheque was drawn in the ordinary course of business between the bank and the customer, and the bank was unaware of the sequestration, and had no reason to believe that the customer's estate had been sequestrated, or was the subject of sequestration proceedings, then the bank incurs no liability by honouring the cheque.[85]

The making of a winding-up order terminates a bank's authority to honour the cheques of a company customer.[86] Moreover, where a company is wound up by the court, any disposition of the company's property made after the commencement of the winding-up is, unless the court orders otherwise, void.[87] (A winding-up commences at the time of the presentation of the petition for winding up, unless the company has earlier passed a resolution for voluntary winding up, in which case the date of the resolution is the crucial date.[88]) Thus while the bank should incur no liability for honouring cheques in ignorance of any winding-up proceedings, matters may be different if, without the sanction of the court, it continues to honour cheques once it is aware of those proceedings.[89]

---

[80] [1993] 3 All E.R. 789.
[81] SI 1999/2083.
[82] *per* Millet J. in *Re Charge Card Services Ltd* [1987] Ch. 150 at 166.
[83] Bankruptcy (Scotland) Act 1985, s.31(1).
[84] *ibid.*, s.32(8).
[85] s.32(9)(b)(iii).
[86] *National Westminster Bank Ltd v Halesowen Pressworks and Assemblies Ltd* [1972] A.C. 785.
[87] Insolvency Act 1986, s.127.
[88] s.129.
[89] *Re Gray's Inn Construction Co Ltd* [1980] 1 W.L.R. 711.

### (iv) Closing the account

A bank's authority to honour cheques is withdrawn by either party closing the account. The customer need give no notice, but should be aware that any cheques not yet presented when the account is closed must be dishonoured by the bank. The bank must however give reasonable notice, and cheques drawn prior to notice being given must be honoured.[90]

### (v) Other duties of banks

#### (i) To recognise signature/advise of forgeries

It has already been seen that a bank cannot debit its customer's account if it pays a cheque upon which his signature has been forged. Moreover, in *Weir v National Westminster Bank plc*[91]; it was suggested that the bank is supposed to recognise its customer's signature, with the result according to Lord Hope that:

> "a bank owes a duty to its customer to detect forgeries and to advise its customer if it comes to its attention in the course of the operation of that account that the signature of the customer on cheques drawn on that account had been forged."

However, the First Division was adamant that this was as far as the duty extended, so that the bank did not have to recognise the forgery of the customer's signature in any other context, *e.g.* as an indorser. On the other hand, it also held that the bank was bound to recognise the signature of the customer's agent when he was the sole signatory on the account—in this case a solicitor operating a client's account under power of attorney.

#### (ii) Confidentiality

A bank must not disclose details relating to a customer's account to third parties. According to Atkin L.J. in *Tournier v National Provincial and Union Bank of England*,[92] the duty:

> "must at least extend to all transactions that go through the account, and to any securities given in respect of the account; and in respect of such matters it must extend beyond the period when the account is closed or ceases to be an active account."

He continued that the duty extends to information obtained other than from the account, if its source was the relationship between the bank and customer. Yet Bankes L.J. in the same case[93] identified four exceptions to the duty:

(1) Where disclosure is compelled by law (as *e.g.* where directed to do so by a court). This exception applies even where the customer has given an express instruction not to disclose.[94]
(2) Where there is a public duty to disclose (as where it suspects a crime has been committed)
(3) Where the interests of the bank demand disclosure. It is thought that this would relate to situations where the commercial standing of the bank would otherwise be at risk. It would not embrace situations where disclosure of information relating to a customer would make money for the bank.
(4) Where the customer has given express or implied consent to disclosure. The banking industry for many years proceeded on the assumption that customers give implied

---

[90] *King v British Linen Co* (1899) 1 F. 928.
[91] 1993 S.C. 515 at 523G.
[92] [1924] 1 K.B. 461 at 485.
[93] At 472–473.
[94] *Christofi v Barclays Bank plc, The Times,* July 1, 1999, CA.

consent to the provision of references, provided the request comes from another bank. But in *Turner v Royal Bank of Scotland*[95] the Court of Appeal held that there was no such implied consent.

Is a bank obliged to inform a customer when it has disclosed matters pertaining to his account? English authority suggests that the answer is negative when the customer is under criminal investigation,[96] but the Privy Council has indicated that a customer should be informed where disclosure has been ordered in civil proceedings, unless the public interest or the bank's own interests dictate otherwise.[97]

### (d) Duties of customer

A customer is under a duty to inform the bank as soon as he becomes aware of forgeries or fraud pertaining to his account, and will not be able to prevent the bank debiting his account in respect of sums paid by the bank as a result of a breach of this duty.[98] It is actual knowledge which matters in this context, the courts having resisted any attempt to extend this principle to cover situations where the customer should have been aware of forgeries or fraud.[99] He is also under a duty not to draw a cheque so as to facilitate alteration of the sum to be paid, although this duty does not seem to extend to alteration of the payee's identity.[1] A customer is not under a duty to check bank statements so as to detect frauds,[2] nor more generally to report facts which would lead a reasonable person to suspect fraud.[3]

## 5.15.  PROMISSORY NOTES

The other form of instrument recognised by the Act is a promissory note. Section 83(1) defines a promissory note as:

> "an unconditional promise in writing made by one person to another signed by the maker, engaging to pay, on demand or at a fixed or determinable future time, a sum certain in money to, or to the order of a specified person or to bearer"

Certain elements of that definition are identical to the definition of a bill of exchange and indeed s.89(1) provides that the provisions of the Act which apply to bills also apply "with the necessary modifications" to promissory notes. The major difference between the two instruments, is that a promissory note features a promise to pay, not an order to a third party to pay. Thus there is no drawee or acceptor, so that any provisions regarding acceptance are inapplicable.[4] The maker of a note is treated as an acceptor of a bill—*i.e.* the person primarily liable on the instrument, and the first indorser as the drawer of an accepted bill—*i.e.* a person who is jointly liable with the "acceptor" (the maker of the note) in case of dishonour.[5] Any subsequent indorser is just like an indorser under a bill. A note need not use the word "promise",[6] but must nonetheless include a clear promise to pay, not merely a statement that a

---

[95] *The Times,* April 17, 1999, CA.
[96] *Parry-Jones v Law Society* [1969] 1 Ch. 1.
[97] *Robertson v Canadian Imperial Bank of Commerce* [1994] 1 W.L.R. 1493.
[98] *Greenwood v Martin's Bank Ltd* [1933] A.C. 51; *Orr v Union Bank of Scotland* (1854) 1 Macq. 513.
[99] *Price Meats Ltd v Barclays Bank plc* [2000] 2 All E.R. (Comm.) 346.
[1] See respectively *London Joint Stock Bank v Macmillan* [1918] A.C. 777; *Slingsby v District Bank* [1932] 1 K.B. 544, CA.
[2] *Tai Hing Cotton Mill Ltd v Liu Chong Hing Bank Ltd* [1986] A.C. 80.
[3] *Patel v Standard Chartered Bank* [2001] Lloyd's Rep. Bank. 229.
[4] s.89(3).
[5] s.89(2).
[6] *McTaggart v MacEachern's J F,* 1949 S.L.T. 363 at 365.

certain amount is payable, from which a promise to pay might be inferred.[7] So an IOU is not a promissory note. The most familiar example of a promissory note payable to the bearer is, of course, a banknote. But a banknote issued by the Bank of England (and by the Scottish banks under £5) is not just a note but legal tender.[8]

Although the above definition speaks of a promise made by one person to another, it is possible to create a note by promising to pay oneself a certain sum, and then indorsing the document. But the document is not a note, until it is indorsed.[9] If it is indorsed specially, it becomes a note payable to the named indorsee. If it is indorsed generally, it becomes a note payable to the bearer. Again, although as with a bill, a note which promises anything other than the payment of money is not valid,[10] s.83(3) indicates that a note is not invalid simply because it also pledges collateral security, e.g. giving the payee security over some part of the maker's property, as well as promising the payment of money. Also like a bill, s.84 states that a note is not effective until delivered to the payee or bearer. Section 84(1) provides that a note may be made by two or more makers, their liability being either joint or joint and several, depending on its tenor. This is in contrast to a bill, where the liability of acceptors, where there is more than one, would always be joint.[11] Where liability is joint, then each obligee is liable pro rata,[12] while joint and several liability sees each obligee liable for the entire sum. Section 84(2) provides that a note which runs "I promise to pay", but is signed by two or more persons, creates joint and several liability. A note which runs, "We promise to pay", probably creates only joint liability.

It may be remembered that, under s.45, a bill payable on demand must be presented for payment within a reasonable time, if the drawer is not to be discharged. There is no such rule with regard to the maker of a note. Nevertheless, s.86(1) states that a demand note must be presented for payment within a reasonable time of indorsement, if the indorser is not to be discharged. The reason for the difference is that notes are often intended to be used, not as negotiable instruments, but as continuing securities. Where such is the character of a particular note, this may influence the determination of what might be a reasonable time in a particular case.[13] To be a holder in due course under a bill, one must take it before it is overdue, and under s.36(3), a demand bill may be so regarded when it appears on the face of it to have been in circulation for an unreasonable length of time. However, in the same circumstances, by virtue of s.86(3), a note would not be deemed to be overdue, so that its holder could enforce it against all prior parties. Section 87(2) renders presentment for payment necessary to make an indorser liable, i.e. before the holder can proceed against an indorser he must be able to show that he has first sought payment from the maker. Section 87(2) states that presentment for payment is not usually necessary to make the maker liable, although if in its body the note expresses itself to be payable at a particular place, it must be presented there to render the maker liable. The view has been taken that a note is only payable at a particular place, if this is expressed "in the terms of the actual contract to pay which is contained in the note",[14] e.g. if the note reads "I promise to pay John Smith on demand at my office in 975 Bath Street, Glasgow, £5,000". A statement somewhere on a note, "payable at my office in 975 Bath Street, Glasgow, £5,000", does not make the note payable at that place.[15] By the same token, if a note is only payable at a particular place, s.87(3) insists that it must be presented there to render any indorser liable.

Under s.88, by making a note the maker promises to pay it according to its tenor, and is precluded from denying to a holder in due course the existence of the payee and his capacity to indorse.

---

[7] *Akbar Khan v Attar Singh* [1936] 2 All E.R. 545, PC.
[8] Currency and Bank Notes Act 1954.
[9] s.83(2).
[10] *Dickie v Singh*, 1974 S.L.T. 129.
[11] *Re Barnard* (1886) 32 Ch. D. 447.
[12] *Coats v Union Bank of Scotland*, 1929 S.L.T. 477.
[13] s.86(2).
[14] *Re British Trade Corporation Ltd* [1932] 2 Ch. 1 at 9.
[15] *Stevenson v Brown* (1902) 18 T.L.R. 268.

## 5.16. MODERN PAYMENT MECHANISMS

It would be short-sighted to conclude this discussion of payment instruments without acknowledging that nowadays cheques and other bills of exchange are increasingly being supplanted by other types of payment order in terms of popular use. Thus payment is often arranged through:

- Bank giro credit transfers, whereby an individual completes a form instructing that the bank transfer a specific sum of money to the account of a named payee. The individual requesting the transfer must provide the bank with the sum in question to allow the transfer to be made.
- Standing orders, whereby a customer of a bank directs the bank to pay a specific amount to a designated individual at regular intervals. The relevant form will authorise the bank to debit the customer's account, but the bank is under no obligation to make the payment if there are insufficient sums in the account.[16]
- Direct debits, whereby a customer supplies a creditor with a form to be tendered to the former's bank, authorising the bank to pay to the creditor such sums as the creditor should demand.

Yet commonplace as these payment systems have become, authority on their precise legal basis is very scarce. It is safe to say that they are not negotiable instruments. It will be remembered that s.3(1) of the Act defines a bill of exchange as "an unconditional order in writing addressed by one person to another, signed by the person giving it, requiring the person to whom it is addressed to pay on demand or at a fixed or determinable future time a sum certain in money to or to the order of a specified person or to bearer". While each of these instructions may meet certain requirements of that definition, they are probably not payable "on demand or at a fixed or determinable future time". Nor are they payable "to the order" of the beneficiary, and they are unlikely to be regarded as orders.[17] It is also clear that they do not have assignative effect in the same way as a bill of exchange. The relationship of banker and customer is that of debtor and creditor. While the presentation of a cheque has the effect that the right to repayment owed by the bank to the customer is assigned to the holder of the cheque, up to the value of the cheque,[18] this is not the effect of these other payment instructions.[19] Rather the relationship between banker and customer as regards these payment instructions is that of principal and agent.[20] The bank owes no duties to the beneficiary.[21] It should be remembered that the legal basis of payments via credit cards and debit cards is analysed in the chapter on consumer credit.

---

[16] *Whitehead v National Westminster Bank Ltd, The Times,* June 9, 1982.
[17] *The Brimnes* [1975] 1 Q.B. 929, CA.
[18] *British Linen Bank v Carruthers* (and see the discussion in para. 5.9.).
[19] *Mercedes Benz Finance Ltd v Clydesdale Bank plc,* 1997 S.L.T. 905.
[20] *ibid.,* and see *Royal Products Ltd v Midland Bank Ltd* [1981] 2 Lloyd's Rep. 194.
[21] *Wells v First National Commercial Bank* [1998] P.N.L.R. 552, CA.

# Chapter 6

# CAUTIONARY OBLIGATIONS AND OTHER RIGHTS IN SECURITY

## 6.1. INTRODUCTION

While payment for goods and services may occur on receipt, our economy operates very largely on the basis of credit. The granting of credit, of course, involves the risk that the creditor will not be paid. Insolvency law tends to operate on the basis of equal treatment, and therefore equal misery, for creditors. But generally the law of insolvency does not disturb the rights of secured creditors. This chapter deals with the various ways someone who is owed money can, at least to some extent, be assured of receiving payment. Previous chapters have already looked at hire-purchase, conditional sale and reservation of title clauses, all of which are, in one sense, rights in security. There is no need to consider these again. These are security rights over corporeal moveable property, created by contract. Contract can create security rights over incorporeal moveable property and over heritage, while certain security rights over corporeal moveable property arise by operation of law. The situation where a third party guarantees a party's performance of a contractual obligation—described by Scots law as a cautionary obligation—can also be regarded as a right in security. Each will be considered below. It can be appreciated that rights in security provide creditors with some extra security beyond the personal obligation of the debtor that repayment will be made, whether by granting them some sort of right in property, or by providing a personal guarantee from a third party. No personal obligation undertaken by the debtor, however expressed, can ever create a right in security.[1]

---

[1] *Graham & Co. v Raeburn & Verel* (1895) 23 R. 84.

# (1) CONTRACTUALLY CREATED RIGHTS

## 6.2. General Duties of Creditors

Whatever the form of security, the creditor is subject to certain general duties. So, if the debt is paid, then he must restore the exact property which was provided in security, unless there is express or implied agreement to the contrary.[2] Secondly, he must not merely take care of the property, but take reasonable care to protect the interests of the debtor. Thus where a creditor held shares in a company in security, and new shares were offered to existing shareholders on very advantageous terms, he was found liable in damages to the debtor for failing to communicate that offer to the debtor.[3] He must also take into account the interests of the debtor when selling the property, and a sale may be interdicted if these interests are clearly being disregarded.[4] When selling, he is in a fiduciary position, and so may not purchase the property himself unless authorised to do so by the agreement between the parties,[5] or by statute.[6] Finally, when there are two creditors who hold a security over property belonging to the debtor, and the creditor who has priority also has a security over other property of the debtor, that creditor (known as the catholic creditor) must have regard to the interests of the other creditor (known as the secondary creditor). So, if the catholic creditor chooses to enforce only the catholic security to the prejudice of the secondary creditor, as where the sale of that property yields only sufficient funds to meet the claim of the former, rendering the latter's security worthless, the secondary creditor may demand an assignation of the security over the other property.[7] This account is premised on the catholic creditor having no interest in retaining that security. If he has such an interest, as where the property is being held as security for more than one debt, then the secondary creditor has no such rights.

# (2) RIGHTS OVER CORPOREAL MOVEABLES

## 6.3. Pledge

This arises when the owner of corporeal moveables places them in the hands of his/her creditor to be retained until the obligation is satisfied.[8] If the debt is not repaid, the creditor will be entitled to sell the property. Pledge is not competent in relation to other forms of property.[9]

### (a) The necessity of delivery

For any right in security to be created over corporeal moveables, delivery of the property to the creditor is crucial.[10] As Lord Trayner puts it in *Pattison's Tr v Liston*[11]

---

[2] *Crerar v Bank of Scotland*, 1922 S.L.T. 335, HL.

[3] *Waddell v Hutton*, 1911 1 S.L.T. 223.

[4] *Kerr v McAthur's Trs.* (1848) 11 D. 301.

[5] *Taylor v Watson* (1846) 8 D. 400.

[6] *Ferguson v Rodger* (1895) 22 R. 643.

[7] *Littlejohn v Black* (1855) 18 D. 207.

[8] Bell, *Principles*, s.203.

[9] *Christie v Ruxton* (1862) 24 D. 1182.

[10] Although the D.T.I. Consultation Paper, *Security over Moveable Property in Scotland* (1994) suggested the creation of a new form of security over moveables, which would have been made effective, not by possession, but by registration in a register of security interests. The security was proposed to extend to certain forms of incorporeal moveable property termed receivables, *i.e.* sums due in respect of goods or services rendered in the course of business.

[11] (1893) 20 R. 806 at 813, but if physical delivery is impossible, as in the case of underground pipes, it may be that a written assignation would be enough to give the debtor a preference, in the event of the debtor's bankruptcy: *Darling v Wilson's Tr* (1887) 15 R. 180 at 183.

"It is quite certain that an effectual security over moveables can only be effected by delivery of the subject of the security."

It is not enough that the debtor is obliged to deliver the moveables to the creditor.[12] That creates merely a personal right, rather than a real right to the moveables which would be effective against a liquidator or a trustee in bankruptcy. Nor can it be argued that the debtor holds the moveables as a trustee for the creditor[13] Equally, sham sales whereby what are essentially security transactions are presented in the form of actual sales—as where a debtor "sells" certain goods to his creditor, but retains possession and use thereof—are not valid either as sales or as rights in security[14] Moreover, the attempt to extend a heritable security over moveables held on the property in question will fail, due to the fact that the debtor retained possession of the moveables.[15]

Yet, while delivery is vital, it may be actual, symbolic or constructive. Actual delivery is straightforward, and would embrace the handing over to the creditor of the keys to the premises where the moveables are stored[16] However, delivery must be to the creditor *qua* creditor, and not in some other capacity, so that when keys were delivered to the creditor in his capacity as the debtor's agent no pledge was created[17] Symbolic delivery occurs where the creditor is given documents of title to the moveables, as where delivery occurred when the creditor was given a bill of lading (see para. 4.33.) in respect of certain goods[18] Constructive delivery occurs where the keeper of the goods is instructed by the debtor to hold them on behalf of the creditor. It is not enough for the debtor to assign possession to the creditor, if this is not intimated to the keeper[19] Moreover, the keeper of the goods must be an independent third party and not the employee of the debtor, for then the goods effectively remain in the debtor's hands, and there can be no delivery[20] It follows that there can be no delivery simply by the debtor indicating that he henceforward holds the goods on behalf of the creditor[21] Naturally there can be no delivery until the goods have been ascertained or have come into existence,[22] but goods may be regarded as having been constructively delivered from the point that they are ascertained or have come into existence.[23]

At common law, it would appear that the insistence upon the creditor's possession of the property as being necessary to establish the right, precludes the possibility of a pledge being created simply by documents of title to the property being pledged[24] Nonetheless, the Factors Act 1889 allows a mercantile agent who is in possession of goods or documents of title thereto with the owner's consent, to pledge those goods by pledging documents of title thereto[25] Similarly, s.25(1) of the Sale of Goods Act 1979 directs that where a person who has agreed by buy goods, obtains with the seller's consent possession of the goods or documents of title thereto, any pledge by such individual (or a mercantile agent acting for him) to a person acting in good faith and without notice of the original seller's rights, will have the same effect as if the "seller" were a mercantile agent in possession of goods or documents of title thereto with the owner's consent. It seems to follow from the above that such a person can pledge the goods not merely in the normal way, but also by pledging documents of title thereto. By contrast, s.24 of

---

[12] *Bank of Scotland v Hutchison, Main & Co Ltd Liquidators*, 1914 1 S.L.T. 111, HL.

[13] *ibid.*

[14] *Jones & Co's Tr. v Allan* (1901) 9 S.L.T. 349; and see s.62(4) of the Sale of Goods Act 1979.

[15] *Stiven v Cowan* (1878) 15 S.L.R. 422.

[16] *West Lothian Oil Co Ltd v Mair* (1892) 20 R. 64.

[17] *Pattison's Tr v Liston* (1893) 20 R. 806.

[18] *Hayman v McLintock*, 1907 S.C. 936.

[19] *Inglis v Robertson & Baxter* (1898) 6 S.L.T. 130, HL.

[20] *Anderson v McCall* (1866) 4 M. 765.

[21] *Boak v Megget* (1844) 6 D. 662.

[22] *Hayman & Son v McLintock* (1907) 15 S.L.T. 63.

[23] *Pochin & Co v Robinows and Marjoribanks* (1869) 7 M. 622; *Black v Incorporation of Bakers* (1867) 6 M. 136.

[24] Compare *Hamilton v Western Bank of Scotland* (1856) 19 D. 152, with *North-Western Bank Ltd v Poynter, Son and Macdonalds* (1894) 2 S.L.T. 311; and see para. 4.33..

[25] ss.2–3, and see *Inglis v Robertson & Baxter* (1898) 6 S.L.T. 130, HL. especially the views of Halsbury L.C.

that Act indicates that where a seller of goods remains in possession of the goods or documents of title thereto, any pledge by him (or a mercantile agent acting for him) to a person acting in good faith and without notice of the previous sale, has the same effect as if the person pledging the goods were expressly authorised by the owner to do so. Since in this case the seller in possession is clothed with the authority of the owner, he can validly pledge the goods, but not documents of title thereto. It is submitted that the matter is not altered by the seller in possession using a mercantile agent. It may be added that, apart from such specialities, an ostensible pledge made by someone who is not the owner of the goods nor the properly authorised agent of the owner, cannot be effective.[26]

### (b) Obligations of the creditor

The creditor must take reasonable care of the property pledged, and will be liable for damage thereto caused by his negligence or that of his employees.[27] Otherwise, he is not liable for accidental damage to that property, unless he retains it unlawfully.[28] His right expires with loss of possession,[29] but it has been held that possession is not lost merely because he gives pledged jewellery to his family to wear.[30] In the same case it was confirmed that while he is not entitled, unless otherwise agreed, to use the property, breach of this term will usually not warrant termination of the contract. It is submitted, however, that matters might be otherwise if that use materially reduced the value of the property. English authority has even suggested that, while it is a breach of contract for the creditor himself to pledge the goods, that breach does not justify rescission.[31] If he does use the goods, he would be in the position of a hirer, and liable to the debtor accordingly.[32] If the goods are lost when being used, then the creditor will be wholly liable.[33]

## 6.4. PLEDGES UNDER THE CONSUMER CREDIT ACT 1974—PAWN

If a debtor who is not a body corporate obtains credit of up to £25,000 by pledging an article, that constitutes a pawn under the Consumer Credit Act 1974.[34] The relevant provisions of the Act replace the old Pawnbrokers Acts. The pawnee must give the pawnor a receipt in the prescribed form in return for the article.[35] Failure to do so is an offence, as is taking an article in pawn from a person whom the pawnee knows to be, or who appears to be and is, a minor.[36] A pawn is redeemable at any time within six months after it is taken, or during such longer period as is agreed by the parties.[37] If the pawn has not been redeemed by the end of this period, then it continues to be redeemable until the pawn is realised by the pawnee selling it.[38] This is subject to an exception where the credit does not exceed £75 and the redemption period is six months. In such cases property passes to the pawnee at the end of that period, and

[26] *Mitchell v Heys and Son* (1894) 1 S.L.T. 590.
[27] *Dominion Bank v Bank of Scotland* (1889) 16 R. 1081.
[28] *Fraser v Smith* (1899) 6 S.L.T. 335.
[29] Bell, *Principles*, s.206.
[30] *Wolifson v Harrison*, 1978 S.L.T. 95.
[31] *Donald v Suckling* (1866) L.R. 1 Q.B. 585.
[32] *Wolifson v Harrison*, 1978 S.L.T. 95.
[33] See Holt J. in *Coggs v Barnard* (1703) Ld. Raym. 909 at 913.
[34] ss.8(1)–(2), 189(1).
[35] s.114(1); and see Consumer Credit (Pawn-Receipt) Regulations 1983 (SI 1983/1566).
[36] ss.114(2), 115.
[37] s.116(1)–(2).
[38] s.116(3).

redemption is no longer possible.[39] No special charge may be made for redemption beyond the end of the redemption period, and charges for the safe-keeping of the pawn cannot be levied at a higher rate beyond the end of that period.[40]

A pawn is redeemed by the pawnor surrendering the pawn-receipt and paying the amount owing, although the pawnee need not deliver the pawn to the bearer of the receipt if he knows or has reasonable cause to suspect that the bearer is not the owner nor authorised by the owner to redeem it.[41] A pawnee who delivers or refuses to deliver the pawn in accordance with these provisions is not liable in delict.[42] If the person entitled to redeem has lost the pawn-receipt, he may redeem the pawn by instead tendering the prescribed form of statutory declaration or (where the pawnee agrees and the credit does not exceed £75) written statement.[43] A pawnee who refuses without reasonable cause to allow redemption commits an offence.[44]

Once the end of the redemption period is reached, the pawnee may seek to sell the pawn.[45] To be entitled to do so, the pawnee must give the pawnor not less than the prescribed period of notice, indicating in that notice the asking price.[46] He must then give details of the sale, its proceeds and expenses. Those proceeds (*i.e.* the amount raised minus expenses) may be sufficient to discharge the debt, and any surplus should be paid to the pawnor.[47] Otherwise, the size of the debt is merely diminished.[48] If the pawnor alleges that less than the true market value was raised, the pawnee may seek to prove that reasonable care was taken to obtain the true market value. If he fails, then the proceeds of sale will be treated as if the true market value were raised.[49] In other words, if, for example, a debt of £8,000 is secured by an article worth £10,000, but the pawnor fraudulently or negligently conducts the sale so that it realises only £5,000 (minus expenses of say, £500), instead of the pawnee being treated as still owing £3,500, he would be regarded as being owed £1,500 by the pawnor. A very similar provision deals with the situation where the pawnor alleges that expenses of sale were unreasonably high.[50]

It is of course the case that any pawnee who takes goods on pawn covered by the Act requires to be licensed (see para. 3.3.). Any pawnee who enters into such an agreement without being licensed commits an offence, while the agreement is not enforceable against the pawnor without an order from the Office of Fair Trading.[51]

## 6.5. BONDS OF BOTTOMRY AND *RESPONDENTIA*

These securities represent exceptions to the fundamental principle that security over corporeal moveables cannot be given without possession. A bond of bottomry is granted over a ship, a bond of *respondentia* over its cargo.[52] They can only be resorted to in order to raise a sum of money, which is absolutely necessary to permit the ship to complete its voyage, and which cannot otherwise be raised. If more than one bond is granted, then priority is determined by

---

[39] s.120(1)(a).
[40] s.116(4).
[41] s.117(1)–(2).
[42] s.117(3).
[43] s.118; and see Consumer Credit (Loss of Pawn-Receipt) Regulations 1983 (SI 1983/1567).
[44] s.119.
[45] s.121(1); and see Consumer Credit (Realisation of Pawn) Regulations 1983 (SI 1983 No. 1568).
[46] s.121(2).
[47] s.121(3).
[48] s.121(4).
[49] s.121(6).
[50] s.121(7).
[51] ss.39–40.
[52] See generally Bell, *Principles*, ss.452–456.

the date at which each is granted, the later having priority. The bondholder's claim has priority over ordinary creditors, but not over the wage claims of master and crew.[53] The money lent by the bondholder is lost, if the ship (or cargo in the case of a bond of *respondentia*) fails to reach its destination. Such bonds can be granted by the shipowner (or cargo owner in the case of a bond of *respondentia*) or his agent, but may be granted by the master of the ship, even if not authorised to do so, if the ship is in a foreign port, is unable to proceed unless the money is raised, if that money cannot be raised on the owner's personal credit, and if the master is unable to communicate with the owner.[54] If the sum raised is not repaid on the ship/cargo's arrival at its destination, the bondholder can, on application to the court, sell the ship/cargo (both if both sorts of bonds have been granted).[55] If the master of the ship, acting as agent for its owner, grants a bond of *respondentia,* the latter will be liable to the cargo owner should the cargo be thus sold.[56] It is safe to say that the conditions under which these bonds used to be granted having passed, they are now almost unheard of.

## 6.6.   STATUTORY MORTGAGES AND CHARGES

It is also now the case that various statutes provide for the creation of rights in security over particular types of corporeal moveable property. None of these rights depend on possession. Thus the Merchant Shipping Act 1995 provides[57] for the creation of a mortgage over a registered ship, or over a share in such a ship. Such a mortgage must itself be registered (in the Register of British Shipping) to be effective.[58] More than one such mortgage may be created over a particular ship (or share), and the priority of such mortgages being determined by the order in which they are registered.[59] It is important to note, however, that such mortgages yield in terms of priority to bonds of bottomry and maritime liens.[60] If the debt is not paid, the mortgage holder is empowered to sell the ship, but if there are other holders with priority, then he needs either their concurrence or a court order to be able to sell.[61] In similar fashion, it is also possible to create mortgages over registered aircraft.[62]

Companies (but not individuals or unincorporated bodies) may create a form of security known as a floating charge.[63] Detailed consideration thereof belongs to a text on company law, but it presents certain interesting features. In particular, when created, applies to all property owned by the company, whether heritable or moveable, but does not specifically attach to any item.[64] This means that property can be freely bought and sold by the company, with any property sold ceasing to be subject to the charge, and any property acquired becoming subject to the charge. This will continue to be the case until the charge is discharged by payment of the debt, or until the charge crystallises. A charge crystallises either when the company goes into liquidation,[65] or where the charge holder appoints a receiver.[66] The holder may appoint a

---

[53] *The Daring* (1868) L.R. 2 Adm. 260.

[54] *Miller & Co v Potter, Wilson & Co* (1875) 3 R.105; *Dymond v Scott* (1877) 5 R.196.

[55] *Lucovich, Petr.* (1885) 12 R. 1090.

[56] *Anderston Foundry Co v Law* (1869) 7 M. 836.

[57] s.16.

[58] Sch. 1, para. 7.

[59] *ibid.*, para. 8.

[60] *The Halcyon Isle* [1981] A.C. 221.

[61] Sch. 1, paras 9.

[62] Civil Aviation Act 1982 s.86 and Mortgaging of Aircraft Order 1972 (SI 1972/1268).

[63] Companies Act 1985, s.462(1). Industrial and Provident Societies may also grant floating charges, by virtue of s.3 of the Industrial and Provident Societies Act 1967. The D.T.I. Consultation Paper, *Security over Moveable Property in Scotland* (1994) suggested that persons other than companies be permitted to grant floating charges over their moveable property (subject to certain excepted classes of moveables).

[64] See Buckley L.J. in *Evans v Rival Granite Quarries* [1910] 2 Q.B. 979 at 999.

[65] Companies Act 1985, s.463(1).

[66] Insolvency Act, s.53(7).

receiver either on the occurrence of the events specified by the deed creating the charge as entitling him to do so, or on the occurrence of any of a number of other events which, broadly, indicate an inability to repay the loan.[67] When a charge crystallises, the effect is to constitute the holder as a holder of a fixed security over each and every item of property, moveable or heritable, which the company then owns.[68–69] In other words, at that point the charge ceases to float and attaches to all the company's property.

A charge is created by the execution of an appropriate deed, and its registration within 21 days of execution in the Register of Companies[70] If not registered within this period, the charge has no effect.[71] More than one floating charge may be created by a company, and their priority will generally be determined by the order in which they are registered, although charges which arrive for registration in the same post will be ranked equally.[72] The terms of the deed may prohibit the creation of further charges and fixed securities, and/or determine the order of ranking of charges and fixed securities.[73] It is therefore possible for the holders of existing charges and securities to agree that a newly created charge shall have priority. However, a fixed security which arises by operation of law (see paras 6.9. to 6.10.), rather than through agreement, will always have priority over a charge, whatever a ranking agreement may say.[74] Moreover, unless this is affected by a ranking agreement, a fixed security created by contract before the charge has attached will have priority over the charge.[75] After the holder of such a fixed security, the holder of the charge also ranks behind, in the following order[76]:

- anyone who has effectually executed diligence on any item of property subject to the charge;
- creditors in respect of all liabilities, charges and expenses incurred by the receiver;
- the receiver in respect of his liabilities, expenses and remuneration;
- any preferred creditor (see para. 8.32.).

It can be seen then that, despite the advantages of a floating charge in allowing the company to trade freely, without the restrictions imposed by the creation of fixed securities, it is generally more advantageous to hold a fixed security than a floating charge. On the other hand, the holder of a fixed security cannot appoint a receiver. For this reason, holders of fixed securities may also insist on the grant of a floating charge.

## 6.7. RIGHTS OVER INCORPOREAL MOVEABLES

Generally, a right in security may be created over any form of incorporeal moveable property, except for alimentary rights and rights involving a substantial element of *delectus personae*.[77] So debts, shares, rights under insurance policies, copyright, patents and trade marks may all be the subject of security. There are usually two steps necessary to constitute the security. The first is the assignation of the right by the owner to the security holder. Without this no security right

---

[67] *ibid* s.52(1).
[68–69] *ibid.* s.53(7); and see *Forth & Clyde Construction Co Ltd v Trinity Timber & Plywood Co Ltd,* 1984 S.L.T. 94. Indeed, depending on how the agreement is phrased, it may extend to property coming into the company's hands after that date: *Ross v Taylor,* 1985 S.L.T. 387.
[70] Companies Act 1985, s.410(2).
[71] *ibid.*
[72] *ibid.,* s.464(4).
[73] *ibid.,* s.464(1).
[74] *ibid.,* s.464(2); and see *Grampian Regional Council v Drill Stem (Inspection Services) Ltd,* 1994 S.C.L.R. 36.
[75] Insolvency Act, s.60.
[76] *ibid.*
[77] *Paterson v Baxter* (1849) 21 S.J. 125.

can be created. So where a solicitor persuaded a client to take out a life assurance policy to cover cash advances, paid all the premiums, and retained the policy "in security", it was held that he had no right to the proceeds in the absence of assignation.[78] Assignation creates a personal right against the granter of the security,[79] but the assignee requires to intimate the assignation to the "debtor" in the relevant obligation. As Lord Dunpark puts it in *Gallemos Ltd v Barratt Falkirk Ltd*:[80]

> "Intimation of an assignation to the debtor is the equivalent of delivery of a corporeal moveable and is necessary to complete the title of the assignee."

So in *Strachan v McDougle*[81] in order to provide security for a loan made by M, S assigned to her the rights under an insurance policy on his life. Yet no valid security was created because the assignation had not been intimated to the insurance company. This meant that while M had a personal right against S in respect of receiving the proceeds of the policy, a creditor who had done diligence on the policy had a prior claim to the proceeds.

Forms of assignation are provided by the Transmission of Moveable Property (Scotland) Act 1862, but these need not be followed, and indeed no particular form of words is required, as long as there is expressed a clear intention to make an immediate assignation.[82] Lack of such a clear intention, or any indication that the assignation should be made in the future will be fatal.[83] The same Act indicates how intimation should be made, but intimation may be implied from circumstances which suggest that the "debtor" cannot be unaware of the assignation, such as where the assignee takes court action or does diligence against him based on the assignation.[84] The "debtor" may be personally barred from arguing that there has been no intimation, where he has acted upon the assignation, *e.g.* by making payments to the assignee.[85] Intimation is excused where the assignee is also the "debtor".[86] The fact that intimation is highly impractical will not excuse failure to intimate. So where a company assigned the right to the uncalled capital on its shares, the fact that intimation had not been made to each individual shareholder meant that there was not a valid right in security.[87]

The assignee in enforcing his rights against the debtor stands in the shoes of the assignor—*assignatus utitur iure auctoris*. So the assignee gets no better right than the assignor, and any defence which would succeed against the latter will succeed against the former. So where a life assurance policy was void as a result of a misrepresentation by the insured, it was similarly unenforceable by his assignee.[88] Moreover, if a debt was extinguished by compensation prior to assignation, it cannot be enforced by the assignee.[89] But an assignee is not affected by a latent trust.[90]

Of course in relation to certain types of property, there is no "debtor", *e.g.* patent. This of course means that intimation is not possible. However, in certain cases, such as patents and trade marks, the assignation will only create a personal right against the assignor until the assignation is registered in the appropriate public register.[91] Again, the right to a share in a company can only be established by the registration of a transfer of that share in the company's

---

[78] *Wylie's Ex. v McJannet* (1901) 4 F. 195.
[79] See *Campbell's Trs. v Whyte* (1884) 11 R. 1078.
[80] 1990 S.L.T. 98 at 101.
[81] (1835) 13 S. 954.
[82] *Carter v McIntosh* (1862) 24 D. 925.
[83] *Gallemos Ltd v Barratt Falkirk Ltd*, 1990 S.L.T. 98; *Bank of Scotland v Hutchison, Main & Co Ltd*, 1914 1 S.L.T. 111, HL.
[84] *Whyte v Neish* (1622) Mor. 854.
[85] *Livingston v Lindsay* (1626) Mor. 860.
[86] *Russell v Earl of Breadalbane* (1831) 5 W. & S. 256.
[87] *Liquidator of the Union Club Ltd v Edinburgh Life Assurance Co* (1906) 14 S.L.T. 314.
[88] *Scottish Widows' Fund and Life Assurance Society v Buist* (1876) 3 R. 1078.
[89] *Shiells v Ferguson, Davidson & Co* (1876) 4 R. 250.
[90] *Redfearn v Ferrier and Somervail* (1813) 1 Dow 50.
[91] Patents Act 1977, ss.31–33 (Register of Patents); Trade Marks Act 1994, ss.22–24 (Register of Trade Marks).

own register of shareholders.[92] By contrast, there is no register in respect of copyright, so that a simple assignation would be sufficient to create a real right.[93]

## 6.8. HERITABLE SECURITIES

Often a debtor's most valuable property is heritage—land and buildings. Section 9(1) of the Conveyancing and Feudal Reform (Scotland) Act 1970 (the Act) created a new form of security, known as the standard security. Since 1970, the standard security is, by virtue of s.9(3) of the Act, the only competent form of heritable security for a debt. Such a security may be created over any estate or interest in land which is capable of being owned or held as a separate interest and to which a title may be recorded in the Register of Sasines.[94] So a security may be created not only on property owned by the giver of the security, but over a lesser interest such as a lease, so long as title thereto is recordable. Debt is defined by s.9(8)(c) to include not only fixed but also fluctuating amounts, as well as an obligation *ad factum praestadum, i.e.* an obligation to carry out a task, such as the completion of a building project.

A standard security must be in either of two prescribed forms, depending whether the personal obligation of repayment is included in the deed (Form A), or constituted in a separate instrument (Form B).[95] To give the holder a real as opposed to merely a personal right, the security must be properly executed and duly recorded.[96] There are standard conditions contained in Sch. 3, which s.11(2) applies to every standard security. These may be varied by the parties, save for the conditions as to sale, foreclosure or redemption.[97] The conditions deal with such matters as the debtor's obligations to maintain and repair the property, to complete unfinished buildings, not to demolish or alter buildings without the creditor's consent, to pay rates, etc. to insure the subjects, not to let the subjects. They also deal with the circumstances when the debtor is to be regarded as in default and the creditor's rights in that case, and with the creditor's right to call up the security. These standard conditions can affect third parties in that if a debtor does grant a lease without the creditor's consent, the lease can be reduced by the creditor, unless the creditor knew at the time when the security was granted that the lessee had a real right or at least a right which could be made real.[98]

### (a) Transfer

A standard security may be transferred in whole or in part via an assignation in conformity with one of the two forms prescribed by Sch. 4, and on recording the assignation the security (or the assigned part) becomes vested in the assignee as if it had been granted in his favour.[99] Except as otherwise stated therein, an assignation conveys to the assignee the benefit of any additional security for the debt, the right to recover any expenses incurred by the creditor, and the benefit of any steps the creditor took to enforce the security.[1]

---

[92] Companies Act 1985, ss.183–186; and see *Guild v Young* (1884) 22 S.L.R. 520.

[93] Copyright, Designs and Patents Act 1988, s.90.

[94] s.9(2), (8)(b). There is an exception in that such a security cannot be created over an entailed estate, but this is of no practical consequence, and all entailed estates are in any event due to be disentailed under ss.48–50 of the Abolition of Feudal Tenure etc (Scotland) Act 2000.

[95] s.9(2) and Sch. 2.

[96] See *American Express Europe Ltd v Royal Bank of Scotland (No. 2)*, 1989 S.L.T. 650; and s.11(1).

[97] s.11(3).

[98] See *Trade Development Bank v Warriner and Mason (Scotland) Ltd*, 1980 S.L.T. 223; *Trade Development Bank v David W Haig (Bellshill) Ltd Trade Development Bank v Crittall Windows Ltd*, 1983 S.L.T.510.

[99] s.14(1). The assignee only obtains a real right on recording: see *Sanderson's Trs. v Ambion (Scotland) Ltd*, 1994 S.L.T. 645.

[1] s.14(2); and see *Watson v Bogue (No. 1)*, 2000 S.L.T. (Sh. Ct) 125.

## (b) Ranking

It is possible for a debtor to grant more than one standard security over the same property. The basic rule is that the security which is first recorded has priority, although it is open to the parties to regulate the order of preference by agreement.[2] Obviously, the ranking of a prior security cannot be altered without the agreement of the holder of that security. However when a security holder receives notice of the creation of a subsequent security (or of the outright assignation or conveyance of the debtor's interest), his security is restricted to[3]:

- existing advances,
- further advances he is contractually obliged to make,
- interest on any such advances,
- expenses and outlays reasonably incurred in exercising any power conferred by the security.

If, after receiving such notice, the creditor does make any advances that he is not contractually obliged to make, it is probable that those advances are still covered by the security, but rank behind the advances of the second security holder. Accordingly, unless the security subjects are very valuable, or the sums secured relatively small, any such further advances may only be secured in a theoretical rather than a practical sense.

## (c) Competition

The holder of a standard security may find himself in competition with the holders of other forms of security, and of creditors who have sought to do diligence on the property. Thus a creditor may seek to inhibit the debtor from alienating his heritable estate. If a debtor has been inhibited prior to his granting of the security, that security has no effect against the inhibitor, who may indeed reduce it.[4]

On the other hand, an inhibition granted after the security has no effect on the security.[5]

Generally, the insolvency of the debtor has no effect on secured creditors. So a trustee in bankruptcy, or a liquidator may sell the secured property only with the consent of the secured creditor, unless a sufficient amount is obtained to discharge the security, while an administrator or receiver must obtain that consent or else seek the authority of the court to sell.[6] In all cases, the secured creditor has preference in terms of any amount realised. The relationship between fixed securities and floating charges is discussed in para. 6.6. above.

## (d) Default

Where a debtor is in breach of some obligation arising out of the security, and that default may be remedied, the creditor may serve a notice calling on the debtor to remedy the default within a month.[7] The debtor, if aggrieved by any requirement of the notice, has 14 days to object to the court, which may uphold the notice, or vary it, or set it aside in whole or in part.[8] Should the debtor fail to comply with the notice, then the creditor may look to sell, or carry out necessary repairs, or apply to the court for a decree of foreclosure.[9] Where a notice is served, the debtor or proprietor may redeem the security by giving notice at any time before an enforceable contract has been concluded for the sake of the subjects.[10] As an alternative to

---

[2] See *Scotlife Homes (No. 2) Ltd v Muir,* 1994 S.C.L.R. 791, and s.13(3)(b).

[3] s.13(1).

[4] *Baird and Brown v Stirrat's Tr.* (1872) 10 M. 414.

[5] *Campbell's Trs v De Lisle's Exrs.* (1870) 9 M. 252.

[6] See variously, Bankruptcy (Scotland) Act, s.39; Companies Act 1985, s.623(4), Insolvency Act 1986, ss.16, 61.

[7] See Standard Conditions 9(1)(b) and s.21. For the form of the notice, see Sch. 6, Form B.

[8] s.22.

[9] See Standard Conditions 10(2), (6) and (7).

[10] s.23(3).

serving a notice of default, the creditor may instead apply directly to the court for a warrant to exercise any of the remedies available when the debtor fails to comply with a calling-up notice (see below).[11] This opens up a wider range of remedies.[12] Such an application is mandatory where the reason for the debtor's default is the fact that the proprietor of the subjects is insolvent.[13] The debtor and the proprietor will usually be one and the same, but that is not necessarily the case.

## (e) Calling-up notice

Where the creditor wishes the debt to be paid, or in default thereof, to exercise a power of sale or any other statutory power, he must serve a calling-up notice on the proprietor(s).[14] The debtor must be given at least two months to pay, although the debtor may agree to a shorter period of notice, or waive the right to notice altogether.[15] If the debtor does not comply with the notice, that amounts to default, permitting the creditor to exercise the statutory default powers[16]—*i.e.* selling, carrying out necessary repairs, entering into possession and recovering rents, letting, applying to the court for a decree of foreclosure. Often a creditor who faces default on the part of the debtor must consider whether to serve a calling-up notice or a default notice. Although the former contemplates a longer period of notice, it may not be objected to by the debtor, and opens up a wider range of remedies. Nor is there any reference to a power to redeem when a calling-up notice has been served. Nonetheless, it has been held that the debtor's ordinary right to redeem under s.18 by giving two months notice is not affected by the service of a calling-up notice.[17] It has also been held that there is no reason why the creditor should not serve a calling-up notice and a default notice together.[18]

## (f) Residential property

Where the security is over "an interest in land used to any extent for residential purposes"[19] the provisions regarding calling-up and default are subject to significant qualification as a result of the Mortgage Rights (Scotland) Act 2001. Where a creditor has served a calling-up notice, or notice of default or applied to the court to be permitted to exercise any of the remedies available when the debtor fails to comply with a calling-up notice, an application may be made to the court for the suspension of the creditor's rights.[20] Not only the debtor may make this application, but also:[21]

(1) the proprietor (if not the debtor),
(2) a non-entitled spouse, if the subjects are a matrimonial home,
(3) a person living with the debtor or proprietor as their *de facto* spouse, even if of the same sex.

In all these cases, the subjects must be that person's sole or main residence. In addition, a person under (iii) may also apply if[22]:

---

[11] s.24; see Standard Conditions 9(1)(c).

[12] *Bank of Scotland v Fernand,* 1997 S.L.T. (Sh. Ct.) 68; but see *Skipton Building Society v Wain,* 1986 S.L.T. 96.

[13] See Standard Condition 9(1)(c). For what amounts to insolvency in this context, see Standard Condition 9(2).

[14] s.19, and see *Hill Samuel & Co Ltd v Haas,* 1989 S.L.T. (Sh.Ct.) 68. For the form of the notice, see Sch. 6, Form A.

[15] s.19(10). If the house is a matrimonial home in terms of the Matrimonial Homes (Family Protection) (Scotland) Act 1981, the debtor may not agree to waive or shorten the period of notice without the written consent of the non-entitled spouse.

[16] Standard Conditions 9(1)(a) and 10.

[17] *G Dunlop & Son's J F v Armstrong,* 1994 S.L.T. 199, where the power was said to be exercisable right up to the point of the conclusion of a contract of sale, subject to liability for payment of the expenses incurred by seeking to sell.

[18] *Bank of Scotland v Millward,* 1994 S.L.T. 901.

[19] Mortgage Rights (Scotland) Act 2001, s.1.

[20] *ibid.*

[21] s.1(2).

[22] s.1(2)(d).

- the subjects are still their sole or main residence, though no longer that of the debtor or proprietor,
- they lived with the debtor or proprietor for at least six months prior to the departure of the debtor or proprietor, and
- the subjects are the sole or main residence of a person under 16, who is their child and the child of the debtor or proprietor. A child includes any stepchild or person treated by the couple as their child.[23]

An application must be made before the expiry of the relevant period of notice or before the conclusion of the court proceedings.[24] The rights of the creditor are then suspended until the application is determined.[25]

The court may suspend the creditor's rights to such an extent, for such period, and subject to such conditions as it thinks fit, but will only do so where it considers it reasonable in all the circumstances, having regard in particular to:

- the nature of and reasons for the default,
- the applicant's ability to remedy the default within a reasonable period of time,
- any action taken by the creditor to assist the debtor to fulfil those obligations,
- the ability of the applicant and any other person residing at the subjects to secure reasonable alternative accommodation.[26]

## (g) The creditor's rights

As indicated above, the full range of rights available to the creditor on default are, carrying out necessary repairs, entering into possession and recovering rents, letting, selling the subjects, and applying to the court for a decree of foreclosure. Nothing need be said about the first of these. A creditor who takes possession is entitled to recover any rents due from tenants, as from the date of entering into possession. He is not entitled to any arrears of rent.[27] He may indeed himself grant a lease of the whole or part of the subjects for up to seven years, or for a longer period on application to the court.[28] He also has assigned to him all rights and obligations of the proprietor under the lease or in relation to the management or maintenance of the subjects.[29] It has been held that while an obligation to contribute to common repairs (such as where the subjects form part of a tenement) may thus be transmitted, the creditor does not inherit liability for repairs which have already been done.[30]

The most important right is undoubtedly that of sale of the subjects. It has been held that this power does not confer an unfettered discretion, and the creditor must have regard to the interests of the debtor when exercising it. In particular, if the value of the property sold is likely to exceed the debt, the creditor must account for that surplus to the debtor. Therefore, if he intends to sell in a way which will result in there being no surplus, he may be interdicted by the debtor.[31] The creditor, under s.25, may sell by private bargain or public roup, and must advertise the sale and take all reasonable steps to ensure that the price is the best that can be reasonably obtained. If the creditor fails in these duties, he may be liable in damages to the debtor, but the onus of proving such failure will be a difficult one to discharge,[32] and even

---

[23] s.1(3).
[24] s.1(4), but see s.1(5).
[25] s.1(7)–(8).
[26] see generally s.2.
[27] *UCG Bank Ltd v Hire Foulis (In Liquidation)*, 1999 S.C. 250.
[28] 1970 Act, s.20(3).
[29] s.20(5).
[30] *David Watson Property Management Ltd v Woolwich Equitable Building Society*, 1992 S.L.T. 43, HL.
[31] *Armstrong, Petitioner*, 1988 S.L.T. 255 at 258, *per* Lord Jauncey.
[32] Compare *Royal Bank of Scotland v A and M Johnston*, 1987 G.W.D.1–5, with *Bank of Credit v Thompson*, 1987 G.W.D.10–341, and *Associated Displays Ltd v Turnbeam Ltd*, 1988 S.C.L.R. 220.

proven failure will not necessarily result in an award of damages unless loss is also proven.[33] In *Dick v Clydesdale Bank plc*[34] the creditor was alleged to have caused a loss to the debtor by advertising land for agricultural use, when it could have yielded a considerably higher price had it been sold for commercial use. This argument was rejected, as no planning permission had been granted for such use, and the creditor was not obliged to emphasise the development potential of the land. Lord Hope opined[35]:

> "In the ordinary case the creditor may be regarded as having fulfilled the duties imposed upon him in regard to the marketing of the subjects, if he takes and acts upon appropriate professional advice . . . [I]t is clear that the creditor is entitled to sell the security subjects at a time of his own choosing, provide he has taken all reasonable steps to ensure that the price at which he sells is the best that can be reasonably obtained at the time . . . [He] is not to be subjected to the risk of challenge simply on the theory that the subjects may have had a greater value than was realised by the sale. What matters is the reality of the market place in which the subjects were exposed when he decided to sell."

This was of course a case where the debtor's argument about the property having a higher value was purely speculative. It has been acknowledged that the creditor will be liable if he sells in a way which clearly is unlikely to achieve the best price[36] The proceeds of sale will be applied in the following order of priority and any surplus is payable to the owner:[37]

- the expenses of the sale,
- sums due under prior securities being redeemed,
- the sum due under the standard security and securities of equal ranking,
- sums due under postponed securities according to their ranking.

The right of foreclosure sees the creditor who has failed to find a buyer at a price sufficient to cover the amount due, taking over ownership of the subjects. It is only available[38]:

- when the creditor has exposed the subjects for sale by public roup at a price not exceeding the sum due under the security and any security of prior or equal ranking, and has failed to find a buyer, or
- he has failed to obtain that price, but has managed to sell part of the subjects for a sum below that price.

In such circumstances, he may apply to the court for a decree of foreclosure, not earlier than two months from the date of the first exposure to sale.[39] He must lodge in court a statement setting out the amount due under the security, and satisfy the court that this amount is not less than the price at which the property has been exposed, or part of it sold.[40] The application must be served on the debtor, the proprietor (if a different person), and any other heritable creditor.[41] The court may[42]:

- allow the debtor or proprietor a period of up to three months in which to pay the amount due,

---

[33] See *Davidson v Clydesdale Bank plc* 2002 S.L.T. 1088, where a failure was established, in that the subjects were sought to be advertised for sale, emphasising their attractive nature and location, but making no reference to the valuable mineral deposits to be found thereon. Yet there was held to be no loss, as the working of the minerals would have reduced the amenity of the property, so that no more would have been obtained through selling the property by reference to the minerals.

[34] 1991 S.C. 365.

[35] At 370–371.

[36] *Bisset v Standard Property Investment plc*, 1999 G.W.D. 36–1253.

[37] s.27.

[38] s.28(1).

[39] *ibid.*

[40] s.28(2).

[41] s.28(3).

[42] s.28(4).

- order the exposure of the subjects at a price fixed by it—the creditor may bid in that event,
- grant the decree of foreclosure.

That decree, when duly recorded, has the effect of vesting the subjects in the creditor, disburdening them of the standard security and all postponed securities and diligences, and giving the creditor the same right as the debtor to redeem securities of prior and equal ranking.[43] In other words, the creditor takes the property free of securities of lower ranking, since the sale would not have realised enough money to have met any of these claims anyway, but the property is still affected by other securities. The debtor still owes the creditor to the extent that the debt exceeds the value at which the property is deemed to be taken over.[44] It should be remembered that foreclosure is only available when the creditor sought to sell by public roup. It is not competent when the subjects are advertised for private sale.

## (h) The effect of the Consumer Credit Act 1974

Where the sum secured is less than £25,000, the 1974 Act may also apply. The provisions of the Act do not apply to heritably secured loans made by banks, building societies, insurance companies and local authorities.[45] Otherwise the form and content of agreements must comply with the statutory regulations[46] (see para. 3.6.). Moreover, s.58(1) of the 1974 Act states that, before the creditor sends an unexecuted regulated agreement to be secured on land to the debtor for his signature, the creditor must first give the debtor a copy of the unexecuted agreement, containing a notice in prescribed form indicating the debtor's right to withdraw from the agreement and how that is exercisable. Under s.58(2), the withdrawal provisions do not apply to a mortgage agreement or an agreement relating to a bridging loan. Moreover, a creditor who intends to serve a calling up or default notice, must first serve a default notice under the 1974 Act[47] (see para. 3.8.).

# (3) RIGHTS IN SECURITY ARISING BY OPERATION OF LAW

Certain security rights over moveables arise by operation of law, without the need for agreement by the parties. These are essentially liens, whereby a creditor in possession of the debtor's moveable property may retain it as security for payment, and hypothecs, whereby a creditor obtains a security over the debtor's moveables without possession thereof.

## 6.9.   LIEN

It has already been seen how an unpaid seller has, by virtue of s.39(1)(a) of the Sale of Goods Act 1979, a right of lien over the goods, so long as they remain in his possession (see para. 1.12.). This right is created by statute, being unknown to the common law. The typical common law lien arises where a person who has rendered services to another is entitled to

---

[43] s.28(6).
[44] s.28(7).
[45] s.16.
[46] Consumer Credit (Agreements) Regulations 1983 (SI 1983/1553).
[47] ss.87–88.

retain that other's moveables until he is paid for those services, or at least paid damages for breach of contract.[48] The right of lien is thus based on possession. So where engineers were brought in to work on a ship which remained under the control of its owners, there was no possession and hence no lien.[49] A distinction is sometimes made between true possession and mere custody. So a company secretary did not have a lien over its books and papers which were in his hands, as he held them on behalf of the company, rather than them having been entrusted to him for a particular task.[50] He may have had custody of this material, but the company had never relinquished possession. Moreover possession must be conferred by the owner of the property, or at least by someone entitled to confer possession, rather than by, say, a hirer.[51] And that possession must have been obtained legitimately, not as a result of mistake or fraud.[52] The right of lien is lost when possession is lost, unless possession is lost through improper means.[53] It is further argued that the right cannot revive once possession has been lost simply by the creditor resuming possession, but this is probably only true in relation to a special lien.[54] If possession is relinquished as regards part of the goods, the right of lien can still be exercised in relation to the remainder.[55] And of course a creditor may relinquish physical custody without relinquishing legal possession, *e.g.* by giving custody to a third party.[56] Although the right *prima facie* entitles the creditor only to retain possession until payment is made, it is open to him to apply to the court for a warrant to sell the property.[57] Equally, the owner may also seek such a warrant where the creditor's retention of the property threatens his commercial interests, although the creditor has a preferential interest in the sum thus realised.[58] A lien is subject to the general equitable control of the courts, who may release the property subject to such conditions as they may determine.[59]

## (a) Special Liens

Liens are either general or special. The normal form of lien is the special lien, which is based on the simple premise that if A carries out work for B on particular goods entrusted to him by B, he is entitled to retain those goods until he is paid for his services.[60] However, he is not entitled to retain other property belonging to B as security for that debt.[61] By contrast, under a general lien the creditor is entitled to retain any of the debtor's property which he holds as security for general indebtedness to him. General liens are exceptional and thus recognised only in relation to a number of long established categories,[62] although a general lien might also arise as a result of usage of a particular trade,[63] or more unusually under the express terms of a contract.[64] The most common form of special lien is that of the person who repairs goods, but it would also extend to anyone who does any work on goods, as in the case of a miller,[65] or to

---

[48] *Moore's Carving Machine Co v Austin* (1896) 33 S.L.R. 613; but the lien probably does not extend to the cost of storing the property while awaiting payment: *Carntyne Motors v Curran,* 1958 S.L.T (Sh. Ct.) 6.

[49] *Ross and Duncan v Baxter & Co* (1885) 13 R. 185.

[50] *Barnton Hotel Co Ltd v Cook* (1899) 7 S.L.T. 131.

[51] *Lamonby v Arthur G Foulds Ltd,* 1928 S.L.T. 42.

[52] *Louson v Craik* (1842) 4 D. 1452.

[53] Bell, *Principles,* s.1415.

[54] *ibid.,* s.1416; and see *Morrison v Fulwell's Tr.* (1901) 9 S.L.T. 34; *London Scottish Transport Ltd v Tyres (Scotland) Ltd,* 1957 S.L.T. (Sh. Ct.) 48; *Hostess Mobile Catering v Archibald Scott Ltd,* 1981 S.L.T. (Notes) 125.

[55] *Gray v Wardrop's Trs.* (1851) 13 D. 963.

[56] *Renny v Kemp* (1841) 3 D. 1134.

[57] *Gibson and Stewart v Brown & Co* (1876) 3 R. 328.

[58] *Parker v Brown & Co* (1878) 5 R. 979; where the condition of the goods was deteriorating.

[59] *Garscadden v Ardrossan Dry Dock Co,* 1910 S.C. 178.

[60] *National Homecare Ltd v Belling & Co Ltd,* 1994 S.L.T. 50.

[61] *Findlay v Waddell,* 1910 1 S.L.T. 315.

[62] *Laurie v Denny's Tr.* (1853) 15 D. 404.

[63] *Strong v Philips & Co* (1878) 5 R. 770.

[64] *Anderson & Co's Tr. v Fleming* (1871) 9 M. 718.

[65] *Chase v Westmore* (1816) 5 M. & S. 180.

anyone who does work in relation to goods, as in the case of a storer[66] or carrier (see para. 4.7.). Indeed the right will arise in relation to property which is placed in a person's hands so that certain work can be done, even if that work is not done directly in relation to that property. So an accountant, who is given papers and other documents by his client so that a particular piece of work can be done, has a special lien over that material.[67]

## (b) General Liens

It is not proposed to cover the minutiae of general liens, and in particular it is inappropriate to cover the innkeeper's lien in a work of this kind. Still, such liens are recognised as extending to solicitors, bankers and factors.

## (i) Solicitors

A Scottish solicitor[68] has a lien over all of his client's papers in his hands in order to cover the whole of the account with the client, even though the account has nothing to do with a particular document.[69] It covers all disbursements and expenses incurred on behalf of the client in the ordinary course of business as a solicitor, but does not extend to cash advances made to a client.[70] Nor does it entitle the solicitor to retain money given to him by the client for a particular purpose which has been frustrated.[71] In the insolvency of the client, the solicitor must deliver up any title deed or other document of the client, but this is without prejudice to the right of lien.[72] Similarly, the order of distribution of a bankrupt estate laid down by s.51 of the Bankruptcy (Scotland) Act 1985 is specifically expressed not to affect the right of lien.[73] The effect is to render the solicitor as a preferred creditor, although relevant authority suggests that his preference is postponed to that of outlays, remuneration and expenses of the interim and permanent trustees (and probably of a petitioning creditor).[74] Again, the solicitor's security extends to the whole estate,[75] so that his claim must yield to that of any creditor who has a security over a specific item of property. Subject to these points however, the solicitor's claim would be preferred to that of any unsecured creditor (see also para. 8.32.). It is also the case that the solicitor's claim is postponed to that of any heritable creditor, who has recorded his security.[76] The solicitor's lien, of course, cannot be claimed against a third party who has a right to the papers,[77] unless that third party's right derives from the client, but even this is subject to an exception in that if the solicitor also acts for the third party, he is barred from exercising the lien against that party, unless he had previously made the party aware that he intended to enforce the lien.[78] It has also been held that, while a solicitor, who has been given papers in order to conduct a court action, cannot withhold the papers if they are required for the prosecution of that action,[79] he can retain them if they are required for the initiation of an action.[80]

---

[66] *Laurie v Denny's Tr.* (1853) 15 D. 404.

[67] *Meikle and Wilson v Pollard* (1880) 8 R. 69.

[68] No lien extends to the account of an English solicitor, unless a Scottish solicitor has paid it or become liable for it on his client's behalf—*Liquidator of Grand Empire Theatre v Snodgrass,* 1932 S.C. (H.L.) 73.

[69] *Paul v Meikle* (1868) 7 M. 235.

[70] *Christie v Ruxton* (1862) 24 D. 1182.

[71] *Middlemas v Gibson,* 1910 S.C. 577.

[72] Bankruptcy (Scotland) Act 1985, s.38(4); and see s.144 of the Insolvency Act 1986 in the context of liquidation.

[73] s.51(6)(b).

[74] *Miln's J.F. v Spence's Tr.,* 1927 S.L.T. 425.

[75] *Rorie v Stevenson* (1908) 15 S.L.T. 870.

[76] Conveyancing (Scotland) Act 1924 s.27; Land Registration (Scotland) Act 1979, s.29(2).

[77] See *e.g. Weir and Wilson Ltd v Turnbull and Findlay* (1911) 2 S.L.T. 78.

[78] *Gray v Graham* (1855) 2 Macq. 435.

[79] *Callman v Bell* (1793) Mor. 6255.

[80] *Yau v Ogilvie & Co,* 1985 S.L.T. 91.

## (ii) Bankers

A banker has "a general right to retain all unappropriated negotiable instruments belonging to the customer in [his] hands for securing his balance on the general account".[81] In other words, he has a lien over any negotiable instrument (bills of exchange including cheques, promissory notes, etc.) which the customer has lodged with him for the purpose of collecting the proceeds and crediting the customer's account. If they are lodged for some other purpose, such as for safekeeping,[82] or for the bank itself to purchase them at a discount,[83] then no lien arises.

## (iii) Factors

Factors or mercantile agents have a general lien over all of their employer's property, including money, which comes into their hands in the course of their employment.[84] A mercantile agent is defined by s.1(1) of the Factors Act 1889 as someone "having in the customary course of his business as such agent authority either to sell goods or to consign goods for the purpose of sale, or to buy goods, or to raise money on the security of goods. However, in this context a factor would embrace anyone who buys property, makes advances or incurs liability on behalf of the principal.[85] Thus auctioneers and stockbrokers are entitled to this lien, whereas a factor in the sense of the manager of an estate is not.[86] The lien covers not only advances made and expenses and liabilities incurred in the course of employment, but also any salary or commission due.[87] It does not cover debts which may be due to the factor in another capacity.[88]

# 6.10. HYPOTHEC

A hypothec is a right of security over moveables which remain in the possession of the debtor. Certain security rights which can be created by contract such as aircraft mortgages, ship mortgages, bonds of bottomry and bonds of *respondentia* are in essence conventionally created hypothecs (see paras 6.5. to 6.6.). However hypothecs can also arise by operation of law. The types of such hypothecs which are relevant in the present context, are maritime hypothecs, and those which may be claimed by landlords and solicitors.

## (a) The landord's hypothec

A landlord has a hypothec over moveables on the premises, *e.g.* house furniture, or equipment and stock on business premises, to secure up to a year's rent. Although the hypothec does not *prima facie* extend to property on the premises not owned by the tenant,[89] it will extend to property which a third party has knowingly allowed to enter the premises for the tenant's use and enjoyment.[90] So Lord President Clyde opines it in *Dundee Corporation v Marr*[91]:

---

[81] *per* Lord President Inglis in *Robertson's Tr. v Royal Bank of Scotland* (1890) 18 R. 12 at 16.

[82] *Leese v Martin* (1873) L.T. 17 Eq. 224; but see *Robertson's Tr. v Royal Bank of Scotland* (1890) 18 R. 12.

[83] *Borthwick v Bremner* (1833) 12 S. 121.

[84] Bell, *Principles*, s.1445.

[85] *Glendinning v Hope* (1911) 2 S.L.T. 161, HL.

[86] See *Miller v Hutcheson and Dixon* (1881) 8 R. 489; *Glendinning v Hope* (1911) 2 S.L.T. 161, HL, *Macrae v Leith* (1913) 1 S.L.T. 273.

[87] *Sibbald v Gibson* (1852) 15 D. 217.

[88] *Miller v McNair* (1852) 14 D. 955.

[89] See *Bell v Andrews* (1885) 12 R. 961 (hypothec did not cover a piano owned by the tenant's daughter), *Pulseometer Engineering Co Ltd v Gracie* (1887) 14 R. 316 (pumps owned by a third party and displayed for sale on the premises not affected by the hypothec).

[90] *Rudman v Jay* (1908) 15 S.L.T. 853.

[91] 1971 S.C. 96 at 100.

"This right of hypothec covers in general all goods in the possession of the tenant in the premises, whether he owns them or has hired them from a third party. For that third party is presumed to know the law and therefore is presumed to have consented to the landlord's right of hypothec over them when he delivers the articles into the possession of the tenant . . ."

So in that case, the hypothec extended to a jukebox on the premises, which was rented from a third party, and it has also been held to cover beer kegs within a public house belonging to a brewery rather than the tenant[92]

In some ways the hypothec is like a floating charge in that it does not attach to the moveables to which it potentially extends until it is enforced. This means that the tenant can dispose of or add to the property held on the affected premises until that point. The hypothec is enforced by the landlord raising an action of sequestration for rent within three months of the end of the period in respect of which the claim is brought. The sheriff court has exclusive jurisdiction to entertain such an action[93] It is competent to secure up to a year's rent, but in respect of further arrears the landlord is simply an unsecured creditor[94] It is indeed possible to extend the security to cover the payment of the next instalment of rent due, if the landlord can show the sheriff cause why that should be done.[95]

Of course, the value of the security could be significantly reduced, or perhaps even rendered worthless, if the tenant, prior to sequestration for rent being granted, were able to strip the premises. Thus a landlord who fears that the tenant or the owner of the goods may seek to remove certain goods, may seek to interdict removal, or seek a warrant to have goods removed returned[96] Nonetheless, such remedies are to be regarded as exceptional, and a landlord who seeks them without giving notice to the other party does so periculo petentis, i.e. at his own risk. Thus if such a remedy is sought without notice to the other party, and subsequently turns out to have been unnecessary, the landlord will be liable in damages.[97] Once sequestration for rent is granted, anyone who removes any of the property subject to the security will be liable to the landlord for its value. Indeed, it has been suggested that a third party removing property in bad faith is liable for the whole of the rent due[98] It is no defence for an individual to say that they bought an item from the tenant in ignorance of the sequestration, although such an individual may ask the court to order that the tenant's property be sold off first in the hope that enough might be raised thereby to meet the landlord's claim and the expenses of the sequestration.[99]

At common law, the hypothec does not however, extend to clothing in ordinary use, nor to money, bills or bonds.[1] Moreover, the hypothec does not arise in relation to articles exempt from attachment in terms of s.11(1) of the Debt Arrangement and Attachment (Scotland) Act 2002, nor any article which is kept in a dwelling house, and which is not a non-essential asset in terms of Pt 3 of that Act[2] (for details of the sort of property thus excluded see para. 8.19.). That Act impacts on this area in other ways:

- by insisting that no action be taken to enforce a hypothec on a Sunday, Christmas Day, New Year's Day, or any other day prescribed by the rules of court, nor (unless a

---

[92] *Scottish and Newcastle Breweries Ltd v City of Edinburgh DC,* 1979 S.L.T. (Notes) 11.
[93] *Duncan v Lodijensky* (1904) 11 S.L.T. 684.
[94] *Young v Welsh* (1833) 12 S. 233.
[95] *Duffy v Gray* (1858) 20 D. 580.
[96] *Nelmes & Co v Ewing* (1883) 11 R. 193.
[97] See, *e.g. Gray v Weir* (1891) 19 R. 25.
[98] *Jack v McCaig* (1880) 7 R. 465.
[99] See *Ryan v Little,* 1910 S.C. 219; *McIntosh v Potts* (1905) 13 S.L.T. 108.
[1] Bell, *Principles,* s.1276.
[2] s.58(2).
[3] ss.12, 58(1).

sheriff has given prior authority) at any time other than between the hours of 8am and 8pm.[3]
- Where a caravan, houseboat, or other moveable structure owned by the tenant is the only or principal residence of a third party, by allowing either of those parties to apply to the sheriff for its release from the hypothec.[4]
- By insisting that it is not competent to enter a dwelling house to enforce a hypothec, unless there is a person present who is over 16 and able to understand the proceedings, or the tenant has been given days day's notice of intended entry. (the sheriff may dispense with the requirement to give notice, on cause shown.).[5]
- By allowing the tenant to apply to the sheriff for the return of any article on the basis that it is not subject to the hypothec, or that its auction would be unduly harsh.[6]

## (b) Solicitor's Hypothec

A solicitor who has incurred costs in conducting litigation on a client's behalf, has a hypothec over any expenses awarded to the client, and may move for a decree for those expenses in his own name as agent disburser. The result of this is that payment of the expenses to the client does not affect his claim, and the claim is effectual even if the client has been sequestrated or been subject to diligence prior to it arising.[7] Should the solicitor permit the decree for expenses to be awarded in the client's name, he may still assert his right by giving notice to the other party, but in this case someone who has already done diligence on the client's estate would have a prior claim.[8] It might be thought that the creditor's right would not arise where the action is abandoned or settled by the client, but it has been held[9] that a solicitor is entitled to have himself sisted as a party to the action in order to obtain a decree for expenses:

- where a finding of expenses has already been made,[10]
- where expenses follow as a necessary consequence of a previous interlocutor,
- where the parties have settled in order to defeat his claim.

At common law the hypothec only extends to expenses, but in terms of s.62(1) of the Solicitors (Scotland) Act 1980, a court can give a solicitor a charge over any property recovered by an action in order to secure his costs.

## (c) Maritime liens

Despite their designation these "liens" are really hypothecs, as they do not depend on possession of the ship to which they attach. A maritime lien is "a privileged claim on a vessel in respect of a service done to it, or an injury caused by it".[11] The right is ultimately enforceable by the sale of the ship under the authority of the court. As far as liability for damage is concerned, the negligent handling of the ship itself must cause the damage (to property or persons) for the lien to arise.[12] Thus, where in a storm, ship A ran aground because the crew of ship B cut her mooring ropes in order to avoid a collision, the owners of ship B had no lien over ship A, as "the ship" had not caused the damage.[13] As far as services are concerned, a

---

[4] ss.17, 58(1).
[5] ss.48, 58(1).
[6] ss.52(3), 58(1).
[7] See *Black v Kennedy* (1825) 4 S. 124; *Hunter v Pearson* (1835) 13 S. 495; *Pollard v Galloway and Nivison* (1881) 9 R. 21.
[8] *Stephen v Smith* (1830) 8 S. 847.
[9] In *McLean v Auchinvole* (1824) 3 S. 190.
[10] As in *Ammon v Tod* (1912) 1 S.L.T. 118, where decree, including expenses, had been given in favour of the client, but the other party had appealed, and the parties had then settled.
[11] *per* Gorel Barnes J. in *The Ripon City* [1897] P 226 at 242.
[12] *The Veritas* [1901] P. 304.
[13] *Currie v McKnight* (1896) 4 S.L.T. 161, HL.

seaman has a lien for his wages, whether or not he has a contract with the owner,[14] and if the proceeds of the sale of the ship are insufficient to discharge the claim, he has a secondary lien over the freight (see para. 4.40.), albeit not over the cargo.[15] Although this is a common law right, s.39(1) of the Merchant Shipping Act 1995 precludes a seaman from contracting out of his right to wages, while s.41 provides that the master of the vessel has the same rights and remedies for his remuneration and all disbursements or liabilities properly made or incurred by him on account of the ship as a seaman has for his wages. To be properly made, a disbursement would have to be made on the owner's behalf, within the scope of the master's authority.[16] So disbursements made on another's behalf, *e.g.* a charterer, would not fall within the lien.[17] Those who effect repairs and supply necessaries to a ship have a lien if this is done in a foreign port, but they have no lien if such things are done in a port within the UK.[18] A salvor has a lien,[19] and indeed would have a lien properly so called if he retained actual possession of the ship.[20] A maritime lien has priority over a ship mortgage and a subsequent possessory lien, but defers to an existing possessory lien.[21] Often a number of individuals will hold a maritime lien over a ship. Generally, the last person to render a service has priority over other holders of maritime liens.[22] However, a lien in respect of damage done by the ship will have priority over all other liens,[23] save for subsequent salvage liens.[24] This means that prior salvage liens defer to damage liens, but they will otherwise be preferred to all other liens.[25] Liens for wages are preferred to liens for a master's disbursements.[26]

# (4) CAUTIONARY OBLIGATIONS

## 6.11.   INTRODUCTION

There are three parties involved in cautionry—the cautioner, the creditor and the principal debtor. In a cautionary obligation the cautioner promises the creditor that, if the principal debtor fails to pay a certain sum or fulfil a certain obligation (the principal debt), then he (the cautioner) will pay or fulfil. In other words, cautionry is a form of guarantee. It is thus a form of security for a creditor, albeit taking the form of a right against a person (the cautioner) rather than a right in property

## 6.12.   NATURE OF CAUTIONRY

It may help understand the nature of cautionry, if it can be contrasted with other obligations to which it bears some similarity. So a representation as to credit, which is an assurance made by

---

[14] *The Castelgate* [1893] A.C. 38.
[15] *The Mary Ann* (1845) 9 Jur. 94. Someone who is claiming for damage done similarly has a secondary claim to the freight: *The Willem III* (1871) 3 A. & E. 487.
[16] *The Castelgate* [1893] A.C. 38.
[17] *ibid.*
[18] *Clydesdale Bank Ltd v Walker and Bain*, 1925 S.L.T. 676. Indeed *Constant v Christensen* (1912) 2 S.L.T. 62, insists that there is no lien for necessaries even if supplied in a foreign port.
[19] *The Bold Buccleugh* (1851) 7 Moo. P.C.C. 267.
[20] *Mackenzie v Steam Herring Fleet Ltd* (1903) 10 S.L.T. 734.
[21] See *The Athena* (1923) 14 Ll. L. Rep. 515, HL; *The Russland* [1924] P 55.
[22] *The Lyrma (No. 2)* [1978] 2 Lloyd's Rep. 30.
[23] *Currie v McKnight* (1896) 4 S.L.T. 161, HL.
[24] *The Inna* [1938] P. 304.
[25] *The Lyrma (No. 2)* [1978] 2 Lloyd's Rep. 30.
[26] *The Mons* [1932] P. 109.

A to B that C is creditworthy (perhaps up to a certain defined limit) in order that C can obtain money, credit or goods from B, is not a cautionary obligation as long as A does not bind himself to pay any debt incurred by C.[27] Similarly, a letter of comfort whereby A indicates to B that it his policy to ensure that any obligation undertaken by C is discharged, but falls short of accepting any legal obligation to perform that obligation, is certainly not a cautionary obligation.[28]

## (a) Third party pledge

The arrangements considered above do not amount to cautionry because they fall short of offering any guarantee of performance. One might regard property being pledged by a third party as security for the repayment of a debt as not amounting to a cautionary obligation for a more fundamental reason—the fact that it is a property based security, rather than the undertaking of a personal obligation of performance.[29] Yet it was decided in *Hewitt v Williamson*[30] that the granting of the standard security for the debts of a third party could be a cautionary obligation. This was not a proper cautionary obligation, however, but a cautionary obligation in a broad sense, which was not subject to certain basic rules pertaining to cautionary obligations—*e.g.* the rule that the cautioner is freed by any material alteration in the obligation between the creditor and principal debtor to which he does not consent (see para. 6.20.). Indeed, Lord Macfadyen admitted that he would not have regarded the granting of the security as a cautionary obligation at all, but for the decision in *Smith v Bank of Scotland*[31] in which the House of Lords treated just such an arrangement as a cautionary obligation. It has been pointed out[32] that, although it is not apparent from the report in *Smith*, Mrs Smith had undertaken personal liability for her husband's debts, and was thus a cautioner, the granting of the standard security being thus intended to secure not her husband's debts, but the cautionary obligation. So there is no need, as a result of *Smith*, to treat third party pledges as cautionary obligations. Nonetheless, subsequent cases[33] have continued to do so, with the result that it is difficult to insist that they are not cautionary obligations, whether this makes theoretical sense or not. Still, such pledges should only be regarded as cautionary obligations in a broad sense". Accordingly, In other words, they should be treated as cautionary obligations only in the sense that the creditor is subject to the duty of good faith as elaborated in *Smith* (see para. 6.16.). Otherwise they should not be regarded as cautionary obligations, and in particular, the "cautioner" should not be regarded as providing a personal guarantee of the debt.

## (b) Accessory obligation

One other way of distinguishing cautionry from other similar obligations is that a cautionary obligation is an accessory rather than an independent obligation in that it always requires the

---

[27] See *Park v Gould* (1851) 13 D. 1049. If such a representation turned out to be false, then any contract which it induced, *e.g.* a cautionary obligation induced by the creditor's statement as to the debtor's financial standing, would be voidable: *Royal Bank of Scotland v Greenshields,* 1914 1 S.L.T. 74. Again, if it were negligently made, it might render the maker delictually liable, should the other party rely on it: *Hedley Byrne & Co v Heller* [1964] A.C. 465.

[28] See *Kleinwort Benson v Malaysia Mining Corporation Bhd* [1989] 1 W.L.R. 379; 1 All E.R. 785, CA. where a statement by a parent company to a creditor of its subsidiary to the effect that it was its policy to ensure that the subsidiary was in a position to meet its liabilities was held not to impose any legal liability. However compare *Chemco Leasing SpA v Rediffusion plc* [1987] 1 F.T.L.R. 201; *Re Atlantic Computers plc* [1995] B.C.C. 696.

[29] So in *Braithwaite v Bank of Scotland,* 1999 S.L.T. 25. Lord Hamilton opined (at 30C-D) that,
"a cautionary obligation is one in which A grants to C a personal obligation to make payment to C in the event of the default of B to make such payment. Such an obligation is to be distinguished from that in which identified or identifiable property is made available by A to C, whether in the form of real security or otherwise, against the failure of B to pay his debts to C . . . Arrangements ancillary to the granting of real security over identified or identifiable property or made for similar purposes in relation to such property are likewise to be so distinguished."

[30] 1998 S.C.L.R. 601.

[31] 1997 S.L.T. 1061. And Lord Hamilton in *Braithwaite* suggested (at 30B) that as a result of *Smith*, "the concept of cautioner and cautionry may be invoked in relation to any circumstance in which A exposes himself or his property in security of the debts of B to C".

[32] In Professor Gretton's perceptive Commentary on *Hewitt*, 1998 S.C.L.R. 616–618.

[33] *e.g. Forsyth v Royal Bank of Scotland,* 2000 S.L.T. 1295; *Royal Bank of Scotland v Clark,* 2000 S.C.L.R. 193.

presence of a principal debt. As Lord Justice-Clerk Ross puts it in *City of Glasgow DC v Excess Insurance Co Ltd*[34]:

> "The obligation of a cautioner is not an independent obligation, but is essentially conditional in its nature, being properly exigible only on the failure of the principal debtor to pay at the maturity of his obligation."

It is thus the absence of a principal debt which thus distinguishes cautionry from contracts such as insurance and indemnity. So in *Milne v Kidd*[35] an obligation to purchase shares if they did not reach a certain price was held to be a contract of indemnity rather than caution. Equally, in the English case of *Sutton & Co v Grey*,[36] G had contracted that he would have one-half of any commission earned as a result of introducing clients to S & Co, and in return would bear one-half of any loss sustained through such clients. It was held that this was a contract of indemnity rather than guarantee, Lord Esher M.R. observing:

> "The test is whether the defendant is interested in the transaction . . . or whether he is totally unconnected with it. If he is totally unconnected with it, except by means of his promise to pay the loss, the contract is a guarantee; if he is not totally unconnected with the transaction, but is to derive some benefit from it, the contract is one of indemnity."

Again, if party A orders goods for party B on the understanding that A will pay for them, that is not cautionry, since A is undertaking the primary obligation, rather than guaranteeing an obligation undertaken by B. As the Lord President says in *Stevenson's Tr v Campbell & Sons*[37]:

> "If two come to a shop and one buys and the other . . . says, 'Let him have the goods, I will be your paymaster' . . . this is an undertaking as for himself and he shall be intended to be the very buyer."

The same might be said of delegation, where instead of A guaranteeing B's obligation to C, C consents to A taking over responsibility for performance of that obligation.[38]

Indeed, even if the function of a contractual arrangement is to guarantee the performance of another contract, if the obligation under that arrangement is independent in form, it will not be regarded as a cautionary obligation. This is the position with the various arrangements which have emerged in modern times whereby a party secures performance of a contract by agreeing with a bank (typically for a consideration) that the bank will make a payment, if the party entitled to performance indicates that the other party to the contract has defaulted. These arrangements are styled, performance bonds, performance guarantees or demand guarantees. Potter L.J. explains it in Cargill International SA v Bangladesh Sugar and Food Industries Corporation[39]:

> "Such a bond is a guarantee of performance. That is not to say that it is a guarantee in the sense that it has all the normal incidents of a contract of surety; it is of course a contract of primary liability as far as the bank which gives it is concerned."

They are not regarded as guarantees, since they are usually payable if certain conditions are met, irrespective of whether default in the contract "guaranteed" can be established. Lord Denning M.R. remarks that a bank which gives a performance bond[40]:

---

[34] 1986 S.L.T. 585 at 588G.

[35] (1869) 8 M. 250; It is sometimes difficult in practice to determine whether a particular contract is intended to be an indemnity or a guarantee: see *Heald v O'Connor* [1971] 1 W.L.R. 497.

[36] [1894] 1 Q.B. 285 at 288.

[37] (1896) 23 R. 711 at 714.

[38] *Morrison v Harkness* (1870) 9 M. 35.

[39] [1998] 1 W.L.R. 461 at 468G.

[40] In *Edward Owen Engineering Ltd v Barclays Bank International Ltd* [1978] Q.B. 159 at 171. It would appear that if liability under a performance bond is made contingent upon failure of the party in the main contract to perform—the interpretation which tends to be imposed on such arrangements by the Scottish courts—then the bond will nonetheless be regarded as a cautionary obligation. See *City of Glasgow District Council v Excess Insurance Co Ltd*, 1986 S.L.T 585; *Royal Bank of Scotland Ltd v Dinwoodie*, 1987 S.L.T 82; *Trafalgar House Construction (Regions) Ltd. v General Surety and Guarantee Ltd* [1995] 3 All E.R. 737; H.L.

"must honour it according to its terms. It is not concerned in the least with the relations between the supplier and the customer; nor with the question whether the supplier has performed his contractual obligation or not; nor with the question whether the supplier is in default or not."

As will be seen (see para. 6.19.), the nature of cautionry as an accessory obligation generally has the effect that if the principal debt is unenforceable, then so too is the cautionary obligation.[41] The validity of an independent obligation on the other hand, will not usually be affected by the invalidity of another contract. An illustration is provided by the English case of *Yeoman Credit Ltd v Latter*.[42] A finance company agreed to sell a car to a young person on hire-purchase. L agreed to cover the company against loss under the contract. When the young person defaulted, L argued that because of the way loss was defined under his (L's) contract with the finance company it was in essence a guarantee. Accordingly, as the main contract was invalid due to the young person's lack of capacity, the guarantee was also invalid. The Court of Appeal, however, held that the contract was an indemnity, and thus unaffected by the potential invalidity of the young person's contract with the finance company.

# 6.13.  CONSTITUTION AND FORM

A cautionary obligation can be formed in the same way as any other contract. In particular, a general offer to enter into a cautionary obligation is valid and can be enforced by anyone who acts on it. Thus in *Fortune v Young,* 1918 S.C. 1, Y gave F a letter indicating that he would guarantee the repayment of any money advanced to F, up to a certain sum. The Inner House held that this guarantee could be enforced by any person who chose to lend money to F. Equally, where an offer to provide caution has been made to an individual, it is possible to constitute the obligation simply by acting on that offer.[43]

The creation of a cautionary obligation may be complicated by the fact that there are to be co-cautioners. Where it is intended that there should be more than one cautioner, the assumption is that each enters into the obligation on the basis that either all become cautioners for the whole sum or none. Thus in *Scottish Provincial Insurance Co v Pringle*[44] money was lent only on condition that repayment be guaranteed by four individuals. Three of the four signed the document, but the principal debtor forged the signature of the fourth. It was held that none of the co-cautioners was bound. Lord Wood noted[45]:

"The subscription of any one was *per se* of no binding efficacy. It was only by the combination of the subscriptions of all, that the subscription of each could come to be of obligatory force."

Similarly, in *Ellesmere Brewery Co v Cooper*[46] where one of four guarantors added the words "£25 only" to his signature, this was held to release all the guarantors from any obligation.

---

[41] However, see *Swan v Bank of Scotland* (1835) 2 Sh. & Macl. 67, HL; *Garrard v James* [1925] Ch. 616.

[42] [1961] 1 W.L.R. 828. It should be noted, however, that a very similar result was reached in *Stevenson v Adair* (1872) 10 M. 919, where a cautionary obligation was enforced despite the lack of capacity of the principal debtor, since the cautioner was aware of the lack of capacity when entering into the obligation. The seeming exception to the principle that the principal debt is unenforceable, then so too is the cautionary obligation, is explicable in terms of personal bar. In *Yeoman* the fact that Latter was aware of the lack of capacity was one of the factors which helped the court reach the conclusion that the contract was intended to be one of indemnity rather than guarantee.

[43] *Wallace v Gibson* (1895) 22 R. (H.L.) 56.

[44] (1858) 20 D. 465. See also *Paterson v Bonar* (1844) 6 D. 987. But this is not the rule in judicial cautionry, *i.e.* caution required in relation to court proceedings: *Simpson v Fleming* (1860) 22 D. 679.

[45] At 471.

[46] [1896] 1 Q.B. 75.

Following the repeal of the Mercantile Law Amendment (Scotland) Act 1856, s.6, there is no longer any requirement that cautionary obligations should be in writing,[47] unless a cautionary obligation is a gratuitous unilateral obligation not undertaken in the course of a business—as many will be. In this case by virtue of s.1(2)(a)(ii) of the Requirements of Writing (Scotland) Act 1995 the obligation would require to be in writing and subscribed by the cautioner. If these requirements of form were not met, the obligation would still be valid if the creditor has acted (or refrained from acting) in reliance on the obligation with the knowledge and acquiescence of the cautioner, been affected to a material extent as a result of such action, and would be adversely affected to a material extent if the obligation were invalid.[48]

It should also be noted that if security for a regulated agreement under the Consumer Credit Act 1974 is provided in the form of a guarantee or indemnity, such guarantee or indemnity must be in writing,[49] and properly executed. This means that it must be in the form prescribed by regulations,[50] must embody all the terms of the security,[51] and must be signed by the guarantor,[52] who must get a copy of both the regulated agreement and the security agreement.[53] If the agreement is not in writing or is not properly executed, it cannot be enforced except by order of the court.[54]

If someone signs in a representative capacity a document constituting a cautionary obligation, the courts will be slow to assume that he intends to undertake personal liability.[55]

## 6.14. PROPER AND IMPROPER CAUTIONRY

Proper cautionry arises where the fact that the cautioner is bound as cautioner appears clearly on the face of the deed by which they are bound.[56] In improper cautionry the principal debtor and cautioner appear to be bound jointly as co-debtors, although their true relationship can either be discerned from a closer reading of the deed,[57] or the creditor is otherwise aware that one party acts in reality as cautioner[58]. Where two parties appear to be bound jointly as co-debtors, and the creditor is not aware that, as between themselves, the parties have agreed that one is the principal debtor and one is his cautioner, that is not a cautionary obligation. Thus, whatever the rights of those individuals *inter se*, the cautioner is not entitled to the rights of a cautioner *vis-à-vis* the creditor.[59]

The point of the distinction was that, although an improper cautioner, once that relationship was established to exist, was entitled to all the normal rights of a cautioner,[60] only a proper cautioner was entitled to the benefit of discussion and the benefit of division.[61] The benefit of

---

[47] Although that provision will continue to apply to cautionary obligations entered into before August 1, 1995. For an account of its effect, see E. A. Marshall, *Scots Mercantile Law* (3rd ed., 1997), para. 8.42.

[48] Requirements of Writing (Scotland) Act 1995, s.1(3)–(5).

[49] Consumer Credit Act 1974, s.105(1).

[50] s.105(4)(a); Consumer Credit (Guarantees and Indemnities) Regulations 1983 (SI 1993/1556).

[51] s.105(4)(b).

[52] Consumer Credit (Guarantees and Indemnities) Regulations 1983 (SI 1993/1556), reg. 4.

[53] ss.105(4)(d), 105(5).

[54] s.105(7).

[55] *Montgomery Litho Ltd v Maxwell,* 1999 S.L.T. 1431.

[56] Bell, *Principles* s.247.

[57] As in *Paterson v Bonar* (1844) 6 D. 987, where, despite the parties appearing to be jointly and severally liable to a bank under a credit account, the fact that only one party could operate the account showed that the others were cautioners. And in *Scottish Provincial Insurance Co v Pringle* (1858) 20 D. 465, despite several persons accepting joint and several liability for a loan, the fact that one had assigned a life assurance policy to pay debt on his death, indicated that he was the true debtor, and the others cautioners.

[58] *Jackson v McIver* (1875) 2 R. 882.

[59] *Union Bank of Scotland v McMurray* (1870) 7 S.L.R. 596.

[60] *Mackenzie v Macartney* (1831) 5 W & S 504, HL.

[61] Bell, *Commentaries,* I, 365.

discussion allowed the cautioner to insist that, in the event of default, the creditor should first take all reasonable steps to enforce the debt against the principal debtor, including obtaining a degree against the debtor and doing diligence thereon, before proceeding against the cautioner. However, that right was removed by s.8 of the Mercantile Law Amendment (Scotland) Act 1856, unless it is expressly provided for "in the instrument of caution". Thus, failing such provision, a creditor need not pursue the debtor before enforcing the cautionary obligation against the cautioner.[62] Section 8 speaks of "payment of the debt", thus raising the possibility that it does not apply where the principal debt is an obligation of performance, so that the benefit of discussion would still be available in such a case.[63] The benefit of division dictates that each co-cautioner is only liable for his *pro rata* share of the debt (not counting insolvent cautioners), and cannot be asked to pay unless all co-cautioners are similarly asked.[64] In improper cautionry each cautioner is jointly and severally liable with the principal debtor for the entire sum.[65]

## 6.15. EFFECT OF MISREPRESENTATION, ETC.

### (a) By creditor

As a cautionary obligation is a contract, if it is induced by the creditor's misrepresentation, undue influence or force and fear, or by facility and circumvention, it is rendered void or voidable as appropriate.[66] Equally, a cautionary obligation may be rendered void by essential error.[67] *Royal Bank of Scotland v Ranken*[68] makes it clear that any misrepresentation must be material, and also induce the cautioner to enter into the obligation. Thus in that case, where one cautioner was actually aware of the true position, he remained bound, whereas another cautioner who was misled was entitled to avoid the obligation. Nonetheless, it remains the case that a creditor is under no duty to disclose material facts of which the cautioner may be ignorant.[69] Yet there is a duty of disclosure if the circumstances of the arrangement between the debtor and the creditor are unusual, and not what the cautioner would expect.[70] Moreover, if the creditor does volunteer any information, whether spontaneously or in answer to a question, he must give a full and fair representation of the situation. The contract may be avoided if he misleads the cautioner by revealing only part of the true situation.[71] Equally, he must disclose the true position, if he becomes aware that the cautioner is labouring under a material misapprehension.[72] It is submitted that the creditor is not entitled to decline to answer, if asked a specific question by the cautioner.[73]

---

[62] *Morrison v Harkness* (1870) 9 M. 35; *Sheldon and Ackhoff v Milligan* (1907) 14 S.L.T. 703; *Scottish Metropolitan Property v Christie,* 1987 S.L.T. (Sh. Ct.) 18.

[63] See *Johannesburg Muncipal Council v D Stewart & Co (1902) Ltd,* 1909 S.C. 860; but see the views of Lord Shaw in 1909 S.C. (H.L.) 53 at 57.

[64] Bell, *Principles,* ss.62, 267, but see *McArthur v Scott* (1836) 15 S. 270.

[65] *Richmond v Graham* (1847) 9 D. 633.

[66] See *Smith v Bank of Scotland* (1829) 7 S. 244; *Forbes v Forbes's Trs.,* 1957 S.L.T. 346; *Sutherland v W M Low & Co* (1901) 9 S.L.T. 91.

[67] *Bennie's Trs. v Couper* (1890) 17 R. 782.

[68] (1844) 6 D. 1418, see especially Lord Jeffrey at 1437.

[69] *Young v Clydesdale Bank* (1889) 17 R. 231.

[70] See *Hamilton v Watson* (1845) 4 Bell's App. 67, especially Lord Campbell at 103.

[71] *Falconer v North of Scotland Banking Co* (1863) 1 M. 704; and see Lord Clyde in *Smith v Bank of Scotland,* 1997 S.L.T. 1061 at 1065L.

[72] *Royal Bank of Scotland v Greenshields* (1914) 1 S.L.T. 74; and see Lord Clyde in *Smith v Bank of Scotland,* 1997 S.L.T. 1061 at 1065L–1066A.

[73] *Young v Clydesdale Bank* (1889) 17 R. 231 at 244, *per* Lord Shand; *Royal Bank of Scotland v Greenshields* (1914) 1 S.L.T. 74 at 75, *per* Lord McKenzie; But *cf. Wallace's Factor v McKissock* (1898) 25 R. 642 at 653, *per* Lord McLaren.

## (b) By debtor

As long as the principal debtor is not acting as the creditor's agent,[74] the traditional approach of Scots law has been to insist that the debtor's misrepresentation or undue influence does not affect the validity of the cautionary obligation, unless the creditor is aware of that misrepresentation, etc.[75] However, as Lord Clyde has pointed out in *Smith v Bank of Scotland*[76] "the rule is not absolute". So while, the normal rule applies in relation to a fraudulent misrepresentation, where fraud is involved, the creditor cannot enforce the obligation unless he has given valuable consideration, *e.g.* lent the debtor money on the strength of the obligation.[77] Moreover, Lord Clyde cites with approval English authority to the effect that a creditor will not be entitled to enforce the cautionary obligation, even if unaware of the debtor's fraud, if a reasonable person would have suspected that fraud had occurred.[78] More general contractual principles would render void a cautionary obligation induced by force and fear exercised by the debtor.[79] It is also the case that where the creditor is in breach of the duty of good faith, he will be unable to enforce the obligation if the debtor has been guilty of misrepresentation, etc. The duty of good faith will be considered in the next paragraph.

## 6.16. THE DUTY OF GOOD FAITH

The facts of *Smith v Bank of Scotland* appeared unexceptional. Mrs Smith claimed that she had been induced to guarantee her husband's business debts as a result of his misrepresentation and undue influence. However, as these vitiating factors were unknown to the creditor, the law would have seemed clearly to indicate that the validity of the cautionary obligation could not be challenged. Yet in practically identical circumstances, the guarantee would have been unenforceable because of the doctrine of constructive notice as explained by the House of Lords in *Barclays Bank plc v O'Brien*[80] This indicates that in circumstances where the creditor is aware that the surety (cautioner) reposes trust and confidence in the debtor in financial matters, the creditor will be put on his inquiry, and fixed with constructive notice of the debtor's misrepresentation and undue influence. In other words, the creditor will be regarded as aware ·of any such misrepresentation or undue influence. This, of course, was not the law of Scotland, as was recognised by the Inner House in *Smith*.[81]

Yet, in the House of Lords, Lord Clyde indicated that he had[82]:

> "not been persuaded that there are sufficiently cogent grounds for refusing the extension to Scotland of the development which has been achieved in England by the decision in *Barclays Bank plc v O'Brien*."

It is clear then that a major change was to be effected in the law for reasons of policy. However, while it was one thing to import the result in the *O'Brien* case, importing the principle on which it rested would be more problematic, constructive notice being derived from the English law of equity, and having no proper counterpart in Scots law. Lord Clyde therefore

---

[74] In which case the fraud, etc. is attributable to the creditor: see *Mair v Rio Grande Rubber Estates Ltd,* 1913 S.L.T. 166, HL.

[75] *Young v Clydesdale Bank* (1889) 17 R. 231.

[76] 1997 S.L.T. 1061 at 1065I.

[77] *Clydedale Bank v Paul* (1877) 4 R. 626 at 628–629, *per* Lord Shand.

[78] 1997 S.L.T. 1061 at 1065J–K; The English case is *Owen and Gutch v Homan* (1853) 4 H.L.C. 997, especially the views of Lord Cranworth L.C. at 1035–1036.

[79] *Trustee Savings Bank v Balloch,* 1983 S.L.T. 240.

[80] [1994] 1 A.C. 180.

[81] 1996 S.L.T. 392.

[82] 1997 S.L.T. 1061 at 1067K.

preferred to rest the decision on the principle of good faith, which he saw as underpinning the examples, considered in the previous paragraph, of situations where the creditor is disabled from enforcing the obligation.[83] It is of course the case that many specific rules might be said to be rooted in a broad concept such as good faith, but it is not usually open for parties seeking relief to refer generally to "good faith" or "equity" or "justice". Lord Clyde therefore required to provide some practical content to the doctrine of good faith in this context. Thus where "the circumstances of the case are such as to lead a reasonable man to believe that owing to the personal relationship between the debtor and proposed cautioner the latter's consent may not be fully informed or freely given", the creditor must "warn the potential cautioner of the consequences of entering into the proposed cautionary obligation and to advise him or her to take independent advice'.[84] If the creditor fails in this duty, he is not in good faith.

It was not clear from Lord Clyde's speech whether any failure to act in good faith disabled the creditor from enforcing the obligation, whether or not the debtor had acted wrongfully. However, subsequent cases have made it clear that the cautioner would require to prove not only a breach of good faith by the creditor, but also an actionable wrong by the debtor, before the cautionary obligation may be impugned.[85] Subsequent cases have also clarified the range of relationships where the duty of good faith imposes an obligation on the creditor to warn and advise the potential cautioner. So these include not only husband and wife, but also parent and child—at least where the parent is the cautioner.[86] Moreover:

> "the rule can apply even in circumstances where the person who is in a close personal relationship with the cautioner is not himself the borrower, provided he has an interest to use the personal relationship to prevail upon the cautioner to agree to act as such, and the existence of that relationship is known to the creditor. Thus in *Smith* the actual principal debtor appears to have been a firm of which the pursuer's husband was a partner, rather than the pursuer's husband as an individual."[87]

Moreover, while the principle will not normally arise where a shareholder or director is asked to guarantee a company's debts, it can arise if, for example, a son persuades his mother to guarantee the debts of a company in which she holds shares and which he runs.[88] Given the intention to assimilate Scots law to that of England in this area, English decisions are presumably also instructive in this context. Thus *O'Brien* itself tells us that the principle extends to every case "where there is an emotional relationship between cohabitees" (whether heterosexual or homosexual), or wherever the "surety reposes trust and confidence in the principal debtor in relation to his financial affairs", as long as the creditor is aware of such facts.[89] So it has been applied in the case of a non-cohabiting couple, who enjoyed "a stable sexual and emotional relationship of long standing',[90] while in another English case it was applied where an employee was persuaded to guarantee the debts of her employer's business.[91] Nonetheless, if the obligation secured is for the cautioner's benefit as much as that of the debtor, then the duty of good faith does not arise. So, if a mother has a substantial interest in the company which is run by her son,[92] there is no need to advise or warn her. Nor is there any duty of good faith owed where a husband and wife jointly guarantee a loan made to both of them.[93]

---

[83] *ibid.*, at 1066B.
[84] *ibid.*, at 1068F–I.
[85] See *Braithwaite v Bank of Scotland*, 1999 S.L.T. 25 at 33B–C; *Wright v Cotias Investments Inc*, 2000 S.C.L.R. 324 at 332E–F.
[86] *Wright v Cotias Investments Inc*, 2000 S.C.L.R. 324.
[87] *ibid.*, *per* Lord McFadyen at 335C.
[88] *ibid.*
[89] [1994] 1 A.C. 180 at 198c–f, *per* Lord Browne-Wilkinson.
[90] *Massey v Midland Bank plc* [1995] 1 All E.R. 929 at 933c–d, *per* Steyn L.J.
[91] *Credit Lyonnais Bank Nederland N V v Burch* [1997] 1 All E.R. 144.
[92] As was the case in *Cotias*.
[93] *Ahmed v Clydesdale Bank plc*, 2001 S.L.T. 423.

## (a) The duty of good faith—independent legal advice

In practice, institutional lenders have proved reluctant to assume the responsibility of explaining in detail to potential cautioners the implications of entering into the transaction, and instead have refused to proceed until they have confirmation that any potential cautioner is legally advised.[94] It has indeed been held that the creditor's duty of good faith is discharged if it appears that the potential cautioner has independent legal advice. Thus in *Forsyth v Royal Bank of Scotland*[95] Lord Macfadyen opined that if the cautioner had her own legal advisor, the bank need take no steps at all to advise her, observing:

"The creditor is entitled to assume that a granter of a standard security who has the benefit of a solicitor acting for her will thereby have the benefit of separate advice, and that advice will cover at least all the ground which he would, in the absence of a solicitor have had to cover in order to preserve his good faith. Since he is entitled to make that assumption, the creditor is not in breach of the requirements of good faith if he does nothing himself to advise or warn the granter of the security"

Moreover, if the solicitor also acts for the bank, it is for the solicitor to decide whether a conflict of interest precludes him advising the cautioner. If so, it is for the solicitor and not the bank to advise her to seek independent advice, and the bank is entitled to assume that this has been done[96] The focus of the law is on the creditor's behaviour. So if he believes on reasonable grounds that a cautioner has received independent advice, he does not fail to act in good faith by taking no further steps[97] On the other hand, if the situation was not clear, the bank could not be in good faith unless it inquired further[98] It has also been held[99] that where a solicitor, although advising the bank, also believed himself to be acting for the cautioners, that belief could be imputed to the bank as his principal, thus ensuring that the bank acted in good faith. It was further held that the bank was not in breach of duty to a cautioner, simply because her co-cautioner (in this case her husband) failed to pass on the advice he received from the solicitor.

Since *O'Brien* the House of Lords in England[1] has insisted that it is for the bank to satisfy itself that a potential guarantor has been properly advised. This means that the bank should ask the potential guarantor for the name of the solicitor advising her or him, and indicate that it will require written confirmation that the solicitor has explained the nature of the obligation and its practical implications before proceeding with the obligation. The bank should not proceed with the obligation without this confirmation. Their Lordships added that where the bank did not want to assume the responsibility of explaining the debtor's financial affairs to the potential guarantor, it would have to supply the solicitor acting for her with the financial information necessary for that purpose, and will require the debtor's consent to reveal that information. If that consent were not forthcoming, again the bank should not proceed with the obligation. This seems to go a lot further than the duty of good faith as interpreted in the Scots

---

[94] This has been judicially recognised, see *Royal Bank of Scotland v Etridge (No. 2)* [2001] 4 All E.R. 449 at 478g, *per* Lord Clyde.

[95] 2000 S.C.L.R. 61 at 75C.

[96] *ibid.*, at 75D.

[97] *Broadway v Clydesdale Bank plc*, 2000 G.W.D. 19–763.

[98] *ibid.*

[99] *Broadway v Clydesdale Bank plc (No. 2)* 2001 G.W.D. 14–552. But a solicitor's knowledge will not be attributed to the bank where he deliberately misrepresents the position to the bank: see *Thomson v Royal Bank of Scotland*, 2002 G.W.D. 18–592.

[1] *Royal Bank of Scotland v Etridge (No. 2)* [2001] 4 All E.R. 449.

[2] *Clydesdale Bank plc v Black*, 2002 S.C.L.R 857, see especially Lord Marnoch at 872D-873A; Lord Sutherland observes at 876C:

"I do not consider that any inference can be drawn from what Lord Clyde said in either *Smith* or *Etridge* that he was of the opinion that in Scotland there was or should be a duty to investigate how far the written warnings and advice had been seen, understood and followed up by a guarantor and thereby 'satisfy' themselves that all was well."

courts, and indeed the Inner House has confirmed that the decision is not to be regarded as having altered the law of Scotland.[2]

## 6.17. EXTENT OF THE CAUTIONER'S LIABILITY

Cautionary obligations must be construed *contra proferentem*, the *proferens* in this case being the creditor.[3] Thus while the court will try to ascertain the true intention of the parties, and this may involve taking into account general commercial practice,[4] the extent of the cautioner's knowledge,[5] "the factual matrix and in particular the transactional context of the guarantee",[6] and reading the obligation as a whole,[7] any ambiguities will be resolved in favour of the cautioner.[8] So in *Harmer & Co v Gibb*[9] the cautioner guaranteed payment for all goods: "as you may from time to time sell and deliver to M . . . up to a value of £200." This was held to impose upon the cautioner a liability to ensure payment for up to £200's worth of goods, and not a liability for the total amount owed by the debtor, subject to a limit of £200. The debtor owed £300 and the creditor held a security over the debt to the value of £120. Had the latter construction prevailed, the cautioner would have been liable for the whole amount of the debt, minus the security (£300—£120 = £180). But under the former construction he was liable for only £200, minus the proportion of the security which the amount guaranteed bore to the whole debt. In other words, since he had guaranteed two-thirds of the debt, he was entitled to two-thirds of the security (£120 × 2/3 = £80). So his ultimate liability was £200 − £80 = £120.

Similarly, where a cautioner guarantees all advances to be made to a particular debtor, up to a given limit, then unless the contrary is clearly expressed, the obligation will be interpreted as not extending to any advance made subsequent to the limit being reached, rather than guaranteeing the entire debt subject to a stated maximum limit of liability.[10] Two consequences follow from the former interpretation. First, any payment made by the debtor to the creditor once the limit is reached, goes towards reducing the cautioner's ultimate liability (see para. 6.19.).[11] Secondly, once the cautioner has paid the creditor the amount guaranteed, he can seek to recover from a bankrupt debtor's estate. The reasoning behind this is that as he has paid in full that part of the debt he has undertaken to guarantee, his obligation to the creditor is fully discharged (see para. 6.19.). Were the alternative interpretation to be applied, the cautioner would not be regarded as having discharged his obligation until the principal debt is paid in full. Accordingly, the cautioner would not be entitled to seek to recover from the debtor unless the creditor had received full payment.[12]

Finally, the cautioner's liability can never exceed that of the principal debtor. This was shown in *Jackson v McIver*[13] where M had lent the debtor £300, taking in return a blank promissory note signed by the debtor and J. When the debtor defaulted, J having become bankrupt, M

---

[3] *Aitken's Trs. v Bank of Scotland*, 1945 S.L.T. 84 at 89, *per* Lord Justice Clerk Cooper.

[4] *Calder & Co v Cruikshank's Tr.* (1889) 17 R. 74.

[5] *Bank of Scotland v Wright* [1991] B.C.L.C. 244.

[6] *Waydale Ltd v DHL Holdings (UK) Ltd (No 2)* 2001 S.L.T. 224 at 232A, *per* Lord Hamilton.

[7] *Huewind Ltd. v Clydesdale Bank plc*, 1996 S.L.T. 369 at 372.

[8] *Baird v Corbett* (1835) 14 S. 41 at 47; *Tennant & Co v Bunten* (1859) 21 D. 631 at 634, *per* Lord Cowan.

[9] (1911) 2 S.L.T. 211.

[10] *Bank of Scotland v MacLeod*, 1986 S.L.T. 504. It is possible that the obligation will take the form of a guarantee of any advances made to the debtor, once a certain figure has been exceeded. Again this could be subject to a limit. So if the cautioner guarantees advances over £800,000, subject to a maximum liability of £1million, that guarantee is not effective until £800,000 and the limit of his liability is reached once £1,800,000 has been advanced: *Huewind Ltd. v Clydesdale Bank plc*, 1996 S.L.T. 369.

[11] *Cuthill v Strachan* (1894) 1 S.L.T. 527.

[12] *Harvie's Trs v Bank of Scotland* (1885) 12 R. 1141.

[13] (1875) 2 R. 882.

sought to fill in the note for £2,000, hoping that if that sum were claimed from J's estate, the dividend would yield £300. It was held that, as J was effectively guaranteeing the repayment of £300, he was a cautioner, so that the maximum M could claim from his estate was £300. Lord Gifford stated[14]:

> "Cautionry is an accessory obligation, and the accessory can never be bound for more than the principal. Cautioners in a cash credit bond . . . can never be liable for more than the balance due by the principal, although the bond *ex facie* may be for a much larger amount."

It should be noted that the above principle is qualified to the extent that the cautioner will additionally be liable for any expenses reasonably incurred in seeking to enforce the principal debt against the debtor.[15]

## 6.18. THE RIGHTS OF CAUTIONERS

We have already observed that certain rights (benefits of division and discussion, see para. 6.14.) derive from proper cautionry. What other rights do cautioners have?

### (a) Relief

A cautioner is entitled to call on the principal debtor to relieve him of liability, even if the debt is not yet due.[16] Moreover, when the debt is due, he may demand that the debtor pays it.[17] Alternatively, he may himself pay the principal debt as soon as it falls due.[18] When the cautioner has paid the principal debt, then he is entitled to recover the amount paid, including any expenses he has incurred, from the principal debtor.

> "Cautioners on making payment of the debt, or any portion of the debt, have a right to relief and indemnification against the principal debtor to the full extent to which they have been answerable for him. This right of relief . . . arises *de iure* without any formal assignation by the creditor."[19]

The right of relief prescribes after five years from the date of payment of the debt.[20] Additionally, where the debtor is insolvent, and the cautioner has properly paid the debt or is liable to do so, he may retain any property of the debtor as may be in his hands, and may plead compensation in respect of any money debt he owes the debtor.[21]

Where there is more than one cautioner, then unless each is bound only for a specific part of the debt,[22] any who has paid more than his share may seek relief to that extent from the other cautioner(s).[23] In deciding the amount of such relief insolvent cautioners are not counted. Thus

---

[14] At 885.

[15] *Struthers v Dykes* (1847) 9 D. 1437.

[16] *Doig v Lawrie* (1903) 10 S.L.T. 523; assuming this is not inconsistent with the terms of the cautionary obligation, see Lord Kinnear in *Roughead v White* (1913) 1 S.L.T. 23 at 27.

[17] *Cunningham v Montgomerie* (1879) 6 R. 1333.

[18] *Gray v Thompson* (1847) 10 D. 145. A cautioner seeking relief, having paid the debt before it is due, might be met by the plea that there was no reasonable obligation or necessity to pay it: *Owen v Bryson* (1833) 12 S. 130.

[19] *per* Lord Cameron in *Smithy's Place Ltd v Blackadder,* 1991 S.LT 790 at 795C–E.

[20] *ibid*.

[21] *McPherson v Wright* (1885) 12 R. 942.

[22] In which case no relief arises: see *Morgan v Smart* (1872) 10 M. 610.

[23] *Marshall & Co v Pennycook* (1908) 15 S.L.T. 581. It does not matter that the cautioners were bound in different deeds, or were originally unaware of each other's existence: *McPhersons v Haggarts* (1881) 9 R. 306; *Union Bank of Scotland v Taylor*1925S.L.T. 583, especially Lord President Clyde at 586. However no right of relief is owed to a cautioner who has paid the debt, when there was no obligation or necessity to do so: *Henderson v Paul* (1867) 5 M. 628.

in *Buchanan v Main*[24] where two out of five co-cautioners were insolvent, when two other cautioners had paid the principal debt, they were entitled to require the fifth cautioner to contribute one-third of the debt. This of course presupposes that the cautioners are each bound equally. Yet what might happen if, for example, two cautioners guaranteed repayment of an overdraft, one subject to a limit of £5,000, the other subject to a limit of £10,000, and the overdraft stands at £3,000 when one of the obligations is enforced? The Scottish cases have not really addressed this point, but English authority witnesses the application of either the maximum liability[25] or independent liability[26] approaches. The former insists that the ratio of liability is determined by the maximum liability each cautioner might have under his obligation. As this is £10,000 and £5,000 respectively, it is clear that these cautioners must always bear any liability in the ratio of 2:1, and this ratio must apply whatever the overall liability may be. The independent liability approach determines the ratio by asking what liability would each cautioner bear, if he alone guaranteed the obligation. In the above scenario, each cautioner would be liable for £3,000, so that they should therefore bear that liability equally. However, if the sum due were £7,500, then as the first cautioner would be liable for the whole of that sum, and the liability of the second would be restricted to £5,000, the proportion in which they should share that liability among themselves would be $^{75}/_{50}$, or 3:2. Therefore if the first cautioner paid £7,500, he would be entitled to recover two-fifths of that—£3,000—from the other.

## (b) Assignation

Where the cautioner has paid the principal debt *in full*, he can demand from the creditor an assignation of the debt, as well as any security for it, or diligence done on it.[27] Such security must have been granted by the debtor. The right does not extend to securities granted by to the creditor by third parties.[28] If the creditor holds the security over two debts, then he is entitled to retain it despite the cautioner paying the principal debt if the other debt is unpaid,[29] unless the second debt is incurred subsequent to the cautioner paying the principal debt.[30]

## (c) Sharing in Securities

All cautioners are entitled to share any security granted by the debtor to a co-cautioner, even if that security is granted after the cautionary obligations have been undertaken,[31] unless they have agreed that they should not have the benefit of that security.[32] The principle does not apply to securities granted by a third party.[33] There is also authority for the view that the principle may not apply when co-cautioners have limited the amount for which they are liable, but this seems to depend on them being regarded as having guaranteed separate, specific sums[34]—a relatively unusual construction.

## (d) Ranking in Bankruptcy

If the principal debtor is bankrupt, and the creditor is paid in full by the cautioner, then the cautioner is entitled to rank on the principal debtor's estate for the amount paid. However, if

---

[24] (1900) 3 F. 215.
[25] *Ellesmere Brewery Co v Cooper* [1896] 1 Q.B. 75.
[26] *American Surety of New York v Wrightson* (1910) T.L.R. 603.
[27] *Ewart v Latta* (1863) 1 M. 905.
[28] *Gordon's Trs v Young* (1910) 1 S.L.T. 134.
[29] *Sligo v Menzies* (1840) 2 D. 1478.
[30] *Fleming v Burgess* (1867) 5 M. 856.
[31] *Steel v Dixon* (1881) 17 Ch. D. 825.
[32] *Hamilton & Co v Freeth* (18890 16 R. 1022.
[33] *Scott v Young,* 1909 1 S.L.T. 47.
[34] *Lawrie v Stewart* (1823) 2 S. 327. See also *Morgan v Smart* (1872) 10 M. 610.

the creditor has ranked upon the principal debtor's estate, and then obtained payment of the remainder of the debt from the cautioner, the cautioner has no right to a ranking because of the rule that the same debt cannot be ranked twice on the bankrupt estate.[35] Where some limit is placed on the amount guaranteed, much will depend on the construction imposed on the obligation. Where the cautioner is seen as having guaranteed the whole of the obligation, albeit subject to a maximum liability, then the cautioner is not entitled to rank, and remains liable (up to his limit) to the creditor for any shortfall after the latter has ranked.[36] On the other hand, if the cautioner is regarded as having guaranteed a specific part of the principal debt, then payment up to the limit will entitle the cautioner to rank for that amount. Alternatively, if the creditor has already ranked on the debtor's estate and obtained a dividend, the cautioner is entitled to deduct the amount of that dividend from the amount otherwise owed to the creditor. So in *Veitch v National Bank of Scotland*[37] V had imposed a limit of £1,500 on his guarantee. Ultimately, the amount of the principal debt was around £6,000, while the dividend saw creditors being paid £2 for every £3 they were owed, so that the creditor received around £4,000, thus leaving £2,000 still owing. It was held that the debt should be regarded as, in effect, two debts—£1,500 which was covered by the guarantee, and £4,500 which was not. The £4,000 paid by way of dividend could be regarded as paying two-thirds of both debts, *i.e.* £1,000 of the £1,500 guaranteed, and £3,000 of the £4,500 not guaranteed. Therefore since £1,000 of the £1,500 guaranteed had already been repaid by way of dividend, the cautioner's liability was limited to £500, even though the creditor was still owed £2,000.

It has also been held[38] that if the cautioner pays the amount for which he is liable before the debtor becomes insolvent, the creditor is limited to ranking for the amount remaining unpaid, leaving the cautioner to rank for the amount he has paid. It would be open to the creditor to prevent this result by drawing up the obligation so as to make it clear that, whenever the cautioner pays, only the creditor is entitled to rank on the debtor's estate, the cautioner being precluded from ranking.

# (5) TERMINATION OF THE CAUTIONARY OBLIGATION

## 6.19. TERMINATION BY EXTINCTION OF THE PRINCIPAL DEBT

The accessory nature of the cautionary obligation is reflected by the fact that the extinction of the principal debt necessarily entails the extinction of the cautionry obligation. There are several ways in which this may occur.

### (a) Discharge of the principal debtor

If the creditor releases the principal debtor from his obligation without the cautioner's consent, the latter is in turn released from his obligation[39] Thus in *Aitken's Trs v Bank of Scotland*[40] a father guaranteed his son's overdraft to the extent of £500. When the overdraft reached £2,000 the bank sued the son for repayment. He repaid £1,500, and confident that the remaining £500 was covered by the guarantee, the bank allowed a decree of *absolvitur* to be pronounced against

---

[35] *McKinnon v Monkhouse* (1881) 9 R. 393.

[36] *Harvie's Tr v Bank of Scotland* (1885) 12 R. 1141.

[37] (1907) 14 S.L.T. 800.

[38] In *McKinnon's Tr. v Bank of Scotland* (1915) 1 S.L.T. 182.

[39] It follows that if the cautioner's consent to discharge is obtained, then he is not released, and that consent may be expressed through a term in the contract, or given at the time of discharge, or even thereafter: *Fleming v Wilson* (1823) 2 S. 296; *Wright's Trs v Hamilton's Trs* (1834) 12 S. 692.

[40] 1945 S.L.T. 84.

him. This was held to be tantamount to discharging the debtor, and the cautioner was released from liability.

There are two exceptions to the above rule. One is statutory.[41] The other arises where the creditor simply agrees not to sue the principal debtor, while expressly reserving his remedies against the cautioner—a *pactum de non petendo.*[42] In this situation, however, the cautioner's right of relief against the principal debtor is preserved. The creditor's arrangement with the debtor may be expressed in terms of an absolute discharge, and yet be construed as a *pactum de non petendo,* as long as his remedies against the cautioner are reserved.[43]

## (b) Novation etc.

The cautioner is discharged by novation, *i.e.* where the existing principal debt is extinguished and a new one substituted.[44] The same result flows from the substitution of a new principal debtor. However in *De Montfort Insurance Co plc v Lafferty,*[45] De Montfort acted as cautioner for an obligation owed to L by a local authority. Later under what was termed a deed of novation L released the local authority from that obligation, which was transferred to a company. However, L could still demand payment from the local authority of any sum not paid by the company. Lord Penrose.[46] took the view that the contention that the deed of novation created a new agreement, did not reflect the reality of the transaction. Nothing about the transaction was altered, and in particular the principal debtor was not released from any obligation unless that obligation were performed by another. Accordingly, the granting of the deed of novation did *not* release De Montfort. Finally, while an offer to guarantee any transaction the debtor might enter into with A, cannot generally be taken up by B,[47] the assignation of an existing principal debt to a new creditor will not usually release the cautioner.[48]

## (c) Compensation

A plea of compensation can be taken by the cautioner, if when the creditor seeks to have the cautioner pay the principal debt, he owes money to either the cautioner or the debtor.[49] Alternatively, if the creditor pleads the debt guaranteed in compensation for a debt or debts due by him to the principal debtor, that will extinguish the cautionary obligation.[50]

## (d) The rule in Clayton's case

That rule[51] is that in the case of a current account between debtor and creditor, in the absence of appropriation, the earliest credit item is set against the earliest debit item. So in *Deeley v Lloyd's Bank Ltd*[52] D guaranteed X's overdraft. When the overdraft reached £1,000 D

---

[41] Thus under s.60(1) of the Bankruptcy (Scotland) Act 1985, a cautioner will not be freed by the debtor's discharge under the Act, nor by the creditor voting for, or assenting to, or not opposing such discharge, or any composition (see para. 8.35.).

[42] See *e.g. Muir v Crawford* (1875) 2 R. (H.L.) 148, where it was also noted that the cautioner does not need to be informed of the a *pactum de non petendo.*

[43] *Aitken's Trs v Bank of Scotland,* 1945 S.L.T. 84 at 90, *per* Lord Justice-Clerk Cooper.

[44] *Commercial Bank of Tasmania v Jones* [1893] A.C. 313. But the acceptance of additional obligations by the debtor is not novation, and thus will not release the cautioner, as long as the original obligation remains enforceable: *Hay and Kyd v Powrie* (1886) 13 R. 777.

[45] 1998 S.L.T. 535.

[46] At 538F.

[47] see *e.g. Bowie v Watson* (1840) 2 D. 1061.

[48] *Waydale Ltd v DHL Holdings (UK) Ltd,* 2001 S.L.T. 224.

[49] *Bechervaise v Lewis* (1872) L.R. 7 C.P. 372.

[50] See Lord Ormidale in *Hannay & Sons' Tr. v Armstrong Bros & Co* (1875) 2 R. 399 at 414.

[51] As expressed in *Devaynes v Noble, Clayton's Case* (1816) 1 Mer. 529 at 572.

[52] [1912] A.C. 756. For Scottish illustrations of the principle see *Royal Bank of Scotland v Christie* (1839) 1 D. 745; *Cuthill v Strachan* (1894) 21 R. 549.

intimated that he would not guarantee any further advances. The overdraft continued to run for some time, with X paying in significant sums of money, but also withdrawing ever larger sums. When the bank eventually sought to enforce the guarantee, the overdraft stood at several thousand pounds. Yet D was held not to be liable, since as soon as X had paid sums amounting to £1,000 into the account, the guarantee was extinguished. Yet as noted above, the principle only applies in relation to current accounts, and only where payments are not appropriated. While current accounts are not entirely confined to the banking industry,[53] normal trading accounts between businesses, or between tradesmen and their customers, are not regarded as current accounts, even if advances are sometimes made thereunder.[54] It is always open to the debtor to indicate how he wishes a payment to be applied,[55] and in the absence of any such indication, the creditor is entitled to make that decision.[56] So it is only where neither the debtor nor creditor has made any appropriation that there is room for the rule to operate.[57] The creditor may always preclude the operation of the rule by a term in the contract, while in practice, this situation is avoided by the creditor closing the existing account once the obligation is withdrawn, and opening a new account.

### (e) Prescription

If the principal debt prescribes, then the cautionary obligation should also fall.

## 6.20.　TERMINATION BY THE ACTIONS OF THE CREDITOR

The cautionary obligation can similarly be extinguished by certain behaviour on the part of the creditor. The recognised categories thereof are considered below, and of course on the application of basic contractual principles a cautioner may always be released by the creditor's failure to comply with a specific undertaking of the cautionary obligation.[58] Whether the creditor owes a more general duty to the cautioner is doubtful. Certainly, Lord Ross, observes in *Lord Advocate v Maritime Fruit Carriers Ltd*[59]:

> "I am not prepared to hold that a creditor in Scotland owes no duty to act reasonably in a question with a guarantor".

Equally, Lord Low[60] suggests that if during the currency of a continuing obligation, circumstances come to the attention of the creditor which materially affect the risk which the cautioner has undertaken, and which would have dissuaded the cautioner from undertaking that risk, the creditor is bound to communicate these to the cautioner. Moreover, Lord Salvesen[61] suggests that the principle which demands that the creditor under a guarantee of fidelity disclose to the cautioner material information regarding the employee whose fidelity is guaranteed, probably also applies to the case of a bank:

> "making further advances to the credit of a secured account after knowledge that the person to whom the advances were made had become insolvent or had been guilty of

---

[53] See the unusual case of *McKinlay v Wilson* (1885) 13 R. 210.

[54] *Hay & Co v Torbet* (1908) 15 S.L.T. 627; *Dougall v Lornie* (1899) 7 S.L.T.145.

[55] As in *Buchanan v Main* (1900) 8 S.L.T. 297.

[56] *Jackson v Nicoll* (1870) 8 M 408. So it is therefore open for a creditor to appropriate a payment to an unsecured debt rather than a secured debt: *Anderson v North of Scotland and Town and County Bank* (1909) 2 S.L.T. 262.

[57] *Westminster Bank Ltd v Cond* (1940) 46 Com. Cas. 60.

[58] See *Clydebank and District Water Trustees v Fidelity and Deposit Co of Maryland* (1915) 2 S.L.T. 357, HL.

[59] 1983 S.L.T. 357 at 360.

[60] *Brittania Steamship Insurance Association Ltd v Duff*, 1909 2 S.L.T. 193 at 195.

[61] *Bank of Scotland v Morrison*, 1911 1 S.L.T. 153 at 156; speaking of *Snaddon v London, Edinburgh and Glasgow Assurance Co Bank of Scotland* (1902) 10 S.L.T. 410.

dishonesty. Such a proceeding might well be characterised as unfair dealing towards the cautioner, sufficient to free him from responsibility for advances made after the debtor's misconduct had been disclosed to the bank."

Apart from the fact that the last case is extrapolating from a duty of disclosure under what is essentially a contract of insurance, the problem with the views expressed in all of these cases is that they are essentially *obiter*. Moreover, the attempt to create some sort of general duty of the creditor to act fairly or reasonably runs into the difficulty that this seems to be at odds with the way in which the relationship between the creditor and cautioner has developed in the cases as a whole. The law has tended to recognise very specific duties owed by the creditor to the cautioner, and even the recently established duty of good faith operates within defined limits, and has a specific content (see paras 6.15. to 6.16.).

What are the categories of case where the creditor's behaviour is recognised as releasing the cautioner?

## (a) Giving time

This occurs where the creditor legally disables himself from demanding immediate payment when the principal debt falls due. Simply failing to press for immediate payment is not "giving time" in this technical sense.[62] An example of giving time is provided by the case of *C & A Johnstone v Duthie*[63] where the fact that the creditor had accepted payment from the debtor in the form of two bills of exchange payable three months from their date was held to have released the cautioner. Lord Kinnear noted[64]:

"The reason why the giving of time discharges the cautioner is because he is thereby deprived of the chance of considering whether he will have recourse to his remedy against the principal debtor or not, and because it is then out of his power to operate the same remedy against him as he would have had under the original contract."

The case further confirmed that the it was not necessary to show actual harm to the cautioner for this result to follow, nor indeed would proof of actual benefit to the cautioner through giving time constitute a defence. However, as Lord President Inglis points out in *Calder & Co. v Cruikshank's Tr*[65]:

"There is a broad distinction taken in all cases between the guarantee of a particular debt of a certain amount, to be paid at a certain time, and a general guarantee for the price of goods sold or for money advanced or the like. In the former case if a creditor innovates or alters the relation of debtor and creditor in any essential point, he liberates the cautioner. In the latter case that result by no means follows."

In particular, to quote Lord Justice Clerk Moncrieff in *Stewart, Moir and Muir v Brown*[66]:

"[The cautioner] necessarily, by the generality of the obligation, leaves the principal debtor and creditor free to arrange the details of their transactions as they think fit, provided these are not at variance with the ordinary custom of merchants."

It may be added that a cautioner will not be released if he has consented to time being given,[67] or if the creditor has expressly reserved his rights against him.[68]

---

[62] *Hamiltons's Exr. v Bank of Scotland* (1913) 1 S.L.T. 296.
[63] (1892) 19 R. 624.
[64] At 629.
[65] (1889) 27 R. 74, at 80.
[66] (1871) 9 M. 763, at 766.
[67] *Hamiltons's Exr. v Bank of Scotland* (1913) 1 S.L.T. 296.
[68] As the cautioner will be entitled to enforce the debt against the debtor, see *Muir v Crawford* (1875) 2 R. (H.L.) 148; *Huewind v Clydesdale Bank plc*, 1996 S.L.T. 369.

## (b) Alteration of principal debt

Any alteration of the contract between the creditor and principal debtor without the cautioner's consent will release the latter. So in *N. G. Napier Ltd v Crosbie*[69] an agreed increase of the amount of the debtor's weekly repayment liberated the cautioner from the obligation. Lord Guthrie observed[70]:

> "The rule of law is well settled that if a creditor agrees with the principal debtor to a material alteration of the contract without the consent of the cautioner, the cautioner is discharged ... The rule is founded on equitable considerations. If a cautioner has accepted liability for another's obligations under a contract, it would be unjust that he should be held bound if the effect of an alteration of the creditor's agreement with the principal debtor would be to increase the amount of his liability or to modify to his prejudice the conditions of his liability."

As this principle operates on the basis that the cautioner should not be bound to guarantee an obligation other than that to which he agreed, if the alteration of the contract between the creditor and principal debtor occurs before the cautionary obligation is entered into, it can obviously have no effect on that obligation[71] The excerpt from the judgment of Lord President Inglis in *Calder & Co v Cruikshank's Tr*,[72] quoted in the section on giving time (above) might tend to suggest that the principle does not apply in cases of general guarantees. However, the better view is that it does apply so as to ensure that the cautioner does not end up guaranteeing something quite different from that which he has undertaken, but given the nature of the guarantee, it is impossible to predict the precise content of what is covered by the guarantee.

Obviously, if the cautioner has agreed to guarantee the debt of the principal debtor on the basis that it is fixed at or will not exceed a certain sum, he will be released if that sum is exceeded. It has also been argued that where the cautioner has fixed a limit on the amount guaranteed, he should be released if the creditor advances sums beyond that limit. The basis of this argument is that although the cautioner is protected by the limit, he is prejudiced by the creditor continuing to lend money beyond that guaranteed, as the bigger the debt, the more likely it is that the debtor will default. This argument has been rejected however.[73]

## (c) Discharging a co-cautioner

It goes without saying that one mode of termination is by the creditor formally discharging the cautioner, but the Mercantile Law Amendment (Scotland) Act 1856, s.9, states:

> "Where two or more parties become bound as cautioners ... any discharge granted by the creditor ... to any one of such cautioners, without the consent of the other cautioners, shall be deemed and taken to be a discharge granted to all the cautioners; but nothing herein contained shall be deemed to extend to the case of a cautioner consenting to the discharge of a co-cautioner who may have become bankrupt."

However, the above only applies where the co-cautioners are jointly liable, not where they have each guaranteed repayment of a separate sum. So in *Morgan v Smart*,[74] a debt of £105 was guaranteed by B and S, B to the extent of £70 and S to the extent of £35. It was held that the discharge of B did not affect the liability of S. It is probably the case that the principle does not apply where the creditor in discharging a co-cautioner expressly reserves his rights against the

---

[69] 1964 S.L.T. 185.
[70] At 138.
[71] *Hewitt v Williamson*, 1999 S.L.T. 313.
[72] (1889) 27 R. 74, at 80.
[73] *Bank of Scotland v MacLeod*, 1986 S.L.T. 504; *Huewind Ltd v Clydesdale Bank plc*, 1995 S.L.T. 392.
[74] (1872) 10 M. 610.

cautioner.[75] The last clause of the provision appears to make little sense. What is meant by saying that the provision does not apply if a cautioner agrees to the discharge of a bankrupt co-cautioner? The answer is that the drafters probably intended to use the word "creditor" instead of "cautioner", *i.e.* to provide that a cautioner is not released where the creditor discharges a co-cautioner who is bankrupt.

### (d) Giving up securities

Given that a cautioner who pays the debt is entitled to the assignation of any security held by the creditor over the debt, a creditor who voluntarily gives up any such security, releases the cautioner to the extent of the value of that security.[76] The same applies where the creditor fails to make a security effectual,[77] but not where the creditor merely fails to obtain a security which the cautioner anticipated he would have.[78] The fact that the cautioner obtains only partial release reflects the extent to which the cautioner is prejudiced by the creditor's conduct. If, however, the creditor has agreed with the cautioner to retain or have recourse to a particular security, its release amounts to a breach of contract, entirely liberating the cautioner.[79] It remains an open question in Scotland whether the creditor in realizing a security owes a duty of care to the cautioner, so as to minimize the latter's liability.[80]

## 6.21.   TERMINATION BY THE CAUTIONER

Clearly, where a cautioner guarantees a specific transaction, he cannot withdraw from it on his own initiative. Nor may he withdraw from a continuing guarantee, to which he has committed himself for a specified period, before the end of that period.[81] Yet, if a guarantee is of a continuing nature, with no time limit expressed, the cautioner is entitled at any time to inform the creditor that he will not guarantee future advances.[82] The cautioner may then give reasonable notice to the principal debtor to oblige the latter to obtain the cautioner's discharge by the creditor (usually by paying all sums due under the guarantee.[83])

## 6.22.   TERMINATION BY OPERATION OF LAW

### (a) Under the contract

If the obligation is granted for a specific transaction or for a specific period of time, then the completion of that transaction or the expiry of that period without any failure by the debtor will

---

[75] This is certainly so in England—*Thompson v Lack* (1846) 3 C.B. 540;—and has *obiter* support in Scotland—*Morton's Trs. v Robertson's J.F.* (1892) 20 R. 72 at 78, *per* Lord McLaren.

[76] *Sligo v Menzies* (1840) 2 D. 1478.

[77] *Fleming v Thomson* (1826) 2 W & S. 277.

[78] *Bank of Ireland v Morton (No. 2)* 2002 G.W.D. 38/1244.

[79] *Drummond v Rannie* (1836) 14 S. 437.

[80] See *L.A. v Maritime Fruit Carriers Co Ltd*, 1983 S.L.T. 357 There is authority for that view in England: see *Standard Chartered Bank Ltd v Walker* [1982] 1 W.L.R 1410, CA. But *cf. Downsview Nominees Ltd v First City Corp.* [1993] A.C. 295. The English cases however indicate that the creditor is entitled to accord primacy to his own interests in realising the security (see *China and South Sea Bank Ltd v Tan* [1990] 1 A.C. 536, PC.), and assuming he takes care to obtain a reasonable price when doing so, he cannot be challenged on the basis that it would have been more advantageous to the guarantor to have realised at a different time (see *AIB Finance Ltd v Debtors* [1998] 2 All E.R. 929).

[81] *Spence v Brownlee* (1834) 13 S. 199.

[82] *Buchanan v Main* (1900) 8 S.L.T.297.

[83] See *Doig v Lawrie* (1903) 10 S.L.T. 523.

terminate the obligation, and the cautioner will not be taken to have guaranteed any further advances by the creditor.[84]

## (b) Death

If the contract does not provide otherwise, the death of either the principal debtor or creditor releases the cautioner in respect of any debt not then due, but he remains liable for existing debts. Thus in *Woodfield Finance Trust (Glasgow) Ltd v Morgan*[85] M guaranteed the payments by P on an 139 week T.V. rental contract. After 65 weeks P died owing several weeks arrears. The creditor pursued M for the arrears and for the remaining payments under the contract. M was held liable for the arrears, but not for any sum due after P's death.

On the other hand, the death of a cautioner has no effect on his liability. So if he has guaranteed repayment of a specific debt, his estate will be liable to carry out that obligation. Indeed, if a continuing guarantee is for a definite period, then the cautioner's estate remains liable for sums advanced after his death up to the date of expiry of that guarantee. If such a guarantee is for an indefinite period, it will remain in force until his representatives intimate that it is withdrawn[86] The problems which this rule may create can be exacerbated by the fact that the creditor is under no duty to inform the representatives of the existence of the obligation. So in *British Linen Co v Monteith*[87] a creditor was entitled to enforce a guarantee against representatives 14 years after the death of the cautioner. Lord Deas stated,[88]:

> "It is said there is great hardship in holding representatives liable who may never have heard of the obligation. It may be so. But who is to blame for this? The granter of the obligation, who left no trace of it in his repositories? or the bank officers who may or may not have heard of his death? I think that the duty lies on the debtor, who binds his representatives, to keep them informed that he has done so, rather than upon the creditor, who receives and relies on the obligation."

Yet there are suggestions[89] that a creditor who is aware that such representatives are ignorant of the obligation, but nonetheless allows them to dispose of the estate, may be personally barred from enforcing the obligation.

## (c) Change in the constitution of a firm

The Partnership Act 1890 s.18 states:

> "A continuing guaranty or cautionary obligation given either to a firm or to a third person in respect of the transactions of a firm is, in the absence of any agreement to the contrary, revoked as to future transactions by any change in the constitution of the firm to which, or of the firm in respect of the transactions of which, the guaranty or obligation was given."

This would embrace not only the assumption of a new partner, and the retirement of an existing partner, but also the incorporation of the firm as a company,[90] so that conversion into a limited liability partnership should arguably have the same effect.

---

[84] *Scott v Mitchell* (1866) 4 M. 551.

[85] 1958 S.L.T. (Sh.Ct.) 14.

[86] Or possibly only until the representatives advise the creditor of the death. Certainly in England notification of the death has been enough to terminate the obligation without any need to intimate that the guarantee is withdrawn: see *Coulthart v Clementson* (1879) 5 Q.B.D. 42.

[87] (1858) 20 D. 557.

[88] At 562.

[89] *per* Lord Justice Clerk Moncrieff in *Caledonian Banking Co v Kennedy's Trs* (1870) 8 M. 862 at 868.

[90] See respectively, *Spiers v Houston's Exrs* (1829) 3 W. & S. 392; *Royal Bank of Scotland v Christie* (1841) 2 Rob. 118; *Hay & Co v Torbet* (1908) 15 S.L.T. 627.

## (d) Prescription

A cautionary obligation may prescribe if no relevant claim nor acknowledgement of the existence of the obligation has been made within five years of it becoming enforceable.[91] The crucial question then is when the obligation becomes enforceable. Normally, it will become enforceable on default by the debtor, so that failure to act on the obligation within five years of that default will see the obligation prescribe.[92] But much depends on the terms of the obligation itself. In *Royal Bank of Scotland v Brown*[93] the cautioners undertook to pay "on demand" all sums due by a company to the bank. The bank had made a claim in the company's liquidation in 1969, but had failed to recover anything. It was not until 1974 that payment was demanded from the cautioners, and not until 1979 that an action was raised to enforce the cautionary obligation. It was argued that as the obligation became enforceable in 1969 it must have prescribed. It was held however, that the words "on demand" in the obligation meant that the obligation did not become enforceable until a demand for payment was made. No such demand had been made since 1974, so that the prescriptive period had not yet run by the time the action was raised.

---

[91] See Prescription and Limitation of Actions (Scotland) Act 1973, s.6(1)–(3), Sch. 1, para. 1(g), Sch. 2, para. 2; *Royal Bank of Scotland v Brown*, 1983 S.L.T. 122.

[92] See *City of Glasgow DC v Excess Insurance Co Ltd,* 1986 S.L.T. 585, especially Lord Justice Clerk Ross at 588G.

[93] 1983 S.L.T. 122.

# Chapter 7

# INSURANCE

## 7.1. INTRODUCTION

An insurance policy is a contract between the insurer and the insured. As a result, many of the principles which govern insurance contracts are those which apply to any type of contract. However, insurance contracts are also governed by specific principles which are only applicable in an insurance context. Other relevant sources of regulation are informal, such as the Statement of General Insurance Practice commented on below.[1]

What is the nature of insurance? The following definition of the contract of insurance was provided by Channell J. in *Prudential Insurance v IRC*[2]:

> "It must be a contract whereby for some consideration, usually but not necessarily for periodical payments called premiums, you secure to yourself some benefit, usually but not necessarily the payment of a sum of money, upon the happening of some event . . . [T]he event should be one which involves some amount of uncertainty. There must be either uncertainty whether the event will ever happen or not, or if the event is one which must happen at some time there must be uncertainty as to the time at which it will happen."

This chapter will concern itself with the way in which the law governs the insurance contract, rather than the detailed statutory regulation of the operation of the insurance industry.[3]

## 7.2. TYPES OF INSURANCE

The principles of insurance may differ according to the type of insurance taken out by the insured. In indemnity insurance, the insured is indemnified for his or her loss, but never more

---

[1] See paras 7.4.(b)(vi) and 7.5.(d) below.

[2] [1904] 2 K.B. 658 at 663.

[3] Although reference to the Financial Ombudsman Service (which has swallowed up the Insurance Ombudsman Bureau, and various other such schemes) may afford an individual insured a remedy where the law offers none.

than fully indemnified.[4] Indemnity insurance can be contrasted with life assurance, where the insurer pays an agreed sum either on the insured's death if the policy is a whole life policy, or on a specific date where the policy is a term policy. The chapter will, in the main, concentrate on general principles of insurance law, rather than aspects which are specific to particular types of indemity insurance, *e.g.* fire or marine insurance.

Indemnity insurance may also be either first party or third party. First party insurance covers the insured against damage to his or her property, and an example of this would be a home contents insurance policy. Third party insurance, as the term suggests, covers the insured's liability to a third party. The difference between first and third party insurance can be illustrated by considering motor insurance. The insured may take out first party insurance to cover personal injury to him or herself and property damage in the form of damage to his or her car. He or she must also take out third party insurance against his or her liability for property damage or personal injury caused to another road user.[5] Such insurance will only cover the insured where he or she is actually legally liable to the third party. Before any payment could be made by the insurer under such a policy, the injured party would have to prove that the insured was delictually liable.

In the motor insurance context, the role of the Motor Insurers' Bureau should be briefly mentioned. This body, which is funded by all authorised motor insurers, undertakes liability in certain situations by virtue of an agreement with the Secretary of State for Transport. The main thrust of the protections provided by the Bureau is to ensure that claims for injury or death caused by uninsured or untraceable drivers are met.[6] The Bureau is also liable for any loss caused by an uninsured driver where a judgment in favour of the injured third party is not met within seven days.

## 7.3.   INSURABLE INTEREST

The insured must have a financial interest in the event which is insured against, which interest is known as an insurable interest. This principle was originally introduced to prevent persons using insurance policies for the purposes of gaming or wagering.[7] It was thought to be contrary to public policy to permit a person to take out insurance over the life of another person where the insured had no financial interest in the life assured. This rule is part of the common law and was described by Bell as follows[8]:

> "It is essential to the contract of insurance that there shall be a subject in which the insured has an interest, a premium given or engaged for, and a risk run."

If the insured has no insurable interest, then the insurance contract is treated as an illegal contract, and the insured may be prevented from recovering the premiums which he or she has paid.[9]

Certain statutes also require the presence of an insurable interest, and these are commented on below.

---

[4] See the definition provided by Brett L.J. in *Castellain v Preston* (1883) 11 Q.B.D. 380 at 386.

[5] Road Traffic Act 1988, ss.145(3)(a) and 143(1).

[6] See Motor Insurers' Bureau (Compensation of Victims of Untraced Drivers) Agreement, November 22, 1972; Motor Insurers' Bureau (Compensation of Victims of Uninsured Drivers) Agreement, December 21, 1987; and *White v White* [2001] W.L.R. 481, HL.

[7] Gambling contracts, or *sponsiones ludicrae*, are particular types of illegal contracts and therefore not enforceable, see *Stair Memorial Encyclopedia,* Vol. 15, paras 763 *et seq.*

[8] Bell, *Principles*, s.457.

[9] For Scots law on the availability of unjustified enrichment remedies in the context of an illegal contract, see L. J. Macgregor, "Illegal Contracts and Unjustified Enrichment" (2000) E.L.R. 19.

## (a) Life assurance[10]

The Life Assurance Act 1774 provides that the insured must have an insurable interest in the life assured:

> "[No] insurance shall be made by any person or persons, bodies politick or corporate, on the life or lives of any person or persons or on any other event or events whatsoever, wherein the person or persons for whose use, benefit, or on whose account such policy or policies shall be made, shall have no interest, or by way of gaming or wagering . . ."[11]

Although the 1774 Act does not define insurable interest, it limits the insured's recovery to ". . . the amount of value of the interest of the insured in such life or lives . . ."[12] This implies that the insured can recover only his or her financial interest in the life assured. It is assumed that an insured has an insurable interest in his or her own life,[13] and in the life of his or her spouse.[14] The effect of the Married Women's Policies of Assurance (Scotland) Act 1880 should be noted here. This Act permits a married woman to take out a policy on the life of her husband for her own benefit.[15] It also provides that where a husband or wife takes out a life policy on his or her own life for the benefit of his or her spouse or children (or both) the policy is deemed to be held by the insured in trust for the spouse or children.[16] Parents owe to their children an obligation of aliment,[17] and this financial interest means that children have an insurable interest in the lives of their parents. Children have no corresponding obligation to aliment their parents, and so parents have no insurable interest in the lives of their children. Outwith these defined classes of relationship, the insured would have to possess a financial interest in the life insured to have an insurable interest.[18]

The 1774 Act is, unfortunately, ambiguous on the issue of the time at which the insurable interest must exist.[19] This issue was considered by the court in *Dalby v India & London Life Assurance Co.*[20] In this case, four policies of insurance, worth a total of £3,000, had been taken out with the plaintiff's company, Anchor Life, over the life of the Duke of Cambridge. Anchor Life then reinsured[21] the policies with the defendant insurance company. The insured then cancelled the policies, but Anchor maintained the reinsurance policy in place. When the Duke died, Dalby claimed under the reinsurance policy. The defendants argued that the plaintiff's insurable interest in the Duke's life had ceased when the insured had cancelled the policies. However, it was held that it was sufficient if the insurable interest existed at the time at which the insurance contract was entered into and there was no requirement that it continue in existence until the time of the loss. In the opinion of Parker B. to hold otherwise would mean

---

[10] The term "assurance" is sometimes used where the policy-holder insures his or her life, the holder being referred to as the "assured." This may be because ". . . death is assured of happening, the risks covered by other insurances are not," see J. Birds and N. Hird, *Modern Insurance Law*, (5th ed., 2001) at 10. These terms are not used in this chapter, where all references are to "insurance" and the "insured".

[11] Life Assurance Act 1774, s.1.

[12] Life Assurance Act 1774, s.3.

[13] *Griffiths v Fleming* [1909] 1 K.B. 805 at 821, *per* Farwell L.J. This right does not extend to engaged couples nor to cohabitees: see N. Leigh-Jones, J. Birds and D. Owen (eds), *MacGillivray on Insurance Law*, (10th ed., 2003) para. 1–93.

[14] *Wight v Brown* (1845) 11 D. 459.

[15] Married Women's Policies of Assurance (Scotland) Act 1880, s.1.

[16] Married Women's Policies of Assurance (Scotland) Act 1880, s.2 as amended by the Married Women's Policies of Assurance (Scotland) Amendment Act 1980, s.1. There is no requirement that the policy be delivered or intimated to the beneficiaries.

[17] See Family Law (Scotland) Act 1985, s.1(1)(c).

[18] Where the employer has a financial interest in the life of an employee, the employer may also have an insurable interest in that life: see *Turnbull & Co v Scottish Provident Institution* (1896) 34 S.L.R. 146.

[19] See ss.1 and 3.

[20] (1854) 15 C.B. 365.

[21] Insurer A may enter into a contract of insurance with insured B. Reinsurance occurs where insurer A insures the risk which it has undertaken in terms of that policy with a different insurer, insurer C.

that an insured would pay a fixed premium during the course of insurance policy, but the amount of his or her eventual claim would be uncertain, depending upon a recalculation of his or her insurable interest at the time of the death of the life assured.[22]

## (b) Indemnity insurance

Although this point is not clear from the terms of the Act itself, the 1774 Act has been interpreted as not applying to indemnity insurance.[23] Nevertheless, it is clear that the insured in indemnity insurance must have an insurable interest as a result of the operation of Scots common law.[24] This rule also logically follows from the nature of indemnity insurance given that, as explained above, the insured must have suffered a financial loss in order to have a valid claim. The insurable interest must exist at the date of the loss, but it is probably the case that it need not exist at the time of entering into the insurance contract.

Care must be taken in identifying the insured's exact financial interest in the event insured against. In *Fehilly v General Accident Fire and Life Assurance Corporation Ltd*[25] a tenant had sought to insure its interest in the subjects of let, a ballroom in Stirling. When the building was destroyed by fire, the tenants sought to recover from the insurer the value of the building at the time of destruction. The insurer argued that the tenant's insurable interest was restricted to the market value of the lease. The tenant failed in its attempt to recover the full value of the building on the basis that it did not have an insurable interest in the full value of the building. This was because, in terms of the repair clause of the lease, the tenant was only obliged to maintain the subjects in the condition in which they were in when the lease was entered into, and not fully to reinstate the building in the event of it being destroyed.[26] The tenant's insurable interest was limited to the market value of the lease.

The insured must have an insurable interest in any heritable property which he or she seeks to insure. Where the insured has a right to the property which is less than outright ownership, care must be taken to ensure that he or she actually has a sufficient insurable interest. Problems have occurred due to the distinction which is made between the legal personality of a limited company and that of its shareholders.[27] In *Gowan v Jeffrey Associates*[28] Mr Gowan was the director and sole shareholder of a company, had signed personal guarantees covering the company's indebtedness, and was owed a substantial amount of money by the company both through a loan and for work which he had carried out on the company's behalf. He decided to purchase the business premises, and, as part of his plans, insured the premises against fire. He entered into the insurance contract at a time when no contract had been entered into for the purchase of the premises. It can be seen, therefore, that, although Mr Gowan had no contractual or other right to the premises, he had a great deal to lose should they be destroyed. When the premises were, in fact, destroyed by fire, he claimed under the insurance policy. The defenders argued that he had no insurable interest and refused to meet his claim. Lord Hamilton followed pre-existing House of Lords authority[29] to find that the pursuer had no insurable interest. He was clearly dissatisfied with the authorities which led to this result, and he noted that those authorities had not been followed in Canada where a wider test has been adopted. Under this version of the test, which depends upon the insured's "factual expectancy," where the insured has a "moral certainty"[30] of profit or loss, then this is sufficient to provide

---

[22] (1854) 15 C.B. 365 at 403.

[23] *Mark Rowlands v Berni Inns Ltd* [1985] Q.B. 211 at 227, *per* Kerr L.J.; *Siu Yin Kwan v Eastern Insurance Ltd* [1994] 2 A.C. 199 at 211, *per* Lord Lloyd.

[24] Bell, *Principles*, s.457.

[25] 1982 S.C. 163.

[26] 1982 S.C. 163 at 169–170, *per* Lord Cowie.

[27] *Salomon v Salomon & Co* [1897] A.C. 22.

[28] [1998] S.C.L.R. 619.

[29] In particular, *Macaura v Northern Assurance Co Ltd* [1925] A.C. 619, a decision of the House of Lords in a Northern Irish appeal.

[30] See *Lucena v Craufurd* (1806) 2 Bos. & Pul. (N.R.) 269 in which Lawrence J. (at 300–303) set out a wide test for insurable interest. His view on this point was not shared by his colleagues on the bench, and the wider test was not applied in *Macaura v Northern Assurance Co Ltd* [1925] A.C. 619.

him or her with an insurable interest. Reform is clearly required in order to avoid unfair results such as that which occurred in *Gowan v Jeffrey Associates*.

Problems may also arise due to the manner in which partnerships currently take title to heritable property.[31] In *Arif v Excess Insurance Group Ltd*[32] it was held that Arif, who was a partner of a firm which ran a hotel business and the holder of the insurance policy covering the hotel, did not have an insurable interest in the hotel. This was because the heritable proprietor of the hotel was another one of the partners of the firm. To avoid this result, the property would require to be insured in the firm name.

### (c) Marine insurance

An insurable interest is also required in a marine context. The Marine Insurance Act 1906, s.4, provides that contracts of insurance by way of gaming or wagering are void, and that a contract of marine insurance is deemed to be one of gaming or wagering where the insured has no insurable interest.[33] The Act also makes it clear that the insurable interest need exist only at the time of the loss and not at the time when the insurance contract is entered into.[34]

The Marine Insurance Act 1906 is thought to have codified the pre-existing common law. The Act is therefore often referred to in non-marine cases as illustrative of the common law.

## 7.4.  Good Faith, the Duty of Disclosure and Misrepresentation

### (a) The general duty of utmost good faith

Whether parties to a contract are bound by general duties of good faith in Scots law is currently a controversial issue which cannot be explored here.[35] In an insurance context, the duty, which applies to both parties to the contract,[36] is often described as being of "utmost" good faith or *uberrima fides*.[37] Lord Mansfield's judgment in *Carter v Boehm*[38] is usually identified as the source of this principle.[39] Although he confirmed that the duty is a reciprocal one,[40] his explanation of the rationale of the rule focuses mainly on the insured:

> "Insurance is a contract of speculation. The special facts, upon which the contingent change is to be computed, lie most commonly in the knowledge of the insured only: the underwriter trusts to his representation, and proceeds upon confidence that he does not

---

[31] As discussed above at para. 9.2., a firm was previously unable to take feudal tenure to property in its own name, see Bell, *Commentaries*, II, 508 and so title was taken in the name of the partners as trustees for the firm. This position is amended by the Abolition of Feudal Tenure etc (Scotland) Act 2000, s.70.

[32] 1986 S.C. 317.

[33] Insurable interest is defined in s.5(1) and (2).

[34] Marine Insurance Act 1906, s.6(1).

[35] See *Smith v Bank of Scotland*, 1997 S.C. (H.L.) 111 at 121 *per* Lord Clyde; A. D. M. Forte (ed.), *Good Faith in Contract and Property* (1999).

[36] *Life Association of Scotland v Foster* (1873) 11 M. 351 at 359, *per* Lord President Inglis; *Banque Financière de la Cité v Westgate Insurance* [1991] 2 A.C. 249.

[37] Gloag, *op cit.*, pp.496–507. Examples of other contracts *uberrimae fidei* identified by Gloag include cautionary obligations and proposals to enter into partnerships; *Life Association of Scotland v Foster* (1873) 11 M. 351 at 359, *per* Lord President Inglis.

[38] (1766) 3 Burr. 1905.

[39] See also Marine Insurance Act 1906, s.17: "A contract of marine insurance is a contract based on the utmost good faith, and, if the utmost good faith is not observed by either party, the contract may be avoided by the other party.".

[40] *Carter v Boehm* (1766) 3 Burr. 1905 at 1909, *per* Lord Mansfield.

keep back any circumstance in his knowledge to mislead the underwriter into a belief that the circumstances does not exist, and to induce him to estimate the risque, as if it did not exist."[41]

In other words, certain facts which may be material to the insurer's assessment of the risk are known only to the insured and must therefore be disclosed by him or her. Such a duty to disclose is the most important aspect of the wider duty of good faith and is considered below.

## (b) The duty of disclosure

### (i) An aspect of the duty of good faith

Like the duty of good faith, the duty of disclosure is mutual although very few cases exist which analyse the duty as it applies to the insurer.[42] The fact that the duty of good faith is wider in ambit than the duty of disclosure can be illustrated by considering particular aspects of both duties. The duty of good faith applies at all times during the insurance contract, including during negotiations, during the currency of the insurance contract and when a claim is made.[43] By contrast, the duty of disclosure applies during negotiations, but only up until a binding insurance contract is formed.[44] It revives at the time of renewing the contract where the contract is renewed annually[45] but there is no obligation on the insured to disclose factors increasing the risk during the period of insurance.[46] If the parties enter into litigation related to the insurance contract, then both the duty of good faith and the duty of disclosure terminate with the raising of proceedings.[47]

Currently, there is a great deal of dissatisfaction with the duty of disclosure. It is thought that it places an onerous obligation on the insured[48] and in this respect goes beyond the formulation of the general duty of good faith originally set forth by Lord Mansfield.[49] Some argue that, in a modern context, it is inappropriate for the insured to be placed under such an onerous duty where the insurer probably relies more on the wealth of information available from actuaries and experts in deciding whether or not to accept to insure the risk. The consequences of a breach of the duty of disclosure are severe. The "innocent" party has an option to avoid the contract *ab initio*.[50] There is no right to damages.[51] If the contract is avoided, any losses already paid out by the insurer to the insured must be repaid by the insured, and all premiums must be

---

[41] *Carter v Boehm* (1766) 3 Burr. 1905 at 1909, *per* Lord Mansfield.

[42] Although see *Banque Keyser Ullman SA v Skandia (U K) Insurance Co Ltd* [1990] 1 Q.B. 665 at 772, *per* Steyn J.

[43] The existence of the duty of good faith at the time when a claim is made was confirmed by Lord Penrose in *Fargnoli v G A Bonus plc*, 1997 S.C.L.R. 12 at 23. The extent of the duty which applies at the time of making a claim may be less than that which applies at the commencement of the contract, see *Manifest Shipping v Uni-Polaris Insurance Co (the "Star Sea")* [2001] 1 All E.R. 743.

[44] *Ionides v Pacific Ins Co* (1871) L.R. 6 Q.B. 674. It is common for insurance policies to extend the duration of the duty by stating that the insurer will not be bound until the first premium is received by the insurer, see MacGillivray, *op. cit.*, para. 17–20.

[45] *Law Accident Insurance Society v Boyd*, 1942 S.C. 384; *Lambert v Co-operative Insurance Society Limited* [1975] 2 Lloyd's Rep. 485; MacGillivray, *op. cit.*, para. 17–21. The General Insurance Practice Statement, para. 1(b) requires insurers to include a prominent notice on the existence of the duty of disclosure in the proposal form, and this is extended to renewal notices by para. 3.

[46] Although exceptionally, failure to disclose facts which dramatically increase the risk may be regarded as a breach of the continuing duty of utmost good faith: see *The Litsion Pride* [1985] 1 Lloyd's Rep. 437. The same is true of the insurer: see *The Good Luck* [1990] 1 Q.B. 818, CA. reversed on different grounds by the House of Lords [1992] 1 A.C. 233. Moreover, the insurer may seek to impose such an obligation through the use of an "increase of risk" clause.

[47] *Manifest Shipping Co Ltd v Uni-Polaris Shipping Co Ltd (the "'Star Sea")* [2001] 2 W.L.R. 170, HL.

[48] See MacGillivray, *op. cit.*, paras 17–92—17–97.

[49] See R. Hasson, "The doctrine of *uberrima fides* in insurance law—a critical evaluation" (1969) 32 M.L.R. 615; Birds and Hird, *op. cit.*, p.102.

[50] *Joel v Law Union & Crown Insurance Co* [1908] 2 K.B. 863; Marine Insurance Act 1906, s.17. Avoidance is retroactive, and the contract is therefore treated as though it had never existed.

[51] *Banque Financière de la Cité v Westgate Insurance* [1991] 2 A.C. 249 at 280, *per* Lord Templeman.

refunded by the insurer to the insured under the principles of unjustified enrichment. The remedies are therefore likely to have a more severe effect on the insured than on the insurer.[52] A good example of the operation of these rules may be found in *Banque Financière de la Cité v Westgate Insurance*.[53] Essentially, due to a massive fraud, an insurance policy covering a transaction came nowhere near meeting the losses arising therefrom. This fraud was known to the insurer, but not disclosed to the insured. The insured could have rescinded in response to that breach of duty, but that would have left it considerably worse off, as the proceeds of the policy at least covered some of its loss. What it realistically required was damages to cover the remainder of its loss, and by denying the insured damages, the law left it without an effective remedy. By contrast, an insurer will almost never have an interest in seeking damages from an insured, as it does not stand to suffer a loss as a result of the contract. For an insurer the most disadvantageous aspect of the contract is having to meet the insured's loss under the policy. If the insurer is entitled to withhold that performance in response to the insured's breach of duty—the remedy the law actually affords it—this is an ideal situation. It can be seen then, that by treating the parties equally in this respect, the law gives to the insurer the remedy which benefits it most, and to the insured no effective remedy at all.

### (ii) Actual knowledge of the insured

Where the insured is an individual, the duty will only encompass matters which are within the actual knowledge of the insured. He or she cannot be expected to disclose matters of which he or she is unaware.[54] The operation of this principle is seen in *Economides v Commercial Union Assurance plc*.[55] The Court of Appeal refused to allow the insurance company to avoid liability on the basis that the insured had indicated that the value of the contents of his home was £16,000, when it was far higher. The court pointed out that the insured was operating on the basis of information provided to him by his father, genuinely thought he was telling the truth, and was under no obligation to establish the true position. The question is more complex in its application to corporate actors, where it is thought that the company's knowledge is the knowledge of those who ". . . represent the directing mind and will of the company, and who control what it does".[56] It is also relevant to consider the terms of the Marine Insurance Act 1906, s.18(1), which provides that the insured is deemed to know every circumstance which, in the ordinary course of business, ought to be known by him or her. This section has, however, been interpreted restrictively by the courts.[57]

### (iii) "Materiality"

Section 18 of the Marine Insurance Act 1906 provides that:

> ". . . the assured must disclose to the insurer, before the contract is concluded, every material circumstance which is known to the assured . . . Every circumstance is material which would influence the judgment of a prudent insurer in fixing the premium or determining whether he will take the risk."[58]

As stated above, this Act codified the common law. This provision is therefore relevant beyond the marine insurance context, subject however to the fact that, as is explored below, a different test applies in Scotland in relation to life assurance. Section 18 is ambiguous as regards the

---

[52] See Davidson, Insurers—"Duty of Disclosure and Duty of Care", 1988 S.L.T. (News) 73.

[53] [1991] 2 A.C. 249.

[54] *Joel v Law Union & Crown Insurance Co* [1908] 2 K.B. 863 at 884, *per* Fletcher Moulton L.J.; *Hearts of Oak Building Society v Law Union Insurance* [1936] 2 All E.R. 619 at 625, *per* Lord Goddard.

[55] [1998] Q.B. 587.

[56] MacGillivray, *op. cit.*, paras 17–7—17–8.

[57] MacGillivray, *op. cit.*, para. 17–8.

[58] Marine Insurance Act 1906, s.18(2).

actual extent of influence which the non-disclosure must have on the hypothetical prudent insurer. Effectively, there are two possible interpretations of this section: first, that the fact which was not disclosed would have had a decisive influence on the prudent insurer (the "decisive influence" test); or second, that the fact is one which would have had an effect on the mind of the prudent insurer. This question was considered by the Court of Appeal in *Container Transport International Inc and Reliance Group Inc v Oceanus Mutual Underwriting association (Bermuda) Ltd*[59] in which Kerr L.J., referring to the prudent insurer, stated:

> "The word 'influence' means that the disclosure is one which would have had an impact on the formation of his opinion and on his decision-making process in relation to the matters covered by s.18(2)."[60]

The issue was then considered in the important House of Lords case, *Pan Atlantic Insurance Co v Pine Top Insurance Co Ltd.*[61] The decisive influence test was rejected by a narrow majority[62] in the House of Lords, despite a forceful dissenting opinion from Lord Lloyd. There is therefore no need to prove that the prudent insurer would have acted in a different manner had he known of the fact. One need only prove that it was one factor which he or she would have taken into account. The House of Lords added a further requirement, namely, that the *actual* insurer must prove that the failure to disclose the relevant fact induced him or her to enter into the contract before he or she can use it as a basis for avoiding liability. Their Lordships applied this requirement because inducement is an aspect of the general law of contract on misrepresentation.[63] So, while the rejection of the decisive influence test might seem to balance the scales against the insured, the requirement of inducement might appear to tip them significantly in the other direction, especially as it might be thought a difficult task to show that non-disclosure of a single fact induced the insurer to contract. However, the Court of Appeal in *St Paul Fire & Marine Insurance Co v McConnell Dowell Construction Ltd*[64] makes it clear that a presumption in favour of inducement exists, and that non-disclosure need only be one of the inducing factors, not the sole inducing factor. It is therefore for the insured to prove that the failure to disclose had no effect on inducing the insurer to contract, a most difficult task.[65]

The resulting position on materiality is a complex one. The test rests on non-disclosure of facts which would be considered material by a prudent insurer, not those which would be considered material by the actual insured. The insured is therefore expected to assess what a business-person with expertise in insurance practice would consider to be material. This is an assessment which an individual insured may be wholly unqualified to make. It is doubtful whether the additional requirement of actual inducement will improve the position of the insured. Although insurers tend to plead misrepresentation and non-disclosure interchangeably, the two concepts differ, particularly where the misrepresentation is innocent.[66] In misrepresentation one can honestly believe that what one states is true but, because the representation is, in fact, false, a misrepresentation is made. In non-disclosure, the insured knows the truth but fails to appreciate that he or she should disclose the particular fact to the insurer. As has also been pointed out, the test requires us to consider whether the insurer has been induced by a fact of which he or she was unaware.[67] The difficulty of proving a causal link,

---

[59] [1984] 1 Lloyd's Rep. 476.

[60] [1984] 1 Lloyd's Rep. 476 at 492.

[61] [1995] 1 A.C. 501.

[62] 3:2.

[63] See also *Gaelic Assignments Ltd v Sharpe*, 2001 S.L.T. 914.

[64] [1995] 2 Lloyd's Rep. 116.

[65] See *Marc Rich v Portman* [1997] 1 Lloyd's Rep. 225 where the past failure of the insurer to take material facts into account did not overcome the presumption in favour of inducement.

[66] See Birds and Hird, *op. cit.* p.97; see also Lord President Normand's analysis of the difference between the two concepts in *Zurich General Accident and Liability Insurance Co Ltd v Leven*, 1940 S.C. 406 at 415.

[67] See Birds and Hird, *op. cit.*, p.112.

given that what has occurred is an omission to act, has no doubt prompted the presumption in favour of inducement, leaving the insured with the near impossible task of rebuttal.

*Pan Atlantic* has not received a full analysis in Scottish case law yet, but it is suggested that Scots law would be likely to follow the case. The policy of ensuring uniformity of approach in insurance matters in Scotland and England is an important one.

Scots law differs from English law on the issue of materiality in life insurance contracts. This is as a result of the case of *Life Association of Scotland v Foster*.[68] The insured had been asked by the insurer whether she had a rupture and had answered in the negative. She later died as the result of a rupture, and it was discovered that, at the time at which she was asked this question, she had a small swelling on her groin which was a symptom of rupture. She was, however, completely unaware that this was a symptom of rupture. The First Division held that the insurer could not avoid the insurance contract for non-disclosure given that Mrs Foster, not having any medical knowledge, could not have known that the swelling was material. Lord President Inglis expressed the duty of disclosure in life assurance contracts as follows:

> "His duty is carefully and diligently to review all the facts known to himself bearing on the risk proposed to the insurers, and to state every circumstance which any reasonable man might suppose could in any way influence the insurers in considering and deciding whether they will enter into the contract."[69]

Thus, the duty is framed by reference to what the reasonable man in the position of the insured would consider to be material, not what the prudent insurer would consider to be material. Although Lord President Inglis appeared to suggest that the reasonable insured test applied in all types of insurance, it was recently confirmed in *Hooper v Royal London General Insurance Co Ltd*[70] that the reasonable insured test applied only to cases of life assurance, and that the prudent insurer test was the test applicable in all other types of insurance. Lord Justice-Clerk Ross explained his reasoning by reference to the difference between life assurance and all other types of insurance. In life assurance, the questions asked relate to "personal matters" which are often "peculiarly within the knowledge of the assured" and "are not capable of assessment on any objective basis."[71] He contrasted this position with indemnity insurance where the answers to the questions asked can be objectively ascertained.[72] As a result, Scots law applies a more lenient test to the insured in life assurance cases compared to English law.

### (iv) Matters excluded from the duty of disclosure

Four specific classes of information are excluded from the duty of disclosure both under the common law and in terms of the Marine Insurance Act 1906. First, the insured need not disclose any circumstance which diminishes the risk.[73] Thus, in *The Dora*,[74] it was unnecessary to disclose the fact that a yacht would spend a large proportion of its time in the builders' yard, because it was at less risk there than it was at sea.[75]

Secondly, the insured need not disclose any circumstance which is known or presumed to be known to the insurer, which includes matters of common notoriety or knowledge, and matters which the insurer, in the ordinary course of business, ought to know.[76] An example of this exclusion can be found in *Cohen, Sons & Co v Standard Marine Insurance Co Ltd*.[77] In this case

---

[68] (1873) 11 M. 351.
[69] (1873) 11 M. 351 at 359.
[70] 1993 S.L.T. 679.
[71] 1993 S.L.T. 679 all at 683.
[72] 1993 S.L.T. 679 at 683.
[73] Marine Insurance Act 1906, s.18(1).
[74] [1989] 1 Lloyd's Rep. 69.
[75] [1989] 1 Lloyd's Rep. 69 at 89–90, *per* Phillips J.
[76] Marine Insurance Act 1906, s.18(2).
[77] (1925) 21 Lloyd's Rep. 30.

the insurers were held unable to avoid the policy on the grounds that the insured had failed to disclose that an obsolete battleship under tow had no steam power to assist steering, because it was regarded as well-known that such vessels often went to sea in this condition.

Thirdly, the insured need not disclose any circumstance which is waived by the insurer.[78] The case law suggests that a waiver might occur where the answer given by the insured ought to have put the insurer on his or her inquiry. As Lord Esher M.R. explained in *Asfar & Co v Blundell*[79]:

> "But it is not necessary to disclose minutely every material fact . . . [T]he rule is satisfied if he discloses sufficient to call to the attention of the underwriters in such a manner that they can see that if they require further information they ought to ask for it."

In *Mann MacNeil & Steeves Ltd v Capital and Counties Insurance Company Ltd*[80] the insured disclosed that the ship was wooden with motor engines. As such, it was dangerously liable to fire damage, and the insurers ought to have been put on their inquiry to ask what cargo it was carrying. They failed to do so, thus failing to find out that the cargo carried was petrol. They were therefore held to have waived their knowledge of that fact and were unable to avoid the policy.[81]

Fourthly, there is no duty to disclose any circumstance which it is superfluous to disclose by reason of any express or implied warranty.[82] Warranties, which are considered in more detail below, are fundamental terms of the contract in an insurance context. Thus, where the insurer can rely on the insured warranting, or, in effect, guaranteeing, the veracity of a particular fact or facts, there is no need to rely on the duty of disclosure.[83]

Ordinarily convictions which are relevant to the risk insured against should be disclosed. However, the insured is not under an obligation to disclose convictions which are "spent" under s.4(3)(a) of the Rehabilitation of Offenders Act 1974. Convictions resulting in a prison sentence of more than two and one-half years can never become spent under the Act. It may be the case, however, that after the passage of a significant period of time, no conviction would be considered to be material.[84]

Waiver may also arise due to the nature of the proposal form. The insurer does not, by asking particular questions, waive his or her right to disclosure of any material outside the ambit of those questions. The insured's duty of disclosure is an onerous one and is not so easily displaced. However, a particular question may require to be answered in some detail. Under normal principles of interpretation of contracts, requesting detailed information may indicate a waiver of the right to information not covered by the question. As an example, a particular question may request details of losses suffered in the previous five years. This would tend to suggest that the insurer has waived his or her right to disclosure of any losses outwith this period even if those losses would otherwise be considered to be material.[85] It is also possible that an answer provided by the insured is either incomplete or of such a nature as to put a reasonable insurer on his or her inquiry. Waiver may be established if the actual insurer fails to pursue the particular matter with the insured.[86]

---

[78] Marine Insurance Act 1906, s.18(3).

[79] [1896] 1 Q.B. 123 at 129.

[80] [1920] 124 L.T. 778.

[81] See in particular, [1920] 124 L.T. 778 at 781, *per* Atkin L.J.

[82] Marine Insurance Act 1906, s.18(3)(d).

[83] *The Gunford Ship Co Ltd v Thames and Mersey Marine Insurance Co Ltd*, 1910 S.C. 1072 at 1084, *per* Lord President Dunedin.

[84] *Zurich General Accident and Liability Insurance Co Ltd v Leven*, 1940 S.C. 406 at 416, *per* Lord President Normand.

[85] See Birds and Hird, *op. cit.*, p.108.

[86] *Container Transport International Inc v Oceanus Mutual Underwriting Assoc (Bermuda) Ltd* [1984] 1 Lloyd's Rep. 476 at 511–512, *per* Parker L.J.; *Cohen, Sons & Co v Standard Marine Insurance Co Ltd* [1925] 21 Lloyd's Rep. 30.

## (v) The impact of agency on disclosure

Under agency principles, a principal is deemed to be aware of facts which are known to his or her agent provided that the agent acquired the knowledge in the course of carrying out the principal's business.[87] An example of the operation of this principle in an insurance context can be found in *Cruikshank v The Northern Accident Insurance Co Ltd*[88] where the proposal form contained the question "Are there any circumstances which render you particularly liable to accident?" The insured dictated the response to the insurer's agent: "Slight lameness from birth". The insurers sought to avoid payment of a claim on the basis that the insured had failed to disclose the fact that he was extremely lame. The insurers were held unable to avoid payment because the extent of the lameness must have been visible to the insurer's agent when he met with the insured.

It is, however, not always clear whether the principal is the insurer or the insured. It has been held that the agent is acting on behalf of the insured, not the insurer, in the completion of the proposal form.[89] This is because it is the insured's duty to complete the proposal form, and, if he or she asks the agent to complete it, then that agent does so on the insured's behalf.[90] The agent may act for the insurer and the insured at the same time. He or she may act as the insurer's agent, for example, in the acceptance of the risk under a cover note[91] whilst being treated as the insured's agent for the purposes of disclosure.[92] It is possible that a clause which has this effect may be challenged by an insured under the Unfair Terms in Consumer Contracts Regulations 1999.[93]

## (vi) Statement of General Insurance Practice

Certain protections relating to the duty of disclosure are provided by the Statement of General Insurance Practice 1986. Where the proposer is an individual, a statement must be prominently displayed on the form warning the proposer of the consequences of failure to disclose and indicating that, if the proposer is in any doubt as to the materiality of any fact, he or she should disclose it. It binds the insurer to ask clear questions on issues which insurers have generally found to be material and prevents the insurer from repudiating liability on grounds of non-disclosure of a material fact which the policyholder could not reasonably have been expected to disclose.

Although these provisions provide some protection, it should be borne in mind that they relate only to individual proposers and do not assist businesses, small or otherwise. They also only bind insurance companies who are either members of the Association of British Insurers or of Lloyd's.

## (c) Misrepresentation

An insurance contract, like any other contract, can be reduced where one of the parties can prove that he or she was induced to enter into it as a result of an operative misrepresentation.[94] The doctrine of misrepresentation is not as important in an insurance context as it is in other types of contract. There are several reasons for this. The insurer is perhaps more likely to rely on the insured's wide duty of disclosure. Additionally, the contract can only be reduced where the insured has made a representation prior to the conclusion of the contract. Due to the use of

---

[87] Marine Insurance Act, 1906, s.19.
[88] (1895) 23 R. 147.
[89] *McMillan v Accident Insurance Co,* 1907 S.C. 484; *Arif v Excess Insurance Group Ltd,* 1986 S.C. 317 at 319.
[90] *McMillan v Accident Insurance Co,* 1907 S.C. 484 at 490–491, *per* Lord Justice-Clerk Macdonald.
[91] *Stockton v Mason* [1978] 2 Lloyd's Rep. 18.
[92] *Arif v Excess Insurance Group Ltd,* 1986 S.C. 317.
[93] SI 1999/2083; see Sch. 2, para. 1(n) and see para. 7.11. below.
[94] See the definition provided by H. MacQueen and J. Thomson, *Contract Law in Scotland,* (2000) para. 4.59.

"basis of the contract" clauses, which are discussed below, statements made by the insured are elevated to the level of contractual terms rather than representations.[95] If the insurer can rely on the insured's breach of an actual term of the contract, there is no need to take the perhaps more difficult route of proving a misrepresentation, where the onus of proof on the issue of inducement lies on the insurer.[96]

## (d) Fraudulent claims

Where the insured makes a claim which is fraudulent, the insurer is under no liability to meet that claim. The making of a fraudulent claim also rules out any valid claim which the insured might have made in relation to the same incident. As explained by Sir Rodger Parker:

> "On what basis can an assured who asserts, for example, that he has been robbed of five fur coats and some valuable silver, when he has only been robbed of one fur coat and no silver, be allowed, when found out, to say, "You must still pay me for the one of which I was truly robbed"?; I can see none and every reason why he should not recover at all."[97]

A similar approach was adopted by Lord Penrose in the Scottish case of *Fargnoli v G A Bonus plc*.[98] Lord Penrose also considered the more complex issue of the effect of a fraudulent claim on an earlier honest claim under the same policy. The insurers sought to avoid liability for damage caused to a restaurant by fire on the basis that a second fire had been wilfully caused by the insured. The insurance policy provided that, where a fraudulent claim had been made by the insured, "all benefit" of the insurance policy was to be forfeited by the insured. The insurers argued that the insured's fraud rendered the policy retrospectively void. Lord Penrose applied familiar principles of Scots contract law to find against the insurers. Relying on *Lloyd's Bank v Bamberger*[99] he explained that a material breach of contract permits the innocent party to rescind, but does not ". . . absolve parties from primary obligations already due for performance at the time of the rescission."[1] The subsequent fraud by an insured would not, therefore, permit an insurer to avoid liability in relation to an earlier honest claim. The clause in this particular case was not expertly drafted, and it was construed *contra proferentem*, or against the interests of the party putting forward the clause, *i.e.* the insurer.[2] There might therefore be some doubt as to whether a more carefully drafted clause could render the policy retrospectively null, although one would imagine that the courts would seek to avoid such a conclusion. Where the insured is a consumer, such a clause might also be struck at by the Unfair Terms in Consumer Contract Regulations 1999.[3]   Given that the effect of a fraudulent claim is not to render the policy retrospectively null, the insured is not bound to pay back any insurance proceeds received from previous claims made under the policy.

There may be no bar to recovery where the party guilty of fraud and the party making the claim under the policy are distinct legal persons. Thus, in *Bank of Scotland v Guardian Royal Exchange*[4] where the benefit of an insurance policy was extended to a bank which was the

---

[95] For the distinction between terms and representations, see McBryde, *op. cit.*, at 5–45—5–53; MacQueen and Thomson, *op. cit.*, paras 3.14–3.19.

[96] The misrepresentation route is even less attractive to insurers in England in the wake of *Economides v Commercial Union Assurance Co plc* [1997] 3 All E.R. 636, in which it was held that it was sufficient if the insured honestly believed that what he had said was true and that there was no further requirement that he have reasonable grounds upon which to base his honest belief. As a result of this case, misrepresentation in insurance law differs from other types of misrepresentation in English law. In Scots law, a misrepresentation which induces a contract renders it voidable, even if the misrepresentor has an entirely reasonable belief in the truth of the statement made by him or her.

[97] *Orakpo v Barclays Insurance Services* [1995] L.R.L.R. 443; and see *The Aegon* [2002] 1 W.L.R. 616, CA.

[98] 1997 S.C.L.R. 12.

[99] 1993 S.C. 570.

[1] *Fargnoli v GA Bonus plc*, 1997 S.C.L.R. 12 at 22, *per* Lord Penrose.

[2] *Fargnoli v GA Bonus plc*, 1997 S.C.L.R. 12 at 21, *per* Lord Penrose-22; see also *Bass Brewers Ltd v Independent Insurance Co Ltd*, 2002 S.C. 67 for the meaning of *contra proferentem*, see p.256, n.14, below.

[3] SI 1999/2083; see Sch. 2, para. 1(b) See also para. 7.11. below.

[4] 1995 S.L.T. 763.

security-holder over the subjects, the fact that the owner of the subjects had burned down the subjects did not disentitle the bank from claiming under the policy. The nature of the bank's interest was determined as a matter of construction of the policy, and was held to be an independent right and not one which derived from the owner.

## 7.5. THE PROPOSAL FORM

### (a) Warranties

#### (i) Definition

The term "warranty" when used in an insurance context refers to a fundamental term of the contract. The meaning of warranty can be illustrated by reference to the Marine Insurance Act 1906:

> "A warranty . . . means a promissory warranty, that is to say, a warranty by which the assured undertakes that some particular thing shall or shall not be done, or that some condition shall be fulfilled, or whereby he affirms or negatives the existence of a particular state of facts."[5]

The Marine Insurance Act 1906 also details the consequences of breach of a warranty by the insured:

> "A warranty . . . is a condition which must be exactly complied with, whether it be material to the risk or not. If it be not so complied with, then, subject to any express provision in the policy, the insurer is discharged from liability as from the date of the breach of warranty, but without prejudice to any liability incurred by him before that date."[6]

In order to create a warranty, no special form of words is required. Rather, ". . . any form of words expressing the existence of a particular state of facts as a condition of the contract . . ." is sufficient.[7] Nevertheless, the language used must quite clearly indicate that a warranty was intended.[8] Normal rules of contractual interpretation apply to the construction of insurance warranties.[9]

#### (ii) Past/present facts, or as to future facts

In certain cases, the insured will only warrant past or present facts. It is, however, possible to warrant that a state of affairs will prevail throughout the duration of the insurance contract. The latter type of warranty is known as a promissory or continuing warranty. In *Woodfall & Rimmer v Moyle*[10] one of the questions in the proposal form asked, "Are your machinery, plant and ways properly fenced and guarded and otherwise in good order and condition?" to which the insured answered, "Yes". It was held that the insured had not made a continuing warranty, in other words, he had not bound himself to ensure that the obligations contained in the

---

[5] s.33(1).

[6] Marine Insurance Act 1906, s.33(3). The consequences of breach of a warranty are considered in further detail at para. 7.5.(iv) below.

[7] *Dawsons Ltd v Boninn* [1922] S.C. (H.L.) 156 at 166, *per* Viscount Findlay.

[8] *Dawsons Ltd v Boninn* [1922] S.C. (H.L.) 156 at 165–167, *per* Viscount Findlay.

[9] See *Hussain v Brown* [1996] 1 Lloyds Rep. 627, *per* Saville L.J. in the context of his discussion of promissory warranties, for which see below.

[10] [1942] 1 K.B. 66.

question were fulfilled throughout the period of the insurance. The question was interpreted rather as being designed to provide the insurers with a picture of both the existing condition of the machinery and the type of person with whom they were dealing.[11] A similar result was reached in *Kennedy v Smith & Ansvar Insurance Co Ltd.*[12] In this case the insured had completed the proposal form together with an "Abstinence and Membership Declaration" indicating that he was a total abstainer from alcohol and had been so since birth. The defenders provided insurance cover to abstainers at reduced premiums. While driving his car home from a bowls competition with two of his friends, the party had stopped at a local pub and the insured had had one (or perhaps one and a half) pints of lager. When they continued the journey home, the insured's car had careered on to the wrong side of the dual carriageway, and both the passengers were killed. The defenders refused to pay out under the claim, arguing that, at the time of the accident, the abstinence declaration was false because the insured was under the influence of alcohol. The First Division held that the declaration of abstinence did not cover the insured's future behaviour, Lord President Emslie commenting:

> ". . . if insurers seek to limit their liability under a policy by relying upon an alleged undertaking as to the future prepared by them and accepted by the insured, the language they use must be such that the terms of the alleged undertaking and its scope are clearly and unambiguously expressed or plainly implied and that any such alleged undertaking will be construed, *in dubio, contra proferentem.*"[13]

As he indicates, because a continuing warranty may place a relatively onerous obligation on the insured, such warranties must be very clearly expressed. An ambiguity will lead to the term being interpreted *contra proferentem*, or against the party putting forward the clause.[14] As Lord President Inglis explained in *Life Association of Scotland v Foster*:

> "This rule, founded on plain justice, is quite settled in practice. Insurance companies have the framing of their contracts in their own hands. They may make such conditions as they please, but they are bound so to express them as to leave no room for ambiguity. They must be construed . . . in the sense in which the agreement would be understood by a layman who was about to enter upon an insurance transaction."[15]

Where the warranty is drafted using the present tense, it is unlikely that it will be interpreted as a continuing one.[16]

The effect of a breach of a warranty will differ depending upon whether it is classed as relating to past/present facts or future ones. If a warranty as to past/present facts is breached, then the breach is considered to have occurred when the insurance contract was entered into, and the insurance contract will be avoided *ab initio*. Breach of a warranty as to the future will discharge the insurer from liability from the date of the breach, but he or she will remain liable for claims arising prior to the breach.[17]

## (iii) Warranties of opinion

The insured may grant a warranty of opinion, effectively meaning that he or she warrants that facts are true to the best of his or her knowledge or belief. Should this be the case, he or she

---

[11] [1942] 1 K.B. 66 at 71, *per* Lord Greene M.R.

[12] 1976 S.L.T. 110. See also *Hussain v Brown* [1996] 1 Lloyd's Rep. 627.

[13] 1976 S.L.T. 110 at 116–117, *per* Lord President Emslie.

[14] For an example of a warranty being construed *contra proferentem*, see *Provincial Insurance Co v Morgan* [1933] A.C. 240. Views differ on the exact meaning of the *proferens*, see Gloag, *op. cit.*, at 400–401; McBryde, *op. cit.*, paras 8–34—8–39; MacQueen and Thomson, *op. cit.*, para. 3.47.

[15] *Life Association of Scotland v Foster* (1873) 11 M. 351 at 358, *per* Lord President Inglis. In the second sentence in this quote, the Lord President quotes Chief-Justice Cockburn in *Fowkes v The Manchester, etc Assurance Association*, 31 L.J.Q.B. 153.

[16] *Woolfall & Rimmer v Moyle* [1942] 1 K.B. 66.

[17] This is clear from the wording of s.33(3) of the Marine Insurance Act 1906 quoted above.

will only be in breach where he or she has been either dishonest or reckless in providing an answer. Thus, in *McPhee v Royal Insurance Co Ltd*[18] the insured completed a proposal form by adding the dimensions of the cabin cruiser which he was seeking to insure. The form contained a declaration that the information was provided to the best of his knowledge and belief. Rather than measuring the vessel himself, he telephoned the previous owner of the vessel and, having obtained the dimensions from him, inserted them into the proposal form. It transpired that these dimensions were incorrect and the insurers sought to avoid liability when the vessel was destroyed on the basis that the answers were not true to the best of the proposer's knowledge and belief. In holding that a material misstatement had been made, Lord Robertson explained:

> "To give true answers to the best of a person's knowledge and belief . . . means that he who gives the answers must have a reasonable basis for his knowledge and belief, and must not act recklessly in giving them."[19]

### (iv) Effect of a breach of warranty

Because a warranty is a fundamental term of the insurance contract, it should follow that a breach of that warranty entitles the insurer to rescind[20] the insurance contract. The effect of rescission should be the termination of the contract. However, s.33(1) of the Marine Insurance Act 1906 (quoted above) indicates that the effect of a breach of warranty is merely to discharge the insurer from liability. The insurance contract therefore remains in existence. Although there may appear to be little difference between these two possibilities, in some cases the outcome could be very different depending upon which analysis is adopted. If the insurer is merely discharged from liability and the contract remains in force, then other claims unrelated to the breach of warranty may require to be met by him or her, and other clauses of the contract may remain in effect. If the contract is rescinded, then such claims would not be possible.

The actual effect of a breach was recently considered by the House of Lords in *Bank of Nova Scotia v Hellenic Mutual War Risks Association (Bermuda) Ltd, "The Good Luck."*[21] The facts of the case are complicated. In essence, the owner of the ship insured it with the defendant insurers. The owners then mortgaged the ship to the plaintiff bank, and assigned the benefit of the insurance to that bank. The insurers undertook to notify the bank promptly if the insurers ceased to insure the ship. The ship sailed into the Arabian Gulf, which constituted a breach of warranty. It was hit by Iraqi missiles and became a constructive total loss. The insurers, having discovered the breach of warranty, failed to inform the bank. The bank, believing that the ship was covered by insurance, made further advances to the owners which would not have been made had the bank been aware that the ship was no longer insured. The bank sued the insurers for breach of their undertaking. In the House of Lords, Lord Goff interpreted s.33(1) of the Marine Insurance Act 1906 as providing that, where the insured was in breach of a promissory or continuing warranty, the insurer was automatically discharged from liability. The insurer did not have the option to decide whether or not to treat the insurance as at an end. Rather than relying on the promissory warranty as a fundamental term of the contract, and therefore a "condition" in normal English legal terminology, he stated that compliance with a warranty was a condition precedent to the attaching of the risk.[22] Thus, the non-fulfillment of the condition precedent through breach of the warranty effectively discharged the insurer from liability.

---

[18] 1979 S.C. 304.

[19] 1979 S.C. 304 at 339.

[20] Whereas English cases refer to the insurer's right to repudiate, the correct term in Scots law is rescind, given that the insured and not the insurer is in breach.

[21] [1992] 1 A.C. 233.

[22] [1992] 1 A.C. 233, Lord Goff at 262–263. Condition precedent, although a term which is widely used in Scotland, is an English term, for which the Scottish equivalent is suspensive condition: see H. MacQueen and J. Thomson, *op. cit.*, para. 3.59; McBryde, *op. cit.*, paras 5—35—5—40.

The effect of this complex case for Scots law is difficult to state, not least because of the use of English legal concepts, some of which have no parallel in Scots law. Although the case involved marine insurance, there is no indication that the principles would be inapplicable to other types of insurance. If Lord Goff's approach is followed in Scotland, then the effect of a breach of warranty is not to enable the insurer to rescind the contract as a whole, but only to release him or her from liability. Difficulties remain however. His references to the insurer being automatically discharged from liability sit uneasily with the insurer's ability to waive the breach of warranty.[23] This would suggest an option to rescind rather than an automatic discharge. It is clear, however, that where the insurer is released from liability, the insured is entitled to repayment of his or her premiums, unless he or she had made a non-disclosure or misrepresentation which was fraudulent.[24]

Aside from the actual effect of breach, it is clear that there is no requirement on the part of the insurer to prove that the breach of warranty itself caused the loss before the insurer is discharged from liability.[25] In other words, the statement made may be immaterial to the risk and yet the insurer will nevertheless be discharged from liability.

### (b) Basis of the contract clauses

As stated above, no special form of words is required in order to create a warranty. It was previously very common to elevate each statement provided by the proposer on the proposal form to the level of a warranty by using a basis of the contract clause. Such a clause, which is normally located at the bottom of the proposal form, indicates that each of the questions and answers provided forms the basis of the contract between insurer and proposer. The effect on the insured is draconian. Because warranties must be strictly complied with, any inaccuracy in the information provided could discharge the insurer from liability.[26] Although such practices have been described as ". . . mean and contemptible,"[27] in a relatively recent Scottish case the validity of such clauses was recognised as part of the operation of the principle of freedom of contract.[28] That case, however, involved a contract between two businesses. The use of basis of the contract clauses where the insured is an individual has been tackled by the Statement of General Insurance Practice as is discussed below.

### (c) Clauses descriptive of the risk

In certain cases, what appears to be a warranty has been interpreted as a clause descriptive of, or delineating the risk, perhaps in an attempt to temper the consequences for the insured. Thus, where a particular term has not been complied with, if it is treated as a warranty, the insurer is discharged from liability. If it is treated as descriptive of the risk, the insurer will not be "on risk" during the period when the clause is not being complied with. Once the insured complies with the clause again, the insurer will revert to being "on risk." The consequences for the insured are therefore far less serious where the clause is treated as being descriptive of the risk rather than as a warranty. A clause which is descriptive of the risk may also be referred to as an exception from cover.[29]

---

[23] Marine Insurance Act 1906, s.34(3).

[24] See *Anderson v Fitzgerald* (1853) 4 H.L. Cas. 484. It should be noted, however, that the policy may validly provide for forfeiture of the premiums in cases where no fraud is involved: see *Kumar v Life Assurance Corp of India* [1974] 1 Lloyd's Rep. 147.

[25] *Dawsons v Boninn*, 1922 S.C. (H.L.) 156.

[26] See also *Standard Life Assurance Co v Weems* (1884) 11 R. (H.L.) 48 at 50, *per* Lord Blackburn.

[27] *Glicksman v Lancashire & General Insurance Co Ltd* [1927] A.C. 139 at 144, *per* Lord Wrenbury.

[28] *Unipac (Scotland) Ltd v Aegon Insurance Co plc*, 1996 S.L.T. 1197 at 1202 (opinion of the court).

[29] See *Provincial Insurance v Morgan* [1933] A.C. 240, in which the insured had stated on a proposal form that the lorry to be insured would carry coal. He also signed a declaration stating that his answers were the basis of the contract. On the day on which it was damaged, the lorry had been carrying both coal and timber, although all of the timber had been delivered at the time of the accident. The insurers sought to avoid liability because the insured had failed to comply with the conditions as to goods carried. Lord Rutherford and Lord Wright in the House of Lords were of the opinion that the statements were not warranties but merely descriptive of the risk, an approach which had been taken by the Court of Appeal. The result of this approach was that the insurer was not on risk when the lorry was carrying timber, but was on risk once all of the the timber had been delivered. The remaining judges in the House of Lords decided the case as a matter of interpretation of a promissory warranty.

## (d) Statement of General Insurance Practice

The Statement of General Insurance Practice has tackled the abuse of warranties. It provides that any basis of the contract clause should be restricted to completion according to the proposer's knowledge and belief.[30] Thus, only warranties of opinion are possible in such situations. It also prevents statements as to past or present fact from being converted into warranties[31] and prevents the insurer from repudiating a policy on grounds of a breach of warranty or condition where the circumstances of the loss are unconnected with the breach "unless fraud is involved."[32] Although these provisions provide the proposer with some protection, they are subject to the limitations already detailed, namely that they only protect individuals and only bind certain insurers.

## (e) Notice

The policy may impose a time limit on the insured within which he or she must notify the loss. Whether the insured has complied with the requirements of the policy in relation to notice is essentially a question of interpretation of the insurance policy. In one case, the insured or his personal representatives were bound to provide notice of an accident ". . . as soon as reasonably possible after it has come to the knowledge of the insured or of the insured's representative . . ."[33] The insured died in an accident in India, and, although her personal representatives were informed of her death within one month of the accident, a year had passed before they discovered the existence of the insurance policy and intimated the loss to the insurance company. They were found to have notified the insurers timeously, Roche J. explaining that ". . . all existing circumstances must be taken into account . . ."[34] This included the means of the administratrix' knowledge of the policy. A similar approach has been taken by Lord Denning, who approved the interpretation of "immediate" as "with all reasonable speed considering the circumstances of the case."[35] However, when the clause imposes a specific time limit for notification, this type of liberal approach is not open. So in one case the accident and injuries received were to be notified within 14 days, and a failure to do so meant that the insured was not entitled to recover even though the injury forming the basis of the insured's claim did not develop for a further eight months.[36] It is probable that such clauses are challengeable (where the insured is a private individual) under the Unfair Terms in Consumer Contracts Regulations 1999.[37] It has also been held that notification of damage by the owners of property did not remove the need for separate notification by the holders of a standard security over the property, who had insured their interest with the same company.[38]

## 7.6. Repayment of the Premium

Where the risk under the policy is not run, and the insurer was therefore never going to be liable to pay, he or she is usually bound to return the premium to the insured. Otherwise the insured has paid the premium for nothing. As Lord Mansfield explained:

---

[30] Statement of Insurance Practice 1986, para. 1(a).
[31] Statement of Insurance Practice, 1986, para. 1(b).
[32] Statement of Insurance Practice, 1986, para. 2(b)(iii).
[33] *Velest's Administratrix v Motor Union Insurance Company Ltd* [1925] 2 K.B. 137.
[34] [1925] 2 K.B. 137, at 142.
[35] *Farrell v Federated Employers Insurance Association Ltd* [1970] 3 All E.R. 632 at 635 where he approves the approach of Fletcher Moulton L.J. in *Re Coleman's Depositories Ltd and Life and Health Insurance Association* [1907] 2 K.B. 798. See also *Jacobs v Coster* [2000] Lloyd's Rep. I.R. 506, CA.
[36] *Cassel v Lancashire & Yorkshire Accident Insurance Co Ltd* (1885) T.L.R. 495.
[37] SI 1999/2083; see Sch. 2, para. 1(b). See also para. 7.11. below.
[38] *Bass Brewers Ltd v Independent Insurance Co Ltd,* 2002 S.C. 67.

> "Equity implies a condition that the insurer shall not receive the price of running a risque, if he runs none . . . If the risque is not run, though it is by the neglect or even the fault of the party insuring, yet the insurer shall not retain the premium."[39]

So if the insurance policy is void, perhaps because the insured has been guilty of misrepresentation or non-disclosure, then the premium should be repaid, unless perhaps the insured's conduct is considered to be fraudulent.[40] The premium may also be recoverable because the insured lacks an insurable interest, or because of breach of warranty on the part of the insured. If the insured has breached a promissory warranty, it may be the case that premiums paid up to the time of breach cannot be recovered, whereas premiums paid after the date of breach are recoverable, on the basis that the risk was run up to the point where the warranty was breached. It is, however, very common in practice for insurance policies to provide that all premiums will be forfeited by the insured in situations of breach of warranty, whether promissory or otherwise. Although there is an argument that such forfeiture clauses may operate as penalty clauses,[41] well-established authority suggests that they are enforceable.[42] Still, it is probable that such clauses are challengeable (where the insured is a private individual) under the Unfair Terms in Consumer Contracts Regulations 1999.[43]

If the insured has been at fault in entering into an insurance contract which is considered to be illegal, then he or she will be barred from recovering the premiums. Taking out an insurance policy on the life of another where the insured has no insurable interest is considered to be illegal under the Life Assurance Act 1774 and so the premiums would not be repayable.[44] Where the insured is innocent of any illegal conduct, for example because she was fraudulently induced by the insurer to enter into an illegal insurance policy, the premiums are repayable.[45]

## 7.7. INDEMNITY

### (a) General principle

The importance of the indemnity principle was commented on by Brett L.J. in *Castellain v Preston*[46]:

> "The very foundation . . . of every rule which has been applied to insurance law is this, namely, that the contract of insurance contained in a marine or fire policy is a contract of indemnity, and of indemnity only, and that this contract means that the assured, in case of a loss against which the policy has been made, shall be fully indemnified, but shall never be more than fully indemnified. That is the fundamental principle of insurance, and if ever a proposition is brought forward which is at variance with it, that is to say, which either will prevent the assured from obtaining a full indemnity, or which will give to the assured more than a full indemnity, that proposition must certainly be wrong."[47]

---

[39] *Stevenson v Snow* (1761) Burr 1237 at 1240, *per* Lord Mansfield.

[40] *Anderson v Fitzgerald* [1853] 4 H.L. Cas 484.

[41] *Kumar v Life Insurance Corporation of India* [1974] Lloyd's Rep. 147 at 154, *per* Kerr L.J. On penalty clauses see McBryde, *op. cit.*, paras 22–144 *et seq*; H. MacQueen and J. Thomson, *op. cit.*, paras 6.47–6.51.

[42] *Standard Life Assurance Co v Weems* (1884) 11 R. (H.L.) 156; *Sparenborg v Edinburgh Life Assurance Co* [1912] 1 K.B. 195.

[43] SI 1999/2083; see Sch. 2, para. 1(d). See also para. 7.11. below.

[44] s.1.

[45] *Hughes v Liverpool Victoria Legal Friendly Society* [1916] 2 K.B. 482.

[46] (1883) 11 Q.B.D. 380.

[47] (1883) 11 Q.B.D. 380 at 386.

In that case, the indemnity principle was applied in a situation where the insured had signed a contract to sell his house shortly before it was destroyed. Under the specific contract entered into,[48] he was entitled to recover the full value of the house from the purchaser, even though the house had been destroyed. It was held that he could not also recover the value of the house from the insurer because this would have the effect of over-compensating him.

The insured's loss is calculated at the time of the loss. *Prima facie* value will be determined by the cost of reinstatement or restoration where the subjects have not been fully destroyed. However, the rule may be displaced if it can be proved that the subjects actually had a different value at the time of the loss. Thus, in *Leppard v Excess Insurance Co,*[49] a cottage was insured for "full value" which was defined as "the amount which it would cost to replace the property in its existing form should it be totally destroyed." The owner had, shortly before the cottage was destroyed by fire, been seeking to sell it at a price of £3,000. It was held that the lower price represented the market value and was therefore the amount recoverable. Full reinstatement value was not recoverable given that this would have permitted the plaintiff to recover more than his actual loss. It should be borne in mind that the insurance policy may also contain an excess clause which will have an effect on what the insured can recover. Such clauses bind the insured personally to bear a specific percentage of the loss.

The terms of the policy may lead to a departure from the indemnity principle. In particular, the value of the subjects may be specifically stated in the policy. Such a value will conclusively determine the amount recovered by the insured, regardless of whether it exceeds the actual value of the subjects at the time of the loss. As an example, in *Elcock v Thomson*[50] the subjects had been partially damaged. The insured was able to recover a percentage of the agreed value, notwithstanding the fact that this was several times the actual value of the subjects.

A further departure from the indemnity principle occurs in policies which supply "new for old" where the insurer provides the subject's replacement rather than its market value, or bears the cost of repair or reinstatement. The insurer may seek to deduct a proportion of the cost of repair on the basis that repairing an item may actually increase its value.

The concept of underinsurance may also have an impact on the amount recoverable by the insured. This issue is covered by the Marine Insurance Act 1906:

> "Where the assured is insured for an amount less than the insurable value or, in the case of a valued policy, for an amount less than the policy valuation, he is deemed to be his own insurer in respect of any uninsured balance."[51]

As a result, where the insured is underinsured, he or she can recover only the proportion of the sum insured which the damage bears to the value of the subjects. Thus, if subjects worth £2,000 are insured for only £1,000, and suffer £600 damage, then the insured can recover only £300 (50 per cent of the loss). However, this principle only applies in marine insurance. In non-marine cases the insured is entitled to recover the full extent of his or her loss, notwithstanding the fact that he or she was underinsured. An insurer can avoid this result by inserting an "average" clause which would, in effect, apply the same principle to non-marine situations. Average clauses, although common in commercial insurance, are rare in policies over domestic heritable property.

## (b) Subrogation

### (i) General principle

The principle of subrogation is a consequence of the principle of indemnity and cannot, therefore, arise in cases of life insurance. It is often stated to involve two separate rules. Firstly,

---

[48] This is, of course, an English case. In Scotland the common law rule which provides that risk passes on conclusion of missives would normally be amended in missives.

[49] [1979] 2 All E.R. 668.

[50] [1949] 2 K.B. 755.

[51] Marine Insurance Act 1906, s.81.

as stated in *Castellain v Preston*, the insured must never be more than fully indemnified.[52] Thus, the insured cannot profit from his loss, and any profit which he or she does make is payable to the insurer. Secondly, where the insurer has indemnified the insured, the insurer is entitled to all the insured's rights as regards third parties in respect of the loss itself and any sums which the insured may receive which diminish the loss. The insurer takes the place of, or "stands in the shoes of" the insured in relation to the insured's rights against third parties. As Brett L.J. observed in *Castellain v Preston*:

> ". . . as between the underwriter and the assured the underwriter is entitled to the advantage of every right of the assured, whether such right consists in contract, fulfilled or unfulfilled, or in remedy in tort . . . or in any other right . . . legal or equitable."[53]

The sections which follow analyse both aspects of subrogation as they operate in practice.

### (ii) Insurer must sue in the name of the insured

It is clear that the insurer once subrogated to the rights of the insured, must sue in the name of the insured. The insurer cannot sue in its own name, as would be the case where the insured had assigned its rights to the insurer. This was recently confirmed by Lord President Rodger:

> " . . . where the insured is subrogated to the rights of the assured, it must raise any action in the name of the assured. As Lord Goff explained in his speech in *Esso Petroleum* at p.878F–H (p.663E–F), the payment by the insurer indemnifying the assured does not have the effect of transferring the assured's rights to the insurer and so the insurer cannot simply go ahead and itself raise actions based on those rights. Nonetheless, because the insurer has indemnified the assured, the law gives it the right to insist that the assured should authorise it to use the assured's name in proceedings against third parties. If need be, the insurer can take proceedings to compel the assured to grant the necessary authority."[54]

### (iii) Insurer's right arises only when the insured has been compensated by the insurer

It is clear that the insurer must have actually paid the insured before the insurer can be subrogated to the rights of the insured. An example of this principle can be found in the case of *Scottish Union and National Insurance Co v Davis*[55] in which Davis's car had been damaged when a coping stone fell from a building, striking the car. He took the car to a garage for repair, and the garage made three, ultimately unsuccessful, attempts at repair, before Davis eventually took the car away. In the meantime, the garage sent their bill direct to the insurers who paid the bill without first checking that the insured's car had been satisfactorily repaired. Davis managed to recover compensation in tort from the owners of the building in settlement of his claim against them. When the insurers claimed to be entitled through subrogation to this sum their claim failed. This was because the insurers had not indemnified Davis in respect of his loss.

### (iv) Any defect in the insured's title to sue will similarly affect the insurer

Given that subrogation is simply a mechanism which allows the insurer to enforce the rights of the insured, where the insured's title to sue a third party is defective in some respect, this

---

[52] (1883) 11 Q.B.D. 380 at 386, *per* Brett L.J., quoted above; *Yorkshire Insurance Co Ltd v Nisbet Shipping Co Ltd* [1962] 2 Q.B. 330 at 339–340, *per* Diplock J.

[53] (1883) 11 Q.B.D. 380 at 388, *per* Brett L.J., cited with approval by Lord Jauncey in *Esso Petroleum Co Ltd v Hall Russell & Co Ltd*, 1988 S.L.T. 1123 at 1140L, HL.

[54] *Caledonia North Sea Ltd v London Bridge Engineering Ltd*, 2000 S.L.T. 1123 at 1140, *per* Lord President Rodger, referring to the speech of Lord Goff in *Esso Petroleum Co Ltd v Hall Russell & Co Ltd*, 1988 S.L.T. 874.

[55] [1970] 1 Lloyd's Rep. 1.

defect will also affect the insurer. In *Simpson & Company v Thomson*[56] two vessels belonging to the same owner collided and one sank. The owner paid a sum into court to compensate the various parties who had suffered a loss as a result of the collision and who therefore had a claim against him under the Merchant Shipping Acts. The owner's insurers paid the owner and then tried to claim a proportion of the fund paid into court. They were unsuccessful because the only action which the insured had, as the owner of a damaged ship, was an action against himself, as the negligent party. It being impossible for the insured to sue himself, there was no action for the insurers to be subrogated to.

It has been argued that an insurer was not entitled to be subrogated to the insured's right recently on the basis that where the loss was met by the insurer, there was no loss and therefore no right to which to be subrogated. As was to be expected, that argument was entirely rejected, it being pointed out that the same argument could be used by any party who was potentially liable to an insured, leaving no room at all for the principle of subrogation to operate.[57]

### (v) *Where more than one person is interested in the same property*

Particular problems arise in commercial leases where the landlord generally controls the insurance of the subjects, recovering the cost of the premiums from the tenant either by direct re-imbursement or through a service charge. The policy may, for example, cover the subjects against damage by fire. The subjects may, however, be destroyed by a fire which is caused by the negligence of the tenants. The insurers will compensate the landlords as owners of the subjects in terms of the insurance policy. The insurers may then seek to be subrogated to the landlord's rights against the negligent party, namely the tenant. If this principle were permitted to operate, then the tenant would be in the position of having paid for the insurance and yet being liable for the cost of repairing the damage caused to the subjects. This result can be avoided by insuring in joint names of the landlord and the tenant, or obtaining for the tenant a waiver by the insurers of their subrogation rights. The tenant's interest in the subjects may also be noted on the insurance policy, although this is the least certain method of protecting the tenant. Even if such mechanisms were not employed, the courts may construe the lease as disclosing no intention to impose ultimate liability on the tenant through the exercise of subrogation rights.[58] This was the outcome in *Mark Rowlands v Berni Inns Ltd*[59] where the court was clearly influenced by the particular terms of the lease, specifically: that the landlord was obliged to use insurance proceeds to rebuild the subjects; that the tenant was not liable to repair damage caused by any of the insured risks; and that the insurance was for the benefit of both the landlord and the tenant.

### (vi) *Co-insurance cases*

Where several parties are insured under the same insurance policy, and damage is caused by the negligence of one of those parties, the insurer cannot be subrogated to the rights of the other insured against the negligent party. Thus in *Petrofina (UK) Ltd v Magnaload*[60] an insurance policy had been taken out to cover the construction and extension of an oil refinery. The insured was defined as the main contractors, sub-contractors and various other parties involved in the construction. Damage was caused by the negligence of one of the sub-contractors. The insurers settled a claim by one of the insured parties, and then brought a claim against the negligent sub-contractors, claiming to be subrogated to the insured party's

---

[56] (1877) 5 R. (H.L.) 40.

[57] *Caledonia North Sea Ltd v London Bridge Engineering Ltd,* 2000 S.L.T. 1123 at 1134A–1136A, *per* Lord President Rodger, affirmed by 2002 S.L.T. 278, HL.

[58] See also *Barras v Hamilton,* 1994 S.L.T. 949.

[59] [1986] Q.B. 211.

[60] [1984] Q.B. 127 See also *Hopwell Project Management Ltd v Ewbank Preece Ltd* [1998] 1 Lloyd's Rep. 448; *Fraser Pile & Dredge Ltd v Can-Dive Services Ltd* [2000] 1 Lloyd's Rep. 199.

right. It was held that the insurers could have no right of subrogation against a negligent party who was also an insured under the same insurance policy. In *Petrofina* the denial of subrogation rights seems to be based on the necessity to avoid circuity of action. In other words, if the insurers used subrogation rights against the negligent insured, the latter could then claim indemnity against the insurers. More recent cases have, however, suggested that the prohibition is to be explained by reference to an implied term of the contract of insurance excluding subrogation rights in these circumstances.[61]

### (vii) Extent of subrogation rights

If the subjects are underinsured, then the insured may seek to recover any shortfall from the negligent party. The issue here is whether the insurer is entitled to exercise subrogation rights once he or she has paid out the insurance proceeds (albeit that these are less than the insured's loss), or whether the insurer is only entitled to do so once the insured has been fully compensated, including retaining any shortfall the insured has recovered from the negligent party. It appears that the former is the correct analysis: the insurer can exercise his subrogation rights once he has indemnified the insured regardless of whether the insured's actual loss exceeds the amount of the insurance proceeds.[62]

This question was analysed in *Lord Napier and Ettrick v Hunter*[63] where Lord Templeman in the House of Lords used the following figures to illustrate the issue. He assumed that the loss suffered by the insured was £160,000. The insurers were only liable to meet £125,000 of this amount, and the policy contained an excess of £25,000. The insurers paid the insured £100,000 of insurance proceeds. The insured also recovered £130,000 from the third party liable for the loss. The question considered was whether the insured was entitled to retain £60,000 of the amount recovered from the third party, which, when added to the £100,000 insurance proceeds would fully compensate him for his total loss of £160,000, or whether the insurer was entitled to a greater proportion of the amount recovered from the third party, leaving the insured under-compensated. He indicated that the latter alternative was the correct one. Because there was an excess of £25,000, the insured was considered to be his own insurer for this amount. The insured would be entitled to retain a proportion of the £130,000 recovered from the third party. This would be his uninsured loss (£60,000) minus the excess (£25,000), namely £35,000. The insurers were entitled to the balance of £95,000 (£130,000 minus £35,000). Thus the insured would not be fully compensated for his loss. In the aftermath of this case, it is clear that where a policy contains an excess clause, the insurer is entitled to recover everything that he or she can through subrogation, before the insured can recover any of the excess from the third party.

The *Napier* case considered the effect of an excess clause rather than the problem of underinsurance. However, Lord Templeman also considered the problem of underinsurance and indicated that the insured is considered to be his own insurer for any loss above the sum insured against.[64]

In rare cases there may be a profit left over after subrogation rights have been exercised by the insurer. If that is the case, the insured is entitled to retain such a profit. The insurer's subrogation rights extend only to the amount which they have paid to the insured, and not to any profit over and above that indemnification. In *Yorkshire Insurance Co Ltd v Nisbet Shipping Co Ltd*[65] a vessel insured for £72,000 was sunk as a result of the negligence of the Canadian government. The insurer paid to the insured £72,000 in terms of the insurance policy. The insured thereafter successfully sued the Canadian government. However, between payment of

---

[61] *National Oilwell Ltd v Davy Offshore Ltd* [1993] 1 Lloyd's Rep. 582; *Co-operative Retail Services Ltd v Taylor Young Partnership Ltd* [2000] 2 All E.R. 865; and see Davidson, "Limited Interests in Property, Covenants to Insure and Subrogation"—1994 S.L.T. (News).

[62] *Lord Napier and Ettrick v Hunter* [1993] A.C. 713.

[63] [1993] A.C. 713.

[64] [1993] A.C. 713 at 730, *per* Lord Templeman.

[65] [1962] 2 Q.B. 330.

the insurance proceeds and the court action, the pound had been devalued. When the payment made by the Canadian government following the court action was transmitted to London, it amounted to almost £127,000. The insured accounted to the insurer the sum of £72,000 only. In an action by the insurer in which it sought payment of the remaining £55,000, it was held that the insurer's right was limited to recovery from the insured of the sum paid by the insurer to the insured. Although this case was decided on the operation of the Marine Insurance Act 1906,[66] there is no reason to suppose that it does not represent a general rule.

## (c) Double insurance and contribution

### (i) General principles

It is open to the insured to insure his or her property with as many insurers as he or she wishes. The principle of indemnity will operate to ensure, however, that the insured is not over-indemnified for his or her loss. The insured, in the event of a loss, may choose which insurer to claim against. Although that insurer cannot argue that other insurers are similarly liable, once he or she has paid the claim, he or she can demand that the other insurers contribute their share of the loss.[67] Contribution is stated to be subject to further conditions, namely: the insurances must cover the same subjects; the policies must cover the same risks; the same interests must be covered; and the policies must be enforceable.[68]

The legal basis of the right to contribution is not clear. It cannot arise from contract given that the insurers do not have a contractual relationship with one another. In older cases it is identified as an equitable principle,[69] whereas, in a modern context, it has been suggested that its purpose is the avoidance of unjust enrichment.[70]

Contractual clauses play an important role in this area, and their impact on the general rules of contribution is considered below.

### (ii) Calculating ratios of contribution

The rules for determining the amounts of contribution to be paid by each insurer are complex, and may often depend upon insurance practice rather than any legal rule. There are two possible approaches. The simpler approach, known as the "maximum liability" approach, dictates that each insurer will pay the proportion of the loss which the sum he or she has insured bears to the total of all sums insured. This approach can be seen in property insurance where the sum insured by different insurers is likely to be the same. The alternative approach is known as the "independent liability" approach. This approach assumes that there has been no double insurance before calculating the individual insurer's liability as normal. That amount is then assessed as a proportion of all of the insurance taken out by the insured, in order to calculate the contribution payable by that particular insurer (see para. 6.18. for practical examples of how these approaches operate.)

The right to claim contribution is not confined to cases of co-insurance. In one case,[71] an insurer was found entitled to a 100 per cent contribution from a party who had agreed to indemnify the insured against loss arising from a contract between the insured and that party. On the effect of contribution, Lord Rodger commented:

> "If the insurers and defenders were properly to be regarded as co-obligants on an equal footing in a joint and several obligation to indemnify the pursuers, the insurers would

---

[66] In particular, s.79(1).

[67] *Sickness and Accident Assurance Association Ltd v General Accident Assurance Corporation Ltd* (1892) 19 R. 977.

[68] *Legal and General Assurance Society Ltd v Drake Insurance Co Ltd* [1991] 2 Lloyd's Rep. 36 at 38, *per* Lloyd L.J and 44, *per* Ralph Gibson L.J.

[69] *Legal and General Assurance Society Ltd v Drake Insurance Co Ltd* [1991] 2 Lloyd's Rep. 36 at 42, *per* Nourse L.J.

[70] Birds and Hird, *op. cit.*, p.316.

[71] *Caledonia North Sea Ltd v London Bridge Engineering Ltd*, 2000 S.L.T. 1123; affirmed 2002 S.L.T. 278, HL.

indeed have a right to relief to the extent of a contribution of their *pro rata* share from the defenders. That is the position which the law has adopted in respect of double insurance where two insurers are liable to indemnify the assured in the events which have happened. Reflecting the commercial reality and the practical understanding of insurers, the law treats the matter as if there were really only one insurance and the insurers are seen as co-obligants, each liable to bear a one-half share of the liability."[72]

Applying those principles to the facts of the particular case he commented:

". . . if, as I have held, both the insurers and the defenders in the present cases are under an obligation to indemnify the pursuers but, as between the defenders and the insurers, the defenders should bear the ultimate liability, then the insurers have a right to total relief from the defenders. It follows that the defenders have no corresponding right of relief against the insurers. In other words, the insurers are like the cautioner who can bring an action of relief to recover the whole of his expenditure from the principal debtor but is not subject to any obligation of relief towards the principal debtor."[73]

It may be added that this case serves to emphasise the distinction between the right to contribution, which is the insurer's own independent right of relief, and his or her right to subrogation, where he or she stands in the place of the insured to enforce the latter's right, in this case a right of indemnity.

### (iii) "Rateable proportion" clauses

As stated above, where the insured chooses to claim against a particular insurer, it is not open to that insurer to argue that other insurance policies have been taken out over the same risk in order to avoid full payment of the claim. He or she must meet the claim and only then proceed to claim a contribution from the other insurer. Contractual clauses, known as "rateable proportion" clauses, are used by insurers to avoid this result. Such a clause states that the insurer will only be liable for a rateable proportion of the insured's loss and no more. Assuming that each of the insurers insuring a specific risk has used such a clause, the burden then falls on the insured to claim the relevant proportion from each insurer. Despite having used a rateable proportion clause, the insurer may nevertheless pay the insured's claim in full, perhaps because the existence of further insurance was unknown to the insurer. If the insurer later becomes aware of other insurance, he or she may seek to recover a contribution from that insurer.

### (iv) Contribution where the second insurer is not liable to the insured

Difficulties may arise where the second insurer would have had a defence against paying out a claim to the insured. Does the existence of this defence mean that the first insurer will be unable to recover a contribution from the second insurer, or will a contribution be payable nevertheless? This specific question was considered in the case of *Legal and General Assurance Society Ltd v Drake Insurance Co Ltd*[74] in which a motorist had taken out two policies, both of which included clauses making it a condition precedent to liability that the insured notify the insurer of an incident which might give rise to a claim. When an accident did occur, the insured only notified and claimed against one insurer who paid out in full. There was thus a breach of the second insurance contract, namely the failure to provide that insurer with notice of the accident. It was held that, although the second insurer was not liable to the insured, the first insurer did have an enforceable right of contribution against the second insurer. The Court of

---

[72] *Caledonia North Sea Ltd v London Bridge Engineering Ltd,* 2000 S.L.T. 1123 at 1141–1142, *per* Lord President Rodger.
[73] *Caledonia North Sea Ltd v London Bridge Engineering Ltd,* 2000 S.L.T. 1123 at 1142, *per* Lord President Rodger.
[74] [1991] 2 Lloyd's Rep. 36.

Appeal appeared to base its decision on this point on equitable considerations. Their Lordships indicated that questions of contribution should be considered at the time of the loss. In their opinion, in this case, both insurers were potentially liable at the time of the loss.[75] The cover lapsed due to the failure of the insured to notify the second insurers of the accident. It follows that the cover could not lapse until after the loss had occurred. However, the second insurer was ultimately found not liable to make payment of any contribution. This was because the first insurer's policy contained a rateable proportion clause. Given that there were two insurance policies in force, the first insurer's liability was limited to one half of the loss. It is part of the principle of contribution that the first insurer who pays a claim must pay under a legal liability and not "voluntarily." Because the first insurer was considered to have paid the full amount "voluntarily," no contribution was payable by the second insurer. The first insurer was, however, able to recover some of the claim which it had paid out. It was entitled to reclaim one-half of its payment from the insured. This leads to the unusual result that an insured who has, effectively, paid two premiums ends up recovering only half of his or her loss.

The *Drake* decision was questioned in the later case of *Eagle Star Insurance Co v Provincial Insurance plc*.[76] In particular, doubt was cast on the suggestion that the relevant time for assessing questions of contribution was the time of the loss. The Privy Council suggested that the correct time for this assessment was the date of any judgment against the insurer who pays a claim to the insured. It does not, however, call into question the principle that the insurer claiming contribution must not pay a claim "voluntarily."

### (v) Clauses disclaiming liability where double insurance occurs

Insurance companies seek to avoid the problems of double insurance by using contractual terms which provide that, if the insured has taken out a second policy to cover the same risk as the first policy, the insurers are not liable under the first policy. However, both insurance policies may contain such a clause, which has the effect of leaving the insured with no cover whatsoever. This situation has been considered in several cases, most notably in *Weddell v Road Transport and General Insurance*.[77]

In the course of explaining why such clauses could not operate to deny the insured any cover, Rowlatt J. commented:

> "In my judgment it is unreasonable to suppose that it was intended that clauses such as these should cancel each other . . . with the result that, on the ground in each case that the loss is covered elsewhere, it is covered nowhere. On the contrary the reasonable construction is to exclude from the category of co-existing cover any cover which is expressed to be itself cancelled by such co-existence, and to hold in such cases that both companies are liable, subject of course in both cases to any rateable proportion clause which there may be."[78]

Although the motivation behind this decision is clear, the reasoning is less clear. Where Rowlatt J. refers to "intention" he is not referring to contractual intention, given that there is no contractual relationship between the two insurers. It may simply be that, as a matter of policy, the courts are not willing to allow the insured to be left without cover.

As might be expected, insurers developed amended exclusion clauses to avoid the result in *Weddell*. In *Steelclad Ltd v Iron Trades Mutual Insurance Co Ltd*[79] each of the policies contained the following clause:

---

[75] [1991] 2 Lloyd's Rep. 36 at 38, *per* Lloyd L.J.
[76] [1993] 3 All E.R. 1.
[77] [1932] 2 K.B. 563.
[78] [1932] 2 K.B. 563 at 567, *per* Rowlatt J.
[79] 1984 S.L.T. 304.

"The Company shall not be liable for any loss or damage which is insured *or would but for the existence of this policy* be insured by any other policy."[80]

Referring to the "critical words" of this clause Lord Stott commented:

"They would appear to have been expressly designed to meet this situation and to close the door to the escape route open to the court in *Weddell*."[81]

An Extra Division of the Inner House decided that the policies would not have cancelled one another out in any event because the wording of the relevant clause in one policy was not sufficiently wide to refer to the other policy. The court could, therefore, have avoided analysing the legal position where both policies use similar exclusion clauses. It did not, however, avoid the issue and, following *Weddell*,[82] indicated that such clauses would not cancel one another out. Lord Hunter explained:

"Each of these conditions, regarded separately, would appear to have a sensible and reasonable content. But when they co-exist they would, if applied absolutely literally, produce the absurd and inequitable result that the pursuers are not, and never at any time were, entitled to be indemnified under either policy . . . In that situation, I do not feel compelled to apply the absolutely literal construction . . ."[83]

## 7.8.   PROXIMATE CAUSE

The insurer will not be liable for the insured's losses unless those losses were actually caused by the risks insured against. However, as in other areas, in insurance law identifying the cause of a loss is a difficult exercise. In marine insurance in terms of the Marine Insurance Act 1906,[84] and in other types of insurance by virtue of the common law,[85] the court must identify the "proximate cause". Lord Shaw summed up the difficulties of the assessment of causation in *Leyland Shipping Co Ltd v Norwich Union Fire Insurance Society Ltd* as follows:

"The chain of causation is a handy expression, but the figure is inadequate. Causation is not a chain, but a net. At each point influences, forces, events, precedent and simultaneous, meet; and the radiation from each point extends infinitely. At the point where these various influences meet it is for the judgment as upon a matter of fact to declare which of the causes thus joined at the point of effect was the proximate and which was the remote cause. What does 'proximate' here mean? To treat proximate cause as if it was the cause which is proximate in time is, as I have said, out of the question. The cause which is truly proximate is that which is proximate in efficiency."[86]

Thus, the proximate cause is not necessarily the last cause or event. At this stage, as is apparent from the above quote, the practice was to select one cause as "the" proximate cause from a number of competing causes. In more recent times, it has been recognised that there may be

[80] Author's emphasis.

[81] *Steelclad Ltd v Iron Trades Mutual Insurance* [1983] S.L.T. 347 at 348, *per* Lord Stott.

[82] 1984 S.L.T. 304 at 307, *per* Lord Hunter and at 310, *per* Lord Robertson. See also Davidson, "Double Insurance Exclusion of Liability and Justice", (1986) 54 S.L.G. 3.

[83] 1984 S.L.T. 304 at 308, *per* Lord Hunter.

[84] Marine Insurance Act 1906, s.55(1).

[85] *Gray v Barr* [1971] 2 Q.B. 554 at 567, *per* Lord Denning M.R. and Salmon L.J. at 579; *Wayne Tank and Pump Co Ltd v Employers Liability Assurance Corporation Ltd* [1974] Q.B. 57 at 66, *per* Denning M.R.

[86] 1918 A.C. 350 at 369, *per* Lord Shaw. See also *Yorkshire Dale SS Co Ltd v Minister of War Transport* [1942] A.C. 691 at 706, *per* Lord Wright.

several concurrent proximate causes rather than one important proximate cause. Thus in *J. J. Lloyd Instruments Ltd v Northern Star Insurance Co Ltd*[87] the concurrent causes of the damage to a ship were found to be its unseaworthiness and adverse sea conditions, only the latter of which was a risk covered by the policy. The Court of Appeal took the view that, where there is no express exclusion of liability, the insured is entitled to recover where there are concurrent causes, at least one of which is an insured risk.[88] It follows from this approach, however, that where liability for one of the concurrent causes is excluded, the insurer will not be liable.[89]

Where human action is involved, it is assumed that such action and not the insured risk is the proximate cause of the loss. An exception to this principle occurs where human action has been taken to avoid the risk. An example of this exception is found in *Johnstone v West of Scotland Insurance Co*[90] where the house next door to the insured subjects was damaged by fire. A dangerously unstable gable which had been left standing was removed on the instructions of the Dean of Guild. During removal the gable fell on to the insured subjects and destroyed them. Even though the actual damage had been caused as a result of intentional human action, it was held that the proximate cause remained damage by fire. As this was insured under the policy, the insurers were held liable.

The wording of the actual policy may limit the insured's rights in this area. It is common for the policy either to stipulate that the damage must be caused "directly or indirectly" by the insured risk or exclude a proximate cause using this expression. In *Coxe v Employers' Liability Assurance Corp Ltd*[91] liability was excluded where death was directly or indirectly caused by war. The insured was hit by a train whilst walking along an unlit railway line on his way to inspect sentries guarding the line. It was held that, because he had been acting in pursuance of his military duties, his death had been indirectly caused by war, and that the insurers were not, therefore, liable.

## 7.9. PUBLIC POLICY

It is of the essence of insurance contracts that the insured cannot deliberately cause the loss insured against. As Lord Atkin explained:

> "The fire assured cannot recover if he intentionally burns down his house, nor the marine assured if he scuttles his ship, nor the life assured if he deliberately ends his own life. This is not the result of public policy, but of the correct construction of the contract."[92]

Public policy has a role in this area nevertheless. The insured may be prevented from recovering the insurance proceeds where the insured's act in seeking to cause the loss is criminal, immoral or contrary to public policy. The principles governing this area are those which normally apply to illegal contracts.[93] The insured is not entitled to profit from his or her own wrong.[94]

---

[87] [1987] 1 Lloyd's Rep. 32.

[88] Lawton L.J. describes this as "settled law," see *J. J. Lloyd Instruments Ltd v Northern Star Insurance Co Ltd* [1987] 1 Lloyd's Rep. 32 at 36.

[89] *Wayne Tank and Pump Co Ltd v Employers Liability Assurance Corporation Ltd* [1974] Q.B. 57.

[90] (1828) 7 S. 52.

[91] [1916] 2 K.B. 629.

[92] *Beresford v Royal Insurance Co* [1938] A.C. 586 at 595, *per* Lord Atkin. Although see the exceptional case of *Gordon v Rimmington* (1807) 1 Camp. 123. During the Napoleonic war, the captain of a ship set fire to her rather than allowing her to be captured by the French. The insurers were held liable to meet the insurance claim notwithstanding the captain's deliberate action in destroying the ship.

[93] L.J. Macgregor, "*Pacta Illicita*" in K. G. C. Reid and R. Zimmermann, (eds) *A History of Scottish Private Law* (2000), at 129.

[94] This principle is often expressed using the maxim *ex turpi causa non oritur actio*. If the act committed by the insured is actually criminal, the commission of that act need only be proved on the balance of probabilities and not beyond reasonable doubt: see *Sodden v Prudential Assurance Co Ltd*, 1999 S.C.L.R. 367.

In one of the most famous cases in this area, *Beresford v Royal Insurance Co*,[95] the insured committed suicide with the express purpose of obtaining for his personal representatives the benefit of five insurance policies. A clause of the policy provided that the policy would be void if the insured committed suicide within the period of one year from its commencement. The insured committed suicide after this period had elapsed. Lord Atkin indicated that there were two issues to be determined in such cases: firstly, the contract must be interpreted using normal principles of interpretation, and, secondly, the court should determine whether the contract was one which could be enforced in a court of law.[96] Although as a matter of construction of the insurance contract the insurers were bound to meet the claim,[97] the contract was not enforceable for reasons of public policy. He explained: " . . . the absolute rule is that the Courts will not recognize a benefit accruing to a criminal from his crime."[98]

In accordance with established principles relating to illegal contracts, illegal acts committed in the course of performance of an otherwise legal contract may not have the effect of denying the insured his claim.[99] If the insured has contravened a statute, the court will identify what it considers to be the purpose of that statute and determine whether enforcing the contract would be contrary to that purpose.[1]

## 7.10.  ASSIGNATION AND THIRD PARTY RIGHTS

The insurance policy forms a contract between the insured and the insurer and, therefore, normal rules of privity of contract prevent third parties who have suffered a loss caused by the conduct of the insured claiming under that policy. Not being parties to that contract, such third parties have no right to sue under the policy, even if the policy is taken out by the insured with the express purpose of covering such a liability. The Third Parties (Rights Against Insurers) Act 1930 acts to temper the strict operation of the rules of privity of contract. Before the passing of the Act, if the insured became bankrupt, the proceeds of any insurance policy would be paid to the insured's trustee in bankruptcy. It therefore formed part of the general assets to be distributed to the insured's creditors. The 1930 Act prevents the insurance proceeds from being dissipated in this way. In effect, it allows a third party who has a valid claim against an insured who has become bankrupt to proceed directly against the insurer.[2] It thus operates as a statutory assignation of the insured's rights under the insurance policy to the injured third party, giving that third party a preferred status in comparison with the insured's other general creditors.

Because the Act operates a statutory form of assignation, the third party can obtain no better right against the insurer than that of the original insured. The third party "stands in the shoes of" the insured in any action against the insurer. This principle leads to certain practical restrictions in the operation of the Act. The insured's liability to the third party must be established before the third party has any right under the Act.[3] Additionally, any defence which the insurer could have raised against the insured can similarly be raised against the third party.[4] However, the insurer is not barred from challenging the insured's liability to the third party

[95] [1938] A.C. 586.

[96] This approach is also adopted in *Gray v Barr* [1971] 2 Q.B. 554.

[97] [1938] A.C. 586 at 596, *per* Lord Atkin and at 602, *per* Lord MacMillan.

[98] [1938] A.C. 586 at 599, *per* Lord Atkin.

[99] See *Euro-Diam Ltd v Bathurst* [1990] 1 Q.B. 517, applying *St John's Shipping Corp v Joseph Rank Ltd* [1957] 1 Q.B. 267.

[1] *St John's Shipping Corp v Joseph Rank Ltd* [1957] 1 Q.B. 267, and see Davidson, "Unauthorised Insurers and Prohibited Contracts", 1986 J.R. p.38.

[2] Third Parties (Rights Against Insurers) Act 1930, s.1(1).

[3] *Saunders v Royal Insurance plc*, 1998 S.C.L.R. 1118.

[4] *Saunders v Royal Insurance plc*, 1998 S.C.L.R. 1118.

simply because the insurer decided not to defend the third party's action against the insured.[5] The Act has been interpreted as protecting the third party's rights only where he or she has suffered a loss through either the negligence of, or a breach of contract by, the insured.[6] It does not assist a third party who is seeking to claim professional fees, such as, for example, legal fees, under an insurance policy taken out by the insured.[7] These limitations were recognised in a recent joint consultation paper by the English and Scottish Law Commissions.[8] No legislation has, to date, implemented the recommendations of the Law Commissions.

Provided that the policy itself contains no prohibition on assignation, it is open to the insured to assign his or her interest in the insurance policy. Where the policy insures the life of the insured, it does not matter that the assignee has no insurable interest in the life of the insured.[9] This is because the insurable interest need only exist at the time when the insurance policy is taken out.[10] In indemnity insurance, however, the insured must have an insurable interest at the date of the loss. As a result, the subjects insured must also be assigned or transferred to the assignee so that the assignee can meet this requirement.

The assignee following assignation obtains no better right under the insurance policy than the insured.[11] An example of the operation of this principle can be seen in *Scottish Equitable Life Assurance Society v Buist*[12] in which the insured's actual state of health and his addiction to alcohol had not been disclosed to the insurers. The policy was then assigned before the insured died at the age of 30. Because the assignee could obtain no better right under the policy than the insured, the insurers were found entitled to avoid the assignee's claim for payment. It should be noted that, in common with other incorporeal rights, the insured, in addition to assigning his or her right to the policy, must intimate the assignation to the insurer.[13]

## 7.11.   THE UNFAIR TERMS IN CONSUMER CONTRACTS REGULATIONS 1999

Insurance contracts were not subject to the controls applied by the Unfair Contract Terms Act 1977.[14] Such contracts are, however, included within the ambit of the Unfair Terms in Consumer Contracts Regulations 1999.[15] A full discussion of the effect of the Regulations is outside the ambit of this chapter, but certain points can be made about their effect within an insurance context.

The Regulations only protect consumers, who are defined as natural persons not acting for the purposes of a trade, business or profession.[16] They are also aimed at standard form contracts, and so would embrace any term of an insurance contract which had not been individually negotiated.[17]

---

[5] *Cheltenham & Gloucester plc v Sun Alliance and London Insurance plc*, 2001 S.C.L.R. 671.

[6] *Tarbuck v Avon Insurance plc* [2001] 2 All E.R. 503.

[7] *Tarbuck v Avon Insurance plc* [2001] 2 All E.R. 503.

[8] *Third Parties (Rights Against Insurers) Act 1930*, (Law Commission Consultation Paper No. 272; Scottish Law Commission Consultation Paper No. 184, July 2002.).

[9] *Brownlee v Robb*, 1907 S.C. 1302.

[10] *Dalby v India & London Life Assurance Co* (1854) 15 C.B. 365.

[11] This is due to the operation of the principle *assignatus utitur jure auctoris*, or the assignee exercises the right of his or her cedent.

[12] (1877) 4 R. 1076.

[13] See *Strachan v McDougle* (1835) 13 S. 954 where an unintimated assignation was defeated by an arrestment.

[14] Unfair Contract Terms Act 1977, s.15(3)(a)(i).

[15] SI 1999/2083 as amended by the Unfair Terms in Consumer Contracts (Amendment) Regulations 2001, SI 2001/1186 (hereinafter "1999 Regulations") implementing Directive 93/13. See also the earlier implementation of the Directive in SI 1994/3159.

[16] 1999 Regulations, reg. 3(1).

[17] 1999 Regulations, reg. 5(1).

Two particular protections provided by the Regulations can be singled out as relevant in an insurance context. First, regulation 7 requires that any written term of the contract should be in plain and intelligible language, with any doubt as to interpretation being resolved in favour of the consumer.[18] The use of the word "plain" tends to suggest that such contracts should be intelligible to the normal lay-person. Insurance contracts often fall short of this standard, and it is the view of the Office of Fair Trading that a term which is obscure could be unfair for that reason alone.[19] Secondly, the terms of the contract are subjected to a fairness test under reg. 5. There are two exceptions to this protection.[20] The first provides that the fairness test does not apply to any term which concerns the adequacy of the price as against the services supplied. Thus, it would not be possible to assess the fairness of the premium in an insurance contract. Secondly, the fairness test does not apply to a term which defines the main subject-matter of the contract (unless it is not expressed in plain and intelligible language[21]). Some guidance on what would comprise the main subject matter of the contract in an insurance context can be drawn from recital 19 of the preamble to the Directive. It suggests that in insurance contracts ". . . terms which define or circumscribe the insured risk and the insurer's liability . . ." fall within the scope of that phrase. Thus, many of the most important terms of an insurance contract would not be subject to the fairness test. However, it is submitted that a "basis of the contract clause", which would allow an insurer to escape liability because of a non-material misstatement by the insured in the proposal form[22] is not such a term, and so is potentially subject to the Regulations. The same would be true of a term which deems every term of the contract to be material.[23] Somewhat surprsingly, the Office of Fair Trading has conceded that a term which excludes liability if the loss is covered by another policy[24] does define the risk.

A term is unfair if "contrary to the requirements of good faith, it causes a significant imbalance in the parties' rights and obligations arising under the contract, to the detriment of the consumer".[25] A term which is unfair is voidable at the consumer's instance.[26]

---

[18] See *Re Drake Insurance plc* [2001] Lloyd's Rep. I.R. 643.

[19] *Unfair Contract Terms Bulletin* No. 4, p.22; and see *Kindlance Ltd v Murphy,* 1997, unreported, High Court of Northern Ireland.

[20] 1999 Regulations, reg. 6(2).

[21] See *Pearl Assurance plc v Kavanagh,* 2001 C.L.Y. 3382.

[22] As in *Dawsons Ltd v Bonnin,* 1922 S.C. (H.L.) 156, discussed in para. 7.5.

[23] See the views of Lord Greene M.R. in *Zurich General Accident and Liability Insurance Co Ltd v Morrison* [1942] K.B. 53 at 58.

[24] As discussed in para. 7.8, under the heading of contribution, see OFT, *Unfair Contract Terms Bulletin* No. 5, p.116.

[25] 1999 Regulations, reg. 5(1). Terms will usually be unfair if they give the insurer an unfair advantage, see reg. 6(1) and Sch. 2.

[26] 1999 Regulations, reg. 8.

# Chapter 8

# PERSONAL INSOLVENCY

## 8.1. INTRODUCTION

This area of the law concerns itself with the sequestration of an insolvent debtor's estate—its removal and deposit in the hands of a neutral third person, its realisation and ultimate distribution amongst the creditors of the estate. This may occur, either through the granting of a voluntary trust deed for creditors, or through judicial sequestration—the process whereby an individual is made bankrupt, following an application to the court. The law in this area is mainly statutory, being governed by the Bankruptcy (Scotland) Act 1985 (as amended).

The Act, which largely gave effect to SLC Report No. 68 (1982) on "Bankruptcy and Related Aspects of Insolvency and Liquidation", represented a major revision and restatement of the Scots law of bankruptcy, repealing the Bankruptcy Acts of 1621 and 1695 and the Bankruptcy (Scotland) Act 1913. Among the reforms introduced by the Act were:

(1) the introduction of the office of interim trustee, with an interim trustee requiring to be appointed in every judicial sequestration;

(2) the requirement that a permanent trustee be appointed or elected in every judicial sequestration;

(3) the requirement that trustees be qualified insolvency practitioners;

(4) the making available of funds from the public purse to meet the expenses of judicial sequestration, where the estate was insufficient to meet these;

(5) the removal of the requirement for public examination of the debtor;

(6) the imposition of certain restraints on the permanent trustee's power to sell the family home;

(7) the introduction of new rules regarding gratuitous alienations and unfair preferences;

(8) the automatic discharge of the debtor three years after the date of sequestration (unless a deferment were granted);

(9) the introduction of the concept of the protected trust deed.

The Act itself, however, was subject to significant reform within 10 years of coming into effect, through the agency of the Bankruptcy (Scotland) Act 1993. The main reason for this second measure was the unforeseen consequences of reforms designed to remove much of the stigma from bankruptcy, together with the provision of public funding to meet trustees' fees and outlays where the assets of the estate were insufficient for that task. This meant that whereas before there was little point in seeking to sequestrate a debtor who had very few assets, it suddenly became a very attractive option—at least for insolvency practitioners. The availability of the trust deed route to sequestration, also made it a very straightforward option, in that a debtor could sign a trust deed and the trustee could immediately petition for sequestration without involving a creditor. Thus a totally unexpected explosion in the number of sequestrations resulted, with a staggering increase in the cost to the public purse. The 1993 Act then addressed these problems by:

(a) making it possible for the Accountant in Bankruptcy to act as interim and/or permanent trustee and effectively ensuring that he will be so appointed in most cases where the estate is insufficient to meet the expenses of sequestration. In this way, greater public control is exercised over the cost of sequestration process;

(b) the creation of a new scheme for summary administration of small estates, whereby a streamlined and thus less costly procedure may be followed;

(c) the imposition of greater restrictions on the right of a trustee under a trust deed to petition for sequestration;

(d) making it more difficult for debtors to seek sequestration without the concurrence of creditors;

(e) making it easier for debtors to seek sequestration via the device of the protected trust deed, in the hope that there would be more resort to this route, avoiding the costs and procedural complexities of judicial sequestration.

This chapter will consider the process of sequestration under the Act. At the time of writing, the Act is due to be amended in a peripheral way by the Insolvency Scotland Regulations 2003. The Regulations intend to bring the law better into line with the EC Insolvency Regulation 1346/2000 on cross border insolvency proceedings. It will be assumed that the 2003 Regulations are in force. The E.C. Regulation has direct effect in all Member States, so that its provisions have the force of law in Scotland, and the Act has to be read subject thereto.

A detailed examination of the provisions of the Regulations is beyond the scope of this work. However, they contemplate that although the main insolvency proceedings can only be held in the Member State where the debtor has the "centre of his main interests" (his domicile or main place of business), secondary proceedings may be held in any state where he has an establishment, and are restricted to assets in that state. The sequestration process described in this chapter may thus constitute the main insolvency proceedings or secondary proceedings, depending on where the debtor has the centre of his main interests. While generally anyone who is entitled to request the opening of such secondary proceedings under the law of that state may still do so, only creditors who are established in that state or whose claims arise from the operation of that establishment can instigate such proceedings. The liquidator (a trustee in bankruptcy would qualify to be regarded as a liquidator) in the main proceedings may also request such proceedings. The liquidator in the secondary proceedings may recover assets taken to another Member State after his appointment, but is otherwise confined to acting within his own state. However, the main proceedings will be effective in every Member State, and the liquidator therein will be able to act in every such state, requiring only a certified copy of his appointment. He is entitled to publish public notice of his appointment, and register it in any public register. If there are already secondary proceedings in operation when he is appointed, he cannot override such proceedings, but may participate in them. Indeed, he may request that those proceedings or the process of realisation therein be stayed. He may also propose composition in those proceedings, or request that proceedings which fall short of sequestration, be converted to full sequestration proceedings. Liquidators are bound to communicate and co-operate with each other, and the liquidator in any secondary proceedings must give the liquidator in the main proceedings an early opportunity to submit proposals. Any surplus in secondary proceedings must be transferred to the main proceedings. A creditor based in a Member State may make a claim in any other, and must be notified of any proceedings and associated legal requirements. He may claim in his own language, although he may be required to provide a translation, and must provide any necessary supporting information and documentation. In Scottish proceedings, if a trustee has to give notice to or provide a copy of a document to the court or the Accountant in Bankruptcy, the trustee shall give such notice or copies to any Member State liquidator appointed in relation to the debtor.[1]

## 8.2. THE ACCOUNTANT IN BANKRUPTCY

Before examining the rules governing judicial sequestration, it is worth noting the role of an official who guarantees some degree of public oversight of the process. The Office of Accountant in Bankruptcy was created in 1856, and from 1889 to 1993 was coincident with that of Accountant of Court. The two offices are now separate, testifying to the increased significance of the office following the 1993 Act. The functions of this official are as follows[2] (all references are to the 1985 Act, as amended):

- the supervision of the performance of those involved in the sequestration process;
- the maintenance of a register of insolvencies;
- the preparation of an annual report;
- the reporting of suspected offences to the Lord Advocate.

### (a) Supervisory role of the accountant

The Accountant supervises the performance of interim and permanent trustees and of commissioners. This is not generally a directive role, although in cases where a certificate of summary administration has been granted, he may give directions to the permanent trustee.[3] He issues "Notes for Guidance for Interim and Permanent Trustees", and occasionally updates these notes (the latest edition is 1999.). These notes provide checklists of documents to be sent to him by interim and permanent trustees. The Accountant investigates complaints against interim and permanent trustees and commissioners. Where he takes the view that anyone subject to his supervision has failed without reasonable excuse to perform any duty, he shall report the matter to the court, which may remove the individual from office or impose another appropriate sanction.[4] If he has reasonable grounds to suspect that anyone subject to his

---

[1] s.48A(2).
[2] See Bankruptcy (Scotland) Act 1985, s.1A.
[3] Sch. 2A, para. 3.
[4] s.1A(2).

supervision has committed an offence, he must report the matter to the Lord Advocate.[5] The Accountant does not supervise the performance of trustees under trust deeds.

### (b) The accountant as interim/permanent trustee

An important innovation introduced by the 1993 Act is that where a nominated trustee is not appointed as interim trustee (see para. 8.9.), the court shall appoint the Accountant to act as interim trustee.[6] (It is also possible for the Accountant to act as permanent trustee.) Needless to say, the Accountant may delegate any of his functions to his staff or in relation to "his functions in respect of the sequestration of the estate of any debtor" may appoint agents.[7] Thus he may sub-contract the conduct of certain sequestrations to qualified insolvency practitioners for a fixed fee.

## 8.3.　WHO CAN BE SEQUESTRATED?

The following categories of entity may be sequestrated in terms of ss.5 to 6 of the Act:

- living debtors[8];
- deceased debtors;
- trusts;
- partnerships and limited partnerships, including in both cases dissolved partnerships;
- bodies corporate, but not companies under the Companies Acts;
- unincorporated bodies, *e.g.* clubs and trade unions.

## 8.4.　WHO CAN PETITION FOR SEQUESTRATION?

### (a) Living debtors

Who can petition for the sequestration of a debtor? The possibilities are the debtor himself, if certain conditions are met (see the next sub-paragraph), or a qualified creditor or qualified creditors if the debtor is apparently insolvent (see below), or the trustee under a trust deed, if certain conditions are met (see below).[9] A qualified creditor is someone who, at the date of presentation of the petition, is owed at least £1,500, while qualified creditors are at that date in aggregate owed at least £1,500.[10] Contingent or future debts or amounts payable under confiscation orders do not count.[11] Additionally in insolvencies with a cross border element, a petition may also be brought by a temporary administrator[12] (within the meaning of Art. 38 of

---

[5] s.1A(3).
[6] s.2(6).
[7] s.1B.
[8] Debtors must be sequestrated individually, unless one is sequestrating a firm or association. It is therefore not competent to bring a single petition to sequestrate spouses who are not in partnership: *Campbell v Dunbar,* 1989 S.L.T. (Sh. Ct) 29.
[9] s.5(2).
[10] s.5(4). In determining whether the £1,500 threshold is reached, interest and the expenses of doing diligence are both taken into account: *Arthur v SMT Sales and Service Co Ltd,* 1999 S.C. 109.
[11] *ibid.*
[12] s.5(2)(ba).

the EC Insolvency Regulation 1346/2000) or by a liquidator[13] (within the meaning of Art. 3(1) of that Regulation).

It should also be noted that the Debt Arrangement and Attachment (Scotland) Act 2002 creates a national debt arrangement scheme to enable multiple debts to be paid in accordance with a debt arrangement programme over a period of time. This witnesses a debtor, having obtained the advice of a money adviser, applying to the Scottish Ministers for approval of a debt arrangement programme.[14] No creditor may found on any debt owed by a debtor whose debts are being paid under an approved debt arrangement programme in presenting or concurring in the presentation of a petition for sequestration.[15] This relates not only to debts covered by the programme, but to any other debt, provided the creditor has received proper notice of the approval of the debt arrangement programme.[16]

## (b) Petitions by the debtor

What are the conditions under which a debtor may petition for his own sequestration? A debtor[17] can always petition with the concurrence of a qualified creditor or qualified creditors[18]—but see the previous sub-paragraph re the limitation imposed by the Debt Arrangement and Attachment (Scotland) Act 2002. The requirement of agreement by a significant creditor or body of creditors offers some safeguard against the debtor petitioning against the interests of his creditors. Alternatively, the debtor may petition without such concurrence if,[19]:

(1) he owes at least £1,500 at the date of presentation of the petition; *and*
(2) sequestration has not been awarded against him during the previous five years (to guard against the, possibly mythical, individual who employs serial, self-arranged sequestration as a means of escaping from his debts); *and*
(3) he is either apparently insolvent (see para. 8.5.); or he has handed over his estate to a trustee under a voluntary trust deed for the benefit of his creditors, and the trustee has tried unsuccessfully to make the trust deed protected (see para. 8.38).

The culmination of these conditions aims, once again, to protect against debtors petitioning against the interests of their creditors.

## (c) Petitions by a trustee under a voluntary trust deed

As an alternative to sequestration, a debtor can seek to place his estate in trust for the benefit of his creditors. However, such an arrangement may not work as well as hoped. So the trustee can petition if either the debtor has failed to comply with an obligation under the trust deed with which he could reasonably have complied, or with any instruction or requirement reasonably given to or made of him by the trustee for the purposes of the trust deed.[20] Alternatively, the trustee can petition simply on the basis that it would be in the best interest of the creditors that sequestration be awarded.[21]

---

[13] s.5(2)(bb).
[14] See Debt Arrangement and Attachment (Scotland) Act 2002, ss.2–3.
[15] s.4(3).
[16] s.4(5).
[17] It has been held that it is incompetent for someone with power of attorney to sign for the debtor, and it was doubted whether any mandatory could be authorised to apply for sequestration: *Toni, Petitioner,* 2002 S.L.T. (Sh. Ct) 159.
[18] Bankruptcy (Scotland) Act 1985, s.5(2A).
[19] s.5(2B).
[20] s.5(2C)(a).
[21] s.5(2C)(b).

## (d) Deceased debtors

If it is sought to sequestrate the estate of a deceased debtor, the petition may be made by[22]:

- the executor or a person entitled to be appointed as such; or
- a qualified creditor or qualified creditors;
- or the trustee under a voluntary trust deed.

As sequestration in these circumstances may simply be a means of paying off creditors on the estate, if an executor or trustee petitions, it is not necessary that the debtor is insolvent, and the petition may be presented at any time.[23] Nor is there any need to show insolvency when a qualified creditor or qualified creditors petition at least six months after the debtor's death.[24] However if a qualified creditor or qualified creditors petition before that date, the debtor must have been apparently insolvent within the four months prior to his death.[25]

## (e) Trusts

If it is sought to sequestrate a trust, the petition may be made by[26]:

- a majority of the trustees with the concurrence of a qualified creditor or qualified creditors, or
- a qualified creditor or qualified creditors if the trustees are apparently insolvent.

## (f) Partnerships

If it is sought to sequestrate a partnership or limited partnership, the petition may be made by[27]:

- the partnership itself with the concurrence of a qualified creditor or qualified creditors; (The Partnership Act 1890, s.24(8), states that while ordinary matters connected with the partnership business can be decided by a majority of the partners, no change in the nature of that business can be made without the consent of all existing partners. Thus in the absence of special agreement in the partnership deed, such a step would require the assent of all partners); or
- a qualified creditor or qualified creditors, if the firm has been apparently insolvent within the four months prior to the petition.

## (g) Bodies corporate or unincorporated

If it is sought to sequestrate a body corporate or unincorporated body, the petition may be made by[28]:

- a person authorised to act on its behalf with the concurrence of a qualified creditor or qualified creditors; or
- a qualified creditor if the body has been apparently insolvent within the four months prior to the petition.

---

[22] s.5(3).
[23] s.8(3)(a).
[24] s.8(3)(b)(ii).
[25] s.8(3)(b)(i).
[26] s.6(3).
[27] s.6(4).
[28] s.6(6).

## 8.5. APPARENT INSOLVENCY

It will have been seen above that in a number of circumstances a petition is only competent if the debtor has been "apparently insolvent". The term insolvency has a number of meanings. So-called absolute insolvency arises where the debtor's total liabilities exceed his total assets. It is entirely possible for someone to be in this condition for a considerable period of time without evident financial difficulty, as an individual may be able to pay his debts as they fall due, while suffering from significant underlying insolvency. Absolute insolvency does not lead directly to sequestration, although it is not without legal significance in this context, as it is a pre-condition for common law challenges to gratuitous alienations and fraudulent preferences (see para. 8.23). Simple or practical insolvency occurs when a debtor is unable to pay his debts as they fall due. It may arise merely because the debtor is facing liquidity problems, and so is not necessarily indicative of absolute insolvency, although the two can obviously co-exist. Simple insolvency is not the same thing as apparent insolvency, although it often quickly leads to apparent insolvency. Simple insolvency is what is required for the exercise of the possessory remedies of unpaid sellers under the Sale of Goods Act 1979. By contrast, apparent insolvency is a term of art created by the 1985 Act to describe a number of situations which are broadly indicative of serious financial problems on the part of the debtor, and which thus may be regarded as establishing a *prima facie* case for sequestration. Thus for the debtor apparent insolvency can be constituted by any of the following circumstances[29]:

(1) Actually being sequestrated—where a petition is presented by a debtor with the concurrence of a qualified creditor, it is possible that he may not have been apparently insolvent before that point.

(2) Being adjudged bankrupt in England, Wales or Northern Ireland.

(3) Giving notice to his creditors that he has ceased to pay his debts in the ordinary course of business.

(4) Granting a voluntary trust deed for his creditors. (But where the debtor petitions for his own sequestration without the concurrence of a qualified creditor or qualified creditors, neither (3) or (4) is indicative of apparent insolvency.[30] This provision is clearly designed to prevent a debtor arranging his own sequestration via a self created act of apparent insolvency.

(5) Being served with a charge for payment and the expiry of the days of charge (14) without payment. A charge is a formal requisition of payment served by a sheriff officer.

(6) Allowing 14 days to elapse without payment following the attachment or seizure of moveables in pursuance of a summary warrant for the recovery of rates or taxes, Attachment is a new form of diligence which is introduced by s.10 of the Debt Arrangement and Attachment (Scotland) Act 2002 to replace poinding, and which sees corporeal moveables owned by the debtor frozen in his own hands prior to possible removal and auction. It has been held that an arrestment of wages does not amount to a seizure of moveables.[31]

(7) A decree of adjudication being granted on any part of his estate. Adjudication is a form of diligence whereby heritable property owned by the debtor is vested in a creditor via a decree granted by the Court of Session until redeemed by payment of the debt.

(8) The selling of his effects under a sequestration for rent. Sequestration for rent is a type of diligence to recover rent. It takes the form of a sheriff court action and may ultimately lead to the sale of the tenant's property.

---

[29] s.7(1).
[30] s.5(2B)(c).
[31] *Mackay Petr,* 1996 S.C.L.R. 1091.

(9) The making of a receiving order against him in England or Wales.

The fact that diligence is being done on the estate is usually a good indicator of insolvency, but diligence is not invariably attributable to insolvency, such as where diligence results from a stubborn refusal to pay a particular debt. Similarly, although a solvent debtor would not normally grant a voluntary trust deed for his creditors, this may occasionally happen, *e.g.* as a safeguard against a debtor's improvidence. Therefore, none of the circumstances outlined in (4) to (9) create apparent insolvency, if it can be shown that the debtor was able and willing to pay his debts as they fell due, or would have been so willing but for being subject to a restraint, confiscation or charging order.

    (10) a creditor in respect of a liquid debt of at least £750 (or an aggregate of liquid debts amounting to at least that sum) having served on the debtor by personal service via an officer of the court, a notice in prescribed form[32] requiring him either to pay the debt of find security for its payment, and three weeks having expired from that service without payment being made, or the debtor intimating to the creditor by recorded delivery that he denies that there is a debt or that the sum claimed is immediately payable.

A debt is liquid when the amount is settled and it is immediately payable. The three week time period is strictly enforced, even though it may bear harshly on ordinary individuals, and a debtor who fails to record his objection as required may find that he is precluded from challenging the liquidity of the debt.[33] The prescribed form of notice demands that clear evidence of the existence of the debt be attached thereto. If this is not done, the debtor's apparent insolvency is not properly constituted, and sequestration as a result may not be competent.[34] It has also been held that the effect of serving a notice under this provision prevents that creditor seeking sequestration under (5).[35]

    Under (1) and (2) the debtor's apparent insolvency continues until his discharge, while otherwise it continues until he becomes able to pay his debts and pays them as they become due.[36]

    A partnership may be apparently insolvent either through its own apparent insolvency, or through the apparent insolvency of a partner for a debt of the firm.[37] An unincorporated body may be apparently insolvent if, in respect of a debt of the body, someone representing the body or someone holding its property as a fiduciary is apparently insolvent.[38]


## 8.6.   THE MECHANICS OF A PETITION

The first thing to be asked is whether the Scots courts have jurisdiction to award sequestration. They will have jurisdiction if the debtor habitually resided or had an established place of business in Scotland during the year prior to the presentation of the petition or the death of the debtor.[39] As regards a firm, body corporate, or unincorporated body, it must either have had an established place of business in Scotland during the year prior to the presentation of the petition, or have been constituted or formed under Scots law and at any time carried on business in Scotland.[40] The latter criterion allows the sequestration in Scotland of an entity

---

[32] Bankruptcy (Scotland) Regulations 1985, SI 1985/1925, Form 1.
[33] *Guthrie Newspaper Group v Gordon*, 1992 G.W.D. 22–1244.
[34] *Lord Advocate v Thomson*, 1994 S.C.L.R. 96.
[35] *Unity Trust Bank v Ahmed*, 1993 S.C.L.R. 53.
[36] s.7(2).
[37] s.7(3)(a).
[38] s.7(3)(b).
[39] s.9(1) and (4).
[40] s.9(2).

which no longer operates in Scotland, or which has long ceased to operate at all. Where a Scots court has jurisdiction to sequestrate a firm, then it also has jurisdiction to sequestrate any partner thereof, even though it might not otherwise have jurisdiction over him[41] In the case of a limited partnership, an extra requirement is that it must be registered in Scotland.[42] A petition must state, so far as this is within the petitioner's knowledge, whether the debtor has his main place of business in another state, and if the petitioner is aware that a liquidator has been appointed in relation to the debtor in another Member State, he must send a copy of the petition to that liquidator.[43] Business means the carrying on of any activity, whether for profit or not,[44] so that "place of business" will have a much wider meaning than might be anticipated. A petition may be presented to the Court of Session or the sheriff court in any sheriffdom where the residence or place of business is situated.[45] The provisions as to jurisdiction are now subject to EC Insolvency Regulation 1346/2000.

The petitioner must send a copy to the Accountant on the day of presentation of the petition,[46] and if this is not done sequestration cannot be granted.[47] Additionally, when the debtor is a petitioner he must present a statement of assets and liabilities along with the petition, and furnish the Accountant with a copy of this statement along with the copy of the petition.[48] Again, failure in this obligation will prevent the petition being granted,[49] while if the debtor without reasonable excuse:

(1) fails to send the statement to the Accountant; or
(2) fails to disclose a material fact therein; or
(3) makes a material misstatement therein,

he commits a criminal offence.[50]

## 8.7. THE AWARD OF SEQUESTRATION

When the preconditions for sequestration are met, it must be awarded "forthwith", the court having no discretion in the matter.[51] Obviously, if there is doubt as to whether those preconditions are indeed met, or whether a defence to the petition has been established, and some enquiry has to be made into the facts, the proceedings may be continued or even sisted, despite the requirement that the award be made "forthwith".[52] Moreover, in *Chris Hart Business Sales Ltd v Campbell*[53] the petition was not granted in light of an interim interdict preventing the petitioner seeking the debtor's sequestration.

### (a) Petition presented by debtor

Where a petition is presented by a debtor the court will make the award unless cause is shown why sequestration cannot competently be awarded, and shall make the award if satisfied[54]:

---

[41] s.9(3).
[42] Bankruptcy (Scotland) Regulations 1985, SI 1985/1925, para. 12(3).
[43] s.6A.
[44] s.73.
[45] s.9(1) and (4).
[46] s.5(6); but see *Scottish & Newcastle Breweries plc v Harvey-Rutherford,* 1994 S.L.T (Sh. Ct) 61.
[47] s.12(1) and (3).
[48] s.5(6A).
[49] s.12(1).
[50] s.5(9).
[51] See *e.g. Sales Lease Ltd v Minty,* 1993 S.L.T. (Sh. Ct) 52 at 54.
[52] s.12(1) and see *e.g. Royal Bank of Scotland plc v Forbes,* 1988 S.L.T. 76.
[53] 1993 S.C.L.R 383.
[54] s.12(1).

(1)  that the petition has been presented in accordance with the provisions of the Act;
(2)  that the requirements relating to copies of the petition and the statement of assets and liabilities (discussed in the previous paragraph) have been fulfilled;
(3)  that either of the conditions permitting a debtor to petition without the concurrence of a creditor (as described in para. 8.4.) are satisfied.

## (b) Petition presented by creditor/trustee

Where the petition is presented by the creditor or a trustee the court shall make the award if satisfied[55]:

(1)  that if the debtor has not appeared, proper citation has been made, (In such cases the debtor will be cited to appear before the court to show cause why sequestration should not be granted[56]);
(2)  that the petition has been presented in accordance with the provisions of the Act;
(3)  that the requirements relating to copies of the petition are satisfied;
(4)  in the case of a creditor, the requirements as to apparent insolvency have been fulfilled;
(5)  in the case of a trustee, that the matters averred in his petition are true (see *Petitions by A Trustee Under a Voluntary Trust Deed* under para. 8.4.).

However sequestration will not be awarded if either[57]:

(a)  cause is shown why it is not competent, or
(b)  the debtor forthwith pays or satisfies the debt in respect of which he became apparently insolvent and any other debt he owes to the petitioner and any concurring creditor (or produces written evidence of payment/satisfaction, or gives or shows sufficient security for such debt(s)).

As regards showing sufficient security for a debt, in *Clydesdale Bank plc v Grantly Developments*[58] the firm sought to resist the petition presented by the bank on the basis that the bank already held standard securities over the property of the firm. Lord Nimmo-Smith reacted as follows[59]:

> "I have found some difficulty in following this argument. [T]he Act makes it clear that the debtor can only escape an award of sequestration if he forthwith . . . pays the debt or gives or shows that there is sufficient security for the *payment* of the debt . . . [A] standard security is only sufficient security if it is capable of realisation forthwith and will accordingly result in payment of the whole debt without undue delay."

Again in *Commissioners of the Customs and Excise v Zaoui*[60] Lord Prosser stated:

> "The sufficiency of any security must be demonstrated to the satisfaction of the court *forthwith*. I think the word can be read as having somewhat more scope than the word "immediately", but I cannot envisage it as covering more than a matter of days . . . Once a debtor appears before the court to show cause why sequestration should not be awarded, the statute requires him to do so at that hearing, although perhaps with some brief deferment or continuation. More fundamentally . . . I am satisfied that the offering of security is not the giving of security."

It is obviously possible for petitions to be presented in respect of the same debtor in different sheriffdoms, or in a sheriffdom and the Court of Session, or indeed by different individuals in

---

[55] s.12(3).
[56] s.12(2).
[57] s.12(3)A.
[58] 2000 S.C.L.R 711.
[59] at 777F–778A.
[60] 2001 S.L.T. 201 at 206C–D.

the same sheriffdom. If the debtor, or anyone petitioning for sequestration (or concurring in that petition) becomes aware that another such petition is before a court, or sequestration has been awarded, or analogous proceedings are under way, he must bring that to the notice of the court as soon as possible.[61] Failure to do so might lead to that individual being made liable for the expenses of the petition, or in the case of the debtor to a criminal conviction.[62] The court may then of its own motion, or at the instance of an interested party, allow the petition to proceed or sist or dismiss it.[63] Additionally, the Court of Session has the power, of its own motion, or at the instance of an interested party, to order that petitions be heard together, or to direct a sheriff to sist or dismiss a petition.[64]

### (c) Date of sequestration

Where the debtor presents the petition, the date of sequestration will be the date of the award.[65] Where a creditor or trustee presents, the date will be the date on which the court grants warrant to cite the debtor.[66] Where more than one warrant is granted, the date of the first will be the date[67] It is vitally important to know the date of sequestration, as many of the consequences of sequestration operate from, or by reference to that date.[68]

## 8.8. RECALL OF SEQUESTRATION

While a petitioner or a concurring creditor may appeal against the refusal to award sequestration, a decision to award sequestration is not subject to appeal.[69] However, in certain circumstances the award may be recalled. A petition for recall must be presented to the Court of Session, and may be presented by the debtor, any creditor or other person having an interest, the interim or permanent trustee, or the Accountant.[70] The court may recall the award if it is satisfied that in all the circumstances, including those arising after sequestration, it is appropriate to do so.[71] This clearly gives the court considerable discretion, and Lord Prosser has suggested that recall should be granted if it can be done "without apparent prejudice to creditors".[72] However, given that there are generally good reasons why sequestration was granted in the first place, this may be difficult to establish.[73] The Act lists three specific grounds on which sequestration may be recalled, without prejudice to the court's general power to recall. These are[74]:

- The debtor has paid his debts in full or provided sufficient security for their payment. It would not be sufficient for the debtor to aver that such payment could be made or security be provided.[75]

---

[61] s.10(1).
[62] *ibid.*
[63] s.10(3)(a).
[64] s.10(3)(b).
[65] s.12(4)(a).
[66] s.12(4)(b).
[67] *ibid.*
[68] See McBryde, *Bankruptcy* (2nd ed., 1995), para. 5.03.
[69] s.15(3)–(4).
[70] s.16(1).
[71] s.17(1).
[72] *Button v Royal Bank of Scotland plc,* 1987 G.W.D. 27–1019.
[73] See, *e.g. Grantly Developments v Clydesdale Bank plc,* 2002 G.W.D. 11–339, where an Extra Division held that it was not a good ground for recall that the debtor insisted that he had no assets, this being a matter which the process of sequestration was designed to ascertain.
[74] s.17(1)–(2).
[75] *Martin v Martin's Tr.,* 1994 S.L.T. 461.

- The majority in value of the creditors reside in a country other than Scotland, and it is more appropriate that the debtor's estate be administered there.
- One or more other awards of sequestration of the estate or analogous awards have been granted.—Where a petition is presented in such a case, the court may decide to recall the other award(s).

Where recall is sought under any of these three specific grounds, no time limit applies to the presentation of the petition, although the deeper into the process presentation is made, the less likely the petition is to be granted.[76] Otherwise, the petition must be presented within 10 weeks of the award of sequestration,[77] although in cases where justice so demands the court may allow presentation beyond that period through exercising the *nobile officium*.[78]

The court may refuse to recall the award, or order that the sequestration continue subject to such conditions as it thinks fit.[79] Recall restores the debtor and any other person affected by the sequestration so far as possible to the same position he would have been in had sequestration not been awarded,[80] and the court has the power to make any order necessary to achieve this.[81] Nonetheless, if a period of prescription was interrupted by the presentation of the petition for sequestration, the recall of an award does not affect that interruption.[82] Nor does the recall invalidate any transaction entered into prior to the recall by the interim or permanent trustee with a person acting in good faith.[83] The court on recall must make provision for payment of the outlays and remuneration of the interim and (where relevant) the permanent trustee. It may either direct that the payment be made out of the debtor's estate or require the petitioner for sequestration to pay.[84] It may also direct that payment of the expenses of a petitioning or concurring creditor be made out of the debtor's estate.[85] The question of whether the court could impose a personal liability on the debtor to pay the outlays and remuneration of the permanent trustee, should his estate be inadequate for that purpose, was considered in *Hall v Crawford*[86] The majority of the court took the view that it was not open to the court to impose personal liability in terms of s.17(3)(a), although it was also thought[87] that the court's power under s.17(3)(c) to make such further order as it considers necessary and reasonable would entitle it to impose such liability. Lord Marnoch opined[88]:

> "the real 'moral' to be derived from the case is that a trustee should impose a motion for recall of sequestration unless and until he is satisfied that . . . he will be in a position to pay for his outlays and remuneration 'out of' the funds in his hands, or alternatively that he has made some other secure arrangement for their payment."

In addition to the provisions outlined above, a non-entitled spouse who has occupancy rights in the matrimonial home under the Matrimonial Homes (Family Protection) (Scotland) Act 1981 may apply for a recall on the basis that the purpose of the sequestration was wholly or mainly to defeat those occupancy rights.[89] The 1981 Act confers occupancy rights upon a spouse who is not permitted or entitled to occupy the matrimonial home, and s.41 gives the right of recall to such a spouse, in order to deal with the possibility that the other spouse might seek to thwart

---

[76] *Van Overwaele v Hacking and Paterson*, 2002 S.C. 62.
[77] s.16(4).
[78] *Wright v Tennent Caledonian Breweries Ltd*, 1991 S.L.T. 823.
[79] s.17(6).
[80] s.17(4).
[81] s.17(3)(c).
[82] s.17(5)(a).
[83] s.17(5)(b).
[84] s.17(3)(a).
[85] s.17(3)(b).
[86] 2002 S.C.L.R. 464.
[87] See Lord Marnoch at 472B.
[88] at 472B-C.
[89] s.41(1).

those rights by arranging for his own sequestration. A permanent trustee must intimate the sequestration to any such non-entitled spouse within 14 days of the issue of the act and warrant.[90] The non-entitled spouse may then petition for recall within 40 days of the issue of the act and warrant (see previous paragraph) or 10 weeks of the award of sequestration. The court may instead of granting recall make any other order as it thinks fit to protect the occupancy rights.[91]

It remains theoretically possible for the Court of Session to exercise its common law power to reduce an award of sequestration, but it would not be appropriate if recall were competent, and it is difficult to imagine a situation where reduction would be appropriate, but recall would not be available.[92] It will not be considered if the petitioner has allowed a significant period of time to elapse.[93]

# (1) THE SEQUESTRATION PROCESS

## 8.9. APPOINTMENT OF THE INTERIM TRUSTEE

The first step in any sequestration will be the appointment of the interim trustee to take over the administration of the debtor's estate. Normally the petition will nominate the interim trustee, and the court under s.2(1) will usually appoint that person if he fulfils the following conditions[94]:

- is resident within the jurisdiction of the Court of Session;
- is a qualified insolvency practitioner;
- has given a written undertaking to act as interim trustee, and where no permanent trustee is elected, as permanent trustee.

Where the petition is presented by a creditor or trustee then the court may appoint an interim trustee before sequestration is awarded, provided that the debtor consents or cause is shown,[95] e.g. the need to safeguard the estate.

In all cases if no interim trustee is appointed as described above, the court will appoint the Accountant to act as interim trustee.[96] In cases where it is obvious that the available assets will be insufficient even to meet the outlays and remuneration of the interim trustee, it is most unlikely that a private insolvency practitioner would be willing to accept nomination. In such cases the Accountant will inevitably be appointed.

Where the interim trustee dies in office, the court will appoint a new interim trustee, on the application of the debtor, a creditor or the Accountant.[97] An interim trustee (not the Accountant) who wishes to resign may apply to the court for authority to do so, and the court shall grant such an application if it is satisfied[98]:

(1) that, for whatever reason, legal or practical, he is unable to act, or
(2) that he has so conducted himself that he should no longer continue to act.

The interim trustee may also be removed by the court on either of the above grounds on the application of the debtor, a creditor or the Accountant,[99] or following upon a report to the

---

[90] *ibid.*
[91] s.41(1)(b)(ii).
[92] *Wright v Tennent Caledonian Breweries Ltd,* 1991 S.L.T. 823.
[93] *Arthur v SMT Sales and Service Co Ltd,* 1999 S.C. 109: 12 years after the award of sequestration.
[94] s.2(3).
[95] s.2(5).
[96] s.2(2), (6)(b).
[97] s.13(5).
[98] s.13(2)–(3).
[99] *ibid.*

court by the Accountant that he has failed to perform any of his duties without reasonable excuse.[1] In the last case, the court shall appoint a replacement on the application of the Accountant.[2] Otherwise, it will automatically appoint a replacement.[3]

## 8.10.   THE FUNCTIONS OF THE INTERIM TRUSTEE

The interim trustee is there essentially to look after the estate until a permanent trustee is appointed to carry through the sequestration process to its conclusion. His formal functions are[4]:

(1)  to safeguard the estate pending the appointment of a permanent trustee;
(2)  to ascertain the reasons for the debtor's insolvency and the circumstances surrounding it;
(3)  to ascertain the state of the debtor's liabilities and assets (to this end the debtor must supply the trustee with a statement of his assets and liabilities, containing, inter alia, a list of his assets and liabilities and a list of his income and expenditure.[5] Where the debtor has petitioned for his own sequestration he is required to submit such a statement with the petition.[6] Therefore in such a case he need merely send this statement to the trustee not more than seven days after the appointment.[7] Otherwise, he must prepare a statement from scratch and send it to the trustee not more than seven days after the latter has informed him of his appointment.[8] A debtor who, without reasonable excuse, fails to furnish the interim trustee with a statement, or fails to disclose a material fact therein, or make a material misstatement therein, will be guilty of a criminal offence.[9] It may seem strange that the debtor is required to detail his income and expenditure in a statement of his assets and liabilities, but the inclusion of this information allows creditors to assess whether it might be worthwhile to press for the debtor to make a contribution from income.);
(4)  to administer the sequestration process pending the appointment of a permanent trustee;
(5)  to supply the Accountant with such information as is necessary to enable him to discharge his functions. This last function persists even after he has ceased to act in the sequestration.[10]

## 8.11.   THE POWERS OF THE INTERIM TRUSTEE

The interim trustee is granted extensive powers to ensure the interim preservation of the debtor's estate. First, a general power to direct the debtor as to the management of the estate is conferred.[11] If the debtor thinks any such direction is unreasonable, he may apply to the court,

---

[1] s.1A(2).
[2] s.13(1).
[3] s.13(2), (4).
[4] s.2(4).
[5] s.73(1); Bankruptcy (Scotland) Amendment Regulations 1993 (SI 1993/439).
[6] s.5(6A)(a).
[7] s.19(1).
[8] s.19(2).
[9] s.19(3).
[10] s.2(4)(e).
[11] s.18(1).

which may set aside the direction or substitute its own, although the debtor must comply with the original direction until the appeal is finally determined.[12] The aforementioned general power is supplemented by a number of specific powers. These include the power to[13]:

(1) require the debtor to deliver up money, valuables, business or financial documents;
(2) place anything mentioned in (1) in safe custody;
(3) require the debtor to deliver up perishable goods, and arrange for their sale or disposal (while generally the sale of any property is a function restricted to the permanent trustee, the need for this exception is obvious.);
(4) make an inventory or valuation of the debtor's property;
(5) require the debtor to implement any transaction the debtor has undertaken, *e.g.* a beneficial contract;
(6) effect or maintain insurance policies in respect of the debtor's business or property;
(7) carry on the debtor's business and borrow money in so far as such borrowing is necessary to safeguard the estate;
(8) close down the debtor's business.
(9) request the supply of gas, electricity, water or telecommunications services for the purposes of the debtor's business.[14]

Moreover, he can ask the court for a warrant to enter and search the debtor's home or business premises (but not elsewhere) to search for and take possession of money, etc. which warrant the court may grant on cause shown.[15] More generally, the court, on the trustee's application, may grant such other order to safeguard the estate as it thinks appropriate.[16] Thus in *Scottish & Newcastle plc, Petitioner*[17] the court authorised the sale of licensed premises—a power which only the permanent trustee would normally have. The debtor is guilty of an offence if he fails without reasonable excuse to comply with any direction or requirement or obstructs the interim trustee in any search.[18]

The interim trustee may also request the debtor to appear before him to give information in relation to the debtor's assets, his dealings with them, or his conduct in relation to his business or financial affairs.[19] Equally he may request the debtor's spouse or any other person he thinks can give him such information to supply that information.[20] If he thinks it necessary, he may apply to the sheriff for an order requiring the debtor, the spouse or such other person to appear before the sheriff for private examination.[21]

## 8.12. DUTIES OF THE INTERIM TRUSTEE

Where the petition is not presented by the debtor, the interim trustee must inform the debtor of his appointment as soon as practicable,[22] and must in any case advertise his appointment in the Edinburgh Gazette.[23] Once the interim trustee receives the statement of assets and liabilities referred to in para. 8.10., he shall prepare a statement of the debtor's affairs,

---

[12] s.18(4).
[13] s.18(2).
[14] s.70.
[15] s.18(3)(b).
[16] s.18(3)(c).
[17] 1992 S.C.L.R. 540.
[18] s.18(5).
[19] s.20(4)(a).
[20] s.20(4)(b).
[21] s.20(4).
[22] s.2(7).
[23] s.15(6); Bankruptcy (Scotland) Regulations 1985 (SI 1985/1925), para. 16.

indicating whether the assets are likely to be able to pay any dividend whatever in respect of preferred, ordinary and postponed debts[24] (see para. 8.32.). This requires him to estimate the value of the debtor's assets, and the value of the probable expenses of the sequestration. Not less than four days before the statutory meeting (see below) the interim trustee (unless he is the Accountant) must send the Accountant a copy of both the aforesaid statements, together with written comments as to the causes of the insolvency and the extent to which the conduct of the debtor may have contributed thereto.[25] Such comments attract absolute privilege.[26]

The interim trustee must call a statutory meeting of creditors within 60 days of the award, or such longer period as the sheriff may allow, at a place and time determined by him.[27] Not less than seven days before the meeting he shall notify any known creditor and the Accountant of the meeting, inviting the submission of claims not already submitted.[28] Where the interim trustee is the Accountant, this may well be because no private insolvency practitioner has been willing to accept appointment, due to fears that the available assets might be insufficient even to meet his outlays and remuneration. In such cases creditors are most unlikely to receive anything from the estate, so that the statutory meeting is fairly pointless, serving only to prolong the process and increase its expense. So where the interim trustee is the Accountant, he may intimate to the creditors that he does not intend to hold the meeting.[29] However, any creditor can request that the meeting be held, and if a quarter in value so request, the meeting must be held.[30] Where the meeting is not held the inevitable effect is that, as no permanent trustee is elected, the Accountant or his nominee becomes permanent trustee.[31]

## 8.13. THE STATUTORY MEETING

Where the statutory meeting is held, it must be chaired, at least to begin with, by the interim trustee.[32] The quorum is a single creditor entitled to vote.[33] If no such creditor attends, then the interim trustee (unless he is the Accountant) must forthwith notify the Accountant and report to the sheriff, who shall thereupon appoint him as permanent trustee.[34] Where, in such a case, the Accountant is the interim trustee, he must forthwith report to the sheriff,[35] and he or his nominee automatically becomes the permanent trustee.[36] In both these cases the modified procedure under Sch. 2 applies[37] (see para. 8.37.). The same result follows if the meeting is attended by creditors, but no permanent trustee is elected.[38]

When the meeting is attended by creditors, the first task of the interim trustee is to accept or reject in whole or in part the claim of each creditor (and to convert any claim stated in foreign currency into sterling).[39] Acceptance (partial or otherwise) of a claim determines a creditor's entitlement to vote at the meeting.[40] Having decided which claims he will accept, the interim

---

[24] s.20(1).
[25] s.20(2).
[26] s.20(3).
[27] s.21(1), (1A).
[28] s.21(2).
[29] s.21A(2).
[30] s.21A(5).
[31] s.21B.
[32] s.23(1).
[33] Sch. 6, para. 12.
[34] s.24(4).
[35] s.24(3A).
[36] s.25A(1).
[37] ss.24(5), 25A(3).
[38] s.24(3A), (4).
[39] s.23(1)(a).
[40] s.23(2).

trustee shall invite the creditors to elect one of their number as chairman, although failing such election, he remains in the chair.[41]

Thereafter, the interim trustee makes available for inspection the statement of assets and liabilities prepared by the debtor (see para. 8.10.), and the statement of the debtor's affairs prepared by himself (see para. 8.12.).[42] He must answer to the best of his ability any questions put by the creditors, and must consider any representations they make,[43] *e.g.* in regard to possible gratuitous alienations by the debtor. As a result of what he has heard, he may decide that it is necessary to revise the statement of the debtor's affairs,[44] and if he does so, he must send as soon as possible a revised copy to every creditor of whom he is aware.[45] Finally, once again in light of what he has heard, he must once more express an opinion as to whether the assets are likely to be able to pay any dividend whatever in respect of preferred, ordinary and postponed debts.[46]

At the conclusion of the meeting, the creditors shall proceed to the election of the permanent trustee (see para. 8.15.).[47] The result is determined by a majority of creditors or their mandatories.[48] Although otherwise entitled to vote at creditors' meetings no postponed creditor (see para. 8.32.) may vote in the election of the permanent trustee, and nor may any creditor whose debt is acquired (unless by succession) after the date of the sequestration.[49] The debtor cannot be elected as permanent trustee.[50] Nor can the Accountant,[51] nor anyone whose interests are opposed to the general interests of the creditors.[52] Additionally, in order to be eligible for election, an individual must reside in Scotland,[53] be a qualified insolvency practitioner,[54] and give a written undertaking to act.[55]

If a permanent trustee is elected, the meeting (or any subsequent meeting of creditors) may elect between one and five of their number as commissioners (see para. 8.26.), to supervise and advise the trustee.[56] There do not have to be commissioners, and there cannot be any in a sequestration under Sch. 2[57] (see para. 8.37.).

## 8.14.  INTERIM TRUSTEE—TERMINATION OF FUNCTIONS AND DISCHARGE

If the interim trustee is not to become the permanent trustee, he must on the latter's confirmation hand over everything relating to the sequestration, and thereupon shall cease to act.[58] Within three months of such confirmation, the interim trustee shall[59]:

> (1) submit to the Accountant his accounts of his intromissions (if any) with the estate and a claim for his outlays and remuneration; and

---

[41] s.23(1)(b).
[42] s.23(3)(a).
[43] s.23(3)(b).
[44] s.23(3)(d).
[45] s.23(5).
[46] s.23(3)(c).
[47] s.24(1).
[48] Sch. 6, paras 11, 13.
[49] s.24(3).
[50] s.24(2)(a).
[51] s.24(2)(f).
[52] s.24(2)(c).
[53] s.24(2)(d).
[54] s.24(2)(b).
[55] s.24(2)(e).
[56] s.30(1).
[57] Sch. 2, para. 6.
[58] s.26(1).
[59] s.26(2).

(2) send to the permanent trustee (unless he himself has become the permanent trustee) a copy of the above submission.

His accounts are audited by, and the actual amount of outlays and remuneration payable determined by, the Accountant, although such determination may be appealed to the sheriff by him, the permanent trustee, the debtor or any creditor.[60] When the interim trustee receives a copy of the Accountant's determination he may apply to the Accountant for a discharge, which the latter may grant or refuse, subject to the right of the interim trustee, the permanent trustee, the debtor or any creditor to appeal to the sheriff.[61] The grant of a discharge discharges the interim trustee from all liability (other than liability for fraud) in the exercise of his functions.[62]

## 8.15. ELECTION/APPOINTMENT OF THE PERMANENT TRUSTEE

While the main function of the interim trustee is to safeguard the estate, the arrival of the permanent trustee heralds the beginning of the process of sequestration proper. There must be a single permanent trustee. The office cannot be held jointly.[63]

If the meeting elects a permanent trustee, the interim trustee must forthwith report to the sheriff.[64] The debtor, any creditor, the interim trustee, the permanent trustee or the Accountant may within four days of the meeting object to the sheriff concerning the election.[65] If there is a timeous objection, the sheriff shall forthwith give the parties an opportunity to be heard thereon, and shall give his decision,[66] which shall be final.[67] If he sustains the objection, the sheriff shall order the interim trustee to arrange a new meeting to elect the permanent trustee.[68] If he does not sustain the objection, or if no timeous objection is made, the sheriff shall forthwith confirm the elected person as permanent trustee.[69]

In all cases where the permanent trustee is appointed rather than elected, then unless the sequestration is proceeding on streamlined basis under a certificate of summary administration, a somewhat modified procedure will apply under Sch. 2 of the Act[70] (see para. 8.37.).

## 8.16. RESIGNATION/DEATH OF PERMANENT TRUSTEE

A permanent trustee must apply to the sheriff if he wishes to resign office, and authority to do so can only be given on two grounds: inability to act or misconduct.[71] The same applies to an interim trustee.[72] If a permanent trustee (other than the Accountant) dies, it is the duty of the commissioners (see para. 8.26.), or the Accountant if there are none, to call meeting of creditors to elect a new trustee.[73] The same is true if the trustee is permitted to resign, except where the application has been granted subject to the election of a new permanent trustee, in

---

[60] s.26(3)–(4); and see s.26A where the Accountant is the interim trustee.

[61] s.27(1)–(4).

[62] s.27(5).

[63] *Commissioners of the Inland Revenue v MacDonald*, 1988 S.L.T. (Sh. Ct.) 7.

[64] s.25(1)(a).

[65] s.25(1)(b).

[66] s.25(3).

[67] s.25(5).

[68] s.25(4)(b).

[69] s.25(2), (4)(a).

[70] ss. 24(5), 25A(3).

[71] s.28(1).

[72] s.13(2).

[73] s.28(2)(a).

which case the resigning permanent trustee must himself call a meeting of creditors to elect a new trustee.[74] Where the Sch. 2 procedure applies, the Accountant or his nominee may apply to the sheriff for his appointment in place of a deceased or resigning trustee.[75]

## 8.17. Functions of Permanent Trustee

The functions of the permanent trustee include[76]:

- to recover, manage and realise the debtor's estate, wherever situated;
- to distribute the estate among the creditors according to their respective entitlements;
- to ascertain the reasons for the debtor's insolvency and the circumstances surrounding it;
- to ascertain the state of the debtor's liabilities and assets, (this and the previous function are shared with the interim trustee, and might be seen as a continuation of the investigatory aspect of the sequestration process. It should be remembered, however, that the main purpose of the process is the recovery and distribution of the estate, so such investigations should be pursued no further than is necessary to safeguard the interests of the creditors.);
- to provide an accurate record of the sequestration process through maintaining a sederunt book into which all key documents are inserted (he must also give the debtor and all creditors known to him written notice that the book is available for inspection at an address specified by him.[77]);
- to keep regular accounts available for inspection by all interested parties;
- to supply the Accountant with such information as the Accountant considers necessary to enable him to discharge his functions under the Act. (This last function persists even after he has ceased to act in the sequestration.)

## 8.18. Vesting of the Estate in the Permanent Trustee

While the interim trustee has certain powers to deal with the debtor's estate, the latter remains the owner of that estate. However when the permanent trustee is appointed,[78] or his election confirmed by the sheriff,[79] the sheriff-clerk issues his act and warrant. By virtue of that act and warrant the debtor is divested of his entire estate, which vests in the trustee as at the date of sequestration.[80] So in relation to heritage, the act and warrant has the same effect as a decree of adjudication in favour of the permanent trustee,[81] while in relation to moveables where delivery or possession or intimation of its assignation would normally be required to complete title, such delivery, possession or intimation will be deemed.[82] Vesting includes all powers the

---

[74] s.28(2)(b).
[75] Sch. 2, para. 3(2).
[76] s.3.
[77] s.56A(4)(b)(ii).
[78] Sch. 2, para. 2.
[79] s.25(2).
[80] s.31(1)(a). This is not incompatible with Art. 1 of Protocol 1 of the ECHR: see *Krasner v Dennison*, [2001] Ch. 76, CA.
[81] s.31(1)(b).
[82] s.31(4).

debtor might have had in relation to the estate,[83] and any dealing with the estate by the debtor is ineffective in a question with the permanent trustee.[84]

## (a) Acquirenda

Moreover, any estate which the debtor acquires after the date of sequestration and prior to discharge, e.g as a result of inheritance, similarly automatically vests in the permanent trustee. The Act provides in s.32(6):

> "any estate wherever situated which (a) is acquired by the debtor on a relevant date, and (b) would have vested in the permanent trustee if it had been part of the debtor's estate at the date of sequestration, shall vest in the permanent trustee for the benefit of the creditors at the date of acquisition, and any person who holds any such estate shall, on production of a copy of the act and warrant certified by the sheriff clerk confirming the permanent trustee's appointment, convey or deliver the estate to the permanent trustee: Provided that—
>
> > (i) if such a person has in good faith and without knowledge of the sequestration, conveyed the estate to the debtor . . ., he shall incur no liability to the permanent trustee except to account for any proceeds of the conveyance which are in his hands."

In *Rankin's Tr. v H C Somerville & Russell*[85] R was sequestrated in February 1991 and the permanent trustee appointed in 1991. R's father died in January 1992, and the firm of solicitors dealing with the estate, paid over the residual estate to her in October 1992, although they were aware of her sequestration. They claimed to be justified in doing so, as they had not seen the trustee's act and warrant which was not exhibited to them until July 1996. Lord Macfadyen disagreed, observing[86]:

> "It is in my view clear the acquirenda vest in the permanent trustee at the date of acquisition, provided two conditions are satisfied, namely that the acquisition occurred on a relevant date, and that the property would have vested in the permanent trustee if it had been part of the debtor's estate at the date of sequestration. If these conditions are satisfied, nothing more is required to perfect the trustee's right. A statutory transfer of property takes place by virtue of the concurrence of those circumstances, and without any further procedure. On that transfer taking place, it follows that any holder of the property who would otherwise have been under an obligation to convey, deliver or pay the property to the debtor ceases to be under that obligation, and comes under a substitute obligation to hold the property for, and await the claim of the permanent trustee. From that it follows that if the holder in fact conveys, delivers or pays the property to the debtor, he thereby wrongfully disposes of the property which belongs to the permanent trustee for the benefit of the creditors. In that situation the permanent trustee is entitled to seek the appropriate remedy against the former holder. If the property which has been paid away to the debtor is cash, that remedy will be a money claim.
>
> If the defenders' contention is correct until the moment of production of the certified copy act and warrant to the holder arrives, the holder is under no obligation to pay the trustee and remains under obligation to pay the debtor . . . But it is clear that s.32(6)(i) is concerned with protecting a holder who has paid the acquirenda away before production to him of the certified copy act and warrant, since there could be no question of the

---

[83] s.31(8); *e.g.* exercising voting rights under shares which were part of the debtor's estate: *Cumming's Tr. v Glenrinnes Farms Ltd,* 1993 S.L.T. 904.
[84] s.32(8).
[85] 1999 S.L.T. 65.
[86] At 71F–72C.

holder acting "without knowledge of the sequestration" once the act and warrant had been produced to him. Thus if the defenders' contention as to the construction of s.32(6) is correct, the proviso is providing a defence to a liability which could never arise. The only context in which the proviso is necessary to protect the holder acting in good faith and without knowledge of the sequestration is one in which s.32(6) would otherwise give rise to the possibility of liability to the trustee attaching to the holder in consequence of a disposal of the acquirenda carried through before sight of the act and warrant.

. . . [Thus] production of the certified copy act and warrant is not part of the machinery for creating or perfecting the trustee's right to the acquirenda, nor a necessary step to render unlawful any payment to the debtor. I do not consider that there is any force in the defenders' submission that that construction deprives the second part of s.32(6) of all content. It sets up the evidential role of the certified copy act and warrant as sufficient to satisfy the holder of the permanent trustee's entitlement, and thus provides a procedure for vindication of the permanent trustee's already fully constituted right to the property."

A debtor must immediately inform the permanent trustee of any *acquirenda,* failing which he commits an offence,[87] and may not validly deal with this property.[88] Naturally, anything acquired with *acquirenda* also vests in the trustee.[89]

## (b) Tantum et tale

The permanent trustee effectively gains the same rights as the debtor to the estate, and is thus subject to any limitations which affected the debtor.[90] Moreover, the Act specifically states that the right of any secured creditor is preferable to the rights of the permanent trustee, and that the vesting of the estate in the permanent trustee does not defeat a landlord's hypothec.[91]

## (c) Specialities of moveable property

The permanent trustee acquires the debtor's entire moveable estate, including any rights to payment which the latter may have, *e.g.* a right to claim rent.[92] However, there is a difference between acquiring rights and undertaking onerous obligations, such as that of a tenant under a lease, and the permanent trustee will not be liable for such obligations unless he adopts the contract[93] (see para. 8.22.). Again, while it has been noted above that where delivery or possession or intimation of its assignation would normally be required to complete title to moveables, such delivery, possession or intimation will be deemed,[94] where some further step is necessary to complete title, *e.g.* registration, the title of the permanent trustee is not perfected until that step occurs,[95] and the rights of the permanent trustee may be defeated if a third party registers title first.[96]

## (d) Damages

If damages awarded to the debtor form part of the estate then they will vest in the permanent trustee. More importantly, a trustee can raise an action in respect of patrimonial loss suffered

---

[87] s.32(7).

[88] *Alliance and Leicester Building Society v Murray's Tr.,* 1994 S.C.L.R. 19.

[89] *Royal Bank of Scotland plc v Macgregor,* 1998 S.C.L.R. 923: property acquired by a loan taken out after the date of sequestration vests in the trusteee, albeit subject to security granted in relation thereto.

[90] *Heritable Reversionary Co Ltd v Millar* (1892) 19 R. (H.L.) 43.

[91] s.33(2)–(3).

[92] *Mitchell's Tr. v Pearson* (1834) 12 S. 322.

[93] *Myles v City of Glasgow Bank* (1879) 6 R. 718; *McDonald's Trs v Cunningham,* 1997 S.C.L.R. 986.

[94] s.31(4).

[95] *Cumming's Tr. v Glenrinnes Farms Ltd,* 1993 S.L.T. 904.

[96] *Morrison v Harrison* (1876) 3 R. 406.

by the debtor.[97] On the other hand, it has always be recognised that a right to sue for *solatium* is a right purely personal to the debtor, so that only the debtor can raise such an action.[98] Yet as soon as an action to recover *solatium* is raised, the right to any damages paid (or indeed to any sum received in settlement of the claim) vests in the permanent trustee, even if damages (or the amount agreed on) are only paid after the debtor is discharged.[99] It is specifically provided that an award under the Criminal Injuries Compensation Scheme does not vest in the permanent trustee.[1] Obviously, if damages are paid in respect of the wrongful dismissal of the debtor from employment, they will vest in the permanent trustee. Actual remuneration from employment counts as income and so will not vest.

A question arises in relation to payment in lieu of notice. If this is regarded as remuneration from employment, it will not vest, but if it were to be treated as liquidated damages, then it might be argued that it should vest. It is suggested that redundancy payments, compensation for unfair dismissal and other compensation in respect of the infringement of employment rights are equivalent to damages and thus should vest. The same argument might be made in respect of contractual compensation on dismissal, *e.g.* contractually enhanced redundancy payments, or *ex gratia* payments. It has to be recorded, nonetheless, that the Notes by the Accountant in Bankruptcy for the Guidance of Interim and Permanent Trustees refer[2] to the case of *Patrick McGrail*, heard in Glasgow Sheriff Court on August 10, 1990, in which certain of the above matters were discussed. The trustee in that case conceded that payment in lieu of notice did not vest. The sheriff held that the statutory redundancy payment was alimentary in nature, so did not vest, but that both a contractually enhanced redundancy payment and an *ex gratia* payment did vest.

### (e) Pensions

Under occupational pension schemes the fund from which the pension is payable is not owned by the debtor, so that where he receives any sum (including a lump sum) from an occupational pension, it is treated as income and so will not vest in the permanent trustee. Nonetheless, if the permanent trustee thinks the amount is excessive he may seek a voluntary contribution from the debtor or an order from the court that the excess be paid to him (see next paragraph). A personal pension usually takes the form of an annuity purchased by a fund invested and owned by the debtor, so that although payments take the form of income, that income derives from the estate vested in the permanent trustee (the pension fund). Thus traditionally, personal pensions have vested in the permanent trustee.[3] Yet, as a result of reforms effected by ss.11-13 of the Welfare Reform and Pensions Act 1999, personal pensions no longer so vest in sequestrations awarded after May 29, 2000. It may be added that when s.16 of that Act is brought into force the permanent trustee may, in terms of ss.36A–36C of the 1985 Act, seek a court order to recover excessive contributions to pension schemes (whether personal or occupational), contributions being deemed excessive if they so appear in light of the debtor's circumstances, or if they were made for the purpose of putting assets beyond the reach of creditors.

### (f) Contingent interests

The permanent trustee even takes over contingent interests of the debtors. Section 31(5) provides:

> "Any non-vested contingent interest which the debtor has shall vest in the permanent trustee as if an assignation of that interest had been executed by the debtor and intimation thereof made at the date of sequestration."

---

[97] *Muir's Tr. v Braidwood*, 1958 S.C. 169.
[98] *Watson v Thompson*, 1991 S.C. 447.
[99] *Coutt's Tr. v Coutts*, 1998 S.C.L.R. 729.
[1] Criminal Injuries Compensation Act 1995, s.7(2).
[2] At para. 6.23.1.
[3] See *Rowe v Sanders* [2002] 2 All E.R. 800.

In *Stuart's Tr. v H. J. Banks & Co Ltd*[4] the debtor prior to sequestration had entered into a contract with B & Co whereby he was to receive commission in respect of introducing purchasers of land to them. The amount of the commission would depend on the final purchase price, and would become due only when missives had been concluded. Missives were not concluded until after his discharge from sequestration. It was held that entitlement to payment arose when the work was done, being a non-vested contingent interest, based on the contingency that missives would be concluded. It therefore passed to the trustee, who was entitled to the commission even though it was paid after sequestration.

### (g) Specialities of heritable property

The act and warrant vests heritable property in the permanent trustee, but he does not acquire a real right in the property until his title is properly registered. Thus in *Fleming's Tr. v Fleming*[5] Lord Sutherland noted:

> "It is clear . . . that the effect of vesting of the bankrupt's estate in the trustee is that he gets a personal right only, and if there is a prior disponee of heritable property, a race to the register will result."

In that case the debtor lived in the matrimonial home to which title had been taken in the name of himself and his wife and to the survivor of them. When he died, it was held that as the permanent trustee had not registered his act and warrant, he (the trustee) did not have a real right to the debtor's share of the house, which passed to the debtor's wife under the special destination.

Lord Sutherland continued[6]:

> "There is no inequity in this result as, if a trustee wishes to protect his position against the possibility of the death of the debtor giving rise to the automatic infeftment of the substitute, all the trustee has to do is register his act and warrant in the appropriate register and this will give him a real right which will defeat the right of the substitute . . . [I]f he omits to do so he must take the consequences."

However, this was ultimately of little benefit to the widow because[7]:

> "The share passing under the special destination can only be taken with such qualifications as could be pleaded against the institute. The substitute takes no greater right than that possessed by the institute. The institute's share was vested in the trustee and was liable for the debtor's debts . . . On the death of the debtor his share passed under the special destination with the same qualifications."

In other words, the widow obtained her husband's share of the property, but could be sued for its value.

The other side of the coin is that if heritage has been sold by the bankrupt prior to sequestration, but the purchaser does not register his title before the trustee acquires a real right to the bankrupt's estate, that heritage will vest in the trustee rather than the purchaser. This result was upheld in *Burnett's Tr. v Grainger,*[8] the Inner House explicitly confining the rule in *Sharp v Thomson,*[9] which would have favoured the purchaser, to situations where there is a contest between a purchaser and a receiver under a floating charge.

---

[4] [1998] S.C.L.R. 1109.
[5] 2000 S.C. 206 at 209C.
[6] *ibid.*
[7] 212B–C, See also *Halifax plc v Gorman's Tr.,* 2000 S.L.T. 1409.
[8] 2002 S.L.T. 699.
[9] 1997 S.C. (H.L.) 66.

## 8.19.   ESTATE EXCLUDED FROM VESTING

Certain estate is exempted from vesting—

### (a) Property held in trust

Property which the debtor holds in trust for another is specifically excluded from vesting.[10] Thus in *Council of the Law Society v McKinnie*[11] the First Division held that funds held in a solicitor's client account were held in a fiduciary capacity, and thus were immune from vesting. This rule will apply as long as property or funds held in trust (or at least the assets into which they have been converted) can be identified.[12] If trust property cannot be identified, the rule cannot be applied,[13] although the court will allow funds held in trust to be recovered, if they have been paid, along with other monies, into an account which is in credit.[14]

### (b) Income

Income received by the debtor vests in the debtor unless it is income derived from estate vested in the permanent trustee.[15] Thus if the debtor's mother provides for the rents from properties she owns to be paid to the debtor, he may retain that money. But rents from properties the debtor owns counts as income derived from the estate vested in the permanent trustee, and thus also vest in the permanent trustee. Moreover, if the permanent trustee considers the debtor's income to be excessive, he may apply to the sheriff for an order that the excess be paid over to him.[16] The sheriff will allow the debtor a suitable amount to provide for his aliment and "relevant" obligations. Those obligations are his alimentary obligations, any obligation to make a periodical allowance to a former spouse and any obligation to pay child support maintenance under the Child Support Act 1991.[17] The sheriff need not allow the debtor sufficient income to allow him to comply with a previous court order relating to aliment or periodical allowance.[18] In other words, if having worked out the amount the debtor requires to aliment himself, the sheriff is then faced with the plea that the debtor is also bound to pay his ex-wife £1,000 per month by way of periodical allowance, he may decide to allow all of that sum or only part of it. The sheriff has complete discretion here, and is not bound by any formula, but should determine a suitable amount balancing the interests of the debtor and the creditors.[19] Should the debtor's circumstances change, he, the permanent trustee, or any other interested person may apply to the sheriff for the variation or recall of the contribution order.

Creditors cannot use diligence to attach the debtor's income in respect of pre-sequestration debts.[20] It would seem to follow that income can be attached in respect of post-sequestration debts. In this context, diligence includes the making of a deduction from earnings under the Child Support Act 1991. Other deductions from money which would otherwise be payable to the debtor do not amount to diligence.[21]

In *Accountant of Court v Halifax plc*[22] Lord Penrose rejected the contention of the defenders, who had issued free shares to a bankrupt despite a claim by the Accountant in Bankruptcy

---

[10] s.33(1)(b).
[11] 1993 S.L.T. 238.
[12] *Newton's Exix v Meiklejohn's J F*, 1959 S.L.T. 71; *Smith v Liquidator of James Birrell Ltd*, 1968 S.L.T. 174.
[13] *Hofford v Gowans*, 1909 1 S.L.T. 153.
[14] *Mags of Edinburgh v McLaren* (1881) 8 R. (H.L.) 140.
[15] s.32(1).
[16] s.32(2).
[17] s.32(3).
[18] *ibid.*
[19] *Brown's Tr. v Brown*, 1995 S.L.T (Sh. Ct) 2.
[20] s.32(4).
[21] *Mulvey v Secretary of State for Social Security*, 1997 S.L.T. 753.
[22] 1999 S.C.L.R. 1135 at 1143F–1144B.

(acting as permanent trustee) that they were his, to the effect that the shares were income and not *acquirenda*. Lord Penrose noted:

> "In my opinion, the expression 'income' is not apt to include a price paid, in whatever form, to a debtor effectively to accept the substitution of a different creditor on a subsisting loan. It is clear that the property would be acquirenda . . . If the vesting day under the transfer agreement was earlier than the date of sequestration . . . the right to shares would be part of his estate on sequestration. If there remained some unfulfilled requirement . . . . the right would be properly described as contingent, and s.31(5) would apply. If any requirement had to be performed by the bankrupt personally, s.64 would oblige him to do that act and there would be power in the sheriff to order performance if need be."

But the House of Lords has held in *Mulvey v Secretary of State for Social Security*[23] that the permanent trustee has no interest in social security benefits paid to the debtor. Accordingly, the deduction by the Secretary of State of sums from the debtor's income support to cover loans earlier made from the social fund could not be equated with a creditor withholding money due to the debtor on the basis of compensation. (The trustee could normally object to compensation being pleaded, as it allows that creditor to benefit unfairly.)

It may be assumed that assets the debtor acquires from income do not vest in the permanent trustee.

### (c) Property exempted from attachment

Property kept outwith a dwellinghouse in respect of which attachment is incompetent by virtue of s.11 of the Debt Arrangement and Attachment (Scotland) Act 2002, does not vest in the permanent trustee.[24] This covers:

(1) any implements, tools of trade, books or other equipment reasonably required by the debtor in the practice of his profession, trade or business (not exceeding in aggregate value £1,000);
(2) any vehicle, the use of which is reasonably required by the debtor as above (not exceeding £1,000 in value);
(3) a mobile home which is the debtor's only or principal residence;
(4) any tools or other equipment reasonably required for keeping in good order and condition any garden or yard adjacent to or associated with a dwellinghouse in which the debtor resides.

Similarly, property kept in a dwellinghouse which is not a non-essential asset for the purposes of Pt 3 of the Debt Arrangement and Attachment (Scotland) Act 2002, does not vest in the permanent trustee.[25]

None of the following can be non-essential assets:

(a) clothing reasonably required by the debtor or any member of the debtor's household;
(b) any implements, tools of trade, books or other equipment reasonably required by any member of the debtor's household in the practice of their profession, trade or business (not exceeding in aggregate value £1,000);
(c) medical aids or equipment reasonably required by the debtor or any member of the debtor's household;
(d) books or other articles reasonably required for the education or training of the debtor or any member of the debtor's household (not exceeding in aggregate value £1,000);

---

[23] 1997 S.L.T. 753.
[24] s.33(1)(a).
[25] s.33(1)(aa).

  (e)  toys of a child who is a household member;
  (f)  articles reasonably required for the care or upbringing of such a child;
  (g)  the following articles in the dwelling reasonably required for the use of the debtor or
     a member of his household, namely beds; bedding; household linen; chairs; settees;
     tables; food; lights and fittings; heating appliances; curtains; floor coverings; anything
     used for cooking, storing or eating food, anything used to clean the house or clean,
     mend, dry or press clothes; refrigerators; items of domestic safety; tools used to
     repair or maintain the house or household articles; furniture used to store clothing,
     bedding, household linen, articles used to clean the house, or utensils used to cook
     and eat food; computers and accessory equipment; microwave ovens; radios; tele-
     phones; televisions.

It can thus be appreciated that most standard household items do not vest.

## (d) Property excluded under the proceeds of Crime Act 2002

The 2002 Act provides for the confiscation of the assets of persons convicted of criminal offences. It is not proposed to go into the detail of this rather arcane area. However, among the devices it employs are confiscation orders, restraint orders which interdict individuals from dealing with any realisable property held by them, and orders appointing enforcement and director's receivers in England and Northern Ireland and enforcement administrators in Scotland to manage affected property. Essentially, property affected by any such order will not be regarded as part of the debtor's estate at the date of sequestration.[26] However where an order is quashed or discharged, or where a surplus remains after satisfaction of that order, the relevant property or surplus will vest in the permanent trustee.[27] Where sequestration has already been awarded, no property which is part of the estate, nor any of the debtor's income which has been ordered to be paid to the permanent trustee, can be affected by any order under the 2002 Act.[28]

## 8.20.  RECOVERY OF ESTATE AND DOCUMENTS

Although the estate automatically vests in the permanent trustee, he must take practical steps to ingather it. Thus, as soon as possible after being confirmed in office, the permanent trustee should take possession of the estate and any document in the debtor's possession or control which relates to his assets or his business or financial affairs.[29] He is also entitled to have access to and copy all documents relating to such matters which have been sent by the debtor to a third party, and if access is obstructed, he may apply to the sheriff for an order that the person obstructing should cease to obstruct.[30] Similarly, he may require delivery of any title deed or document of the debtor held by a third party, but this is subject to any right of lien the third party may have over the deed or document.[31] Bell indicates that a lien gives the holder preference over all creditors, whether secured or not, and the deeds or documents may only be recovered by paying the debt or finding security for its payment.[32] Any person who damages, conceals or removes from Scotland any part of the estate or any document which relates to the debtor's assets or business or financial affairs may commit an offence.[33]

---

[26] Proceeds of Crime Act 2002, s.420(2); but to obtain a good title to heritage, the restraint order must be recorded in the Land Register or Register of Sasines before the award of sequestration: s.420(3).
[27] 1985 Act, ss.31A–31C.
[28] Proceeds of Crime Act 2002, s.421.
[29] 1985 Act, s.38(1)(a).
[30] s.38(2)–(3).
[31] s.38(4).
[32] *Commentaries* (7th ed.), ii, 108.
[33] s.67(2).

## 8.21.  INFORMATION AND EXAMINATIONS

The permanent trustee may require information to carry out his functions, and is given extensive powers to enable him to secure it. Thus he may request the debtor or any other person to appear before him to give information regarding the debtor's assets, the debtor's dealings with them, or the conduct of the debtor's affairs.[34] Moreover, if he considers it necessary (*i.e.* where informal meetings have not yielded the information sought), then the permanent trustee can apply to the sheriff for a private examination of any such person.[35] (It may be remembered that the interim trustee has similar powers to require information or seek a private examination before the sheriff: see para. 8.11.) Although, the permanent trustee need not indicate what he hopes to discover through the examination,[36] the granting of the application appears to lie at the sheriff's discretion.[37] Alternatively, the permanent trustee can apply to the sheriff for a public examination of any such person as mentioned above, and must do so if so requested by the Accountant, the commissioners (see para. 8.26.), or one quarter in value of the creditors.[38] Although such an application should normally be made not less than eight weeks before the end of the first accounting period (see para. 8.27.), it can be made at any time on cause shown.[39] If the application is properly made, it must be granted by the sheriff.[40]

An individual will be ordered to appear for private or public examination not earlier than eight days nor later than 16 days after the order, at a time specified in the order,[41] although if that individual is prevented from attending for any good reason, the sheriff may appoint a commissioner to conduct the examination.[42] (This is a commissioner in the sense of a person who takes evidence on commission, rather than one of the creditor commissioners who supervise the trustee.) Outside of this speciality, an individual who fails, without reasonable excuse, to appear commits an offence.[43] On the application of the permanent trustee, the court, if satisfied that this is necessary to secure the attendance of the relevant individual at the examination, may grant a warrant for his arrest and delivery to the place of examination.[44] Either the sheriff or the commissioner may order any individual to produce any document in his custody or control relating to the debtor's assets, his dealings with them, or his conduct in relation to his business or financial affairs, and to deliver a copy to the permanent trustee.[45]

The main differences between a private and public examination, apart from the latter being held in open court,[46] are that:

- when the sheriff makes an order for a public examination, the permanent trustee must publish notice thereof in the Edinburgh Gazette, sending a copy to every known creditor (and to the debtor if he is not the person being examined), and informing them of their right to participate in the examination[47];
- whereas at a private examination only the permanent trustee (or a solicitor or counsel acting for him), or the debtor if he is not the person being examined, may question the relevant individual, in a public examination any creditor may ask questions.[48]

---

[34] s.44(1).
[35] *ibid.*
[36] *Park v Robson* (1871) 10 M. 10.
[37] s.44(2).
[38] s.45(1)(a)–(b).
[39] s.45(1).
[40] s.45(2).
[41] ss. 44(2), 45(2).
[42] s.46(2).
[43] ss. 44(3), 45(4).
[44] s.46(1).
[45] s.46(4).
[46] s.45(2).
[47] s.45(3), and Bankruptcy (Scotland) Regulations 1985 (SI 1985/1925), Form 7.
[48] s.47(2).

Questions are confined to matters relating to the debtor's assets, his dealings with them, or his conduct in relation to his business or financial affairs.[49] The legal adviser of the witness may not ask questions in order to clarify his client's evidence, but may object to questions which stray beyond the permissible issues.[50] The sheriff (and presumably the commissioner) may also ask questions, although this is not explicitly stated in the Act.[51] Examinations before a sheriff are on oath,[52] so that perjury becomes possible, while refusal to answer invites a finding of contempt, although in *Paxton v HMA*[53] it was held that such a finding was not open where the refusal to answer occurred when the examination had continued after the sheriff had left the bench. The witness is not excused from answering a question merely because the answer may incriminate him, or on grounds of confidentiality.[54] Nonetheless, his evidence is not admissible against him in any subsequent criminal proceedings, other than proceedings in respect of perjury.[55] This implies that the evidence may be admissible against him in subsequent civil proceedings. A public examination may be sought in order to impress upon the witness how serious the issue may be, but may also serve to alert all and sundry that the sequestration may not be proceeding entirely smoothly.

In this context it may also be noted that the permanent trustee can also seek a private examination of a creditor or other person regarding the amount or validity of the creditor's claim.[56]

## 8.22.   MANAGEMENT OF THE ESTATE

Although the main function of the permanent trustee is to realise the estate and distribute the proceeds amongst the creditors, in order to protect the estate he may have to manage it, sometimes over an extended period of time. To begin with, however, as soon as possible after being confirmed in office, he must consult with the commissioners (see para. 8.26.), or the Accountant if there are no commissioners, regarding the exercise of his functions.[57] Moreover, he must comply with general or specific directions given by[58]:

- the creditors (*i.e.* a majority in value of those voting at a creditors' meeting). A trustee might seek such a meeting specifically in order to receive directions in relation to issues where he is reluctant to proceed on his own initiative; or
- the court at the behest of the commissioners; or
- the Accountant if there are no commissioners.

The only exception to the above is that directions given by the creditors or the Accountant may be ignored if the permanent trustee has to sell perishable goods, and he believes that compliance would adversely affect the sale[59].

Certain specific powers are conferred on the permanent trustee, but if there are commissioners the exercise of those powers requires their consent or that of the creditors or the court.[60] It would appear that no consent is required where there are no commissioners. These powers are:

---

[49] *ibid.*
[50] *Holmes Petitioner,* 1988 S.L.T. (Sh. Ct) 47.
[51] *ibid.*
[52] s.47(1).
[53] 1984 S.L.T. 367.
[54] s.47(3).
[55] s.47(3)(a). Although a witness may not be forced to disclose any information received from a person who is not being examined, where it is confidential between them: s.47(3)(b).
[56] s.48(5)–(6).
[57] s.39(1).
[58] *ibid.*
[59]  s.39(6).
[60] s.39(2).

- to carry on the debtor's business. (the business may have certain contracts which, if performed, may significantly benefit the estate, or which if not performed may increase its liabilities. The continuation of the business may also make it easier to sell with its goodwill intact);
- to bring, defend or continue any legal proceedings relating to the estate;
- to create a security over any part of the estate (it may be that he needs to borrow money in order to run the business);
- to make payments or incur liabilities in order to acquire property which is the subject of a right or option (*e.g.* exercising the right to buy shares at specially discounted rates, which he knows he will be able to resell at a profit).

The permanent trustee may adopt any contract entered into by the debtor prior to sequestration if he considers that adoption would be beneficial, unless such adoption is excluded by the express or implied terms of the contract.[61] Many contracts expressly prohibit adoption in this context, or give a party a right not to allow adoption, or more generally exclude assignation. Where a contract involves an element of *delectus personae* in relation to the debtor, then adoption is impliedly excluded.[62] The permanent trustee may equally decline to adopt any contract.[63] If the permanent trustee declines to adopt, then this is quite likely to amount to a breach of contract, giving the other party a claim for damages, which may be considered in the sequestration.[64] However, a court will not order the trustee to implement the contract.[65] A party who invokes a right to elect to terminate the contract on the debtor's sequestration has no claim against the estate.[66] If the permanent trustee does adopt, he will generally become personally liable for performance, including obligations which had arisen prior to vesting.[67] The permanent trustee may equally enter into new contracts, if he considers that to do so would be beneficial.[68] Such a step is very likely where he is carrying on the debtor's business. The permanent trustee will certainly become personally liable for performance of such new contracts.[69]

There may be other pitfalls for an unwary trustee. The case of *Vale Sewing Machines v Robb*[70] involved a liquidator, but would seem equally applicable to a case of personal insolvency. The company in liquidation had among its assets certain goods which were subject to a retention of title clause. The seller of these goods left the liquidator in no doubt that, as the company still owed money on these goods, property therein had not passed to it. Nonetheless, the liquidator proceeded to resell the goods. He was held personally liable to the owner. The sheriff added[71]:

> "The defender indicated to me that the proceeds of sale have been placed in a suspense account pending resolution of this action. The action is raised against him personally and the decree is one on which he alone is personally liable. He is not entitled to apply any part of the liquidation funds to satisfy that decree as they would amount to a misappropriation of funds held for the general body of creditors."

Just because a contract is allowed to continue for some time before being terminated does not mean it is adopted. So in *Lindop v Stewart Noble & Sons Ltd*[72] the fact that an employee had continued in employment for almost four weeks before being dismissed did not mean that his

---

[61] s.42(1).
[62] *Anderson v Hamilton & Co* (1875) 2 R. 355.
[63] s.42(1).
[64] *Crown Estate Commissioners v Liquidators of Highland Engineering Ltd,* 1975 S.L.T. 58.
[65] *ibid.*
[66] *Buttercase v Geddie* (1897) 24 R. 1128.
[67] *Dundas v Morison* (1857) 20 D. 225.
[68] s.42(4).
[69] *Mackessack & Son v Molleson* (1886) 13 R. 445.
[70] 1997 S.C.L.R. 797.
[71] at 800B.
[72] 1997 S.C.L.R. 889.

contract was adopted. Generally, enforcing rights under a contract which involve no element of performance does not infer adoption, *e.g.* the collection of money due under the contract,[73] or even suing upon the contract.[74] Adoption will not be inferred even if the trustee takes limited steps to protect the position of the estate, so that the lease of a farm was not adopted, simply by the trustee involving himself in its running prior to sale.[75] But where a trustee invoked a term in a lease obliging the landlord to purchase sheep, that was held to be an adoption allowing the landlord to invoke reciprocal obligations in the lease.[76] If the trustee fails to indicate an intention to adopt within a reasonable time, then he will be held to have abandoned the contract.[77] If the other party wishes a clear decision on adoption, he may write to the trustee requesting a decision.[78] The trustee then has 28 days from the receipt of the request (or such longer period as the court may allow) to adopt or refuse to adopt the contract.[79] If the trustee does not reply in writing to the request within the period allowed, he is deemed to have refused to adopt the contract.[80]

## 8.23. CHALLENGEABLE TRANSACTIONS

In seeking to deal with the debtor's estate, the permanent trustee may discover that the debtor had disposed of parts of it prior to sequestration. The law of bankruptcy could not operate effectively if there was no means of challenging disposals which had the effect of unfairly prejudicing the body of creditors. Accordingly, procedures for challenge are laid down. It should be noted, however, that no decree to reduce a gratuitous alienation or unfair preference can be granted under the Act in respect of property which is the subject of the "tainted gift" provisions of the Proceeds of Crime Act 2002.[81]

### (a) Gratuitous alienations

Under s.34(1) such transactions may be challenged in the Court of Session by a creditor, the permanent trustee, the trustee under a protected trust deed, or the judicial factor on a deceased's estate. The essence of a gratuitous alienation is that the debtor has simply given up some part of his estate. It must be shown that there has been a transfer of the debtor's property (including a cash payment), or a renunciation of a right,[82] as where a debtor gave up his right to the assignation of a lease.[83] In the context of corporate insolvency, it has been held that the giving of a guarantee amounts to an alienation.[84] An alienation will be challengeable if made to an associate of the debtor within five years of the date of the debtor's sequestration (or of his death, or the granting of a protected trust deed).[85] If made to any other person, the relevant period is two years.[86] The term associate is defined[87] so as to embrace a wide variety of

[73] *Mitchell's Trs v Pearson* (1834) 12 S. 322.
[74] *Sturrock v Robertson's Tr.,* 1913 S.C. 582.
[75] *McGavin v Sturrock's Tr.* (1891) 18 R. 576.
[76] *Craig's Tr. v Lord Malcolm* (1900) 2 F. 541.
[77] *Crown Estate Commissioners v Liquidators of Highland Engineering Ltd,* 1975 S.L.T. 58.
[78] s.42(2).
[79] *ibid.*
[80] s.42(3).
[81] Proceeds of Crime Act 2002, s.422.
[82] 1985 Act, s.34(2)(a).
[83] *Ahmed's Tr. v Ahmed (No. 2),* 1993 S.L.T. 651.
[84] *Jackson v Royal Bank of Scotland plc,* 2002 S.L.T. 1123.
[85] s.34(3)(a).
[86] s.34(3)(b).
[87] s.74.

individuals who are seen as having close ties, emotional or financial with the debtor. So an associate may be:

(1) a spouse, including any former or reputed spouse;
(2) certain relatives of the debtor or his spouse (including any former or reputed spouse), *i.e.* any direct ancestor or descendant, any sibling, uncle, aunt, niece or nephew, in all cases, treating an illegitimate child as legitimate, treating any adopted child as a natural child, and treating any half blood relationship as of the whole blood;
(3) the spouse (including any former or reputed spouse) of any such relative;
(4) business partners and their associates, a firm itself being an associate of any of its members;
(5) the debtor's employer or employee (and for this purpose any director or other officer of a company is treated as its employee);
(6) a company if the debtor alone, or the debtor and his associates control it. A company is an associate of another company if the same person controls both, or a person controls one and his associates (or he and his associates) control the other. Equally, a company may be an associate of another company if a group of two or more person controls each company, and the groups either consist of the same persons or their associates. Control occurs where the directors of a company (or of another company which controls the first) are accustomed to act in accordance with the instructions of a person or group, or where a person or group is entitled to exercise or control the exercise of one third of the voting power at any general meeting of the company (or of another company which controls the first).

A mere friend of the debtor, no matter how close, or even a fiancee is not an associate.

In order to determine when an alienation took place, the Act[88] directs that this shall be when the alienation became completely effectual. In relation to moveables this is taken to be the date of delivery, while in relation to heritage, it is taken to be the date of recording of the disposition.[89] The same argument must also apply to any transaction where some form of registration is necessary to complete title.

There are three absolute defences to a challenge.

(a) that at any time after the alienation, the debtors assets exceeded his liabilities.[90]

The Act attempts to open to challenge alienations by individuals who are plainly insolvent. Thus alienations during periods of temporary insolvency are not challengeable.

(b) that the alienation was for adequate consideration.[91]

In other words, that the alienation was not gratuitous at all. In *McFadyen's Tr. v McFadyen*[92] it was that held that the term "consideration" should be accorded its ordinary meaning as something of value given in return for something else. In that case, a mother purchased a house for her son and paid all the running costs. He then having transferred title to her gratuitously, it was held that this amounted to a gratuitous alienation, as her contribution of the price and payment of the costs could not be treated as consideration. In similar fashion in *Matheson's Tr. v Matheson*[93] Lord Marnoch held consideration could not be provided in respect of a disposition of a house by a husband to his wife by a number of past gifts she had made to him. A payment cannot be treated as amounting to consideration if it was not so intended at the

---

[88] s.34(3).
[89] See respectively *Craiglaw Developments Ltd v Wilson*, 1997 S.C.L.R. 1157; and *Grant's Tr. v Grant*, 1986 S.L.T 220.
[90] s.34(4)(a). If this defence is pleaded, clear evidence of this fact must be provided: *Lombardi's Tr. v Lombardi*, 1982 S.L.T. 81.
[91] s.34(4)(b).
[92] 1994 S.L.T. 1245.
[93] 1992 S.L.T. 685.

time. On the other hand, the fact that a disposition of heritage narrates that it is for "love, favour and affection" does not prevent the debtor seeking to prove that in reality adequate consideration was given.[94]

In *Cay's Tr. v Cay*[95] a husband who had given a large sum of money to his wife sought to argue that adequate consideration had been provided by her undertaking to aliment him Predictably, this argument received short shrift from Lord McCluskey, who opined[96]:

> "It cannot be maintained that this transfer of funds effected any alteration in the defender's obligation to aliment the debtor or in the debtor's corresponding legal right to demand such aliment. The legal rights of the defender and debtor *inter se* in relation to aliment remained after the transfer of funds exactly as they had been before. Accordingly, it cannot be said that the transfer of funds constituted a consideration in the form of a newly created legal right to be enjoyed by the debtor against the defender."

In regard to determining whether the consideration is adequate when genuine consideration is supplied, Lord Cullen observes in *Lafferty Construction v McCombe*[97]:

> "I do not take the view that it is for the defender to establish that the consideration was the best which could have been obtained in the circumstances. On the other hand, the expression 'adequate' implies the application of an objective standpoint. he consideration should be not less than would reasonably be expected in the circumstances, assuming that persons in the position of the parties were acting in good faith and at arms length."

In this context, the Second Division in the *Cay* case was prepared to concede that consideration could be found in an undertaking by Mrs Cay to assume liability for certain of her husband's debts, but held that as the alienation was inadequate since that liability could not exceed £20,000, while the alienation was in the region of £35,000. Again, in *Kerr v Aitken*[98] a husband and wife jointly owned a house and a further parcel of land, the latter being subject to a standard security in favour of a bank. He sought to argue that consideration for his otherwise gratuitous alienation of his half of the house in favour of her was supplied by her waiving her right of relief against him should the bank enforce the standard security to recover the amount of his overdraft. The argument was rejected because there was no suggestion that a right of relief against him was worth anything.

    (c) That the alienation was a permitted gift, *i.e.* a birthday, Xmas or other conventional gift, or charitable donation (but in this last case not to an associate).[99]

Any such gift or donation will still be open to challenge if not "reasonable", obviously a significant qualification in this context. A donation is charitable if made for any charitable, benevolent or philanthropic purpose, whether or not this is regarded as charitable within the meaning of any rule of law.[1]

If an alienation is successfully challenged, then the court shall grant decree of reduction or order restoration of property to the estate or such other redress as may be appropriate.[2] Nevertheless, a third party who has acquired any property in good faith and for value shall not be prejudiced.[3] Thus where a third party is involved, it may be most appropriate to order the original recipient of the alienation to pay over to the estate the proceeds of the sale to the third

---

[94] *Nottay's Tr. v Nottay,* 2001 S.L.T. 769.
[95] 1998 S.C.L.R 456.
[96] at 461B–C.
[97] 1994 S.L.T. 858 at 861D.
[98] [2000] B.P.I.R. 278.
[99] s.34(4)(c).
[1] s.34(5).
[2] s.34(4).
[3] *ibid.*

party. But where a third party is not involved, restoration would seem to be the main remedy, if possible. In *Short's Tr. v Chung*[4] S sold to C two flats in Glasgow in October 1986 for £2,500 each. C gifted them to his wife in May 1987 and S was sequestrated in June 1987. A valuer acting for the permanent trustee valued the flats as at October 1986 at £6,500 and £7,000. The Lord Ordinary decided that the alienations were not for adequate consideration and granted reduction of the transactions. Mrs C was not protected as she had not given value for the property. Mrs C then appealed on the basis that the remedy of reduction was inequitable as, due to the rise in property prices, it allowed the debtor's estate to benefit by more than the difference between the sum paid and the actual market value of the property at the time of sale. She contended that the appropriate remedy would have been to order her to pay £8,500 (the difference between the sum paid and the actual market value of the property at the time of sale). The Second Division responded as follows[5]:

> "It is clear that the general purpose [of s.34] is to provide that as far as possible any property which has been improperly alienated should be restored to the debtor's estate. In the case of a disposition of heritable property this can easily be done by reduction of that disposition. We consider that the reference to 'such other redress as may be appropriate' is not intended to give the court a general discretion to decide a case on equitable principles, but is designed to enable the court to make an appropriate order in a case where reduction or restoration of the property is not a remedy which is available."

Equally, in the Cay case It was argued on behalf of Mrs Cay that she should not be obliged to repay the whole £35,000, as she had used the money partly to pay off £20,000 of her husband's debts. The Second Division followed its previous line that s.34(4) does not "create any general discretion to decide on equitable principles to order something less than a full return of the alienated property".[6] Nor was there any room for the doctrine of set off to apply, as "there was no *concursus debiti and crediti*".[7]

By contrast, in *Nottay's Tr. v Nottay*[8] the debtor's spouse, having been given certain equipment by the debtor, was asked to pay for it by the trustee. She argued that, as she had sold it on, but had been compelled to sue the buyer for payment, the trustee should really be seeking the return of the property from the buyer. Lord Clarke said,[9] that the case:

> "is distinguishable from *Short* and *Cay*, where the relevant property could be reconveyed by reduction of the relevant disposition. In the present case, the property is moveable, has been sold to a third party, and the whereabouts of the goods are unknown. It is also nothing to the point that the second defender may not herself have received consideration for the goods, if there was a gratuitous alienation in terms of s.34. The pursuer is entitled to seek appropriate redress from her which, in this case, would appear to be the value of the goods in question."

## (b) Unfair preferences

Such a transaction may be challenged in the same court and by the same categories of person as in regard to gratuitous alienations above.[10] To be challengeable, the preference must have occurred no more than six months before the date of sequestration (or the date of granting of a protected trust deed, or the date of death if sequestration of the appointment of a judicial factor

---

[4] 1991 S.L.T. 472.
[5] at 476K. For a final twist in the tale of this saga, see *Short's Tr. v Keeper of the Registers of Scotland,* 1996 S.C. (H.L.) 1; and *Short's Tr. v Chung (No. 2),* 1997 S.C.L.R. 1181.
[6] at 464B.
[7] at 463C.
[8] 2001 S.L.T. 769.
[9] at 774C–D.
[10] s.36.

follows within 12 months of death).[11] A preference is unfair if a creditor is preferred to the prejudice of the general body of creditors.[12] An example might be the granting of a security to an hitherto unsecured creditor, but a simple payment of a debt might in certain circumstances suffice. An interesting example from the corporate sphere is found in the case of *Baillie Marshall Ltd (in liquidation) v Avian Communications Ltd*[13] where A Ltd acquired the business of B Ltd for a consideration which included the payment of B Ltd's trade creditors, but not their other creditors, with the aim of preserving the goodwill attached to B Ltd's business.

Certain transactions cannot be challenged.

(1) Any transaction in the ordinary course of trade or business.[14]

In *Nordic Travel Ltd v Scotprint Ltd*[15] Lord Cameron adopts the following definition thereof:

> "a transaction which it would be usual for a creditor or debtor to enter as a matter of business in the circumstances . . . uninfluenced by any belief on the part of the creditor that the debtor might be insolvent."

So the payment of debts as they fall due would be in this category, as would the delivery of orders to customers. But returning goods to a supplier because of fears that the account would not be paid would not be, and would therefore amount to an unfair preference.[16] In *Balcraig House's Tr. v Roosevelt Property Services Ltd*[17] some four months before the date of sequestration a firm which ran a hotel "sold" its contents to a company, although the firm continued in possession of these goods. The consideration for this transaction was said to be a sum of money which the company had loaned the firm four years earlier, but which had never been repaid. Lord Maclean took the view that this transaction was an unfair preference as the debtor was in effect voluntarily transferring assets to one creditor in respect of a debt already incurred. Even if it were a true sale, it could not be seen as within the ordinary course of the firm's business as a hotel.

(2) Any payment in cash in respect of a debt then payable—unless there is collusion.[18]

It follows that cash payment of a debt not yet due would amount to a preference.[19] Payment by banker's drafts, cheques or other bills of exchange amounts to cash payment.[20] But it is would normally be an unfair preference for a debtor to indorse to a creditor a bill drawn up in his favour.[21] As far as collusion is concerned, Lord President Emslie defines it thus in the *Nordic* case[22]:

> "The creditor who has been preferred has been apprised of the debtor's situation and duties, and enters into a transaction with him for the purpose of deceiving and defeating the rest of his creditors."

and,

> "There is no authority for the view that the word 'collusion' is apt to include a creditor's knowledge of the insolvency of the debtor at the time of payment. The word . . . is intended to refer to participation by the creditor whose co-operation is necessary to achieve the result, in some device or transaction designed particularly to confer upon him a preference which would itself be [unfair]."

---

[11] s.36(1).
[12] *ibid.*
[13] 2002 S.L.T. 189.
[14] s.36(2)(a).
[15] 1980 S.C. 1 at 29.
[16] *Morton's Tr. v The Fifeshire Auction Co Ltd,* 1911 1 S.L.T. 405.
[17] 1994 S.L.T. 1133.
[18] s.36(2)(b).
[19] *Whatmough's Tr. v British Linen Bank,* 1932 S.C. 525 at 543, *per* Lord President Clyde.
[20] *Whatmough's Tr. v British Linen Bank,* 1934 S.C. (H.L.) 51.
[21] *Horburgh v Ramsay* (1885) 12 R. 1171; but see *Watson v Young* (1826) 4 S. 507.
[22] at 11 and 19.

(3) A transaction where the debtor and the other party undertake reciprocal obligations—*nova debita*.[23]

An example would be where a party demands security in return for advancing money to the debtor—but not where the debtor grants a security in relation to a loan that has already been made. In *Thomas Montgomery & Sons v Gallacher*[24] the suppliers of G became concerned by his tardiness in failing to pay his account on the proper date. Accordingly in return for agreeing to continue to supply him, they persuaded him to grant a heritable security over his trade premises. That security was stated to be "in respect of credit facilities presently granted to me and for future credit facilities". Lord Stewart took the view that transactions entered into after this agreement were *nova debita* and thus validly covered by the security. The granting of the security in respect of existing transactions would, however, have been an unfair preference. Yet the issue did not arise since G had continued to make payments in respect of goods supplied, and on the basis of the rule in *Clayton's* case, see para. 6.19. it was assumed that such payments should be ascribed to the earlier transactions, with the result that these earlier debts had been settled.

In *Nicoll v Steelpress (Supplies) Ltd*[25] (a case decided under the equivalent provisions of the Insolvency Act 1986) S Ltd became worried when one of the companies it supplied fell further and further behind in the payment of its account. Accordingly, it arranged that it would only continue to supply the company if each order was met by a payment which would go some way towards clearing off the existing debt—*e.g.* on one occasion goods invoiced at under £350 were released in exchange for a cheque for £10,500. It was held that this amounted to an unfair preference. An Extra Division of the Inner House opined[26]:

> "The principle is that the consideration given to the debtor in the transaction cannot be less than full value to qualify for the exception. Strict equivalence is necessary in that the debtor's estate must not be diminished as a result of the transaction."

Once again, this exception does not apply where there is collusion.[27]

(4) The grant of a mandate to pay over arrested funds, as long as there has been a decree for payment or a warrant for summary diligence, and that decree/warrant has been proceeded by an arrestment on the dependence or followed by an arrestment in execution.[28]

The result of a successful challenge is identical to a successful challenge of a gratuitous alienation. The facts of *Baillie Marshall Ltd (in liquidation) v Avian Communications Ltd*[29] (a case decided under the equivalent provisions of the Insolvency Act 1986), are related above. The liquidator sought damages from the company which had bought the liquidated company's business in return for, *inter alia*, the payment of the latter's trade creditors. The measure of damages sought represented the amount which the other creditors would have received by way of dividend, but for the transaction. It was held that such an action was not competent. Relying on cases decided in relation to gratuitous alienations under the bankruptcy legislation, Lord Kingarth took the view that restoration of property is the primary remedy envisaged by the statute, and the words "or such other redress as may be appropriate", should be construed as relating to redress of the same general character, and not as giving the court a general equitable jurisdiction.

### (c) Challenging gratuitous alienations/fraudulent preferences at common law

Any creditor has the right to challenge a gratuitous alienation at common law and by virtue of s.34(8) this right of challenge is extended to the permanent trustee (as well as a trustee under a

---

[23] s.36(2)(c).
[24] 1982 S.L.T. 138.
[25] 1992 S.C.L.R. 332.
[26] at 338B.
[27] s.36(2)(c).
[28] s.36(2)(d).
[29] 2002 S.L.T. 189.

protected trust deed or any judicial factor). For a challenge to succeed at common law, it must be shown not only that the alienation was gratuitous, but that it prejudiced lawful creditors, and most importantly, that at the time of the alienation the debtor was absolutely insolvent or was made so by the alienation and is still absolutely insolvent at the time of challenge. Absolute insolvency (as opposed to apparent insolvency—see para. 8.5.) occurs when the debtor's liabilities exceed his assets.

In much the same way s.36(6) gives a permanent trustee (as well as a trustee under a protected trust deed or any judicial factor) the same right to challenge a fraudulent preference at common law. Despite the use of the term fraudulent, there is no need for an actual dishonest intention to be shown. The criteria are that the transaction was a voluntary act of the debtor,[30] undertaken when he was absolutely insolvent and knew himself to be so,[31] which transaction preferred one creditor to the prejudice of others.[32] Although the debtor must be aware of his insolvent state, the state of knowledge of the preferred creditor is irrelevant. As Lord Justice Clerk Hope puts it in *McCowan v Wright*[33]

> "The creditors are equally injured—the prejudice to them is the same, whether the receiver at the time knew that the security was a fraud against them or not; and if it was a fraud . . . it does not become less so that he did not at the time know it was a fraud."

While Lord President Emslie notes in *Nordic Travel Ltd v Scotprint Ltd*[34]:

> "The creditor's knowledge of his debtor's absolute insolvency at the time when the debtor performs an act in his favour is quite irrelevant in deciding whether or not the act is a fraudulent preference. If a particular act by an insolvent debtor to his creditor is per se unobjectionable and lawful, I am unable to see how his creditor's mere knowledge of his insolvency can make it objectionable and unlawful."

Defences (1)–(3) considered in the previous sub-paragraph in relation to unfair preferences apply in this context also.

If the appropriate conditions are met, then a transaction might be challenged as a gratuitous alienation or fraudulent preference whenever it occurred—*i.e.* the time limits laid down by the Act do not apply. A transaction can indeed be challenged prior to the commencement of the sequestration process, although obviously it would be a creditor rather than the permanent trustee who would make such a challenge.

Finally, it should be remembered that whether a transaction is being challenged at common law or under statute, the court cannot recover money or property from a defender who is outside Scotland.[35]

## (d) Capital sum payable on divorce

While a decree ordering the transfer or property and/or the payment of a certain sum on the debtor's divorce could hardly be described as either a gratuitous alienation or unfair preference, it may appear unduly generous with the benefit of hindsight. Thus if, within five years of the order, the debtor's estate has been sequestrated, or he has granted a trust deed which has become protected, or he has died and within 12 months after his death he has either been sequestrated or a judicial factor has been appointed to administer his estate, the appropriate person (the permanent trustee, the trustee under the trust deed, or the judicial factor) may request the court to recall an order.[36] It must be shown that the debtor was

---

[30] See Lord President Emslie in *Nordic Travel Ltd v Scotprint Ltd,* 1980 S.C. 1 at 10.
[31] *McCowan v Wright* (1853) 15 D. 494.
[32] *ibid*.
[33] (1853) 15 D. 494 at 498.
[34] 1980 S.C. 1 at 14.
[35] *Reid v Ramlort Ltd, The Times,* October 14, 1998, HL.
[36] s.35(1)–(2).

absolutely insolvent at the date of the order, or was so rendered by the order.[37] (A debtor is absolutely insolvent where her/his liabilities are greater than her/his assets.[38] The court, having regard to all the circumstances, including the financial and other circumstances of the person against whom the order would be made, may order repayment of the whole or part of the sum paid, the retransfer of the whole or part of any property transferred, or payment of the whole or part of the proceeds from the sale of property.[39]

## (e) Excessive pension contributions

While any sums paid to the debtor from an occupational or personal pension schemes do not vest in the permanent trustee, such amounts obviously derive to some extent from contributions made to such schemes by or on behalf of the debtor. It is therefore possible that during the period leading up to the sequestration, the debtor may have been investing considerable sums in such a scheme to safeguard his ultimate pension position, to the detriment of his creditors. For that reason the permanent trustee may apply to the court in such circumstances.[40] If the court is satisfied that the debtor's rights under the scheme are to any extent derived from excessive contributions, it may make such order as it thinks fit for restoring the position to what it would have been had the excessive contributions not been made.[41] Such an order may in particular require those responsible for the scheme to pay over an amount to the trustee, and/or to reduce the benefits paid by the scheme to the debtor or to any other person, *e.g.* a dependant of the debtor, where these benefits derive from the rights of the debtor.[42] The maximum amount that may be ordered to be paid is the amount of the excessive contributions, or the value of the debtor's rights under the scheme, whichever is the lesser.[43] Before it can make an order, the court must be satisfied that the making of the excessive contributions has unfairly prejudiced the creditors,[44] and in so deciding shall consider whether any contributions were made for the purpose of putting assets beyond the reach of creditors, and whether contributions appear excessive in view of the debtor's circumstances when they were made.[45] In deciding when whether contributions are excessive, no account is to be taken of any debit on the debtor's benefits on account of pension sharing.[46] In other words, the court is not allowed to take into account that a debtor has to share a pension with an ex-spouse in working out whether contributions were excessive.

## (f) Extortionate credit transactions

It is not unknown for debtors who are sinking deeper into financial difficulties to enter into very unwise credit transactions. The permanent trustee can challenge any credit transaction entered into within three years prior to the date of sequestration on the basis that it is extortionate.[47] A credit transaction is extortionate if, having regard to the risk accepted by the credit supplier, its terms required grossly exorbitant payments to be made, or it otherwise grossly contravened the ordinary principles of fair dealing.[48] It will be presumed that a transaction is extortionate, and so it will fall to the credit supplier to prove the contrary.[49]

---

[37] s.35(2).
[38] s.73(2).
[39] s.35(2).
[40] s.36A(1).
[41] s.36A(2).
[42] s.36A(2)–(3).
[43] s.36B(4).
[44] s.36A(2)(b).
[45] s.36A(6).
[46] s.36A(3)–(4).
[47] s.61(2).
[48] s.61(3).
[49] *ibid.*

These criteria are essentially the same as those applied in order to determine whether a credit bargain is extortionate in terms of s.138 of the Consumer Credit Act 1974 (see para. 3.9.), so case law thereunder may be instructive. Where the court finds a credit transaction to be extortionate, it may do any one or more of the following things[50]:

- set aside the obligation in whole or in part;
- vary the terms of the obligation or any associated security;
- require repayment to the permanent trustee of any sums paid by the debtor;
- require the surrender to the permanent trustee of any property held as security for the purposes of the transaction;
- direct accounts to be taken between any persons.

Again, these powers are very similar to those of the court under s.139 of the Consumer Credit Act 1974. Obviously any money or property returned under this provision vests in the permanent trustee.[51] While the sequestration process is in operation neither the debtor nor the permanent trustee can ask that an extortionate credit agreement be reopened under s.139 of the Consumer Credit Act 1974.[52] Remedy lies in the hands of the permanent trustee exercising the rights described above, perhaps in conjunction with the provisions relating to gratuitous alienations and unfair preferences.[53]

## 8.24. REALISATION OF THE ESTATE

While the permanent trustee may have to manage the estate, his main concern will be to sell it off, including any debts owing to the estate.[54] Any part of the estate may be sold either by public sale or private bargain.[55] However, it is incompetent for the permanent trustee, or any associate of his, or a commissioner to purchase any part of the estate.[56] The meaning of the term "incompetent" in this context is not clear. It may be that s.39(8) is intended as a qualification of s.39(7), which recites that the validity of the title of any purchaser shall not be challengeable on the ground that there has been a failure to comply with s.39. If so, then it is possible that s.39(8) intends to suggest that such sales are void, with the result that any purchaser from the permanent trustee etc cannot obtain a good title. It must also be remembered that a permanent trustee is a fiduciary.[57] Thus, if for example, a trustee were to sell part of the property of the estate to another, on the understanding that the property would then be resold to the trustee, such a transaction would be voidable at common law, and the trustee liable in damages to the estate.[58]

The permanent trustee may sell heritage despite it being subject to an inhibition, although that inhibition will remain in effect to preserve a preference in the ranking of the creditor's claim.[59] Where heritage is subject to a security then either the permanent trustee or the secured creditor may sell. Generally, once the permanent trustee has intimated his intention to sell, the secured creditor may not take steps to sell the property, and vice versa.[60] Nonetheless, if either party, has intimated his intention to sell, then delays unduly in doing so, the other may seek the

---

[50] s.61(4).
[51] s.61(5).
[52] s.61(6).
[53] ibid.
[54] s.39(5).
[55] s.39(3).
[56] s.39(8).
[57] York Buildings Company v Mackenzie (1795) 3 Pat. 378.
[58] Fraser v Hankey & Co (1847) 9 D. 415; Whyte's Tr. v Burt (1851) 13 D. 679.
[59] s.31(2).
[60] s.39(4)(b).

authority of the court to proceed with the sale himself.[61] Moreover, the permanent trustee may not sell heritage without the concurrence of any secured creditor, unless he obtains a sufficiently high price to discharge the securities.[62] The Accountant in Bankruptcy counsels[63]:

> "[T]he trustee should ensure that any offer which he proposes to accept is more than sufficient to cover not only the expenses of the sale and conveyancing, including a fee to cover the trustee's own time costs in connection with the transaction, but also full settlement with the secured creditor . . . [U]nder no circumstances will the Accountant pass any of these expenses . . . as a proper charge against other funds held for the general body of creditors."

There may also be difficulties if the permanent trustee wishes to sell the family home. This is the place where immediately before the date of sequestration the debtor's spouse (with or without the debtor) or former spouse resided, or the debtor resided with a child of the family.[64] The width of the definition means that more than one residence could qualify as the family home. A child of the family includes any child or grandchild of the debtor, his spouse, or former spouse, as well as any person who has been brought up and accepted as if s/he were the child of any of those individuals.[65] The actual age of the child is irrelevant.[66] The inspiration of the provisions in this area is the recognition that, while it is obviously not acceptable that the debtor's family should continue indefinitely to occupy accommodation of a high standard while his creditors await payment, nonetheless, the family could experience genuine hardship through the immediate sale of their home.[67] Accordingly, the permanent trustee requires to obtain the consent of the spouse or debtor, and if that cannot be obtained, the authority of the court, if he wishes to sell.[68] (The debtor's consent need only be sought, if living with a child of the family, but not a spouse, or former spouse.) It will be seen that the Act protects the interests of the family. There is no need to seek any consent or authority if the debtor occupies a house alone or with someone, *e.g.* a lover or parent, who is not part of the family. Nor indeed is consent required when a child occupies a house alone.

Where the permanent trustee is unable to obtain the necessary consent, and is obliged to apply to the court, the court will take into account all the circumstances of the case, including[69]:

- the needs and financial resources of the spouse/former spouse or any child of the family,
- the length of time the home has been used as a residence by any of the above individuals,
- the interests of creditors.

The court then may decide to refuse the application. It might do so, for example, when the amount which might be secured from the sale would be modest in comparison with the dislocative effect of the sale on the family, but in extreme cases applications have been refused even where the family home was the debtor's major asset, in light of the trauma which sale might cause.[70] Even if the court authorises the sale of the home, it may postpone the granting of the application for up to 12 months or grant it subject to conditions.[71] In *McMahon's Trs v McMahon*[72] it was held that such conditions could validly include the payment of part of the

---

[61] s.39(4)(c).
[62] s.39(4)(a).
[63] Notes for Guidance of Interim and Permanent Trustees, paras 6.11.2. and 6.12.1.
[64] s.40(4)(a).
[65] s.40(4)(b).
[66] *ibid.*
[67] *Report of the Review Committee on Insolvency Law and Practice* (1982) Cmnd. 8858, para. 1118.
[68] s.40(1).
[69] s.40(2).
[70] See *e.g. Gourlay's Tr. Petr,* 1995 S.L.T. (Sh. Ct) 7; but compare *Salmon's Tr. v Salmon,* 1989 S.L.T. (Sh. Ct) 49.
[71] s.40(2).
[72] 1997 S.C.L.R. 439.

proceeds of sale to certain of the debtor's dependants. It may be noted that the court must take into account the same factors, and has the same powers where the permanent trustee raises an action for the division and sale of the family home (which would be required if the house were not owned solely by the debtor), or an action to obtain vacant possession, *i.e.* eviction.[73] It might be added that the above safeguards only apply where the permanent trustee wishes to sell the family home. There are no such safeguards where a secured creditor exercises the right to sell the property over which it has security, even if that property is a family home.

Following upon the realisation of the estate, the permanent trustee would proceed to distribute it as directed by the Act. The order of distribution is considered at para. 8.32. in the section dealing with creditors, which now follows.

# (2) THE CREDITORS

This treatment, having so far considered the subject from the standpoint of the debtor or permanent trustee, now turns to look at sequestration from the perspective of the creditors. Before considering the relationship of creditors to the sequestration process, it is useful to consider the impact that pre-sequestration activities may have on that process, *i.e.* the relationship between sequestration and diligence.

## 8.25.  SEQUESTRATION AND DILIGENCE

Obviously, when an individual is in financial difficulties and his/her creditors are not receiving payment, one or more creditors may be tempted to do diligence on the debtor's estate in order to obtain payment. Diligence is of course the process whereby the debtor's property is attached in order to facilitate recovery of his debts. The main forms of diligence are arrestment and attachment of moveables and inhibition and adjudication in relation to heritage. The point of doing diligence is of course to give a creditor a preferential right to the asset(s) upon which diligence is done. If a number of creditors seek to do diligence upon a certain asset, priority tends to be determined in terms of the date on which diligence was done—the earlier a creditor did diligence the more advantageous his position. Yet the law of personal insolvency is premised on the basis that creditors are treated fairly and, for the most part, equally. That aim would hardly be served if a creditor could ensure full payment simply by being the first to rush to diligence. Accordingly, there are special rules regarding diligence.

### (a) Equalisation of diligence and apparent insolvency

Certain rules apply to diligence even though outwith the context of the sequestration process. Thus all arrestments and attachments executed within the period 60 days before the constitution of apparent insolvency (see para. 8.5) and four months thereafter are treated as if they had been executed on the same date.[74] So, if an act of apparent insolvency is committed on July 31, any diligences done during the period between June 1 and November 30 are treated as if they had been done on the same day. The result of course is that they are all ranked equally. This is known as equalisation of diligence, and ensures equal treatment of creditors. The Act also states that if there is any judicial process relating to the arrestments or attachments, any creditor who can produce liquid grounds of debt or a decree for payment

---

[73] s.40(3).
[74] s.75(1)(b), Sch. 7, para. 24(1).

within the aforesaid period is entitled to share equally in the assets affected by the diligence.[75] The above example is very straightforward. Yet if an individual is experiencing financial difficulties, more than one instance of apparent insolvency may arise, so that there may be overlapping equalisation periods. This can give rise to issues of great complexity to which the current law provides no obvious solution.[76]

It may be noted that none of the above provisions apply to an earnings arrestment, a current maintenance arrestment, or a conjoined arrestment order.[77] This is because there can only be one earnings arrestment and current maintenance arrestment effective against a debtor at any one time. If any other creditor wishes to share in the earnings of a debtor, a conjoined arrestment order must be sought.

Equalisation of diligence does not apply to inhibitions, which by their nature do not attach to a specific asset. All adjudications before or within a year and a day after an effectual adjudication are equalised.[78] There is no connection with insolvency.

## (b) Diligence and sequestration

As might be expected, actual sequestration has an effect on diligence. Thus, broadly speaking, any diligence done within 60 days prior to the date of sequestration or any time thereafter is effectively cut down.[79] So no arrestment or attachment within the aforesaid period is effectual, and any estate so arrested or attached, or the proceeds of sale thereof must be handed over to the permanent trustee.[80] There is no need for arrestment or attachment to be subsisting at the date of sequestration.[81] If the estate has been arrested or attached during the crucial period, it or the proceeds of its sale must be handed over, even if the arrestment or attachment has been withdrawn or otherwise fallen.[82] There is no suggestion under the Act that a third party who has acquired an estate in good faith from the arresting/attaching creditor may retain it. Therefore, the permanent trustee should be able to demand that such a third party hands over the estate. The arresting/ attaching creditor is nonetheless entitled to certain expenses to be paid from the estate or the proceeds of its sale, *i.e.* expenses incurred[83]:

- in obtaining the extract of the decree or other document on which the arrestment or attachment proceeded;
- in executing the arrestment or attachment;
- in taking any further action in respect of the diligence.

None of the above provisions applies to an earnings arrestment, a current maintenance arrestment, a conjoined arrestment order, or deductions from earnings orders under the Child Support Act 1991.[84] Yet sequestration terminates such arrestments and orders, although the interim or permanent trustee must apply for the recall of a conjoined arrestment order.[85]

In similar vein, no inhibition within the crucial period is effective.[86] As inhibition does not attach to specific assets, no provision is made for the handing over of any estate to the permanent trustee, nor for the creditor to recover any expenses in connection with the inhibition. However, the permanent trustee acquires any right of challenge competent to the

---

[75] Sch. 7, para. 24(3).
[76] See Scottish Law Commission Discussion Paper on the Equalisation of Diligences (1988) No. 79, paras 5.42.—5.53.
[77] Sch. 7, para. 24(8).
[78] Diligence Act 1661, Adjudications Act 1672.
[79] s.37.
[80] s.37(4).
[81] *ibid*.
[82] As to the previous law see *Johnston v Cluny Estates Tr.,* 1957 S.L.T 293.
[83] s.37(5).
[84] s.37(5A).
[85] Debtors (Scotland) Act 1987, ss.72 and 66.
[86] s.37(2).

inhibitor and any right the inhibitor would have to receive payment for discharging the inhibition.[87] Again, no poinding of the ground (required to give a heritable creditor security over moveables on the subjects) is effectual within the crucial period, save in respect of certain interest.[88] Finally, adjudication after the date of sequestration is incompetent.[89]

While sequestration does not itself amount to diligence,[90] the Act treats it as having the effect of the appropriate form of diligence. Thus s.37(1) recites that, as from the date of sequestration, the award of sequestration has the effect in relation to any dilgence done of:

- a duly recorded decree of adjudication on the debtor's heritable estate, and
- an arrestment in execution and decree of furthcoming, an arrestment in execution and warrant of sale, and a completed poinding,

in favour of the creditors according to their respective entitlements. In other words, it is as if each creditor did the appropriate form(s) at the date of sequestration. This has significant consequences where the date of sequestration occurs within four months of the constitution of apparent insolvency. Since, as described above, all arrestments and attachments executed within the period 60 days before the constitution of apparent insolvency and four months thereafter are treated as if they had been executed on the same date, all arrestments and attachments within that period will be equalised with the sequestration itself, and so will effectively be cut down. This is illustrated by *Stewart v Jarvie*.[91] Diligence was done on October 16, 1936, apparent insolvency constituted on November 27, 1936. Sequestration was awarded on January 4, 1937. It can be appreciated then that diligence was done more than 60 days prior to the date of sequestration, so that it was not automatically cut down. Nonetheless, the sequestration did occur within four months of the constitution of apparent insolvency, and the diligence was executed less than 60 days prior to that latter date, so that the diligence was equalised with the sequestration and the creditor concerned gained no priority over the other creditors in the sequestration. Lord Fleming explained the matter thus[92]:

> "It is important to note that, on the one hand, the appellant's arrestment was used within 60 days prior to the constitution of [apparent insolvency], and that, on the other hand, sequestration took place within four months thereafter . . . Applying [the legislation] to the case in hand, the result is that on January 4 the sequestration is to be regarded as equivalent to an arrestment used for behoof of all the creditors equally. And accordingly the appellant's claim for a preference over the other creditors must be dealt with on the footing that, in addition to the arrestment he used on October 16, there was also used for the behoof of the general body of the creditors, an arrestment on January 4 . . . The appellant is not entitled to any preference over the other creditors, for his arrestment and their arrestment are equalised. The appellant is entitled to be ranked on the arrested fund for the amount of his claim, but equally all the other creditors are entitled to be ranked thereon *pari passu* with him for the amount of their respective claims."

Of course, if diligence has been effected too early to be struck down by the sequestration, it remains effective. It may well be that the effect of the diligence is to transfer ownership of the asset concerned to the creditor. If however, ownership is retained by the debtor, the asset will vest in the permanent trustee and the diligence is treated as a security over the asset.

---

[87] s.37(3).
[88] s.37(6).
[89] s.37(8).
[90] *G & A Barnie v Stevenson*, 1993 S.C.L.R. 318.
[91] 1938 S.C. 309.
[92] at 312.

## 8.26. THE CREDITORS' SUPERVISION OF THE INSOLVENCY PROCESS—COMMISSIONERS

It is possible for the creditors to elect from among their fellows commissioners to advise and supervise the interim and permanent trustees.[93] When sequestration was a process controlled by the creditors, election of the commissioners was mandatory. Now, however, there need not be commissioners (and often none will be elected), while it is not permitted to have commissioners in any sequestration where the permanent trustee is appointed rather than elected.[94] They may be elected at the statutory meeting of creditors or at any subsequent meeting of creditors, and there may any number of commissioners from one to five at any one time.[95] They will be elected by those creditors who are qualified to elect the permanent trustee[96] (see para. 8.13.). To qualify for election individuals must be creditors or mandatories of creditors. A mandatory is someone a creditor has authorised in writing to represent him at a meeting.[97] (The creditor must lodge that authorisation with the trustee prior to the meeting.[98]) Certain individuals are disqualified—the debtor; an associate (see para. 8.23.) of the debtor or of the permanent trustee; a person who holds an interest opposed to the general interests of creditors—and should a commissioner become such a person, he is no longer entitled to continue in that role.[99] A commissioner may resign at any time,[1] and may be removed from office:

- by the creditors at a meeting called for that purpose[2];
- if an elected permanent trustee is replaced by an appointed permanent trustee[3];
- where he is a mandatory, by the creditor recalling the mandate, and intimating that recall in writing to the permanent trustee[4];
- by the court, following on a report by the Accountant that he has failed without reasonable excuse to perform his legal duties.[5]

The general functions of a commissioner are to supervise the intromissions of the permanent trustee with the estate and to advise him.[6] They are subject to certain mandatory duties. Thus, when they become aware that the permanent trustee has resigned, died or been removed from office by the sheriff, they must call a meeting of creditors to elect a replacement.[7] Within six weeks of the end of an accounting period (see next paragraph), they must determine the amount of outlays and remuneration payable to the permanent trustee and may audit his accounts.[8] They must consider any offer of composition reported by the permanent trustee and decide whether it should be placed before the creditors.[9] In addition, their consent is required if the permanent trustee is[10]:

- to carry on the debtors business,

---

[93] s.4.
[94] Sch. 2, para. 6.
[95] s.30(1).
[96] ss.24(3), 30(1).
[97] Sch. 6, para. 11(1).
[98] Sch. 6, para. 11(2).
[99] s.30(2).
[1] s.30(3).
[2] s.30(4)(b).
[3] Sch. 2, para. 6.
[4] s.30(4)(a).
[5] s.1A(2).
[6] s.4.
[7] See ss.28(2)–(3), 29(5)–(6).
[8] s.53(5).
[9] Sch. 4, paras 4–5.
[10] See ss.39(2), 48(3), 52 and 65(1).

- to bring, defend or continue any legal proceedings relating to the estate,
- create a security over any part of the estate,
- make payments or incur liabilities in order to obtain property which is the subject or a right, option or power, which is part of the estate,
- to allow claims other than in proper form,
- to vary the length of an accounting period, other than the first,
- to pay preferred debts earlier than would otherwise be the case,
- to postpone payment of a dividend to the ordinary creditors,
- to refer any claim or question to arbitration,
- to compromise any claim.

There are also powers which they may exercise at their discretion:

- to inspect the permanent trustee's accounts at all reasonable times[11];
- to require the permanent trustee to apply to the sheriff for an order for the public examination of the debtor or other relevant person[12];
- to dispense with the taxation of an account in respect of legal services incurred by the permanent trustee[13];
- to require the permanent trustee to call a meeting of commissioners, or to call a meeting of commissioners themselves if the permanent trustee fails timeously to respond to such a request.[14]

Although the permanent trustee must "have regard" to advice offered by the commissioners,[15] and consult with them regarding the recovery, management and realisation of the estate,[16] he need not take that advice. Nonetheless, the commissioners may apply to the sheriff for the permanent trustee to be given directions as to such matters, with which directions he must comply.[17] The Act also provides that where a "person having an interest" is dissatisfied with any act, omission or decision of the permanent trustee, he may apply to the sheriff who can confirm, annul or modify any such act or decision, or give the permanent trustee such directions as he thinks fit.[18] It is submitted that a commissioner is a "person having an interest". As a last resort commissioners may apply to the sheriff for the permanent trustee's removal from office.[19] The performance of commissioners is itself subject to the supervision of the Accountant, who must report any suspected offences committed by a commissioner to the Lord Advocate.[20] If the Accountant considers that a commissioner has failed without reasonable excuse to perform a legal duty, he must report this to the court, who may remove the commissioner from office, or censure him, or make such other order as seems appropriate.[21]

Commissioners owe fiduciary duties to the debtor and creditors.[22] While a commissioner is specifically precluded from buying any part of the estate,[23] he might also be liable in respect of any transaction related to the estate from which he might benefit, or which might be inimical to interests of the debtor and/or creditors. Moreover, a commissioner must act gratuitously and is not even entitled to expenses. Indeed, if a commissioner also acts as solicitor for the permanent trustee, he may recover his outlays only, and cannot charge for his legal services.[24] If the

---

[11] s.3(1)(f).
[12] s.45(1).
[13] s.53(2A).
[14] Sch. 6, paras 17–18.
[15] s.3(2).
[16] s.39(1).
[17] *ibid.*
[18] s.3(7).
[19] s.29(1).
[20] s.1A(1), (3).
[21] s.1A(2).
[22] *Campbell v Cullen*, 1911 1 S.L.T. 258.
[23] s.39(8).
[24] *Geddes' Tr.* unreported, April 6, 1985.

permanent trustee pays fees to such a commissioner, the Accountant will hold him personally liable to the estate for such a sum.[25]

## 8.27. SUBMISSION OF CLAIMS

Although a few creditors may become commissioners, and the law of diligence will impact on many creditors, all creditors will be interested in submitting claims on the estate and receiving some sort of payment. Claims must be submitted in the prescribed form,[26] which requires details of each debt, and any security for a debt, and must be signed by the creditor or his agent. A claim must be accompanied by an account or voucher which constitutes *prima facie* evidence of the debt.[27] However any failure to meet such requirements can be sanctioned by the interim trustee,[28] or by the permanent trustee, but in this latter case if there are any commissioners, it requires their consent.[29] Moreover, the Act states that a creditor who neither resides nor has a place of business in the UK may be permitted to submit an informal claim in writing.[30] Indeed, where the interim trustee knows where such a creditor resides or has a place of business, then he must write to him to inform him of his right to make a claim—unless he has already done so in notifying him of the statutory meeting.[31] A claim may be stated in foreign currency, where a court order, contract or bill of exchange requires payment to be made in that currency.[32] The claim will be converted into sterling at the rate of exchange for that currency at the mean of the buying and selling spot rates prevailing in the London market at the close of business on the date of sequestration.[33] It is an offence for a creditor to submit a false claim, account or voucher (subject to a defence that he neither knew nor had reason to believe that it was false), and for the debtor who knows of such an offence to fail as soon as is practicable to report it to the trustee in office.[34] The submission of a claim interrupts the running of prescription,[35] and bars any enactment relating to the limitation of actions.[36]

A creditor may submit a claim at or before the statutory meeting in order to be entitled to vote at that meeting,[37] and if this claim is accepted by the interim trustee, it does not require to be resubmitted in order to be entitled to vote in subsequent meetings, nor to be entitled to share in dividends.[38] So it is very common for a creditor to submit a claim before the statutory meeting, not because he intends to vote at or even be present at that or any other meeting, but simply to secure his right to share in dividends. While a claim under a confiscation order under the Proceeds of Crime Act 2002 may not be submitted to the permanent trustee,[39] there seems to be no bar upon such a claim being submitted to the interim trustee. It may be noted that a liquidator appointed in relation to the debtor in another Member State is deemed to be a creditor.[40] Where a creditor has lodged a claim in more than one set of proceedings in the EU, there are rules to ensure that his vote is not double counted and that he does not receive a double payment.[41]

---

[25] *Notes by the Accountant for the Guidance of Interim and Permanent Trustees,* para. 7.7.
[26] s.22(2)(a), Bankruptcy (Scotland) Regulations 1985 (SI 1985/1925), Form 5.
[27] s.22(2)(b).
[28] s.22(2).
[29] s.48(3).
[30] s.22(3)(b).
[31] s.22(3)(a).
[32] s.22(6), s.48(7); Bankruptcy (Scotland) Regulations 1985 (SI 1985/1925), para. 6.
[33] s.23(1)(a), s.49(3); Bankruptcy (Scotland) Regulations 1985 (SI 1985/1925), para. 7.
[34] s.22(5), s.48(7).
[35] Prescription and Limitation (Scotland) Act 1973, s.9(1).
[36] s.22(8).
[37] s.22(1).
[38] s.48(2).
[39] Proceeds of Crime Act 2002, s.420(4).
[40] s.48A(1).
[41] s.48A(3)–(6).

Although a claim accepted by the interim trustee does not require to be resubmitted, the permanent trustee may take a different view of its validity. If a creditor does not submit a claim at or before the statutory meeting, then in order to be entitled to vote at any meeting, he must submit a claim at or before that meeting, and to be entitled to participate in a dividend, a claim must be submitted not later than eight weeks before the end of an accounting period.[42] Again, once a claim is made, it does not require to be resubmitted.[43] Accounting periods are usually successive periods of 26 weeks running from the date of sequestration, although the length of any period after the first may be varied by the permanent trustee in conjunction with the commissioners, or with the Accountant if there are no commissioners.[44] A creditor who has submitted a claim may always subsequently submit a further claim specifying a different amount,[45] save that a secured creditor may not in such a claim specify a different value for his security if the permanent trustee has required him to discharge, convey or assign it in accordance with the Act.[46]

## 8.28. WHAT MAY BE CLAIMED

Generally, a creditor may claim the amount owed plus interest due at the date of sequestration.[47] As to interest after the date of sequestration see para. 8.32.

### (a) Debts due after the date of sequestration

If a debt is due after the date of sequestration, then it is simply treated as due at that date, but subject to deduction of interest at the higher of the prescribed rate at the date of sequestration and the rate which would otherwise apply to that debt.[48] Where the debt is due significantly after the date of sequestration, this approach can severely reduce its amount.

### (b) Secured creditors

A creditor who holds a security over any part of the debtor's estate should deduct the value of the security (as estimated by him) from the claim, unless he surrenders it for the benefit of the estate (or undertakes to do so in writing).[49] Although the creditor estimates the value of the security, the trustee may at any time after the expiry of 12 weeks from the date of sequestration require the creditor to discharge the security, or convey or assign it to the trustee, on payment of the value so specified.[50] The amount of that payment is then deducted from the debt. The fact that the trustee can discharge the security by paying the creditor what the latter says it is worth obviously discourages the creditor from undervaluing a security in order to maximise the amount of his claim. Unless the trustee has already exercised this power, it is always open for a creditor to resubmit a claim, based on a different estimate of the value of the security.[51] Since the Act focuses on securities over the debtor's estate,[52] it follows that any security held by the creditor over another's estate, *e.g.* a parent of the debtor, or security in the form of a cautionary obligation, is not deducted from the claim.

---

[42] s.48(1).
[43] s.48(2).
[44] s.52(2).
[45] s.22(4), s.48(4).
[46] s.48(4), Sch. 1, para. 5(2).
[47] Sch. 1, para. 1(1).
[48] Sch. 1, para. 1(2).
[49] Sch. 1, para. 5(1).
[50] Sch. 1, para. 5(2).
[51] s.48(4).
[52] s.73(1).

## (c) Aliment or periodical allowance

Claims for arrears of aliment or periodical allowance in respect of the period prior the date of sequestration can only be made if due by virtue of a court decree or written agreement, and if in the case of a spouse (or an ex-spouse claiming for a child) the parties were living apart during the period to which the claim relates.[53] Such claims arising after the date of sequestration cannot be allowed at all,[54] and would have to be made against the debtor himself.

## (d) Contingent debts

A contingent debt "is a debt which has no existence now but will only emerge and become due upon the occurrence of some future event".[55] That event may never occur, but even if it is bound to occur, its exact date cannot be determined. Where the existence or amount of a debt depends upon a contingency, the creditor may choose either to wait until that contingency has arisen, or have the debt valued by the permanent trustee, or by the sheriff if there is no permanent trustee.[56] Where the debt is valued by the permanent trustee, any interested party may appeal to the sheriff, who may affirm or vary that valuation.[57] The amount of the valuation determines the amount of the creditor's claim. The risk that the creditor runs in submitting to valuation is that the debt may be under-valued, while the risk of waiting for the contingency to arise is that it may not arise. In relation to contingent creditors Lord President Inglis observes in *Mitchell v Scott*[58]

> "If . . . contingent creditors, *i.e.* those whose debts are not yet payable and may never become payable, were not entitled to claim in the sequestration, their debts would be gone forever, because the bankrupt's discharge would finally put an end to them."

In *Crighton v Crighton's Tr.*[59] the husband of the debtor, having raised an action of divorce (in which he claimed a capital sum) some time before the debtor was sequestrated, was granted a divorce and awarded a capital sum of £157,000 after the date of sequestration. The trustee rejected his claim on the basis that it only emerged after sequestration. However, both the sheriff and sheriff-principal held that the trustee had to accept the claim as being a contingent debt due by the debtor at the date of sequestration. Sheriff-Principal Hay opined[60]:

> "The debtor's obligation to the claimant to share the matrimonial property fairly with him . . . arose at the latest when he raised the action of divorce and craved payment of a capital sum . . . From that point on . . . the debtor was under a contingent liability to pay the claimant whatever capital sum might be awarded."

## (e) Debts due under composition contracts

Although a sequestration may be ended by a composition contract (see para. 8.35.), the sequestration may revive if that contract fails. In such a case, each creditor may resurrect his original claim, less any amount actually paid under the composition contract.[61]

## (f) Claims against partners for partnership debts

Partnerships may be sequestrated without the sequestration of individual partners, and vice versa. However, while a firm is not liable for the debts of individual partners incurred as

---

[53] Sch. 1, para. 2.
[54] Sch. 1, para. 2(i)(b).
[55] *per* Lord Watson in *Fleming v Yeaman* (1884) 9 App. Cas. 966 at 976.
[56] Sch. 1, para. 3.
[57] Sch. 1, para. 3(3).
[58] (1881) 8 R. 875 at 879.
[59] 1999 S.C.L.R. 16.
[60] at 22C.
[61] Sch. 1, para. 4.

individuals, individual partners do have a residual liability for the debts of the firm, *i.e.* if the firm proves unable to pay its own debts, creditors may proceed against individual partners.[62] Thus a partner may ultimately be sequestrated in respect of the firm's debts. Since a creditor must first seek to obtain whatever he can from the firm before turning to its partners, the Act provides that a creditor proceeding against the estate of an individual partner in respect of the debt of the firm must deduct the value of his claim against the firm from his claim against the partner.[63] That value is estimated by the creditor himself, but that estimate need not be accepted by the trustee. Firms may have a great number of partners, and a creditor may be simultaneously pursuing claims against a good many partners. Yet the value of such claims do not have to be deducted.

## 8.29.  CO-OBLIGANTS

It may be the case that a creditor can require someone other than the debtor to pay a debt, as where the debtor is jointly and severally liable with one or more persons, or where someone is a cautioner for the debt. Usually such a co-obligant will have a right of relief against the debtor. However, special rules apply in the context of sequestration. Thus the common law prohibition against double ranking will apply. So, for example, a cautioner who has been required to pay all or any part of the principal debt normally has a right of relief against the debtor.[64] That would mean if the cautioner pays the whole of the principal debt, he may make a claim in the sequestration. (Indeed the Act itself indicates that a co-obligant who has paid the debt may obtain, at his own expense, an assignation of the debt, and thereafter, claim, vote and obtain a dividend.[65]) However, if the creditor makes a claim in the sequestration, and then pursues the cautioner for the remainder of the principal debt, the latter may not make a claim in the sequestration in respect of the sum he had had to pay, as it is unfair to the creditors that what is essentially the same debt should be allowed to rank twice on the estate.[66]

The Act also regulates the rights of co-obligants. Thus while the common law envisaged various ways in which a co-obligant could be released by the actions of the creditor, it is now provided that a co-obligant is not freed from liability by the discharge of the debt, or by the creditor voting, or drawing a dividend, or assenting to (or at least not opposing) a composition or the debtor's discharge.[67] Where a co-obligant holds a security over the debtor's estate, he must account for it to the permanent trustee so as to put the estate in the same position as if he had paid the debt and then had his claim accepted after deducting the value of the security.[68] This provision, deals with the situation where, for example, a cautioner holds a security over the debtor's estate. If the creditor, makes a claim against the debtor's estate and receives a dividend, he will pursue the cautioner for the remainder of the debt. As noted above, the cautioner in such a scenario may not make a claim in the sequestration in respect of the sum he has had to pay, because of the rule against double ranking. But if he is allowed to enforce his security against the estate, the rule against double ranking is to some extent avoided. The provision prevents this by effectively depriving him of the benefit of the security.

---

[62] Partnership Act 1890, s.9. A creditor has no claim against an individual partner unless the firm is unable to pay: see *Brickmann's Tr. v Commercial Bank* (1901) 38 S.L.R. 766.

[63] Sch. 1, para. 6.

[64] *Smithy's Place Ltd v Blackadder*, 1991 S.L.T. 790.

[65] s.60(3).

[66] *Mackinnon v Monkhouse* (1881) 9 R. 393.

[67] s.60(1).

[68] s.60(2).

## 8.30. BALANCING OF ACCOUNTS

Sometimes a creditor will also owe money to the debtor. Clearly, the creditor would prefer not to pay the debtor in full and then make a claim for the full amount he is owed by the debtor, as he is likely to be able to recover only a fraction of the latter sum. Rather he would wish to set off the sum he owes against the sum owed by him, so that he either is treated as owing the balance due to the debtor, or else he can make a claim for the balance owing to him. This is permitted in the context of insolvency,[69] and indeed an illiquid debt may be set off against a liquid debt,[70] so that the creditor may set off a future or contingent debt owed by the debtor against a liquid debt owed by him.[71] Moreover, it is open to a creditor who has a claim which is partly preferential or partly secured, to choose to set off the debt owed by him against any part of his claim which is neither preferential or secured.[72] One major qualification is that a debt arising before insolvency may only be set off only against a debt similarly arising,[73] and equally a debt arising after insolvency may only be set off only against a debt also arising after insolvency.[74] It has been said that[75]:

> " bankruptcy law presupposes reciprocal obligations which are both existing at the time of the declaration of insolvency, although only one of them is, it may be, immediately exigible. It has no application to the case of a new obligation arising after bankruptcy or declaration of insolvency."

In this context the meaning of insolvency is rather vague. It would appear that sequestration proceedings need not actually have commenced, and that indeed a party is insolvent if his "pecuniary responsibility and circumstances had materially altered to the worse",[76] although the mere fact that a party is experiencing losses is insufficient, if there is no suggestion that his liabilities exceed his assets, or that he is experiencing difficulty in meeting his liabilities when they fall due.[77]

It may be noted that if a creditor has claimed in the debtor's sequestration, a co-obligant of the debtor cannot attempt to set off any right of relief he may claim against the debtor against any debt which he may owe the debtor.[78] Consider the example, of a debt which is reinforced by a cautionary obligation. If the creditor makes a claim against the debtor's estate and receives a dividend, he will pursue the cautioner for the remainder of the debt. The cautioner in such a scenario may not make a claim in the sequestration in respect of the sum he has had to pay, because of the rule against double ranking. But if he is allowed to set off his right of relief against a debt which he would otherwise have to pay to the debtor's estate, that estate is diminished and the rule against double ranking is to some extent avoided. Thus the rule against double ranking precludes such set-off. If the Crown is a creditor, set-off cannot be allowed in respect of any claim for taxes, duties or penalties, nor can any claim for the repayment of taxes, duties or penalties be set off against any other claim by the Crown.[79] Otherwise set-off is generally available when the debts in question relate to the same government department, although the leave of the court is required if the Crown is to be allowed to plead set-off when different government departments are involved.[80] Leave is usually given.[81] It has been

---

[69] See *Ross v Ross* (1895) 22 R. 461 at 465, *per* Lord McLaren.
[70] See *Scott's Trs v Scott* (1887) 14 R. 1043 at 1051, *per* Lord President Inglis.
[71] *Hannay & Sons Tr. v Armstrong & Co.* (1877) 4 R. (H.L.) 43.
[72] *Turner v IRC,* 1994 S.L.T. 811.
[73] *Taylor's Tr. v Paul* (1888) 15 R. 313.
[74] *Liquidators of Highland Engineering v Thomson,* 1972 S.C. 87.
[75] *Asphaltic Limestone Concrete Co v Corporation of Glasgow,* 1907 S.C. 463 at 474, *per* Lord McLaren.
[76] *Paul & Thain v Royal Bank of Scotland* (1869) 7 M. 361 at 364, *per* Lord Ormidale.
[77] *Busby Spinning Co Ltd v BMK Ltd,* 1988 S.C. 70 at 72–73, *per* Lord Cullen.
[78] *Anderson v Mackinnon* (1876) 3 R. 608.
[79] Crown Proceedings Act 1947, s.35(2)(b).
[80] Crown Proceedings Act 1947, s.35(2)(c)–(d).
[81] *Smith v Lord Advocate,* 1980 S.C. 227.

suggested (*obiter*) that if the Crown is due to return any sum as a gratuitous alienation or unfair preference, it would be unfair to the creditors as a whole to allow this to be set off against debts due to the Crown.[82]

## 8.31.  ADJUDICATION OF CLAIMS

Turning now to how claims are dealt with, it may be noted that at the commencement of any meeting of creditors the permanent trustee accepts or rejects the various claims. This determines the right of any creditor to vote at the meeting.[83] The permanent trustee will only accept or reject claims for the purpose of paying a dividend if there are funds available, but where he engages in such adjudication, he must do so not later than four weeks before the end of the relevant accounting period.[84] The two types of adjudication have no bearing on each other. As noted above (para 8.27.), a claim must be submitted not later than eight weeks before the end of that accounting period in order to be considered, but it should be remembered that once a claim is made, it does not require to be resubmitted.[85] Thus a claim may well have been submitted during an earlier accounting period, or indeed submitted to the interim trustee at the beginning of the sequestration. If the permanent trustee requires to be satisfied as to the amount or validity of a claim, he may ask the creditor or any other person whom he believes to have such evidence to produce further evidence, and if that individual refuses or delays in doing so, the trustee may apply to the sheriff for an order for his private examination before the sheriff.[86] If the permanent trustee rejects a claim in whole or in part, he must forthwith inform the creditor of his reasons.[87] A claim may be referred to arbitration or compromised, but if there are commissioners, they must consent.[88] Both the debtor and any aggrieved creditor may appeal to the sheriff against the decision to accept or reject a claim, or to give a claim a particular ranking.[89] Where the acceptance or rejection is for the purpose of determining the right of a creditor to vote at a meeting, an appeal must be made within two weeks of that decision.[90] Where the acceptance or rejection is for the purpose of determining the right of a creditor to share in a dividend, an appeal must be made not later than two weeks before the end of the relevant accounting period.[91] Where a creditor appeals against an adjudication, the debtor may not demand to be sisted as a party to the proceedings in order to argue that the trustee made the correct decision.[92]

## 8.32.  DISTRIBUTION OF ESTATE

At the end of each accounting period, the permanent trustee will distribute such assets as he has managed to realise during that period to cover certain expenses and to pay dividends to those creditors whose claims he has accepted. Broadly speaking, the Act accords priority to the

---

[82] *John E Rae (Electrical Services) Linlithgow Ltd v LA,* 1994 S.L.T. 788 at 791, *per* Lord Clyde.
[83] s.49(1).
[84] s.49(2).
[85] s.48(1)–(2).
[86] s.48(5)–(6).
[87] s.49(4), (7).
[88] s.65(1).
[89] s.49(6).
[90] s.49(6)(a).
[91] s.49(6)(b).
[92] *McGuiness v McGuiness' Tr.,* 1993 S.C.L.R. 755.

expenses of the sequestration itself, with certain debts being seen as more deserving and others as less deserving than the great mass of ordinary debts. It may also be remembered that the Act does not affect the rights of secured creditors nor of creditors who may have a lien over title deeds.[93] Effectively, a secured creditor will receive the value of his security before the estate benefits from the asset realised. Subject to these points, the estate will be distributed in the following order[94]:

- the outlays and remuneration of the interim trustee;
- the outlays and remuneration of the permanent trustee[95];
- where the debtor was deceased at the date of sequestration, deathbed and funeral expenses reasonably incurred, and expenses reasonably incurred in administering the deceased's estate (unreasonable expenses are treated as ordinary debts, while any such expenses in relation to a debtor who dies after the date of sequestration do not count as debts in the sequestration);
- the expenses of a petitioning or concurring creditor;
- preferred debts (but not interest thereon up to the date of sequestration), ordinary debts;
- interest on preferred debts and interest on ordinary debts after the date of sequestration;
- postponed debts.

Where funds are insufficient to pay any of the above classes of debt in full, the creditor will be paid a rateable proportion,[96] *e.g.* if the funds available will only pay 20 per cent of the ordinary debts, then each ordinary creditor will receive 20 per cent of his claim. In the unlikely event of all the above debts being paid in full, any surplus will be paid to the debtor,[97] although if the sequestration amounts to secondary proceedings in a cross-border insolvency, any surplus must be transferred to the main proceedings in another EU state.[98] A surplus includes any kind of estate, but not an unclaimed dividend.[99]

## (a) Preferred debts

Certain debts must be paid in full before any ordinary creditor receives anything. These used to include certain debts due to the Inland Revenue and Customs and Excise, and certain social security payments, but now mainly comprehend certain payments due to employees. More specifically, they are[1]:

- contributions to occupational pension schemes and state scheme premiums;
- European Coal and Steel Community levies and surcharges;
- certain payments ordered under the Reserve Forces (Safeguard of Employment) Act 1985;
- accrued holiday pay up to the date of sequestration, where the employment has been terminated (whether before or after that date);
- arrears of wages for up to four months prior to the date of sequestration—subject to a maximum of £800 per employee. Arrears of wages beyond the limit would be treated as an ordinary debt. It is not clear whether the limit refers to gross or net wages. Wages is defined so as to include certain payments due under statute when the employee is absent from work for good cause.

---

[93] s.51(6).
[94] s.51(1).
[95] See McBryde, *op. cit.*, paras 16–104 to 16–120.
[96] s.51(4).
[97] s.51(5).
[98] s.51(5A).
[99] s.51(5).
[1] Sch. 3.

(If anyone advances money to pay arrears of wages or holiday pay, they will have a preferential claim, if the money was in fact used to pay the employee and he would have had a preferential claim.) In relation to all the above categories, if the debtor was deceased at the date of sequestration, then the crucial date is the date of death rather than the date of sequestration.

## (b) Postponed debts

Obviously these are debts which can only be paid when every other claim is met in full. As it is not unusual for ordinary creditors to receive nothing, it may be appreciated that it is very rare for postponed creditors to receive anything. Postponed debts are[2]:

- a loan to the debtor in return for a share of the profits of his business, which is postponed to the claims of other creditors under s.3 of the Partnership Act 1890. Such a person has to some degree tied himself to the fortunes of the debtor's business. As he will benefit more than an ordinary creditor if the business prospers, it is fair that he should have a lower priority than an ordinary creditor if the business struggles;
- a loan made by the debtor's spouse;
- the creditor's right to anything vesting in the permanent trustee as a result of a successful challenge of a gratuitous alienation (or to the proceeds of the sale of such a thing).

## 8.33. EFFECT OF SEQUESTRATION ON THE DEBTOR

Turning from the creditors to consider the effect of sequestration on the debtor, it can be observed that various effects have already been noted, such as the vesting of his estate and any *acquirenda* in the permanent trustee, and his prohibition from dealing with the estate; the possibility that he might be ordered to contribute excess income to the trustee; his duty to co-operate with the trustee; his liability to examination, and the possibility that he may commit certain offences. However, there remain certain effects of the process which are yet to be discussed, primarily certain general offences which might be committed by the debtor, and his disability from holding certain offices and carrying on certain professions.

Section 67 enumerates the general offences which the debtor may commit. These are:

- during the relevant period, making a false statement to a creditor or someone concerned in the administration of his estate regarding his business or financial affairs, unless he neither knew nor had reason to believe that the statement was false;
- during the relevant period, damaging or removing from Scotland any part of his estate or document relating to his assets or his business or financial affairs, unless he can show that he did not do so with intent to prejudice the creditors;
- failing to return to Scotland in compliance with a court order after the date of sequestration;
- during the relevant period, falsifying a document relating to his assets or his business or financial affairs, unless he can show that he had no intention to mislead the permanent trustee, a commissioner or any creditor;
- failing to report to the relevant trustee such a falsification by a third party within a month of becoming aware thereof;
- during the relevant period, making a gratuitous alienation or unfair preference, unless he can show that he did not do so with intent to prejudice the creditors;

---

[2] s.51(3).

- during the year leading up to the date of sequestration, otherwise than in the ordinary course of business, pledging or disposing of property obtained on credit, unless he can show that he did not do so with intent to prejudice the creditors. (this offence can only be committed if he is engaged in trade or business);
- during the two years leading up to the date of sequestration, failing to keep or preserve such records as are necessary to give a fair view of the state of his assets or his business or financial affairs, unless he can show that such failure was neither reckless nor dishonest. (again this only applies if he is engaged in trade or business, and no offence is committed if his unsecured liabilities at the date of sequestration did not exceed £20,000[3]);
- obtaining credit to the extent of £250 without advising the other party that he has been sequestrated and is not yet discharged.

Under s.67 "the relevant period" is the period commencing one year before the date of sequestration and concluding with the debtor's discharge.

Looking briefly at the disabling effects of sequestration, it may be observed that, for example, certain professions may not be practised by undischarged bankrupts, most notably that of solicitor,[4] and certain public offices, such as acting as a Member of either House of Parliament, are closed to them,[5] while it is actually an offence for an undischarged bankrupt to act as a director of a company or be involved in its promotion, formation or management, except with the leave of the court.[6] Again, s.33(1) of the Partnership Act 1890 indicates that, subject to the contrary agreement of the partners, a partnership is dissolved by the bankruptcy of any partner, while a company's articles of association will usually remove a director from office if he becomes bankrupt.[7] The last example serves as a reminder that all manner of contractual disqualifications or terminations may result from insolvency.

## 8.34.  DISCHARGE OF THE DEBTOR

### (a) Automatic discharge of the debtor

Given the above effects of sequestration, the debtor will obviously be concerned to know when he can obtain a discharge. Under the previous legislation, the debtor had to apply to the court for a discharge. Thus through ignorance, impecuniosity, reluctance to appear before a court, or just sheer inertia, many bankrupts did not make that application and thus remained forever undischarged. Accordingly, the Act contemplates that a debtor will be automatically discharged three years after the date of sequestration, unless a creditor or the permanent trustee has applied to the sheriff for a deferment.[8] A debtor who has been discharged may apply to the Accountant for a certificate, which the Accountant must grant if satisfied of the discharge.[9] Such a certificate is not necessary for a discharge, but might provide useful evidence of the fact of discharge. Although the Act allows for deferment, it does not seem to envisage early discharge. Still, Professor McBryde[10] suggests devices whereby an early discharge may be obtained.

---

[3] Bankruptcy (Scotland) Regulations 1985 (SI 1985/1925), para. 9.
[4] Solicitors (Scotland) Act 1980, s.18(1).
[5] Insolvency Act 1986, s.427. See also Enterprise Act 2002, s.268.
[6] Company Directors Disqualification Act 1986, s.11(1).
[7] That would be the effect of art. 81(b) of Table A—Companies (Tables A to F) Regulations 1985 (SI 1985/805). Table A is a set of model articles, which may be adopted in whole or in part by a company, but which will apply automatically if a company does not register articles: Companies Act 1985, s.8.
[8] s.54(1), (3).
[9] s.54(2); Bankruptcy (Scotland) Regulations 1985 (SI 1985/1925), Form 8.
[10] *op. cit.*, para. 18.45.

## (b) Deferment

The permanent trustee or any creditor may seek to prevent the debtor's automatic discharge by making an application for its deferment, and *prima facie* in order to be valid such an application must be made within two years and nine months of the date of sequestration.[11] However, a sheriff is entitled to overlook defective procedure,[12] and in so doing may extend or waive any time limit under the Act.[13] It has therefore been held that a court may extend the above time limit.[14] Where an application is received timeously, but cannot be disposed of within the three year period, it appears that the discharge is effectively suspended until the determination of the application.[15] If it is not received timeously, there seems to be some dispute as to whether the discharge is effectively suspended until the determination of the application for the court to extend the time limit (and if that application is successful, until the determination of the application proper),[16] or whether an interim discharge might be granted.[17] On receipt of the application, the sheriff shall order a copy to be served on the debtor, and (if the application is made by a creditor) on the permanent trustee[18]. He shall also order the debtor within 14 days to lodge a declaration that he has made[19]:

(1)  full and fair surrender of his estate,
(2)  full disclosure of claims he is entitled to make against others,
(3)  delivery to the interim/permanent trustees of every document relating to the estate or his affairs.

Failing the timeous lodging of such a declaration, the sheriff must automatically grant a deferment for a period not exceeding two years.[20] If the declaration is lodged, then there will be a hearing not earlier than 28 days after that lodging, and the sheriff will order the applicant to notify the debtor and (if appropriate) the permanent trustee (or the Accountant if the permanent trustee has been discharged) of the date of the hearing.[21] The permanent trustee (or the Accountant if the permanent trustee has been discharged) shall then lodge not later than seven days before the date of the hearing a report on the debtor's assets and liabilities, his financial and business affairs, his conduct in relation thereto, and on the sequestration and his conduct in the course of it.[22] The debtor, the applicant and any creditor may make representations at the hearing. The sheriff will then either dismiss the application, or grant a deferment for a period not exceeding two years, subject to the right of the applicant or the debtor to appeal against that decision within 14 days of it being made.[23] Yet although the Act says nothing about the grounds for granting a deferment, the sheriff will not take this course unless good cause is shown,[24] and an applicant must clearly set out in the application the grounds on which deferral is sought.[25] Deferment has been granted on the basis of the debtor's obstructive behaviour,[26] and (arguably unnecessarily) where the trustee wished to sist himself to a reparation action by the debtor.[27] If deferment is granted, the debtor can nonetheless petition

---

[11] s.54(3).
[12] s.63(1)(a).
[13] s.63(2)(c).
[14] *Pattison v Halliday*, 1991 S.L.T 645.
[15] *Clydesdale Bank plc v Davidson*, 1994 S.L.T. 225.
[16] *Whittaker's Tr. v Whittaker*, 1993 S.C.L.R. 718.
[17] *Pattison v Halliday*, 1991 S.L.T 645.
[18] s.54(4)(a).
[19] s.54(4)(b).
[20] s.54(4).
[21] s.54(5)(a)–(b).
[22] s.54(5).
[23] s.54(6).
[24] *Crittal Warmliffe Ltd v Flaherty*, 1988 G.W.D. 22–930.
[25] *Chowdhury's Tr. v Chowdhury*, 1996 S.C.L.R. 948.
[26] *Nicol's Tr. v Nicol*, 1996 G.W.D. 10–531.
[27] *Watson v Henderson*, 1988 S.C.L.R. 439.

at any time for a discharge, provided he lodges the declaration.[28] A hearing will then be held in much the same way as described above.[29] The refusal of a petition is no bar to subsequent petitions. Equally, a further deferment may be applied for not later than three months before the end of the period of deferment, so that theoretically if such applications continue to be made, the discharge may be postponed indefinitely.[30]

## (c) Effects of discharge

There are three main effects:

(1) The debtor ceases to be disqualified from the various offices and professions which are not open to undischarged bankrupts;

(2) any estate acquired by the debtor after discharge vests in him, rather than the permanent trustee, although it should be remembered a contingent interest which is acquired by the debtor before discharge, but does not vest until after discharge, will continue to vest in the permanent trustee[31];

(3) the debtor is discharged from all debts due at the date of sequestration, with the following exceptions[32]:

    (a) any liability to pay a fine or penalty to the Crown, including payment under a confiscation order,

    (b) any liability to forfeiture of bail money under s.1(3) of the Bail (Scotland) Act 1980,

    (c) any liability incurred by reason of fraud or breach of trust,

    (d) any liability to pay aliment or a periodical allowance on divorce (where these cannot be included in a claim in the sequestration),

    (e) any liability to pay child support maintenance,

    (f) any liability in respect of a student loan.[33] A student loan is not treated as a debt in a sequestration.

Of course, discharge cannot prejudice the rights of a secured creditor.[34] Moreover, it should be remembered that the discharge of the debtor does not necessarily end the sequestration, which may continue for some time thereafter.[35] Thus the obligation to co-operate with the permanent trustee continues after discharge.[36] Nor does discharge reinvest the debtor in his former estate, unless he is discharged through composition[37]—see next paragraph. It may also be noted that discharge relates only to debts as at the date of sequestration, not to debts incurred after that date.

## 8.35. DISCHARGE ON COMPOSITION

A composition contract, whereby a debtor is relieved of liability for his debts in return for part payment, may be used as an alternative to sequestration. But it is possible for a debtor who has been sequestrated to obtain early discharge through composition, this process being known as

---

[28] s.54(8).
[29] *ibid.*
[30] s.54(9).
[31] s.31(5).
[32] s.55(1)–(2).
[33] Education (Student Loans) Act 1990, Sch. 2, para. 6.
[34] s.55(3).
[35] *Henderson v Bulley* (1849) 11 D. 1473.
[36] s.55(2)(e).
[37] *Buchanan v McCulloch* (1865) 4 M. 135.

judicial composition, and being governed by the Act.[38] The process cannot begin until the act and warrant is issued to the permanent trustee.[39] An offer would be made to him, which he would then communicate to the commissioners (or if there are none to the Accountant),[40] who would decide whether the offer should be placed before the creditors. A positive decision would be prompted by the view that the offer—which must be at least 25p in the £—will be timeously implemented, and by satisfaction with the caution or other security[41] to be provided for its implementation.[42] If it is placed before the creditors, and a majority in number and at least two thirds in value accept, the sheriff is asked to approve the composition and discharge the creditor.[43] The sheriff then fixes a hearing at which the creditors may make representations.[44] If, having heard these and examined the appropriate documents, he judges that the required majority has approved and that the offer is reasonable, he shall make an order approving the composition.[45] Once various formalities are complied with, he shall then make an order discharging the debtor and the permanent trustee,[46] whereupon the sequestration ends and the debtor is reinvested in his estate.[47] However, if any creditor can satisfy the Court of Session that there has been or is likely to be a default in payment, or that for any reason the composition cannot be proceeded with without undue delay or without injustice to the creditors, or at all, it may recall the sheriff's order, with the effect that the sequestration revives.[48] Only two offers of composition may be made during the course of a sequestration.[49]

## 8.36.  THE END OF THE SEQUESTRATION PROCESS

The approval of a composition offer, as described above, leads to the conclusion of the sequestration. The permanent trustee shall submit to the commissioners (or to the Accountant if there are none) his accounts for audit, along with a claim for his outlays and remuneration.[50] Where such documents are sent to the commissioners, a copy must be sent to the Accountant.[51] The permanent trustee must also take all reasonable steps to ensure that the interim trustee (if a different person) has also sent such documents.[52] The permanent trustee then lodges with the sheriff clerk a declaration that all necessary charges in connection with the sequestration have been paid or satisfactory provision made in respect of their payment, while a bond of caution or other security must be lodged by or on behalf of the debtor.[53] As explained in the previous paragraph, once these documents have been lodged, the sheriff makes an order discharging the debtor and the permanent trustee.[54]

If a sequestration is not ended by composition, in one sense it never ends. It has already been seen that the discharge of the debtor does not end the sequestration, and nor will the discharge of the trustee. If, following such discharge, significant new assets appear, it is open to

---

[38] s.56 and Sch. 4.
[39] Sch. 4, para. 1(1).
[40] Sch. 4, para. 2.
[41] See Sch. 4, para. 1(2).
[42] Sch. 4, para. 3.
[43] Sch. 4, paras 5–6.
[44] Sch. 4, para. 7.
[45] Sch. 4, para. 6.
[46] See Sch. 4, paras 9–11.
[47] Sch. 4, para. 16.
[48] Sch. 4, para. 17.
[49] Sch. 4, para. 15.
[50] Sch. 4, para. 9(1)(a); and see para. 9(1A) where the Accountant is the trustee.
[51] ibid.
[52] Sch. 4, para. 9(1)(b).
[53] Sch. 4, para. 10.
[54] Sch. 4, para. 11.

appoint a new trustee.[55] Nonetheless, in most cases the discharge of the trustee will mark a practical end to the sequestration.[56] This will usually be sought when the estate has no further assets which are capable of being realised, and any funds available to the trustee are not sufficient to justify a further distribution.

When the permanent trustee has made the final division of the estate, and inserted his final audited accounts in his sederunt book, he must deposit unapplied balances and unclaimed dividends in an appropriate bank or institution, and send the Accountant the deposit receipt and a copy of the audited accounts.[57] At the same time as sending these documents he may apply to the Accountant for a discharge.[58] It is not necessary to apply for a discharge, but it will mean that he is discharged from all liability to the creditors (other than for fraud) in respect of the exercise of his functions.[59] Such discharge would also cover any period during which he acted as interim trustee.[60] The permanent trustee shall notify the debtor and all creditors known to him of his application, informing them that they are entitled within 14 days to make representations to the Accountant regarding the application.[61] In light of the documents submitted and any representations made, the Accountant will either grant or refuse the discharge, notifying the permanent trustee, the debtor and any creditors who have made representations.[62] Any of these parties may, within a further 14 days, appeal against the decision to the sheriff, whose decision will be final.[63]

Where the Accountant acts as permanent trustee the procedure is very similar, except that the Accountant obviously will not apply to himself for a discharge.[64] Instead, he must send to the debtor and all creditors known to him, a copy of his determination of his fees and outlays, and a notice informing them that[65]:

(1)  he has started the procedure leading to his discharge, and
(2)  they may within 14 days appeal to the sheriff against his determination and/or discharge.

Once more, the decision of the sheriff will be final.[66] Where no appeal is made or an appeal is refused, the Accountant will be discharged.[67]

## 8.37.  STREAMLINED PROCEDURES

This chapter has concerned itself with standard sequestrations. However, where the assets involved are very small, expedited procedures are available which are aimed at reducing administration and costs. The first applies to so-called "small assets" cases under Sch. 2. The second is the certificate of summary administration under Sch. 2A. Almost invariably those cases where Sch 2A applies will also be subject to the provisions of Sch. 2.

---

[55] *Northern Heritable Securities Investment Co v Whyte* (1888) 16 R. 100.
[56] *Buchanan v McCulloch* (1865) 4 M. 135.
[57] s.57(1)(a)–(b).
[58] s.57(1)(c).
[59] s.57(5).
[60] *ibid*.
[61] s.57(2).
[62] s.57(3).
[63] s.57(4), (4A).
[64] s.58A.
[65] s.58A(4).
[66] s.58A(6).
[67] s.58A(7).

## (a) Small assets cases

The designation of "small assets" cases is actually rather misleading, as the size of the estate does not directly determine the applicability of the procedure. Rather, the Sch. 2 procedure applies in certain circumstances, which tend broadly to indicate that the estate is probably (but not necessarily) small. The procedure thus applies:

(1) Where the Accountant is the interim trustee but does not call a statutory meeting, with the result that he becomes the permanent trustee.[68]
(2) Where the Accountant is granted a certificate of summary administration.[69]
(3) where no creditor attends the statutory meeting or the meeting fails to elect a permanent trustee, so that appointment is made by the court.[70]
(4) where no permanent trustee is elected to replace one who dies, resigns, or is removed but not replaced.[71]
(5) in cases of summary administration, unless the permanent trustee has been elected.[72]

It can be seen that the crucial factor for the application of the procedure is the fact that the permanent trustee is appointed rather than elected.

The main differences in small assets cases are[73]:

- procedures for replacing a permanent trustee who dies, resigns or is removed, are streamlined;
- there are no commissioners, and if an ordinary sequestration becomes a Sch. 2 sequestration, any commissioners cease to hold office;
- if the Accountant is the permanent trustee, he need not consult or obtain the consent of anyone regarding the recovery, management or realisation of the estate, while if anyone else is the permanent trustee, he needs only the consent of the Accountant;
- the Accountant's consent is needed for examination of the debtor;
- if the Accountant is the permanent trustee, a streamlined procedure applies to the preparation of accounts, the determination of fees and outlays, and appeals against such determination.

## (b) The certificate of summary administration

This device was introduced by the Bankruptcy (Scotland) Act 1993 to reduce the burden on the permanent trustee in certain cases. This time the procedure is specifically related to the size of the estate, in that a certificate must be granted if the aggregate amount of unsecured liabilities does not exceed £20,000, and the aggregate amount of assets (excluding heritage and property not vesting in the permanent trustee) does not exceed £2,000.[74] Application may be made:

(1) by the Accountant not later than seven days after the award of sequestration on a debtor's petition[75]—but an application will not be granted where there is already in office an interim or permanent trustee who is not the Accountant[76];
(2) by the Accountant where, as interim trustee, he does not call the statutory meeting of creditors[77];

---

[68] ss.21B(2), 25A(3).
[69] ss.23A(4), 25A(3).
[70] ss.24(3A), 25A(3), 24(4)–(5).
[71] ss.28(5), 29(8).
[72] Sch. 2A, para. 5.
[73] See Sch. 2, paras 3–9.
[74] s.23A(1)–(2).
[75] s.12(1A).
[76] s.23A(9).
[77] s.21B(2).

(3) by the interim trustee where the meeting is called but no creditor attends or no permanent trustee is elected[78];

(4) by the interim trustee in his report of the statutory meeting to the sheriff after a permanent trustee has been elected.[79]

It can be appreciated that except in (4) it is envisaged that the Accountant will act as permanent trustee under the certificate. It should also be remembered that except in (4) the Sch. 2 procedure will apply to such a sequestration.

The debtor, any creditor, the permanent trustee or the Accountant may apply at any time for the withdrawal of the certificate.[80] If anyone but the permanent trustee applies, the applicant must send a copy of the application to the permanent trustee, who must report to the sheriff on the circumstances of the sequestration.[81] If it appears to the sheriff that summary administration is no longer appropriate, he shall withdraw the certificate.[82]

Essentially, the effect of the certificate is to confer upon the permanent trustee discretion to perform his duties only to the extent he considers it to be of financial benefit to the estate and in the interests of creditors.[83] Thus, for example, the permanent trustee may curtail investigations or the pursuit of assets if there is little point in engaging therein, and no creditor can take him to task. He is subject to directions from the Accountant, and must obtain from the debtor every six months a written account of his current state of affairs.[84]

## 8.38. PROTECTED TRUST DEEDS

Having considered the formalities of the sequestration process, it may be useful to deal briefly with some alternatives to sequestration. Creditors may enter into all manner of informal arrangements with debtors rather than press for sequestration. Such arrangements however, typically do not prevent any creditor deciding to opt for sequestration at any time. Again, it was observed earlier that a composition contract, whereby a debtor is relieved of liability for his debts in return for part payment, may be used as an alternative to sequestration (as opposed to judicial composition which ends the sequestration process). This will of course only bind those creditors who become party to the contract, while their rights are restored should the debtor default. Traditionally, perhaps the most popular alternative to sequestration is for the parties to arrange that the debtor simply places his estate, or an agreed part thereof, in trust for the benefit of the creditors. This procedure is quicker, cheaper and more straightforward, while from the debtor's point of view none of the disabilities in terms of holding office, etc. ensue. The process is also almost entirely private. Yet the Act does not ignore private trust deeds altogether. Whatever the trust deed may say, the Act allows the debtor, the trustee or any creditor to require that the trustee's accounts are audited and his remuneration fixed by the Accountant.[85] Equally, it permits a trustee to record certain notices in the Register of Inhibitions and Adjudications, extends the provisions of Sch. 1 to valuation of claims (unless the deed provides otherwise), and stipulates that the submission of a claim to a trustee shall bar any provisions relating to limitation of actions.[86] Moreover, in terms of the Insolvency Act 1986, any individual who acts as a trustee without being a qualified insolvency practitioner

---

[78] ss.24(3B), 24(4A).
[79] s.25(2A).
[80] s.23A(5).
[81] s.23A(6).
[82] s.23A(7).
[83] Sch. 2A, para. 1.
[84] Sch. 2A, paras 2–3.
[85] Sch. 5, para. 1.
[86] Sch. 5, paras 2–4.

commits a criminal offence.[87] In the main, however, none of the statutory obligations and sanctions apply, and in particular gratuitous alienations and unfair preferences cannot be challenged. Nor is there anything to prevent any dissident creditor undermining the process at any time by seeking to do diligence on the estate or indeed petitioning for sequestration. If sequestration is granted, which of course it should be, given that the granting of a trust deed for creditors is an act of apparent insolvency allowing any creditor to petition,[88] the trustee under the deed must hand over the estate to the permanent trustee.[89] It should indeed be remembered that the trustee under a deed may himself petition for sequestration if the trust deed process does not go according to plan.[90] It was to deal with some of these disadvantages that the concept of a protected trust deed was introduced.

How does a trust deed become protected? Certain requirements must be met. First of all, the trustee must be a person who would not be disqualified from acting as the permanent trustee were the debtor to be sequestrated.[91] This means that, *inter alia*, he requires to be a qualified insolvency practitioner. Secondly, the trust deed having been delivered to him, the trustee must publish a notice in the prescribed form in the Edinburgh *Gazette,* also sending to every known creditor within one week thereof a copy of that notice and of the deed.[92] The trust deed then becomes protected unless, within five weeks of the publication of the notice, the trustee has received written objections from a majority in number or at least one third in value of the creditors, and as long as once the five weeks has expired the trustee sends a copy of the deed to the Accountant with a certificate indicating that it is a true copy, and that he has not received the requisite number of objections.[93] Any creditor who has received the notice, but does not object, is treated as having acceded to the deed.[94]

The main effects of a trust deed becoming protected are as follows:

- An objecting creditor, or a creditor who did not receive the notice, has no higher right to recover the debt than an acceding creditor.[95] If the deed is properly drawn up this should mean that no creditor can sue or do diligence. It is however provided that an objecting creditor, or a creditor who did not receive the notice, may present a petition for sequestration within six weeks of the *Gazette* notice.[96] The court will award sequestration if it considers it to be in the best interests of the creditors.[97] Moreover, such a creditor may present a petition for sequestration at any time on the grounds that distribution of the estate is unduly prejudicial to any creditor or class of creditors.[98] In this case the court will award sequestration if it considers that the ground is established.[99]

- The debtor cannot petition for sequestration.[1]
- The trustee or any creditor can challenge an unfair preference[1] or gratuitous alienation,[2] while the former can also challenge an order for the payment of a capital sum on divorce.[3]

---

[87] ss.388(2)(b), 389(1).
[88] ss.5(2)(b), 7(1)(c)(i).
[89] *Salaman v Rosslyn's Trs* (1900) 3 F. 298.
[90] s.5(2)(c), 5(2C).
[91] Sch. 5, para. 5(1)(a); and see s.25(2).
[92] Sch. 5, para. 5(1)(b)–(c).
[93] Sch. 5, para. 5(1)(d)–(e).
[94] Sch. 5, para. 5(2).
[95] Sch. 5, para. 6(a).
[96] Sch. 5, para. 7(1)(a).
[97] Sch. 5, para. 7(2).
[98] Sch. 5, para. 7(1)(b).
[99] Sch. 5, para. 7(3).
[1] Sch. 5, para. 6(b).
[2] s.36(1), (4) and (6).
[3] s.34(1), (2) and (8).
[4] s.35(1)–(2).

# Chapter 9

# PARTNERSHIP

## 9.1. INTRODUCTION

### (a) Importance of partnerships

The importance of the partnership or firm as a business entity cannot be over-stated.[1] A recent study indicated that there are almost as many partnerships as there are trading companies in the UK.[2] It is a common misconception to think of the firm as a small business entity. Whilst, as a general rule, the number of partners in a partnership is limited to 20 specific legislative provisions permit certain professionals to exceed that limit, for example, solicitors, accountants and stockbrokers.[3] Moreover, while a firm may have few partners, it may have many employees. Some firms employ thousands of people, and are more significant organisations than many companies.

### (b) Why choose a partnership?

There are many reasons why a partnership as a business entity may be more attractive than a limited liability company. One of the most important advantages is that of privacy of financial information. Firm accounts can remain private, in contrast to the stringent requirements for preparation and publication of annual accounts for a limited company. The creation of a partnership does not involve the same degree of formality and expense as is involved in the creation of a limited company. Flexibility in management is also possible due to the fact that there are few rules which govern the creation and running of a firm. Each partner may participate in the management of the firm or include more detailed rules in the partnership agreement setting up a management structure.[4]

---

[1] See below, at para. 9.2.(a), on the usage of the terms "partnership" and "firm".

[2] The DTI Small and Medium Enterprise (SME) Statistics for the UK 1998 (August 1999), Table 23 indicates that, at the beginning of 1998 there were 684,645 partnerships and 723,325 companies, cited in "Partnership Law: A Joint Consultation Paper" (Law Com. Consultation Paper No. 159, Scot. Law Com. D.P. No. 111, 2000), para. 1.4.

[3] Companies Act 1985, ss.716(1) and 716(2)(a)–(c) and Limited Partnership Act 1907, s.4(2). The Department of Trade and Industry has the power to extend this exemption to other partnerships by statutory instrument.

[4] See 1890 Act, s.24(5), which states as a general rule that every partner may take part in the partnership business. Like most of the provisions of this Act, this rule may be excluded by the written partnership agreement.

On the other hand, trading as a limited company may be more attractive to a particular business. The most obvious advantage is limited liability itself. As is explored in more detail later in this chapter, partners are jointly and severally liable for the debts of the firm.[5] However, the advantage of limited liability for companies is often more illusory than real. It is common for banks to require directors of companies to provide personal guarantees for the debts of the company.[6] Other advantages of choosing the limited liability company include the ability to grant a floating charge, which is not available to the firm,[7] and easier transfer of ownership through the buying and selling of shares. There is also no limit on the number of shareholders in a company.

The comparison of the advantages and disadvantages of partnerships as opposed to limited companies must be modified following the passing of the Limited Liability Partnership Act 2000, ("LLP Act 2000"). The adoption of the Limited Liability Partnership ("LLP") as a business format opens the benefit of limited liability to individual partners and brings with it other advantages which are characteristic of a limited company, for example, the ability to grant a floating charge. The law relating to LLPs is considered later in this chapter.

It is important to note that the LLP Act 2000 did not repeal the main pre-existing piece of legislation governing partnerships, the Partnership Act 1890("the 1890 Act"), nor the less important Limited Partnership Act 1907. The LLP Act 2000 simply creates a new type of partnership which the partners may or may not choose to adopt. It remains as important now as it was prior to the passing of this Act to analyse the provisions of the 1890 Act. This Act sought to codify the pre-existing common law rules in Scotland and England and applies to both jurisdictions.

Recent developments in partnership law are not limited to the LLP Act 2000. The Scottish and English Law Commissions completed a major review of partnership law on July 31, 2000.[8] Although no legislation has as yet been enacted as a result of this review, it seems likely that partnership law in Scotland and England will be subject to radical amendment in the not too distant future.

## 9.2. THE NATURE OF A PARTNERSHIP

### (a) Definition of a partnership

The 1890 Act defines a partnership as: ". . . the relation which subsists between persons carrying on a business in common with a view of profit."[9] Limited companies are excluded from that definition,[10] although a limited company may become an individual partner in a partnership.[11] "Business" is defined as including every trade, occupation, or profession.[12]

---

[5] 1890 Act, s.9.

[6] See J. Freeman and M. Godwin, "Incorporating the Micro Business: Perceptions and Misperceptions" published in A. Hughes and D. Storey, *Finance and the Small Firm* (1st ed., 1994) pp.232–281 where they indicate that 54 per cent of respondents taking part in their research said that directors currently provided personal guarantees, principally to banks, cited in Joint Consultation Paper No. 159/111, (above n.2), para. 1.11.

[7] Although the Limited Liability Partnership created by the Limited Liability Partnership Act 2000 has the ability to grant floating charges: see below, para. 9.6.(b)(xi).

[8] Joint Consultation Paper No. 159/111, (above n.2).

[9] 1890 Act, s.1(1).

[10] 1890 Act, s.1(2)(a).

[11] A partnership so formed does not, however, avoid the requirement of preparation and publication of accounts, see Partnerships and Unlimited Companies (Accounts) Regulations 1993 (SI 1993/1820).

[12] 1890 Act, s.45.

Although this point is not abundantly clear from the definition, a partnership is clearly a contractual relationship created through agreement.[13] Merely describing a business as a partnership will not necessarily be sufficient to create a partnership.[14] The question of whether a partnership exists can only be answered by considering all the relevant facts. The agreement may either be express or may arise by implication from the parties' conduct. If the latter, the court will examine all relevant facts in order to make an inference as to the true intention of the partners.

Several further points can be made concerning the definition. Given that the business must be carried on in common, a partnership requires a minimum of two persons. Despite the reference to profit, there is no requirement on the partners to make an actual profit. All that is required is that the partners carry on business ". . . with a view of profit." Clubs and charitable organisations with no intention of making a profit do not, therefore, fall within this definition.

The partnership may have been formed to carry out one single transaction or purpose. Such arrangements, which are more usually referred to as joint ventures, are simply types of partnership and are governed by the 1890 Act in the same way as any other partnership.[15]

A recent case suggests that the time of commencement of the partnership is not necessarily the moment when the partnership begins trading, but rather the time when the partners come together to embark on the activity in question.[16] In this case the partnership was formed to run a restaurant. Activities such as fitting out the premises and purchasing equipment were held to have been partnership activities, even though the restaurant had, at the relevant time, not commenced trading.

The 1890 Act makes use of both the terms "partnership" and "firm." The definition in s.1 tends to suggest that the term "partnership" should be used to describe the actual relation subsisting between the partners, whereas s.4 indicates that the word "firm" is the correct term to apply to the collective entity of "partnership." Usage of these terms in the 1890 Act is, however, inconsistent and does not reflect the pattern set out in these sections. This may simply reflect the fact that it is difficult to isolate the two separate meanings when discussing the whole area of partnership. This chapter seeks, as far as possible, to conform to the terminology set out in ss. 1 and 4 of the 1890 Act.

The 1890 Act provides guidelines in s.2 to assist in the determination of whether a firm has or has not been formed.

## (i) Guideline 1

"Joint tenancy, tenancy in common, joint property, common ownership or part ownership does not of itself create a partnership . . ."[17] This principle is illustrated in *Sharpe v Carswell*[18] in which Sharpe's widow sought to obtain compensation for her husband's death aboard a fishing vessel. She argued that Carswell was her husband's employer and therefore that compensation was due under the Workman's Compensation Act 1906. Carswell argued that because Sharpe had held shares in the fishing boat, Sharpe was necessarily a partner and not an employee. It was held that mere ownership of shares did not, without more, render the deceased a partner and Mrs Sharpe successfully proved her entitlement to compensation.

---

[13] *Pooley v Driver* (1877) 5 Ch. D. 458 at 471–472, *per* Jessel M.R. The joint consultation paper indicates that this is part of the common law of England and Scotland and is ". . . so fundamental that it need not be expressed", Joint Consultation Paper No. 159/111, (above n.2), para. 5.18.

[14] *Inland Revenue Commissioners v Williamson* (1928) 14 Tax Cas. 335 at 340, *per* Lord President Clyde.

[15] *Mair v Wood,* 1948 S.C. 83 at 86, *per* Lord President Cooper.

[16] *Khan v Miah* [2000] 1 W.L.R. 2123; [2001] 1 All E.R. 20; [2001] All E.R. (Comm.) 282.

[17] 1890 Act, s.2(1).

[18] 1910 S.C. 391.

## (ii) Guideline 2

"The sharing of gross returns does not of itself create a partnership . . ."[19] The application of this principle can be seen in a case on very similar facts to *Sharpe v Carswell*.[20] The fact that one person in a fishing business, Clark, was remunerated through a share of gross earnings was not of itself sufficient to establish the existence of a partnership. Importantly, Clark did not contribute to running capital, nor would have been liable if the business had made any losses.

## (iii) Guideline 3

"The receipt by a person of a share in the profits of a business is prima facie evidence that he is a partner in the business, but the receipt of such a share . . . does not in itself make him a partner in the business or liable as such . . ."[21] There may be reasons other than partnership why an individual may receive payments out of the profits of the business. He or she may be a creditor receiving repayments of a debt in instalments[22] or may have made a loan to the firm in terms of which the rate of interest payable varies with the firm's profits.[23]

## (b) Separate legal personality of the firm

One important difference between the law of Scotland and that of England, embodied in the 1890 Act, is that in Scotland a firm has a legal personality which is distinct from the partners of whom it is composed.[24] There are many practical implications of this rule. In Scotland, contracts may be entered into in the name of the firm and the firm can sue and be sued.[25] The rule does, however, have limitations. Although the firm can become a tenant under a lease of heritable property, in practice, the lease is granted to the partners as trustees of the firm.[26] It was previously the case that a firm could not hold title to feudal property. A recent legislative amendment has now removed this anomaly.[27]

As already stated, the individual partners are jointly and severally liable for debts of the firm which were incurred whilst he or she was a partner.[28] The obligation of the partner towards the firm is accessory in nature. In this respect it resembles a cautionary obligation.[29] A debt due by the firm must first be constituted against the firm, for example, by obtaining a court decree against the firm, before any of the partners may be found individually liable. Once the debt has been constituted against the firm, any one partner may be liable for the whole amount of the

---

[19] 1890 Act, s.2(2).

[20] *Clark v Jamieson,* 1909 S.C. 132.

[21] 1890 Act, s.2(3).

[22] 1890 Act, s.2(3)(a). See *Alna Press Ltd v Trends of Edinburgh,* 1969 S.L.T. 186; *Dollar Land (Cumbernauld) Ltd v C I N Properties Ltd,* 1996 S.L.T. 186 at 195–196, *per* Lord Coulsfield. When the case was appealed to the Inner House and House of Lords, partnership issues were not judicially considered: see 1997 S.L.T. 260, 1998 S.L.T. 992.

[23] 1890 Act, s.2(3)(d).

[24] 1890 Act, s.4(2). This section does not apply in England.

[25] Bell, *Commentaries,* II, 508. Where the firm name includes the names of the partners the firm can sue and be sued in its own name: see *Forsyth v Hare and Company* (1834) 13 S. 42. Where the firm uses a descriptive name, the names of three partners (or two if there are only two partners) must be added where the action takes place in the Court of Session: *Antermony Coal Company v Wingate* (1866) 4 M. 1017 at 1018–1019, at 1020 *per* Lord President McNeill, Lord Curriehill and at 1022, *per* Lord Ardmillan. This latter rule does not apply in the sheriff court, see r.5.7.1. Ordinary Cause Rules 1993. Despite the lack of a separate legal personality in England, in practice the firm is usually entitled to raise and defend court proceedings in its own name.

[26] *Moray Estates Development Co v Butler,* 1999 S.C.L.R. 447.

[27] For the previous position, see Bell, *Commentaries,* II, 508. To get round this difficulty, title was taken in the name of the partners as trustees for the firm. The position has been amended by the Abolition of Feudal Tenure etc (Scotland) Act 2000, s.70.

[28] 1890 Act, s.9.

[29] *Mair v Wood,* 1948 S.C. 83 at 86, *per* Lord President Cooper. The obligation of the partner is not entirely analogous to a cautionary obligation. The partner's liability is joint and several whereas co-cautioners would be bound only for a proportionate share of the debt.

debt, with a right of relief from the other partners and the firm itself. In practice, it is possible and indeed common for the firm and the individual partners to be sued in the same action.

It is difficult to apply the concept of a separate legal personality to the relationship of partnership because of its contractual nature. Contracts such as partnership involve *delectus personae.* This expression is used to denote the type of contract where one party is relying on the special skill of another party. The choice of and reliance on that party's special skill implies the exclusion of performance of the obligation by another party.[30] Thus, in theory at least, it follows that any change in the membership of a partnership should bring the old firm to an end, and create a new firm.[31] The assets of the old firm can then be taken on by the new firm together with its obligations. One might argue, therefore, that the separate legal personality of the firm after the change in membership is a different legal personality from that which existed prior to the change. To counter that argument, one could point to the fact that it is possible for partners to provide, in a written partnership agreement, that the separate legal personality of the firm continues notwithstanding a change in the membership of the partnership.[32] This might indicate that the legal personality of the original firm survives the change in the membership. Further support for this view can be obtained if one considers the situation of the retiral of one partner, where the remaining partners are carrying on the same business. In such a situation, the partners are not simply able to ignore the pre-existing partnership agreement, unless they unanimously agree to do so. Again, this would suggest that the legal personality of the pre-existing firm continues. This whole issue is, unfortunately, subject to doubt.[33]

In practice, the provisions of the 1890 Act often act to temper the otherwise inequitable results which would ensue if an entirely new firm was created with each change in membership.[34] One of the benefits for Scotland of the introduction of the LLP Act 2000 is the clarification of the doubt surrounding the principle of separate legal personality, at least in the context of LLPs.

## (c) Business Names Act 1985

A firm may trade under the name of the existing partners, or under those names with certain minor additions,[35] or using the corporate names of corporate partners.[36] Should the firm wish to adopt a descriptive name as opposed to one using the partners' surnames, then the Business Names Act 1985 applies. Certain names are prohibited under the Act and the use of others is subject to the prior approval of the Secretary of State.[37] Partnerships falling within the controls of the 1985 Act must include the name of each partner on business documents[38] and an address for each of the partners for service of partnership documents.[39] This information must also be displayed at any place of business of the partnership[40] or supplied to those requesting such information.[41] Breach of these provisions can result in either civil or criminal sanctions.[42]

---

[30] McBryde, *Contract* (2nd ed., 2000) paras 12–42—12–43.

[31] As is the position in England, see *Lindley & Banks on Partnership*, (2000, 18th ed.), para. 3–04.

[32] See also 1890 Act, s.33(1) which allows the partners to agree that the firm will not be dissolved on the death of a partner.

[33] See Joint Consultation Paper No. 159/111, (above n.2), paras 2.10 and 2.35.

[34] See ss.17, 36.

[35] The additions are the forenames and initials of the partners and the letter "s" if there is more than one partner sharing the same surname.

[36] Business Names Act 1985, s.1(1)(a).

[37] Business Names Act 1985, ss.2 and 3.

[38] Business Names Act 1985, s.4(1)(a)(i).

[39] Business Names Act 1985, s.4(1)(a)(iv). The Act exempts partnerships of over 20 partners from the requirements of s.4(1)(a) subject to certain controls: see s.4(3).

[40] Business Names Act 1985, s.4(1)(b).

[41] Business Names Act 1985, s.4(2).

[42] Business Names Act 1985, ss.5 and 7.

## 9.3. RELATIONSHIPS BETWEEN PARTNERS AND THIRD PARTIES

The rule that any change in the membership of the partnership creates a new firm would obviously create unacceptable results in practice. The partnership could avoid payment of its debts simply by changing its membership. The 1890 Act contains provisions governing the liability of partners in specific instances of change of membership. These provisions, like many of the other provisions of the Act, provide a "fall-back" position only, and may be excluded in a written partnership agreement.

### (a) Liability of an incoming partner for prior acts of the firm

The 1890 Act provides that a person who is admitted as a partner into an existing firm does not thereby become liable to the creditors of the firm for anything done before he became a partner.[43] That person may, however, be held to have accepted such liability. This is because a presumption exists to the effect that, where a new firm takes on the whole assets, stock and business of an old firm it also takes on the whole liabilities of the old firm.[44] The mere addition of one new partner may not rebut this presumption, and the incoming partner may find him or herself liable as a partner of that new firm. In *Heddle's Exx v Marwick & Hourston's Trustee*,[45] at the same time as emphasising that whether a new partnership has been formed by a change in membership is a question which must be determined on the facts and circumstances of each individual case, Lord Shand indicated that the presumption might be rebutted where a new partner had paid a large sum of capital into the partnership. His view was borne out in a later case in which the presumption was overturned in those particular circumstances.[46]

### (b) Liability of a retiring partner

The 1890 Act provides that a partner who retires from a firm does not thereby cease to be liable for partnership debts or obligations incurred before his retirement.[47] An interesting example of the operation of this rule occurred in *Welsh v Knarston*.[48] A solicitor's firm received instructions in relation to a client's claim for personal injury compensation. The firm failed to raise an action, and the client's action became time-barred. After the instructions were received, but before the action became time-barred, two of the partners left the partnership, thus, in theory, dissolving the partnership. In the subsequent action for negligence by the client against the firm and the partners thereof, the two partners argued that they were not liable, because, although they had been partners at the time when the instructions were received, they had left the firm prior to the point at which the client's claim had become time-barred. It was held that each of the partners was under a continuing obligation to raise the action and that this liability survived the dissolution of the partnership.

### (c) Agency of partners

In Scotland partners are agents of the firm, and thus many of the rights and duties which apply between principal and agent apply in a similar manner between the firm and the partners.[49]

---

[43] 1890 Act, s.17(1).

[44] *Heddle's Exx v Marwick & Hourston's Trustee* (1888) 15 R. 698.

[45] (1888) 15 R. 698.

[46] *Thomson and Balfour v Boag & Son*, 1936 S.C. 2 see, in particular, Lord President Normand at 10, where he approves Lord Shand's opinion in *Heddle's Exx v Marwick & Hourston's Trustee* (1888) 15 R. 698. See also *Miller v MacLeod*, 1973 S.C. 172.

[47] 1890 Act, s.17(2).

[48] 1972 S.L.T. 96.

[49] See *Mair v Wood*, 1948 S.C. 83 at 87, *per* Lord President Cooper. Partners are not agents of one another. In English law a partner cannot be an agent of the firm because the English firm lacks legal personality, see Joint Consultation Paper No. 159/111, (above n.2), para. 2.12.

The partner's role as agent is expanded upon in s.5 of the 1890 Act which provides partners with a type of implied authority. In other words, his or her authority is defined by reference to the authority which it would be usual for the partner to have in the particular business carried out by the partnership.[50] Whilst acting within the confines of this authority, a partner has the ability to bind the firm unless the partner has no authority to act and the person with whom he or she is dealing either knows that he or she has no such authority or does not know or believe him or her to be a partner.[51]

### (d) Liability for wrongs

If a partner, by a wrongful act or omission, causes loss or injury to another person who is not a partner, the firm is liable for that wrongful act provided that the wrongful act occurs either when the partner is acting in the course of the business of the firm or the partner has the authority of his co-partners.[52] This rule, embodied in s.10 of the 1890 Act, makes the firm vicariously liable for certain actions of the partner. Some doubt has been caused due to the slightly ambiguous wording of s.10. The ambiguity surrounds the type of situations in which the partner will have "the authority of his co-partners." This phrase could mean either that the firm is liable where the general act which the negligent partner was carrying out was authorised by the partnership, or is liable only where the specifically wrongful action was so authorised.[53] If the correct interpretation is the latter of these meanings, then the ambit of the firm's vicarious liability will be much narrower.

It is important to note that, in terms of s.10, the firm is only vicariously liable where the person injured is not a partner. Thus, in a famous case, one partner in a fishing business was injured when he fell through a hole in the deck caused by the removal by one of his co-partners of boards in the deck. Whilst applying s.10 to find that the firm was not liable, Lord Keith stated that partners act as agents for the partnership, "But as between themselves the partners are really in the position of principals."[54]

The firm may also be liable to make good losses caused where partnership funds have been misappropriated by a partner.[55] The firm is liable in two types of situations: first, where one partner, acting within the scope of his apparent authority receives money or property of a third person and misapplies it;[56] and, secondly, where the firm in the course of its business receives such money or property and it is misapplied by one of more of the partners while it is in the custody of the firm.[57] The reference to apparent authority in the former situation indicates that one should analyse the question from the perspective of the third party only, not taking into account any limitations on the partner's authority which have not been communicated to third parties.[58]

## 9.4. RELATIONS OF THE PARTNERS TO ONE ANOTHER

Normally, one would expect the written partnership agreement to govern the partners' relations *inter se*. If this is not the case, the 1890 Act provides a set of rules as a "fall-back" position. It is

---

[50] See para. 2.3. above.
[51] See para. 2.4.(c) above.
[52] 1890 Act, s.10.
[53] See the discussion in the *Stair Memorial Encyclopaedia,* Vol. 16, para. 1043.
[54] *Mair v Wood,* 1948 S.C. 83 at 87, *per* Lord Keith at 90.
[55] 1890 Act, s.11. See *New Mining and Exploring Syndicate Ltd v Chalmers and Hunter,* 1912 S.C. 126.
[56] 1890 Act, s.11(a).
[57] 1890 Act, s.11(b).
[58] See para. 2.4.(b) above.

possible for the partnership agreement to be amended, although the consent of all of the partners is required for this purpose.[59] If the written agreement includes provisions which should govern a particular situation, it is not possible to prove that an oral variation of the agreement has taken place given that variations of a written agreement require to be made in writing.[60]

## (a) Fiduciary duties/requirements of good faith

A partner is subject to stringent duties towards his or her fellow partners. It is sometimes said that such duties arise due to the fiduciary nature of the relationship,[61] although a partner could equally be described as being subject to duties of utmost good faith.[62] The standard of the duty of care which individual partners owe primarily to the firm and secondarily to the other partners in the exercise of partnership business is subject to doubt. Older authorities indicate that the standard is the subjective one of the diligence which he or she would show in the conduct of his or her own affairs.[63] A recent Scottish case suggests that the standard is the lower, more objective standard of reasonable care only, although the extent of that duty may vary depending on the circumstances of the case.[64]

Many of the more particular aspects of the partner's duties are contained in the 1890 Act. Certain of the duties are owed by an individual partner to the other partners, and others are owed by that individual partner to the firm as a whole.

### (i) Duty to account

In terms of s.28 of the 1890 Act an individual partner owes a duty to render true accounts and full information of all things affecting the partnership to any partner or his legal representative.[65] This section, with its reference to "all things affecting the partnership" clearly imposes a wide duty. A partner is therefore under a duty to disclose details of any acts which he or she carried out in competition with the partnership[66] or any payment which the partner has received in contravention of his or her duties as a partner. The appropriate action for enforcement of this duty is an action of accounting on the part of the firm in which the partner would be forced to account to the firm for any payments made in breach of his or her duty.[67] The partner may also be liable in damages for breach of duty.[68]

### (ii) Duty not to make a secret profit

This duty, which is expressed in s.29(1) of the 1890 Act, is owed by the individual partner to the firm as a whole. Again, it is drafted widely, covering benefits ". . . derived from any transaction concerning the partnership, or from any use by him of the partnership property, name, or business connection." The duty also applies to transactions undertaken after dissolution of the partnership by the death of a partner, and before the affairs of the partnership have been wound up.[69]

---

[59] 1890 Act, s.19.
[60] *Starrett v Pia*, 1968 S.L.T. (Notes) 28.
[61] *Adam v Newbigging* (1888) 13 App Cas 308.
[62] See para. 7.4.(a) above for the duty of utmost good faith in an insurance contract.
[63] Stair, *Institutions*, I,16,7; Erskine, *Institutes*, III,3,21 referring to Justinian, *Institutes*, III,25,9.
[64] *Ross Harper & Murphy v Banks*, 2000 S.L.T. 699 at 702–703, *per* Lord Hamilton. A similar debate on the extent of the standard of care exists in the context of agency and mandate: see *Stair Memorial Encyclopedia* (2002 Reissue) "Agency", paras 23 and 87.
[65] 1890 Act, s.28.
[66] Conduct of this type would also be caught by s.30 of the 1890 Act, commented on below.
[67] *Smith v Barclay*, 1962 S.C. 1.
[68] *Ferguson v Mackay*, 1985 S.L.T. 94.
[69] 1890 Act, s.29(2); *Laird v Laird* (1855) 17 D. 984.

## (iii) Duty not to compete with the firm

A version of this duty is expressed in s.30 of the 1890 Act, which requires partners acting in a business of the same nature as the firm, without the consent of his partners, to account for and pay over to the firm all profits made by him in that business.[70]

## (iv) Expulsion of a partner

Even a majority of the partners cannot expel a partner unless a power to do so has been included in the written partnership agreement.[71] Where such a power exists, the partners are bound to exercise it in accordance with the requirements of good faith. A good example of these requirements is found in the English case of *Blisset v Daniel*.[72] One of the partners, Blisset, received notice that he had been expelled from the partnership. Although the written partnership agreement contained a power in favour of the majority to expel, it did not require the partners either to hold a meeting to discuss the expulsion or to give to the expelled partner reasons for the expulsion. Blisset had recently had an argument with another partner, Vaughan, because Vaughan had attempted to foist his son on the partnership as a manager despite the son's evident lack of qualifications. Blisset had objected to the son's appointment. Blisset was expelled by notice, but was given no reasons for the expulsion, nor was a meeting called to discuss the expulsion. It was held that the power to expel must be exercised in good faith and for the good of the partnership as a whole. As these requirements had not been met in this case, the expulsion was void. Further evidence of the lack of good faith was found in the fact that the partners had persuaded Blisset to sign a set of accounts at a time when it had been agreed that Blisset would be expelled, but when he was unaware of this.

If the power to expel is not contained in the written partnership agreement, the only other solution for the partners is to dissolve the partnership.

## (b) Management of partnership affairs

The partners are bound by general duties of good faith in relation to the management of the firm. Thus, where certain partners from two branch offices of a solicitors' firm left the firm, taking with them client files to set up a new firm in competition with the old firm in offices very close to the original branch offices, it was held that the partners had breached their fiduciary duties not to damage the partnership which they were leaving.[73] The court noted, in particular, that they had no right of ownership over the client files, and had severely inconvenienced the partnership by taking such files. The leaving partners were found liable in damages which were calculated by reference to the profit made in breach of their partnership duties rather than by reference to the loss suffered by the partnership.

The 1890 Act contains rules in s.24 governing the management of partnership affairs which apply where the written partnership agreement is silent. Every partner is entitled to take part in the management of the firm.[74] Importantly, the rules provide that all partners may share equally in the capital and profits of the firm, and must contribute equally to the firm's losses.[75] Thus, if the partners intend to take different percentages of drawings from the profits of the firm, this would require to be specifically provided for in the written agreement. In a recent English Court of Appeal case, Nourse L.J. indicated, albeit *obiter*, that this section created an entitlement for each partner to share equally in the capital of the firm, regardless of the amount of capital individually contributed by that partner either at the commencement of the

---

[70] *Pillans Bros v Pillans* (1908) 16 S.L.T. 611.
[71] 1890 Act, s.25.
[72] (1853) 10 Hare. 493.
[73] *Finlayson v Turnbull (No. 1)*, 1997 S.L.T. 613.
[74] 1890 Act, s.24(5).
[75] 1890 Act, s.24(1).

partnership, or the commencement of his or her membership as a partner.[76] In his view, however, this presumption could be easily rebutted through proof of an implied agreement that final shares of capital would correspond to original contributions of capital. This slightly unusual result of s.24(1) is often avoided in practice by appropriate drafting in the written partnership agreement. Not surprisingly, this section is one of the provisions of the 1890 Act highlighted by the Law Commissions as requiring amendment.[77]

Individual partners have a right to an indemnity from the firm where that partner has made payments or incurred personal liabilities in the ordinary and proper conduct of the business of the firm.[78] This indemnity also extends to acts done to preserve the business or property of the firm.[79]

Section 24, of the 1890 Act also provides that no partner is entitled to remuneration for acting in the partnership business.[80] Although this assumes that partners are always remunerated through a share of the profits, this is, in fact, not the case. It is very common, particularly in the legal profession, for certain partners to be salaried partners only. As a result of the terms of s.24, the ability to create a salaried partner would require to be specifically included in the written partnership agreement. Generally, the concept of a salaried partner is a problematic one, particularly given that it is not contained in the 1890 Act.[81] The main difficulty lies in the fact that it will not be obvious to those outside the partnership that a salaried partner is any different from any other partner. He or she is thus being "held out" to the outside world as a partner. As a result of s.14 of the 1890 Act, such a partner will be liable to third parties who have given credit to the firm as a result of that partner's representations. Although the written partnership agreement will probably contain an indemnity provision in favour of the salaried partner, it would be preferable for the salaried partner to be protected by the 1890 Act itself.

Differences arising as to the ordinary matters connected with partnership business may be decided by a majority of the partnership[82] provided that all partners are present and able to express a view.[83] Where there is an equal split, case law suggests that those pressing for continuation of the *status quo* will prevail.[84] There are exceptions to this principle of majority rule, however. No change in the nature of the partnership business may be made[85] nor may any partner be introduced without the consent of all existing partners.[86]

Partners making payments or advances to the firm beyond the amount of capital which it is agreed that he or she will contribute are entitled to interest on those advances at the rate of 5 per cent.[87] Interest is not payable to individual partners on the amounts of capital which it is agreed that he or she will contribute until the profits have been ascertained.[88]

## (c) Partnership property

Difficult questions may arise as to whether property is owned either by one or more partners as individuals, or is, in fact, partnership property. This can be an important question, particularly where valuation of a partner's share in the partnership is concerned either on dissolution of the partnership or on the death of that partner. If the written partnership agreement fails to define exactly what is partnership property, then use can be made of the definition contained in the

---

[76] *Popat v Shonchhatra* [1997] 1 W.L.R. 1367 at 1372–1373, *per* Nourse L.J.
[77] Joint Consultation Paper No. 159/111, (above n.2), paras 12.16—12,17.
[78] 1890 Act, s.24(2)(a).
[79] 1890 Act, s.24(2)(b).
[80] 1890 Act, s.24(6).
[81] See Styles, "The Salaried Partner," (1994) 39 J.L.S.S. 254.
[82] 1890 Act, s.24(8).
[83] *Const v Harris* (1824) Turn. & R. 496 at 525, *per* Lord Chancellor Eldon.
[84] *Donaldson v Williams* (1833) 1 Cr. & M. 345.
[85] 1890 Act, s.24(8).
[86] 1890 Act, s.24(7).
[87] 1890 Act, s.24(3).
[88] 1890 Act, s.24(4).

1890 Act, namely. "[a]ll property and rights and interests in property originally brought into the partnership stock or acquired, whether by purchase or otherwise, on account of the firm, or for the purposes and in the course of the partnership business . . .".[89] The Act further provides that all such property must be "held and applied by the partners exclusively for the purposes of the partnership, and in accordance with the partnership agreement."[90] A further section states that property bought with money belonging to the firm is deemed to have been bought on account of the firm, unless the contrary attention appears.[91]

Because partnership property is owned by the firm as a separate legal person[92] only the firm has an insurable interest in that property for insurance purposes.[93] Thus, partnership property must be insured in the name of the partnership and not in the name of an individual partner or partners.

It may also be important to identify partnership property for diligence purposes. The creditor of a partner as an individual may arrest the partner's share in the partnership in the hands of the firm.[94] The partner's asset is a share in that partnership, and so what is being arrested is an incorporeal right. Case law suggests that specific property cannot be arrested, but rather only the interest of the partner in any surplus assets once realised.[95]

In theory, a partner's share in the partnership is assignable using the same method by which other incorporeal moveable rights are assigned, namely by assignation followed by intimation to the firm.[96] However, the partnership contract may be one which involves *delectus personae*, in which case an individual partner could not assign his or her share in the partnership without the consent of the other partners.[97] Unless the consent of the other partners has been obtained, the assignee is not entitled to interfere in the management or administration of the partnership business, nor require any accounts of the partnership transactions, nor inspect partnership books.[98] His or her only entitlement is to the share of the profits which would otherwise be due to the assigning partner, and he or she must accept the account of profits agreed to by the other partners.[99]

## 9.5. DISSOLUTION OF THE PARTNERSHIP

The word "dissolution" can be used to describe a number of different situations in partnerships. It may, for example, be used to describe the situation where the firm is wound up completely, or where a change in the membership of the partnership terminates the old firm and creates a new firm. In this section dissolution other than by a court is considered separately from dissolution by a court.

---

[89] 1890 Act, s.20(1).

[90] 1890 Act, s.20(1).

[91] 1890 Act, s.21. See *McNiven v Peffers* (1868) 7 M. 181; *Davie v Buchanan* (1880) 8 R. 319; *Hardie's Exx v Wales* (OH), March 26, 2003.

[92] As explained above, the ability of the firm either to take a tenancy to heritable property under a lease or to take title to heritable property is complex. These factors are, in effect, limitations on the separate legal personality of the firm.

[93] *Arif v Excess Insurance Group Limited,* 1986 S.C. 317.

[94] Bell, *Commentaries*, II 536; Erskine, *Institutes*, III 3, 24.

[95] *Parnell v Walker* (1889) 16 R. 917; Erskine, *Institutes*, III 3, 24.

[96] cf. *Hill v Lindsay* (1846) 8 D. 472 which suggests that intimation to each partner is required.

[97] See 1890 Act, s.24(7).

[98] 1890 Act, s.31(1).

[99] 1890 Act, s.31(1).

## (a) Dissolution other than by the court

### (i) Rescission of the partnership agreement

A right to rescind the partnership agreement arises where one partner has been induced, for example, by fraud or misrepresentation, to enter into the partnership. Section 41, of the 1890 Act refers to three specific rights of the rescinding partner which he or she may have in addition to any other rights on rescission. First, the rescinding partner has a lien or right of retention over the surplus of partnership assets after satisfaction of the partnership liabilities.[1] This right covers any payment made by the partner into the partnership for the purposes of purchasing a share in the partnership or contributing capital.[2] Secondly, the rescinding partner stands in the place of a creditor of the firm for any payment made by him or her in respect of partnership liabilities.[3] Thirdly, he or she has a right to be indemnified by the person guilty of the fraud or making the representation against all debts and liabilities of the firm.[4] As would be the case in other instances of fraudulent or negligent misrepresentation, damages may be available.[5] The right to rescind may still be present where no fraud is involved, but *restitutio in integrum*, as a normal condition of the operation of rescission, must be possible.

### (ii) Dissolution by notice

Where no fixed term was agreed upon for the duration of the partnership the partnership is known as a partnership at will and, it may be dissolved by notice by one of the partners to all of the other partners.[6] Where there is a written partnership agreement, notice will usually be given in writing, although this is not a requirement of the 1890 Act. It has been held that an intention to dissolve can be implied from the circumstances as a whole, including the actings of the partners.[7] The Act does not specify the amount of notice required, or even that it should be a reasonable period.[8] Dissolution is effective as from the date of the notice, or, if the notice is undated, the date of communication of the notice.[9]

### (iii) Dissolution by expiry of the term

A partnership entered into for a specific term will be dissolved on the expiry of that term.[10] Joint ventures will be dissolved once the adventure or undertaking has been terminated.[11] Where the partnership was originally entered into for a fixed term, but the partners continue to act as though a partnership were in existence after the expiry of the term, without settling the affairs of the firm or entering into a new agreement, the partnership will become a partnership at will and therefore terminable on notice by one partner to all of the other partners.[12] The rights and duties of the partners under the new partnership will be the same as those which applied under the old partnership so far as these are consistent with the incidents of a partnership at will.[13]

---

[1] 1890 Act s.41(a).

[2] 1890 Act, s.41(a).

[3] 1890 Act, s.41(b).

[4] 1890 Act, s.41(c).

[5] For fraudulent misrepresentation, see J. Thomson, *Delictual Liability* (2nd ed., 1999), p.51; for negligent misrepresentation see Law Reform (Miscellaneous Provisions) (Scotland) Act 1985, s.10. See also *Ferguson v Wilson* (1904) 6 F. 779.

[6] 1890 Act, s.26(1).

[7] *Jassal's Exx v Jassal's Trustees,* 1988 S.L.T. 757.

[8] Erskine, *Institute*, III 3, 26; Bell, *Commentaries*, II 522, 523.

[9] 1890 Act, s.32.

[10] 1890 Act, s.32(a).

[11] 1890 Act, s.32(b).

[12] 1890 Act, s.27(1).

[13] 1890 Act, s.27(1).

## (iv) Dissolution by death or bankruptcy

The 1890 Act provides that the death or bankruptcy of any partner dissolves the partnership.[14] This provision is, however, subject to the agreement of the parties and the opportunity would almost invariably be taken to amend this default rule. The written partnership agreement may, for example, provide that the partners have the option to continue the partnership after the death of one partner.[15] In one unusual case, the deceased's personal representatives became partners on the partner's death.[16]

## (v) Dissolution by illegality

The 1890 Act contains a statutory expression of the general rule against illegal contracts. A partnership is dissolved by the happening of any event which makes it unlawful for the business of the firm to be carried on or for the members of the firm to carry it on in partnership.[17] As an example, a partnership will be dissolved if the outbreak of war renders the partnership agreement illegal. In one case a partnership agreement was rendered illegal by the outbreak of war with Germany because the partners of the firm were an English company and a German company.[18] After the war was over, it was held that the German company was entitled to a share of the profits made by the partnership after dissolution when the English company continued to carry on the business using capital contributed by the German company.

## (b) Dissolution by the court

### (i) Permanent incapacity

A partner may petition for dissolution of the partnership where one of the other partners is subject to mental incapacity or has become permanently unable to perform his part of the partnership.[19] It is not open to a representative of the partner affected by the mental incapacity to use this section to petition for dissolution. The petition can only be brought by one of the other partners. It is open to the court to refuse the petition, as happened in one case where the partner suffering from mental incapacity had the option not to participate in the management of the partnership.[20]

### (ii) Prejudicial conduct

A partner may petition for the dissolution of the partnership on the grounds that another partner has engaged in conduct which, in the opinion of the court, is calculated prejudicially to affect the carrying on of the business.[21]

---

[14] 1890 Act, s.33(1).

[15] *W. S. Gordon & Co Ltd v Thomson Partnership*, 1985 S.L.T. 122.

[16] *Hill v Wylie* (1865) 3 M. 541.

[17] 1890 Act, s.34.

[18] *Stevenson & Sons v AG Für Cartonnagen-Industrie* [1918] A.C. 239, HL.

[19] 1890 Act, s.35(a) and (b). In relation to mental incapacity, s.35(a) retains for Scotland the original definition which appeared in the 1890 Act, whereas the definition was amended and updated for England. Given that the Act contains an out-dated definition, the partnership agreement should take the opportunity to define the types of mental incapacity which would dissolve the partnership.

[20] *Eadie v MacBean's Curator Bonis* (1885) 12 R. 660.

[21] 1890 Act, s.35(c). The standard of behaviour expected of a partner may be high. In *Carmichael v Evans* [1904] 1 Ch. 486, the partnership agreement provided that partners could be expelled for "scandalous conduct detrimental to the partnership business" or for committing "any flagrant breach of the duties of a partner". The court upheld the expulsion of a partner who was convicted of travelling on a train without a ticket, classing the crime committed as one of dishonesty.

### (iii) Breach of contract

The 1890 Act also provides that a petition for dissolution can be made where one of the partners ". . . wilfully or persistently commits a breach of the partnership agreement" or conducts himself in such a manner that it would not be reasonably practicable for the remaining partners to carry on the partnership with him.[22]

### (iv) Loss

If the partnership can only be carried on at a loss, then this constitutes a ground of dissolution by the court.[23] Raising a petition under this section will probably be relatively straightforward where all partners are agreed that the business can only be carried out at a loss. If this is not the case, then the task of assessing whether it can only be carried on at a loss falls to the court, which may not find such a question easy to determine.

### (v) Just and equitable

If a court considers that circumstances have arisen which, in the opinion of the court, render it just and equitable that the partnership be dissolved, then the court may decree a dissolution.[24] This section tends to be used as a "catch-all" ground where the circumstances do not clearly fall within any of the other subsections of s.35.

Where the problem lies in the conduct of one partner alone, then, unless expressly provides the partnership agreement for the expulsion of an individual partner, the court has no power simply to expel that partner, thus allowing the remaining partners to continue the business. It must dissolve the partnership as a whole.

## (c) Partners' continuing authority to wind up partnership affairs following dissolution

Despite the fact that the partnership has been dissolved, in terms of s.38 of the 1890 Act, the authority of each partner continues in order to allow the partners to wind up the affairs of the partnership and complete unfinished transactions, but not otherwise.[25] It appears that the partners do not by virtue of this section become parties to contracts with the firm, and therefore that those contracts do not remain in force.[26] The partners retain authority simply for the limited purposes referred to in s.38.

The lease of partnership property deserves specific mention in this context. The lease itself is likely to state that it lapses on dissolution of the partnership. Alternatively, it may state that assignation is permitted prior to dissolution. The general rule, which follows from the treatment of the partnership as a separate legal person, is that the lease will terminate when the partnership is dissolved.[27] There are exceptions to this rule, one of which is that the lease may continue if it is assignable. In *Lujo Properties Ltd v Green*[28] the tenants under a lease were a firm of solicitors which was dissolved when one of the partners left the partnership. The landlords attempted to hold the individual partners liable for the remainder of the rent notwithstanding the dissolution of the partnership. In theory, the lease should have been terminated by the dissolution of the partnership. It was held, however, that because the lease

---

[22] 1890 Act, s.35(d). See also *Thomson Petitioner* (1893) 1 S.L.T. 59.

[23] 1890 Act, s.35(e).

[24] 1890 Act, s.35(f).

[25] 1890 Act, s.38. This is consistent with the rule that the authority of an agent can continue despite the death or incapacity of the principal for as long as necessary to complete transactions for the principal, see para. 2.9.(f) above.

[26] *Inland Revenue Commissioners v Graham's Trustees*, 1971 S.C. (H.L.) 1 *per* Lord Reid at 121.

[27] *Inland Revenue Commissioners v Graham's Trustees*, 1971 S.C. (H.L.) 1.

[28] 1997 S.L.T. 225.

was assignable, it would revive on assignation to a new tenant. In the absence of such an assignation, the individual partners were held liable under s.38 for the rent due for the unexpired term of the lease.

## (d) Partners' rights in respect of application of partnership property

On dissolution of the partnership, every partner is entitled to have the property of the partnership applied in payment of the debts and liabilities of the firm.[29] Surplus assets available after payment of debts and liabilities will be valued so that sums representing each partner's share in such assets can be distributed amongst the partners.[30] Although it would be preferable for the partnership to be wound up by the remaining partners, an individual partner or his or her representatives is entitled to apply to the court to wind up the business and affairs of the partnership.[31]

The 1890 Act contains provision for repayment of a premium, as opposed to a partner's capital contribution, which a partner paid in order to join the partnership,[32] although payment of such premiums appears to be rare in a modern context.

Particularly difficult problems may arise in connection with the calculation of the individual share due to a retiring partner or to the representatives of a deceased partner. The method of calculation may be governed by the written partnership agreement. The partner's share may be calculated by reference to the amount standing at the individual partner's credit in the balance sheet of the partnership accounts for the previous year. However, valuation of capital assets can be problematic. Difficulties may arise because the balance sheet may refer to the value of a partnership asset at its date of acquisition by the partnership, rather than its current market value. The court will require to ascertain, as a matter of interpretation of the partnership agreement, whether the partners intended that the assets should be valued at their current market values or at any other value detailed in the accounts. The difficulties surrounding this question can be illustrated by contrasting two cases.

In *Clark v Watson*[33] the partnership agreement provided that, on the death of one partner, all partnership property was to become the property of the remaining partner and that the representatives of the deceased partner were to be paid a sum which would include amounts representing goodwill, a share of the partnership profits up to the date of death, and the capital standing at the credit of the deceased partner in the "accounts" of the partnership. No further definition of the "accounts" of the partnership was contained in the agreement. The heritable property owned by the partnership was entered in previous annual accounts at its original cost plus the cost of renovations and improvements, a value which was far less than its market value at the time of death. It was held that, in view of the lack of specification on which accounts were to be used, a balance sheet should be drawn up detailing the market values of all property at the date of the partner's death. The deceased partner's share would therefore be calculated using current values. This case can, however, be contrasted with *Thom's Exx v Russel and Aitken*.[34] The partnership agreement provided for payment to the deceased partner's representatives of the ". . . share standing at his credit in the capital of the firm as may be determined by the partnership auditors." "Capital" was interpreted as meaning the book value of the capital, *i.e.* the value appearing in the accounts or balance sheet. The court could find no basis on which to order revaluation of the assets of the firm to obtain their market values at the date of death. The share payable to the deceased partner's representatives was not, therefore, calculated using up-to-date market values of the partnership assets. Clearly, much depends on the court's interpretation of the written partnership agreement. To avoid such unpredictable results, careful drafting covering valuation of partnership assets is required.

---

[29] 1890 Act, s.39.
[30] 1890 Act, s.39.
[31] 1890 Act, s.39.
[32] 1890 Act, s.40.
[33] 1982 S.L.T. 450.
[34] 1983 S.L.T. 335.

Section 44, which can be amended in the written partnership agreement, sets out a number of rules governing the final distribution of assets. In relation to losses, it provides:

> "Losses, including losses and deficiencies of capital, shall be paid first out of profits, next out of capital, and lastly, if necessary, by the partners individually in the proportion in which they were entitled to share profits."[35]

Thus, losses are borne by the individual partners not in proportion to the percentages of capital which they originally contributed to the partnership, but rather in proportion to the percentages of profits which they were entitled to draw from the partnership. It may also be noted that because of the firm's separate legal personality, the estate of the firm may be sequestrated under the Bankruptcy (Scotland) Act 1985 (see paras 8.2.–8.3).

## 9.6.   LIMITED LIABILITY PARTNERSHIPS

### (a) The Limited Partnerships Act 1907

The 1907 Act created the first opportunity in the UK for partners to avoid the general rule of joint and several liability for the debts of the firm. The type of partnership created by this Act was not particularly popular and there are many possible reasons for this. It may be because, under the 1907 Act, not all of the partners can avoid joint and several liability. There must be at least one "general partner", who remains liable for all the debts of the firm.[36] Another possible reason is that, within a year of the Act being passed, the private company was introduced, a business entity which proved to be particularly popular.[37] However, the Act remains in force and appears to be here to stay.[38] In a recent joint consultation paper published by the English and Scottish Law Commissions, its amendment rather than its repeal was recommended.[39] It remains popular for agricultural tenancies in Scotland and its attractive tax regime has led to its widespread use in the venture capital industry and in property investment.[40]

The general principles of partnership law, embodied mostly in the 1890 Act apply to partnerships formed under the 1907 Act except as amended by the latter Act.[41] The limited partnership therefore has separate legal personality in Scotland, but not in England.

### (i) Definition

The limited partnership[42] is limited to 20 members, at least one of which must be a general partner who remains liable for all the debts and obligations of the firm and at least one of which is a limited partner.[43] The limited partner is able to contribute capital or property to the partnership,[44] but is not entitled to take part in the management of the firm nor does he or she

---

[35] 1890 Act, s.44(a).

[36] Limited Partnerships Act 1907, ("the 1907 Act"), s.4(2).

[37] See Companies Act 1907.

[38] Companies House has estimated that there are 3,555 limited partnerships in Scotland: see Limited Partnerships Act 1907: A Joint Consultation Paper, ("Joint Consultation Paper"), Law Commission Consultation Paper No. 161, Scottish Law Commission Discussion Paper No. 118, September 28, 2001, para. 1.3.

[39] Joint Consultation Paper No. 161/118.

[40] Joint Consultation Paper No. 161/118, paras 1.5–1.6 and 4.49.

[41] 1907 Act, s.7.

[42] The 1907 Act uses the term "limited partnership" to describe the type of partnership created by the Act. This should not be confused with the limited liability partnership, or LLP, created by the Limited Liability Partnership Act 2000, commented on below.

[43] 1907 Act, s.4(2). A body corporate may be a partner in a limited partnership, see 1907 Act, s 4(4).

[44] 1907 Act, s.4(3).

have the power to bind the firm.[45] If the limited partner takes part in management, then he or she becomes liable for the debts and obligations of the partnership incurred during the period when he or she was involved in management.[46] Thus the limited partnership is attractive to those who would like to finance a firm without being held jointly and severally liable for the firm's debts.

The Act contains an ambiguous exception to the limited partner's prohibition from participation in management. It states that the limited partner is entitled to inspect the books of the firm and ". . . examine into the state and prospects of the partnership business, and may advise with the partners thereon."[47] The exact meaning of the phrase "advise with" remains subject to doubt, but it appears that it does not mean seek to influence or persuade management in its conduct of the firm.[48]

The limited partner must not draw out any of his or her capital during the continuation of the partnership.[49] If he or she does so, he or she becomes liable for the debts and obligations of the firm up to the amount withdrawn.[50]

## (ii) Incorporation

The limited partnership can only be created through registration with the Registrar of Companies.[51] This contrasts with the position under the 1890 Act where a partnership may arise simply as a matter of agreement between the partners, whether express or implied. If the requirements of the 1907 Act in relation to registration are not complied with, then a partnership under the 1890 Act is created with each partner being a general partner.[52]

The Act contains no provision to de-register a limited partnership, and this may mean that the register contains references to defunct limited partnerships. Curiously, and in contrast to partnerships created under the 1890 Act or the limited liability partnership under the Limited Liability Partnership Act 2000, the choice of a name for a limited partnership is unregulated.

## (iii) Management

The Act provides a set of default provisions governing management of the limited partnership which, like those contained in s.24, of the 1890 Act, may be amended by the express or implied agreement of the partners.[53] The matters covered are the same as those referred to in s.24, but amended to reflect the limited partner's lesser importance in management matters. Thus, differences as to ordinary matters concerned with the partnership business are decided by a majority of the general partners,[54] implying that the limited partner could participate if the matter at issue was an extraordinary rather than an ordinary one.[55] It is possible to introduce a new partner without the consent of the limited partner[56] although the consent of all the general partners to the introduction will still be required.[57] Although the limited partner is not entitled to dissolve the partnership[58] he or she does have more freedom than a normal partner in

---

[45] 1907 Act, s.6(1).
[46] 1907 Act, s.6(1).
[47] 1907 Act, s.6(1).
[48] See Joint Consultation Paper No. 161/118, (above n.38), para. 4.12, citing R. C. I'Anson (ed.), *Lindley and Banks on Partnership*, (1995, 17th ed.) para. 31–04, n.17.
[49] 1907 Act, s.4(3).
[50] 1907 Act, s.4(3).
[51] 1907 Act, ss.5, 8 and 13 to 15.
[52] 1907 Act, s.5.
[53] 1907 Act, s.6(5).
[54] 1907 Act, s.6(5)(a).
[55] See Joint Consultation Paper No. 161/118, (above n.38), para. 4.23.
[56] 1907 Act, s.6(5)(d).
[57] This arises by virtue of the 1890 Act, s.24(7).
[58] 1907 Act, s.6(5)(e).

certain respects, reflecting his or her role as an investor rather than a full partner. The other partners are not entitled to dissolve the partnership simply because the limited partner has permitted his share to be charged in some way,[59] and the limited partner may assign his or her share in the partnership with the consent of the general partners.[60]

### (iv) Dissolution

Whereas the death or bankruptcy of a general partner will dissolve the limited partnership[61] the death or bankruptcy of a limited partner will not have this effect.[62] The mental incapacity of the limited partner is not a ground for dissolution of the limited partnership unless his or her share cannot be otherwise ascertained and realised.[63] In the event of the dissolution of the limited partnership, its affairs are wound up by the general partners unless the court otherwise orders.[64]

## (b) The Limited Liability Partnership Act 2000

### (i) Introduction

The Limited Liability Partnership Act 2000 introduced a new form of partnership. Unlike partnerships governed by the 1890 Act, partners in an LLP, or members as they are known under the 2000 Act, are not subject to unlimited personal liability for the firm's debts. Several factors had pointed towards the need for a new type of partnership. The consultation documents which preceded the 2000 Act[65] indicated that, in the government's opinion, partnerships imposing unlimited liability were no longer appropriate in a modern context. It was considered that unlimited liability was more appropriate in small partnerships, characterised by agency and good faith. In such partnerships, partners could "keep a close eye" on the standard of work carried out by their fellow partners. Modern partnerships may operate on a global scale, and, where one of the statutory exceptions applies, have in excess of 20 partners. Where that is the case, it is inappropriate to expect partners to exercise such a supervisory function. Much of the impetus for reform has come from the accountancy and other professions who were concerned at the level of damages awards for professional negligence.[66] Despite the fact that pressure for the introduction of LLPs arose most acutely in the context of large professional partnerships, the new LLP is not limited to such partnerships.

The new LLP could be described as a hybrid between a partnership and a company. Certain advantages of the traditional partnership have been retained, broadly those which relate to internal management, such as the flexibility in management and favourable tax treatment.[67] Externally, *i.e.* when one considers the LLP from the stand-point of third parties, the LLP is more akin to a company. The characteristics of a company adopted by an LLP most obviously include limited liability, but also the ability to grant floating charges. These new benefits have, however, come at a price. The insolvency regime applicable to companies is applied to LLPs

---

[59] 1907 Act, s.6(5)(c).

[60] 1907 Act, s.6(5)(b).

[61] 1890 Act, s.33(1).

[62] 1907 Act, s.6(2).

[63] 1907 Act, s.6(2). Like the equivalent provision under the 1890 Act, this provision has not been amended for Scotland since the passing of the original Act. The terminology used is therefore out-of-date.

[64] 1907 Act, s.6(3).

[65] See DTI Consultation Paper, *Limited Liability Partnerships—a new form of business association for professions*, February 1997 (URN 97/597); Draft Bill and Regulations, September 1998 (URN 98/874); Revised Draft Bill and Regulations, July 1999 (URN 99/1025); DTI Consultation on *Regulatory Default Provisions Governing the Relationship Between Members*, February 2000 (URN 00/617); and *Revised Regulatory Default provisions*, May 2000 (URN 00/865).

[66] See *e.g. ADT Limited v BDO Binder Hamlyn* [1996] B.C.C. 808, in which the partners were held jointly and severally liable for an award of £65 million, only £31 million of which was covered by professional indemnity insurance.

[67] LLP Act 2000 ss.10 and 11.

with necessary amendments. Additionally, the LLP is subject to the same administrative requirements as apply to companies in relation to registration, and preparation and registration of annual accounts and an annual return. Thus, in comparison with the traditional partnership, the LLP does not have the benefit of secrecy of financial arrangements and is subject to higher administrative costs.

## (ii) Relevant legislation

The Act came into force on April 6, 2001. The 2000 Act stipulates that the body of partnership law (found mostly in the Acts of 1890 and 1907) will not apply to LLPs.[68] The effect of the 2000 Act is to introduce a new and different type of partnership in addition to those which are already possible under the Acts of 1890 and 1907. Nevertheless, the "flavour" of the 1890 Act can be seen in many of the provisions contained in the 2000 Act.[69]

The legislation used to introduce the LLP is not user-friendly. The 2000 Act is relatively short, and the vast majority of the important provisions is found in two sets of regulations: the Limited Liability Partnerships Regulations 2001[70] which applies to Great Britain; and the Limited Liability Partnerships (Scotland) Regulations 2001[71] which applies to Scotland only.[72] The Regulations apply provisions of companies legislation to LLPs by reference. Thus, the substantive provisions cannot be understood simply by reading the Regulations. Reference to the companies legislation as a whole is required, read subject to the minor amendments enacted by the Regulations to tailor the companies legislation to LLPs.

## (iii) Name

The LLP is subject to the same requirements as a company in relation to the use of a name.[73] A unified register of names now exists, governing both companies and LLPs.[74] It is the responsibility of the persons forming the LLP to check the register to ensure that the name that they have selected has not already been used either by a company or an LLP. The LLP cannot use a name that is already used by a company,[75] nor one which, in the opinion of the Secretary of State, would constitute a criminal offence,[76] is offensive,[77] or gives the impression that the LLP is connected with HM government or with a local authority.[78] If the Registrar registers an LLP with a name which is too similar to another LLP or a company already on the register, the Registrar may, within 12 months of registration, direct the LLP to change its name within such period as is specified by the Registrar.[79]

The name of an LLP must be followed by "Limited Liability Partnership" or the permitted abbreviations "llp" or "LLP."[80]

A change in the name of the LLP will require the lodging of a form with the Registrar of Companies which is signed by the designated member[81] and submitted together with a fee of

---

[68] 2000 Act, s.1(5).

[69] See *e.g.* the default provisions governing the mutual rights and duties of the partners at Pt VI, regs 7 and 8 of the GB Regulations, or the agency provisions in the 2000 Act, s.6.

[70] SI 2001/1090, hereinafter "the GB Regulations".

[71] SI 2001/128, hereinafter "the Scottish Regulations".

[72] The need for a separate set of Scottish Regulations arises due to the fact that certain insolvency matters are devolved to the Scottish Parliament.

[73] Companies Act 1985, s.714.

[74] 2000 Act, Schedule Pt I.

[75] 2000 Act, Schedule, Pt 1, para. 3(1)(b).

[76] 2000 Act, Schedule, Pt 1, para. 3(1)(c).

[77] 2000 Act, Schedule, Pt 1, para. 3(1)(d).

[78] 2000 Act, Schedule, Pt 1, para. 3(2).

[79] 2000 Act, Schedule, Pt 1, para. 4(2). The period of 12 months is extended to five years after registration where the LLP has provided information for the purposes of registration which is misleading, see 2000 Act, Schedule, Pt 1, para. 4(3).

[80] 2000 Act, Schedule Pt I, para. 2(1).

[81] See para. 9.6.(b) below for the meaning of "designated member".

£20.[82] The Registrar will then issue a certificate of change of name and the change will be effective from the date of the certificate.[83]

Where the LLP trades using a name which is not its registered name, the controls of the Business Names Act 1985 also apply. Such controls are commented on above, in the context of traditional partnerships.[84]

## (iv) Definition and incorporation

The LLP is described in the 2000 Act as a "new form of legal entity"[85] and a "body corporate."[86] It is specifically stated that the LLP has legal personality separate from its members[87] and that is has unlimited capacity.[88] This status cannot arise until the LLP has been registered, or, using the language contained in the legislation, incorporated. In other words, unlike an ordinary partnership which may arise simply through the creation of a relationship without registration, an LLP can only be created through registration.

Before an LLP can be incorporated, by virtue of s.2(1)(a), two or more persons associated for carrying on a lawful business with a view to profit must subscribe an incorporation document.[89] The subscribers must complete the relevant form and lodge it with the Registrar of Companies.[90]

This incorporation document contains information such as the name of the LLP,[91] the address of its registered office,[92] and the names and addresses of each of the persons who are to be members of the LLP on incorporation (although such members may be legal persons such as incorporated companies or Scottish partnerships, rather than natural persons).[93] It also identifies the designated and non-designated members.[94] The form is signed by each of the members and also by a solicitor or agent acting for the members in the formation of the LLP, and is submitted by one of those persons to the Registrar together with a registration fee of £95. In addition to the incorporation document, that person must also deliver to the Registrar a statement confirming that the requirements of s.2(1)(a) have been complied with, i.e. that the partnership comprises two or more person associated for carrying on lawful business with a view of profit.[95] The partnership agreement itself need not be registered and is therefore not available to the public. Thus, although members of the public are provided with a degree of protection through the ability to ascertain the identities of the members, secrecy is maintained as regards the internal management of the LLP.

Provided that the incorporation form is in order, the Registrar will issue a certificate of incorporation which bears the date of incorporation, the LLP's registered number and indicates that the LLP is a limited liability partnership.[96] Because the LLP only comes into existence once the Registrar has issued a certificate of incorporation, only once this has occurred may the LLP commence trading.

Despite the fact that the LLP may only be incorporated if it has two members, if membership falls below two, the LLP will continue to exist until it has been dissolved using the

---

[82] 2000 Act, Schedule, Pt I, para. 4(1) and para. 5.
[83] 2000 Act, Schedule, Pt I, para. 5(3)(b).
[84] See para. 9.2.(c)
[85] 2000 Act, s.1(1).
[86] 2000 Act, s.1(2).
[87] 2000 Act, s.1(2).
[88] 2000 Act, s.1(3).
[89] 2000 Act, s.2(1)(a).
[90] If the registered office is located in Scotland, then the form should be lodged with the Registrar in Scotland, 2000 Act, s.2(1)(b). The same provisions apply *mutatis mutandis* for an LLP with its registered office in England.
[91] 2000 Act, s.2(2)(b).
[92] 2000 Act, s.2(2)(d). The LLP must have a registered office at all times: see 2000 Act, Schedule, Pt II, para. 9(1).
[93] 2000 Act, s.2(2)(e).
[94] See para. 9.6.(b)(vii) below for the meaning of "designated member".
[95] 2000 Act, s.2(1)(c).
[96] 2000 Act, s.3.

relevant winding up procedures contained in the 2000 Act. If one member alone continues to trade for more than six months, he or she becomes jointly and severally liable with the LLP for the debts of the LLP contracted during that period.[97]

## (v) Annual return

The LLP is subject to the same legislation which applies to companies in relation to completing and lodging with the Registrar of Companies an annual return and annual accounts.[98]

## (vi) Changes in membership

A member may cease to be a member as a matter of agreement between the members, through death or through dissolution of the LLP.[99] He or she may also cease to be a member by giving "reasonable notice" to the other members.[1] "Reasonable notice" is not defined in the Act, although the members may have taken the opportunity to define this expression in the written partnership agreement. Any person may, after incorporation of the LLP, become a member by agreement with the existing members.[2]

Where any person becomes or ceases to be a member, notification must be made to the Registrar on the relevant form within 14 days.[3] This form must be signed by the designated member,[4] and by a new member if the change is the appointment of that new member. Any changes in the name or address of an existing member must also be notified to the Registrar within 28 days.[5] Again, the relevant form must be signed by both the member it relates to and a designated member. Failure to comply with these requirements constitutes an offence on the part of the LLP and also on the part of every designated member[6] unless he or she can show that he or she took all reasonable steps to ensure that the requirements were complied with.[7]

## (vii) "Designated" members

On incorporation of the LLP, the form must indicate which members are designated and which are non-designated members.[8] A designated member is a member who has the same legal responsibilities as the other members, but has additional administrative responsibilities. His or her duties include ensuring that the LLP complies with the LLP legislation, notifying the Registrar of changes in membership or names and addresses of members, preparing the annual return, appointing an auditor, signing the annual accounts and delivering them to the Registrar, and acting on behalf of the LLP where it is being wound up or dissolved. There must be at least two designated members at any given time.[9]

If two designated members are not identified on the incorporation form, then all members of the LLP are automatically designated members.[10] Once a member ceases to be a member of the LLP, his or her status as a designated member also terminates.[11]

---

[97] Companies Act 1985, s.24 as amended by the GB Regulations, reg. 4 and Sch. 2, Pt 1.
[98] Companies Act 1985, s.363 as amended by the GB Regulations, reg. 4 and Sch. 2, Pt 1.
[99] 2000 Act, s.4(3).
[1] 2000 Act, s.4(3).
[2] 2000 Act, s.4(2).
[3] 2000 Act, s.9(1)(a).
[4] For the meaning of "designated member" see para. 9.6.(b)(vii) below.
[5] 2000 Act, s.9(1)(b).
[6] 2000 Act, s.9(4). For the meaning of "designated member" see para. 9.6.(b)(vii) below.
[7] 2000 Act, s.9(5).
[8] 2000 Act, s.8(1).
[9] 2000 Act, s.8.
[10] 2000 Act, s.8(2).
[11] 2000 Act, s.8(6).

## (viii) Relationship of members

The general rule is that the internal management of the LLP will be determined as a matter of agreement between the members.[12] A partnership agreement made prior to the enactment of the 2000 Act may continue to govern a partnership once it becomes an LLP through registration under the 2000 Act.[13]

As was the position under the 1890 Act, default provisions govern internal management where the partners have not covered a specific issue in their partnership agreement.[14] Such provisions are very similar to those which are contained in the 1890 Act which have already been commented on.[15]

Each of the members is an agent for the LLP[16] and rules which are similar to those contained in the 1890 Act apply in relation to the implied authority of the member.[17]

## (ix) Liability of individual members for negligence

In the case of a partnership governed by the 1890 Act, a client who suffers a loss due to the negligent work of a partner has remedies in both contract and delict. The contractual remedy was available primarily against the firm as a separate legal entity, but also against the individual partners who are jointly and severally liable in terms of s.4(2) of the 1890 Act. The delictual remedy is available against the negligent partner under normal principles of delictual liability for pure economic loss.[18]

In the case of LLPs, the contractual route against an individual partner is no longer available. The only contractual remedy which exists is against the LLP as a separate legal entity. This is because the contract exists between the LLP as a separate legal entity and the client. The client has no contractual remedy against the members individually, given that they are not jointly and severally liable with the LLP. The partner simply acts as an agent of the LLP.[19] The client retains his or her delictual remedy against the member who has been negligent. This action is dependent upon the usual criteria required to impose professional negligence liability, such as the assumption of responsibility by the partner/member and reliance by the client.[20] This delictual action is therefore the only action which is available to the client against an individual partner in the context of an LLP.

## (x) Execution of documents

The Scottish Regulations insert new provisions into the Requirements of Writing (Scotland) Act 1995 relating to the execution of documents.[21] A document is signed by the LLP if it is signed on its behalf by a member of the LLP.[22] In order to benefit from a statutory presumption as to authenticity of the execution of the document, it must either be subscribed by two members,[23] or the single member's subscription must be witnessed.[24]

---

[12] 2000 Act, s.5(1)(a).

[13] 2000 Act, s.5(2).

[14] GB Regulations, Pt VI, regs 7 and 8.

[15] See 1890 Act, s.24 and para. 9.3.

[16] 2000 Act, s.6(1).

[17] 2000 Act, s.6(2) and see 1890 Act, s.5: see para. 9.3.

[18] *Hedley Byrne & Co v Heller & Partners* [1964] A.C. 456; *Williams v (1) Natural Life Health Foods Ltd and (2) Richard Mistlin* (1998) 1 W.L.R. 830.

[19] 2000 Act, s.6(1). The terms of the legislation which set out the agency relationship are very similar to those which were contained in the 1890 Act.

[20] *Hedley Byrne & Co v Heller & Partners* [1964] A.C. 456; *Williams v (1) Natural Life Health Foods Ltd and (2) Richard Mistlin* (1998) 1 W.L.R. 830.

[21] See Requirements of Writing (Scotland) Act 1985, Sch. 2, para. 3A, inserted by the Scottish Regulations Sch. 4, para. 5.

[22] Requirements of Writing (Scotland) Act 1985, Sch. 2, para. 3A(1).

[23] Requirements of Writing (Scotland) Act 1985, Sch. 2, para. 3A(5)(1A).

[24] Requirements of Writing (Scotland) Act 1985, Sch. 2, para. 3A(5).

## (xi) Securities and floating charges

An LLP has the ability to grant securities and floating charges, which must be registered with the Registrar of Companies in the same way as those granted by companies.[25]

## (xii) Insolvency

As stated above, in return for the benefit of limited liability, LLPs became subject to the more stringent insolvency rules applying to companies. This is achieved through the application of the relevant provisions of the Insolvency Act 1986 to LLPs with minor amendments.[26] Thus, LLPs can enter into voluntary arrangements, or be subject to procedures such as administration, receivership and voluntary and compulsory winding up.

If the LLP is wound up, present and past members who have agreed to be liable to contribute to the assets of the LLP in the event of liquidation will be liable to the extent so agreed.[27] In this respect, an LLP is similar to a company limited by guarantee. Aside from such agreement, an individual member may become liable for the debts of the LLP when it is wound up under what has become known as the "claw-back" provisions. A member of an LLP, or any person who has been a member within the period of two years prior to the winding up of the LLP, may be liable to contribute towards claims of creditors if he or she withdrew any property of the LLP during that period.[28] The form of the withdrawal makes little difference—the provisions will apply to withdrawals in the form of shares of profits, salaries, repayment or payment of interest on a loan to the LLP or any other withdrawal.[29] "Property" is also widely defined as any asset of the LLP.

The salary of a salaried partner could be construed as a relevant withdrawal of property, leaving the salaried partner liable to pay back his salary. This is perhaps an improvement on the regime under the 1890 Act where a salaried partner could be subject to unlimited liability, although hopefully indemnified by the other partners. However, it seems surprising that the opportunity was not taken in the context of the LLP legislation to reduce the liability of a salaried partner.

In order to achieve such a "claw-back", a liquidator, where the LLP is in insolvent liquidation, must apply to the court for an order. The liquidator must prove that, at the time of the withdrawal, the member knew or had reasonable grounds to believe that the LLP was unable to pay its debts[30] or knew or had reasonable grounds to believe that the LLP would become unable to meet its debts as a result of that withdrawal taken together with any other withdrawals made (or contemplated) at the same time. Therefore, it is not sufficient for the member simply to check that the withdrawal that he or she is making does not place the LLP in the position of being unable to pay its debts. That member must also check whether any other members have made relevant withdrawals at the same time as his or her withdrawal which, collectively, would have this effect on the LLP.

If the court is satisfied that these conditions are met it may issue a declaration that the member should contribute to the assets of the LLP in such a manner as it thinks fit. However, the court is not entitled to make such a declaration unless the member knew or ought to have concluded that after each withdrawal there was no reasonable prospect that the LLP would avoid going into insolvent liquidation.

The Scottish Regulations apply to LLPs the provisions of the Insolvency Act 1986 previously applicable to companies in relation to fraudulent and wrongful trading.[31]

---

[25] Companies Act 1985 ss.410, 462, 463, 466, 486 and 487 as amended by the Scottish Regulations, reg. 3 and Sch. 1. See also Insolvency Act 1986 ss.50–72 as amended by the Scottish Regulations, reg. 4(1) and Sch. 2.

[26] See 2000 Act, s.14 and Insolvency Act 1985, s.50–72 as amended by the Scottish Regulations, reg. 4(1) and Sch. 2.

[27] Insolvency Act 1986, s.74 as amended by the GB Regulations, reg. 5 and Sch. 3.

[28] Insolvency Act 1986, s.214A as amended by the Scottish Regulations, reg. 4(2) and Sch. 3.

[29] Insolvency Act 1986, s.214A(2)(a) as amended by the Scottish Regulations, reg. 4(2) and Sch. 3.

[30] Insolvency Act 1986, s.123(1)(c) as amended by the Scottish Regulations, reg. 4(2) and Sch. 3.

[31] Insolvency Act 1986, ss.212–215 as amended by the Scottish Regulations, reg. 4(2) and Sch. 3.

## (xiii) Disqualification

Members of LLPs can be disqualified in the same way as directors of companies through the application of the Company Directors' Disqualification Act 1986 to members of LLPs.[32] A member of an LLP can be disqualified from acting either as a member or as a director of a company. Similarly, a disqualified company director can hold neither role.[33]

---

[32] Company Directors Disqualification Act 1986, as amended by the GB Regulations, reg. 4(2) and Sch. 2, Part II.
[33] ibid.

# Chapter 10

# COMMERCIAL DISPUTE RESOLUTION

## 10.1. INTRODUCTION

A work of this kind would be incomplete without some indication of the means by which commercial disputes are resolved. Since this work has followed the traditional approach of elaborating the rights conferred and obligations imposed on parties by the law, the first thought a reader may have is that parties may resort to the courts whenever disputes arise. Yet disputes may not directly relate to the parties' rights and obligations, or may not do so exclusively, while it is possible for the parties to achieve a rights-based determination of their dispute without involving the courts. Accordingly, while litigation is commonly resorted to, parties may prefer to settle a dispute via arbitration, or seek more consensual means of resolving disputes such as mediation. All will be considered below. It should also be borne in mind that parties may to some extent safeguard themselves against defective performance by the other party through devices such as liquidated damages clauses and retention of title clauses, while the essential principle of Scots contract law that allows a party to withhold performance in response to the other's breach may also offer some recourse.

# (1) LITIGATION

## 10.2. WHY LITIGATE?

Taking litigation, as the paradigmatic form of legal dispute resolution, as our starting point, the question might be asked why a party might wish to litigate in the first place. The short answer is, of course, that litigation is the primary means provided by the legal system whereby a party might vindicate his rights. Yet, litigation may often be regarded as a last resort. This is due to a variety of factors. First, litigation is public, and matters revealed in litigation, not to say the very fact of litigation itself, can be damaging to the commercial interests of the parties. Secondly, litigation, especially in the adversarial Scottish system, may be harmful to the commercial relationship between the parties in cases where this is an issue of importance. Thirdly, litigation can be immensely protracted. Fourthly, it can also be very costly. Finally, it is designed (as it is inevitably must be) to resolve the legal issue between the parties without reference to their wider interests.

## 10.3.  JURISDICTION:

Assuming that a party decides to litigate, the first issue is whether the court has jurisdiction to entertain his claim. It may be that its jurisdiction has been contractually excluded, as where he finds that he is a party to an arbitration clause. Such a clause may be ignored by the parties, but if the other party pleads its existence, the court is usually bound (see para. 10.16.) to decline jurisdiction.[1] The same is probably not true of clauses which seek to commit the parties to attempt non-binding forms of dispute resolution.[2] More fundamentally, however, the court may not have jurisdiction to begin with. Thus a court may not have jurisdiction because of the nature of the relief sought—certain remedies (*e.g.* inhibition) may only be sought in the Court of Session—or because of the value of the claim—claims below £1,500 (scheduled to rise to £5,000) are confined to the sheriff court. Alternatively, no Scottish court may have jurisdiction. While it is always possible for parties to invoke the jurisdiction of the Scottish courts in cases where they would not otherwise have jurisdiction,[3] generally there must be a connection between Scotland and the dispute or at least one of the parties. The main ground of jurisdiction is the domicile of the defender,[4] *i.e.* residence in the case of an individual,[5] the registered office or other official address where central management or control is exercised in the case of a corporation or association.[6] Other situations where the courts might have jurisdiction include where Scotland is the place of performance of the contract,[7] where proceedings relate to moveable property situated in Scotland,[8] where they arise out of the operations of an offshoot of a business or undertaking which is situated in Scotland,[9] or if interdict is sought to restrain a wrong committed in Scotland.[10]

Where the contract is a consumer contract, a consumer domiciled in Scotland may bring proceedings against the other party in Scotland,[11] and (with certain exceptions[12]) may only have proceedings brought against him in Scotland.[13] A consumer contract has a specialised definition in this context. First, it is a contract concluded by a person for a purpose outside his trade or

---

[1] *Sanderson v Armour & Co*, 1922 S.C. (H.L.) 117.
[2] Compare *Paul Smith Ltd v H. & S. International Holding Inc* [1991] 2 Lloyd's Rep. 127; and *Halifax Financial Services Ltd v Intuitive Systems* [1999] C.I.L.L. 1467; with *Hooper Baillie Associated v Natcon Group Pty* [1992] 28 N.S.W.L.R. 194.
[3] Civil Jurisdiction and Judgments Act 1982, Sch. 8, r.5.
[4] *ibid.*, Sch. 8, r.1.
[5] *ibid.*, s.41.
[6] *ibid.*, s.42.
[7] *ibid.*, Sch. 8, r.2(2).
[8] *ibid.*, Sch. 8, r.2(9).
[9] *ibid.*, Sch. 8, r.2(6).
[10] *ibid.*, Sch. 8, r.2(10).
[11] *ibid.*, Sch. 8, r.3(3)(b).
[12] *ibid.*, Sch. 8, rr.2(9), 4.
[13] *ibid.*, Sch. 8, r.3(4).

profession,[14] so that a business may sometimes qualify to be regarded as a consumer.[15] Secondly, it must be a contract for a loan repayable in instalments,[16] or a sale of goods by credit,[17] or any other contract for the supply of goods or services, but in this last case only if the consumer concluded the contract in Scotland.[18] Finally, transport and insurance contracts are excluded.[19]

The issue of the law applicable to the contract has no effect on jurisdiction. Thus if a ground of jurisdiction is established, the Scottish courts will hear a case, even though the contract is governed by a foreign law such as English law.

## 10.4. REMEDIES

It is a characteristic of adjudicatory forms of dispute resolution that remedies may be sought. Most of the remedies available through litigation, are also available through arbitration, albeit that in certain cases the arbitral tribunal may require the assistance of a court to enforce an award against a recalcitrant party. So in both cases, a party may submit a claim for payment or a claim (or counterclaim) for damages, or even ask for an interdict or specific implement. However, whereas it is always open to a party to litigate (unless that right is barred by an agreement to arbitrate), arbitration is not open unless the parties have bound themselves to arbitrate. Equally, only a court can compulsorily sist a third party to the proceedings, or order arrestment of the defender's funds on the dependence of the action, and only the Court of Session can grant inhibition or reduction of a deed.

## 10.5. WHICH COURT?

If the parties have determined on litigation as the means of settling their dispute, the next question is in which court should the pursuer raise the action. The choice will be between the Court of Session and the appropriate sheriff court. The value of the claim may dictate the answer, as the Court of Session cannot entertain any claim which does not exceed £1,500 (scheduled to rise to £5,000), exclusive of interest and expenses, so that such claims must be heard in the sheriff court.[20] By contrast, there is no upper limit on the value of claims which may be heard in either court. So it is entirely possible for claims involving many millions of pounds to be heard in the sheriff court. Whether a pursuer will choose to bring a case in the sheriff court or not will depend on a variety of factors such as his perception of the complexity of the issues and his judgment as to the court best able to handle these, whether he feels counsel should be involved, and considerations of convenience, cost and time. Obviously, if the point is one in relation to which there is likely to be an appeal or a series of appeals—as where a point of fundamental importance is being decided for the first time—the Court of Session might be regarded as more likely to deliver an authoritative answer, while the ladder of appeals from there is shorter than from the sheriff court.

This is not a book on civil procedure, so what follows is a very summary account of how a case might be dealt with in both the sheriff court and the Court of Session.

---

[14] *ibid.*, Sch. 8, r.3(1).
[15] *Chris Hart (Business Sales) Ltd v Niven*, 1992 S.L.T (Sh. Ct) 68.
[16] *ibid.*, Sch. 8, r.3(1)(a).
[17] *ibid.*, Sch. 8, r.3(1)(b).
[18] *ibid.*, Sch. 8, r.3(1)(c).
[19] *ibid.*, Sch. 8, r.3(2).
[20] Sheriff Court (Scotland) Act 1907, s.7.

## 10.6. ORDINARY ACTIONS IN THE SHERIFF COURT

To raise an ordinary action in the sheriff court, the pursuer serves an initial writ on the other party.[21] That party has 21 days from the date of service to respond, failing which the pursuer can request a decree in absence.[22] If the other party does timeously intimate an intention to defend, he has 35 days from the date of service of the writ to lodge written defences with the court.[23] If the defences lodged disclose no real defence, the pursuer may apply for a summary decree.[24] Otherwise, the case will call in court for the first time in an options hearing, which will occur no earlier than 10 weeks after the expiry of the above mentioned 21-day period.[25] The writ and any defences may be adjusted at any time up to 14 days before the hearing.[26] An options hearing is so called, because the sheriff has a number of options open to him, and should select that which should expedite the case.[27] The available options include:

- setting a date for a proof, *i.e.* a hearing at which the parties can lead evidence in support of their respective cases;
- giving the parties further time to adjust their pleadings;
- setting a date for a debate on a point of law which he considers ought to be decided before evidence is led—so if for example, the defender argues that the pursuer's case is legally irrelevant, *i.e.* even if the facts alleged are proved they disclose no cause of action, then there may be some sense in determining this issue in order to decide whether a proof would serve any purpose;
- setting a date for a proof before answer—this might arise when a point of law has been raised, but the sheriff feels unable to answer it until he has heard the facts- for example the defender may deny supplying goods which suffered from the defect alleged by the pursuer, but plead that even if this were true, the defect in question would not be sufficient to render the goods unsatisfactory. A sheriff may well feel unable to pronounce on the issue of satisfactory quality until the facts are established.

If the case is going to proof, parties will be expected to lodge any production (usually documents) on which they have founded in their pleadings,[28] while there are procedures which enable parties to recover documents or other property held by the other party or by a third party. Naturally, each side may call whichever witnesses it chooses, and such witnesses can be forced to attend and (subject to issues of privilege) to testify, on pain of contempt, although it is possible to admit affidavit evidence. Usually, a good many facts are agreed or admitted, and so need not be the subject of proof. A proof may be spread over a number of days, sometimes separated by significant periods of time. An appeal lies either to the sheriff principal, or directly to the Inner House, and any appeal may ultimately be taken to the House of Lords. Appeals are not restricted to points of law.

## 10.7. SUMMARY CAUSES IN THE SHERIFF COURT

Introduced in 1976, the summary cause procedure is a streamlined version of that described above, which is utilised when the amount sought is no more than £1,500 (scheduled to rise to

[21] Ordinary Cause Rules 1993, (SI 1993/1956), r.3.1.
[22] rr.3.6., 7.
[23] r.9.6.
[24] r.17.
[25] r.9.12.
[26] r.9.8.
[27] r.9.12.
[28] r.21.

£5,000), but above £750 (scheduled to rise to £1,500). The summons is completed via a pre-printed form, requiring a statement of the details of the claim.[29] If the other party wishes to defend the claim, he must state that defence in his response to the summons.[30] There are no extensive written pleadings, and thus little scope for adjustment of pleadings. Essentially, as long as the broad details of the claim and defence are clear, the issue can proceed to proof. At that stage, the sheriff may dismiss the claim because it is clearly incompetent, or he clearly lacks jurisdiction.[31] Otherwise, he must seek to negotiate a settlement between the parties, and only if settlement cannot be achieved will he proceed to try the case.[32] If the sheriff is satisfied that the key facts of the case are in essence agreed, he may decide the case at its first hearing, without going to proof.[33] There is no scope for debating a point of law prior to proof. If he so chooses, at the first calling of the case a party may represent himself or be represented by an authorised lay person rather than a solicitor or advocate, while the sheriff may even permit lay representation at the proof.[34] The sheriff may give his decision verbally at the proof or in writing within 28 days thereafter.[35]

The streamlined procedure obviously makes the process quicker and less expensive. Other factors also contribute to minimising expense. Thus evidence is not recorded but noted by the sheriff himself,[36] court dues are lower, as are the fees recoverable as judicial expenses, while although the rules relating to the citing of witnesses and the lodging of productions are essentially the same as in relation to an ordinary action, the modest sums at stake would tend to make parties reluctant to incur significant costs in presenting their cases. An appeal lies on a point of law to the sheriff principal, with a further, very limited, right of appeal to the Inner House, but only if the sheriff principal certifies that the case is suitable for appeal to the Inner House.[37]

## 10.8.   SMALL CLAIMS IN THE SHERIFF COURT

In 1988 an even more streamlined form of procedure was introduced, designed to be still more accessible and less expensive than the summary cause procedure. This was the small claims procedure and it operates when no more than £750 (scheduled to rise to £1,500) is sought. A small claim is essentially a variant of a summary cause and the procedures are very similar. However, the small claims procedure is premised on the view that the pursuer (and possibly the defender) will represent himself, (although legal representation is permitted), so that the sheriff is intended to take a very active role in the conduct of the case. Thus, although the pursuer must still provide the defender with fair notice of his claim,[38] it is the sheriff who is required to identify the issues in the case.[39] Moreover, he is entitled to conduct hearings entirely as he sees fit, without regard to the normal rules of evidence and procedure, while the rules specifically state that a hearing shall be conducted as informally as the circumstances of the claim permit".[40] It is fair to say that not every sheriff is pleased to have this type of freedom.[41] A small claim is initiated in much the same way as a summary cause, but where the

---

[29] Summary Cause Rules 2002, S.S.I. 2002 No. 132, r.4.
[30] r.8.1.
[31] r.8.3.1.
[32] r.8.3.2.
[33] r.8.3.3(d).
[34] r.2.
[35] r.8.18.
[36] r.8.13.
[37] r.25.
[38] Small Claims Rules 2002, S.S.I. 2002 No. 133, r.4.2.
[39] r.9.2.2(a).
[40] r.9.3.2.
[41] See Sh Nicholson in *Kuklinski v Hassell*, 1993 S.L.T. (Sh. Ct) 23.

pursuer is an individual, the sheriff clerk will himself arrange for the service on the summons on the defender.[42] If the claim is disputed, the defender so indicates by completing the relevant part of the form and returning it to the sheriff clerk.[43] If no response is lodged by the date indicated on the form, then the pursuer may request a decree.[44] If a timeous response is lodged, disputing the claim, there will then be a hearing. At that hearing the sheriff may dismiss the claim because it is incompetent or he lacks jurisdiction.[45] Otherwise, he must seek to negotiate a settlement between the parties, and only if settlement cannot be achieved will he proceed to decide the case.[46] He should "if possible" reach a decision on the information before him,[47] although it is possible for an evidential hearing to be held if absolutely necessary. Should there have to be such a hearing, the sheriff shall indicate what has to be proved, and what sort of evidence is necessary.[48]

Witnesses may be cited in any hearing, but a party is responsible for the expenses of any witness he calls and for securing the attendance of such witnesses.[49] The small claims procedure takes into account the fact that the prospect of having to pay the other side's expenses if the case is lost deters individuals from going to law. Thus a sheriff may not award expenses if a claim does not exceed £200.[50] Otherwise expenses cannot exceed £75[51] unless against a defender who has no real defence.[52] An appeal can be taken to the sheriff principal on a point of law, but no further appeal is possible.

## 10.9. COURT OF SESSION ACTIONS

An ordinary action in the Court of Session is initiated when a summons drawn up in prescribed form is submitted along with the requisite fee.[53] If the summons meets the requirements of form, it will be signetted, which authorises service on the defender.[54] Once a period of 21 days from the date of service has elapsed, the pursuer can lodge the summons with the court for calling, and must do so within a year and a day of the expiry of the aforementioned period.[55] Once the case appears on the calling list, the defender has three days to intimate to the court that he intends to appear to contest the action.[56] He has seven days from the actual date of calling to lodge written defences in the prescribed form.[57] The pursuer receives a copy of the defences, and he must then lodge the open record within 14 days of the date the defences were lodged (or the period for lodging defences expired).[58] The open record is a document which records the details the pursuer's case and any defences. There is then a period of eight weeks within which the parties may adjust their pleadings on the open record.[59] At the end of that period the record closes, and within four weeks thereafter the pursuer must lodge the closed record.[60] The options are then that:

---

[42] Sheriff Courts (Scotland) Act 1971, s.36A.
[43] r.9.1.
[44] r.8.1.
[45] r.9.2.1.
[46] r.9.2.2(b).
[47] r.9.2.3(c).
[48] r.9.2.4(b).
[49] r.17.4.1.
[50] Sheriff Courts (Scotland) Act 1971, s.36B(1); and see Small Claims Scotland Order 1988, SI 1988/1999.
[51] Sheriff Courts (Scotland) Act 1971, s.36B(2).
[52] Sheriff Courts (Scotland) Act 1971, s.36B(3).
[53] See Rules of the Court of Session, SI 1994/1443, r.13.1.–2.
[54] r.13.5.
[55] r.13.7.
[56] r.17.
[57] r.18.
[58] r.22.1.
[59] r.22.2.
[60] r.22.3.

- the court fixes a date for a proof;
- the court fixes a date for a proof before answer;
- the case is scheduled for a debate on a point of law arising from the proceedings.[61]

Where a proof is held, there are of course rules regarding the citation of witnesses and the lodging of productions. An appeal lies to the Inner House (and ultimately to the House of Lords). Appeals are not restricted to points of law.

## 10.10. COMMERCIAL ACTIONS IN THE COURT OF SESSION AND SHERIFF COURT

As an alternative to ordinary procedure in the Court of Session there exists a special procedure for commercial actions. A commercial action is an action arising out of or concerned with any transaction or dispute of a commercial or business nature.[62] The relevant *Practice Note*[63] made it clear that the dispute need not necessarily be contractual, and provides the following non-exhaustive list of examples: actions related to the construction of a commercial and mercantile document; sale or hire-purchase of goods; the export or import of merchandise; carriage of goods; insurance;[64] banking; financial services; mercantile agency; mercantile usage or custom of trade; a building, engineering or construction contract; commercial leases. It has also been held that proceedings relating to insolvency would be regarded as commercial,[65] and actions relating to any of the branches of the law considered in this book would surely be commercial. That being said, a dispute involving a consumer would not be regarded as commercial, and rather surprisingly the court has regarded intellectual property disputes as not suitable for the commercial action procedure.[66]

It is important to realise that "commercial" cases are not automatically assigned to this procedure. It is for the pursuer to elect to invoke it by using the words "commercial action" in the summons.[67] The summons can be less detailed than that employed in an ordinary action as long as it provides details of the orders the pursuer seeks, identifies the parties and the transaction from which the dispute arises, provides a summary of the circumstances from which the dispute arises, indicates the legal grounds of the action, and appends any documents founded upon or referred to in the summons.[68] The procedure regarding the service of the summons, the indication of an intention to defend, and the lodging of defences resembles that in an ordinary action. However, the form of defences should reflect the streamlined form of the summons, it being enough if the areas of dispute can be identified from the defences.[69] Again, any documents founded upon or referred to should be appended.[70] The case will first call in court at a preliminary hearing, which will occur within 14 days of the lodging of defences.[71] A party may apply for the action to be withdrawn from the commercial action procedure at or before this hearing, but not thereafter.[72] (It is also possible at any stage of an ordinary action to

---

[61] r.22.3.5.

[62] r.47.1.2.

[63] P.N. No. 12 of 1994.

[64] See *Unipac (Scotland) Ltd v Aegon Insurance Co (U.K.) Ltd,* 1996 S.L.T. 1197.

[65] *Rankin's Trs v HC Somerville & Russell,* 1999 S.L.T. 166.

[66] *Birt v Celtic plc* CA 54/95, referred to in Clancy, Murray and Wadia, "The New Commercial Cause Rules", 1997 S.L.T. 45.

[67] r.47.3.1.

[68] r.47.3.2.

[69] r.47.6.

[70] *ibid.*

[71] r.47.2.

[72] r.47.9.

apply for it to be treated as a commercial cause.[73]) Whereas in an ordinary action the parties effectively determine how the litigation progresses, the judge in a commercial action is entitled and indeed expected pro-actively to manage the procedure.[74] Thus he has a wide range of orders at his disposal, and in particular may[75]:

- order either party to provide more detail in the pleadings;
- order the disclosure of witnesses and relevant documents (and the recovery of the latter);
- order to be lodged in process a list of witnesses, any document, any report from a person of skill, any affidavit or any witness statement;
- order the action to proceed to a hearing on the merits without further procedure;
- make any order he thinks fit for the speedy determination of the action,

and generally may make any such order subject to a time limit. It should be observed that the judge will be a specially selected commercial judge,[76] and that commercial actions can be heard throughout the year, including periods when the court is in vacation.[77]

The emphasis at the preliminary hearing is on clarifying the issues between the parties and thus the best way of proceeding. It tends to take the form of an informal round table discussion, and wigs and gowns are not worn.[78] If the judge decides against proceeding immediately to a hearing on the merits, he will fix a date for a procedural hearing in order to decide what procedure is most apt for the determination of the case, and in particular the nature and extent of debate or proof required.[79] At least three days in advance of the procedural hearing, each party must provide advance notice of his proposals for further procedure, and if he proposes a debate, he must indicate what should be debated.[80] Advance notice must also be given of the witnesses each party proposes to call and the matters to which they are to speak, and he must lodge any report of a skilled person on which he intends to rely.[81] The procedure generally aims at full advance disclosure of each party's case, and to minimise the time spent on debates. At the hearing, after considering the submissions of the parties, the judge decides whether the case should go to debate or be sent for proof.[82] If the case goes to debate or proof, then the judge instead of waiting to hear the parties, may direct that written arguments be submitted in advance of the hearing.[83] Moreover, if a proof is ordered, then it is for the judge to decide what needs to be proved and how.[84] And if invited to by the parties, he may dispense with any oral hearing, and determine the matter on the basis of written submissions.[85] With its emphasis on expedition, pro-active case management by the judge, and immense procedural discretion, it can thus be appreciated that the commercial procedure represents a radical departure from traditional Court of Session procedure.

The commercial action procedure is to some degree mirrored in the sheriff court, where a special commercial procedure will be available only if the relevant sheriff principal has so directed.[86] The same sort of transactions are comprehended, although actions relating to consumer credit transactions are specifically excluded.[87] Again, the pursuer must specifically

---

[73] r.47.10.
[74] r.47.5.
[75] r. 47.11.
[76] r.47.2.
[77] r.10.7.
[78] P.N. No. 12 of 1994.
[79] r.47.11.3.
[80] r.47.12.1.
[81] ibid;.
[82] r.47.12.2(a). Unlike in an ordinary action, a party may not insist on a debate: *Highland and Universal Properties Ltd v Safeway Properties Ltd,* 1996 S.C. 424.
[83] r.47.12.2(b).
[84] r.47.12.2(c), (d) (g).
[85] r.47.12.2(h).
[86] Ordinary Cause Rules 1993 (SI 1993/1956), r.40.1.3.
[87] r.40.1.2.

elect for this procedure,[88] although either party may apply to have an ordinary cause transferred to the commercial procedure[89] By the same token, the sheriff must transfer a commercial action to the ordinary cause procedure if at or before the case management conference (see below), the parties submit a joint motion to that effect, or one party makes such a motion, and the sheriff is of the view that either detailed pleadings are required to enable justice to be done between the parties or other circumstances warrant such an order.[90] Expedition is once more a key objective of the procedure, and the sheriff is empowered to make any order he this fit for the progress of the case.[91] Where the construction of a document is the only matter in the dispute, no pleadings or pleas in law require to be included in the initial writ.[92] Generally the initial writ need only indicate the nature of the dispute, the grounds of action and the remedy sought,[93] while defences must be in the form of answers which allow the extent of the dispute to be indentified, and must include the defender's pleas in law.[94] The case management conference is at the centre of any defended action under the commercial procedure. In it the sheriff "shall seek to secure the expeditious resolution of the action."[95] The sheriff generally has the same sort of powers as the judge at the procedural hearing in a commercial action.[96]

# (2) ARBITRATION

## 10.11. INTRODUCTION TO ARBITRATION

As an alternative to litigation, the parties may seek a binding resolution of their dispute via arbitration, or indeed be obliged to do so because of an arbitration clause in the relevant contract. Arbitration essentially sees the determination of the issue(s) between the parties by a third party—the arbiter, whose decision takes the form of a formally binding award. There are two legal regimes applicable to arbitration in Scotland (leaving aside statutory forms of arbitration), in that international commercial arbitrations held in Scotland are subject to the UNCITRAL Model Law on International Commercial Arbitration (adopted into Scotland by s.66 and Sch.7 of the LR(MP)(S) Act 1990). The two regimes overlap, in that the Model Law is not a complete law and thus requires to be supplemented by existing domestic law in those areas where it is silent. It is indeed possible for parties to a dispute which is neither international nor commercial to invoke the provisions of the Model Law.[97] Any arbitration involving a non-Scots party will be international, so many disputes arising in the fields covered by this work will be governed by the Model Law, if arbitrated in Scotland. For this reason, an attempt will be made to take account of the Model Law as well as domestic law. Without going into the minutiae of the Model Law, it is safe to say that all the branches of law discussed within this book would be regarded as "commercial", although disputes involving consumers would be excluded.[98] Equally, even if the arbitration involves two Scottish parties, it is still international if their dispute concerns a matter outwith Scotland, or their contract is to be substantially performed outwith Scotland.[99] It may be noted that the Model Law employs the term arbitrator rather than arbiter.

---

[88] r.40.4.
[89] r.40.5.1.
[90] r.40.6.1.
[91] r.40.3.1.
[92] r.40.7.1.
[93] Form G1A.
[94] r.40.9.3.
[95] r.40.12.1.
[96] r.40.12.3.
[97] s.66(4).
[98] Art. 2(g).
[99] Art. 1(3).

## 10.12.   WHY ARBITRATE?

If the parties wish a binding resolution of their dispute, but do not want to go to court, then arbitration is the main alternative. It shares some of the advantages and drawbacks of litigation, though this is not invariably the case. So the procedure employed in arbitration can be very flexible indeed, considerably more flexible than even the most radical forms of court procedure described above. Yet many arbitrations simply ape formal court proceedings. Thus depending on the type of arbitration adopted, arbitration can be considerably more expeditious than court proceedings, or even slower than the most formal proceedings. Equally it can be very inexpensive, or (because of the need to meet the costs of employing an arbiter or arbiters and support staff, together with the ancillary costs of the arbitral proceedings) significantly more expensive than litigation. One of the main advantages of arbitration is the ability to choose the arbiter. Thus the parties may select an individual because of that person's particular knowledge and experience, which they believe will assist him to come to a just decision in the dispute. So while many arbiters are lawyers, others are drawn from a variety of professions. It is indeed possible to have a tribunal of two or more arbiters, so that more than one discipline, or more than one legal culture, is represented, the latter being thought to be particularly important in the context of international arbitration. Again, while court proceedings are public, arbitration is private and (probably) confidential. It is also the case that if enforcement is sought against a losing party abroad, in a number of states an arbitral award is easier to enforce than a foreign court decree. On the other hand, the powers of an arbiter are inevitably less extensive than that of a judge, and the assistance of the court may be required to support the arbitration at various points, possibly including the enforcement of the award. Moreover, if the dispute seeks a definitive view on an issue of general importance, such as the correct interpretation of a widely used standard form contract, then it is better to litigate than arbitrate.

## 10.13.   WHAT MATTERS MAY BE REFERRED TO ARBITRATION?

The broad rule of thumb is that, since the foundation of arbitration is agreement, one may refer to arbitration any issue which can be determined by agreement between the parties. Thus while an arbiter obviously cannot deal with the criminal consequences of fraud, he can be empowered to consider the effect of fraud on the civil relations of the parties.[1] Equally, while the creation and dissolution of a company involves the invocation of state power, and thus can never be within the competence of an arbiter, since the creation and dissolution of a partnership can be effected by agreement, it is possible to empower an arbiter to dissolve a firm. In the same way, while only the state can grant a patent, it is open to parties to agree to refer to an arbiter the question of whether one has infringed the other's patent. The foundation of the arbiter's powers being agreement, the effect of the arbiter's determination is generally confined to the relations between the parties themselves, and cannot impinge on the rights of third parties. Thus while an arbiter may decide, as between A and B, whether property has passed under their contract of sale, no arbiter may actually confer a real right to property. In the particular context of this book, any dispute arising out of the various commercial contracts examined would be arbitrable. As regards bankruptcy, while it is not possible for an arbiter to make an award of sequestration, the permanent trustee is specifically empowered to refer any claim to arbitration.[2]

---

[1] *Earl of Kintore v Union Bank of Scotland* (1865) 4 Macq. 465.
[2] Bankruptcy (Scotland) Act 1985, s.65.

# 10.14. WHO CAN ACT AS ARBITER?

Taking the view that the question of capacity is not really relevant in a work of this kind, the real question is what sort of factors will disqualify an individual from acting as arbiter. Just as the parties are entitled to choose anyone they wish to be their arbiter, so too they may agree in advance that any arbiter must possess (or lack) certain characteristics or qualifications. Thus anyone who does not have the agreed qualifications may be regarded as disqualified and thus challenged and removed, while an award made by such an arbiter is arguably void.[3] Apart from such conventional disqualifications, an individual would be disqualified if he has a financial interest, however minimal, in the dispute,[4] or if he has a close relationship with one of the parties.[5] Equally, if an individual has shown evidence of bias,[6] or being predisposed towards a particular conclusion,[7] that will disqualify, while English authority would suggest that the existence of circumstances which suggest a real danger of bias would be enough to disqualify.[8] However, if a party agrees to the appointment of an arbiter despite being aware of a disqualifying factor,[9] or permits the proceedings to continue without objection after becoming aware of a disqualifying factor,[10] he will be taken to have waived his right to object. Of course, even if that right is waived, evidence of actual bias in the conduct of the arbitration or the making of the award will permit a challenge.

Turning to the Model Law, although it employs its own particular formula, the grounds on which an arbitrator is disqualified are in substance practically identical to those recognised by Scots law.[11] Again, a party may not challenge an arbitrator in whose appointment he participated.[12] One feature of the Model Law is that it imposes a duty on anyone who is approached to be an arbitrator to disclose any factor liable to give rise to justifiable doubts as to his impartiality or independence, a duty which persists throughout the proceedings.[13] Although the Model Law is silent on the consequences of breach of this duty, it may be supposed that it would give rise to an action for damages for breach of statutory duty. Another feature of the Model Law is that it lays down an actual challenge procedure, albeit that this will only apply in the absence of an agreed procedure.[14] This indicates that a party has 15 days from becoming aware of a disqualifying factor or the constitution of the arbitral tribunal to submit a written challenge to the tribunal itself.[15] If the other party agrees with the challenge, the arbitrator will be removed from office. Alternatively the challenged arbitrator may resign. But if neither of these things happens, then the tribunal itself will decide on the challenge. The challenged arbitrator, who may indeed be the sole arbitrator, will participate in that decision. The possibility of abuse, which that seems to involve, is however mitigated by the fact that a party may appeal to the court within 30 days of receiving notice of the rejection of his challenge.[16] The logic of the Model Law is that any party who fails to make a challenge as directed by its provisions must be taken to have waived his right of objection.

---

[3] *Rahcassi Shipping Co SA v Blue Star Line Ltd* [1969] Q.B. 173.

[4] *Sellar v Highland Railway,* 1919 S.C. (H.L.) 19 (small shareholding in one of the parties).

[5] See, *e.g. McDougall v Laird & Sons* (1894) 22 R. 71; *Caledonian Railway Co v Glasgow Corporation* (1897) 5 S.L.T. 200.

[6] *Pekholtz & Co v Russell* (1899) 7 S.L.T. 135.

[7] *ERDC Construction Ltd v H. M. Love & Co (No. 2),* 1997 S.L.T. 175.

[8] *R v Gough* [1993] A.C. 646.

[9] *Buchan v Melville* (1902) 4 F. 620; where one of the parties was appointed arbiter! It is of course another matter if a new disqualifying factor emerges after the appointment has been agreed: *Fleming's Trs v Henderson,* 1962 S.L.T. 401.

[10] *Johnson v Lamb,* 1981 S.L.T. 300.

[11] Art. 12(2).

[12] *ibid.*

[13] Art. 12(1).

[14] Art. 13(1).

[15] Art. 13(2).

[16] Art. 13(3).

## 10.15. ARBITRATION AGREEMENT:

As noted above, the basis of arbitration is agreement between the parties that they should arbitrate. It is now clear that an arbitration agreement need not be in writing,[17] though in practice it almost invariably would be. An agreement to arbitrate may take the form of a free standing submission to arbitration once a dispute has arisen, or a clause in the original contract between the parties indicating that disputes between them should be referred to arbitration. In Scotland the courts are reluctant to hold that parties have agreed to arbitrate unless that was clearly their intention. So whereas in England the courts are generally happy to assume that parties who adopt a standard form contract are bound by an arbitration clause therein,[18] that is not the case in Scotland.[19] *A fortiori*, the Scots courts are reluctant to accept that parties who agree to be bound by the terms of another contract—such as where subcontractors agree to adopt the terms of the main contract—intend to be bound by an arbitration clause in that contract.[20] The Model Law insists that the arbitration agreement shall be in writing, but goes on to indicate that writing is constituted by any exchange of communications which provides a record of the agreement.[21] Indeed, writing can be deemed to exist if there is an exchange of statements of claim and defence in which the existence of the agreement is alleged by one party and not denied by the other.[22] The Model Law also acknowledges the possibility of an arbitration agreement being incorporated from another document, but appears to leave the question of whether such incorporation has occurred to Scots law.[23]

## 10.16. EFFECT OF ARBITRATION AGREEMENT

As Lord Dunedin observes: "If the parties have contracted to arbitrate to arbitration they must go".[24] So, if one party seeks to litigate, and the other pleads the existence of a valid arbitration agreement, then the court will refer the issue to arbitration. Of course, if such a plea is not raised, or if the parties decide that they would prefer to litigate despite the existence of the arbitration agreement, then the court will determine the issue between them.[25] Should one party seek to litigate, the other does not forfeit his right to insist on arbitration merely by entering defences,[26] but if he allows litigation to progress too far he may be held by his conduct to have waived that right.[27] It may also be pointed out that the general; rule suffers a major exception in relation to contracts governed by the Unfair Terms in Consumer Contracts Regulations 1999.[28] Because it is thought that arbitration clauses are often inserted in consumer contracts to deter consumers from enforcing their rights, the cost of arbitrating often being far greater than going to court, especially where special low cost court procedures are available, an arbitration clause will be deemed unfair and thus will not bind the consumer when the amount sought does not exceed £5,000.[29] Turning to the Model Law, it directs that a court

---

[17] Requirements of Writing (Scotland) Act 1995, s.1(1).
[18] *Golodetz v Schrier* (1947) 80 Ll. L. Rep. 647.
[19] *McConnell and Reid v Smith,* 1911 S.C. 635.
[20] *Goodwins, Jardine & Co. v Brand* (1905) 7 F. 995; *Babcock Rosyth Defence Ltd v Grootcon (United Kingdom) Ltd* 1998 S.L.T. 1143.
[21] Art. 7(2).
[22] *ibid.*
[23] *ibid.*
[24] *Sanderson v Armour & Co,* 1922 S.C. (H.L.) 117 at 126.
[25] *Stanley Miller Ltd v Ladhope Developments Ltd,* 1988 S.L.T. 514.
[26] *Presslie v Cochrane McGregor Group Ltd,* 1996 S.L.T. 988.
[27] *Inverclyde (Mearns) Housing Society Ltd v Lawrence Construction Co Ltd,* 1989 S.L.T. 815.
[28] SI 1999/2083.
[29] Arbitration Act 1996, ss.89–91; Unfair Arbitration Agreements (Specified Amounts) Order 1999, SI 1999/2167.

before which an action is brought in a matter which is the subject of an arbitration agreement shall, if a party so requests at any time before the pleadings in the action are finalised, refer the parties to arbitration, unless it finds that the agreement is null and void, inoperative or incapable of being performed.[30] It can be seen that the position is very similar to that at common law. In particular, the court will only refer the dispute to arbitration if one party so requests, and a party can no longer insist on arbitration if he allows the proceedings to continue past a certain stage.

## 10.17.  APPOINTING ARBITERS

Assuming that there is a valid arbitration agreement, the first step in referring a dispute to arbitration is to establish the arbitral tribunal. There are as many ways of doing this as it is possible for human ingenuity to devise. One obvious method would be for the arbitration agreement itself to nominate a particular individual or office holder to act as arbiter should a dispute arise. Another would be for the agreement to require a particular person or body to nominate an arbiter. Alternatively, the parties may simply agree on an arbiter. Or in a two arbiter tribunal, it may be contemplated that each party will appoint an arbiter. Typical modes of constitution of a three arbiter tribunal would be for each party to appoint an arbiter, with the third being appointed by the parties acting together, or perhaps by the other two arbiters acting together. If the procedures for appointing the tribunal break down, then the court can be asked to intervene in certain limited circumstances. Thus if a party to an agreement to refer to a single arbiter refuses to concur in the nomination of an arbiter, and the agreement makes no provision for such an eventuality, or such provision has failed, then a party may request the court to appoint an arbiter.[31] Similarly, if a party to an agreement to refer to two arbiters refuses to name an arbiter, and the agreement makes no provision for such an eventuality, or such provision has failed, then the other party may request the court to appoint an arbiter.[32] However, the court has no power of appointment outside these two specific situations. So it cannot assist when the parties have simply agreed to go to "arbitration", and then prove unable to agree on the nature of their tribunal,[33] unless perhaps trade custom may be invoked to show that a single arbiter or two arbiters must have been intended.[34] Nor can it intervene where the person or institution charged with making an appointment fails to do so,[35] nor where the individual nominated as arbiter in the agreement dies,[36] or declines to act.[37]

The Model Law also deals with the situation where the appointing procedures of the parties break down—and in a more comprehensive way. Thus to begin with, if the parties have not determined the number of arbitrators, it is provided that there shall be a single arbitrator.[38] The parties are free to agree upon an appointments procedure, but if they do not, then if there is to be a single arbitrator and the parties are unable to agree on his identity, he shall be appointed by the court on the request of a party.[39] Similarly, if there is no agreed appointments procedure in relation to a three arbitrator tribunal, then each party shall appoint one arbitrator, and those arbitrators acting together shall appoint the third.[40] Should a party fail to

---

[30] Art. 8(1).
[31] Arbitration (Scotland) Act 1894, s.2.
[32] Arbitration (Scotland) Act 1894, s.3.
[33] *McMillan & Son v Rowan & Co* (1907) 5 F. 317.
[34] See *e.g. Douglas & Co v Stiven* (1900) 2 F. 575.
[35] *Cowie v Kiddie* (1897) 5 S.L.T. 259.
[36] *Bryson & Manson v Picken* (1896) 12 Sh. Ct Rep. 26.
[37] *British Westinghouse Electric and Manufacturing Co Ltd v Provost of Aberdeen* (1906) 14 S.L.T. 391.
[38] Art. 10(2).
[39] Art. 11(3)(b).
[40] Art. 11(3)(a).

appoint an arbitrator within 30 days of being requested to do so by the other party, or should the two arbitrators fail to agree on the third within 30 days of their appointment, a party may request the court to appoint.[41] More generally, where under an agreed appointment procedure, a party fails to act as required, or the parties or two arbitrators fail to reach an agreement expected of them, or a third party or institution fails to perform a function entrusted to it, and no provision is made for such eventuality in the procedure, then any party may request the court to take the necessary measure.[42] Finally, if an arbitrator dies, or resigns or is removed from office, then subject to the contrary agreement of the parties, a substitute must be appointed according to the rules which applied to the appointment of the original arbitrator.[43]

## 10.18.   JURISDICTION

Once the tribunal is established, the arbiter can proceed with the reference. Yet a preliminary question may arise as to whether he has jurisdiction to decide the dispute. That leads on to the further question as to who should determine such questions. The thrust of the Scottish cases is that while it is ultimately for the courts to determine the scope of an arbiter's jurisdiction, in the first instance it is for the arbiter himself to rule on jurisdictional questions.[44] This is not to say that the courts will not occasionally intervene to stop an arbiter proceeding where it is obvious that he has no jurisdiction,[45] but such intervention will only occur in the most extreme cases.[46] An allied question is what effect do events which might vitiate a contract have upon the jurisdiction of an arbiter which is derived from a clause in the same contract? Early views suggested that if a contract was brought to an end, the same must be true of an arbitration clause. Thus, for example, there is some authority to suggest that a party cannot repudiate a contract, and then invoke an arbitration clause in that contract.[47] Yet, given that most disputes concern alleged breaches, it would seem to thwart the intention of the parties that their disputes should be determined by arbitration, if the arbitration clause is robbed of force in such circumstances.[48] Accordingly, the proper position must be that the arbitration clause survives any "terminating" event in order to allow the arbiter to consider the effect of such events on the rights of the parties.[49] English authority even suggests that an arbiter should have authority to consider issues of initial validity and legality of the contract, including whether it might be considered to be void *ab initio*,[50] although there are cases which insist that the illegality of certain types of contract is so indisputable and fundamental that the entire contract including the arbitration clause must be regarded as a nullity.[51] It seems to be agreed that an arbiter cannot have jurisdiction if one party insists that there was never an agreement to begin with.[52]

The Model Law states that the tribunal may rule on its own jurisdiction, including objections regarding the existence or validity of the arbitration agreement, continuing that, for this purpose, an arbitration clause will be treated as an agreement independent of the other terms

---

[41] *ibid.*

[42] Art. 11(4).

[43] Art. 15.

[44] *McCosh v Moore* (1905) 8 F. 31.

[45] See *e.g. Parochial Board of Greenock v Coghill & Son* (1878) 5 R. 732 (court believed there was no question for the arbiter to decide).

[46] *Dumbarton Water Commissioners v Lord Blantyre* (1884) 12 R. 115.

[47] *Municipal Council of Johannesburg v D Stewart & Co,* 1909 S.C. (H.L.) 53.

[48] *Heyman v Darwins* [1942] A.C. 356.

[49] *Scott v Gerrard,* 1906 S.C. 793. See also *James Scott & Sons Ltd v Del Sel* 1923 S.C. (H.L.) 37; (frustration); *Albyn Housing Society Ltd v Taylor Woodrow Homes,* 1985 S.L.T. 309; (prescription).

[50] *Harbour Assurance Ltd v Kansa Ltd* [1993] Q.B. 701.

[51] *Soleimany v Soleimany* [1998] 3 W.L.R. 811.

[52] *Ransohoff and Wissler v Burrell* (1897) 25 R. 284; *Harbour Assurance Ltd v Kansa Ltd* [1993] Q.B. 701.

of the contract, and that a decision by the tribunal that the contract is void will not invalidate the clause.[53] It indicates that a plea that the tribunal has no jurisdiction must be raised no later than the submission of the statement of defence to a claim or counterclaim.[54] Where the plea is that the tribunal had jurisdiction but is exceeding it, must be raised as soon as the matter alleged to be beyond its jurisdiction emerges in the proceedings.[55] In either case, the tribunal may entertain a late plea, if it considers the delay in raising it to be justified.[56] A failure to raise a timeous plea almost certainly precludes a party from challenging the award on grounds of jurisdictional excess, unless the lack of jurisdiction is of such a fundamental nature, *e.g.* that the dispute is of a type not capable or being arbitrated under Scots law, that the award would be regarded as a nullity. The Model Law seems to regard the power of the tribunal to review its own jurisdiction as absolute, at least in the first instance. Thus on the face of it, the tribunal and not the court would have competence to determine even such fundamental jurisdictional objections as the fact that a party denies entering the agreement at all, and this has how it has been interpreted in other states which have adopted the Model Law.[57] However, as under Scots law, the court rather than the tribunal has the final say on the matter. If a party raises a jurisdictional challenge, the tribunal may rule on this separately, or as part of an award on the merits.[58] In the latter case, the aggrieved party may challenge the award on the basis of lack of jurisdiction.[59] In the former case, he may within 30 days of receiving notice of that ruling appeal to the court, whose decision on the matter will be final.[60]

## 10.19. CONDUCT OF PROCEEDINGS

Just as the parties create the arbiter's jurisdiction and define its limits through their agreement, so too they can stipulate how they wish the arbitration to be conducted, whether directly or through the invocation of a particular set of arbitral rules. Otherwise, the arbiter is master of the procedure to be adopted.[61] So, subject to the fact that a party has a right to present his case, the arbiter is entitled to determine the form in which claims and defences should be presented, and whether amendments may be permitted thereto.[62] Again, while an arbiter must always admit enough evidence to enable him properly to carry out his function,[63] he otherwise has a discretion as to the nature and extent of evidence he will receive.[64] Thus in certain cases, such as where the arbiter has essentially been invited to make a judgment based on his own personal knowledge and skill, it may even be open to the arbiter to decline to hear the parties.[65] And unless the parties have indicated otherwise, an arbiter is not bound by the ordinary rules of civil evidence.[66] Of course, as an arbitral tribunal is not a court, the assistance of the court is required if unwilling witnesses are to be cited to attend or documentary or other evidence is to be secured.[67] Moreover, while a party must take the consequences of failing to take advantage

[53] Art. 16(1).
[54] Art. 16(2).
[55] *ibid.*
[56] *ibid.*
[57] *Fung Sang Trading Ltd v Kai Sun Sea Products & Food Co Ltd* [1992] A.D.R.L.J. 93.
[58] Art. 16(3).
[59] Art. 34(2)(a)(iii).
[60] Art. 16(3).
[61] *Holmes Oil Co v Pumpherston Oil Co* (1890) 17 R. 624.
[62] *ERDC Construction Ltd v H. M. Love & Co,* 1996 S.C. 523.
[63] *Holmes Oil Co v Pumpherston Oil Co* (1890) 17 R. 624.
[64] *Mitchell v Cable* (1848) 10 D. 1297.
[65] *Hope v Crookston Bros* (1890) 17 R.868.
[66] *Alston v Chappel* (1839) 2 D. 248.
[67] *Crudens Ltd,* 1971 S.C. 64; Administration of Justice (Scotland) Act 1972, s.1(1).

of an opportunity to present evidence,[68] an arbiter may not make a judgment by default, *i.e.* in those cases where evidence is clearly necessary in order that he may reach a judgment, he is not entitled to make an award if he has no evidence before him at all.[69] An entirely fundamental duty is to treat the parties equally.[70] So while an arbiter is quite within his rights to proceed if a party has the opportunity to attend a hearing but chooses not to do so,[71] ordinarily he should not hear[72] nor inspect[73] evidence in the absence of one of the parties.

Although in theory there would be nothing to prevent the parties agreeing that their arbitration would be open to the public, in practice this is unheard of, and it is submitted that in the absence of agreement to the contrary it is an implied condition of an arbitration agreement that the proceedings are private. There is scant authority in Scotland as to whether, and if so to what extent, matters revealed in the proceedings are confidential, although this is an issue which is much debated in the courts of England and elsewhere.[74] Again, unless the parties say otherwise, it is up to the arbiter to determine the time and location of hearings, and a hearing may be held outwith Scotland if necessary. As many arbiters are not lawyers, they may wish to appoint a legally qualified clerk to advise them on how to proceed. An arbiter has complete discretion whether or not to appoint a clerk,[75] unless perhaps the nature or circumstances of the arbitration makes it obvious that the appointment of a clerk is not contemplated. Although any clerk is the servant of the arbiter,[76] it is the parties who are liable for his remuneration.[77] Any factor which might disqualify an individual from acting as arbiter should also disqualify him from serving as clerk,[78] unless waived by the parties. Similarly, unless the nature or circumstances of the arbitration makes it obvious that such an appointment is not contemplated, an arbiter has discretion to appoint a man of skill to advise him on a particular issue. Again, it is the parties who are liable for the remuneration of this individual[79]

Where there are a number of arbiters, any decision may be made by a majority in the case of disagreement, although in the absence of disagreement it would amount to misconduct to exclude any arbiter from the decision-making process.[80] If there is deadlock, then statute empowers arbiters to nominate an oversman, unless the parties agree otherwise.[81] Indeed, it is possible for the arbiters to appoint an oversman at the outset in case disagreement should arise.[82] Where a dispute does arise, the entire submission to arbitration must be devolved on the oversman, unless the terms of the submission empower the arbiters to make awards on specific issues. In that case, a partial devolution is competent.[83] Any factor which might disqualify an individual from acting as arbiter, should also disqualify him from serving as oversman.[84] If the arbiters are unable to agree on an oversman, or even on a means whereby an oversman might be appointed, any party can ask the court to make the appointment.[85] It is possible for one arbiter to invite the oversman to act, as a situation which might arise where the arbiters are in dispute as to whether they are actually in disagreement.[86] If an oversman has

[68] *Mitchell v Cable* (1848) 10 D. 1297.
[69] *United Collieries v Gavin* (1899) 2 F. 60.
[70] *Mitchell v Cable* (1848) 10 D. 1297.
[71] *Barr v McNaughton* (1852) 15 D. 21.
[72] *McNair's Tr. v Roxburgh and Faulds* (1855) 17 D. 445.
[73] *Earl of Dunmore v McInturner* (1835) 13 S. 356.
[74] See Davidson, *Arbitration* paras 12.08–12.10.
[75] *Fletcher v Robertson* (1918) 1 S.L.T. 68.
[76] *Johnson v Gill*, 1978 S.C. 78.
[77] *McFarlane v Black* (1842) 4 D. 1459.
[78] *Mowbray v Dickson* (1848) 10 D. 1102.
[79] *McLeod v Bisset* (1825) 4 S. 330.
[80] *McCallum v Robertson* (1825) 4 S. 66.
[81] Arbitration (Scotland) Act 1894, s.4.
[82] *Frederick v Maitland and Cunningham* (1865) 3 M. 1069.
[83] *Gibson v Fotheringham*, 1914 S.C. 987.
[84] *Smith v Liverpool, London and Globe Insurance Co* (1887) 14 R. 931.
[85] Arbitration (Scotland) Act 1894, s.4.
[86] *Gibson v Fotheringham*, 1914 S.C. 987.

been appointed at an early stage of the proceedings in case disagreement should emerge, it is common practice for him to sit in on the proceedings along with the arbiters. In such a case, if the submission is ultimately devolved on him, he need not rehear the evidence.[87] Authority is lacking on the position where the oversman is appointed after the parties have been heard. However, the English cases suggest that, while it may be open to an umpire (oversman) to proceed on the basis of the notes of the arbitrators, the evidence must be reheard if either party so insists.[88] It would of course be different if the parties had agreed that the oversman could proceed on the basis of such notes.[89] Although there is no authority on this point, an oversman is surely entitled to remuneration on the same basis as a man of skill. Practically, this issue tends to be avoided, as the fees of any oversman are included in the award of expenses.[90]

Turning to the Model Law, it makes explicit certain points which are implicit in Scots law. Thus Art. 19(1) recites that. "Subject to the provisions of this Law, the parties are free to agree on the procedure to be followed by the arbitral tribunal in conducting the proceedings", while Art. 19(2) continues "failing such agreement, the arbitral tribunal may, subject to the provisions of this Law, conduct the arbitration in such manner as it considers appropriate". Art. 19(2) goes on to make it clear that the tribunal's procedural discretion "includes the power to determine the admissibility, relevance, materiality and weight of any evidence". There are further instances of procedural freedom. Thus it is up to the parties, or failing whom the arbitral tribunal, to decide upon the place of arbitration.[91] Place here is used in the sense of the legal seat of proceedings, rather than the actual physical location of any hearings. Thus if Scotland is chosen as the place of arbitration, the tribunal may nonetheless choose to hold some, perhaps all, of the hearings elsewhere. Again, the parties, or failing whom the arbitral tribunal, may decide the language(s) to be employed in the proceedings,[92] and the tribunal has a discretion as to whether or not any documentary evidence should be translated into the official language(s).[93] However, the freedom of the parties/arbitral tribunal is not unlimited. Two fundamental and mandatory principles of the Model Law are that the parties shall be treated equally and each given a full opportunity of presenting his case.[94] It is not possible for the parties to contract out of this provision, and discretion exercised under the other provisions of the law must be considered in the light of these two principles.

Article 23(1) of the Model Law appears to demand that within the period laid down by the parties, or failing whom the arbitral tribunal, the claimant shall state his claim, the facts supporting it, the points at issue, and the remedy sought, while the respondent shall indicate his defence. Yet the parties may agree otherwise, so that in certain cases the statements of claim and defence may be very rudimentary, and might not even be in writing. Again, subject to contrary agreement, the tribunal may allow either party to supplement his claim or defence during the proceedings, unless it considers this inappropriate in light of the party's delay.[95] Although, subject to contrary agreement, it is at first sight for the tribunal to decide whether oral hearings are necessary, unless the parties have actually agreed that no hearings are to be held, either can demand an oral hearing, as long as such demand is not made at an inappropriately late stage of the proceedings.[96] The parties must be given sufficient advance notice of any hearing or other meeting of the tribunal.[97] Equally all statements, documents or other information supplied to the tribunal by one party must be communicated to the other,

---

[87] *Sellar v Highland Railway Co,* 1918 S.C. 838.
[88] *Re Jenkins* (1841) 1 Dow. 276.
[89] *Re Firth and Howlett* (1850) 19 L.J.Q.B. 169.
[90] *Glasgow Parish Council v United Collieries Ltd* (1907) 15 S.L.T. 232.
[91] Art. 20(1).
[92] Art. 22(1).
[93] Art. 22(2).
[94] Art. 18.
[95] Art. 23(2).
[96] Art. 24(1).
[97] Art. 24(2).

while any expert report or evidentiary document on which the tribunal relies in making its decision must be communicated to both parties.[98] Unless the parties agree otherwise, if there is more than one arbitrator, any decision of the tribunal, including the making of an award, may be reached by a majority.[99] The framers of the Model Law did not contemplate the possibility of a tribunal featuring an even number of arbitrators, and thus the further possibility of a deadlock arising with no majority in either direction. It is submitted that this gap in the law can be filled by the provisions of the Arbitration (Scotland) Act 1894 regarding recourse to an oversman. Art. 29 also provides that procedural questions may be decided by a presiding arbitrator, if so authorised by the parties or all the members of the tribunal. This is obviously a permissive provision. There need not be a presiding arbitrator and cannot be unless there is more than one arbitrator. However, the parties or tribunal may invoke this power to allow purely procedural matters to be dealt with speedily and efficiently.

The Model Law also contains default provisions, which will apply unless the parties agree otherwise, as where they agree upon different default provisions.[1] In all cases, the provisions do not apply if a party shows sufficient cause for his default. Looking at the specific provisions, first, if a party has not timeously stated his claim, the tribunal will terminate the proceedings.[2] Such termination has no effect on the rights of a party, not even on the claimant's right to insist in arbitration in the future. Where a respondent fails timeously to state his defence, the tribunal should continue the proceedings, without treating this failure as an admission.[3] Moreover, where a party fails to appear at a hearing or produce evidence, the tribunal may continue the proceedings and make an award on the evidence before it.[4] In other words, although a party must be given a full opportunity of presenting his case, if he chooses not to, an award may be made against him without him saying a word in his defence or even appearing before the tribunal. The claimant would, however, have to adduce some evidence of his own. The mere failure of the respondent to participate does not allow an award to be made against him.

The Model Law also explicitly confers certain powers upon arbitrators. Thus unless the parties agree otherwise, the tribunal may, at the request of one party, order the other to take such interim measures of protection as it considers necessary in respect of the subject matter of the dispute.[5] It may also require him to provide appropriate security in connection with any such measure.[6] In other words, a tribunal might, for example, order one party to consign the goods which are the subject of the dispute with a third party, to prevent possible damage or destruction, and/or provide a guarantee from a third party that the cost of any damage or destruction will be met. Any such order must take the form of an award in order to facilitate its enforceability.[7] Also, unless the parties agree otherwise, the tribunal may appoint one or more experts to report to it on such specific issues as it may determine,[8] *e.g.* on a technical issue before the tribunal, and may require a party to give the expert any relevant information, or produce or provide access to any relevant goods, documents or other property for his inspection.[9] Again, unless the parties agree otherwise, if a party so requests or the tribunal considers it necessary, the expert shall participate in a hearing after delivering his report.[10] In any such hearing the parties must have the opportunity to question the expert and have their own expert witnesses testify to the points at issue.[11] Finally, the tribunal, or a party with the

---

[98] *ibid.*
[99] Art. 29.
[1] Art. 25.
[2] Art. 25(a).
[3] Art. 25(b).
[4] Art. 25(c).
[5] Art. 17(1).
[6] *ibid.*
[7] Art. 17(2).
[8] Art. 26(1)(a).
[9] Art. 26(1)(b).
[10] Art. 26(2).
[11] *ibid.*

tribunal's approval, may request from the Court of Session or sheriff court assistance in taking evidence or recovering documents.[12]

Consideration of the tribunal's powers may be concluded by considering the circumstances where the tribunal might formally terminate the proceedings. To a certain extent this has already been touched on in that it has been seen that if the claimant has not timeously stated his claim, the tribunal will terminate the proceedings.[13] Additionally, it will terminate the proceedings where the claimant withdraws his claim, unless the other party objects and the tribunal recognises a legitimate interest on his part in obtaining a final settlement of the dispute.[14] A respondent may well prefer the certainty of the final disposal of the dispute through an award, especially where he thinks the claimant's case is weak, to the situation where the claimant may revive the claim at any point in the future. Secondly, the tribunal must terminate the proceedings when the parties agree on their termination.[15] Thirdly, it must terminate the proceedings when it finds that their continuation has become unnecessary or impossible.[16]

## 10.20. RIGHTS, DUTIES AND LIABILITIES OF ARBITERS

Although an arbiter's services were originally rendered gratuitously, it has long been accepted that an arbiter is entitled to remuneration, and that the parties are jointly and severally liable for this.[17] In relation to duties, an arbiter is obliged to carry out the reference unless he has a good reason for resigning, a duty which will be enforced, according to authority, "under penalty of imprisonment".[18] Again, although the courts generally concede that the arbiter has discretion as to how and when to proceed, authority suggests that a party may ask the court to order a plainly dilatory arbiter to proceed.[19] As regards liabilities, the major question is whether arbiters may be sued by the parties for breach of duty. Authority suggests that arbiters are probably immune from suit unless they act in bad faith.[20] The question of arbitral immunity has, however, more recently been considered by the House of Lords in a couple of English cases wherein the Scottish Law Lords featured prominently. Thus in *Sutcliffe v Thackrah*[21] it was held that an architect, who had certified that certain work met the appropriate standard, was not entitled to immunity, as he had not acted "judicially"—judges having complete immunity from suit in respect of the exercise of their function. So it seemed that only arbiters who exercised a judicial function were entitled to immunity, in contrast to arbiters whose task was essentially certification and valuation. Yet in *Arenson v Arenson* and *Casson, Beckman, Rutley & Co*[22] Lord Kilbrandon found it difficult to draw a meaningful distinction between the functions performed by the two categories of arbiter. Moreover, he suggested that the main reason why judges enjoyed immunity was that they were officers of the state charged with providing public justice on behalf of the state. This was not the situation of private arbiters. Therefore, the question of which (if any) arbiters are immune and, if so, when, is now rather uncertain. Thus any arbiter would be well advised to insist on the parties agreeing to grant him immunity.

---

[12] Art. 27.
[13] Art. 25(a).
[14] Art. 32(2)(a).
[15] Art. 32(2)(b).
[16] Art. 32(2)(c).
[17] *McIntyre Brothers v Smith,* 1913 S.C. 129.
[18] *Forbes v Underwood* (1886) 13 R. 465 at 469.
[19] *Watson v Robertson* (1895) 22 R. 362.
[20] *McMillan v Free Church* (1862) 22 D. 1282.
[21] [1974] A.C. 727.
[22] [1977] A.C. 405.

## 10.21.   THE STATED CASE PROCEDURE

At common law, an arbiter was always the final judge of both fact and law. He remains the final judge of fact, but s.3(1) of the Administration of Justice (Scotland) Act 1972 allows a party to request that an arbiter state a case for the opinion of the Court of Session on any question of law arising in the arbitration. The effect of the provision may be excluded by express agreement of the parties in the agreement to refer.[23] It is clear that the phrase agreement to refer should be widely construed, not confined to the original arbitration agreement, but embracing any agreement by which the parties clearly contract out of the provision.[24] An arbiter can only state a case on the application of a party. He may not do so on his own initiative. A case may be stated "at any stage in the proceedings".[25] Thus a case cannot be stated in respect of a point of law arising from the final award, as the making of the award ends the proceedings.[26] This is the result of unfortunate drafting, as it is certainly the case that the stated case procedure is intended to give a party a right to appeal against an award on a point of law. However, in practice such appeals are effectively allowed by the tendency of arbiters to issue proposed findings or a draft award before making a final award.

The procedure is initiated by a party sending a minute to the clerk setting out the point on which the case is applied for.[27] The clerk must send a copy of that minute to every other party, and within 14 days of that minute being sent any other party may lodge a minute with the clerk setting out additional questions, at the same time sending a copy to every other party.[28] Within 21 days of the expiry of that 14 day period, the tribunal shall either decide to state a case or shall refuse to do so.[29] A tribunal which agrees to state a case on certain questions but not others is to that extent refusing to state a case.[30] The bases on which it might refuse are that the question does not arise, or does not require to be decided, or is frivolous.[31] Alternatively, if the application is made before the facts are ascertained, the tribunal may defer consideration of the application until it ascertains the facts.[32] The tribunal's exercise of that discretion may be reviewed by the court if it is clearly unreasonable,[33] but this would only happen in the most extreme case.[34] If the tribunal has so deferred its consideration, it must decide whether to state or refuse to state a case within 14 days of ascertaining the facts, and must intimate that decision to each party.[35]

Whenever the tribunal refuses to state a case, any intimation must be accompanied by a certificate specifying the date of the decision and the reason for refusal.[36] When the refusal occurs after the facts have been ascertained, the tribunal must also provide a note of the proposed findings in fact on which it proposes to base its decision.[37] When the refusal occurs before the facts have been ascertained, the tribunal must also provide a note of, or sufficient reference to, the averments of the parties on which the refusal is based.[38] The party whose application has been refused then has 14 days from the intimation of such refusal to apply to the Inner House for an order requiring the other party to show why a case should not be

---

[23] s.3(1).
[24] *Whatlings (Foundations) Ltd v Shanks & McEwan (Contractors) Ltd,* 1989 S.L.T. 857.
[25] s.3(1).
[26] *Fairlie Yacht Slip v Lumsden,* 1977 S.L.T (Notes) 41.
[27] RCS, r.41.5.
[28] RCS, r.41.6.1.–2.
[29] RCS, r.41.7.1.
[30] *John G McGregor (Contractors) Ltd v Grampian Regional Council,* 1989 S.L.T. 299.
[31] RCS, r.41.7.1(b).
[32] RCS, r.41.7.1(c).
[33] *Shanks & McEwan (Contractors) Ltd v Mifflin Construction Ltd,* 1993 S.L.T. 1124.
[34] *Edmund Nuttall Ltd v Amec Projects Ltd,* 1993 S.L.T. 255.
[35] RCS, r.41.7.2.–3.
[36] RCS, r.41.7.4(a).
[37] RCS, r.41.7.4(b).
[38] RCS, r.41.7.4(a).

stated,[39] serving a copy on the tribunal and every other party. If the other party cannot show why a case should not be stated, the court will order the arbiter to state a case. Where the tribunal agrees to state a case, or is ordered to do so, it must within 14 days of intimating its decision to the parties prepare a case in draft and submit a copy to each party).[40] Generally, the form in which the case is stated is a matter for the tribunal.[41] The opinion of the court binds the tribunal.[42] However, it is not a judgment and thus cannot be appealed to the House of Lords.[43] In arbitrations governed by the Model Law, the stated case procedure does not apply.

## 10.22. THE AWARD

The ultimate end of arbitral proceedings is for the tribunal to decide the issue(s) between the parties in its award, the equivalent of the judgment of a court. The possibility of a draft award as a precursor to a final award was noted in the last paragraph. A draft award is not binding, but there may be awards other than final awards which do bind the parties. Thus one may have an interim award in which the tribunal may find it convenient to deal with one of the issues between the parties, *e.g.* who has the right of possession of certain property for the time being. The essential characteristic of such an award, is that it is always liable to be recalled by a final award. A continuing award deals with an issue, *e.g.* the amount of compensation payable, until some uncertain future date. It differs from an interim award, in that while it may be superseded by a final award, it cannot be recalled by the final award. A part award involves the final determination of one or more of the issues before the tribunal, but not all. It is doubtful whether a tribunal has any inherent power to make such awards,[44] so if the parties think it useful that the tribunal should have power to make interim, continuing or part awards, they should confer that power expressly. As an arbitral award is not among those documents which require to be in writing in terms of the Requirements of Writing (Scotland) Act 1995, it might be suggested that the award requires to be in no particular form. However, it is at least arguable that it is an implied term of the contract between the arbiter and the parties that the award should take the same form as the submission to arbitration,[45] while the parties may lay down expressly the form which the award must take. Where it has been made clear that the award must be signed by the arbiters, it is enough if the majority sign[46]—unless of course the parties have demanded that all arbiters should sign.

Depending on the terms of the submission, an award may determine the rights of the parties,[47] interdict a party,[48] or award specific implement.[49] Yet bizarrely enough an arbiter has no inherent power to award damages.[50] This power must therefore be expressly conferred, otherwise the arbiter must simply decide the question of liability, leaving assessment and award to the court.[51] An arbiter has implied power to award interest on any sum due from the date of award until payment, but cannot award interest from the point of liability until the date of

---

[39] RCS, r.41.8(1)–(3).

[40] RCS, r.41.9(1).

[41] *Gunac Ltd v Inverclyde District Council*, 1983 S.L.T. 130; and for further procedural details, see RCS, r.41.9.—41.16.

[42] *Mitchell-Gill v Buchan*, 1921 S.C. 390.

[43] *John G McGregor (Contractors) Ltd v Grampian Regional Council*, 1989 S.L.T. 299.

[44] *Taylor Wodrow Construction (Scotland) Ltd v Sears Investment Trust Ltd*, 1992 S.L.T. 609.

[45] *Dykes v Roy* (1869) 7 M. 357.

[46] *Love v Love* (1825) 4 S. 53.

[47] *Lumsden v Gordon* (1842) 4 D. 1353.

[48] *Gray v Brown* (1833) 11 S. 353.

[49] *Connal v Coldstream* (1829) 7 S. 726.

[50] *Aberdeen Railway Co. v Blaikie Bros* (1853) 15 D. (H.L.) 20.

[51] *James Scott Ltd v Apollo Engineering Ltd*, 1993 G.W.D. 29–1796.

award unless the parties have expressly conferred this power.[52] The rate of interest is at his discretion.[53] An arbiter does have an inherent power to deal with the question of expenses as part of his award.[54] Moreover, while he has a large measure of discretion as to the award of expenses, that discretion must be exercised judicially, and thus will be reviewable if the decision is patently unreasonable.[55] An award has no force until it has been delivered to at least one of the parties,[56] and it is probably open to an arbiter to refuse to release an award until his fee is paid. Once a final award is made, it binds the parties (although not usually third parties[57]), and is *res judicata* as far as they are concerned[58].

Turning now to the Model Law, its provisions seem to admit the possibility of awards other than final awards being made, without actually authorising the making of such awards.[59] Thus, this would be a matter governed by Scots law as described above. The Model Law does however demand that the award be in writing.[60] It must also be signed by the arbitrators, or at least by the majority of the arbitrators, as long as the reason for the missing signature is stated.[61] One obvious reason would be that a dissenting arbitrator has refused to sign the award, but a signature might equally be missing simply because it is inconvenient for a particular arbitrator to sign. As has been noted above, although the Model Law proceeds on the basis of majority rule when there is more than one arbitrator, the parties can agree that all decisions require unanimity.[62] Yet, even where they have so agreed that an award must be the unanimous decision of the arbitrators, it need only be signed by the majority. Whereas an award need not contain reasons in Scots law, it must state its reasons under the Model Law, unless it is an award on agreed terms, or the parties have agreed that no reasons shall be given.[63] The award is deemed to be made in the place of arbitration (in the sense of its juridical seat), and the award must state that it is made in that place.[64] It must also state the date when it was made.[65] Once it has been made, a signed copy must be delivered to each party.[66]

While a tribunal's authority terminates under Scots law as soon as the award is made, it can be extended under Art. 33 of the Model Law in certain circumstances. So within 30 days of receipt of the award, a party may, with notice to the other, request the tribunal to:

- correct any computational, clerical, typographical or similar error in the award;
- give an interpretation of a specific point or part of the award;
- make an additional award covering claims presented in the proceedings, but omitted from the award (unless the parties agree otherwise).[67]

The 30-day period may be varied by the parties, but not the tribunal. If the tribunal considers the request to be justified, it may make the correction or give the interpretation within 30 days of receiving the request, although it can extend this period if it thinks this is necessary.[68] There is no time limit within which it must make an additional award. It may be noted that the tribunal only has power to give an interpretation of a specific point or part of the award if the

---

[52] *John G McGregor (Contractors) Ltd v Grampian Regional Council*, 1991 S.L.T. 136.
[53] *Farrans (Construction) Ltd v Dunfermilne District Council*, 1988 S.L.T. 466.
[54] *Pollich v Heatley*, 1910 S.C. 469.
[55] *Carnegie v Nature Conservancy Council*, 1992 S.L.T. 342.
[56] *Gray and Woodrop v McNair* (1831) 5 W. & S. 305.
[57] *Mackintosh v Robertson* (1834) 12 S. 321.
[58] *Farrans v Roxburgh County Council*, 1969 S.L.T. 35.
[59] Art. 32(1).
[60] Art. 31(1).
[61] *ibid.*
[62] Art. 29.
[63] Art. 31(2).
[64] Art. 31(3).
[65] *ibid.*
[66] Art. 31(4).
[67] Art. 33(1)–(3).
[68] Art. 33(1), (4).

parties agree to confer that power. On the other hand, the tribunal may, within 30 days of the date of the award, exercise the corrective power mentioned above on its own initiative, without waiting for a party to request it.[69] Any correction, interpretation or additional award must comply with the provisions of the Model Law regarding the form and content of awards.[70]

Under Scots law, if the parties settle the dispute between them, there is no longer an issue for the tribunal to decide. Thus an award on agreed terms is not valid in Scots law.[71] Under the Model Law, if the parties settled the dispute, the tribunal must terminate the proceedings and, if the parties so request, shall record the settlement in the form of an award on agreed terms.[72] One major qualification is that the tribunal need not take this step if it objects to so doing. The tribunal obviously might object to making such an award if, for example, it felt that the settlement was tainted with illegality, but it is not necessary for the tribunal to have any reason for its objection. Any such award must comply with the provisions of the Model Law regarding form and content.[73] It might be asked why the parties would seek such an award if they have reached a settlement. One good reason is that an award is more readily enforceable than a settlement.

## 10.23.  SETTING ASIDE AN AWARD:

Although a party will be bound by an award, the award will obviously cease to be binding if he can challenge it successfully. There are two ways of doing so—by asking that the decree be set aside when action is taken to enforce it, so-called setting aside by exception, or much more commonly by applying directly to the Court of Session to have it set aside. There are a number of grounds on which an award might be set aside. Most of these are common law grounds, but ancient statute also plays a role in that Art. 25 of the Articles of Regulation 1695 indicates that an award may be set aside if "corruption, bribery or falsehood" can be proved against an arbiter. As to the first of these, Lord Neaves opines in *Cameron v Menzies*[74]:

> "It is not easy to define corruption. It is not necessary that arbiter should have been bribed; nor is it necessary that there should be some other form of venality, or gross immorality . . . Corruption may take a milder form. But there must be some pravity of mind; some perversion of the moral feeling, either by interest or passion or partiality."

Bribery would clearly cover ordinary bribery, but would also extend to accepting a gift from one party.[75] Falsehood would embrace deliberate deceit by the arbiter,[76] but not deceit by a party, even if it misleads the arbiter, since the Articles of Regulation are only concerned with the conduct of the arbiter.[77]

### (a) Common law

Turning to common law, there a variety of grounds on which an award might be set aside.

---

[69] Art. 33(2).
[70] Art. 33(5).
[71] *Maule v Maule* (1816) 4 Dow. 363.
[72] Art. 30(1).
[73] Art. 30(2).
[74] (1867) 6 M. 279 at 280.
[75] *Mitchell v Fulton* (1715) Mor. 633.
[76] *Blain v Crawford,* referred to in *Hetherington v Carlyle,* June 21, 1771 F.C.
[77] *Adams v Great North of Scotland Railway Co* (1890) 18 R. 1.

## (i) Award beyond the scope of the submission

Where the arbiter deals with a matter which has not been submitted to him,[78] or purports to exercise a power he does not have,[79] the award may be set aside. The courts do not seem open to the argument that a party may have waived the right to seek the setting aside of the award, by failing to object when it was clear that the arbiter intended to exceed his jurisdiction.[80] Nor does the law admit of the possibility, countenanced by the Model Law (see below), that only the part of the award which exceeds the submission might be set aside.

## (ii) Award does not exhaust the submission

Just as going beyond the submission renders an award liable to being set aside, so too failing to deal with all the matters referred to the arbiter has the same effect.[81] Failing to deal with issues as required by the parties—as where an arbiter is asked to decide how much A is owed by B under a variety of specific heads, but awards a single undifferentiated lump sum, amounts to a failure to exhaust the submission.[82] The option, given by the Model Law, of simply asking the tribunal to deal with the issues it has omitted, is not recognised by Scots law.

## (iii) Award uncertain

If it is impossible to work out what has been decided, then the award must be set aside.[83] However, wherever possible, the court will seek to construe an award so that it makes sense,[84] and it is no barrier to the enforceability of an award that some further calculation is necessary, or some further step need be taken to establish exactly how the award will operate in practice.[85] It is not open to a party to ask the tribunal to interpret its award, as would be possible under the Model Law.

## (iv) Misconduct

This heading does not necessarily mean that the arbiter has engaged in improper behaviour. If, however innocently, he conducts the proceedings otherwise than as agreed by the parties, that is misconduct, and renders the award liable to being set aside.[86] It is also misconduct to fail to adhere to the standards which the law insists must be observed in every arbitration—treating the parties equally,[87] making himself sufficiently aware of the background to the dispute to enable him to perform his function.[88] Moreover, although it is not misconduct to make an error in fact or law, it is probably misconduct blatantly to invent legal principles or relevant facts, and it is certainly misconduct, having sought the opinion of the court on a point of law, to ignore that opinion.[89]

---

[78] *Napier v Wood* (1844) 7 D. 166.
[79] *Carruthers v Hall* (1830) 9 S. 66.
[80] *ERDC Construction v H. M. Love & Co*, 1995 S.L.T. 254.
[81] *Donald v Shiell's Exix*, 1937 S.C. 52.
[82] *Miller & Son v Oliver & Boyd* (1903) 6 F. 77.
[83] *McKenzie v Inverness and Aberdeen Junction Railway Co* (1866) 4 M. 810.
[84] *Patrick v McCall* (1867) 4 S.L.R. 12.
[85] *Paterson v Sanderson* (1829) 7 S. 616.
[86] *Adams v Great North of Scotland Railway Co* (1890) 18 R. (H.L.) 1.
[87] *Mitchell v Cable* (1848) 10 D. 1297.
[88] *Henderson v McGown*, 1915 2 S.L.T. 316.
[89] *Mitchell-Gill v Buchan*, 1921 S.C. 390.

## (v) Award procured by fraud

While fraudulent behaviour on the part of an arbiter is covered by the Articles of Regulation, an award may also be set aside at common law, on the grounds of fraud or concealment by a party[90] or one of his witnesses.[91]

## (vi) Arbiter or oversman disqualified

An award will not be subject to challenge if the parties are aware that any arbiter or oversman is subject to a disqualifying factor, but nonetheless allow the proceedings to progress. However, if such a factor only comes to light when the award is made, then the award is liable to be set aside.[92] It is suggested that the fact that an oversman is subject to a disqualifying factor will be of no consequence unless he has played a role in the making of the award. An award by an oversman has been set aside when one of the arbiters was subject to a disqualifying factor, on the basis that this arbiter might have influenced the judgment of the oversman.[93]

## (vii) Award is not an award

As arbitration in one sense involves the exercise of a judicial function, an award is not properly an award at all, and so is liable to be set aside, if the arbiter has not in reality made a decision, but has rather given effect to an agreement between the parties.[94]

## (b) Model law

Turning to the Model Law, it may first be observed that recourse against an award is permitted only via an action of setting aside raised in the Court of Session or the sheriff court in the sheriffdom in which the defender is domiciled.[95] An exhaustive set of grounds is laid down. These grounds fall into two categories, the first category being grounds in respect of which the party seeking to have the award set aside must provide proof of the grounds. The second category envisages that the court may set the award aside when it "finds" the grounds exist. The grounds in the first category are are set out below.

## (i) First category

### Incapacity of a party

An award may be set aside if the applicant can prove that either party suffered from incapacity.[96] It would appear then that a party may rely on his own incapacity, although it might be argued that having participated in the proceedings, he has thereby waived his right to rely on this ground.[97] Capacity would be determined by the law governing the contract between the parties.[98]

---

[90] *Hong Kong Fire Insurance Co Ltd v Financier Ltd* (1897) 2 S.L.T. 436.
[91] *Calder v Gordon* (1837) 15 S. 463.
[92] *Smith v London, Liverpool and Globe Insurance Co* (1887) 14 R. 931.
[93] *Sellar v Highland Railway Co,* 1918 S.C. 838.
[94] *Maule v Maule* (1814) 4 Dow 363.
[95] Art. 34(1).
[96] Art. 34(2)(a)(i).
[97] Art. 4.
[98] *McFeetridge v Stewart & Lloyds,* 1913 S.C. 773.

## Invalidity of arbitration agreement

An award may be set aside if the applicant can prove that the arbitration agreement was not valid under the law to which the parties subjected it, or, failing any indication thereof, under Scots law.[99] It is rare for an arbitration agreement to specify a governing law. Common law generally assumes that an arbitration agreement will be governed by the law governing the contract.[1] So, if this can be regarded as an implied choice of law, then there will rarely be any need to fall back on Scots law in order to determine whether the arbitration agreement is valid. Again, a party who believes the arbitration agreement to be invalid, but nonetheless allows the proceedings to continue without raising that plea, will almost certainly not be successful in seeking to have the award set aside on this ground.

## Party unable to present case/not given proper notice of proceedings or arbitrator's appointment

An award may be set aside if the applicant can prove that he was not given proper notice of the appointment of an arbitrator or of the arbitral proceedings, or was otherwise unable to present his case.[2] In this context it may be noted that under the Model Law any written communication is deemed to be received if delivered to the addressee personally or at his place of business or residence or mailing address, or if none of these can be found, at his last known place of business, residence or mailing address.[3] Consequently, it is possible for a party to be in complete ignorance of the proceedings, and yet for the award not to be open to challenge on the above grounds. The idea of "proper" notice connotes sufficient notice to allow a party effectively to present his case. A party who does not present his case properly through his own fault, or who simply fails to present his case, cannot rely on the above provision.

## Award exceeds the jurisdiction of the tribunal

An award may be set aside if the applicant can prove that it covers matters beyond the scope of the jurisdiction of the arbitral tribunal.[4] Whereas under Scots common law, the award must be entirely set aside in such circumstances, under the Model Law, if only part of the award exceeds the scope of the jurisdiction of the arbitral tribunal, then only that part need be set aside. As ever, a party who believes that the arbitral tribunal is exceeding its jurisdiction, but nonetheless allows the proceedings to continue without raising that plea, will almost certainly not be successful in seeking to have the award set aside on this ground.

## Arbitral procedure or composition of tribunal is not in accordance with the agreement of the parties or the model law

An award may be set aside if the applicant can prove that the composition of the tribunal or the arbitral procedure is not in accordance with the Model Law or the agreement of the parties.[5] This is the equivalent of setting aside for misconduct at common law. The award may be set aside if the tribunal does not conduct the proceedings as agreed by the parties. Or it may be set aside if the tribunal conducts the proceedings contrary to the mandatory provisions of the Model Law. Where the agreement of the parties is not consistent with mandatory provisions of the Model Law, the latter prevails. In other words, if in the case of such an

---

[99] Art. 34(2)(a)(i).
[1] *Hamlyn & Co v Talisker Distillery* (1894) 21 R. (H.L.) 21.
[2] Art. 34(2)(a)(ii).
[3] Art. 3(a).
[4] Art. 34(2)(a)(iii).
[5] Art. 34(2)(a)(iv).

inconsistency, the tribunal follows the agreement of the parties, the award may be set aside, but if it ignores that agreement and acts as the Model Law dictates, the award is safe.

## Award procured by fraud bribery or corruption

An award may be set aside if the applicant can prove that it has been procured by fraud, bribery or corruption.[6] While the Model Law is, as its name indicates, a model law drafted by UNCITRAL to be adopted into national legislation, this ground appears only in the Scottish version of the Model Law. Its meaning should be relatively straightforward, covering all instances where the award is improperly procured.

### (ii) Second category

The grounds in the second category are set out below.

## Subject-matter not arbitrable under Scots law

The court may set an award aside, if it finds that its subject-matter is not arbitrable under Scots Law.[7] Although the court need not require proof from the applicant in relation to grounds which fall into the second category, it can only set aside an award in the course of setting aside proceedings. Thus the applicant must bring such proceedings before the court can intervene. It is difficult to imagine many commercial matters which are not arbitrable, although certain powers, *e.g.* in the context of sequestration, may only be exercised by the court.

## Award conflicts with public policy

The court may set an award aside, if it finds that it conflicts with public policy.[8] The most obvious application of this provision would be in relation to awards tainted by some sort of immorality or illegality, although the framers of the Model Law considered that it might also cover serious procedural impropriety, substantive injustice, and instances of fraud, bribery or corruption. At the same time, it must be remembered that the Model Law governs international commercial arbitrations held in Scotland. Sometimes the only connection between Scotland and the dispute will be that Scotland is the arbitral forum. It may be that neither of the parties is Scottish, their contract does not concern Scotland, and neither the governing law nor the law applicable to the substance of the dispute is Scottish. In such situations other legal systems have developed an international public policy which is more liberal than domestic public policy. This approach insists that "international" awards should not be open to challenge unless they offend the most fundamental principles of that legal system, and so such awards have been permitted to stand in circumstances in which domestic awards would not.[9] Perhaps the Scots courts would follow suit.

### (iii) Time limits

It is important to note that a time limit is imposed for seeking to have an award set aside under the Model Law—three months from the date when the party seeking to challenge received the award, or if the tribunal had been requested to interpret or correct the award (see above), within three months of that request being disposed of.[10] Thus once that period has elapsed, the award may not be challenged. The one exception to this is where a party seeks to have the

---

[6] Art. 34(2)(a)(v).
[7] Art. 34(2)(b)(i).
[8] Art. 34(2)(b)(ii).
[9] See *e.g.* the English case of *Soinco Saci v Novokuznetsk Aluminium Plant* [1998] 2 Lloyd's Rep. 357.
[10] Art. 34(3).

award set aside on the basis that it has been procured by fraud, bribery or corruption. No limit applies in this instance, and a party may raise setting aside proceedings at any time. It may be added that a court may suspend setting aside proceedings for such period as it thinks fit in order to give the tribunal an opportunity to resume the proceedings or take such other action as will eliminate the grounds for setting aside.[11]

## 10.24.    ENFORCING AN AWARD

It will usually be the case that the party against whom an award is made does not challenge it, but simply acts as it directs. Yet it may happen that such a party, without actually challenging the award, makes no move to abide by it. In such a case, the other party will usually have no option but to apply to the court for the enforcement of the award. The exception is where the submission to arbitration and the award have, with the consent of both parties, been registered for preservation and execution in the books of a sheriff court, or the Books of Council and Session. This will allow the award to be enforced by summary diligence, without reference to a court.[12] Detailed provisions govern the making of an application to either the sheriff court[13] or Court of Session[14] for the enforcement of an award made under the Model Law. A party may seek to resist court enforcement of an award at common law, on the basis that its enforcement would offend public policy.[15] A party may seek to resist court enforcement of an award made under the Model Law largely on the same grounds on which he might ask for the award to be set aside.[16] It is not proposed to deal here with the enforcement in Scotland of awards made outwith this country.

## 10.25.    NON BINDING FORMS OF DISPUTE RESOLUTION

As an alternative to litigation or arbitration, the parties may seek to settle their disputes via procedures which do not result in a binding decision being handed down by a third party. There are various forms of such procedures,

### (a) Negotiation

Most disputes have always been settled by way of negotiation between the parties and/or their representatives. This continues to be the case.

### (b) Mediation and conciliation

While any third party involved in negotiation represents the interests of one of the parties, other forms of dispute resolution witness a third party taking a more independent role, as in mediation and conciliation. The terms are here employed together, as they often appear to be used synonymously, and when used to denote different processes, there seems to be no consensus as to which term describes which process. Mediation and conciliation occupy a

---

[11] Art. 34(4).
[12] *Baillie v Pollock* (1829) 7 S. 619.
[13] Act of Sederunt (Summary Applications Etc) Rules 1999, (SI 1999/929), r.3.12.
[14] RCS, r.62.57.–59.
[15] *Bellshill and Mossend Co-operative Society Ltd v Dalziel Co-operative Society Ltd,* 1957 S.C. 400.
[16] Art. 36.

spectrum. At one end, the mediator/conciliator simply acts as an intermediary between the parties. Alternatively, the mediator/conciliator may take a more active role, perhaps pointing out the strengths and weaknesses in each party's position and/or indicating to each a position, which he believes the other might accept. At the other end of the spectrum the mediator/conciliator actively explores with the parties what they want out of the process, suggesting how their aims might best be achieved, and proactively developing possible solutions. Mediation and conciliation are now offered on a commercial basis by a number of organisations, which generally also train and accredit mediators and conciliators.

## (c) Med-arb

This combines mediation and arbitration, as an individual first acts as mediator, then as arbiter if mediation fails. Alternatively, in some forms of dispute resolution an arbiter might actually attempt to achieve a consensual resolution while the arbitration is proceeding. Such approaches are questionable, as the arbiter's essential neutrality might appear to be compromised.

## (d) Neutral expert

where a dispute involves complex issues of fact, a neutral expert can be employed to analyse the facts in a non partisan way, so that the true picture emerges, and the parties can be aided to settle the dispute.

## (e) Executive tribunal

Sometimes known as a mini-trial, this involves the representatives of the parties making a short, informal presentation of their cases to a panel, which comprises executives from both sides, together with a neutral adviser. The aim is to identify the strengths and weaknesses in each case, and provide some indication of how actual litigation might develop. In order to expedite matters, the parties will have beforehand exchanged the material on which their cases will be based. Following the presentation, the members of the panel seek to achieve a negotiated settlement. The role of the neutral adviser may be confined to promoting settlement, but he will usually provide legal advice during the presentation, and thereafter if negotiations break down, he may suggest the likely outcome of any litigation on the issue, with a view to persuading the parties to reassess their positions.

## (f) Summary jury trial

This is in some respects similar to the executive tribunal. Parties present summary versions of their cases to a mock jury, in order to ascertain its reaction, with a view to being helped to a settlement.

## (g) Ombudsmen

Many industries choose to offer an ombudsman scheme to consumers, and some are indeed legally obliged to do so. Where schemes operate on a voluntary basis, participation is invariably optional, although the great majority of businesses in the industries in question tend to participate. Typically, access to the scheme is free or almost free for consumers. The ombudsman will investigate a consumer's complaint, initially with a view to achieving a settlement. However, if no settlement is possible, the ombudsman will issue a decision which usually binds the business, but not the consumer, leaving the latter free to pursue other remedies if not satisfied. Generally, although there will be an upper limit on the amount of compensation which the ombudsman can award the consumer, he will not be confined by the consumer's strict legal rights. So compensation may be awarded if the business behaved questionably, albeit not illegally.

## 10.26.   WHY RESORT TO ADR?

Leaving aside issues such as counterclaims, in both litigation and arbitration there tends to be a winner and a loser. The dispute between the parties is reduced to a past situation which either did or did not amount to an infringement of a party's legal rights, and for which therefore compensation either is or is not payable. No account is taken of the wider relationship between the parties and their wider interests. This may even mean that a win-lose situation may sometimes become a lose-lose situation. Consider the example of a small software firm which has secured a massive order from a major company. The firm intimates to the company some months before the agreed delivery date that there is no hope of it meeting that date or being able to deliver for a significant period of time. Here is a clear anticipatory breach of contract which would allow the company to rescind and claim damages. Yet let us suppose the firm is on the brink of insolvency. Losing the contract and being sued might put them out of business. The company's claim could be worthless, as any damages awarded would not be practically recoverable, and any resources invested in suing the firm would be thrown away. Indeed, if the company cannot get the very specialised software it requires at the appropriate time, it may risk being unable to fulfil its own contracts, consequently sustaining substantial losses. However, a mediation or negotiation based approach may reveal that cash-flow problems has meant that the firm has been unable to hire sufficient staff to meet its commitments. An early release of part of the sums payable on completion of the contract allows it to recruit the staff and get back on schedule. In return the company receives a discount and favourable rates in respect of further contracts it negotiates with the firm. Thus a lose-lose situation is transformed into a win-win situation. While real life situations may rarely work out so ideally, this example illustrates the possibilities offered by ADR.

It may also be added that ADR processes are invariably private and confidential. Some are very low cost, or even no cost, although those forms which involve meeting the cost of mediation services might conceivably be more expensive than the more streamlined forms of litigation and arbitration. Equally, while ADR is usually designed to be expeditious, it can be extremely protracted, and of course it should always be remembered that the time and expense invested in such processes is ultimately wasted, if no resolution can be reached. Even if a settlement is reached, not all such settlements are binding, so that it is possible that a partly might renege. At least litigation and arbitration can guarantee a binding result. It can also be noted that where there is a marked disparity of power, non-adjudicative processes like negotiation and mediation may operate to the detriment of the weaker party, who might well be better served by insisting on his legal rights.

# INDEX